W9-BUT-906

THE GREENWOOD ENCYCLOPEDIA OF
INTERNATIONAL
RELATIONS

THE GREENWOOD ENCYCLOPEDIA OF
INTERNATIONAL
RELATIONS

VOLUME I
A–E

CATHAL J. NOLAN

Executive Director
International History Institute
Boston University

GREENWOOD PUBLISHING
Westport, CT • London

Library of Congress Cataloging-in-Publication Data

Nolan, Cathal J.
    The Greenwood encyclopedia of international relations / Cathal J. Nolan.
      p. cm.
    Includes bibliographical references and index.
    ISBN: 0–313–30743–1 (set : alk. paper)—ISBN 0–313–30741–5 (v. 1 : alk. paper)—
ISBN 0–313–30742–3 (v. 2 : alk. paper)—ISBN 0–313–32382–8 (v. 3 : alk. paper)—
ISBN 0–313–32383–6 (v. 4 : alk. paper)
    1. International relations—Encyclopedias. I. Title.
JZ1160.N65 2002
327'.03—dc21   2002019495

British Library Cataloguing in Publication Data is available.

Library of Congress Catalog Card Number: 2002019495

ISBN: 0–313–30743–1 (set)
      0–313–30741–5 (vol. 1)
      0–313–30742–3 (vol. 2)
      0–313–32382–8 (vol. 3)
      0–313–32383–6 (vol. 4)

First published in 2002

Greenwood Press, 88 Post Road West, Westport, CT 06881
An imprint of Greenwood Publishing Group, Inc.
www.greenwood.com

Printed in the United States of America

The paper used in this book complies with the
Permanent Paper Standard issued by the National
Information Standards Organization (Z39.48–1984).

10 9 8 7 6 5 4 3 2 1

R
327.03
N78g
v. 1

Sapere aude

For my children,
Ryan Casey and Genevieve Michelle

Contents

Preface

"History," said the American industrialist Henry Ford, "is more or less bunk." Even the great eighteenth-century historian of the Roman Empire, Edward Gibbon, was only slightly more respectful: "history," he declared, is "little more than the register of the crimes, follies, and misfortunes of Mankind." So why bother to consult, let alone write, a multivolume work of international history and international relations such as this? Because history is—whatever Ford thought of it on his good days or Gibbon on his bad ones—the most important of all humanistic inquiries. For modern societies to live with the forces of nature that science has unleashed and that ideological folly or personal vanity threatens to deploy for destructive or oppressive purposes, they first must come to terms with history. Their leaders and citizens alike must understand the ways in which increased material knowledge brings social progress even as it expands conflict and opportunities for war. And they must appreciate that vanity and a lust for power among people of sustained ambition abides still near the center of public affairs and relations among nations and states. In sum, they must realize the profound truth of the matter-of-fact observation, which Albert Einstein once made, that politics is both more difficult, and ultimately far more important, even than nuclear physics.

This work presents readers with the essential continuity of events of their own day with the great ideas, leading personalities, and major developments of the past. Yet, how does any scholar determine what is a key event and who the leading individuals are or identify great-unseen forces and long-term trends that lead to tectonic shifts in the affairs of states and peoples? It is by now axiomatic that historians "know more and more about less and less." That is a particular problem for a work such as this, where the danger lurks of presenting a compendium of "interesting facts" and "more interesting facts," with little coherence and interpretive context. Had a simple compilation of facts been the aim of this work, it might have emerged instead as a multi-author effort wherein dozens of specialists were asked to present their findings about fairly narrow disputes. Instead, it is the work of a single author—albeit, one humbly grateful to hundreds of deeply learned and prolific specialists. Although such an approach presents dangers of interpretive error, it offers opportunities for an expansive exposition that may engage general readers to search out libraries of more specialized histories. Even so, in a work such as this it is more important than usual for readers to know the basis on which historical events and persons were selected for presentation, and the assumptions that underlie its author's judgments about their significance. These criteria and assumptions I have laid out in the paragraphs that follow.

LOGIC OF THE WORK

The first issue to be dealt with is objectivity. In the social sciences and academic history, objectivity springs from conscious emotional, intellectual, and personal detachment from the facts in order to permit them to "speak for themselves." Of course, that is precisely what facts never do. Historical, political, social, and economic statements and assumptions are laden with the values of observers and analysts, even those who honestly strive for detachment rather than merely make a humbug bow in its general direction. This problem is a by-product of the inherent uncertainty of knowledge in these fields. "If you would know history, know the historian" is also sound advice concerning economics and political science. In the final analysis, the best guard against subjective distortion of objective truth is a critical intelligence and skeptical, but not cynical, attitude toward intellectual authority. That does not mean that objective truth is impossible. It does mean, however, that it is hard to attain and that it must never be assumed. In writing this book, I have attempted to achieve a standard of objectivity, which is best summed up in the advice John Quincy Adams lent to all would-be writers of history. "The historian," Adams cautioned, "must be without country or religion." In addition, while alert to issues of human freedom in whatever era, which I must forewarn readers is a high personal value ("if you would know history . . ."), I have tried to avoid reading the values of the present into the past, the better to judge people and events in the light of the imaginative as well as real-world possibilities of their own day.

Passion is also disdained in the modern academy. Yet, it is mostly a virtue in historical writing. One must be scrupulous about facts, of course, and fair-minded. On the other hand, one should not be dispassionate about the Holocaust, or the crimes of Stalin or Mao, or the brutality of the génocidaires who carried out the Rwandan massacres. I have tried, and I hope that I have generally succeeded, to write "without country or religion" in assessing such matters, but that does not mean assuming a position of neutrality on the moral significance of salient people and events. A pose of studied disinterest about the qualities of communism or fascism relative to democracy, or the deeds of Tamerlane, or the meaning of terrorism, is necessarily feigned for any thinking and feeling human being. It is also itself a committed view, whether self-aware that it is so or not. Moreover, to take on a dishonest, because morally masked, position is, to paraphrase Talleyrand, worse than a crime: it would be a mistake. An affectation of detachment from lessons that history teaches about the human condition is both sterile and boring. It is far better for readers to encounter open judgments. On this point, I cleave to the wisdom of the British historian G. M. Trevelyan that in writing about and assessing historical actors and events "the really indispensable qualities [are] accuracy and good faith." Reconstructions of past events and motivations are as accurate as I have been able to make them, though I probably have made errors of fact and interpretation that will require correction in any subsequent edition of this work. As to the rest, I ask readers to accept that I have presented what I believe to be the facts of history, and drawn conclusions about the meaning of those facts, in good faith.

Concerning the comparative length of one entry with another, it is generally true that the further events recede from the present, the more history and historians compress their description. Ideally, that is done because more of the original dross, which always conceals the meaning of human affairs, has been burned away and the right conclusions drawn about what place in the larger story a given historical event or person holds. In reality, it probably more closely reflects a common tendency and need to fix all things in relation to one's own time and point of view. I have made what effort I can to correct for this habit, but I am sure I am as guilty of it as most. As to the length of the overall work, I may only plead in the spirit of Blaise Pascal that I would have written far less, but I did not have the time.

Analytically, this study starts from the straightforward observation that states have dominated international affairs for the past 350 years. Among the nearly 200 states of the early twenty-first century the vast majority are, at most, regional powers or just minor countries. Even so, smaller states sometimes have been quite influential in the larger course of world history, if sometimes solely as objects of aggression or imperial competition. And they are often interesting and important in their own right or concerning issues of regional significance. Thus, all countries currently in existence are covered in this work, as are a large number of extinct nations. Each is treated in an entry that at the least summarizes the main features of its national development and tries to situate the country in the larger contexts of time and region.

It remains true, however, that it is the most powerful states, the major civilizations from which they arise, and the wars in which they are involved that have been the major influences in world history. Even small changes within or among the Great Powers have a more important and long-term impact on world affairs than signal events within or among smaller countries. Comprehensive coverage is thus given to the foreign policies and interactions of the most powerful states and to the dynamics that drive them, including economic, intellectual, political, and social innovation or decay. This includes former Great Powers, now extinct or just declined from the first rank, dating to the Peace of Westphalia (1648) and emergence of the modern states system in seventeenth- and eighteenth-century Europe. Likewise, it is true that even lesser—whether in character or talent—individuals in charge of the affairs of Great Powers have a broad influence on world history and politics. Often, their influence has been weightier than that of even a moral or intellectual titan, if the latter was confined to a Lilliputian land. Therefore, individuals who might be reasonably judged as of little personal consequence are sometimes given their day in this work, owing to the indisputable public consequences of their choices, actions, or omissions while in command of the public affairs of major powers. More than one otherwise mediocre prime minister or president of a Great Power, or unrelieved and appalling dictator, has slipped into significant history via this back door, held ajar for them by the pervasive importance of raw power as a motive and moving force in the affairs of nations. For this reason, most leaders of major powers are profiled, including American, Austrian, British, Chinese, French, German, Indian, Japanese, Ottoman, Russian, and Soviet, along with key military and intellectual figures.

Even the Great Powers pursue grand plans and strategic interests within an international system that reflects wider economic, political, and military realities and upholds certain legal and diplomatic norms. A full understanding of world affairs—which is much more than just relations among states and nations—is incomplete without proper awareness of the historical evolution and nature of this international system (or international society), its key terms, ideas, successes and failures, and the role played in it by numerous nonstate economic and political entities. It is also crucial to appreciate that world affairs manifest cooperative as well as competitive and violent interstate relations and that, since the nineteenth century, complex international relationships have been mirrored in expanding numbers of regional organizations dealing with security, but also economic, social, legal, and even cultural arrangements. Besides the states on the world stage, other actors that demand attention include customs unions, multinational corporations, nongovernmental organizations, and an impressively expanding host—angelic and otherwise—of international organizations. As for individuals, prominent leaders from the lesser powers of Africa, Asia, Australasia, the Americas, and Europe are included according to whether they had a significant impact on international affairs beyond their nation's borders. If they had a major impact on their own society but not on wider affairs, mention of their role is usually made in the national reference alone. Also, United Nations (UN) Secretaries-General are listed, as are many individual Nobel Prize (for Peace) winners.

As with the unique role of the Great Powers, war as a general phenomenon—and great wars among major powers in particular—receives special attention. War is more costly and requires more preparation, effort, sacrifice, ingenuity, and suffering than any other collective human endeavor. There is no greater engine of social, economic, political, or technological change than war and the ever-present threat of war even in times of peace. Moreover, war and the modern state, and the larger international system, clearly evolved together since c. 1500, each greatly influencing the other. World wars—wars that involved most of the Great Powers in determined conflict—greatly compounded these manifold effects. Hence, world wars and protracted Great Power conflicts are covered in detail, including the *Seven Years' War*, the *French Revolution* and *Napoleonic Wars*, *World War I*, *World War II*, and the *Cold War*. Dozens of lesser wars, civil wars, rebellions, and guerrilla conflicts are also recounted, as they constitute a good part of international history and of influential national histories. In sum, war is a major part of international affairs and therefore a core subject of this book.

General developments of world historical significance are also covered, including *industrialization, modernization, telecommunications, total war*, and the *green* and *agricultural revolutions*. Straight historical entries include biographies, major battles, international economic history, national histories, and the history of general international processes and events. Entries attempt to summarize thousands of years when dealing with major civilizations, religions, or economic trends (though with numerous cross references), hundreds of years in the case of the Great Powers and precolonial, colonial, and post-independence history of newer nations. Most listings that are separate from national histories concern the modern era, though some go back much further. The focus is, once again, on the rise of the Great Powers and the course of world civilizations, their formative wars, and their diplomatic, political, and economic relations. This means that the progressive enlargement of the states system through imperial wars, colonialism, and the expansion of commerce and market economics beyond Europe to Africa, Asia, and the Americas has been covered.

In the interest of universality, a serious effort was made to cover regions that, objectively speaking, formed only tributary streams of the riverine flow of world history. Along with something of the flavor of their local histories, it is recounted how such areas were affected by their forced inclusion in the modern state system—often by the *slave trade* or overseas *imperialism*—and by international economic developments. This is particularly true for such areas as the Caribbean, Central America, and the associated states and dependencies of the South Pacific, which are often neglected in more straightforward narrative histories. Along with all modern states, also covered are all extant political entities, whether fully sovereign or not, including *associated states, city-states*, small *colonies, condominiums, dependencies, microstates*, and legal oddities such as the *Sovereign Military Order of Malta* (SMOM). Lastly, a fair number of extinct polities are listed, including former empires, kingdoms, federations, failed states, and political unions, such as *Austria-Hungary*, the *East African Community*, the *Ottoman Empire*, *Senegambia*, the *Soviet Union*, and the *United Arab Republic*, among many others. Also included are colonial-era names and relevant descriptions of all newly independent nations.

Although most summaries are confined to the post-1500 period, national histories may include far distant events if these are generally deemed significant in the evolution and/or historical memory of modern nations or provide intimations of the scope and direction of a given people's posture toward the outside world. For instance, the founding and succession of China's divers dynasties receive extended coverage, partly because their accomplishments and failures importantly illuminate modern China's troubled response to external pressures and its twentieth-century struggle with foreign invasion and internal revolution and partly because China remains deeply cognizant of its long and rich history, and this fact has a strong influence on its contemporary foreign policy behavior. Major intellectual revolutions that have had global historical—including not only intellectual, but also legal and political—significance are also discussed, notably the *Renaissance*, *Protestant Reformation*, and the *Enlightenment*. Although these tumultuous upheavals were originally and primarily European phenomena, they ultimately had profound effects on all international relations down to the present day, such as in their contribution to the development of secularism and the ascendancy of the state as the central principle of political organization. All political revolutions of world historical significance are covered, including the *American Revolution*, the *French Revolution*, the two *Chinese Revolutions* of the first half of the twentieth century, and the several *Russian Revolutions*. Revolutions of more local or regional significance—such as the Cuban, Ethiopian, and Iranian—are also abstracted and their importance assessed.

STRUCTURE OF THE WORK

This work is organized alphabetically. Single-word entries are, therefore, easy and straightforward to locate. But it is not always obvious where a compound term should be listed. For ease of use by readers, compound entries are listed as they are employed in usual speech and writing, that is, in the form in which they are most likely to be first encountered by the average reader. For instance, *natural resources* and *strategic resources* appear, respectively, under N and S rather than R. If readers are unable to find an entry they seek under one part of the compound term, they should have little difficulty finding it under another component of the term or phrase. Additionally, the book is heavily cross-referenced (indicated by italics), with some license taken when cross-referencing verbs to entries, which are actually listed as nouns, such as *annex*, which leads to *annexation*. Readers would be well advised to make frequent use of this feature since cross-references almost always provide additional information or insight on the original entry. Rather than clutter the text unduly with italics, however, common references such as "war," "peace," "surrender," "negotiation," "defeat," "treaty," as well as all country names, have been left in normal font. Yet, all such commonly used terms and all countries have discrete entries. In rare cases, some common terms and specific countries are highlighted, indicating that they contain additional information highly relevant to the entry being perused. To avoid confusion or sending the reader on a fruitless cross-reference search, foreign words and phrases have not been italicized. If they are, then a specific cross-reference to the term or phrase is listed because it has a special and precise meaning for international relations. For example, a textual reference to "the domestic status quo" does not receive italics, whereas "after 1919, Britain was a leading *status quo power*" does, to inform readers that additional information exists under this specialized term. For ease of use, oft-cited acronyms are cross-referenced for quick referral. Thus, *UNGA* redirects browsers to *United Nations General Assembly*, and *WTO* refers readers to the *Warsaw Treaty Organization* and the *World Trade Organization*. Otherwise, entries that readers might have encountered elsewhere in acronym form appear here under the full name of the organization. If a reader does not know the formal title of an international organization, it may be easily located by scanning all entries under the first letter. Thus, if searching for *ECOSOC* without knowing what that acronym stands for, a reader should simply scan entries under E until he or she arrives at *Economic and Social Council (ECOSOC)*. Exceptions to this rule are foreign language acronyms commonly employed in English. These are listed under the acronym itself rather than under a foreign spelling, which is most likely unknown to the English language reader. Hence, the former Soviet security and intelligence agency is listed under *KGB (Komitet Gosudarstvennoy Bezopasnosti)*, rather than the obscure "Komitet."

Crises and wars are inventoried by conventionally accepted names. Readers unsure of a standard name for a war or crisis should simply check a country entry of any known participant. There they will find in the form of a cross-reference the precise term for the entry sought. This method is especially useful for the several wars that even now go by unusual names, or in some cases multiple names, or those conflicts with which a given reader may not be familiar. For instance, someone seeking information for the first time on China's several wars with Japan might reasonably assume that they are called "Chinese/Japanese War(s)" of some given date. In fact, these important conflicts are usually referred to, in English, as the *Sino/Japanese War(s)*. Looking under China or Japan will locate the appropriate cross-reference and guide the reader to the entry that is being sought. Likewise, the several wars involving Israel and various Arab states are listed chronologically under *Arab/Israeli War(s)*, rather than under politically loaded or parochial terms such as "Yom Kippur War" or "Six Day War," although these terms are listed and cross-referenced in consideration of readers who are used to them. In cases of special confusion or a recent change in nomenclature, a guiding cross-reference is listed. For example, the *Iran/Iraq War* was often called the *Gulf War* until that term was usurped by the media for use about the multinational conflict with Iraq over its 1990 invasion and annexation of Kuwait. Readers will find here the entry *Gulf War (1980–1988)*, which explains the shift and redirects them to the newly accepted name of *Iran-Iraq War (1980–1988)*. Below that appears *Gulf War (1990–1991)*, which synopsizes the UN coalition's war with Iraq. Some technical points are as follows:

1. For syntactical reasons, cross-references that begin with a country's name may appear otherwise in the text. For instance, the *invasion of Grenada* may appear in a given sentence, but the entry is found under *Grenada, invasion of*.

2. All civil wars are listed under the country name. Thus, *American Civil War* appears under A and not C. In this case, and some others, the advice of reviewers has been followed to cross-reference wars to their vernacular usages. This allows more general readers to easily find the entries they seek, but has the felicitous side effect of compelling chauvinists or jingoists, of whatever country or stripe, to locate their nation's most boastful conflicts by mere, even humbling, alphabetical order!

3. All dates are from the Common Era (C.E.) unless stated otherwise, in which case the standard designation B.C.E. (Before the Common Era) is used. In cases where ambiguity exists, C.E. is added to ensure clarity.

4. I have for the most part followed the practice of specialists in using the pinyin system for romanizing Chinese personal and place names. However, names that have long become familiar to Western readers under their Wade-Giles form have been left in that form, as in "Chiang Kai-shek" rather than "Jiang Jieshi," with a cross-reference to the pinyin form to avoid causing confusion for younger readers. In some special cases, the alternate form has been provided immediately in parentheses, but this has not been the preferred approach.

SPECIAL FEATURES

Biography

Recent trends in historiography emphasize interactions of whole populations and or social and economic forces. Yet it remains true, as Thomas Carlyle famously noted, that much of international history is accessible through stories of the lives of great men and women caught up in, and to some degree shaping, the tumultuous events of their times. Certainly that remains true of many, even most, states before the nineteenth century and of personal or "charismatic" dictatorships still. Significant lives may serve as beacons, illuminating history. The limitations of space in this work, however, meant that its compact biographies seldom attempt to explain the inner meaning of these extraordinary lives. Readers must explore full biographies to acquire that knowledge and psychological insight into their subject. This work is necessarily limited to the public importance of public lives and is mostly confined to the political sphere, with personal and psychological detail kept to a minimum. Even so, peculiar human elements have not been ignored where they are specially revealing and clearly relevant, as in the mysticism of Nicholas II, the cruelty of Amin, the erratic and callous disregard for life of Mao, the extreme overconfidence of Hitler, or the sadism and near-clinical paranoia of Stalin.

Diplomacy

Entries include key concepts such as *arbitration, conciliation, diplomatic immunity, good offices, mediation,* and *sphere of influence.* Major diplomatic conferences are described, including *Westphalia, 1648; Vienna, 1815; Paris, 1856; Berlin, 1878; Paris, 1919; Washington, 1922; Bretton Woods, 1944; San Francisco, 1945;* and *Helsinki, 1973–1975.* Practices of negotiation, diplomatic functions, and ranks and titles are included. Classic diplomatic terms such as *cordon sanitaire, raison d'état, rapprochement, Realpolitik, Weltpolitik,* and many others are defined and examples of their application provided.

Intelligence

A sampling of major intelligence agencies is included, among them *CIA, KGB, MI5/MI6, Mossad, NSA, STASI,* and *Sûreté,* as well as common terms, jargon, and slang from intelligence tradecraft.

International Law

Listed and defined are numerous international legal concepts, maxims, and specialized terminology, many with illustrative examples, including dozens of entries on subfields such as *international criminal law, international customary law, international public law, laws of war, recognition,* and *sovereignty.* Numerous treaties, from *arms control* to the *Space Treaty* to agreements on the *Law of the Sea* and *Antarctica,* are provided and their terms listed and explained. International law and the attendant politics of *human rights* issues are covered, including *female circumcision, citizenship, refugees, slavery,* and the *slave trade.*

International Organizations (IOs)

All major multilateral bodies and organizations are covered, dating back to the mid-nineteenth century. IOs proliferated with the founding of the *League of Nations* and the *UN.* This work includes entries on all specialized agencies, as well as key committees and commissions of the UN system. There is comprehensive coverage of regional organizations, including several failures, whether organized around economic, political, or security themes. Some prominent nongovernmental organizations are also listed.

International Political Economy

Major economic institutions, such as GATT, IBRD, IMF, and the WTO, and interstate economic associations, such as ASEAN, CARICOM, ECO-WAS, EEC, EU, NAFTA, OECD, and OPEC, have entries. Some historic multinational corporations have been added, such as the *East India Company* and the *Hudson's Bay Company*, and there are more general entries on foreign direct investment and related economic concepts and specialized language, such as *adjustment, balance of payments, debt rescheduling, deficit financing, First Tranche, free trade agreements, oligopoly,* and *structural adjustment.* Also, international economic history is well-covered in entries such as *world depressions,* the *Bretton Woods system,* the *agricultural revolution, industrialization,* and the *gold standard.*

Maps

Multiple maps are available to readers. Some cover world political divisions on a region-by-region basis. Others illustrate major historical conflicts or events, such as the occupation of Germany in 1945, expansion and contraction of the Japanese Empire, and U.S. intervention in Central America and the Caribbean. Some concern long-standing diplomatic and strategic controversies, such as the *Eastern Question* or the *Straits Question.*

Military History

Included are major concepts such as *envelopment, flanking, mobilization, strategy,* and *friction.* Also listed are entries on military ranks and units and a limited set of entries on major weapons systems, conventional and otherwise. Many wars are synopsized, including discussion of their course, causes, and effects. The crucially important events of *World War I* and *World War II* receive extended coverage. Pivotal battles over the past 500 years of world history are highlighted. Generals and admirals of special accomplishment or failure earned discrete biographical entries.

Political Geography

There are entries on every nation, colony, possession, and protectorate, as well as key geographical features, definitions of strategic regions and geographical concepts, and an overview of select geopolitical theories. Significant minority groups are described, such as *Fulani, Ibos, Karen, Kurds,* and *Zulu.* Some nonsovereign regions are cataloged, especially those with secessionist histories, including *Chechnya*, *Ossetia*, *Nagorno-Karabakh*, *Québec*, and *Shaba*. Country entries provide a synopsis history and description of major foreign policies pursued and alliances and may also list core international associations, population levels, and the quality and size of the national military.

Political Science

Included are major concepts, terminology, and translations into plain English of current thinking in this jargon-laden discipline, which also encompasses academic *international relations theory*. This embraces concepts and terms from theoretical subfields such as *dependency*, *deterrence*, *game theory*, *decision-making theory*, *just war theory*, *liberal-internationalism*, *Marxism*, *perception/misperception studies*, *realism*, *strategic studies*, and various *systems theories*. There are also intellectual sketches of key political thinkers on international affairs, among them *Hobbes*, *Bentham*, *Kant*, *Marx*, *Rousseau*, and *Adam Smith*.

Acknowledgments

Dr. Samuel Johnson noted, "The greatest part of a writer's time is spent in reading, in order to write; a man will turn over half a library to make one book." I am keenly aware of that truth and immensely grateful to the hundreds of specialists whose books and articles I have relied upon in such measure. I have not hesitated to add interpretations of my own in areas I know well or where it seemed to me that larger patterns in history were readily apparent and moral and other lessons might be fairly drawn. Even so, writing a work of history such as this is primarily an exercise in synthesis. In a work of this scale and nature, it is simply not possible for a single author to master the primary sources that are the raw ore from which the purer metals of historical truth must be smelted. Instead, my challenge has been to gain sufficient command of the specialty literature in order to provide enough detailed narrative that past events become comprehensible, while also communicating the differing interpretations to which those events may be subject.

If this were a normal monograph, my heavy intellectual debt would be documented in extensive footnotes. That has not proven possible here, since footnotes and related academic paraphernalia would have added several hundred more pages to an already overlong work. However, at the end of longer entries, I have cited direct sources and other recommended books—the latter for various reasons and not by any means always-interpretive agreement on my part. Also, I have added clusters of more general references upon which I have relied in entries of central importance, such as "*war*" or "*international law*" or "*Spanish America*."

Finally, I have prepared and included a Select Bibliography of works consulted. Neither the end citations nor the bibliography are intended to provide a comprehensive listing of the many important works of specialized history available to scholars. My more limited purpose is to point general readers to a mixture of the best, along with the most recent, scholarship in different fields and to expose them to a variety of interpretive points of view. I fully appreciate that a broad work of this nature is necessarily a mere steppingstone to a far richer understanding of international history, which may be gleaned only from a wider reading of those specialized histories. If this work encourages readers to pursue that search for themselves, its purpose will have been achieved.

On a personal note, I need and wish to express my profound gratitude to those who have assisted me in completing this task. I have taken parts of the past seven years to write this work. In that time, I wrote or edited other books, but this one was always on my mind, its demands pervading my reading and thinking, its conclusions seeping into my teaching. My first thanks must go to my editor at Greenwood, Michael Hermann, who is simply the finest editor with whom I have ever worked. In addition to lifting from me all concerns about production values and the usual mundane matters that accompany production of any book, he has been a frequent and always constructive critic and adviser on issues of content.

Several of my colleagues at Boston University must wish that e-mail had never been invented or at least that I had never been introduced to the technology. For their patience with me and forbearance of my many inquiries, and for their counsel, collegiality, and friendship, I am ever appreciative. My thanks and gratitude to Erik Goldstein and David Mayers, both of whom have been extraordinarily supportive of my work. I look forward to many more years together as colleagues and friends, joined now also by my old colleague and friend from the University of British Columbia, Robert H. Jackson. William Tilchin has been prodigiously supportive of this project and as we have worked together on several other conference and book projects. He has read and commented on numerous entries, often saving me from error and always boosting my confidence whenever it sagged, usually during moments when I realized how absurdly huge a task it was that I had set myself. How may I express the fullness of my gratitude to my friend and colleague, William R. Keylor, with whom I had the privilege of cofounding the International History Institute at Boston University and with whom I am honored to work closely on a daily basis? Had I an entry in this book for "gentleman and scholar," it would simply read, "See Bill Keylor," because there would be no need to say more.

Few have read, commented on, corrected, and laughed at (usually in the places intended) more of the text than my dear friend and former colleague, Dr. Carl C. Hodge of Okanagan University College in Kelowna, British Columbia. I am grateful also for comments on selected entries by Dr. Charles Cogan, Senior Fellow at the John F. Kennedy School of Government at Harvard University; Professor Charles Neu, Chair of History at Brown University; and Professor Tom Nichols of the Naval War College. Many other scholars and specialists have read and commented on one entry or another. I have thanked them individually in private and now do so again here. Min Wu, of the International History Institute, has been particularly helpful in confirming and correcting Chinese personal and place names, as has Sijin Cheng of the Department of Political Science. To them, I also extend my sincere thanks.

My wife, Valerie, read all of the book in manuscript form and has been a constant and sage adviser on language, syntax, and Latin throughout its years of writing. As always, she has remained cheerful and supportive even as I spent far too many hours lost in a book on the Mauryan state in India, or Qing China, or Samori Touré, or ensconced in front of the computer. My children, Ryan and Genevieve, continue to fill our home with laughter, wit, and song. At ages eleven and nine, I am deeply grateful for their cheerful presence and companionship.

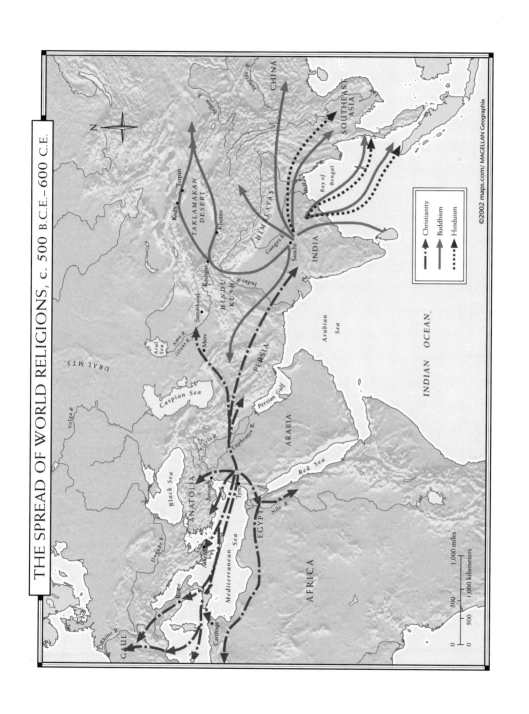

THE SPREAD OF WORLD RELIGIONS, c. 500 B.C.E.–600 C.E.

Christianity
Buddhism
Hinduism

©2002 maps.com/ MAGELLAN Geographix

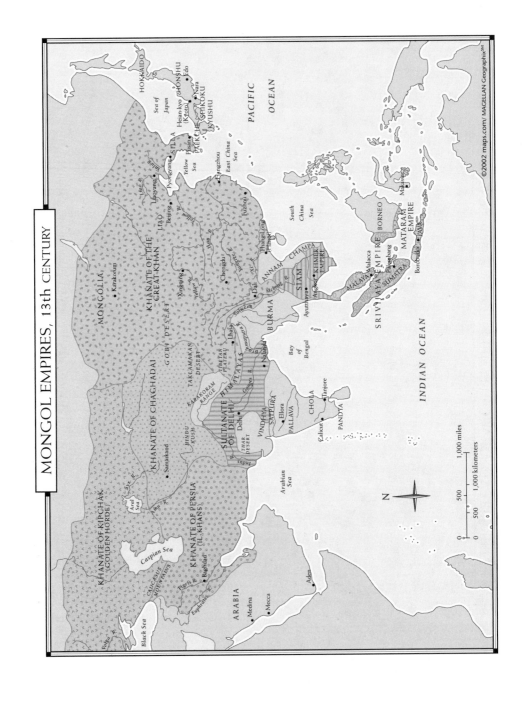

MONGOL EMPIRES, 13th CENTURY

HOKKAIDO

HONSHU
Heian-kyo
(Kyoto) Edo
Nara
SILLA
PAEKCHE SHIKOKU
KYUSHU

Sea of
Japan

Pyongyang
Liaoyang
LIAO
Beijing
Yellow
Sea

Hangzhou

East China
Sea

Fuzhou

MONGOLIA

Karakorum

KHANATE OF THE
GREAT KHAN

GOBI DESERT

Yinchuan
Yellow R.

South
China
Sea

PACIFIC

OCEAN

Chengdu

Dali

ANNAM
Thang Long
(Hanoi)

CHAMPA

SIAM
Ayutthaya
Angkor
KHMER
EMPIRE

BORNEO

Malacca
MALAYA
Palembang
SUMATRA

MATARAM
EMPIRE
Borobudur
Java

Madiun

SRIVIJAYA EMPIRE

KHANATE OF CHAGHADAI

TAKLAMAKAN
DESERT

KARAKORAM
RANGE

Samarkand

HINDU
KUSH

Lhasa
TIBETAN
PLATEAU

HIMALAYAS

SULTANATE
OF DELHI

THAR
DESERT

Delhi
VINDHYA
SATPURA

Ellora
PALLAVA

CHOLA

Tanjore

Calicut
PANDYA

Brahmaputra R.
Ganges R.

BURMA

Bay
of
Bengal

INDIAN OCEAN

KHANATE OF KIPCHAK
(GOLDEN HORDE)

Aral
Sea

Caspian Sea

KHANATE OF PERSIA
(IL-KHANS)

Baghdad

Basra
Euphrates R.

CAUCASUS
MOUNTAINS

Black Sea

Volga R.

ARABIA
Medina
Mecca

Arabian
Sea

Aden

N

0   500   1,000 miles
0   500   1,000 kilometers

©2002 maps.com/ MAGELLAN Geographix℠

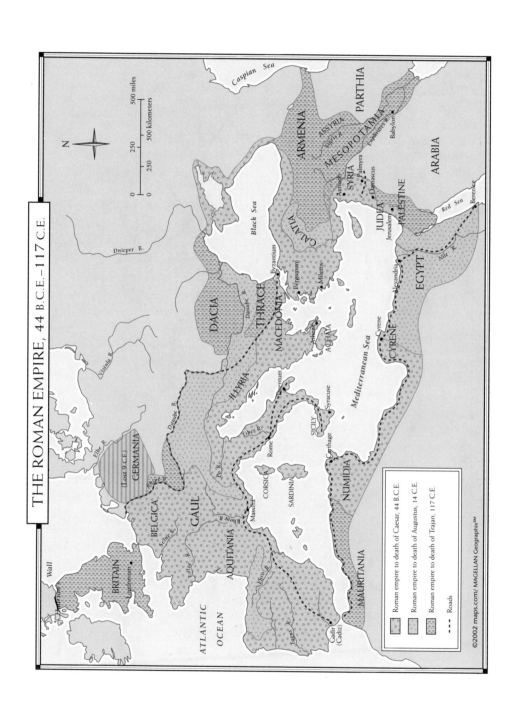

THE ROMAN EMPIRE, 44 B.C.E.–117 C.E.

N

500 miles

500 kilometers

250

250

0

0

ATLANTIC
OCEAN

Wall
Hadrian

BRITAIN
Londinium

Elbe R.

GERMANIA
(Lost 9 C.E.)

BELGICA

Rhine R.

Seine R.

GAUL

AQUITANIA

Vistula R.

Danube R.

DACIA

Dnieper R.

Caspian Sea

Black Sea

Danube R.

ARMENIA

ASSYRIA

Tigris R.

PARTHIA

MESOPOTAMIA

Euphrates R.

Babylon

GALATIA

SYRIA

Palmyra

Antioch

Damascus

JUDEA

Jerusalem

PALESTINE

Red Sea

Berenice

ARABIA

Nile R.

EGYPT

Alexandria

Pergamum

Byzantium

Miletos

THRACE

MACEDONIA

ACHAIA

Athens

Mediterranean Sea

CYRENE

Cyrene

Rhone R.

Po R.

Massilia

Mt.

Loire R.

Rome

Tiber R.

Brundisium

Ebro R.

CORSICA

SARDINIA

SICILY

Syracuse

Carthage

Tagus R.

Cadiz
(Cadiz)

NUMIDIA

MAURITANIA

ILLYRIA

Roman empire to death of Caesar, 44 B.C.E.

Roman empire to death of Augustus, 14 C.E.

Roman empire to death of Trajan, 117 C.E.

Roads

©2002 maps.com/ MAGELLAN Geographix℠

THE SPREAD OF ISLAM, 622 – 750 CE

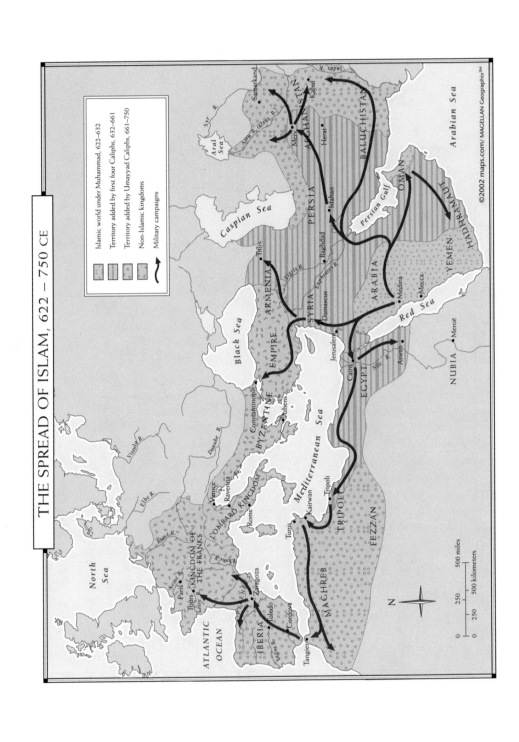

Islamic world under Muhammad, 622–632

Territory added by first four Caliphs, 632–661

Territory added by Umayyad Caliphs, 661–750

Non-Islamic kingdoms

Military campaigns

©2002 maps.com/ MAGELLAN Geographix℠

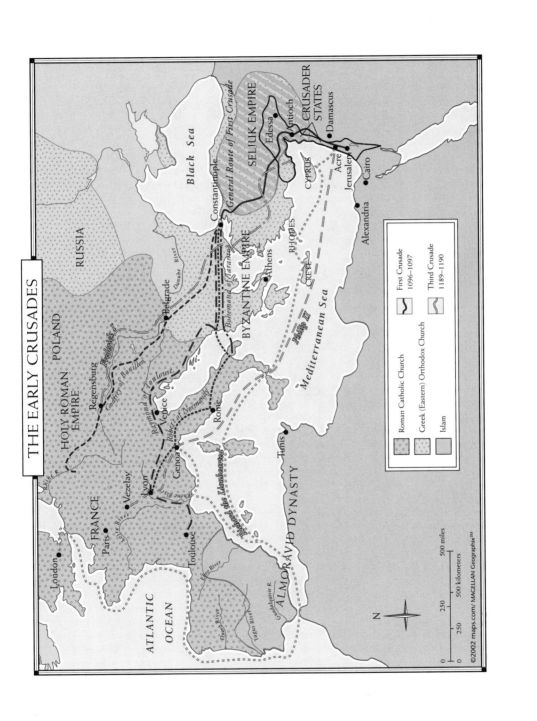

THE EARLY CRUSADES

ATLANTIC OCEAN

London

Paris
FRANCE
Vezelay
Lyon
Toulouse

HOLY ROMAN EMPIRE
POLAND
RUSSIA
Regensburg

Belgrade
Godfrey of Bouillon
Raymond of Toulouse
Venice
Robert of Normandy
Genoa
Rome
Richard the Lionhearted

Tunis

ALMORAVID DYNASTY

Rhône River
Loire River
Kura River
Danube River
Ebro River
Duro River
Tagus River
Guadalquivir R.

Black Sea

Constantinople
Bohemond of Tarantum
BYZANTINE EMPIRE
Athens
Mt.
Philip II

SELJUK EMPIRE
General Route of First Crusade
CRUSADER STATES
Edessa
Antioch
Damascus
Cyprus
Acre
Jerusalem
Cairo
Alexandria
RHODES
CRETE

Mediterranean Sea

N

©2002 maps.com/ MAGELLAN Geographix℠

| 0 | 250 | 500 miles |
| 0 | 250 | 500 kilometers |

Roman Catholic Church	First Crusade 1096–1097
Greek (Eastern) Orthodox Church	Third Crusade 1189–1190
Islam	

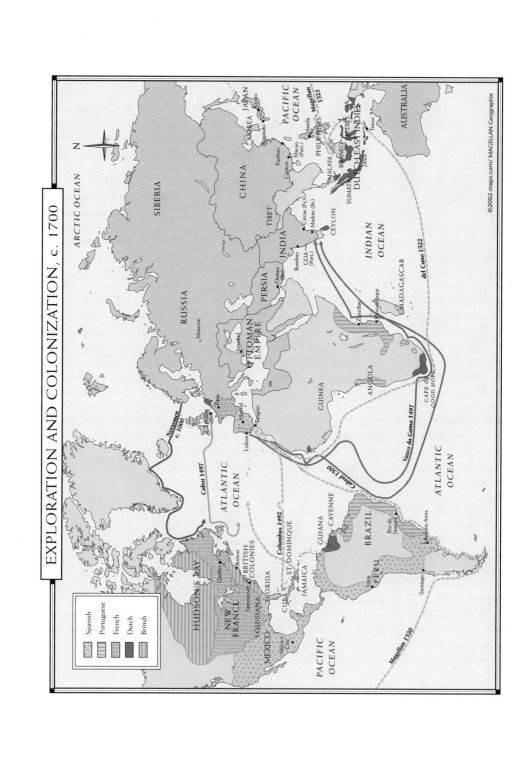

EXPLORATION AND COLONIZATION, c. 1700

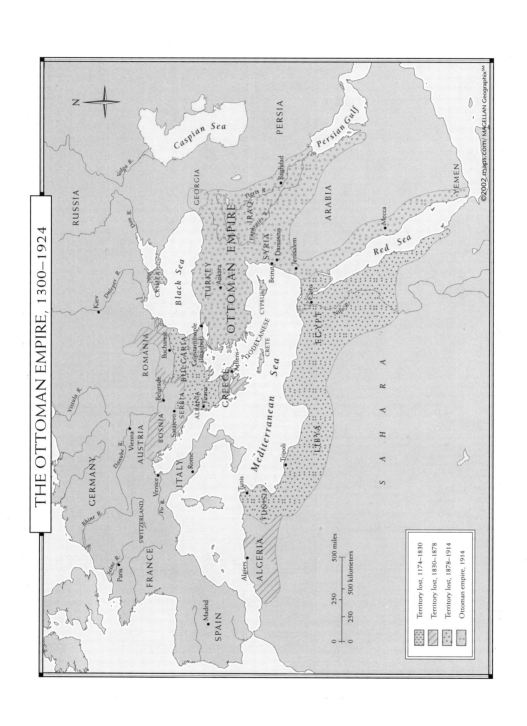

THE OTTOMAN EMPIRE, 1300–1924

Legend:
- Territory lost, 1174–1830
- Territory lost, 1830–1878
- Territory lost, 1878–1914
- Ottoman empire, 1914

©2002 maps.com/ MAGELLAN Geographix℠

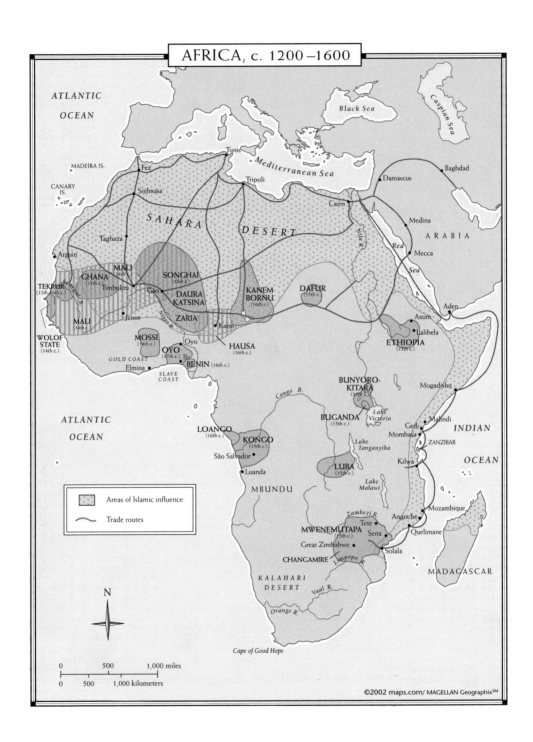

AFRICA, c. 1200–1600

ATLANTIC
OCEAN

Black Sea

Mediterranean Sea

Tunis

Fez

Tripoli

Sijilmasa

Damascus

Baghdad

MADEIRA IS.

CANARY
IS.

Cairo

S A H A R A   D E S E R T

Medina

ARABIA

Taghaza

Arguin

Red

Mecca

Sea

GHANA
(13th c.)

MALI
(14th c.)

SONGHAI
(15th c.)

KANEM-
BORNU
(16th c.)

DAFUR
(15th c.)

Aden

TEKRUR
(11th–16th c.)

Timbuktu

Gao

DAURA
KATSINA

Axum

Lalibela

ETHIOPIA
(13th c.)

MALI
(14th c.)

Jenne

ZARIA

Kano

WOLOF
STATE
(14th c.)

MOSSI
(14th c.)

Oyo

HAUSA
(16th c.)

GOLD COAST

OYO
(17th c.)

Ife

Elmina

BENIN (16th c.)

SLAVE
COAST

BUNYORO-
KITARA
(16th c.)

Mogadishu

ATLANTIC
OCEAN

BUGANDA
(15th c.)

Lake
Victoria

Gedi

Malindi

INDIAN

LOANGO
(16th c.)

Mombasa

ZANZIBAR

KONGO
(15th c.)

Congo R.

Lake
Tanganyika

Kilwa

OCEAN

São Salvador

LUBA
(15th c.)

Luanda

MBUNDU

Lake
Malawi

Mozambique

Zambezi R.

Angoche

Tete

MWENEMUTAPA
(15th c.)

Sena

Quelimane

Great Zimbabwe

Solala

CHANGAMIRE

Limpopo R.

MADAGASCAR

KALAHARI
DESERT

Vaal R.

N

Orange R.

Cape of Good Hope

| | Areas of Islamic influence |
| | Trade routes |

0   500   1,000 miles

0   500   1,000 kilometers

©2002 maps.com/ MAGELLAN Geographix℠

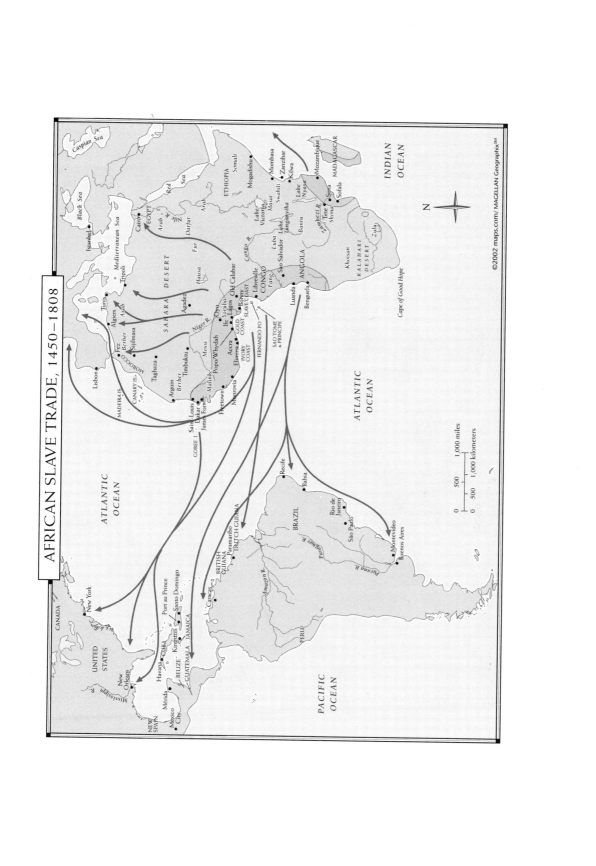

AFRICAN SLAVE TRADE, 1450–1808

©2002 maps.com/ MAGELLAN Geographix℠

THE GROWTH OF RUSSIA, 1598–1796

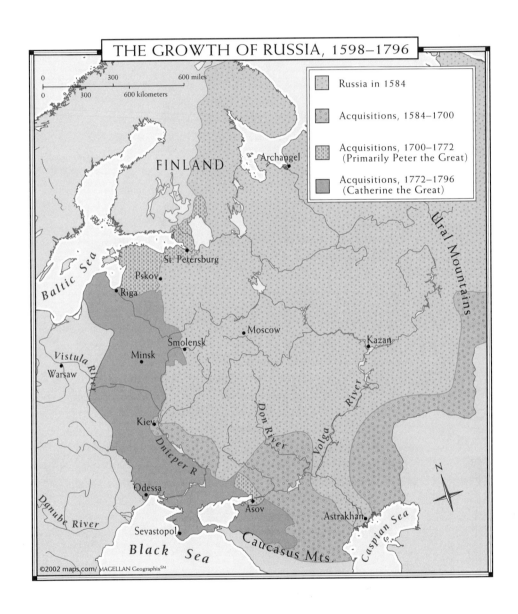

0   300   600 miles
0   300   600 kilometers

Russia in 1584

Acquisitions, 1584–1700

Acquisitions, 1700–1772
(Primarily Peter the Great)

Acquisitions, 1772–1796
(Catherine the Great)

FINLAND

Archangel

Baltic Sea

St. Petersburg

Pskov

Riga

Moscow

Kazan

Ural Mountains

Vistula River

Warsaw

Minsk

Smolensk

Kiev

Don River

Volga River

Dnieper R.

Odessa

Asov

Astrakhan

Caspian Sea

Sevastopol

Danube River

Black Sea

Caucasus Mts.

N

©2002 maps.com/ MAGELLAN Geographix℠

CHINA IN THE QING DYNASTY, 1644–1911

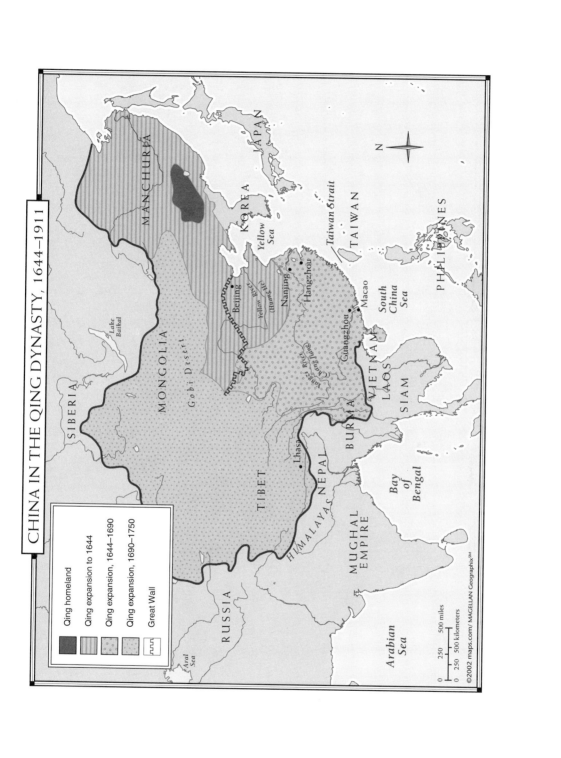

Qing homeland
Qing expansion to 1644
Qing expansion, 1644–1690
Qing expansion, 1690–1750
Great Wall

RUSSIA

SIBERIA

MANCHURIA

KOREA
JAPAN

MONGOLIA

Gobi Desert

Lake
Baikal

Aral
Sea

Yellow River
(Huang He)

Beijing

Nanjing
Hangzhou

Yellow
Sea

Taiwan Strait

TAIWAN

Macao

South
China
Sea

PHILIPPINES

Guangzhou

VIETNAM
LAOS
SIAM

BURMA

Chang Jiang
Yangtze River

Xi Jiang

TIBET

Lhasa

HIMALAYAS
NEPAL

MUGHAL
EMPIRE

Bay
of
Bengal

Arabian
Sea

N

0   250   500 miles
0   250   500 kilometers

©2002 maps.com/ MAGELLAN Geographix℠

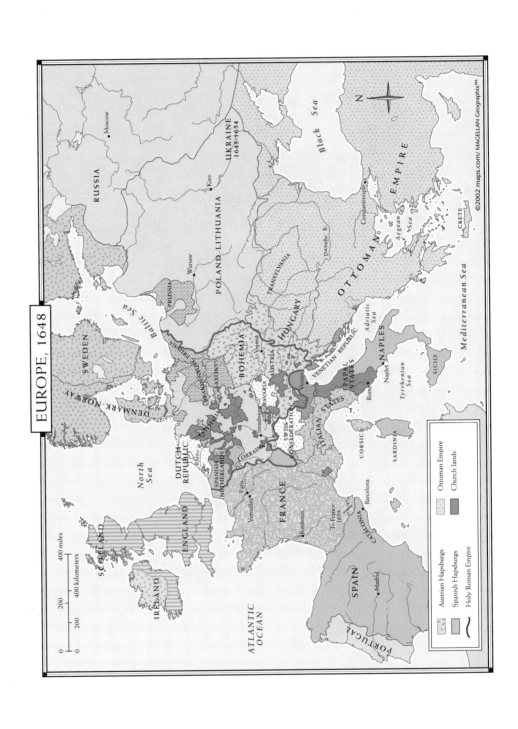

EUROPE, 1648

SCOTLAND

IRELAND

ENGLAND

North
Sea

ATLANTIC
OCEAN

DUTCH
REPUBLIC

SPANISH
NETHERLANDS

Paris •
Versailles •

FRANCE

Bordeaux •

To France
1659

CATALONIA

Barcelona •

SPAIN

• Madrid

PORTUGAL

Rhine •

LORRAINE

Strasbourg •

SWISS
CONFEDERATION

ITALIAN STATES

CORSICA

SARDINIA

PRUSSIA

SWEDEN

DENMARK-NORWAY

Baltic Sea

PRUSSIA

BRANDENBURG

SAXONY

BOHEMIA

Vienna •

AUSTRIA

BAVARIA

Venice •

VENETIAN REPUBLIC

PAPAL
STATES

Rome •

NAPLES

Naples •

Tyrrhenian
Sea

SICILY

RUSSIA

• Moscow

POLAND-LITHUANIA

• Kiev

• Warsaw

UKRAINE
1648–1654

TRANSYLVANIA

HUNGARY

Danube R.

Adriatic
Sea

OTTOMAN EMPIRE

Constantinople •

Black Sea

Aegean
Sea

CRETE

Mediterranean Sea

N

©2002 maps.com/ MAGELLAN Geographix℠

	Austrian Hapsburgs
	Spanish Hapsburgs
	Holy Roman Empire
	Ottoman Empire
	Church lands

400 miles
400 kilometers
0   200   400
0   200

THE FRENCH AND INDIAN WAR, 1754–1763

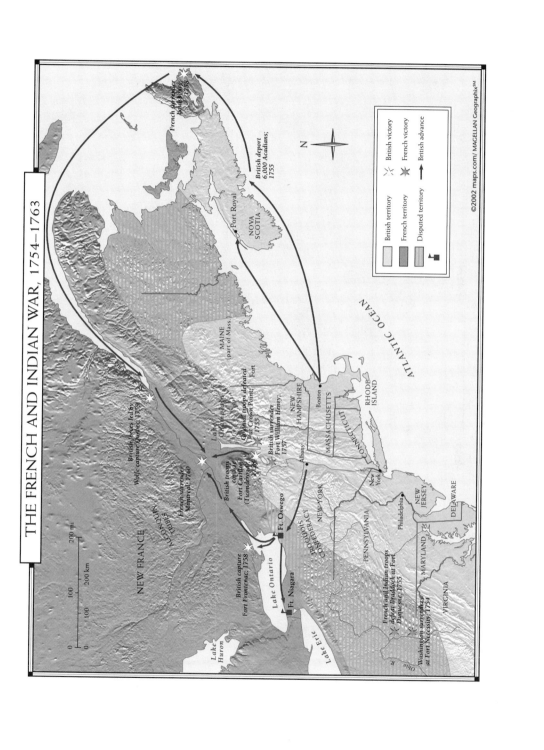

French surrender
Louisburg; 1758

British deport
6,000 Acadians;
1755

Port Royal

NOVA
SCOTIA

MAINE
(part of Mass.)

ATLANTIC OCEAN

N

British victory
French victory
British advance

British territory
French territory
Disputed territory

©2002 maps.com/ MAGELLAN Geographic℠

NEW FRANCE

ALGONQUIN
TRIBES

French surrender
Montreal, 1760

British forces, led by
Wolfe capture Quebec 1759

British troops
capture
Fort Carillon
(Ticonderoga)
1758

British capture
Fort Frontenac; 1758

British surrender
Fort William Henry,
1757

British troops defeated
at Crown Point; Fort
1755

NEW
HAMPSHIRE

Boston

MASSACHUSETTS

RHODE
ISLAND

CONNECTICUT

Ft. Oswego

Lake Ontario

Ft. Niagara

Lake Erie

Lake Huron

IROQUOIS
CONFEDERACY

NEW
YORK

Albany

New
York

PENNSYLVANIA

Philadelphia

NEW
JERSEY

DELAWARE

MARYLAND

French and Indian troops
defeat Braddock at Fort
Duquesne 1755

Washington surrenders
at Fort Necessity, 1754

Ohio R.

VIRGINIA

200 mi.

200 km

0   100

0   100

200

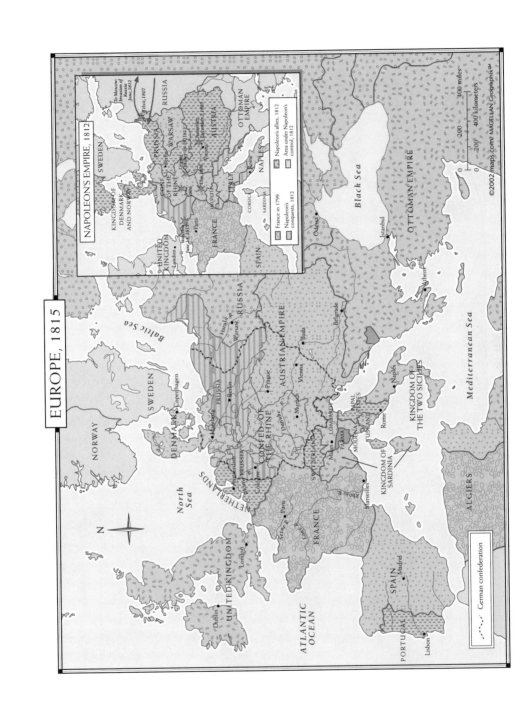

EUROPE, 1815

North Sea

NORWAY

SWEDEN

DENMARK
Copenhagen

Baltic Sea

RUSSIA

PRUSSIA
Berlin

Warsaw

Hamburg

NETHERLANDS
Amsterdam
Cologne

CONFED. OF
THE RHINE

Prague

AUSTRIAN EMPIRE

Buda

Vienna

Belgrade

UNITED KINGDOM
Dublin
London

ATLANTIC
OCEAN

FRANCE
Paris
Seine R.
Loire R.
Marseilles
Rhône R.

SWITZERLAND
Danube R.
Munich

LOMBARDY
Milan
PARMA
MODENA
TUSCANY

KINGDOM OF
SARDINIA

PAPAL
STATES
Rome

KINGDOM OF
THE TWO SICILIES

Naples

SPAIN
Madrid

PORTUGAL
Lisbon

Mediterranean Sea

ALGIERS

Black Sea

OTTOMAN EMPIRE

Athens

N

German confederation

NAPOLEON'S EMPIRE, 1812

SWEDEN

KINGDOM OF
DENMARK
AND NORWAY

UNITED
KINGDOM
London

FRANCE
Paris
Waterloo
June 18, 1815

HELVETIA

CONF.
OF THE
RHINE
Jena
1806

PRUSSIA
Berlin
Leipzig
Oct. 16-19, 1813

DUCHY OF
WARSAW

Austerlitz 1805
Vienna
Ulm 1805

AUSTRIA

Wagram 1809

ITALY

CORSICA
SARDINIA

Rome

NAPLES

SPAIN

RUSSIA

To Moscow:
Invasion of
Russia
June, 1812

Tilsit, 1807

OTTOMAN
EMPIRE

France in 1799

Napoleon's
conquests, 1812

Napoleon's allies, 1812

Area under Napoleon's
control, 1812

0   200   300 miles

0   200   400 kilometers

©2002 maps.com/ MAGELLAN Geographix℠

London
Madrid
Odessa
Istanbul

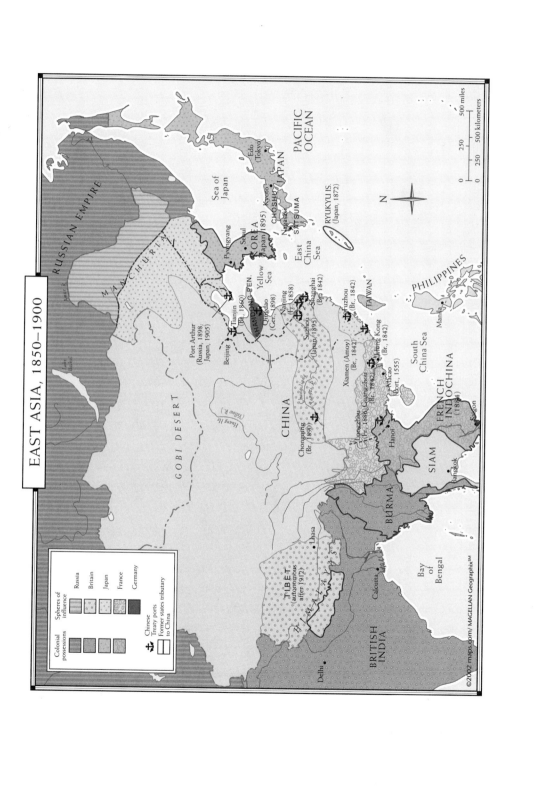

EAST ASIA, 1850–1900

Colonial possessions

Spheres of influence
Russia
Britain
Japan
France
Germany

✠ Chinese Treaty ports

Former states tributary to China

RUSSIAN EMPIRE

MANCHURIA

GOBI DESERT

Huang He (Yellow R.)

CHINA

TIBET (autonomous after 1912)

HIMALAYAS

BRITISH INDIA

Delhi

Calcutta

Bay of Bengal

BURMA

SIAM

Bangkok

FRENCH INDOCHINA (1884)

Saigon

Hanoi

Lhasa

Chongqing (Br. 1890)

Guangzhou (Fr. 1886; Br. 1842)

Macao (Port. 1555)

Hong Kong (Br. 1842)

Xiamen (Amoy) (Br. 1842)

Fuzhou (Br. 1842)

TAIWAN

South China Sea

PHILIPPINES

Manila

Suzhou (Japan, 1895)

Shanghai (Br. 1842)

Nanjing (Tr. 1858)

Ningbo

Yangzi R.

SHANDONG PEN.

Qingdao (Ger. 1898)

Tianjin (Tr. 1860)

Beijing

Port Arthur (Russia, 1898; Japan, 1905)

Yellow Sea

KOREA

Pyongyang

Seoul

Sea of Japan

JAPAN

CHOSHU (1895)

SATSUMA

Nagasaki

Kyoto

Edo (Tokyo)

East China Sea

RYUKYU IS. (Japan, 1872)

PACIFIC OCEAN

Lake Baikal

Lake Aral

N

0   250   500 miles
0   250   500 kilometers

©2002 maps.com/ MAGELLAN Geographix℠

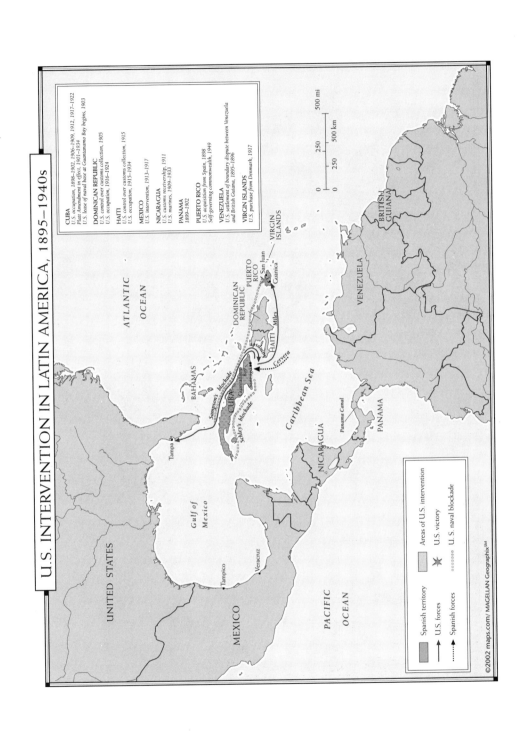

U.S. INTERVENTION IN LATIN AMERICA, 1895–1940s

CUBA
U.S. occupation, 1898–1902, 1906–1909, 1912, 1917–1922
Platt Amendment in effect, 1901–1934
U.S. lease of naval base at Guantánamo Bay begins, 1903

DOMINICAN REPUBLIC
U.S. control over customs collection, 1905
U.S. occupation, 1916–1924

HAITI
U.S. control over customs collection, 1915
U.S. occupation, 1915–1934

MEXICO
U.S. intervention, 1913–1917

NICARAGUA
U.S. customs receivership, 1911
U.S. marines, 1909–1933

PANAMA
1899–1902

PUERTO RICO
U.S. acquisition from Spain, 1898
Self-governing commonwealth, 1949

VENEZUELA
U.S. settlement of boundary dispute between Venezuela and British Guiana, 1895–1896

VIRGIN ISLANDS
U.S. purchase from Denmark, 1917

UNITED STATES

ATLANTIC OCEAN

Gulf of Mexico

MEXICO

Tampico

Veracruz

PACIFIC OCEAN

Tampa

BAHAMAS

Sampson's blockade

Schley's blockade

CUBA

Santiago

Guantánamo

Cervera

HAITI

Miles

DOMINICAN REPUBLIC

PUERTO RICO

San Juan

Guánica

VIRGIN ISLANDS

Caribbean Sea

NICARAGUA

Panama Canal

PANAMA

VENEZUELA

BRITISH GUIANA

	Legend
▨ Spanish territory	▨ Areas of U.S. intervention
→ U.S. forces	✳ U.S. victory
⋯ Spanish forces	▨ U.S. naval blockade

0   250   500 mi

0   250   500 km

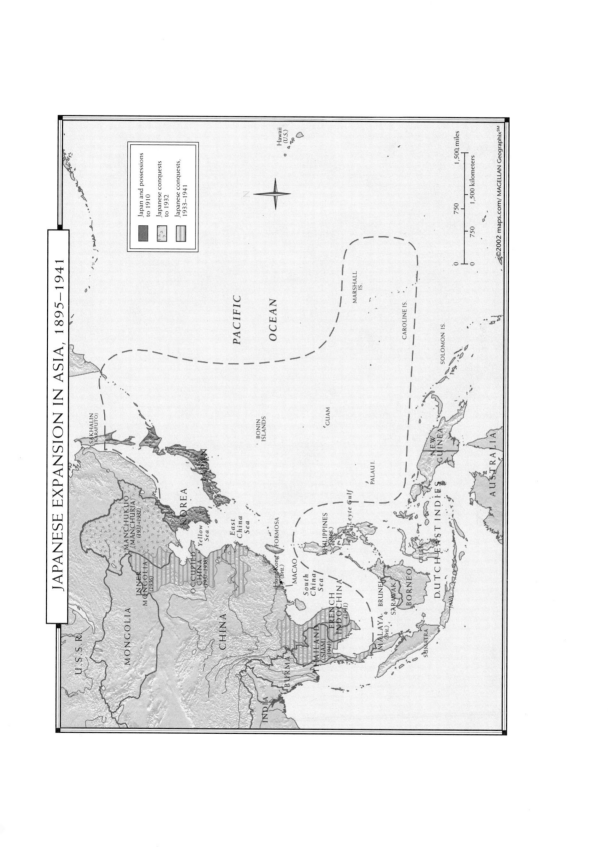

JAPANESE EXPANSION IN ASIA, 1895–1941

Japan and possessions
to 1910

Japanese conquests
to 1932

Japanese conquests,
1933–1941

1,500 miles

1,500 kilometers

0   750

0   750

©2002 maps.com/ MAGELLAN Geographix℠

PACIFIC

OCEAN

Hawaii
(U.S.)

MARSHALL
IS.

CAROLINE IS.

SOLOMON IS.

GUAM

BONIN
ISLANDS

PALAU I.

NEW
GUINEA

AUSTRALIA

SAKHALIN
(KARAFUTO)

U.S.S.R.

MONGOLIA

MANCHUKUO
MANCHURIA
(1931–1932)

INNER
MONGOLIA
(1936)

KOREA

Yellow
Sea

East
China
Sea

OCCUPIED
CHINA
(1937–1939)

CHINA

FORMOSA

Hong Kong
(Brit.)

MACAO

South
China
Sea

Leyte Gulf

PHILIPPINES
(1942)

INDIA

BURMA

THAILAND
(SIAM)
(1941)

FRENCH
INDOCHINA
(1941)

MALAYA
(Brit.)

BRUNEI

SARAWAK

BORNEO

CELEBES

DUTCH EAST INDIES

SUMATRA

JAVA

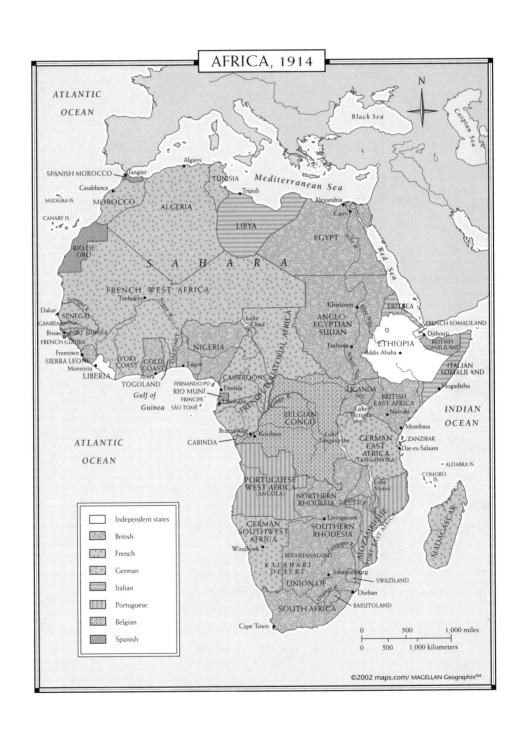

AFRICA, 1914

ATLANTIC OCEAN

Black Sea

Caspian Sea

N

SPANISH MOROCCO
Tangier
Algiers
TUNISIA
Mediterranean Sea
Casablanca
MADEIRA IS.
MOROCCO
ALGERIA
Tripoli
LIBYA
Alexandria
Cairo
EGYPT
Nile R.
Red Sea
CANARY IS.
RIO DE ORO
S A H A R A
FRENCH WEST AFRICA
Timbuktu
Senegal R.
Niger R.
Dakar
SENEGAL
GAMBIA
PORT. GUINEA
Bissau
FRENCH GUINEA
Freetown
SIERRA LEONE
Monrovia
LIBERIA
IVORY COAST
GOLD COAST
Accra
DAHOMEY
TOGOLAND
NIGERIA
Lagos
Lake Chad
Khartoum
Blue Nile
ANGLO-EGYPTIAN SUDAN
Fashoda
White Nile
ERITREA
FRENCH SOMALILAND
Djibouti
ETHIOPIA
Addis Ababa
BRITISH SOMALILAND
ITALIAN SOMALILAND
Mogadishu
Gulf of Guinea
FERNANDO PO
RIO MUNI
PRINCIPE
SÃO TOMÉ
CAMEROONS
Douala
Libreville
FRENCH EQUATORIAL AFRICA
Congo R.
BELGIAN CONGO
UGANDA
Lake Victoria
BRITISH EAST AFRICA
Nairobi
INDIAN OCEAN
Brazzaville
Kinshasa
Lake Tanganyika
GERMAN EAST AFRICA (TANGANYIKA)
Mombasa
ZANZIBAR
Dar-es-Salaam
CABINDA
ATLANTIC OCEAN
ALDABRA IS.
PORTUGUESE WEST AFRICA (ANGOLA)
NORTHERN RHODESIA
Lake Nyasa
COMORO IS.
MADAGASCAR
Zambezi R.
GERMAN SOUTHWEST AFRICA
Windhoek
SOUTHERN RHODESIA
Livingstone
MOZAMBIQUE
PORT. EAST AFRICA
BECHUANALAND
KALAHARI DESERT
Limpopo R.
Johannesburg
SWAZILAND
UNION OF SOUTH AFRICA
Orange R.
Durban
BASUTOLAND
Cape Town

Independent states
British
French
German
Italian
Portuguese
Belgian
Spanish

0   500   1,000 miles
0   500   1,000 kilometers

©2002 maps.com/ MAGELLAN Geographix℠

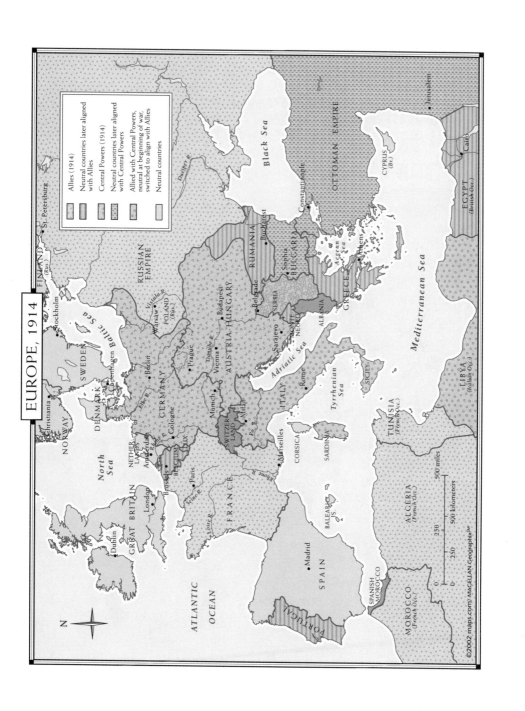

EUROPE, 1914

N

Allies (1914)

Neutral countries later aligned with Allies

Central Powers (1914)

Neutral countries later aligned with Central Powers

Allied with Central Powers, neutral at beginning of war, switched to align with Allies

Neutral countries

ATLANTIC OCEAN

North Sea

Baltic Sea

NORWAY

SWEDEN

DENMARK

Christiania

Stockholm

Copenhagen

FINLAND (Rus.)

St. Petersburg

RUSSIAN EMPIRE

GREAT BRITAIN

Dublin

London

NETHER-LANDS

Amsterdam

Rhine R.

BELGIUM

Brussels

LUX.

Cologne

GERMANY

Berlin

Elbe R.

Warsaw

POLAND (Rus.)

Vistula R.

Dnieper R.

Prague

Munich

Vienna

AUSTRIA-HUNGARY

Budapest

Danube R.

RUMANIA

Bucharest

Black Sea

Paris

FRANCE

Seine R.

Loire R.

Rhône R.

Marseilles

SWITZER-LAND

Milan

Po R.

ITALY

Rome

CORSICA

SARDINIA

Tyrrhenian Sea

SICILY

Adriatic Sea

Sarajevo

Belgrade

SERBIA

MONTE-NEGRO

ALBANIA

BULGARIA

Sophia

GREECE

Athens

Aegean Sea

Constantinople

OTTOMAN EMPIRE

CYPRUS (Br.)

Jerusalem

Cairo

EGYPT (British Occ.)

Mediterranean Sea

SPAIN

Madrid

PORTUGAL

BALEARIC IS.

SPANISH MOROCCO

MOROCCO (French Occ.)

ALGERIA (French Occ.)

TUNISIA (French Occ.)

LIBYA (Italian Occ.)

0   250   500 miles

0   250   500 kilometers

©2002 maps.com/ MAGELLAN Geographix℠

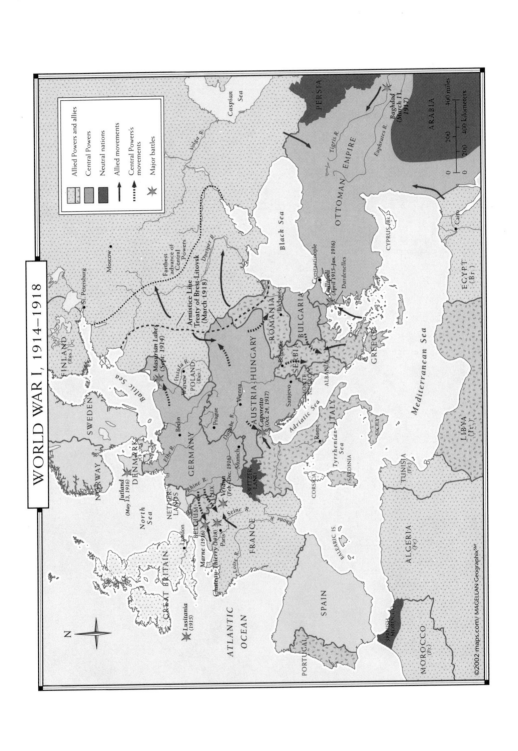

WORLD WAR I, 1914–1918

Allied Powers and allies
Central Powers
Neutral nations
Allied movements
Central Powers's movements
Major battles

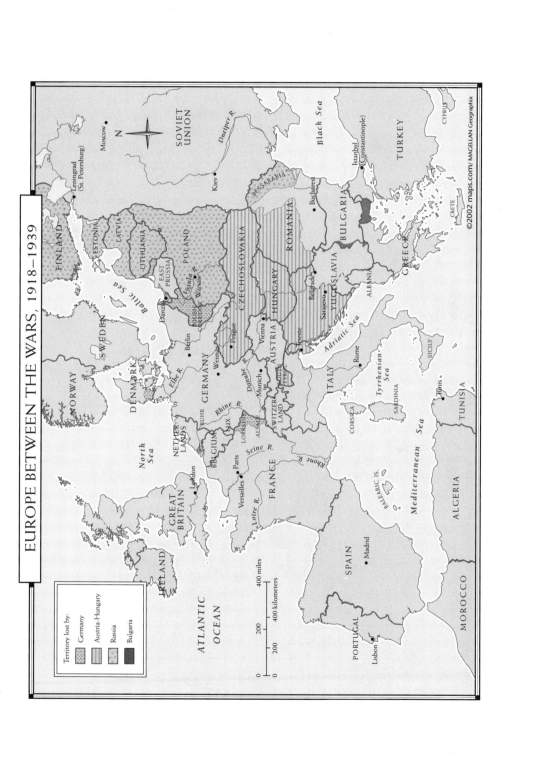

EUROPE BETWEEN THE WARS, 1918–1939

Territory lost by:
Germany
Austria-Hungary
Russia
Bulgaria

©2002 maps.com/ MAGELLAN Geographix

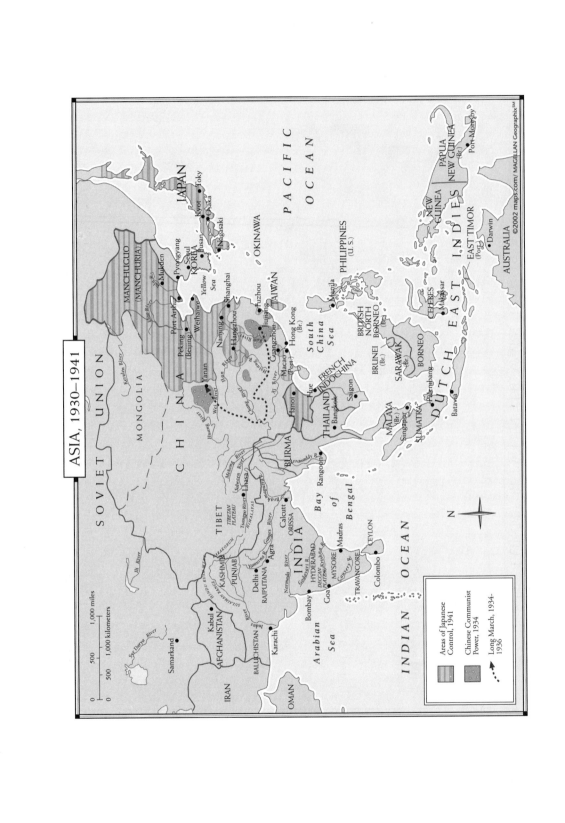

ASIA, 1930–1941

SOVIET UNION

MONGOLIA

MANCHUGUO (MANCHURIA)

CHINA

JAPAN
Tokyo
Kyoto
Osaka
Nagasaki

Pyongyang
Seoul
KOREA
Busan

Mukden
Port Arthur
Peking (Beijing)
Weihaiwei
Tianan
Nanjing
Shanghai
Hangzhou
Fuzhou
Guangzhou
Hong Kong (Br.)
Macao (Port.)

Yellow Sea

TAIWAN

OKINAWA

PACIFIC OCEAN

South China Sea

PHILIPPINES (U.S.)

Manila

NEW GUINEA
PAPUA NEW GUINEA
Port Moresby

©2002 maps.com/ MAGELLAN Geographix℠

FRENCH INDOCHINA
Hue
Hanoi
Saigon

THAILAND
Bangkok

BURMA
Rangoon
Arrawaddy R.

Bay of Bengal

BRITISH NORTH BORNEO (Br.)
BRUNEI (Br.)
SARAWAK (Br.)
BORNEO

CELEBES
Makassar

DUTCH EAST INDIES

MALAYA (Br.)
Singapore
SUMATRA
Palembang
Batavia

EAST TIMOR (Port.)
Darwin

AUSTRALIA

TIBET
TIBETAN PLATEAU
Lhasa
HIMALAYAS

INDIA
Calcutta
ORISSA
HYDERABAD
DECCAN PLATEAU
Madras
MYSORE
Goa
TRAVANCORE
Colombo
CEYLON

KASHMIR
PUNJAB
Delhi
RAJPUTANA
Agra
Bombay

Arabian Sea

INDIAN OCEAN

AFGHANISTAN
Kabul
IRAN
BALUCHISTAN
Karachi
OMAN

Samarkand

N

Areas of Japanese Control, 1941

Chinese Communist Power, 1934

Long March, 1934–1936

0   500   1,000 miles
0   500   1,000 kilometers

WORLD WAR II, EUROPEAN THEATER, 1939–1945

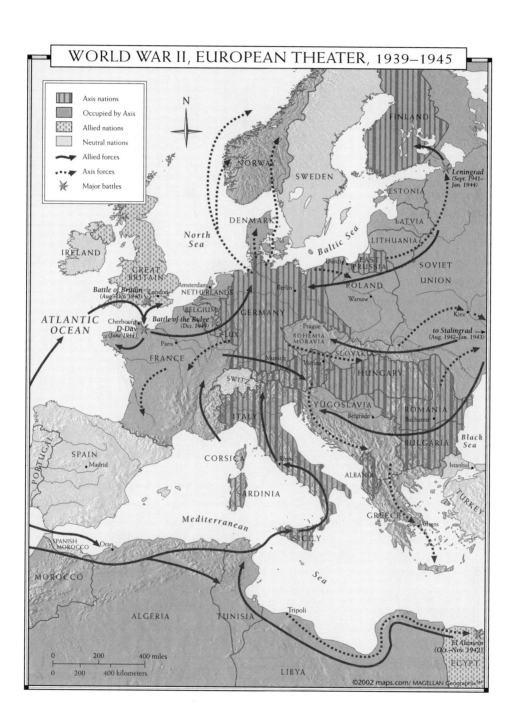

Axis nations
Occupied by Axis
Allied nations
Neutral nations
Allied forces
Axis forces
Major battles

N

FINLAND

NORWAY
SWEDEN
ESTONIA
Leningrad
(Sept. 1941–
Jan. 1944)

DENMARK
Baltic Sea
LATVIA
LITHUANIA

North
Sea
Danzig EAST
PRUSSIA
SOVIET
UNION

IRELAND

GREAT
BRITAIN
Amsterdam
Battle of Britain
(Aug.–Oct. 1940) London
NETHERLANDS
Berlin
POLAND
Warsaw
Kiev

ATLANTIC
OCEAN
BELGIUM
GERMANY
Prague
BOHEMIA
MORAVIA
to Stalingrad
(Aug. 1942–Jan. 1943)

Cherbourg
D-Day
(June 1944)
Battle of the Bulge
(Dec. 1944)
LUX
Paris
Munich
SLOVAKIA
Vienna
HUNGARY

FRANCE
SWITZ.

ITALY
YUGOSLAVIA
Belgrade
ROMANIA
Bucharest

PORTUGAL
SPAIN
Madrid
CORSICA
Rome
BULGARIA
Black
Sea
Istanbul

ALBANIA
SARDINIA

Mediterranean
GREECE
Athens
TURKEY

SPANISH
MOROCCO Oran
SICILY

MOROCCO
Sea

ALGERIA
TUNISIA
Tripoli
El Alamein
(Oct.–Nov. 1942)
EGYPT

LIBYA

0   200   400 miles
0   200   400 kilometers

©2002 maps.com/ MAGELLAN Geographix℠

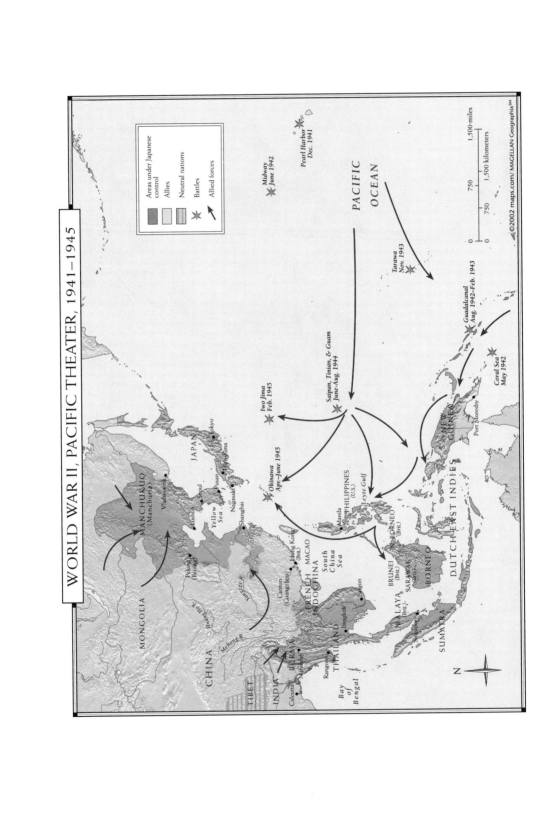

WORLD WAR II, PACIFIC THEATER, 1941–1945

Legend:
- Areas under Japanese control
- Allies
- Neutral nations
- Battles
- Allied forces

©2002 maps.com/ MAGELLAN Geographix℠

MONGOLIA

MANCHUKUO (Manchuria)

CHINA

TIBET

INDIA

Calcutta

BURMA
Mandalay

Rangoon

Bay of Bengal

THAILAND
Bangkok

FRENCH INDOCHINA

Mekong R.

Canton (Guangzhou)

MACAO

Hong Kong (Brit.)

Peking (Beijing)

Yangtze R.

JAPAN

Tokyo

Hiroshima

Nagasaki

Shanghai

Seoul

Pusan

Dairen

Vladivostok

Yellow Sea

South China Sea

Saigon

MALAYA (Brit.)

Singapore

SUMATRA

BRUNEI (Brit.)

SARAWAK (Brit.)

BORNEO (Brit.)

BORNEO

DUTCH EAST INDIES

PHILIPPINES (U.S.)

Manila

Leyte Gulf

NEW GUINEA

Port Moresby

PACIFIC OCEAN

Pearl Harbor
Dec. 1941

Midway
June 1942

Tarawa
Nov. 1943

Guadalcanal
Aug. 1942–Feb. 1943

Coral Sea
May 1942

Saipan, Tinian, & Guam
June–Aug. 1944

Iwo Jima
Feb. 1945

Okinawa
Apr.–June 1945

N

0   750   1,500 miles

0   750   1,500 kilometers

INDEPENDENT STATES TO 1991

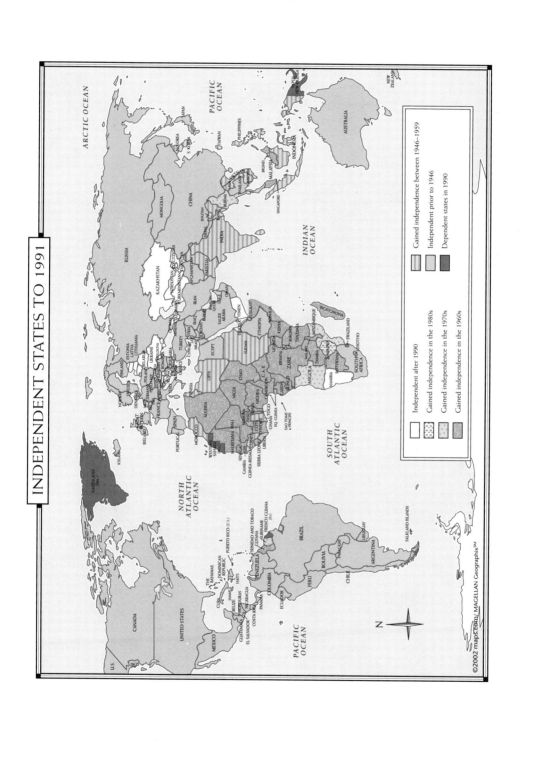

Independent after 1990

Gained independence in the 1980s

Gained independence in the 1970s

Gained independence in the 1960s

Gained independence between 1946–1959

Independent prior to 1946

Dependent states in 1990

©2002 maps.com | MAGELLAN Geographix℠

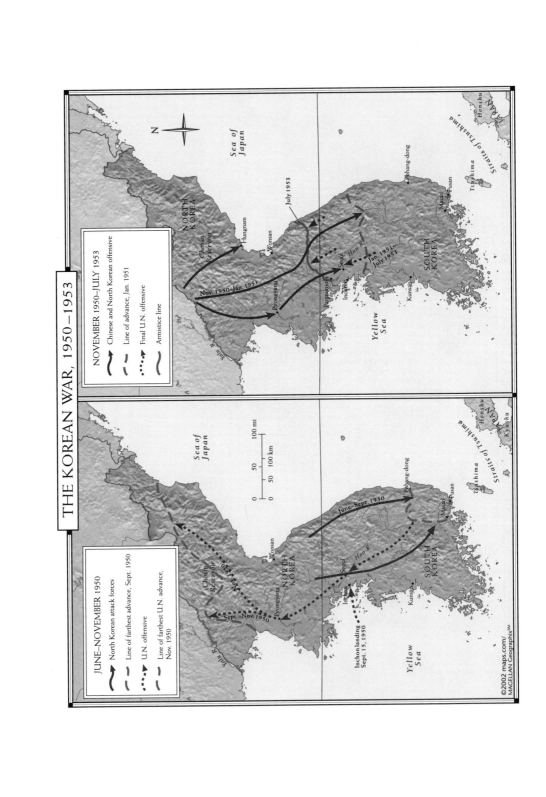

THE KOREAN WAR, 1950–1953

JUNE–NOVEMBER 1950

- North Korean attack forces
- Line of farthest advance, Sept. 1950
- U.N. offensive
- Line of farthest U.N. advance, Nov. 1950

Sea of Japan

Chosin Reservoir

Yalu R.

NORTH KOREA

Wonsan

Pyongyang

Seoul

Han R.

Inchon

Inchon landing
Sept. 15, 1950

Yellow Sea

Kunsan

SOUTH KOREA

Masan

Pusan

Pohang-dong

Sept.–Nov. 1950

June–Sept. 1950

Strait of Tsushima

Tsushima

JAPAN

Honshu

Kyushu

0   50   100 km
0   50   100 mi

©2002 maps.com/
MAGELLAN Geographix℠

NOVEMBER 1950–JULY 1953

- Chinese and North Korean offensive
- Line of advance, Jan. 1951
- Final U.N. offensive
- Armistice line

N

Sea of Japan

NORTH KOREA

Chosin Reservoir

Hungnam

Wonsan

Yalu R.

Nov. 1950–Jan. 1951

Pyongyang

Pyongyang

Inchon

Seoul

Han R.

July 1953

Jan. 1951–
July 1953

SOUTH KOREA

Kunsan

Pohang-dong

Masan

Pusan

Yellow Sea

Strait of Tsushima

Tsushima

JAPAN

Honshu

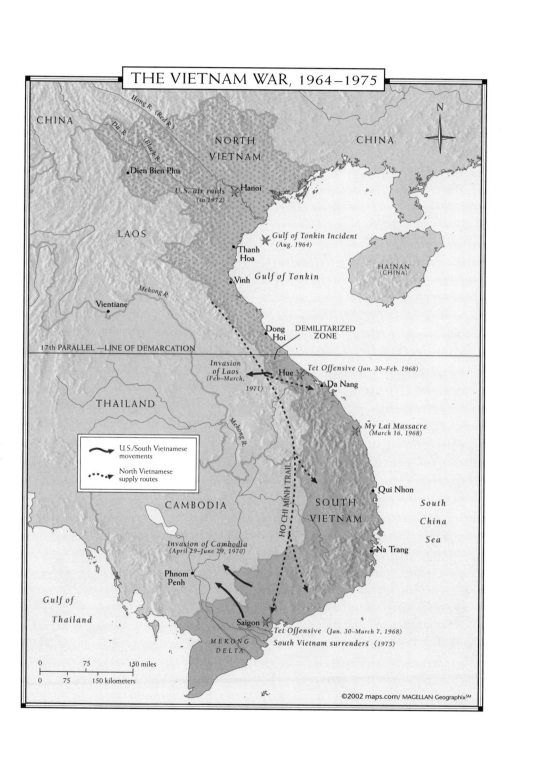

THE VIETNAM WAR, 1964–1975

CHINA

Hong R. (Red R.)

Da R.

Black R.

NORTH
VIETNAM

CHINA

Dien Bien Phu

U.S. air raids
(to 1972)

Hanoi

LAOS

Gulf of Tonkin Incident
(Aug. 1964)

Thanh
Hoa

Vinh Gulf of Tonkin

HAINAN
(CHINA)

Mekong R.

Vientiane

Dong
Hoi

DEMILITARIZED
ZONE

17th PARALLEL —LINE OF DEMARCATION

Invasion
of Laos
(Feb–March,
1971)

Hue

Tet Offensive (Jan. 30–Feb. 1968)

Da Nang

THAILAND

Mekong R.

My Lai Massacre
(March 16, 1968)

U.S./South Vietnamese
movements

North Vietnamese
supply routes

Qui Nhon

South

CAMBODIA

SOUTH
VIETNAM

China

Invasion of Cambodia
(April 29–June 29, 1970)

Sea

Phnom
Penh

HO CHI MINH TRAIL

Na Trang

Gulf of

Thailand

Saigon

Tet Offensive (Jan. 30–March 7, 1968)

South Vietnam surrenders (1975)

MEKONG
DELTA

N

0   75   150 miles

0   75   150 kilometers

©2002 maps.com/ MAGELLAN Geographix℠

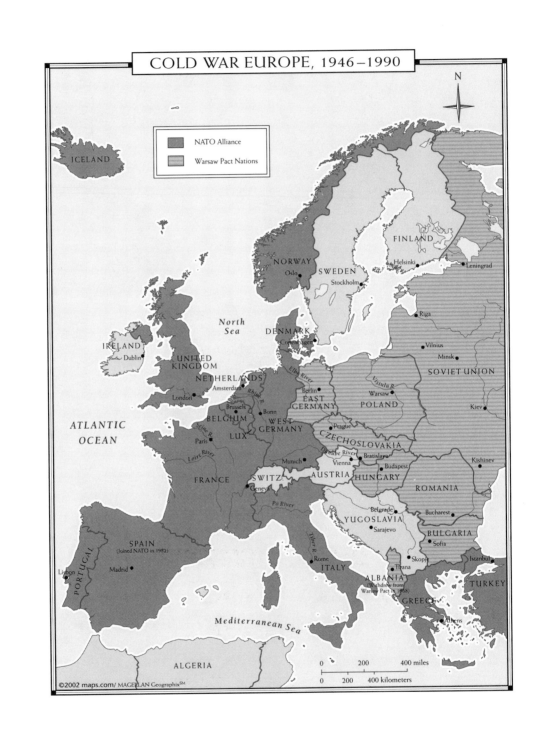

COLD WAR EUROPE, 1946–1990

N

ICELAND

NATO Alliance

Warsaw Pact Nations

NORWAY
Oslo
SWEDEN
Stockholm

FINLAND
Helsinki
Leningrad

North Sea

DENMARK
Copenhagen

Riga

IRELAND
Dublin

UNITED KINGDOM

Vilnius
Minsk

SOVIET UNION

NETHERLANDS
Amsterdam
Elbe River

Berlin
EAST GERMANY

Vistula R.
Warsaw
POLAND

Kiev

London
Brussels
BELGIUM
Rhine
Bonn
WEST GERMANY

ATLANTIC OCEAN

Seine R.
Paris
LUX

Prague
CZECHOSLOVAKIA
Bratislava

Kishinev

Loire River

Munich
Danube River
Vienna
AUSTRIA
HUNGARY
Budapest

ROMANIA

FRANCE
SWITZ.
Geneva

Belgrade
Bucharest

Po River
YUGOSLAVIA
Sarajevo

BULGARIA
Sofia

SPAIN
(Joined NATO in 1982)

Tiber R.
Rome
ITALY

Skopje
Tirana
Istanbul

PORTUGAL
Lisbon
Madrid

ALBANIA
(Withdrew from Warsaw Pact in 1968)

TURKEY

GREECE
Athens

Mediterranean Sea

ALGERIA

| 0 | 200 | 400 miles |
| 0 | 200 | 400 kilometers |

©2002 maps.com/ MAGELLAN Geographix℠

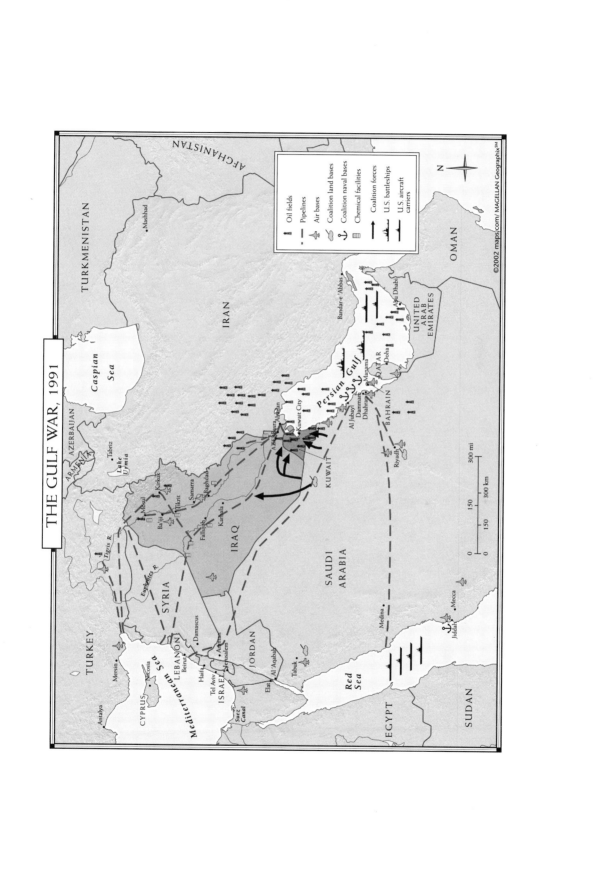

THE GULF WAR, 1991

Legend:
- Oil fields
- Pipelines
- Air bases
- Coalition land bases
- Coalition naval bases
- Chemical facilities
- Coalition forces
- U.S. battleships
- U.S. aircraft carriers

©2002 maps.com/ MAGELLAN Geographix℠

Scale: 0 — 150 — 300 km; 0 — 150 — 300 mi

N

A

abatement. A legal justification for forceful *intervention* by an outside power, or by a regional organization, in what are otherwise considered the *internal affairs* of a neighboring country. Abatement is derived logically and morally from the sole universally accepted justification for the use of force by states: *self-defense*. Abatement amounts to the claim that political or civil unrest or *civil war* (or, more recently, gross and persistent *human rights* abuses) in one state compels military intercession by outsiders to abate an intolerable nuisance caused by a spillover of the unrest, fighting, or refugees into bordering states. Often, claims of a legal right and necessity to abatement are made when national or regional stability is threatened by warfare that spills into neighboring states in the form of *hot pursuit* of fleeing *guerrillas* or when guerrillas take unauthorized refuge or establish military bases across a poorly defended or isolated frontier. The right to abatement also may be invoked in response to financial burdens imposed by massive inflows of refugees fleeing *genocide* or civil war or some other severe economic or political dislocation.

For example, India claimed a need to staunch the inflow of nearly ten million refugees from East Pakistan as justification for its intervention against West Pakistani forces in 1971. Similarly, *NATO* asserted a need to abate *ethnic cleansing* in *Kosovo* when it intervened there in 1999. This claim is, of course, subject to abuse, as when cited as a humbug self-absolution by larger powers when outright aggressing against a smaller neighbor. Two of the most naked examples of such abuse are (1) in 1932 when Japan cited a need to abate violent unrest in Manchuria as justification for its planned invasion of that territory; and (2) in 1939 when the Soviet Union cynically employed the doctrine to justify its invasion of eastern Poland, an act of naked *aggression* flowing from a secret protocol attached to the *Nazi-Soviet Pact*. In public, Moscow asserted that the prior German invasion had created an intolerable situation along its Polish border that required it to intervene, and it promptly did so. More traditionally, the United States has frequently invoked the doctrine of abatement, as in justification of its 1837 cross-border intervention into Canada during the *Caroline Affair*. This claim also attended U.S. intervention in Cuba in 1898; U.S. intervention in Nicaragua in 1909 and subsequently; and the U.S. and Organization of Eastern Caribbean States' *invasion of Grenada* in 1983. *See also armed humanitarian intervention; nonintervention.*

Abbasid Caliphate (750–1258). *See caliph.*

ABC weapons. *See discrete entries on* atomic, biological, *and* chemical weapons, *and* weapons of mass destruction.

Abd al-Aziz ibn Saud (1880–1953). King of Arabia, 1926–1953; founder of Saudi Arabia. He waged a rebellion against Turkish rule, 1901–1915, at the head of the *fundamentalist* sect the *Wahhabi*. He captured Riyadh in 1902. Out of rivalry with *Ibn Ali Hussein* he refused to join *T. E. Lawrence* and the *Arab Revolt*. After *World War I* he again fought against, and defeated, Hussein and other Arab leaders. He invaded the *Hejaz*, 1924–1925, capturing Mecca. He installed the Saud dynasty in Arabia in 1926, becoming king in 1932 (he was *recognized* as King of the Hejaz by Britain in 1927, when he made peace with the *Hashemites*). He oversaw the first *oil* deals with the *West* in the 1930s. He was loyal to the *Allies* in *World War II*.

Abdul Hamid II (1842–1918). Sultan of the *Ottoman Empire*, 1876–1909. He ruled during a period of agonizing decline during which most of Turkey's European territories were stripped away to become independent, under Russian and Austrian pressure. Massacres of some 12,000 Christian Bulgarians by his troops in 1876 roused Europe in opposition, especially *Gladstone*. Hamid was compelled by the *Young Turks* to restore the Imperial constitution of 1876, as the price of his ascension, and to expand representation in the political structures of the empire. In 1878 he was forced to concede independence to Serbia, Montenegro, and Romania and to accept Austrian occupation of Bosnia and Herzegovina. That same year, he suspended the constitution and tried to rule as an *autocrat*. He also reclaimed the title *caliph*, and pandered to his Muslim subjects at the expense of non-Muslims. He probably went so far as to help organize the first *Armenian genocide* in 1895–1896. Still, he enjoyed British support for most of his reign, as London saw his tottering empire as a counterweight to Russian expansion in Central Asia. In fact, this was an illusion, and Hamid mostly presided over decay and decline. In 1908 he was forced to restore the constitution. He attempted a countercoup the next year and was deposed. *See also Atatürk.*

Abkhazia. For more than 1,000 years this region has been joined to Georgia, in some form or other, sharing Georgia's trials under the *Mongols, Tamerlane,* the *Ottoman Empire* and, from 1849, the *Russian Empire.* When Georgia achieved *independence* after the breakup of the *Soviet Union* in 1991, this northwest region attempted *secession,* provoking a *civil war.* The local assembly asked Russia to declare Abkhazia a *protectorate* or *annex* it. In 1993 Russian troops entered as ostensible peacekeepers, but it soon became clear that Moscow was secretly aiding the rebels. *Eduard Shevardnadze* asked for Western help, but by the fall Abkhazia had broken away from effective Georgian control, and most ethnic Georgians were *ethnically cleansed.* An uneasy peace developed when Georgia acceded to a long-term Russian military presence on its internal border with Abkhazia. Russia's interest was access to Abkhazia's strategic Black Sea coastline, a military base, and political leverage over Georgia.

ABM. *See anti–ballistic missile, missile system.*

aboriginal. Issues of social, economic (often concerning land use), cultural, or other concerns that pertain (1) to the *indigenous peoples* of any country; or (2) to the indigenous people of Australia and Tasmania. *See also Aborigines; restitution.*

Aborigines. The original inhabitants of Australia and Tasmania. They arrived in Australia perhaps as long ago as 40,000 years (or even much longer; the evidence is not yet clear), probably from Southeast Asia or Polynesia. They remained primarily hunter-gatherers into modern times and thus were a stateless and widely scattered people when the first Europeans sighted the southern continent. The Aborigines came into extended conflict with white settlers (and law, government, and soldiers) as the latter penetrated Australia's interior continent over the course of the nineteenth century. One-sided warfare meant that many Aborigines died in lopsided battles or outright massacres, though more died of disease imported along with white colonists. The Aborigines of Tasmania were wiped out entirely by 1888. Like most North American Indian tribes, Australian Aborigines were forced onto isolated back-country reserves, a process underway into the 1930s. A generation of Aborigine children was seized from parents by the state and placed with white families in a misguided and ultimately failed attempt at cultural (if not racial) *assimilation.* Aborigines were not granted Australian citizenship until 1948. *Robert Menzies* ensured that they made little social progress into the 1960s. By the 1990s, however, an Aboriginal rights movement was well organized in search of an *apology*, and compensation, for historic wrongs done by the Australian state.

abrogation. Formal nullification of a binding legal commitment between or among states. *See also treaty.*

absentee government. *See government-in-exile.*

absolute advantage. When one state or firm can supply goods or services below the cost of its competitors. *See also comparative advantage; competitive advantage.*

absolute monarch. A *sovereign* unlimited by secular laws or a constitution. *See also absolutism.*

absolute responsibility. The legal doctrine that a state may be held accountable to make amends for harm done to some party, even without being directly guilty of a harmful action that would require payment of *damages*. *See also culpability.*

absolute right. Any international legal right that is held without impediment or restriction.

absolute war. *See Clausewitz; total war.*

absolutism. Unrestrained authority in government—especially of a *sovereign*—but loosely applicable to any tyrannical or *totalitarian* political system. In the heyday of European *state creation*, from the *Protestant Reformation* and the *Peace of Westphalia* to the *Enlightenment*, its legitimizing purpose was domestic political integration under secular authority. After a brief transition period of *enlightened despotism*, absolutism as a basis for political *legitimacy* was displaced by the idea of *popular sovereignty*, starting with the *American Revolution* and, especially, the *French Revolution*. In the seventeenth and eighteenth centuries in continental Europe, *mercantilism* (state monopoly control of all trade and the economy) was absolutism's economic analogue. *See also Akbar; Alexander II; Aurangzeb; Bourbons; Byzantine Empire; Julius Caesar; caliphate; Catherine the Great; Cixi; Frederick the Great; Habsburgs; Hideyoshi; Hirohito; Hongwu; Ivan the Terrible; Justinian; Vladimir Lenin; Louis XIV; Manchus; Mao; mandate of heaven; Mongols; Napoleon I; Nicholas I; Nobunaga Oda; Peter the Great; Roman Empire; Stalin; Tamerlane; Tokugawa Ieyasu; Wanli.*
   Suggested Reading: Paul Monod, *The Power of Kings* (1999).

Abukir Bay, Battle of (August 1, 1798). "Battle of the Nile." British Admiral *Horatio Nelson* tried to intercept the great fleet that carried *Napoleon I* and a French army to Egypt, but he missed it en route. After the French Army disembarked, Nelson located the fleet at idle anchor outside Alexandria and destroyed it. The immediate results of this victory were to cut off Napoleon's army from resupply or return to France and, more importantly, to encourage France's many enemies to join the *War of the Second Coalition*. Longer term, the loss of his fleet bedeviled Napoleon's career and hamstrung his *grand strategy*. The naval superiority achieved by England at Abukir Bay was confirmed and deepened at *Trafalgar*. These twin blows to French naval power allowed Britain to dominate global commerce outside Europe and meant that Napoleon could not invade England, which was free to underwrite a succession of anti-French alliances until final victory over France in 1815.

abuse of rights. An international legal doctrine in which unreasonable exercise of an otherwise legal right may amount to an *illegal act*.

Abwehr. German military intelligence under the *Nazi* regime. During *World War II*, it was headed by Admiral *Wilhelm Canaris*, who used it in part to protect anti-Nazi resisters. Several Abwehr officers were involved in plots against *Hitler*, including the *July Plot* of 1944. That brought the Abwehr under deep suspicion and it was ordered dissolved by *Himmler*, an insatiable personal empire-builder, who absorbed its functions and officers into his *Sicherheitsdienst*.

Abyssinia. The ancient name of Ethiopia, in general disuse after 1945.

Abyssinian War, First (1895–1896). Starting in the 1880s, Italy pressed claims against Abyssinia (Ethiopia) from Italy's base in *Eritrea*, in hopes of linking that northern *protectorate* with their colony of *Italian Somaliland*. In 1889 Abyssinia signed the Treaty of Wichale with Italy, demarcating its border with Eritrea. Italy then asserted that this constituted acceptance by Abyssinia of *protectorate* status, a claim vehemently rejected by Addis Ababa, which saw it more as a mere *friendship treaty*. The dispute led to war in 1895. Abyssinian forces, under Menelik II (c. 1834–1913), decisively defeated an invading army of Italian regulars and colonial troops, at *Adowa* (March 1, 1896). This humiliating loss badly damaged Italy's *prestige*. In the Treaty of Addis Ababa, which followed on October 26, 1896, a somewhat humbled but unrepentant Italy begrudgingly *recognized* Abyssinian independence. Its planned conquest of Ethiopia was thus postponed, until in 1935 *Mussolini* again sent in an invading army. In the interim, Ethiopia not only survived the *scramble for Africa*, it hurried to participate, conquering historically Ethiopian lands to the east and south that had long since been lost to invading Muslims and various Oromo peoples—Galla, Somali, and Dankali nomadic pastoralists.

Abyssinian War, Second (1935–1936). During the early 1930s, from its bases in *Eritrea* and *Italian Somaliland*, Italy progressively encroached on Abyssinian territory along a disputed *frontier* in the *Ogaden*. A border skirmish between Ethiopian and Italian troops occurred at Wal Wal on December 5, 1934. For ten months, tensions built. Britain tried to appease Rome by offering it a strip of Ethiopian land. Italy wanted more, including erasing the shame of *Adowa*, and invaded Ethiopia in October 1935. Italian technological superiority, notably in aircraft and *armor*, and use of illicit *poison gas*, overcame more lightly armed Ethiopian troops. The *Hoare-Laval Pact* (1935) was a hasty attempt to appease Italy at Ethiopia's expense, but it failed. The *League of Nations* denounced Italy as an *aggressor*, but then authorized only limited *sanctions*, specifically excluding *oil* and steel, because Britain and France feared pushing *Mussolini* into an alliance with *Hitler*. In fact, this weak response further discredited the League and its proposed instrument of *collective security*. As one result, Hitler concluded that the West was feeble, speeded his *rearmament* program, and moved more quickly to overturn the international order established by the *Treaty of Versailles*. And Mussolini moved to join him, despite Anglo-French efforts at *appeasement*. When Addis Ababa fell on May 5, 1936, Italy finally possessed the enlarged East African empire it had long coveted, but not for long. Ethiopia was liberated from Italian occupation by British and Ethiopian troops early in *World War II*.

Suggested Readings: G. Baer, *Test Case* (1976); F. Hardie, *The Abyssinian Crisis* (1974).

Acadia. A former French colony spanning what is today much of maritime eastern Canada and parts of Maine. Acadia was first settled by French colonists in 1604. England took control of much of the region after its victory in the *War of the Spanish Succession*, in the *Peace of Utrecht* (1713).When English control was completed in the 1750s, during the *French and Indian War*, most Acadians were summarily expelled (1755 and 1758). After much hardship and death, surviving refugees settled in the *Louisiana* territory (their descendants still live in the rump American state of that name, where the self-referential Cajun is a corruption of the original Acadian). Others longed to return to Acadia, and a few later did so, resettling in what became Canada's maritime provinces in an area still informally called "Acadia." *See also King George's War; King William's War.*

accession. (1) When a state adheres to an already existing *treaty*, which requires prior *consent* of all other *treaty powers*. (2) Taking title to *territory* or political authority. (3) When a *sovereign* legally takes the reigns of power, upon the death or other passage out of power of the previous sovereign. *See also adherence.*

accidental war. (1) The possibility that complex, computer-operated missile and other weapons systems might malfunction and launch an attack that starts a war, without human intention and beyond human control. (2) The idea that war can occur without deliberate choice or action taken by any one decision maker, through mistakes of *perception* as a crisis escalates out of control or through a technical or communications failure. Given the pace of modern events, and the delivery speed and destructiveness of modern weapons, states have become more aware of the need to develop means to reduce the risk of accidental war, particularly among the *Great Powers* and pairings of *nuclear powers.* They have greatly improved communications by setting up direct and secure lines of access among the highest levels of decision makers, and they have developed a wide range of *confidence and security building measures* (CSBMs), though these vary by region and effectiveness. Such measures are intended to provide advance notice of military *maneuvers,* permit direct access by outside observers, provide for inspection of weapons' manufacturing and development facilities to reduce the fear of being caught by surprise by rapid deployment of some new and possibly decisive weapon, and generally aim to reduce tension and elevate trust in relationships that are otherwise less than cordial. Even so, the underlying causes of tension and conflict in many interstate relationships are not addressed by such measures and can still lead to misunderstandings that trigger accidental wars. *See also agent; crisis management; hot line; preventive diplomacy.*

accommodation. (1) In *diplomacy,* and plain English, arriving at a compromise agreement. (2) In *crisis management* theory, *jargon* for a strategy by which a *crisis* is defused by striking limited agreements, which ease the immediate threat of war even though they leave basic issues unresolved. *See also appeasement.*

accord. An agreement between, or among, states. When formal and legally binding, "accord" is simply a synonym for *treaty.*

accretion. Whenever new *territory* is formed by forces of nature, such as spreading alluvial deposits in a river delta or creating an island by oceanic vulcanism, under *international law* it accrues to the state to whose territory it is physically connected, or within whose *territorial sea* it rests. *See also avulsion; thalweg.*

ace. By a convention dating to *World War I,* a fighter pilot with at least five confirmed kills of enemy aircraft. In that war, the greatest German ace was Baron Manfred von Richthofen (the "Red Baron"), with 82 confirmed kills. The top *Allied* fighter pilot was a Canadian, Billy Bishop, with 72 confirmed kills. During *World War II,* the *Luftwaffe* claimed to have hosted more than 3,000 aces, nine of which claimed more than 200 kills each, with two more claiming 301 and 352 victories, respectively. The greatest Allied ace of the war was a Soviet pilot, who attained 62 confirmed kills.

Aceh. An *Islamic* sultanate, independent for 400 years on Sumatra. It was conquered by the Dutch in 1903, after a protracted war. It was incorporated into *Indonesia* after *World War II*. Achenese fought a *guerrilla* campaign against Indonesia rule, c. 1950–1960. In the late 1990s, violence and agitation for independence broke out again.

Acheson, Dean (1893–1971). Assistant U.S. secretary of state, 1941–1945; undersecretary to *George Marshall*, 1945–1947; secretary of state under *Harry Truman*, 1949–1953. Acheson joined the *Department of State* in 1941, at an entry level of central influence. He participated in the Bretton Woods conference in 1944. Acheson helped frame such key policies of the early *Cold War* as the *Marshall Plan*, *containment*, the *Truman Doctrine*, creation of the *North Atlantic Treaty Organization (NATO)*, and U.S. support for Nationalist China after the *Chinese Revolution* (1949). He was instrumental in setting up the *Bretton Woods* international economic system, and he directed postwar economic recovery. He has been heavily criticized for misleading statements about the degree of U.S. support for South Korea, remarks said by some scholars to have failed to discourage North Korea's *aggression*. He vigorously defended the State Department, and—courageously, honorably, but almost certainly also wrongly—his aide *Alger Hiss* from charges of *treason* and being a *Communist* spy. Acheson became a principal target of the worst sort of unprincipled *McCarthyism*—he was called by the hysterically ignorant the "Red Dean." He remained influential behind the scenes until the end of his life, as one of the so-called *Wise Men* of American foreign policy. After the *Tet Offensive*, he advised *Johnson* to pull out of Vietnam. His memoir, *Present at the Creation* (1969), won a Pulitzer Prize.
    Suggested Readings: James Chase, *Acheson* (1998); Gaddis Smith, *Dean Acheson* (1972).

acid rain. High acidic content in rain, caused naturally by volcanoes and artificially by certain industrial pollutants. It can have a devastating impact on flora and fauna. It became a subject of increasing interstate negotiation starting in the 1970s, such as between Canada and the United States, as pollutants crossing international boundaries were seen to transfer the costs of cleanup and recovery from the polluter to neighboring states.

ACP Nations. African, Caribbean, and Pacific states linked to the *European Union* by the *Lomé Conventions*.

acquiescence. When *tacit consent* is inferred from a state's silence on a given matter. *See also consent.*

acquired immune deficiency syndrome (AIDS). A communicable disease medically identified in the early 1980s, though it had been incubating unnoticed for decades before that. In the West it was originally and largely confined to homosexual, hemophiliac, and intravenous drug-using populations, but later made inroads into the general population. Elsewhere, especially in Haiti and sub-Saharan Africa, it infected mainly majority heterosexual populations as a result of poverty, the social dislocation and ravages of multiple wars and their attendant effects of reduced resistance to disease, widespread rape, unprotected prostitution, and because of cultural attitudes resistant to safe sex practices. The *World Health Organization* documented that the majority of cases in the 1990s were in Africa. However, by 2000, AIDS was spreading most rapidly in Asia. After the worldwide influenza of 1919–1920, which killed perhaps 40 million people, AIDS was the greatest global epidemic of the twentieth century, infecting tens of millions of people, mostly in less developed countries. By 2000, 40 percent of people globally with AIDS were children. The epidemic placed strain on the medical systems of most advanced countries, pulling treatment and research dollars away from diseases, which killed many more per capita. AIDS utterly overwhelmed less mature national medical systems in African and other less developed nations. *See also Black Death.*

acquis communautaires. *See deepening vs. widening.*

acquisitive prescription. When legal title to a given *territory* is conceded as a result of its long-term *occupation.*

acta jure gestionis. *See* jus gestionis.

acta jure imperii. *See* jus imperii.

Action Françaises. Founded in 1899 by Charles Maurras (1868–1952) during the *Dreyfus affair*, this extreme *anti-Semitic* organization helped undermine French *national morale* before *World War II*, contributed to the general mood of *defeatism*, and was a mainstay of the *Vichy* regime. *See also fascism.*

action-reaction models. Social science *jargon* for the prosaic—indeed pedestrian—idea, that in politics actions taken by one side call forth reactions from the other. *See also billiard ball model; decision-making theory; game theory; security dilemma.*

active defense. Interception and destruction of enemy forces or weapons before they reach their targets.

active measures. An *intelligence* euphemism for direct action taken to influence events abroad, as opposed to merely gathering information. This may include *assassination*, bribery, *disinformation*, funding political parties or *guerrillas*, and *propaganda*. *See also agent of influence; penetration agent.*

act of state doctrine. Under *international law*, a doctrine denying to municipal courts *jurisdiction* on the legality of acts taken by a foreign power in accordance with the *municipal law* of that foreign power. Thus, states will not usually (legally) permit their courts to hear cases or rule on the merits or validity of foreign laws or on acts by another state taken in accordance with such foreign laws. *See also conflict of laws.*

Act of Union. (1) 1707: An act of Parliament joined Scotland to England, completing a process begun with union of the crowns in 1603 by abolishing the Scottish parliament and naming the combined country *Great Britain*. It also provided for English payment of Scotland's large debt and established *free trade* between England and Scotland. (2) January 1, 1801: The act of Parliament (in London, passed in 1800) by which Ireland was joined to Great Britain, thereby losing its separate Parliament and immediately raising the stakes of the issue of *Catholic emancipation* within Britain. It followed the rising of the *United Irishmen*. Ireland sat 28 Peers and 100 in the House of Commons. *Pitt* pushed it through Parliament, but was unable to obtain Catholic emancipation as hoped and promised, given strong opposition by *George III*. In any case, many Irish never reconciled to what they always regarded as an unnatural act.

act of war. (1) An act of *aggression* constituting a *casus belli*. (2) Any act defined as warlike by the *laws of war*. *See also* casus foederis; jus ad bellum; *just war tradition.*

Acton, Lord, né John (1834–1902). Member of Parliament for Carlow (Ireland); regius chair in modern history at Cambridge University; friend of *Gladstone*, who made him a lord; and incisive student of *power politics*. A Roman Catholic, Acton in 1870 observed firsthand the *Vatican Council*, against which he encouraged secular intervention to forestall the pronouncement of papal infallibility. His most pithy and widely quoted observation, from a personal letter, reads: "power tends to corrupt, and absolute power corrupts absolutely." He said about the ideal of *objectivity* in recording and interpreting facts: "Truth is the only merit that gives dignity to history." On theoretical abstractions, which soon became the bane of modern social science, he wrote: "Writers the most learned, the most accurate in details, and the soundest in tendency frequently fall into a habit which can neither be cured nor pardoned . . . making history into the proof of their theories." *See also* liberté, égalité, fraternité.
Suggested Reading: Roland Hill, *Lord Acton* (2000).

actor. Social science parlance for virtually any player in *international politics*. These are most often *states*, but may be *nonstate actors* such as key *decision makers, ethnic groups, multinational corporations/enterprises*, or *nongovernmental organizations* involved with specific issues of policy or world affairs.

Adams, John (1735–1826). *Federalist* president of the United States, 1797–1801. As a diplomat in Europe during the *American Revolution*, he helped secure financing and alliances that ensured victory for the colonials. He was one of three American commissioners who negotiated the *Treaty of Paris* (1783). After the war, he served with distinction as the first U.S. minister (ambassador) to London. As president, Adams continued *George Washington's* policy of *neutrality*, but also built up the navy to enforce claims to *neutral rights*. Adams was an early opponent of the excesses of the *French Revolution*, and his election was viewed with hostility by the French *Directory*. Along with the *XYZ Affair*, his policy almost brought the United States and France to open war and did lead to the unofficial *Quasi War*. By 1798 the U.S. Navy was persevering against the French, but the main factor securing peace was *Napoleon's* and *Talleyrand's* lack of desire for war and Adams' flexibility and leadership in arranging for peace. Of New England Puritan stock, Adams was irascible and contentious, but scrupulously honest—unlike his successor and bitter political rival, but also his once-and-future friend, *Thomas Jefferson*, whom he had defeated for the presidency in 1796. Jefferson would let the wooden navy that Adams built literally rot in port, for which a high price would be paid against the *Barbary States* and during the *War of 1812*. And again unlike Adams, Jefferson would imprudently set the United States back on a course toward war with the European powers. They both died on July 4, 1826, the 50th anniversary of the Declaration of Independence.

Suggested Reading: David McCullough, *John Adams* (2001).

Adams, John Quincy (1767–1848). Son of *John Adams*; secretary of state, 1817–1824; *Democratic-Republican* president, 1824–1828. He served as a diplomat at various levels in The Hague, Berlin, St. Petersburg, and London, 1794–1802 and 1808–1817, rising to minister (ambassador) at a remarkably young age. He was part of the team that negotiated the *Treaty of Ghent*, ending the *War of 1812*. He drafted the *Monroe Doctrine* and negotiated the transfer of the Floridas from Spain in the *Adams-Onis Treaty* (1819). As president, he sought but failed to obtain concessions from Britain concerning trade with the West Indies. Despite intense personal opposition to *slavery*, he upheld American claims to *neutral rights* against British demands to search U.S. ships that might be transporting slaves. He is usually listed among the most successful secretaries of state, though not presidents, and acknowledged along with *Washington* as framer of the *realist* tradition in American foreign policy. In decrying U.S. *intervention* on behalf of abstract principle, he affirmed early, but not unreasonable, *isolationist* sentiments with a famous admonition that America "goes not abroad, in search of monsters to destroy." His final years were spent as an elected representative in Congress, untiringly fighting to slay the domestic monster of slavery.

Suggested Readings: Samuel Flagg Bemis, *John Quincy Adams and the Foundations of American Foreign Policy* (1949; 1973); Lynn Parsons, *John Quincy Adams* (1998).

Adams-Onis Treaty (1819). *John Quincy Adams* and Ambassador Dom Louis de Onis of Spain agreed to set a formal *boundary* between the United States and *Spanish America* from the Floridas to the Pacific. Adams thus acquired for the United States the East Florida panhandle, West Florida (southern Mississippi, Alabama and Georgia), and the *Oregon Territory*. He gave up only a vague claim to *Texas*, which the United States would later revive anyway. The agreement is also known as the Floridas Treaty and as the Transcontinental Treaty.

Aden. A key port in the Indian Ocean trade. It maintained an independent trade with Kilwa on the Sofala coast of East Africa during the thirteenth through fifteenth centuries. In 1538 Aden was captured by the Ottomans. As Ottoman power declined, British power grew: Aden was *annexed* by Britain in 1833, as a coaling station for the Red Sea trade with Suez, which then linked overland to the Mediterranean. Aden was made a *Crown Colony* in 1937. It became a *protectorate* when London combined several minor *sheikdoms* with the port, but also suddenly (and some say, shamefully) abandoned its security commitment to Aden in November 1967. Aden was later absorbed by the *Marxist-Leninist* state of South Yemen.

Adenauer, Konrad (1876–1967). Mayor of Cologne, 1917–1933; West German chancellor, 1949–1963. In 1933 he was removed from public office by the *Nazis*. He was arrested during the *Night of the Long Knives* but later released. He was arrested a second time after the *July Plot*, but survived until liberated by the American Army. He was reinstated as mayor by the Americans, but dismissed later by the British. After Germany's surrender, he founded and became leader of the *Christian Democratic Union* and in time the first West German chancellor. He worked with the United States and with other Western European countries to rebuild and rehabilitate *West Germany*— for example, by agreeing in 1952 to *reparation* and *restitution* payments to Israel for the *genocide* of Germany's Jews during the *Holocaust*—leading it to full acceptance with its entry into the *North Atlantic Treaty Organization (NATO)* in 1955. This policy was not popular among all Germans, as it required acquiescence to the de facto division of the country. Nevertheless, Adenauer continued to embrace the Western alliance. He agreed to the *Schuman Plan*, Franco-German cooperation, and worked toward European federalism. Under his leadership, West Germany recovered rapidly and became the locomotive of European recovery and prosperity.

As Adenauer foresaw, West Germany was soon a bulwark against Soviet political influence and exerted a magnetic attraction for moribund eastern economies and societies. That reality was dramatized by *East Germany*'s construction of the *Berlin Wall* a year before Adenauer's retirement. Adenauer's greatness lay in dismissing the *Realpolitik* maxim that there could be no permanent friendships among nations, but only a fleeting coincidence of interests. The Kaiserine and Nazi idea that Germany could be at the same time powerful and isolated, he thought, had been a great delusion, which led Germany to utter disaster and national division. Instead, he strove to link Germany with a wider democratic and economic community by economic cooperation, while using rearmament within NATO's commitment to European peace and security to reassert German legitimacy. Thereby, this astute chancellor cemented his own mastery of Germany, secured its commitment to democracy, and provided for its rapid rehabilitation and effective defense.

adherence. Acceptance of a *treaty* by states additional to the original signatories, but with the latter's express *consent*.

***ad hoc* chambers.** *See chambers of the Court.*

adjudication. The settlement of (almost always) nonvital *disputes* through voluntary submission by all parties to a binding judicial decision. *See also arbitration; compulsory jurisdiction; justiciable dispute; limited jurisdiction; mediation; nonjusticiable dispute; political dispute; vital interests.*

adjustment. The way governments use saving, production, and expenditures to correct deficits in *current accounts* and stabilize their *balance of payments*. *See also structural adjustment.*

administration. A synonym for the U.S. *executive* branch or presidency alone, and even then usually used about only the top cabinet and policy officials, not the government as a whole.

administrative detention. *See internment.*

adoption. (1) A doctrine whereby *international laws* are incorporated into *municipal law* by custom or statute, but are not so incorporated automatically. (2) When states *consent* to a *treaty*.

Adowa, Battle of (March 1, 1896). During the *First Abyssinian War* the Italian commander, General Baratieri, was provoked into a premature offensive by aggressive domestic opinion and the prodding of his subcommanders. He therefore sent his invading army of 15,000 Italian regulars and colonial troops to advance in three columns against dug-in Ethiopian positions. The Italians, mainly conscripts and *ascaris* but including several regiments of elite troops, were met by 100,000 Ethiopians led personally by Emperor Menelik II (c. 1834–1913). Most of the Ethiopians were well-armed with repeating rifles, and Menelik also had some 40 artillery pieces manned by an Ethiopian gun corps and some Russian advisers. With both armies running low on food, the Italians attacked in a confused and uncoordinated manner and were de-

feated in detail. They suffered an extraordinary 50 percent casualties, including 5,000 dead and 2,000 taken prisoner. The Ethiopians also took heavy casualties, of about 7,000 dead and 10,000 wounded, but retained the field. Adowa was a humiliation for Italian arms so deeply felt by public opinion that it led to riots in Italy and the fall of the Crispi government. On October 26th, a peace treaty was signed recognizing Ethiopia's independence. The memory of Adowa burned in Italy until *Mussolini* sought to erase it, along with Ethiopia, in the *Second Abyssinian War.* In Ethiopia, however, Adowa Day became the national holiday. *See also Omdurman, Battle of.*

advance. Movement of military forces forward, toward strategic objectives and/or active engagement with the enemy. *See also offensive; retreat.*

adventurism. Rash or reckless pursuit of national ambitions, often *prestige* or *conquest,* which risks war though a victory is highly uncertain. *See also filibuster; Adolf Hitler; Saddam Hussein; Nikita Khrushchev; Wilhelm II.*

advisory opinion. The answer to an inquiry put to an international court by member states. This permits a court to issue general legal opinions or clarifications without a specific case before it.

advisory services. Legal, technical, and other specialized assistance offered to one state by another (or by a *multilateral* agency) to help the weak state meet its treaty obligations, or in the interest of *development.*

Aegis. Complexes of battle-management radar, fire-control systems, and communications systems, deployed on *cruisers* or *destroyers* to defend *carriers* or fleets against missile attack. The United States first developed this technology to defend its navy from ship-to-ship missiles; it later became relevant to advanced *ballistic missile defense.*

aerospace defense. An all-embracing term including measures to defend against aircraft, missiles, or even space-based weapons systems.

affluent society. Advanced, industrial societies that emphasize *consumer goods* and other material satisfactions. The term was coined by economist John Kenneth Galbraith in a 1958 book by the same title.

Afghan Arabs. Originally, non-Afghan *mujahadeen* (mainly, though not exclusively, coming from Arab countries such as Egypt, Saudi Arabia, and Yemen) who went to Afghanistan to fight against the Soviet invasion and the Afghan *communist* regime during the *Afghan-Soviet War.* Upon returning to their own countries many became active in radical *Islamist* opposition movements, and a few joined outright *terrorist* organizations, such as *Egyptian*

Islamic Jihad, *Hamas*, or *al Qaeda*. Others continued their *"jihad"* in other territories where Muslims were at war with non-Muslims, notably in *Bosnia* and *Chechnya*, but also *Palestine*. The term was also used about non-Afghans fighting for al Qaeda, most of whom passed through al Qaeda training camps in Afghanistan before the *September 11, 2001, terrorist attack on the United States*. These men were also predominantly Arabs from Egypt, Algeria, and Yemen, but were joined by numerous Pashtuns from Pakistan, as well as Chinese, Indonesian, Chechnyan, and British Muslims (these mainly Arabs or Indians), and a handful of Western converts, including individuals from Australia and the United States. *See also International Brigades; mercenary.*

Afghan-British Wars. Great Britain feared a potential Russian threat to the Persian Gulf and India, but also desired to control Afghanistan itself. This contest was part of the *Great Game*, a protracted struggle between Britain and Russia for influence in *Central Asia*, along a disputed *frontier* between their respective, expanding empires that stretched from Persia through Afghanistan to Tibet. On the Afghan part of the frontier, three wars were fought between the British in India and Afghanistan.

1838–1842: The first conflict resulted from actions of the *East India Company*, which invaded in 1838 with a force of 16,000 British and *sepoy* regiments. This force captured Kabul in 1839 but could not subdue the countryside. In 1841 the Afghans struck as the British fell back to Peshawar, defeated by the cost of *occupation* and winter weather. During the retreat, which became a panicked rout, the entire force (4,500 troops and 12,000 civilians) was massacred; only one man reached Jallalabad. A punitive expedition returned and retook Kabul, but the country was abandoned again in 1842 in the face of continued resistance. Britain lost nearly 20,000 troops, and the myth of its martial invincibility was broken. To repair the damage, it conquered Sind and the *Sikh* kingdom in Punjab.

1878–1880: Britain invaded Afghanistan after *Alexander II* defeated and annexed the Central Asian Khanates of Bukhara, Khiva, and Samarkand. To Russophobe eyes, Moscow once again appeared to threaten "British India." The Afghans sought but did not receive Russian military aid. They withdrew in the face of initial British victories, but then conducted a sustained *guerrilla war* that trapped the British in the major cities and rendered their control of the country merely nominal. On September 3, 1879, the British resident in Kabul and his entire staff and guard were massacred. A British force returned to the city and carried out brutal atrocities against local Afghans. The bloody cost and savagery of the war helped topple *Disraeli*. A workable peace was arranged in 1880 in which London and the Afghans agreed on sullen, formal inclusion of the country within the British *sphere of influence* in Central Asia.

1919: In the wake of *World War I*, the Afghans rebelled in favor of full independence. Facing other rebellions in Punjab and Ireland, and exhausted by the Great War, the British conceded defeat and *recognized* Afghanistan as an independent state.

Afghanistan. An arid, mountainous, *Islamic* country lying along the historic Central Asian invasion route between *Inner Asia* on one side and India, Persia, and the Middle East on the other. It was first overrun and made part of the Persian Empire in the first millennium B.C.E. For the next thousand years, various north Indian states and the Persian Empire competed to control Afghanistan. With the conversion of Persia to *Islam*, Afghanistan also became progressively Islamicized from the eighth century onward. In the early Middle Ages, Turkic tribes from Central Asia raided and subsequently merged with indigenous Afghan tribes, and both repeatedly raided and sometimes launched full invasions of north India. Then they were themselves overrun by the *Mongol* invasion in the early thirteenth century. Afghanistan was incorporated into the unstable empire of *Tamerlane* during the latter half of the fourteenth century. Unlike his forebear, Tamerlane, who only raided and plundered India and sacked its northern cities, Babur (1483–1530), king of Kabul, invaded India and established the *Mughal Empire* there. This pattern of Afghans raiding outward was reversed when the Emperor *Akbar*, Babur's grandson, captured Kabul in 1581. War with Mughal India waxed and waned during *Aurangzeb's* reign (1658–1701).

An Afghan army toppled the Safavid dynasty in Persia and raided deep into India in 1722. Afghanistan's fractious tribes were loosely united under a single Pathan monarch in 1747, and over the next 10 years the Pathans launched four bloody, plundering invasions of north India, once sacking and pillaging *Delhi*. Thereafter, the Pathans were tied down by frontier warfare with the powerful *Sikh* kingdom of the Punjab, losing Kashmir to the Sikhs in 1819. Afghanistan was a key source of friction, but also a *buffer state*, between Britain and Russia during the nineteenth century's *Great Game*. Afghanistan fought off British conquest in the first of several *Afghan Wars* (1838–1842), but fell under British sway after c. 1857. Even so, it was never fully pacified and fought an additional anti-British war (1878–1880). After a bloody rebellion, it achieved an unruly independence in the 1920s. It then signed a *nonaggression pact* with the Soviet Union. Feudal *emirs* ruled in uneasy coexistence under a loose, central kingdom until 1973, when a *coup* resulted in proclamation of a republic.

Afghanistan was a quiet member of the *Nonaligned Movement* until 1978, when a pro-Soviet coup set up a *Marxist* military regime, drawing Afghanistan into the *Cold War* and generating deep internal opposition and unrest. Fierce resistance to the Afghan Communists provoked a second, Soviet-sponsored coup, then a Soviet invasion in December 1979. Soviet troops and advisers, Afghan Communists, and the secret police of *KHAD* fought and also frequently tortured or simply butchered Afghan *mujahadeen*. The mujahadeen retaliated in kind, seldom taking prisoners. For nine years this was the character of the *Afghan-Soviet War*. The civilian population was caught in the middle and took the greatest number of casualties. The mujahadeen took to the mountains, where they received significant American, Chinese, Pakistani, and Saudi assistance. The *guerrillas* prevailed, and Soviet troops withdrew by 1989. Afghanistan then resumed its traditional *neutrality*. The peace settlement was jointly guaranteed by the United States and USSR, but was rejected by the mujahadeen as long as former collaborators with the Soviets remained in power. The Afghan Communists, who ultimately became just another faction in the civil war, were finally toppled in April 1992.

Elements of the mujahadeen then discarded a United Nations (UN) plan for elections, provoking a renewed *civil war* along factional and tribal lines. UN efforts to mediate proved fruitless, as fighting and casualties became even heavier than during the Afghan-Soviet War. The fighting also moved into Kabul, which had been relatively unscathed to that point. As the factions contended for power, 30,000 were killed in Kabul alone in 1992–1993. Fighting continued throughout the early 1990s, as Afghanistan sank to the status of an utterly ruined and *failed state*—this was the direct and main consequence for Afghanistan of the 1979 Soviet invasion. In 1994 the *Taliban* (a faction of *fundamentalist* mujahadeen, led by erstwhile theology students and backed by Pakistan), launched a *jihad*, which first gave them control of the main Pashtun city of Khandahar, then about two-thirds of the country by 1998. By 2000 they controlled some 95 percent of Afghanistan; having pushed the last military opposition—the Northern Alliance—into an arid, rural pocket of the far north. The Taliban drew financial and political support from only three sources: Pakistani military intelligence (the ISI), *Wahhabi* fanatics in Saudi Arabia, and the very well-financed *terrorist* organization of *Usama bin Laden* known as *al Qaeda*. From these same sources came the serpentine backing and entangling influence of thousands of so-called *Afghan Arabs*, or non-Afghan members of al Qaeda who fought for and alongside the Taliban.

Taliban radicalism isolated Afghanistan from outside influences, including most of the Islamic world. They implemented a puritanical, desert Wahhabism that included severe persecution of women (including a ban on all female work and education) draconian enforcement and summary punishment of violations of *sharia* law by religious police and courts, and trivial tyrannies such as a ban on kite flying, music, pictures, and television. This extraordinarily repressive and atavistic rule drew little world attention until the Taliban displayed a radical cultural iconoclasm, and indeed barbarism, by destroying Afghanistan's remaining *Buddhist* sculptures and monuments, including some several millennia old, which had been designated "world cultural sites" by the United Nations. The Taliban ignored all pleadings, convinced as they were that such art works were "un-Islamic"—and hence forbidden—representations of either human or divine forms.

Taliban support for the anti-Western terrorists of al-Qaeda and for similar fundamentalist guerrillas operating throughout Central Asia, south Russia

17

(Chechnya), and western China (among the Uighurs of Xianjiang Province) set them further at odds with the international community: only Pakistan, Saudi Arabia, and the UAE formally recognized their regime. Then came the *September 11, 2001, terrorist attack on the United States. Under George W. Bush* an American-led and dominated coalition responded with calibrated but devastating *air power* aimed at both al Qaeda and the Taliban. Supporting this primary force were seriatim ground campaigns waged by various Afghan opposition groups, including the Northern Alliance of mostly Tajiks and Uzbeks, the *shi'ite* Hazara of the central highland range who had suffered grievously under the *sunni* Taliban, and various Pashtun and other southern and eastern ethnic groups, which combined in arranging (in many cases, simply by purchasing commanders) the surrender of the entire Taliban regime within less than three months of U.S. entry into the conflict. A coalition government was then installed under UN *Security Council* auspices before the end of 2001. The new government was protected by an International Security Assistance Force composed of troops from over 20 nations, led by Britain on the ground and supported logistically by the United States.

Suggested Readings: Larry Goodson, *Afghanistan's Endless War* (2001); Barnett Rubin, *The Search for Peace in Afghanistan* (1995); Willem Vogelsang, *The Afghans* (2001).

Afghan-Soviet War (1979–1989). A pro-Soviet *coup* in 1978 was partly reversed in a countercoup in 1979. The second coup served as the pretext for a Soviet invasion over Christmas, which brought Babrak Karmal to power in Kabul. What really sparked the invasion, however, was a rebellion by the Afghan garrison in Herat that was brutally put down at a cost of 20,000 lives. For nine years the Soviets fought a brutal campaign against Afghan *guerrillas*, or *mujahadeen*, in which at least one million Afghans died. The mujahadeen received covert assistance from the United States and from Muslim nations, notably Pakistan, which provided weapons, financing, and volunteers. The CIA supplied the ultimately decisive weapons: ground-to-air stinger missiles, which curtailed Soviet *air power* and drove up the cost of the war, and many thousands of mules to haul ammunition and supplies from Pakistan. (The price of mules in the southern United States reached unheard of levels, and supplies grew scarce due to CIA buying.) In 1986 Muhammad Najibullah (head of *KHAD*) replaced Karmal, but fighting continued. A United Nations–arranged *cease-fire* in 1988 led to a phased Soviet withdrawal, with the last *Red Army* troops crossing the Afghan border on February 15, 1989. That was followed by the return home of several million refugees. *See also Brezhnev Doctrine; Carter Doctrine; MI5/MI6; Reagan Doctrine.*

Africa. The world's poorest, as well as second largest and second most populous, continent. Bounded by the Atlantic and Indian Oceans and the Mediterranean Sea, it adjoins Europe and Asia via the Sinai. By convention, it is divided into North Africa, which is predominantly Muslim, Arab, and

Berber, and sub-Saharan Africa, which is predominantly black and divided among Muslims, Christians, and animists. There are also several white *enclaves* dating to the seventeenth century or later, located mainly in the east and south. Sub-Saharan Africa is further subdivided in conventional usage into East Africa, West Africa, and Southern Africa. The continent remains desperately poor and, in some areas, premodern. Unlike North Africa, which was for millennia an integral part of each successive Mediterranean economy, *development* below the Sahara was severely retarded by geography: much of the lower two-thirds of Africa was cut off from contact with world trade routes by the desert, and from the coast by mangrove swamps. In addition, the interior lacked navigable waterways: Africa's great rivers, the Niger, Congo, and Zambezi, are not easy channels to navigate or keep open, even today. Finally, coastal currents and mangrove swamps did not favor oceanic exploration before the fifteenth century. Retardant effects of physical isolation were greatly exacerbated by demographic dislocations caused by widespread internal *slavery*, the later Atlantic and Indian Ocean *slave trades*, endemic ethnic conflict, and frequent and devastating wars. Finally, modern Africa suffered from an unstable political inheritance of fragmented *colonialism*, and in the postcolonial era from extended bad government in a majority of African countries. *See also Sahel; Sudan.*

Suggested Readings: *Cambridge History of Africa*, 8 vols. (1986); J. D. Fage, *A History of Africa* (1995); Roland Oliver, *The African Experience* (1991).

African. A native or citizen of any country in Africa, including the Arab and Berber states of North Africa, the large island of Madagascar, and several small island chains in the Atlantic and Indian Oceans.

African Development Bank (ADB). Headquartered in Abidjan, Côte d'Ivoire, it was founded in 1964 by newly independent African states to assist in their *development* projects and to attract outside capital. It had meager start-up capital, which it concentrated on investment in *infrastructure*. It received occasional infusions from non-African *donor countries*. After 1974 it brought in nonregional members, through the *African Development Fund*. It remains the smallest and least well-funded of the *regional banks*. After 1980 its capital fund expanded greatly as donor nations, and the *International Monetary Fund* and *International Bank for Reconstruction and Development*, used it to channel *structural adjustment* assistance as well as to fund investment and poverty alleviation programs.

African Development Fund (ADF). Set up by the *African Development Bank* in 1974 in response to the *oil shock* of 1973, it includes most African countries as well as more than two dozen nonregional *donor states*. Its main purpose is to provide capital to the poorest African states on the most generous terms possible, such as zero percent interest on 50-year loans, with principal repayment starting after a decade.

African National Congress (ANC). This multiracial, but mostly black, organization was created in 1912 to promote peaceful, democratic reform of South African society. Into the 1940s it had few members, but the introduction of *apartheid* in 1949 changed that. The ANC produced two recipients of the *Nobel Prize* (for Peace): Chief Albert Luthuli (1898–1967) in 1960, and *Nelson Mandela* in 1993. It turned to armed action after the *Sharpeville massacre* in 1960. It made no secret of the joint membership of a number of its senior leaders, such as Joe Slovo, in the South African *Communist Party*, a fact that drew fire from more conservative *Cold Warrior* quarters in the West. The ANC was banned by the apartheid regime in 1961 and many of its leaders, most notably Mandela, imprisoned. It drew money and military support from the *front-line states*, the *Soviet bloc*, and, in its nonmilitary aspects, from a number of Western countries and international aid agencies. Through the 1980s the ANC carried out *guerrilla* attacks from bases in neighboring African states, though its main impact came from political organization in the black townships that surrounded the affluent whites-only cities of South Africa. In 1990 the ANC was legalized ahead of the release of Mandela and negotiations that aimed at a multiracial constitution. The ANC was then drawn into a violent political struggle with unreconstructed whites, *Zulu* supporters of *Inkatha*, and the radicals of the *Pan-African Congress* who rejected any *power sharing*. The ANC prevailed in the first free elections in 1994 and remained the dominant political party in the country into the early twenty-first century.

African socialism. An asserted, romantic, non–class-based concept of *socialism* supposedly peculiar to African traditions. It was a popular notion on the democratic, and later sometimes also apologetic, Left in the 1960s and 1970s. It was trumpeted within Africa mainly by *Nkrumah* of Ghana and *Nyerere* of Tanzania and was still heard faintly calling to the Left in later years. Its core proposition was that African society was inherently and even naturally communal rather than individualistic, and thus also naturally socialistic rather than market-oriented. This claim was used principally to eschew export-oriented *industrialization* and instead focus on forced *collectivization* of *agriculture* and other programs that engaged central planning. It led to a variety of other collectivist economic policies and schemes as well, inter alia in Ghana, Tanzania, Guinea, and under *Mugabe* in Zimbabwe.

At best, the idea arose from a wooly, incomplete, and only partly accurate view of Africa's precolonial history. Although that history had indeed witnessed many communal landholding patterns and pacific social practices, it had also seen far-flung trade and complex markets over many centuries, including well before the arrival of European imperialists, and numerous local wars and indigenous imperial constructions and ambitions. The concept also too conveniently overlooked such indigenous tyrants as *Shaka Zulu* and exploitative empires such as those run by the *Fulbe* or *Ashanti* or the earlier slave empires of *Mali* and *Songhay*. Most of all, it struggled against the larger historical reality that Africa had been integrated into the world economy, for good as well as for ill. That indeed meant that it suffered from unequal economic relationships, but that was a fact that called for international reform and concerted efforts at adjustment rather than futile attempts at economic *autarky*. Even when applied by sincere idealists and relative moderates such as Nyerere, collectivization schemes that presumed a native socialism proved highly coercive and restrictive of many of the very freedoms that Africans had so recently won. *See also Arusha Declaration*; négritude; *pan-Africanism*.

Suggested Reading: Carl G. Rosberg and William Friedland, eds., *African Socialism* (1964).

Afrika Korps. *See Montgomery, Bernard Law; Erwin Rommel; World War II.*

Afrikaner (Boer). A white South African of Afrikaans descent; usually of Dutch or French *Huguenot* lineage, and not including ethnically English whites who settled historically and still live predominantly in the Cape Town area. *See also apartheid; Boer Wars; Great Trek; Orange Free State; Transvaal.*

Afro-Asian bloc. A large *caucus group* operating in the United Nations and other IGOs. It presented a more solid front during the *Cold War* than afterward. *See also Nonaligned Movement.*

Afrocentrism. Viewing world affairs from the point of view of Africa and Africans, usually to the point of exaggeration of the relative importance of Africa in world affairs. *See also ethnocentrism; Eurocentrism;* négritude.

Agadir. A crisis erupted over this Moroccan port in July 1911, when a German gunboat was dispatched to *show the flag* to the French, then expanding across North Africa. The British feared that Germany's intent was to threaten their base at *Gibraltar*. The crisis was resolved, as only *prestige* was at stake, not *vital interests*. Yet it contributed significantly to prewar tension and deepened distrust on all sides. It is sometimes referred to as the Second Moroccan Crisis.

Aga Khan. *See Ismaili.*

agency. In *diplomacy*, when one state acts in behalf of another because the second lacks *representation* or *diplomatic relations* with the government of a third country. This may occur when a small state lacks the resources to maintain diplomatic missions in all other countries, or because it has minimal interaction with a distant country, or when formal relations have been broken as a result of an ongoing dispute but interests exist that require representation. *See also special interest section.*

agent. (1) An element or component of *chemical, biological,* or *nerve weapons.* (2) Any *intelligence* operative, but especially if *covert. See also agent of influence;* agent provocateur; *double agent; illegal agent; legal agent; mole; penetration agent.*

agent of influence. An agent whose task it is to spread *disinformation,* or *propaganda,* by insinuation into a position of influence to affect the decisions of key policymakers. *See also mole; penetration agent.*

agent provocateur. An agent of some *secret police* or *intelligence service* who incites selected persons to actions, which may make them liable to arrest, prosecution, or political defeat.

agent-structure problem. In historical argument, agents of change are frequently identified as key individuals. However, that raises the problem as to where to locate primary *causation.* This is engendered by difficulties in identifying the relative influence of the direct agent of an action or outcome and the deeper *structure* of time, place, and circumstance in which the action occurred and which may have predetermined—or, at a minimum, heavily conditioned—choices available to even the most strong-willed agent. Many serious historical arguments may be reduced, once the passions of the moment are stripped away, to disagreement about whether primary explanatory power resides in the deep structures of a given social setting and the worldview it helps generate or vagaries of otherwise minor events and decisions that have a disproportionate impact on the affairs of nations and peoples. *See also counterfactual; determinism; falsification; historicism; levels of analysis; relativism; volition.*

aggrandizement. An increase in a state's *territory,* usually by *conquest.* If accomplished by one *Great Power* with the agreement of others, it may be accompanied by *compensation.*

aggression. In general, any unprovoked attack aiming at *expansion* or *conquest.* Aggressive war was made illegal in the early twentieth century, despite its definition and identification remaining highly problematical, as in *League of Nations* and *United Nations* (UN) debates. As one result, subsequent aggressors always maintained that they were acting defensively. The idea of aggression assumes that an *international society* exists and that states within this society have certain rights and duties. The unprovoked use of force to strip away one such right, to *territorial integrity,* is deemed to be criminal (indeed, the only state-to-state crime) and justifies the use of force in *self-defense.* It was encoded in *international law* over the course of the twentieth century that nothing but resisting aggression may justify war, that aggressors may be punished by force and their conquests reversed by force, whether applied unilaterally or collectively, and that subsequently they should pay recompense to their victims in the form of *reparations*.

For all that, a precise and binding legal definition of aggression still eludes consensus. Difficulty in definition of "aggression" and even of "war," as best evidenced by the experience of the League of Nations, meant that the terms were avoided when drafting the *United Nations Charter*. Further confusion later arose over the French text, which rendered "armed attack" (*Article 51*) as "aggression armée." The closest approximation of an international legal definition of consensus value comes from a UN Special Committee that adopted a nonbinding sense in 1974, declaring aggression to be the use of force in any manner inconsistent with the terms of the United Nations Charter. It added a list of seven offenses that so qualified, if unprovoked: (1) *incursion, invasion,* or *occupation of territory*; (2) *bombardment*; (3) *blockade* of ports or a coastline, though not if undertaken with UN authority as a *police action*; (4) any unprovoked attack on units of the armed forces of another state, wherever located; (5) use of military bases in a second state to attack a third country, without permission of the second; (6) allowance of unprovoked military action against another state to be taken from one's territory, or otherwise aiding and abetting a second-party aggression; and (7) sending armed *irregulars* or *mercenaries* to attack another state. Although this resolution is useful as a guideline, it is important to note that it was nonbinding, though over time it may acquire some standing in *international customary law*. *See also crimes against peace; indirect aggression; just war tradition.*

aggressor. A state that engages in an unprovoked attack on another or otherwise engages in acts that may be defined as constituting *aggression*. The distinction between aggressor and victim is difficult, but important for triggering the response of third parties under any *collective security* arrangement or even by an alliance, as in 1914, when Italy declined to honor the terms of its alliance with Germany and Austria and remained neutral toward their war with France, Britain, and Russia.

Agincourt, Battle of (1415). *See cavalry; Hundred Years' War.*

agitprop. Agitation and *propaganda* used against targeted countries to stir populations to civil unrest or *rebellion*. This subversive tactic was used by Russian *Marxists* in their domestic political struggles against the Tsarist regime. It was later added to the foreign policy arsenal of the *Soviet Union. See also disinformation.*

agrarian reform. A basic change in a given system of rural landholding (tenure). Reform, which will vary according to local and historical conditions, is essential if a basic economy is to develop beyond mere subsistence to levels of agricultural *productivity* capable of sustaining advanced social and political organization and *industrialization. See also agricultural revolution; Chinese Revolution; famine; French Revolution; Meiji Restoration; Russian Revolution; serfdom; slavery.*

Suggested Reading: Roy Prosterman and J. Reidlinger, *Land Reform and Democratic Development* (1987).

agréation. The formal exchange of diplomats between or among states.

agrément. Formal acceptance of an accredited diplomat by a receiving (host) government.

agricultural revolution. (1) The dramatic increase in agricultural production in Europe in the late seventeenth and early eighteenth centuries, beginning in the Netherlands and other parts of north Europe. It resulted mainly from specialization, but also from shifts in cropping practices and landholding systems and technological innovation. The new productivity in agriculture stimulated *population* growth even while displacing people from the land to rapidly growing cities. It led to rural unrest, urbanization, and urban poverty and propelled Europe's overflow population into colonial enterprises on several continents. Indeed, the subsequent changes in the world economy were underlain by a relative decline in the size of the agricultural sector, accompanied by a simultaneous rise in its *productivity.* This was the essential prerequisite contributing to new accumulations of capital and labor that stimulated the *industrialization* of Europe in the eighteenth and nineteenth centuries and the redistribution of wealth and power among social classes.

On the political level, such changes sometimes resulted in revolutionary upheaval; at other times they led to new social compacts by which different classes shared the fruits of a foreign policy of *imperialism.* American agriculture was commercialized from the first, which greatly enhanced overall economic dynamism. In Asia, a central reason for China's violent internal convulsions in the nineteenth century (*White Lotus* and *Taiping Rebellions*) was *Qing* failure to promote a comparable system of *agrarian reform* and agrarian capitalism. Persistent reliance on outdated peasant landholding and central marketing systems at a time of exponential population growth gave rise to dislocated peasants, banditry, and rebellion, which led to central government weakness and encouraged foreign intervention. (2) A dramatic and astonishing global expansion in farm productivity and output after c. 1940, especially in the United States and Western Europe, based upon industrialization of agriculture and new fertilizers and seed. It had a worldwide impact, raising both population levels and living standards. *See also agriculture; green revolution; militarization.*

Suggested Readings: J. D. Chambers and G. E. Mingay, *The Agricultural Revolution* (1966); E. L. Jones, *The Agricultural Revolution* (1974).

agriculture. One of the strategic sectors of the world economy. *See also agrarian reform; agricultural revolution; CAP; collectivization; famine; FAO; food; GATT; green revolution; Thomas Robert Malthus; neo-mercantilism; Uruguay Round.*

Aguinaldo, Emilio (1870–1964). Philippine patriot. *See also Philippines; Spanish-American War (1898).*

AIC. Advanced industrial country. A self-explanatory, *United Nations* term. *See also First World; LDC; NIC; OECD.*

aid. *Development*, economic, humanitarian, or military assistance from one state to another. Aid is also delivered through multilateral agencies. Private aid is more properly described as charity. The objectives vary with each bilateral relationship, but may include *alliance* or political support, purchase of influence over the recipient's foreign policy, bribery of recipient officials to ensure acceptance of specific projects or contracts, access to markets or market share, development assistance, *postwar reconstruction*, maintenance of economic stability, debt relief, or humanitarian relief. The first significant state-to-state aid in peacetime appeared during the 1890s, when the U.S. government sent famine relief to Tsarist Russia. Most of that aid was private, but the Navy was used to deliver some. After *World War I*, the United States and Canada sent food aid to starving civilians in Belgium. After the *Russian Civil War*, the *American Relief Administration* sent massive food and medical aid to the Soviet Union. Aid became a permanent feature of peacetime international relations during the early *Cold War* when the United States sent massive financial aid to Western Europe under the *European Recovery Program* and additional aid to Japan and launched the *Colombo Plan* and multiple bilateral programs. Other Western countries instituted aid programs in due course, concentrating either on regional programs or on assisting former colonies. The Soviet Union concentrated on military and economic aid to immediate allies and proxies, such as Cuba. In the 1970s cash-rich *OPEC* states set up foreign aid programs, partly to offset the damage done to weak economies by the *oil shocks* they had caused.

By the end of the twentieth century, most developed states used aid in some form as part of their overall diplomacy. Key subcategories are (1) development aid: *soft loans* or grants to assist *LDCs* develop *infrastructure*; (2) economic aid: money or credit given to sustain the economy of a recipient, or meet *balance of payments* problems (Most economic aid is given by the *OECD* nations and by OPEC. There have been repeated efforts to channel aid through multilateral agencies or *regional banks*, but most remains bilateral because donor countries wish to maintain control, no matter what they pledge in public.); (3) humanitarian aid: food, medicine, shelter, or other matériel assistance given to support a civil population in times of national disaster, such as earthquake, flood, or famine, or to alleviate suffering attendant on war; and (4) military aid: money, matériel, or technical advice given to support a recipient's military development, *deterrence*, or wartime operations. It can be given by virtually any state. *See also advisory services; aid burden; donor fatigue; International Bank for Reconstruction and Development; International Monetary Fund; Lend-Lease; NIEO; ODA; tied aid.*

aid burden. The extent to which *aid* draws upon a *donor country's* revenues as a proportion of *GNP*.

aid fatigue. *See donor fatigue.*

Ainu. A minority, indigenous people of northern Japan—Hokkaido and the Kurils. From the eighth to the twelfth century they resisted conquest by the *Shoguns*. For centuries after that, they fought defensive actions against expansionist local *daimyos* such as the Matsume. During 1807–1821, and after 1854, the *bakufu* placed all of Hokkaido under direct administration, forced the Ainu into a *tributary* relationship, and attempted cultural *assimilation*. Disease and poverty led to a drastic decline in Ainu numbers. Along with Okinawans, Koreans, and burakumin (traditional outcasts), the Ainu were widely discriminated against even in post–*World War II*, democratic, and modern Japan.

Aïr, Kingdom of. *See Tuareg.*

Air America. A covert *CIA* supply operation to anti-Communist forces in Indochina, starting in 1959 and ending with U.S. withdrawal in 1972. It was briefly the largest airline in Asia.

airborne infantry/troops. *Infantry* delivered to a battlefield by glider or parachute. In *World War II*, Germany used them in small numbers when invading Norway and Holland (1940), and in a large-scale attack on Crete (1941). German paratroops took heavy casualties in Crete, causing *Hitler* to lose interest. Germany used paratroopers afterward only for such special missions as the rescue of *Mussolini* and in support of regular ground forces. The *Allies* learned the lessons of Crete better than the Germans did and used airborne troops effectively in Sicily, on *D-Day*, and in Holland in late 1944. The United States used paratroops in its invasions of Grenada in 1983 (which a Pentagon spokesman described with the wonderfully convoluted euphemism, "predawn vertical insertion") and Panama in 1989. However, the usually heavy cost in lives and war matériel that can be inflicted on lightly armed parachute units that are even slightly off target or not quickly supported has meant that since World War II they have seldom been used to mount a major assault.

airborne warning and control system (AWACS). Advanced radar and communications equipment based in aircraft. AWACS aircraft spot enemy targets and threats and direct strikes and counterstrikes. They are one of the keys to mounting complex air combat operations.

airburst. The detonation of a *nuclear weapon* at a specific altitude above its target in order to maximize the *blast effect*.

air cavalry. *Infantry* with independent air transport.

aircraft carrier. A large, *capital warship* with a flat deck and concealed hangars, capable of carrying a variety of aircraft. In 1914 the *Royal Navy* conducted the first-ever aircraft carrier–launched air attack, and *escort carriers* were used to guard *convoys* during *World War I*. At the *Washington Naval Conference* the strategic importance of carriers was misunderstood by nearly all involved. Their construction was limited in the final treaties (1922) mainly because it was feared that someone might later seek to convert such large-hulled ships into *battleships*, still thought the most powerful and decisive weapons platforms afloat. In fact, the United States and Japan later converted old battleships and battle cruisers (which also were limited by treaty) into carriers. Most other powers remained reliant on battleships. The new ascendance of the carrier was first demonstrated by the British in 1940, when carrier-launched biplanes sank or damaged several Italian battleships at anchor at Taranto. Japan built the greatest carrier fleet in the world before *World War II* and used it with great success at *Pearl Harbor*. The Japanese Navy lost several carriers early on, however, including four at *Midway*, and lost all its carriers before the war was over. The United States built an astonishing number and array of carriers (90 in 1944 alone), and thereby claimed a naval and naval *air power* preponderance it has yet to surrender. After World War II, several smaller powers maintained carriers, including relatively minor military states such as Canada, until their expense overwhelmed small navy budgets, usually by the beginning of the 1970s. Into the twenty-first century the United States continued to deploy aircraft carrier battle groups as its premier system for projecting power far from its shores and home waters. These were fleets of warships of many types moving under a unified command, all protecting the carrier-based naval air power at their center. *See also Battle of the Atlantic; Coral Sea; Doolittle raid; Gulf War; gunboat diplomacy; Leyte Gulf.*

airdrop. Dropping military or humanitarian relief supplies from the air.

air launched ballistic missile (ALBM). A *ballistic missile* fired from an aircraft, dirigible, or other airborne vehicle.

air launched cruise missile (ALCM). A *cruise missile* fired from an aircraft, blimp, or other airborne vehicle.

air power. The narrow sense of this term is a nation whose air force is in the first rank in terms of numbers and capability, as in "Britain was a major air power in the summer of 1940." A deeper sense suggests an ability to project force with aircraft, or later also with missiles, even into the heartland of an enemy state. Tactical air power is the use of aircraft to destroy the military forces of an enemy or other precise and limited targets, usually in support of one's own ground or naval forces that are seeking to achieve local (battlefield) objectives. Strategic air power involves the use of *strategic weapons* delivered through the air against targets that are themselves of strategic significance. Its central idea is a simple one: strike at the sources of power in the interior of an enemy territory, not just at the forward elements or projection of that power represented by enemy armed forces. The immediate objectives of a strategic strike will vary, but the ultimate objective is always to inflict such massive damage on an enemy's war-making capacity or morale that it will agree to end the war on terms favorable to the attacking power. Strategic attacks, which have proved nearly always ineffective and even counterproductive, aim to demoralize an enemy population or destroy the economic and industrial infrastructure that sustains the enemy's military, or both.

Air power began simply: stationary, tethered balloons were used to spot ground targets and estimate ranges for *artillery* fire during the *War of the First Coalition*, in 1793, and throughout the *Napoleonic Wars*. Balloons were used in similar fashion during the *American Civil War* and the *Franco-Prussian War*. As part of a larger movement at the end of the nineteenth century that sought to place limits on warfare, at the first *Hague Conference* (1899) aerial bombardment from balloons was banned. Balloons were again used as observation platforms for artillery in the first months of *World War I*. Then Germany briefly deployed *Zeppelins* as bombers (1914–1915), including to make raids on London. The first use of fixed-wing aircraft as platforms for weapons was by the Italians in 1911, during a campaign to conquer *Tripoli* (Libya). The potential of this type of air power was only partially realized during World War I. At first, aircraft were employed to supplement balloons, in unarmed and noncombat spotting support of ground and naval forces, to scout enemy positions and direct artillery fire, and at sea to scout for enemy ships and spot for battleship fire. By 1915 fixed-wing *bombers* were deployed, alongside the Zeppelins and observation balloons. That encouraged development of *fighter* interceptors and escorts. By war's end, more than 200,000 military aircraft, of all types on all sides, had been produced and sent into battle, and some 40,000 air crew had been killed.

In several countries at the end of World War I, *isolationists* and some of those who wished to curtail military spending touted air power as a defensive weapon. In contrast, an Italian *fascist*, Giulio Douhet, postulated in "Command of the Air" (1921) that in the next war air power would be strategically decisive and argued in favor of fleets of aircraft to overfly enemy armies and attack the enemy's war factories and cities. Fleets of *strategic bombers* grew from this idea, though rudimentary efforts at strategic bombing had been tried by Germany and Britain from 1917, and several major powers deployed these by the early 1930s. These fleets first showed an ability to inflict damage, and terror, at *Guernica*. Not everyone learned the lessons of air power well, or in time.

Neither before nor during *World War II* did the German *Luftwaffe* or the Japanese Air Force develop a significant strategic bomber force or doctrine, remaining mostly content to use air power in support of ground or naval attacks. Late in the war the Germans developed the first *ballistic missiles*, in the form of the *V-2* rocket, but that was—as its name suggested—a vengeance rather than a war-winning weapon. Until mid-1940 none of the major powers engaged in terror bombing against countries capable of retaliation in kind: the Luftwaffe bombed Warsaw and Rotterdam, but not Paris or London. The *Battle of Britain* changed that. Once *Hitler* retargeted the attack on London and other British cities, in retaliation for Bomber Command having bombed Berlin, Britain developed the doctrine of area bombing. That put to use the only instrument it then had to strike at Germany, to reach into the German heartland to kill workers and level their homes ("dehouse" them, as *Churchill* put it), in an effort to foment a class and popular rising against the *Nazis*. It also was hoped it might avoid the necessity of invading the continent and facing another *Somme*. However, the strategy failed. During much of World War II, Allied bombing of Germany proved far less than effective. A secret wartime study reported that, before navigational equipment improved, just one British night bomber in ten came within five miles of its designated target in Germany. As one historian bluntly and brutally put it: "Bomber Command's crews . . . were dying largely in order to crater the German countryside." On the other hand, the air war tied down hundreds of thousands of German troops and diverted much of Nazi Germany's military effort into servicing antiaircraft guns and crew. More than 50,000 antiaircraft guns were deployed inside Germany alone by 1944. And with improvements in Allied bomb sights and targeting, and then the development of long-distance fighter escorts, the Allies achieved complete *air superiority* later in the war and used it to conduct *thousand bomber raids* and *carpet bomb* German cities. German defenders replied with still larger masses of antiaircraft guns and the first experimental jet fighters, but these latter proved too crude and few in number to make a decisive impact. Still, over the course of World War II the Western Allies lost 22,000 bombers and more than 110,000 air crew in Europe and Asia combined. As lessons were learned, Allied air power proved tactically—

but not strategically—decisive over land and at sea. When used to destroy Axis armies or attack or protect *warships* and *convoys*, it was hugely successful. It helped bring about victory only when backed by the threat or reality of ground invasion, though in the case of Japan an argument might be made that air power delivery of the *atomic bomb* did prove strategically decisive.

During the *Cold War* air power was the primary American instrument of strategic *deterrence*. Its conventional coercive limits were again made apparent to the United States in the *Vietnam War* and to the Soviet Union in the *Afghan-Soviet War*. During the *Gulf War* (1991), controversy continued among specialists over whether it was possible to win a war with air power alone. By the end of NATO's air campaign against Serb forces in *Bosnia* and later in *Kosovo*, doubt about the received wisdom had grown. The exceptionally effective U.S. campaign against the Taliban and al Qaeda in Afghanistan in 2001 then raised anew the possibility that air power in an era of precision munitions might well be decisive, at least when employed by a major against a minor or middle power. Note: Specialists disagree as to whether *aircraft carriers* and *cruise missile-launching submarines* should be classified as elements of air power or *sea power*. *See also ace; first strike; nuclear weapons; smart weapons; total war.*

Suggested Readings: Marc Clodfelter, *The Limits of Air Power* (1989); J. Morrow, *The Great War in the Air* (1993); R. J. Overy, *The Air War, 1939–1945* (1980); A. Stephens, *The War in the Air, 1914–1994* (1994).

air raid. Any attack on ground targets by aircraft, especially if conducted by bombers against an urban target.

airspace. States claim and exercise *sovereignty* not just on but also above and below their territory. Military transit of a country's airspace always requires advance permission. At sea, airspace corresponds to the *twelve-mile limit* or other agreed upon extensions of *jurisdiction*. The rules governing civilian use of national airspace and the principle of free passage through international airspace were set in a 1944 convention that created the *International Civil Aviation Organization* (ICAO). *See also innocent passage.*

air superiority. (1) Tactical: when one side in a battle enjoys clear control of the skies over the battlefield. This usually entails a huge advantage, for instance, by pinning down most movement by the other side and breaking up mass formations, thus contributing greatly to the matter of *victory* or *defeat*. (2) Strategic: when one's own air force has not merely local but also overall, or *theater*, control of the skies.

air-to-air missile (AAM). A *guided missile* fired from an aircraft against enemy planes or *missiles*.

air-to-surface ballistic missile (ASBM). A *ballistic missile* fired from an aircraft at a ground or sea target.

Aix-la-Chapelle, Congress of (1818). Austria, Britain, Prussia, and Russia assembled in this French town for the second meeting of the *Congress system*. France was brought back fully into the *Great Power* fold after its defeat of 1813–1815. Aix settled the contentious question of French *reparations* and confirmed *Napoleon*'s exile to *St. Helena*. Most unusually, it also gave an international guarantee of civil rights to German Jews. Most importantly, Aix marked the beginning of Britain's shift away from the continental powers back toward a policy of *splendid isolation*. London began to return to its tradition of aloofness from continental entanglements in favor of overseas expansion, and it was concerned about restoration of the continental *balance of power*. Britain also opposed any extension of Russian influence into the western half of the continent, which the tsar had eagerly proposed under the guise of intervention to suppress outbreaks of liberal reform and rebellion. *See also diplomatic corps; Holy Alliance.*

Aix-la-Chapelle, Peace of (1748). The treaty that ended both the *War of the Austrian Succession* and, in North America, *King George's War*. It hinted at the *diplomatic revolution* of 1756, as England insisted on a guarantee of Prussia's claim to *Silesia*, already agreed to by Austria at Dresden two years prior. The fortress of Louisbourg in *Acadia* was returned to France, and other North American gains by England reversed, to reflect the wider stalemate. Other than *Frederick the Great* of Prussia, who kept Silesia, no major power was satisfied with the final settlement. *Maria Theresa* of Austria was the most unhappy. And so, they had at it again from 1756 to 1763 in the even more destructive *Seven Years' War*. A pattern was thus set that lasted to the time of *Bismarck* whereby whenever Austria and Prussia were not united by a common enemy, they would fall out over their protracted contest for control of Germany.

Ajaria. A Georgian region that after 1991 sought to secede, but ultimately settled for local *autonomy*. By 2001 the Autonomous Republic of Ajaria was *de facto* independent of Georgia, under Russian military protection.

Akbar (1542–1605). "The Great." Mughal Emperor. An illiterate, in 1562 he wrested control from his harem and regent nurse and launched a new era in Indian history. He sought accommodation with old *Rajput* foes, including hiring some into his military and marrying a Rajput woman, but he could be ruthless too, as when reducing the Rajput city of Chitor and ordering the slaughter of 30,000 of its inhabitants in 1568. Overall, however, he extended broad toleration to his *Hindu* subjects, ended forced conversions to *Islam*, abolished the much hated *jizya* tax on non-Muslims (dhimmîs), and permitted

Hindus to build new temples and shrines. He was a bureaucratic reformer, but his state rested heavily on hard-pressed peasants whom he taxed at a heavy rate. He altered the basis of the Mughal nobility, establishing a base of provincial emirs (mansabdar), whom he then watched over using a vast *intelligence* network of spies and informers in every subdistrict of the empire, supported by regular runners and camel messengers to deliver secret reports directly to him. Akbar donated land in Amritsar to the *Sikhs*, who built the Golden Temple upon it. He distrusted the ulema (Islamic scholars), whom he also alienated by his wide toleration of, and apparent personal interest in, other Indian faiths and by his assault on their tax-protected estates. In 1579 his policies of toleration led to a revolt by Muslim emirs in Afghanistan. Akbar was a restless warrior in charge of an unstable realm: he conquered Gujarat in 1572 and Bengal in 1576; in 1581 he took Kabul, repressing the rebellion and reversing an age-old pattern of invasion; in 1592 he conquered Orissa; and in 1595 he added Baluchistan to his swollen empire. In his old age his son rebelled—a common succession problem for empires rooted in Central Asian cultures and *absolutist* dynasties. Akbar died in 1605 after 47 years on the throne. He may have been poisoned by his son. *See also Panipat, Battles of.*

Akihito (b. 1933). Hesei (Peace) Emperor of Japan. He acceded to the throne in 1989 upon the death of his father, *Hirohito*. In 1993 he apologized to China and Korea for Japan's wartime *aggression* and atrocities, though not sufficiently to appease *public opinion* in those countries.

Aksai Chin. A disputed Himalayan border region claimed by India but occupied by China. *See also Indo-Chinese War; Kashmir.*

Alabama claims. A generic term for a series of disputes between the United States and Great Britain arising principally from the *American Civil War*. The term was taken from a British-built *Confederate* commerce raider (the CSS Alabama), which did great damage to *Union* shipping. The United States sought compensation for the damage. All claims were settled by international tribunal in 1871 and marked an important advance for the principle of *arbitration*. Along with the *Treaty of Washington*, the Alabama settlement signaled a permanent shift from tension and animosity between the United States and Great Britain toward the *rapprochement*, and ultimate *alliance*, which proved critical to the course of world affairs in the twentieth century.

Alamein, Battle of. *See El Alamein, Battle of.*

Alamgir. *See Aurangzeb.*

Alamo. *See Antonio Lopez Santa Anna; Texas.*

Aland Islands. Russia took control of these Baltic islands, along with Finland, when it defeated Sweden in 1809. They were made *neutral* as part of the settlement of the *Crimean War,* in which Moscow was compelled to make multiple concessions. Russia lost its grip on the islands with defeat in *World War I* and descent into the *Russian Civil War.* They were *occupied* by Sweden in 1918, but that provoked an immediate German *intervention.* Germany's defeat later that year sent the issue of ownership to the *Paris Peace Conference.* The *League of Nations* gave the islands to Finland in 1921, but under conditions of permanent *demilitarization* and *autonomy* for their predominantly Swedish population. The Alands were occupied by Nazi Germany, 1941–1944, but reverted to Finland with Germany's defeat in 1945. Finland tried to exempt the Alands from *European Union* rules when negotiating its own admission; the stated reason was that the *Maastricht* treaty threatened Aland *demilitarization* with its promise of a common European defense policy.

Alaska. In 1725 *Peter the Great* sent an exploratory expedition to Alaska. In the nineteenth century, Russia laid claim to large swaths of the west coast of North America, primarily in Alaska (where *Orthodox* missionaries were active after 1823), but including northern California, where a few small settlements were set up. California was not targeted for colonization after declaration of the *Monroe Doctrine,* whereas Alaska was sold to the United States in 1867 for $7.2 million. The purchase was widely ridiculed as "*Seward's* Folly." Canada disputed a portion of Alaska's boundary until *Theodore Roosevelt* took a hard line that compelled the British to make Ottawa back down in 1901. That was the final U.S.-Canadian boundary dispute. *See also Aleutian Islands.*

Albania. Mountainous Albania has most often been part of other people's empires: the ancient Greeks, the *Romans,* and the *Byzantines* all held some or all of modern Albania under their sway. From the eleventh to the thirteenth centuries, coastal Albania was contested ground between the declining power of Byzantium and rising seaborne power of the then-dominant warrior people of Latin *Christendom,* the *Normans.* In the fourteenth century, Albania was overrun by the Serbs. In turn, Serbs and Albanians alike were conquered and ruled by the *Ottoman Empire*—in Albania's case for 500 years, into the early twentieth century. As a result, Albania contains the lion's share of Europe's Muslims (other European Muslims include ethnic Albanians in *Kosovo,* and Serbo-Croatian converts in *Bosnia*).

Albania was conquered by the Turks in stages, partly with the help of Albanian chieftains who allied with the invader against local rivals, though the conquest was fiercely resisted by others. Albania's struggle against conquest was aided by a revolt of local *Janissaries* in 1443, but Albania was finally conquered by *Muhammad II* in 1468. Many Albanians adjusted well to life within the Ottoman Empire, which left many of their local customs and much of traditional authority intact. Some Albanians were prominent in Turkish military service, most notably Ali Pasha (c. 1744–1822), who for many years ran much of Albania as if it were independent of *Constantinople*.

Albania in fact became an independent principality only in 1913, after the *Balkan Wars*—after which it quickly sank into *anarchy* during *World War I*. Nevertheless, its *sovereignty* was widely *recognized* after the war and practically confirmed in 1921 in an agreement among Italy, Greece, and Yugoslavia, which all coveted Albanian territory but could not agree on how to *partition* it. It was proclaimed a republic in 1925, but returned to monarchy under *King Zog I* (r. 1928–1939). Invaded and occupied by Italy in 1939 and Germany in 1940, it was freed by nationalist and communist *guerrillas* in 1944. Under the quixotic, *Stalinist* dictator *Enver Hoxha*, it joined the *Soviet bloc* early in the *Cold War*. A *schism* over *de-Stalinization* led to a break with Moscow in 1958. In 1961 Albania was expelled from COMECON and in 1968 it withdrew from the *Warsaw Pact*. It then supported China and followed a policy of *autarky*. It was the only European country not to sign the CSCE accords in 1975. Hoxha broke with China in 1978, after the death of *Mao Zedong*. This left Albania as Europe's poorest and most repressive country—and along with North Korea—a staunchly Stalinist state. Hoxha died, utterly unmourned, in 1985. Albania was among the last of the *Communist* states to see the old order break down during the upheavals of 1989–1991, and much blood was shed before the Communists were forced out.

Albanian *boat people* crossed as economic *refugees* to Italy in 1991. That year Albania held its first free elections, and *James Baker* was the first U.S. secretary of state to visit and offer political and even military aid, in an extraordinary *reneversement des alliances* considering Albania's recent past. Democracy did not take hold, however, despite U.S. interest and aid. Instead, massive corruption, factionalism, clan loyalty, and several rigged elections followed. In 1993 the United States supplied surplus light arms and equipment to replace obsolete Chinese and Soviet weapons, as Washington and Tirana drew closer together out of shared interest in preventing *ethnic cleansing* by Serbs of ethnic Albanians in *Kosovo*, *Macedonia*, and *Montenegro*. Albania's relations with Greece deteriorated sharply after 1993, for related reasons. The refugee outflow from Albania continued, prompting unilateral Italian intervention from 1997 as one-time Albanian Prime Minister Sali Berisha retreated to his clannish northern stronghold and set himself up as a local *warlord* supporting Kosovo Liberation Army (KLA) guerrillas. As full-scale ethnic cleansing and war broke out in that Yugoslav (Serb) province, hundreds of thousands of ethnic Albanian Kosovars fled into Albania and Macedonia. *NATO's* intervention and continuing presence in the region from 1999 helped stabilize Albania, but it entered the twenty-first century at best a deeply fractured, impoverished, unstable, and in some ways still premodern nation.

Aleutian Islands. An Alaskan archipelago extending toward eastern *Siberia*. During *World War II* the western Aleutians (specifically Attu and Kiska) were occupied by Japan from mid-1942 to mid-1943. They were retaken by the United States after bitter battle and heavy loss of life. That Japanese *occupation* encouraged postwar public acceptance of Alaskan statehood by the lower 48 states.

Alexander of Macedon (356–323 B.C.E.). "The Great." King of Macedon, son of Philip of Macedon (382–336 B.C.E.), conqueror of the *city-state* system of classical Greece. As a youth, he was famously tutored by the philosopher Aristotle. Alexander is not remembered for reigning as a philosopher-king, however; he is recalled for only one thing: conquest. He was the greatest conqueror of the ancient world, and thereby set an example to dazzle the minds of all later conquerors and would-be emulators, from the Caesars of the *Roman Empire* to *Napoleon I*, to schoolboy daydreams of many who later served and expanded the *British Empire* in the eighteenth and nineteenth centuries and worried during the *Great Game* that Russians might march like the Greeks into India, and even *Hitler*. From his base in unified Greece, in 334 B.C.E. he crossed the Straits (Hellespont, or *Dardanelles*) with a Greco-Macedonian army and assaulted the mighty Persian Empire. He easily defeated the first Persian forces sent to stop him and took all of Asia Minor. Thereafter he invaded Syria. In 333 B.C.E. Alexander accomplished what no Greek (or Macedonian) had done before: he destroyed the main Persian Army, at Issus, where it was commanded by no less a personage than the emperor of Persia himself, Darius.

This was the decisive moment of Alexander's life and reign. He did not turn back to govern Greece, which was now secure from its ancient foe, and where he might have ruled as a great law-giver, builder, and civilizer of people and nations. Instead, he chose mere conquest, plunging ever deeper into the building of an empire that could not be sustained in his day, and in fact would not long outlast his death. From Syria he completed *pacification* of the *Levant* and invaded Egypt (332 B.C.E.), where he made a religious trek to an ancient Egyptian oasis shrine and claimed title to the inheritance of the Pharaohs, both divine and secular. Before departing to complete the conquest of Persia, he founded Alexandria on the Mediterranean coast of Egypt. In 331 B.C.E. he returned to Mesopotamia and defeated a regrouped Persian army under Darius at Guagamela. That opened a path through the heart of the Persian empire to India, and Alexander trod along it confidently at the head of his men. The pace of his advance was greatly speeded by the clever innovation of having the Army's supplies accompany along the coast by ship, rather than be carried overland by its men and beasts.

Alexander's despotism grew apace with his success. He crossed into Afghanistan and thence into India (Punjab). These were rich and densely populated lands, and his men—now thousands of miles from home and already burdened with more *plunder* than they could have imagined a few years prior, or carry or spend—refused to continue on a campaign of conquest that no longer had a clear focus or any end in sight. Alexander was thus turned back from the cusp of conquest of the subcontinent and began the long journey home. Behind him, the Mauryan state arose in India in the confused aftermath of his invasion and disruption. The army reached Susa in 324 B.C.E. only after many tribulations and much suffering and death among its cohorts. Convinced by now of his own divinity, Alexander could not convince many others. He died ingloriously of a fever at age 33. No other person in history, save Napoleon, would accomplish so much in war by such a young age, and few did so at any age. His empire looks far more impressive on maps of the ancient world than it was in fact, where it was little more than a narrow path of conquest through sullen alien lands, without cohesion, stability, or governing purpose. It quickly fell apart, divided after his death among quarrelsome generals, resentful and recovering conquered provinces, and always fractious and rebellious Greeks.

Suggested Readings: John Boardman et al., eds., *Oxford History of the Classical World*, (1988–); Robert Fox, *Alexander the Great* (1986); Peter Green, *Alexander of Macedon* (1991).

Alexander I, of Russia (1777–1825). Tsar of Russia, 1801–1825. In his early years Alexander was sometimes called "the Enlightened Despot," because of his education by French philosophes and flirtation with social and constitutional reform; he even corresponded about these issues with *Thomas Jefferson*. Alexander was raised by his grandmother, *Catherine II*, who imparted to him her desire to modernize Russia and link it fully to the West. In contrast, his father (Paul I, "the Mad Tsar") was a brutally stupid ruler whose disastrous reign ended in his *assassination* by a clutch of nobles, and possibly Alexander, in 1801. That act propelled the twenty-four-year-old tsar into supreme power, but left him guilt-ridden at the means used to acquire the throne. Alexander had a mercurial temperament; possibly, he was manic-depressive. In any case, he was subject to prolonged and violent mood swings that alternated between incapacitation and frenetic mysticism.

As tsar, Alexander began well, reforming Russia's bloated and inefficient bureaucracy, seeking to introduce universal education, and reforming the legal code. At first he was also an admirer of *Napoleon*, but over time he learned to despise him. Alexander was drawn by *Metternich* and *Castlereagh*—but mainly, he was provoked by Napoleon himself—into a series of coalition wars against the French tyrant. Alexander's Austrian ally and his own vast armies were decisively defeated in the *War of the Third Coalition*. Alexander then met Napoleon face-to-face at *Tilsit* in 1807 and with him divided Europe and the still warm carcass of Alexander's other erstwhile ally, *Prussia*. In fact, Alexander showed that he had imperial ambitions that nearly matched Napoleon's, even if he lacked the latter's imprudence and all-consuming need to dominate. Alexander now ripped Finland from Sweden, Bessarabia from Turkey, and penetrated yet deeper into Central Asia, following the path cleared by his mother.

Alexander felt deeply and personally betrayed by Napoleon's invasion of Russia in 1812, and thereafter would hear nothing of peace with the French. He joined in the *War of the Fourth Coalition* determined to end Napoleon's rule forever and to expand his own domain in Poland. He was constantly duped and managed by Metternich, who with cutting accuracy said that Alexander was "too weak for true ambition, but too strong for pure vanity." Alexander rode into Paris at the head of a vast army in 1814, a feat of arms long remembered by Russians—when *Stalin* was congratulated at *Potsdam* on his victorious presence in Berlin, he reputedly remarked: "Tsar Alexander got to Paris." Alexander personally attended the *Congress of Vienna*. He extended Russian influence into Central Europe under the guise of a Polish *protectorate* and a conservative coalition with Austria and Prussia, but he never achieved his more visionary objective of a new international order based on conservative and Christian principles. He championed *reaction* against the influence of the *French Revolution*. Five years after *Waterloo* he still had a million men under arms, which he threatened to use to support the messianic aims of the *Holy Alliance*. His reactionary rhetoric, drift into repression at home, military interventions in Poland and Italy, and threat to intervene in far away Latin America in behalf of the principle of *legitimacy* of deposed monarchs all helped push Britain out of the *Congress system* and provoked the United States to proclaim the *Monroe Doctrine*. Alexander was followed into power by his even more deeply reactionary brother, *Nicholas I. See also Alexander II; Ivan III; Nicholas II; Peter I.*

Suggested Readings: P. K. Grimsted, *The Foreign Ministers of Alexander I* (1969); M. Raeff, *Michael Speransky* (1961).

Alexander I, of Yugoslavia (1888–1934). Regent, and later king, of the *United Kingdom of the Serbs, Croats and Slovenes* from 1918 to 1929, when the name was changed to Yugoslavia. He was instrumental in establishing the *Little Entente*, which he wanted to connect to France in a larger security arrangement. While on a diplomatic mission to France in 1934, he was *assassinated* by a Macedonian fanatic.

Alexander II, of Russia (1818–1881). Tsar, 1855–1881. He became tsar at the end of the *Crimean War*, a disaster for Russia, which uncovered its backwardness and finally forced serious reform on its ruling classes. Like *Peter I* before him, Alexander was determined to achieve *modernization* of the Russian economy, government, judicial system, and military, and like Peter, he would largely fail. He initiated a series of great reforms, starting with the most fundamental: *emancipation* of the *serfs*, saying: "Better to abolish serfdom from above than to wait until it begins to abolish itself from below." Legal liberation was enacted without a corresponding grant of land, which hamstrung its economic effects and in some cases left peasants worse off. During Alexander's reign the first signs of a *crisis of rising expectations* appeared in Russia, as liberalization made room for more open dissent among the educated classes. Many intellectuals were frustrated by the paternalism and repression of the Russian state, even as it liberalized. They therefore turned to more radical political theories, including *anarchism* and *Marxism*. Others looked inward, and backward, in the *Slavophile* tradition. More importantly than the changing fashions of intellectual dissent, real class change and class conflict was also on the rise as a result of the *industrialization* that was coming to Alexander's Russia, bringing with it *railways* and new industries, but also rapid growth of new and restless social classes and a rapid expansion of Russia's cities and attendant and rising demands for urban and political reform.

In foreign policy, Alexander was the *Union's* main support during the *American Civil War*, when France and Britain flirted with *recognition* of the *Confederacy*. He wished the Union to serve as a commercial and geopolitical counterweight to Britain, to distract the British from his own designs on the Ottoman Empire. In 1867 he approved the sale of *Russian-America* (Alaska) to the United States. Maintaining amicable relations with *Prussia*, he expanded into the *Balkans* under cover of *pan-Slavism*, and into Central Asia under cover of defending Christians against the Muslim Turks, conquering Samarkand in 1868, Khiva in 1873, and Bukhara in 1876. All of that raised suspicion in London that Alexander's real objective was to capture India. This Anglo-Russian conflict deepened over Afghanistan, in the *Great Game*. Alexander repeatedly used foreign crises to recover Russia's interests lost in the Crimean War and to advance them further: taking advantage of the *Franco-Prussian War*, he repudiated the military limits placed on the Black Sea in 1856; he greatly weakened Turkey in the *Treaty of San Stefano*; and he seized border areas from China during the great dislocation and confusion of the *Taiping Rebellion*. His assassination (by a radical group called Peoples' Will) propelled Russia back into reaction, including officially sanctioned *pogroms*, which ultimately drove two million destitute Jews to emigrate, mainly to the United States. *See also Alexander I; Catherine II; Ivan III; Nicholas I; Nicholas II.*

Suggested Readings: E. Almedingen, *The Emperor Alexander II* (1962); W. Morse, *Alexander II and the Modernization of Russia* (1962).

Alexander III, of Russia (1845–1894). Tsar, 1881–1894. In contrast to his reforming father, Alexander III was a reactionary who increased repression by the *secret police*, permitted *pogroms* against the Jews, and attempted rough *Russification* of Finland and other provinces. This led to deterioration in relations with the United States and other liberal countries. Alexander also presided over an economic boom and managed to avoid serious international conflict. In 1894 he agreed to a Franco-Russian alliance.

Algeciras Conference (1906). An attempt to settle the ongoing dispute that led to the *Moroccan Crisis* of 1905. Contrary to Germany's hopes and expectations, the main significance of the conference was that it brought France and Britain closer and opened a channel between those powers and Russia as well. The conference also authorized France and Spain to police Morocco, which remained under nominal rule by its *sultan*. The Swiss acted as observers. The United States also signed the agreement, but unhelpfully made clear that it would do nothing to enforce its terms. *See also entangling alliances.*

Algeria. In the classical age, before the full expansion of the *Roman Empire*, coastal kingdoms in what is now Algeria were dominated, though not directly ruled, by the Carthaginian Empire. As a result of the *Punic Wars*, Carthage was conquered by Rome (146 B.C.E.).

Within a generation, most of the rest of the North African coast was absorbed by Rome, which also penetrated the interior as far as the fertile zone extended, which at that time was much further than it is today; arable lands were later lost to natural *desertification* and an expanded *Sahara Desert*. Algeria remained a Roman province until the fifth century C.E., when it was lost to Rome by a combination of *Berber* assaults from the deep desert and invasion and conquest by the barbarian Vandals. The *Byzantine Empire* recovered coastal Algeria temporarily in the sixth century, but could not hold it, as *Constantinople* itself faced military pressures from the Persian Empire to the east, new barbarian threats arriving from the north, and then in the seventh and eighth centuries the explosion of *Islam* out of the Arabian desert. *Arab* holy war (*jihad*) rapidly overran all of North Africa. Throughout the *Maghreb*, the new conquerors blended with the Berbers, and various Islamic *caliphates* overlay lingering Roman and Byzantine influences. Over time, this created a syncretic but fundamentally Islamicized and Arabicized culture and society in Algeria, beneath the succession of dynasties (mostly centered in Morocco) that ruled it over the centuries: the Fatamids, Almoravids, Almohads, and Marinds.

In the tenth century an independent Algerian (Berber) dynasty, the Fatamids, arose out of turmoil caused by a combination of desert doctrinal disputes and local political interests. Throughout, Algeria served as one of the termini of the trans-Saharan *slave trade*. With the rise of a Christian empire in Spain during the long *Reconquista*, the Muslim states in North Africa faced a new naval and invasion threat. They responded by developing navies of their own, made up mostly of *galleys* rowed by Christian *slaves*. The small Muslim states were known in Europe as the *Barbary States*. Algiers was one, and for two centuries it was a major port supporting Muslim "Barbary pirate" raids on the lucrative trade of the western Mediterranean up to, during, and after the *Renaissance*. With Spanish power ascendant from 1492, Morocco was able to defend itself, but not Algiers. It therefore turned to the great Islamic power of the Age, the *Ottoman Empire*, for assistance. The price exacted was Turkish *suzerainty*. The city and its hinterland thereafter became the main Ottoman port in the western Mediterranean from 1518. That year, the main *corsair* leader was chased from his base in Algiers by Spanish and Zayanid (the new local dynasty) forces. His brother, Khair al-Din, returned in 1525 as an *Ottoman* pasha and resumed Algiers' corsair ways. He briefly occupied Tunis in 1534. Spain attacked in force in 1541, but was repulsed. Algiers and its hinterland was then ruled by *deys*, in the name of the Ottoman Empire, to the French invasion in 1830.

About 1780 the interior Arab and Berber tribes rebelled under the leadership of *marabouts*. In the first quarter of the nineteenth century, pirating provoked the *Tripolitan War* with the United States and then intervention by the navies of the *Great Powers*. Also during the *Napoleonic Wars*, the deys supplied grain to Napoleon, accumulating a large credit in Paris. In 1815 the *Restoration* government repudiated this debt, starting a prolonged row that—along with France's domestic turmoil and continuing complaints about *piracy*, and the need of a failing monarch, Charles X, to divert attention and domestic unrest with some foreign triumph—culminated in a French invasion, 1830–1832. After the fall of Algiers and Oran to the *Armée d'Afrique*, a fierce *jihad* of desert resistance to the French was led by Abd al-Qadir (1808–1883) from 1832. He was eventually defeated, but managed to stave off conquest and capture for 15 years, during which time he tied down more than 100,000 French and colonial troops. After his capture in 1847, his followers continued the fight at a lower level of intensity into the late 1870s.

Algeria occupied a special place in colonial history as both a kind of French *Siberia*—full of political *exiles*—and a preferred locale of settlement by *colons*: by 1940, one million poor French (and other) colons would migrate to lands forcibly cleared by the French Army. In 1871 Algeria was formally "attached" to France; violent resistance to this act continued until 1879. In 1896 direct rule ended, replaced by a colons-dominated assembly. Algeria was under *Vichy* control during *World War II,* until Anglo-American troops forced a switch to the *Free French* side in 1942. French rule was fully restored in 1945, but local *nationalism* and anticolonial grievances led to the *Algerian War of Independence*, beginning in 1954, which saw cruel and widespread atrocities on both sides. The Algerian revolt brought down the French *Fourth Republic*, already teetering from defeat in Indochina, and returned *Charles de Gaulle* to power. He accepted Algerian independence in 1962 after a *referendum* that received an overwhelming vote for separation from France. That entailed departure of the French colons ("pied noir") and almost led to *civil war* in France itself.

Ahmed Ben Bella (b. 1919) was premier, 1962–1965, and president, 1963–1965. He was an *authoritarian* (especially toward the interior *Bedouin*) and *socialist* at home, broadly *neutral* in the *Cold War*, but active in promoting *decolonization*. During Ben Bella's years in power, Algeria helped train nationalist, anticolonial *guerrillas* from several Middle Eastern and African countries. He was ousted in a *coup*, led by former Front de la Libération Nationale commander Houari Boumédienne (1927–1978), who was dictator until 1978. Boumédienne toed a more neutralist line, accepting aid from the West and the Soviets while opposing any accommodation with Israel. He also sought a *pan-Arab* union in North Africa. Algeria openly broke with the West in 1967 and joined the fight against Israel in the *Third Arab-Israeli War*. During the 1970s and 1980s it developed close ties with the *Soviet bloc*. It opposed Morocco's attempt to annex *Western Sahara*, instead supporting *POLISARIO*. Domestic unrest after 1988 led to a multiparty constitution and attempts to patch relations with the West in the early 1990s. Despite economic distress born of its failed attempt at *self-sufficiency*, followed by collapse of its Soviet ally, Algeria criticized United Nations action against Iraq in the 1990 *Gulf War* and after. When Islamic *fundamentalists* won a first round of elections in 1992, the second was canceled by the military, and emergency rule instituted. This action was not greeted in the West with the same dismay that met canceled elections elsewhere. Algeria accused Iran of funding the militants and broke *diplomatic relations*. It also *recalled its ambassador* from radical, fundamentalist Sudan. By 2000 the Islamic resistance had been repressed, but by extremely brutal means and at an enormous cost in lives and legitimacy: in 1999 the government publicly admitted to 100,000 dead; the actual toll was almost certainly significantly higher.

Suggested Readings: Monir S. Girgis, *Mediterranean Africa* (1987); I. William Zartman and William Habeeb, eds., *Polity and Society in Contemporary North Africa* (1993).

Algerian War of Independence (1954–1962). After the French defeat at *Dien Bien Phu*, Vietnam, Algerian nationalists (the Front de la Libération Nationale, or FLN) fought a *guerrilla* campaign against the French colonial presence that ultimately pitched 100,000 *irregulars* against 500,000 French troops and the one million *colons* (pied noirs) who had settled in Algeria. This campaign so involved the military and engaged the national will that Paris withdrew from control of Morocco and Tunisia, the better to hold onto "l'Algérie française." In 1956 and 1957 the Algerians moved into urban guerrilla warfare in Algiers and other large towns and cities. In 1958 a *mutiny* within the French Army threatened to spread the war to France itself. *Charles de Gaulle* was recalled from the political wilderness, while the FLN set up a *provisional government* in Tunis. De Gaulle put down the mutiny and continued the war, but also offered *autonomy* to Algeria. That sparked a *terrorist* campaign within France and a revolt by French settlers, joined by units of the *Foreign Legion* and the traitorous *Organization de l'armée secrèt* (OAS). Settler and OAS bombs set off in Paris, rising casualties, atrocities, and the general viciousness of both sides shifted French *public opinion* against the war, and Algeria won its independence in July 1962. Perhaps one million Algerians died, along with 30,000 French troops and colons. The war had wider significance too, as inspiration to other *national liberation* movements, including in *southern Africa*. See also *Franz Fanon*.

Algiers. *See Algeria.*

alien. Someone who is foreign born and not a *naturalized* citizen, and therefore owes legal allegiance to another country. A resident/nonresident alien is one who has/has not taken up domicile. Among legal aliens are *diplomats*, *visa* workers, legal immigrants, and *tourists*. An illegal alien is a foreigner who enters without permission. An enemy alien is an alien present or residing in a country with which his or her own is at war. *See also asylum; migration; refugees.*

alignment. The way states are arranged or arrayed vis-à-vis one another, according to their common enemies, *security treaties*, and political interests. *See also alliance.*

Allende Gossens, Salvador (1908–1973). A Chilean *Marxist* who was narrowly elected president in 1970, after three earlier failures (1952, 1958, 1964). He encountered substantial domestic opposition to his program of *nationalizations* and was opposed by several *multinational corporations* whose property his government *expropriated*. He was also firmly opposed by the *Nixon* administration. CIA support for Chilean strikes designed to undermine the Allende government has been confirmed. A CIA role in the 1973 *coup*, during which Allende committed suicide, is widely alleged and may be true, but direct evidence for the charge is still lacking. However, evidence of earlier CIA support for *destabilization* and the overt hostility of the Nixon administration reasonably suggest that the coup may well have had covert U.S. support. In either case, its primary instigators and supporters were Chileans, and not just in the military. The coup led to a repressive *junta* under *Augusto Pinochet* who ruled with an iron, indeed murderous, hand until 1989. In 1990 Allende's corpse was exhumed from the unmarked grave where it was buried by the generals after the coup, and given a *state funeral*. That was done not so much to honor his policies as to commemorate his death while holding, and his defense of, a democratic office.

alliance. A formal agreement among *states*, whether secret or open, in which military and security policy is coordinated with a common *diplomacy*. For the most part, alliances are formed for defensive purposes to mutually enhance the *national security* of members by the simple expedient of combining *deterrent* resources, as in the *Triple Entente*. Alliances may also form to collectively pursue *aggression*, such as did the *Axis*. States may combine in part out of shared ideological goals, as did the members of the *Holy Alliance, Warsaw Pact*, and *NATO*, but this is both a rare and weak bond. More commonly, states ally in spite of ideological differences, as was the case with the *United Nations alliance* in *World War II*. Curiously, *neutral* states sometimes ally to avoid being drawn into alliances; examples include the *League of Armed Neu-*

trality and the *Nonaligned Movement*. It is often asserted by international relation (IR) theorists, usually political scientists, that rigid alliances are a key cause of war because they raise, rather than merely reflect, tensions and exacerbate crises. An oft-cited example in the literature is the *mobilization crisis* preceding *World War I*. Yet, much contrary evidence exists that suggests alliances most often help clarify the intentions of potential adversaries and thereby reinforce *deterrence*. *See also alignment; balance of power; bandwagoning; casus foederis; coalition; collective security; confederation; entangling alliance; entente; league; nonalignment; neutrality; pact; tacit alliance.*
   Suggested Reading: Stephen Walt, *Origins of Alliances* (1987).

Alliance for Progress (1961–1969). An aid and trade initiative for Latin America that revisited the *Good Neighbor policy* of the 1930s. Announced by *John F. Kennedy* in March 1961, it was endorsed by all *OAS* states, except Cuba. It was premised on the idea that the United States had neglected Latin America and on a *takeoff* theory of *development*, which had a powerful Kennedy administration advocate in Walt W. Rostow. The initiative failed because it was simultaneously underfunded and overly ambitious and because of substantive disagreements over the purpose of aid to the region and whether such aid should pursue the goal of promoting democracy. *Richard Nixon* brought it to a formal end.

Allied and Associated Powers. *See Allies (World War I).*

Allied Control Commission. The command structure, or Kommandatura, set up by the four occupying powers in Germany after *World War II*.

Allies (World War I). Common term for the *alliance* that fought against the four *Central Powers* in *World War I*. Its principal members were the *British Empire*, France, Japan, Russia, Serbia, Italy, Belgium, Greece, and Romania, though it numbered fully twenty-eight nations by war's end. The United States insisted upon calling itself an "Associated Power" attached to this alliance, during the war, at the *Paris Peace Conference*, and in the *peace treaties*. The careful wording was to uphold the fiction that the United States had not joined an *entangling alliance*. That was a fine distinction that made no difference. *See also* Entente Cordiale.

Allies (World War II). Common term for the *World War II* alliance that was formally called the "*United Nations*." Its principal members were the United States, the Soviet Union, Britain, and China. Lesser powers included the *Free French* and some forty small nations and territories, of which the more notable were Australia, Belgium, Canada, Greece, Norway, Poland, South Africa, and Yugoslavia (Serbia). Two million troops of the *Indian Army* fought for the *British Empire*. Other than Ethiopians and South Africans, most

Africans who fought did so within various colonial forces. Burmese, Vietnamese, Filipinos, and other Asian peoples were also engaged, in association with larger imperial powers or as *resistance* fighters. The formal name of the alliance was transferred to the postwar security organization founded in 1945 by these victors of World War II.

allocation of resources. How resources are apportioned within an economy. For traditional economists the primary interest is in questions of *efficiency*. Less orthodox views focus on social and *distributive justice*.

ally. (1) A *state* bound by *security treaty* to another state. (2) Less commonly, a state that tacitly coordinates defense policy with another without aid of any *treaty*.

Al-Sabah dynasty. *See Kuwait.*

Alsace-Lorraine. Alsace was seized by France in 1648, as part of the spoils of its victory in the *Thirty Years' War*. Both provinces were the arena of back-and-forth fighting during the wars of *Louis XIV*. France invaded Lorraine during the *War of the Polish Succession* (1733), but did not annex it outright until 1766. After the *Franco-Prussian War*, Alsace and most of Lorraine were ceded to Germany in the *Treaty of Frankfurt* (1871).

Recovery of these lost provinces was the central aim of all French *war plans* before *World War I*, a known fact that influenced *Bismarck's* diplomacy and underlay the strategy of the *Schlieffen Plan*. These provinces witnessed scenes of awful carnage during the *Battle of the Frontiers*. Reunification was achieved by France in the *Treaty of Versailles* (1919). Reclamation of the territories then became a demand of German nationalists. In 1940 the provinces were reannexed by Germany. They were *liberated* and returned to France in 1944. Their continued French status was ensured by the outcome of *World War II* and by Franco-German cooperation within the *European Union*, not to mention the *force de frappe*.

Alwa. Also known as Maquerra. An early medieval *sudanic* and Christian kingdom on the upper Nile (*Nubia*). In the tenth century it was still able to keep *Muslim* traders away from its borders, though it conducted trade with *Mamluk* Egypt. Its king was captured by a Mamluk army in 1316 and replaced by a Muslim ruler. Alwa migrated further south, but was unable to fend off nomadic Arabicized tribes from also migrating southward. It then fragmented into several smaller states, some of which survived into the late fifteenth century.

Amal. A *shi'ite militia* active in the *Lebanese Civil War*, and after, supported by Iran and fiercely opposed to Israel.

Amazon basin. The great drainage basin of the Amazon river system, with its several thousand tributaries. It lies mostly in Brazil but portions are found in nine different countries. After 1980 it became the focus of international environmental concern as *slash and burn* clearing continued, possibly contributing to *global warming* and certainly threatening *biological diversity*. Since 1500, it has also been a place of dislocation and frequently severe mistreatment of *indigenous peoples*.

Amazon Pact. A 1978 treaty signed by most states with territory in the *Amazon basin*: Bolivia, Brazil, Colombia, Ecuador, Guyana, Peru, Suriname, and Venezuela. It aimed at joint development and management of the Amazon basin and at regulation of *water* usage, navigation, transportation, research, and *tourism*.

Amazons. *See Dahomey.*

ambassador. The highest rank of *diplomat*, historically considered the personal representative of a *sovereign* or of the government of a sovereign power. Since the Italian *Renaissance*, ambassadors usually have been resident in their host country. If ad hoc or roving among several posts, they may be called ambassadors-at-large or special ambassadors. Until the seventeenth century, most ambassadors were referred to as ambassadors and procurators, the later term referring to a legal office of specific negotiating power that harkened to ancient Rome. The essential role of an ambassador is to directly and clearly represent the policies and interests of his or her state to a foreign power and to report back to the home government on the political affairs of his or her host country. *See also* chargé d'affaires; *consul; diplomacy; envoy extraordinary; herald; high commissioner; nonresident ambassador; plenipotentiary.*

America. A common alternative to "United States of America." Politically correct persons (for example, academics and editorial writers) wince at this usage, as supposedly exclusive of other nations of the *Americas*.

American Civil War (1861–1865). It broke out after seven *slave states* seceded from the *Union* after the 1860 election of *Abraham Lincoln*, whose ascendancy was seen in the South as presaging the eventual end of the "peculiar institution" of *slavery*. The first seven states were emulated in *secession* by another four states after fighting began. These eleven states (of a total of thirty-three in the prewar Union) formed a new republic, the *Confederate States of America* (CSA). Although secession was triggered by the 1860 election, it sprang from a far deeper conflict between the social values and economies of most slave states—not all slave states departed the Union—and the key industrialized, mercantile, and free-labor Northern states. That conflict had become irreconcilable from the late 1840s with the application for admission of new states after the sudden westward expansion of the United States as a result of the *Mexican-American War*.

On the field of battle the South enjoyed early successes owing to superior morale and early inferior Union generalship. However, over time the natural advantages of the North in numbers of people and industrial capacity were brought to bear and produced a great, though bloody, victory. The war was decided by many factors, but two stand out: (1) a Union naval *blockade* curled around the Confederate coast like an anaconda, an image for which the blockade plan and line was named, and it progressively strangled Confederate trade, aggravating a normal wartime inflation crisis that was further worsened by bad Confederate diplomacy and worse monetary policy; and (2) *attrition* on the battlefield wore down Southern personnel and morale and gave the advantage to the more populous and dynamic North.

The key battles were the successful siege of Vicksburg, which surrendered on July 4, 1863, cutting the Confederacy in half along the line of the Mississippi, and *Gettysburg*, July 1–3, 1863, on whose sanguine fields and corpse-carpeted hills was turned back "the high tide of the Confederacy." Together, those Union victories set the Confederacy on the permanent defensive, while Vicksburg elevated *Ulysses S. Grant* to unified command of all Union forces. Grant then launched, in 1864, his Grand Campaign, a sustained invasion of the CSA heartland. He drove toward Richmond at the head of the Armies of the James and the Potomac, opposed by *Robert E. Lee's* Army of Northern Virginia—the Union named its armies for rivers; the CSA called its after states. Meanwhile, Grant ordered *William Tecumseh Sherman* to drive a second Union army toward Atlanta and Savannah, and sent other, smaller armies to likewise and simultaneously cut into the Confederacy from several directions. Lincoln rejoiced as Grant doggedly drove south, the first general he appointed to command the Army of the Potomac who did not turn back when first beaten and bloodied by Lee, as Grant was at The Wilderness (May 4–7, 1864). Sherman took Atlanta, reached the Atlantic coast, and turned north into the Carolinas, cutting a swath of destruction through the deep Confederacy. Meanwhile, Philip Henry Sheridan also drove south, parallel to Grant, putting the Shenandoah Valley to the torch to deny its forage and crops to Lee and to block the usual Confederate counterattack through the Valley toward Washington and Grant's rear.

These Union armies were not at all like the amateur force that panicked and ran at First Bull Run in 1861. They were swollen with masses of new conscripts, but these were wrapped around a hard core of tough and determined veterans. Such men wanted to end the war and go home, but they also wanted victory. They therefore embraced the much longed-for, and too-long withheld, aggressiveness of their Western commanders and, as they had done under Grant at Vicksburg, again they bisected the Confederacy. A huge pincher movement closed, catching and crushing the rump of Southern forces crowded into a dug-in perimeter around Petersburg and Richmond—though not without a prolonged winter of *trench warfare* that exacted the "last, full measure of devotion" from both sides. During bitter, nonstop fighting over eleven months during 1864–1865, two great armies were never out of contact with each other, as they grappled in a grinding, bloody war of attrition brought about by Lee's decision to entrench against Grant's tenacious effort to take the Southern capital. When Grant finally broke the rebel lines at Petersburg, Lee's rag-tag remnants retreated, and many who had long been loyal to "The Cause" had finally had enough and deserted. Hungry, barefoot troops could run only so far, even for Lee, and they were compelled to surrender at Appomattox Court House (April 9, 1865). Lincoln was shot by a misfit Confederate assassin within the week, dying shortly thereafter, on April 15th. The last remnants of CSA resistance, mainly in the Trans-Mississippi region, surrendered a few weeks later.

The Confederacy lost the war because it failed to secure massive foreign military aid or outright alliance with, not just *diplomatic recognition* by, France and Britain. Conversely, the Union won by forcing the issue militarily, finally bringing to bear superior numbers and industrial capacity under generals of necessary ruthlessness and proven ability. And it won by modifying its diplomacy and curtailing its more principled impulses just enough to placate European sensibilities and forestall outside intervention. The conversion of the war after Lincoln's *emancipation* proclamation (1862) from one to preserve the Union into a war also to end slavery—an evolution that saw slavery as both a moral evil and a strategic asset of the Southern war effort—played an important role in reshaping European public opinion. The ferocity of the war partly reflected that both sides believed they were defending high moral purpose, with roots in the ideals of the *American War of Independence* and the Constitution: the South was persuaded that it fought for *states' rights, nullification*, and a new national liberty; the North was determined to preserve an existing constitutional union of law-abiding and self-governing free men and to uphold a more profound doctrine of natural liberty. Some 620,000 Americans were killed in the Civil War, virtually all of them soldiers, which is still more than in all other American wars combined. Another half-million were maimed in body or mind.

For more than a generation afterward, the majority of Americans had little appetite for *annexation*, seeing the bitter fruits of the Civil War as the harvest of the annexations of the Mexican War. Thus, public opinion opposed acquisition of Cuba or Santo Domingo and commonly called the purchase of *Alaska* "Seward's Folly." The immediate outcome of the Civil War was preservation of the American Union, with all that portended for the defense of civilization in the twentieth century. Surely the war's greatest, most lasting legacy was to expand the original American notion of freedom to whole new classes—and races—of men and women. *See also Alabama claims; Alexander II; contraband; Jefferson Davis; Gettysburg Address; ironclads; King Cotton; Winfield Scott; William Seward; Trent Affair.*

Suggested Readings: Bruce Catton, *The Centennial History of the Civil War*, 3 vols. (1961–1965); Shelby Foote, *The Civil War*, 3 vols. (1958–1974); Ulysses S. Grant, *Personal Memoirs* (1885); James McPherson, *Battle Cry of Freedom* (1988); David Potter, *The Impending Crisis, 1848–1861* (1976).

American Expeditionary Force (AEF). The U.S. armed forces in Europe during *World War I*. When the United States *declared war* on Germany in April 1917, its Navy was world class but its Army numbered fewer than 120,000 men, mostly unequipped with heavy weapons; and its 15,000-man Marine Corps was scattered in the Philippines and Central America. Yet, in March 1918, 320,000 U.S. troops were in France; by August, 1.3 million had arrived. By November, the war was won.

American Relief Administration (ARA). A *famine* relief agency set up after *World War I* to alleviate postwar starvation in Belgium and other parts of Europe, both for humanitarian reasons and to forestall the spread of *Bolshevism*. It was headed, very effectively, by *Herbert Hoover*. During the great famine in Russia from 1921 to 1923, it fed, clothed, and provided medical treatment to tens of millions of Soviet citizens, quite possibly saving the young Soviet regime. *See also Fridtjof Nansen.*

American Revolution (1775–1783). A conflict that began as a minor rebellion but ended as a war of secession from empire by thirteen of twenty-six of Britain's North American and Caribbean *colonies*. (*Upper Canada, Newfoundland*, and Nova Scotia remained loyal, as did all British colonies of the West Indies; *Lower Canada* was effectively *occupied*.) The colonists rebelled for many reasons, among which were efforts to secure greater economic freedom from England's *mercantilist* policies; a desire for enhanced but still limited self-government, which rapidly evolved into demands for full political independence from the crown; a movement to preserve traditional colonial liberties against more direct imperial administration; and population pressures that fed into the powerful desire by new settlers to expand into historic Indian lands in New York and Ohio, then forbidden to white settlement by Indian treaties and alliances with England. The rebellion grew out of the *Seven Years' War* (1756–1763), which, in the *Treaty of Paris* (1763), removed the French threat from North America, thereby reducing colonist need for British military protection. That change also gave rise to demands for Britain to lift old restrictions on further expansion into the vast interior of North America, then still in Indian lands. Imperial policy saw the colonies in larger terms of global empire: London sought an orderly frontier and an end to its American wars and thus continued to deny western expansion to the colonists, knowing full well that further settlement would bring war with frontier Indian nations. In 1763 an order was issued forbidding settlers to cross the Appalachian divide, beyond which the land was to remain in Indian hands. London's alliances with, and perceived protection of, the *Iroquois* and other Indian interests chafed among the settlers as much as, or even more than, the presence of British garrisons and tax collectors.

On the other hand, the victory over France encouraged Lord North's (1732–1779) government to enforce *duties* on American exports it had long neglected, in order to make the colonies pay for the British garrisons that protected them. Although from the American point of view these taxes appeared onerous and the garrisons were burdensome, in fact the average Briton (also subjects of a unitary empire) paid 25 times as much in tax as the average colonist, whose imperial load amounted to about $1.20 per year. That was a fair bargain, in London's view, for having seen off the French and for securing the frontier. Finally, the irritant of the *Navigation Acts* was constant and deep. Fighting broke out with the "shot heard around the world" at Lexington and Concord (April 19, 1775) in Massachusetts, a year before the formal Declaration of Independence by the thirteen colonies (July 4, 1776). Thereafter, the principal contribution made by *George Washington* and the Continental Army and *militia* was to survive, and thereby to sustain the rebellion until Europe's other major powers intervened diplomatically and militarily, for their own reasons, against England. And that is just what happened: defeat of the British under John Burgoyne (1723–1792) at Saratoga (October 17, 1777) was not a decisive military affair in itself, but it permitted Britain's more powerful enemies to *recognize* the "United States" and join the war.

The most decisive battles thus actually took place on the high seas, after France and the Netherlands *declared war* on Britain in 1778 and 1780, respectively, and these powers brought to bear combined navies capable of threatening British commercial and strategic interests more vital than retention of the American colonies. Capping this effort was a major victory on land, over a British army under Charles Cornwallis (1738–1805) at *Yorktown* (October 19, 1781). That said, it was unlikely that Britain could have won after 1780 even had the colonists received minimal or no foreign support: London's *supply lines* were stretched over 3,000 miles of ocean, while the United States was just too large to effectively occupy with an eighteenth century army. After all, it had taken 50,000 troops and many units of American militia to defeat the French in Canada in the 1750s. Once England also faced major hostilities in Europe, the outcome of American independence was ordained. That is why London agreed to the *Treaty of Paris* (1783) on terms far more favorable to the colonists than American arms alone had won in the field or at sea.

As a result of the war, the *British Empire* granted independence to the 13 colonies, and additionally lost to America's allies Florida, Louisiana (east of the Mississippi), Tobago, Minorca, and Senegal (Dakar), though it remained a power in the Americas through retention of the several Canadian colonies and Newfoundland and its most valuable colonies in the Caribbean. It is noteworthy that about one-third of the American population rejected separation from the crown and remained loyal to Britain. Most left, returning to England, resettling in the Caribbean, or moving (many were forcibly expelled) as *United Empire Loyalists* to Upper Canada and Nova Scotia, where their descendants harbored anti-Yankee sentiments for many decades. The new republic treated the old Iroquois Confederacy—including its own Oneida and Tuscaroras allies—as defeated allies of the British, seized Indian lands, and drove most Iroquois into Canadian exile. Despite its complex of local and geopolitical origins, the American Revolution was also the first modern, political war: a conflict over fundamental ideas about governance. Rooted in the *Enlightenment*, it introduced into the real world the notion of mass democracy (which only evolved slowly in America itself after 1783), an idea that agitated the French next, and much of the world over the following centuries.

Suggested Readings: John Alden, *A History of the American Revolution* (1969); Samuel Flagg Bemis, *The Diplomacy of the American Revolution* (1957; 1983); D. Higginbotham, *The War of American Independence* (1977); Richard B. Morris, *The Peacemakers* (1965); Richard B. Morris, *Forging of the Union* (1987); Robert W. Tucker and David Hendrickson, *Fall of the British Empire* (1982).

American Samoa. It was taken over by the United States, 1900–1904, by agreement with Britain, which was *compensated* in the Solomon Islands, and Germany, which received *Western Samoa*. It was administered by the U.S. Navy, which used its superb harbor at Pago Pago until 1951, and then by the Interior Department. Its first elections were held in 1978. It is today an *unincorporated territory* of the United States. Samoans are American *nationals* but not *citizens*, which means they may come and go freely from the mainland and other U.S. *jurisdictions*, but may not vote. Of all American Samoans, by 2000 nearly 70 percent had *migrated* to *Hawaii* or *California*.

American system of manufactures. A term of British origin dating to exhibition at the Crystal Palace in London in 1851, referring to the American innovation of making interchangeable parts of various products by special-purpose machines. "Interchangeability" had been around a long time, as notably in the manufacture of firearms dating to the eighteenth century, at least. But in Europe this process was still carried out by skilled craftsmen who worked with and toward a set of standard measures, which they naturally could only approximate when using hand tools. Very often, in practice this meant that even standardized parts still had to be filed and fitted to the specific machines for which they were intended. The wonder of the "American system," as this early form of *mass production* became known, was that relatively unskilled workers could stamp out highly gauged parts, which even less skilled farmers or workers could easily fit to tools or machines greatly distant from the point of manufacture. The pioneer industries were small arms and farm tool manufacture, which led to innovative marketing through such new systems as mail catalogue and department stores. The British government imported U.S. machines and technology to establish the Enfield Armoury in London during the *Crimean War*, and thereafter all advanced economies adopted variants of the American system.

Suggested Readings: David Hounshell, *From the American System to Mass Production, 1800–1932* (1984); Otto Mayer and Robert Post, eds., *Yankee Enterprise* (1981); Nathan Rosenberg, ed., *The American System of Manufactures* (1969).

American War of Independence. *See American Revolution.*

Americas. North, Central, and South America, and their island extensions. They are named for the Florentine (later naturalized Spanish) cartographer and explorer—he helped map the coast of Venezuela—Amerigo Vespucci (1451–1512). He disputed *Columbus*'s original claim to have discovered the east coast of Asia, arguing correctly that yet another ocean, the Pacific, remained to be crossed. That said, the naming of two continents after him was based partly on misunderstanding of his accomplishments and partly on deliberate fraud. *See also New World.*

Amiens, Peace of (March 25, 1802). A false settlement of Mediterranean issues between Great Britain and France, which amounted to no more than a pause in the long war between those nations. It came about because England was temporarily without continental allies and because *Pitt* was briefly out of power over the issue of *Catholic Emancipation*. Amiens returned some recent conquests to France but allowed retention of certain strategic islands captured from France's allies and *protectorates*. Thus, Britain received Trinidad, which it had captured from Spain, and Ceylon, from the "Batavian Republic" that *Napoleon* controlled in Holland. Malta was to be restored to the Maltese Knights (Britain later reneged on this point), and the *Ionian Islands* were to be returned to Turkey. For the first time in a decade, all of Europe was briefly at peace. However, Napoleon stirred renewed tensions as within just a few months he intervened politically in Germany, Switzerland, and Italy. War between England and France resumed in May 1803.

Suggested Reading: E. Presseisen, *Amiens and Munich: Comparisons in Appeasement* (1978).

Amin, Idi Dada (b. 1926). A Ugandan officer in the British colonial army, and later the Ugandan Army, who took power in 1971 in a *coup* that deposed Milton Obote. He made himself dictator-for-life and conducted an eight-year reign of near-constant butchery, which relied upon and favored his own small, northern Kakwa tribe over most others, especially the historically ascendant Baganda and the Lango tribe, which dominated the army and was Obote's power base. Amin's Kakwa troops lived off murder and *plunder*. To satisfy their greed and shore up his regime, in 1972 he expelled the entire Asian population, bringing Uganda to its economic knees by gutting it of its commercial class. He also promoted Islam (he was a Muslim) against the interest of a predominantly Christian population. Despite these abuses, his theatrical bent for titillating insults aimed at the West played well elsewhere in Africa, among peoples with a grievance against the former colonial powers but who did not suffer him directly. Amin flirted with support for *terrorist* groups and drew financial and military support from Libya. In 1978 the United States imposed *sanctions* on coffee, which severely hurt Amin's regime. He was ousted only after provoking neighboring Tanzania, which he invaded in 1979, provoking *Nyerere* to counterinvade Uganda to the great joy of its oppressed, southern population. Amin fled to Libya, thence to Saudi Arabia, where he lived in comfortable exile. He left behind a *civil war* and *anarchy* from which Uganda took many years to recover. *See also Entebbe raid; Muammar Quadaffi.*

amnesty. Waiver of prosecution of an entire class of offenders (as opposed to a pardon, which is granted to an individual), such as a *prisoners of war*, guerrillas, or government troops who exceeded authority or those involved in *death squads*.

Amnesty International. A global *human rights* monitoring agency made up of hundreds of thousands of private volunteers and a small corps of salaried officers. It works to free *prisoners of conscience* and for the right to a fair trial, and it works against *torture* and capital punishment. Its main tactic is publicity based upon exceptionally careful documentation in annual and occasional reports, which lends its pronouncements a rare credibility in a highly contentious and politicized field. In 1977 it was awarded the *Nobel Prize* for Peace. It has official observer status at meetings of the *UNHRC* and reports also to some regional human rights bodies.

Amritsar massacre (April 13, 1919). It began as an illegal, but entirely peaceful, gathering of 10,000 Indian celebrants on a festival day in a walled garden at Jallianwala Bagh in Amritsar, in Punjab, listening to protestors speak against British rule. The gathering was held despite *martial law* being in effect. Earlier, however, there had been rioting sparked by the arrest of two of *Gandhi's* followers, and several Europeans had been singled out and killed and banks and businesses burned. Brigadier General Reginald Dyer, the local British commander, was determined to demonstrate who was in charge in Punjab, and in India as a whole. He ordered a unit of some 50 *Gurkha* troops to block the exits from the garden, and then he gave them orders to empty their magazines into the unarmed crowd, to "teach a lesson" to all India. In less than ten minutes nearly 1,500 casualties were inflicted, including 379 dead, among them hundreds of women and children (those are the official British figures; Gandhi established an Indian commission that put the death toll at nearly 1,000). Indian opinion was of course both appalled and deeply outraged. *Congress* was galvanized to organize national protests and to reject evermore Britain's claim to any moral authority to govern India.

Dyer was brought before a commission of inquiry in Lahore, where he testified that he gave the order to fire to produce "the necessary moral and widespread effect" of deterrence of future gatherings. He was censured and forced to resign by the commission. Other British opinion was more tolerant: the House of Lords passed a resolution officially commending him for decisiveness, and funds were raised by other officers and elements of a public grateful for his service, to ease the ending of his military career and with it his pension. Years later, Dyer remained unmoved by any moral awareness or contrition. He said that what he had done at Amritsar had been "a jolly good thing." In 1997, in an act intended to represent national contrition, Queen Elizabeth II officially repudiated what Dyer stood for when she laid a wreath and knelt in silent homage in the garden at Amritsar where the innocents had died.

The massacre of the innocents at Amritsar tattered the moral claims Britain made about its good government of India, that it was there to fulfill a "special obligation" to preserve Hindu rights and civilization from a return of Muslim tyranny in some new version of *Mughal* rule, and alternately to preserve Muslims from a tyranny by the Hindu majority. In other words, after Amritsar the days of British rule in India were clearly numbered and everyone but the General Dyers and the imperial press knew it. Gandhi moved to reorganize Congress into a mass political party in 1920 and announced a policy of permanent noncooperation with British rule—starting with a Congress-sponsored school, shops, and British goods *boycott* that September. Congress also now demanded outright independence for India, the very opposite of what Dyer and his supporters had intended or expected would be the result of the "lesson" of the massacre. In sum, the Amritsar massacre was a despicable display of the essential military despotism that underwrote British rule of India and that could not survive such clear exposure. Even so, it is worth recalling that six weeks earlier in Korea (March 1, 1919), Japanese occupation troops had run amok, killing 7,000 and wounding another 150,000 civilian demonstrators.

Amsterdam Treaty (1997). The successor to *Maastricht*, this *European Union (EU)* treaty furthered the idea of a common security and foreign policy and expanded the EU's role in *peacekeeping, humanitarian intervention, crisis management*, and missions of *mediation*.

Amur River. *See Manchuria; Sino-Soviet split.*

Anaconda Plan. *See American Civil War; Winfield Scott.*

analyst. (1) In general (in international relations): Any person who makes considered appraisals of the nature or course of world affairs, often on a professional basis. (2) In intelligence: A person with area, economic, language, scientific, or technical expertise who interprets *raw intelligence.*

anarchical society. A depiction of world politics in which international *anarchy* is significantly muted by decentralized social or societal features that exist in relations among states: *international law, international organization,* moral norms, principles of justice, and the *balance of power. See also classical school; community of nations; world governance.*
   Suggested Reading: Hedley Bull, *The Anarchical Society* (1975).

anarchism. A mid-nineteenth century, libertarian political theory advanced by thinkers such as *Pierre Proudhon* and *Mikhail Bakunin.* It achieved a sizeable following in the late nineteenth and early twentieth centuries. Anarchists saw all states as morally illegitimate because they infringed upon pure freedom. Anarchists looked to replace states with various utopian schemes that were often faintly and/or romantically *socialist*—although most anarchists were bitter rivals of *Marxists*—in their stress on idealized forms of voluntary social and economic cooperation in the absence of overarching political authority. Anarchists saw government, of whatever type, as the principal obstacle to perfect personal *liberty.* Several competing streams of anarchism developed, ranging from effete and sterile academic speculations about ideal stateless societies, to actual experimentation with self-governing collectives, all of which failed, to violent revolutionary idealism that sought the immediate destruction of all states and the states system via direct action such as *assassination* and disruption of public services. Anarchist *terrorists* were active at the end of the nineteenth century. They killed a tsar, an Austrian empress, an Italian king, a French president, a Spanish prime minister, U.S. President *William McKinley,* numerous minor nobility, officials in many countries, and scores of innocent bystanders. Anarchism was important as a dissident movement in prerevolutionary Russia, as a confusing and complicating factor in the *Russian Civil War,* as an intellectual influence in Republican China, and as a mass political movement in Spain before and during the *Spanish Civil War.* Its allure faded rapidly after *World War II,* everywhere save in minor corners of the Academy. At the end of the twentieth century and into the early twenty-first century, unsophisticated youths and street thugs styling themselves as anarchists—which only meant they endorsed a crudely destructive opposition to any public order and seemingly to all efforts at international cooperation and management of *globalization*—made organized appearances at meetings of the *World Trade Organization* and G-7.

anarchy. (1) Domestic: A social and political condition without government or law; this may be theoretical, as in the *state of nature* posited by various *social contract* theories, or actual, as when civil, political, and legal order breaks down into random violence in times of *invasion, occupation,* or *civil war*. (2) International: In the latter half of the twentieth century it became commonplace in academic discourse to proclaim that a condition of legal, moral, and security anarchy is the underlying condition of all *international relations*. It was said that the absence of any central authority over the *sovereign* states means that world politics necessarily approximates the imagined state of nature depicted by *Thomas Hobbes,* among others, in which there is a "war of all against all" and the core problem is the *security dilemma*. Most liberal critics and nearly all historians see all that as a crude view that does not account for common features of interstate cooperation or wider notions of political community such as the *res publica Christiana* previously or *NATO* in the post–Cold War era. They propose instead that modern states exist at the least in an *anarchical society*. In *international relations theory,* the debate is usually framed as one between *realists* and *idealists. See also balance of power; community of nations; English School; failed states; international law; international morality; international organization; international security; international society; laissez-faire; Luddism; national interest; national security; self-help; structural determinism; structure; world community; world governance; world government*.

Anatolia. The broad plateau between the Mediterranean and Black Seas. A key region for the *Ottoman Empire,* it is now the heart of Turkey.

ancien régime. (1) The political and social system of France and Europe before 1789, marked principally by *absolutism* and *mercantilism*. (2) Any era preceding a period of historic, revolutionary political and social upheaval. (3) The European and international order before *World War I,* dominated socially and politically by conservative, *multinational empires,* yet also filled with a sense of unfolding scientific, social, and moral progress. In retrospect, it was an era of enormous building tension among the *Great Powers*. Yet it appeared to most contemporaries that the major problems of human development and politics had already been solved, or soon would be. The shock of destruction that arrived during 1914–1918 was enormous and led to a similarly exaggerated postwar cultural, political, and economic pessimism that lasted until after *World War II* and in many ways ripples through Western culture and history still. *See also* Estates-General; *French Revolution*.
    Suggested Readings: Pierre Goubert, *The Ancien Régime* (1969); E. Williams, *The Ancien Régime in Europe, 1648–1789* (1979).

Andean Common Market (ANCOM). Also known as Andean Group or Andean Pact. A regional economic association agreed to in 1966 and set up in 1969, headquartered in Lima. It includes Bolivia, Chile (withdrew in 1976; rejoined in 1990), Colombia, Ecuador, Peru (withdrew briefly in 1992, but rejoined in 1994), and Venezuela (joined in 1973). Its Foreign Investment

Code was among the more sophisticated, and pragmatic, Southern efforts to regulate MNCs and *foreign direct investment*. In its early days this group was essentially *protectionist*, but under the twin pressures of regional economic rivalry and the *debt crisis* in the 1980s, and reflecting global economic trends, it shifted by the 1990s to *free trade* approaches to *development*. In 1989 it declared as goals nuclear *nonproliferation*, regional development, and some form of political *integration*. In 1994 it agreed to set up a *customs union*.

Andorra, Principality of. A political curiosity surviving from the Middle Ages. *Holy Roman Emperor* Charles II appointed the Archbishop of Urgel to control of Andorra, but this was long disputed by the Comte de Foix. In 1278 a compromise was agreed upon whereby joint *suzerainty* was established. Andorra remained for many centuries a *feudal* holding of the archbishops, for Spain, and on the French side, until 1574, the independent princedom of successive Comte de Foix. The French claim passed to the crown under *Henry IV*, thence to the state with the *French Revolution*. A new constitution in 1993 gave it *independence* and established a constitutional democracy. Although Andorra is self-governing in fact, the Archbishop of Urgel and the president of France are still its titular "co-princes."

Andropov, Yuri Vladimirovich (1914–1984). Soviet leader. He was ambassador to Hungary during the Soviet *invasion* of that country in 1956. He headed the *KGB* from 1967 to 1982, when he was elected general secretary of the *Communist Party* (CPSU). His drawn-out illness and death in February 1984, after just 14 months in office, set off a paralyzing succession crisis. Andropov wanted his friend and protegé *Mikhail Gorbachev* to take over. The old guard elected *Konstantin Chernenko*, who died after just eleven enfeebled and ineffective months in power, and Gorbachev was at last elected.

Andrussovo, Treaty of (1667). After a prolonged conflict between Russia and Poland for possession of the Ukraine in the First Northern War (1654–1660), in this treaty Russia obtained the Smolensk region and eastern Ukraine, including Kiev. Andrussovo was of strategic importance not merely for its further reduction of Polish power, but because it pushed a growing and aggressive Russian state closer to conflict with the *Ottoman Empire* in the Balkans. The settlement was disputed by Poland for another 20 years, but was ratified in a second treaty in 1686.

angary. In *international law*, the right of a *belligerent* to *requisition* or destroy the property of *neutrals* in accord with the doctrine of *necessity*. This must take place on one's own or on enemy *occupied* territory (no violation of the *territorial integrity* of the neutral is permitted) and must be accompanied at some point by full *compensation*. Previously, it included a claimed right to compel neutral ships and crews to carry the belligerent's troops or cargos, but in modern times it has been reserved to property, not persons. On land, there is a special rule concerning railways and rolling stock: under angary, a belligerent may seize neutral rolling stock that crosses onto its territory. However, as a neutral may retaliate by seizing the belligerent's trains on its territory, in practice this right tends to be applied sparingly.

Anglo-American War. *See War of 1812.*

Anglo-Burmese Wars. *See Burma.*

Anglo-Dutch Wars. These were largely naval wars fought over the carriage trade of the North Sea and North Atlantic and over the rich herring fisheries of the Baltic and North Sea. They also had roots in competition but over transoceanic trade, notably in *slaves*, and the logic of distant empires held together by *sea power*. They spurred advances in naval technology, but ended inconclusively, though more to England's advantage than the Netherlands. The animosity these wars engendered was soon overwhelmed by a mutual interest in formal alliance and dynastic *union* against *Louis XIV's* France, in the *Dutch War* of 1672 to 1678.

War of 1652–1654: The conflict was sparked by English insistence upon a right of *visit and search* of Dutch merchant ships in the Baltic, which was reinforced by the *Navigation Act* of 1651 passed by *Cromwell*. In 1653 the Dutch retaliated with a Danish treaty closing much of the Baltic trade to England. Major sea battles were fought at Portland (February 1653) and Gabbard's Shoal (June 1653). The English were sufficiently ascendant after that, they *blockaded* the Dutch coastline; the war ended largely on England's terms and with the Dutch paying compensation for losses.

War of 1664–1667: The Dutch remained a major naval power in the Baltic and North Sea and also challenged England's rising bid for global commercial and naval supremacy, including over the Atlantic *slave trade* and the *spice trade* in the Far East. This second war was thus more far-ranging, with raids and engagements off the African, Caribbean, North American, and South Asian coasts. There were also small land battles in the Netherlands. All the while, the danger of war with France loomed over both England and the Netherlands, as Louis XIV maneuvered anew. The English lost the Four Days Battle, or Battle of the Downs (June 1–4, 1666), to a Dutch fleet. Two months later, an English fleet savaged a Dutch fleet, and so the war went, seesawing back and forth. Then, in 1667, the Dutch sailed boldly up the Thames and caught a royal fleet unawares at anchor, burning and sinking much of it. The war ended with the Treaty of Breda (July 1667), which adjusted the balance of trade in Dutch favor (that is, made it more even-handed than English victory in the first war had left it). There were also colonial swaps: England gained New Amsterdam, which was renamed New York, and Delaware. The Dutch retained Suriname.

Anglo-Egyptian Sudan. Sudan, 1898–1955. This was the period of Sudanese *condominium* under Britain and Egypt, from the slaughter of the *Mahdist* forces at *Omdurman* to independence. Heavy fighting against British rule continued in parts of Sudan into the 1920s. *See also Sudan.*

Anglo-French Entente. *See* Entente Cordiale.

Anglo-German Agreement (1895). Britain transferred *Heligoland* to Germany, as well as a strip of territory that gave *German Southwest Africa* access to the Zambezi River. Germany accepted that Britain had a *protectorate* over *Zanzibar* and recognized other British claims in East Africa.

Anglo-German Naval Agreement (1935). In direct violation of the *disarmament* clauses of the *Treaty of Versailles* and of the *Locarno Treaties*, Britain agreed to German naval *rearmament* up to 35 percent of its own tonnage in *capital warships*. That permitted Germany to lay hulls for more *destroyers*, *cruisers*, and *battleships* than its shipyards could build. The agreement also gave Germany equality with Britain in *submarines*, which later proved the more crucial weapon against Allied surface ships in *World War II*. The main German interest was to engage the British in rejection of the Treaty of Versailles. In that, *Hitler* succeeded. The principal British interest was *appeasement*. As later events proved, that failed miserably, partly by weakening the *Stresa Front*. The agreement reverberated in world capitals since the British had failed to consult their French allies, or the Italians, Americans, or Soviets. In April 1939, Germany renounced the agreement and began to build as many warships as its shipyards could then turn out. *See also Wilhelm Canaris; Karl Dönitz; U-boats; Z-plan.*

Anglo-German naval arms race (1895–1912). A major commitment by Imperial Germany to a naval building program, driven by the interest of Kaiser *Wilhelm II*, led to an expensive and tense naval *arms race* with Great Britain. The most intense phase came after 1900 when Germany passed the Second Naval Law, which aimed at constructing a fleet capable of meeting and blunting the *Royal Navy* in battle. A third phase began with the *Dreadnought* innovation of 1906 in which Germany, then also engaged in an arms race on land with several other major powers, sought to build a fleet that posed risk to Britain's. This significantly contributed to raised international tensions before *World War I*. *See also Anglo-Japanese Alliance/Treaty; John Fisher; Jutland, Battle of; two-power naval standard.*

Anglo-Irish. Descendants of English/Scots settlers, mainly Protestants, living in Ireland. This ethnic minority played a disproportionate role in Irish history, both on the side of *independence* and *republicanism* in the south and in favor of retaining *Ulster*'s ties to the English crown.

Anglo-Irish Treaty (1921). The first treaty between Britain and Ireland in centuries, owing to the historic conquest and occupation of Ireland by England to 1921. In negotiations leading to the treaty, the Irish were represented by *Michael Collins* and Arthur Griffith; *Eamon de Valera* refused to participate. Signing for Britain were *Lloyd George* and *Winston Churchill*, among others. The settlement ended the *Irish War of Independence* by partitioning Ireland into *Ulster* and the *Irish Free State*, while requiring the continuing technical allegiance (via an oath of office) of Irish officeholders to the British Crown. The Dáil Éireann (Irish parliament) split over acceptance of the treaty, voting 64 to 57 in favor. It was then *ratified* by a large majority of the Irish people in a free *referendum*. Hardliners in the *IRA*, reluctantly led by de Valera, rejected the settlement and the oath, along with the *Irish Free State* it created, turning their guns against old comrades during the *Irish Civil War*.

Anglo-Irish War. *See Irish War of Independence.*

Anglo-Japanese Alliance/Treaty (1902). A mutual assistance pact overtly aimed at containing Russia in *Manchuria* and confirming the *territorial integrity* of China and Korea. For London, it precluded a Russo-Japanese alliance in Asia, which had been a concern during the later *Great Game*. And it ended Britain's period of *splendid isolation*, and permitted greater concentration on defense of India and the *Anglo-German naval arms race*. Along with the *Entente Cordiale*, it was part of a British grand scheme to reduce what was increasingly seen in London as serious imperial overcommitment and to recall the legions of the *Royal Navy* to home waters for the defense of Britain itself. For the Japanese, it gained new international *prestige* and respect, opened the way to the surprise attack that started the *Russo-Japanese War*, and was the mainstay of its diplomacy for twenty years. It was redefined in 1905, in Japan's favor, concerning Korea. Renewed for ten more years in 1911, it was replaced by the *Four Power Treaty* in 1922.
Suggested Reading: I. Nish, *The Anglo-Japanese Alliance* (1966).

Anglophone. An English-speaking person or country.

Anglo-Russian Entente (1907–1917). An agreement easing the *Great Game* rivalry between the British and Russian empires in Persia, Afghanistan, and Tibet. It was occasioned by (1) the *Anglo-Japanese Treaty* (1902), which permitted London to focus more on the defense of India; (2) the *Russian Revolution* (1905), which staggered Moscow, forcing it to regather its imperial will and rebuild its political and military strength; and (3) perception of a growing and common threat from Imperial Germany. It established mutual *spheres of influence* in Persia, Afghanistan, and Tibet and settled other outstanding questions dating to the Great Game and *Crimean War*. It included agreement on nominal Chinese control of Tibet and on a British *protectorate* in Afghanistan.

It papered over extant conflicts until these were trumped by a formal Anglo-Russian alliance in September 1914, brought on by the start of *World War I*. Britain remained allied with Russia until the *Bolshevik Revolution* in November 1917, when the old rivalry resumed in Central Asia and a new one broke out in Europe itself. *See also* Entente Cordiale; *Edward Grey; imperial overreach; Triple Entente.*

Angola. Ngola. Portugal's "partnership" with Kongo (*Congo*) and patronage of *Christianity* there lasted only to 1543 and the death of Afonso I. Already by that time Portugal had shifted its main slaving interests southward into Angola. In 1556 a Kongo army was defeated by Ngola enemies, supplied with firearms by Portugal. Kongo thereafter went into a long decline, passed over by the main currents of the *slave trade* and itself raided by Ngola and Yaka—essentially, stateless armed marauders. Portugal began direct colonization of Angola, importing settlers from the home country starting in 1575 and setting them up in a fortified settlement on Luanda Island. A century of Portuguese armed penetration of the interior, in pursuit of slaves rather than territorial conquest, followed. In this effort, the main partners of the Portuguese were the Imbangala, who dominated the Luanda interior slave trade for the next 250 years, selling mainly to Portuguese who transshipped the slaves to Brazil. Colonization of the interior, which to the Portuguese and Imbangala remained simply a vast reservoir of potential slaves, did not occur on a large scale until the twentieth century. The Dutch briefly held Luanda in the seventeenth century (1641–1648), in consequence of their long war with Portugal and Spain—the *Eighty Years' War* (1566–1648)—and competition with Portugal over the slave trade.

Southern Angola was ruled by many small Ovimbundu chieftaincies into the nineteenth century, until slave raiders from *Walvis Bay* penetrated and destabilized the region. Slave raiding slowed when Portugal banned slavery in all its possessions in 1838, but it did not stop for another 20 years. Further east, the Chokwe hunted ivory, and in the nineteenth century overran much of the interior that had been *Lunda*. During the *scramble for Africa*, the Portuguese finally moved decisively inland to forestall other European claims and in so doing extend their essentially *feudal* economic and political structures to new populations of Africans. Portuguese immigration continued even after *World War II*, when most other European states were preparing to abandon their African empires. By the 1960s, 250,000 settlers were in-country and prepared to fight to retain their land and social and racial privileges.

A multi-sided *guerrilla* war for *independence* started in 1961, beginning with massacres of settlers and even more savage Portuguese reprisals against African villagers. A desultory conflict continued for the next two decades. Portuguese rule ended only with a prior *revolution* in Lisbon in 1974. A *civil war* and power struggle followed among the three main groups that had fought the Portuguese. The United States, Zaire (under *Mobutu*), and South Africa backed Jonas Savimbi's UNITA, the Soviets supported the *Marxist-Leninist* MPLA, and an independent FNLA guerrilla army under Holden Roberto fought on without major allies. Although a *Cold War* gloss of *ideology* was painted onto the main factions, at root these groups represented regional and tribal interests, though these differences were exacerbated by the two sides becoming proxies for the larger conflict between the *superpowers*. The MPLA took power in the capital with the help of Cuban troops in 1975—Cuba intervened largely on *Castro*'s own accord, dragging the Soviet Union into Angola with it—and defeated the FNLA by 1979. UNITA retained sections of countryside and its base in the south, while Rhodesia and South Africa sponsored a small guerilla army, called RENAMO. From 1988 to 1991 Cuba withdrew as part of a settlement with South Africa, the United States, and the USSR, which included independence for Namibia in 1990. A peace agreement was signed in 1991 between the MPLA and UNITA.

The MPLA won internationally supervised elections in 1992, but UNITA's Savimbi rejected the results. Russia, Portugal, and the United States jointly warned Savimbi against restarting the war, but he defied them. Heavy fighting resumed in 1993, literally over the heads of United Nations observers. UNITA no longer had foreign backers but still seized or destroyed several important towns. The *Clinton* administration *recognized* the MPLA government, which had abandoned its uncomfortable Marxism, reversing seventeen years of *nonrecognition*. UNITA made major territorial gains before the government resumed the offensive. By September 1993, 1,000 per day were dying, making Angola's war the worst conflict in the world at that time, surpassing even the carnage in *Bosnia*. The MPLA had *artillery* and *armor*, older model Soviet MIGs, and a sizeable army. UNITA's supply lines dried up, but its tribal support remained strong. When neighboring Zaire collapsed into anarchy and foreign intervention in 1998, Angola was drawn into that conflict as well, as Zaire (Congo) had long backed UNITA. By 2000 Angola's relations with Washington were repaired, and U.S. aid was supplied to help fight UNITA and other *warlord* armies.

Suggested Readings: David Birmingham, *Trade and Conflict in Angola* (1966); Gervase Clarence-Smith, *The Third Portuguese Empire, 1825–1975* (1985); Jan Vansina, *Kingdoms of the Savannah* (1966).

Anguilla. This island in the *Lesser Antilles* (Leeward Islands) has been a British colony since 1650. In 1958 it joined the *West Indies Federation*. In 1967 it declared independence, but Britain quietly put down the movement. In 1980 it was administratively detached from St. Kitts and Nevis. It remains a British *dependency*.

Annam. Pacified South. A Viet kingdom, and later a French *protectorate*, situated on the east coast of central *Indochina*. The area was called Annam by the Chinese since the *Tang* dynasty (seventh century).

It frequently intervened in Cambodia, which it sometimes controlled as a *tributary state*, and warred with Siam. It was recognized as an independent kingdom by China after the Tây Són victory in 1789, when Nguyên Huê (Quang Trung, d.1792) became its king. Annam contained the seat of the old imperial capital at Hue. It was split by the 1954 decision of the *Geneva Accords* to divide Vietnam at the 17th parallel. With the military defeat and political *extinction* of the Republic of Vietnam (RVN) in 1975, all historic Annam was incorporated into modern Vietnam. *See also Bao Dai.*

Annan, Kofi (b. 1938). Ghanaian diplomat; *secretary-general* of the *United Nations* (1997–). A career UN civil servant, Annan was the first to rise through the ranks to the top job at the UN. In his early career he was closely involved with issues of *refugees* (especially *internal refugees*). In 1990 he negotiated the release of UN staff and other *hostages* held as human shields by *Saddam Hussein*. In 1993 he was put in charge of all UN *peacekeeping* operations. He was heavily criticized for his weak performance during the 1994 *genocide* in Rwanda. He performed better during complex arrangements in the former *Yugoslavia*, but was taken to task for the UN peacekeepers' failure to prevent a massacre of Bosnian Muslims in Srebrenica in 1995, a city the UN had pledged to protect. In 1997 Annan succeeded fellow African *Boutros Boutros-Ghali* as secretary-general. Accommodating by nature, he worked honestly to secure enhanced *Great Power* cooperation with the UN, especially by China and the United States. However, he badly misread Saddam Hussein, once calling him a "decisive" leader with whom he could work on the issue of weapons inspections (just months before Hussein kicked all UN inspectors out of Iraq). In 1998, at the personal behest of Kofi Annan, a UNGA resolution for the first time called for the eradication of *anti-Semitism*, along with other salient group hatreds. He was less successful in blocking anti-Semitic resolutions at a 2001 UN conference on racism held in Durban, South Africa. Annan was so effective as an administrator and fiscal reformer—rare qualities among secretaries general—that he won praise even from the U.S. Congress, which agreed to pay back dues that had been overdue for many years. In 2001 Annan was reelected for a second five-year term as secretary general.

Following the *September 11, 2001, terrorist attack on the United States*, Annan led UN condemnation of the attack and threw his prestige and support behind U.S. military measures to counteract terrorism. Later that year, Annan was awarded the *Nobel Prize* for peace, jointly with the United Nations as a whole.

annexation. When a state appends, with or without legal sanction, additional territory to itself that previously was claimed by another political authority.

From the Italian *Renaissance* to the great settlement at the *Paris Peace Conference* in 1919–1920, annexation was a commonplace feature of international history. First dynasties, then the *Great Powers*, unilaterally seized and traded territory constrained by little other than threats or *retaliation* by their peers, or cooperated in mutual annexations under the *balance of power* principle of *compensation*. After 1920, when international rhetoric condemned annexation without reference to *popular sovereignty*, the odd stab of conscience led to plebiscites on *self-determination*. Even so, forcible annexations abounded. Some were widely rejected as illegitimate and overturned by the international community when the opportunity ripened: *Nazi Germany's* multiple annexations of 1939–1941, Soviet annexations of the *Baltic States* and other territories during 1939–1940, Indonesia's annexation of *East Timor* in 1975, and Iraq's 1990 annexation of Kuwait. Others were more gray in character: either the claim of the annexing state had some merit or political and military reality was such that reversal proved impossible, whatever the moral merits of the victim's case. This type included India's claim to most of *Kashmir*, China's 1950 takeover of *Tibet*, and Israel's claim to *Jerusalem* and parts of the *occupied territories*.

Anschluss (1938). In its principal usage, this refers to the forced *union* of Austria and Germany by the *Nazis* in March 1938, a union forbidden by the treaties of *Versailles* and *St. Germain*. In 1931 an attempt to establish a simple *customs union* had been blocked by France. In July 1934, Austrian *Nazis* mounted an abortive *coup d'etat*, murdering Chancellor *Dollfuss* in the attempt. The *Putsch* was halted by loyal police and army units led by Kurt von Schuschnigg (1897–1977) and by *Mussolini's* support for Austrian independence and deployment of Italian divisions to the *Brenner Pass*. Strategic collaboration between Italy and Germany after 1936 left Austria badly isolated because France was weakened and defeatist, owing to the ideological conflicts of the *Third Republic*, and Britain was pursuing a policy of *appeasement* of Germany. In 1938 Schuschnigg, now Chancellor of Austria, was summoned to a meeting with *Hitler* in which he was browbeaten and intimidated into accepting Nazi ministers into his government. When Nazi *fifth columnists* sparked anti-Jewish *pogroms* and political riots in favor of Anschluss, the new Nazi minister in charge of police, Seyss-Inquart (1892–1946), did nothing. In a preemptive move, Schuschnigg called for a *plebiscite* on Anschluss with just three days' notice, but then lost his nerve and canceled the vote. On March 11th, Seyss-Inquart implemented Hitler's order to "invite" the German Army across the border; the next day the Anschluss was proclaimed. Britain, France, and Italy did nothing; Schuschnigg and thousands of Austrians were sent to *concentration camps*, and Austria's Jews fell under Nazi rule. A month later Hitler cynically held a plebiscite, which his toadies and propaganda machine reported as voting 99 percent in favor of the Anschluss and of his personal rule as *Führer* of the land of his birth. This easy success greatly enhanced

Hitler's reputation within the *Wehrmacht* and *diplomatic corps*, even as it deepened his already profound contempt for the West. The Anschluss was not reversed until 1945. Austria was then *occupied* by the Allies, formally and separately from Germany, until 1955. Seyss-Inquart was tried at *Nuremberg* and hanged.

Antarctic/Antarctica. The southern polar region/continent. Unlike the *Arctic*, Antarctica is not divided among the states but is instead governed collectively under the *Antarctic Treaty system*. This is possible because, also unlike the Arctic, it has no *indigenous peoples* and remains off-limits to economic exploitation. *See also global commons; whaling.*

Antarctic Circle. The circumpolar line at 23° 28″ north of the South Pole.

Antarctic Treaty (1959). Signed by 12 countries; in effect as of mid-1961. It bans nuclear tests, military activity, economic *exploitation*, and defers all territorial claims to the frozen continent; it is enforced by on-site inspection. It allows scientific research stations as the only permanent installations. The original consultative parties retain full voting rights on all aspects of Antarctic governance. They are subdivided into seven claimant states (Argentina, Australia, Britain, Chile, France, New Zealand, and Norway) and five nonclaimants. Other states have joined the consultative group by also conducting substantial research. All states may adhere as nonconsultative parties. During 1991–1992 the treaty was renegotiated by 33 nations. The main amendment to the original Antarctic *regime* was the Madrid Protocol on Environmental Protection, which banned mining and *oil* exploration for 50 years.

Antarctic Treaty system. The governing legal regime for Antarctica, comprised of the *Antarctic Treaty* and other *conventions* on marine conservation (flora and fauna in 1964, seals in 1972, marine living resources in 1982).

A *moratorium* on mineral exploration and *exploitation* was set in 1977 and extended for 50 years in 1992. In 1988 the *United Nations General Assembly* voted to include the *Secretary-General* in the system, but this was not binding on the original *Treaty States* and essentially they continue to operate in Antarctica outside of the wider UN system. In 1991 an additional and elaborate *protocol* on environmental protection was agreed. These agreements collectively govern the Antarctic according to principles of shared responsibility of the *treaty powers* to ensure nonmilitarization, environmental protection, and scientific cooperation and research. The system is not without its critics: from the late 1980s some *LDCs*, led by Malaysia, proposed reordering the system in line with the *common heritage principle*, which would open it to economic exploitation under a regime of country shares of any profits. Because the states proposing this had little capital, less appropriate technology, and no leverage, the idea drifted off on a free-range floe. From an entirely different quarter, some environmentalist lobbies suggested turning the entire continent into a world conservation park, from which even recreational activity would be banned. *See also whaling.*

Suggested Reading: Arthur Watts, *International Law and the Antarctic Treaty System* (1992).

anti–ballistic missile, missile (ABM). Defensive weapons designed to confuse, deflect, or, in the extreme, shoot down incoming *ballistic missiles*. Proponents of *ballistic missile defense (BMD)* systems said that the claimed success of the Patriot antiaircraft system, converted to defend Israel and Saudi Arabia from Scud missile attacks during the *Gulf War*, showed that ABMs could be used against small, missile-armed powers. Others demurred. Nonetheless, after 1991, advanced research on ABMs resumed in earnest for most major powers. In 1999, Japan and the United States concluded a pact to jointly research an ABM system aimed at blocking potential attacks from North Korea, China, and other powers, and the United States began tests that aimed at a limited deployment by 2005. The clumsy redundancy of the proper term arises grammatically, though not in common usage, since these missiles aim to intercept ballistic missiles, not "ballistics." *See also SDI.*

Anti–Ballistic Missile, Missile (ABM) Treaty (1972–2002). Signed as part of the *SALT I* agreements, it came into force in 1972. It limited the United States and Soviet Union to two *ABM* sites each, one for each capital plus another for a *hard target* such as an *ICBM* silo complex, and to 100 ABM launchers each. An ancillary protocol (1974) cut this to one site apiece. The Soviets built theirs to defend Moscow; the United States started a site to protect part of its land-based *nuclear deterrent*, but abandoned it in 1975 as too expensive and irrelevant to the reigning *strategic doctrine* of *assured destruction*. The *Strategic Defense Initiative* (SDI) program launched by the *Reagan* administration challenged the logic and renewal of the treaty, as did the fact that the Soviets secretly built a battle-ready, phased-array radar at Krasnoyarsk and multiple related sites in violation of the treaty. In 2001 *George W. Bush* argued that the treaty was strategically, technologically, and politically obsolete—a relic of the *Cold War*, which stood in the way of research into a limited *ballistic missile defense* to protect the United States against *rogue states* and *terrorist* threats. He sought from *Vladimir Putin* acceptance by Russia—the *successor state* to the Soviet Union—of mutual termination of the treaty. When Putin declined to agree, on December 13, 2001, Bush exercised his right pursuant to Article XV of the *terms* of the ABM Treaty to declare that further adherence jeopardized America's "supreme instincts," and thereby gave six months notice of *abrogation* of the agreement. *See also MIRV; Strategic Defense Initiative.*

Anti-Comintern Pact (November 25, 1936). A joint declaration by Nazi Germany and Imperial Japan affirming opposition to the *Comintern*. Secret codicils pledged economic and diplomatic, but not military, assistance should either state go to war with the Soviet Union. The soon-to-be Nazi foreign minister, *Joachim von Ribbentrop*, regarded this as a triumph worthy of exchanging German *recognition* of the Japanese *puppet-state* of *Manchukuo*. Italy *adhered* the next year, also recognizing Manchukuo. In 1939, Hungary and Spain signed, followed in 1941 by Slovakia, Rumania, and Bulgaria. Although the pact did little for either Germany or Japan, it made Western powers deeply concerned about German-Japanese collaboration and caused a fusion of perception about the nature of the regimes in Berlin and Tokyo. *See also Axis alliance.*

anti-dumping laws. National laws that ostensibly aim at foreign *dumping*, but are often so specific as to be actually *non-tariff barriers* to trade by legitimate foreign competition. They are part of the *new protectionism*. Regulations against the worst of such laws were included in the *Uruguay Round*, but were weakened in last-minute bargaining.

Antigua and Barbuda. Antigua was discovered by *Columbus* in 1493. It was not finally colonized, however, until 1632, by the British. Antiguan colonists then settled Barbuda in 1661. On both islands, a plantation economy led to extensive *slave labor*. Slavery was abolished in 1834, as part of the larger reform within the *British Empire*. Antigua and Barbuda became an *associated state* within the *Commonwealth* in 1967. They became fully independent in 1981. In addition to ties to Britain, they have connections with the United States and Venezuela. There is some *secessionist* sentiment on Barbuda.

Antilles. *See Greater Antilles; Lesser Antilles.*

antipersonnel weapon. Any weapon designed to kill or maim people, as opposed to disabling equipment.

Antipodes. (1) Upper case: a small island group southeast of, and belonging to, New Zealand. (2) Lower case: any two points diametrically opposite on the Earth's surface. (3) From #2 (and the *Eurocentric* view of sixteenth and seventeenth century explorers of the *South Pacific*): any extremely remote and isolated territory, especially if located in the South Pacific.

antisatellite system (ASAT). Any weapon designed to destroy enemy *satellites*, including antisatellite mines, missiles, and hunter-killer satellites.

anti-Semitism. Although Arabs are also Semites, this term is most often used exclusively to mean animosity to Jews. This virulent, persistent hatred has multiple historical causes: religious bigotry among *Christians* and *Muslims*; social, economic, and professional competition and envy; cultural and ideological scapegoating; and more recently in historical terms, spurious racial theories. The history of the Jewish *diaspora* is complex and lengthy, beyond proper summary here. In essence, the Jews were expelled from Palestine (Judea) by the *Romans* after their defeat in the Jewish War, which broke out in 66 C.E. after an appalling massacre of Jews by Roman soldiers in *Jerusalem*. Emperor Titus (39–81, r. 79–81 C.E.) completed the Jewish War by driving the Jews from their historic homeland (70 C.E.), thus beginning their prolonged and sorrowful diaspora, whose consequences reverberate down through history still. Jews settled in scattered, minority communities in multiple lands throughout the Roman world, especially in North Africa and Anatolia, but much farther afield as well. This was not anti-Semitism on the part of Rome, however—it was the politics of empire and order.

Anti-Semitism as a virulent, specific hatred of Jews for their Jewishness was, until historically recent times, principally a product of Christian civilization. Throughout *Christendom*, Jews were blamed by many, lay and cleric alike, for the *Black Death*, and there were multiple massacres of Jews by Christians—who had parted definitively in doctrine from Judaism in the second century—during the *Crusades* and later, in the *Thirty Years' War* (1618–1648). In each case, Jews were the victims of religious zeal or simply scapegoats for the social and economic turmoil that coursed over the *Holy Roman Empire* and other predominantly Christian lands. Similarly, Jews were blamed by superstitious and ignorant Christians—who also singled out witches and "demon-worshipers"—during other Medieval or early modern episodes of natural calamity or wartime suffering, just as early Christians had themselves once been blamed for natural disasters or ill-fortune in war by pagan Romans concerned that adherents of the new religion did not sacrifice to propitiate the gods in the civic temples.

Jews were forced into ghettos by Muslims as early as 1280 in Moorish North Africa. At different times anti-Semitism was state policy in Spain, Turkey, Poland, Russia, and Germany, usually in the form of proscriptions on the occupations Jews might enter and restrictions on where they could live. Jews were expelled en masse from Spain in 1492, and later also from Portugal, settling mainly in the Pale of Settlement in Poland and western Russia. Those who remained in Iberia under forcible conversions or disguised as Christians ("conversos") became special targets of the *Inquisition*, and in the early seventeenth century they too were expelled from Spain and Portugal. Persecution by *Orthodox* communities also deepened with each famine or political crisis or reform movement in Russia. Thin relief came for some Jews in Eastern Europe when Britain sought legal protections for German Jews at the *Congress of Vienna*. In the late nineteenth century, deteriorating social and political conditions and persecution of Jews in the Ottoman and Russian Empires and in Rumania provoked international protests. After 1882 some two million destitute Jews fleeing *pogroms* in Russia arrived in the United States, becoming an irritant in relations with Britain and Germany, through which these *ref-*

ugees passed, as well as in U.S. relations with Russia, and sparking a rise in anti-Semitism in the United States itself. Protections for Jews were written into the *Minorities Treaties* with east European nations after *World War I*, but proved of paper value only.

In the twentieth century, anti-Semitism took three main forms: (1) hostility to communities of Jews as "alien" elements living within homogenous national societies, even where they had coexisted for centuries as quiet or autonomous minorities; (2) hatred of Jews based on rejection of their asserted right to *self-determination* within the territory of *Palestine*, and after 1948, negative identification of all Jews as morally responsible for policies pursued by Israel; and (3) mythologizing of "the Jew" as a figure of abstract, conspiratorial evil—this variation takes its most peculiar form in Japan, a country with no Jews where anti-Semitism nonetheless has a significant following. Thus, during the 1930s, anti-Semitism fed directly into the rise of *Nazism* in Germany, ultimately leading to the *"final solution"* of the *Holocaust*. Anti-Semitism was not just an important component of the twisted psychological makeup of *Hitler*. It was a prejudice shared by *Stalin*, several other tyrants, and, it must be said, not a few democratic leaders too. Since *World War II*, anti-Semitism has been most important in the politics of the *Middle East*. Formal U.S. concern over anti-Semitism in Soviet society and policy, and continuing mistreatment of Jews in Russia, contributed to the decline of *détente* after 1972. Within the United Nations, an anti-*Zionism* resolution was passed in 1975 with backing from Arab states, but was repealed in 1991 under pressure from the United States. In 1994 the *UNHRC* belatedly added anti-Semitism to its list of condemned, racist attitudes. In 1998, at the behest of *Kofi Annan*, a UNGA resolution for the first time called for eradication of anti-Semitism, along with other salient group hatreds.

Old habits and views die hard, however: in 1998 the Russian *Duma* failed to adopt (107 to 121) a motion condemning remarks made by members of the *Communist Party* accusing unnamed Jews in the media and government, supposedly working with outsiders, for Russia's deepening economic morass. That same year President Mahathir Mohamad gave vent to absurd *anti-Semitic* explanations of the currency speculation and crisis in Malaysia, deflecting all charges of his own government's mismanagement of the economy. And in 2001 an international conference on racism held in South Africa witnessed renewed efforts to identify Zionism as a racist creed and to isolate Israel morally and diplomatically. *See also* Action Françaises; *Aix-la-Chapelle; Alexander II;* Anschluss; *apology; Birobizhan; Catholic Church; Congress of Vienna; Dreyfus affair; Albert Einstein; fascism; Ferdinand and Isabella; genocide; Genocide Convention; Jackson-Vanik amendment; John Paul II; Malaysia; Nuremberg Laws; Pius XII; Poland; Protocols of the Elders of Zion; restitution; Rothschild, House of;* Sonderweg; *Vatican; Lech Walesa.*

Suggested Readings: Michael Curtis, ed., *Anti-Semitism in the Contemporary World* (1985); Richard Levy, *Anti-Semitism in the Modern World* (1991).

antisubmarine warfare (ASW). All passive or active measures that defend against *submarines*. Among others: *convoys*, *destroyers*, surveillance and hunter aircraft, underwater electronic *listening posts*, and hunter-killer task forces, or attack submarines.

antithesis. (1) In general: opposition or contrast; a direct opposite. (2) In Hegelian method: an opposing *thesis* to the original thesis. *See also dialectic; end of history; Marxism.*

apartheid. Separateness. The system of racial segregation of blacks, "coloureds" (mixed race), and Indians from whites that was instituted in 1948 in South Africa and Namibia by the Afrikaner *National Party*, which removed from the constitution those few political rights previously enjoyed by non-whites and substituted a racial dictatorship. Apartheid was rooted in *Calvinist* doctrine isolated from the later *Reformation* and the *Enlightenment,* including a perverse historical reading that held that the *Boers* were the "chosen people" of Africa, destined by the deity to rule over "lesser breeds." Apartheid fed on several centuries of racial and economic warfare in southern Africa that included extermination or enslavement of the Khoi and San, whom the farmer Boers easily overran, and after 1770 near-constant border warfare with the far more powerful *Nguni* peoples whom the Boers encountered once they crossed the Fish River.

After 1949, apartheid's legal and political theorists developed and passed into law *Nazi*-like racial categories and a totalitarian-like *ideology,* instituted a ban on miscegenation, and tried to enforce a shift of the majority black population into absurdly gerrymandered and wholly economically unviable *Bantustans,* enforced by passbook laws to ensure that the races would be geographically segregated. The apartheid state actively suppressed all black and most "coloured" and Indian political and union activity and celebrated the principle of "baaskap," or (white) "boss rule." This was all justified on the theory that the Union of South Africa (Republic of South Africa, after 1961, when it left the *Commonwealth*), comprised distinct nations, each racially defined, and that the people of each nation should live in their own homeland. Fundamentally, this biologically specious and also completely ahistorical thesis was a means of preserving white privileges—political and social, but above all economic—as well as a separate Boer identity, which was otherwise threatened with minority status inside South Africa. The major means to this end was the passbook system, whose enforcement ensured the existence of a large and floating pool of cheap black labor near, but not in, the major cities where only the whites were permitted to reside legally. That led to vast and illegal squatter cities (black townships) outside Johannesburg, Pretoria, and other major centers of employment, which were utterly squalid because they were not supposed to exist and therefore had no tax base or effective government and received few to no social or sanitary services from the South African state.

Apartheid and the appalling conditions it produced in the townships became the focus of a worldwide *human rights* campaign leading first to military, then economic, social, and cultural *sanctions*. This effort was orchestrated among the states primarily through the *United Nations General Assembly*, but also within the Commonwealth and *Organization of African Unity*, as well as bilaterally by most of the major democracies. It was also privately endorsed and pushed by *Nongovernmental Organizations* and many individuals. A 1973 UN convention declared apartheid an international crime, which made no difference to its supporters and did not really aid its victims, though it made a moral point. By the 1980s, increased international sanctions and global shunning of South Africa began to have an effect, wearing not so much on the country's economy as on the psychology of white South Africans, who were made to feel pariahs whenever they traveled abroad and who were excluded from most normal international intercourse such as sports and cultural exchanges—a nicely ironic twist on the notion of separate development.

What made the system unsustainable after 1976 was the growing economic power of the black middle classes inside South Africa, which had also expanded greatly with *industrialization* and *capitalist* development of the whole country. These classes threw up articulate and able leaders within the churches and the *African National Congress* (ANC) who demanded improved social and educational services in the townships, and then led the whole black community in a highly effective economic boycott of white-owned shops in protest against social apartheid (petty segregation of beaches and public facilities). In addition, the black working classes rendered the townships ungovernable by violent resistance to police and the army and by political intimidation of all opponents within the black areas, up to and including murder, often by stoning or worse, by "necklaces" of burning tires. Apartheid was ended in Namibia on May 13, 1989, preparatory to that territory becoming fully sovereign on March 21, 1990. Legal apartheid was revoked in South Africa itself by *de Klerk* in 1991 and was fully dismantled in all legal respects by 1993. Multiparty elections were then held in 1994 and led to the overwhelming election victory of the ANC, with *Nelson Mandela* becoming the first black president of South Africa. *See also passport; recognition.*

Suggested Readings: Roger B. Beck, *History of South Africa* (2000); T.R.H. Davenport and Christopher Saunders, *South Africa: A Modern History* (2000).

apology, in international relations. States have traditionally paid compensation for *damages* under *international law*. Usually, this is accompanied by a quiet though formal acknowledgment of *responsibility*, though sometimes not if *prestige* is also engaged and the issue has caught the public's attention. In the 1990s a new trend began of political rather than legal apology, for historical rather than contemporary deeds. Some states, almost always former *colonies*, began to call for public apologies and sometimes also for *reparations* or *restitution*. The most persistent cases involved Japan, which was hounded by China, South Korea, and other states to apologize for its appalling conduct during *World War II*. Tokyo first did this c. 1995, but it always appeared half-hearted and provoked demands for further apologies and larger reparations. The other major case was a rising demand by African states for apologies from countries on the receiving end of the trans-Atlantic *slave trade* (though not from countries involved in the older Indian Ocean or trans-Saharan slave trades, a morally curious exception that is easier to comprehend financially and in terms of the politics of the G-77).

Among other examples of state-to-state political apology include British Prime Minister Tony Blair apologizing for his country's slow and inadequate response to the mid-nineteenth century Irish potato famine and Pope *John Paul II* apologizing to Jews for the *anti-Semitism* of many *Catholics* and of the Church itself throughout history. *Bill Clinton* gushed apologies in behalf of the United States to almost anyone who asked (Africans, Guatemalans, Vietnamese, among others) and for almost anything done by his predecessors, though not for acts by himself or his administration. Critics of formal state-to-state apology raised several objections. Politically, such statements may be corrupted by a clear tendency for governments to make them from momentary political or even electoral advantage, for prior actions taken and policies pursued by domestic political opponents. Legally, apologies might establish a basis for subsequent monetary claims and thus lead to needless wrangling over international damages. Morally, they appear insincere and trite because they are usually made by people who are not directly responsible for past wrongful acts to people who were not themselves directly harmed. And historically, apologies fail to treat past eras as unique, even discrete, phenomena that need to be understood in their own terms without grafting onto them judgments that derive from contemporary experience and culturally flavored values inapt to the original issues. *See also Aborigines.*

apparat. Party machine. In the *Soviet Union*, this was the network of lower level *Communist Party* functionaries tied by relative privilege and reflected power to the *nomenklatura* and responsible for carrying out in the regions and in local affairs all directives of the *Politburo*. It was the central nervous system of the Soviet body politic, identifying resistance and sending messages back to the muscles (the *KGB*) about *dissidents* and shortages.

Suggested Reading: Igor Lukes and Uri Ra'anan, eds., *Inside the Apparat* (1990).

apparatchnik/apparatchiki. Member(s) of the *apparat*.

appeasement. Pacifying an *aggressor* with concessions, usually territorial; it may include as well concessions on matters of principle. Morally, it challenges the presumption of a duty to resist evil (*aggression*) with the prescription that a higher duty is to seek *peace*. That is a narrow, short-term view, pointing as it does to an *international society* founded not on rights, *sovereign* or otherwise, but on constant readjustments to threats and the naked exercise of *power*. Practically, as a limited tactic within a *balance of power* system, or as an interim measure used to gain time for *diplomacy, rearmament*, or *alliance* building, it may be a viable policy. As such, it formed a tradition within British diplomacy after *Palmerston*, wherein rational *accommodation* of conflicting interests was the preferred form of settlement. Appeasement works only if one's opponent is truly appeasable or if the time gained by short-term concessions to an aggressor is used for the purpose of strengthening one's material or other ability to resist further aggression. If a policy of appeasement simply seeks to avoid war at all costs it is more likely than not to fail and to incur intolerable losses in the process.

The most infamous example of appeasement as both a moral and practical failure was the stance of the United Kingdom and France toward Fascist Italy and Nazi Germany during the 1930s. The first real test came in 1935, when Britain helped undermine the *Treaty of Versailles* by agreeing to the *Anglo-German Naval Agreement*. It was practiced as well toward the Italian assault on Ethiopia and regarding German and Italian assistance to *Franco* and Spanish *fascists* early in the *Spanish Civil War*. Also in 1936, *Hitler* remilitarized the *Rhineland*, and the Western democracies did nothing; appeasement had become habitual. The culmination, and the nadir, of the policy was servile surrender of the *Sudetenland* to Nazi Germany at the *Munich Conference* in 1938. In fact, Hitler was taken aback by this abject surrender: he had expected more opposition from the democracies than he encountered. Munich also encouraged *Stalin* to seek a separate peace with Hitler, culminating in the *Nazi-Soviet Pact*. A qualified appeasement continued through the defeat of Poland and the *phony war* in the West. That dismayed German anti-Nazi resisters and demoralized the French Army, contributing to the *defeatism* that led to the French surrender in 1940. The capitulation of moral principle and real strategic advantage at Munich gave the tactic of appeasement such a bad name that whenever it was later practiced statesmen always called it something else. *See also deterrence; Neville Chamberlain; Winston Churchill.*

Suggested Reading: Stephen Rock, *Appeasement in International Politics* (2000).

application. A claim presented by a state before an international court. If a formal application is made, the full court sits in session. *See also chambers of the Court.*

appreciation. Increase in market value over time.

appropriate technology. Smaller-scale and less sophisticated *technology* than the state-of-the-art variety and therefore is said by its advocates to be more suitable to local economic and social conditions in a *developing nation*. It may be preferred for reasons of easy operation and repair, cheapness, use of a greater amount of *labor* in a labor-rich but *capital*-poor economy, or because it does not disrupt established social patterns. In the 1980s the term was stretched to cover environmentally sensitive technologies as well.

Aquino, María Corazón (b. 1933). President of the Philippines, 1986–1992. After the *assassination* of her husband, opposition leader Benigno Aquino (August 21, 1983), she took over leadership of the main Philippine opposition to *Marcos*. She won the presidency in 1986 in a burst of popular support known as "people's power." She governed weakly, however, barely surviving six *coup* attempts and opposition from within her own *cabinet*. She promised to rule only one term and did not stand for reelection.

Arab. Originally, a nomadic pastoralist (*Bedouin*) people from Arabia. More loosely, any of the Semitic peoples of North Africa, the Arabian peninsula, Palestine, Lebanon, Syria, Iraq, and northern Sudan—excluding *Jews*, who are also a Semitic people historically living in the *Middle East*, but who have a distinct history and faith. Originally located on a strategically sited peninsula that joins the Indian Ocean to the Mediterranean, and the worlds of India and Asia to Europe and Africa, Arabs emerged as a people of world historical significance with the explosion of *Islam* out of the Arabian desert in the seventh century C.E. Ever since, Arabs have been engaged in various struggles with several other of the world's major religions and civilizations. *See also Arab nationalism; Ottoman Empire; and specific Arab countries.*
   Suggested Reading: Albert Hourani, *History of the Arab Peoples* (1997).

Arabian peninsula. A West Asian peninsula constituting Bahrain, Kuwait, Oman, Qatar, Saudi Arabia, the United Arab Emirates, and Yemen. The birthplace of *Islam*, it was under *Ottoman* control for centuries. From 1890 Ottoman control slipped, under British pressure. By 1913 all Arabia had shifted from Ottoman to predominantly British protection. During *World War I* it gave rise to the *Arab Revolt*, but was later subjected to the terms of the *Sykes-Picot agreement*.

Arab-Israeli War, First (May 15, 1948–June 1949). Fighting broke out between Arabs and Jews within *Palestine* in November 1947 and continued as preparations got underway for a *partition* brokered by the United Nations. On April 9th, elements of *Irgun* and the *Stern Gang* encountered heavy resistance at the village of Deir Yassin, after which they massacred 245 civilians. Panic spread among the Arabs, who believed there was a deliberate policy to terrorize them into leaving. Tens of thousands fled. The UN partition plan gave the Jews 55 percent of the land but not *Jerusalem*, which was to be a *free city*. That disappointed Jews, who nonetheless accepted the partition, but outraged Arabs who noted that Jews formed less than one-third of the pre-partition population of all Palestine. (Note: Jews did constitute a small majority in areas allotted to them by the United Nations.) At midnight on May 14th the British *mandate* ended, and the State of Israel was proclaimed as the fulfillment, more or less, of *Zionist* dreams. The next morning Arab armies from Egypt, Iraq, Lebanon, Syria, and *Transjordan* all attacked. The fighting was often hand-to-hand. Although massacres of civilians took place on both sides, it was the Arab population that fled, this time by the hundreds of thousands. (For decades more, most of these refugees and their descendants lived a subsistence life in *refugee camps* because neither Israel nor most Arab states would accept them as permanent residents.) *Cease-fires* were negotiated, starting with Egypt in February 1949. Israel had gained another 21 percent of Palestine, but still had highly insecure borders. *See also Arab Legion; Count Folke Bernadotte; Haganah; Jewish Agency; United Nations Relief and Works Agency.*

Arab-Israeli War, Second (October 29–November 5, 1956). Also known as the Suez War. Beginning in February 1955, *David Ben-Gurion* authorized a campaign of limited military action aimed at compelling the Arab states to make a formal peace with Israel. The Egyptians responded by setting up *fedayeen* units to escalate *frontier* warfare already underway. In September *Nasser* instituted a *blockade* of Israeli shipping through the Straits of Tiran and the Gulf of Aqaba, causing Israel to consider opening the *vital* passage by force. By 1955 France had surpassed even the United States as Israel's main sponsor and, with a U.S. arms *embargo* in place, also as its main supplier of advanced weapons. The first French fighters (Mystères) arrived in April 1956, followed by British tanks and night-fighters. Meanwhile, in June–August 1956, the *Suez Crisis* rapidly developed among Egypt, Britain, and France. In a series of secret meetings France agreed to supply Israel with more advanced weapons to counterbalance a major arms purchase from Czechoslovakia announced earlier by Nasser. On September 1st Israel was informed that France would welcome a joint attack on Egypt. On October 22–24 at Sèvres, British, French, and Israeli representatives met and agreed to intervene in follow-up to an Israeli advance to the Canal under the pretext of separating Israeli and Egyptian forces in the Canal area. Israel therefore attacked on October 29th, seizing *Gaza* and sending tank columns deep into the *Sinai*. Two days later Britain and France piggybacked their attack onto the Israeli thrust, provoking a huge domestic and international outcry against the triple *invasion* and, in particular, fierce American and Soviet opposition. Moscow even hinted at direct military action against Britain and France. All three countries thus were forced to cease operations within a week. The British and French pulled out, utterly humiliated. Israel did better. It returned the Sinai in 1957 after a United Nations *peacekeeping* force was put in place, but it secured its main *war aim* of opening the Strait of Tiran. Also in 1957, Egyptian government returned to Gaza, although the strip remained *demilitarized*. Despite this, another victor (politically speaking) was Nasser: he emerged as a hero in much of the Arab world for standing up to the hated foe in Israel and to the old, imperial powers.

Arab-Israeli War, Third (June 5–10, 1967). It is called by the Israelis the Six Day War. In the ten years since the last war, Israel had developed into a formidable *regional power*. It also had begun to divert the Jordan River to "make the desert bloom." In 1963 that diversion led to frontier clashes with Syria. During January–March 1967, there were again battles between Israeli and Syrian border troops. In April the fighting escalated to tank and air battles. On May 16th, *Nasser* asked for a redeployment of the United Nations *peacekeeping* force in *Sinai*, to enable Egyptian units to move into forward positions; he was told such a partial withdrawal was impossible. Two days later, under *Arab League* pressure, he asked for a total withdrawal of the UNEF. On the 22nd, Egypt closed the Gulf of Aqaba to Israeli shipping. By the 24th, Israel ordered *mobilization* of its *reserves*. In the next week, a flurry of diplomacy made it clear that the Western nations would not open the Gulf for Israel and that the United States, especially, would not be heartbroken should Israel do the job itself. Meanwhile, Nasser and other Arab leaders indulged inflammatory and impolitic rhetoric about "pushing the Jews into the sea." Israel thus began to plan a *preemptive strike*.

In the early hours of June 5th the Egyptian, Jordanian, and Syrian air forces were caught on the ground and largely destroyed. In the subsequent ground fighting the professionalism of the Israeli Army, and *air superiority*, quickly overwhelmed the Arab forces. On June 7th, Jordan was pushed out of East *Jerusalem* and Israel captured the entire *West Bank*, inflicting some 6,000 Jordanian casualties. The next day the Israelis secured *Gaza* and extended their hold on the Sinai to the *Suez Canal*, after ambushing retreating Egyptian units in the Mitla Pass. Egypt's Sinai army lost 15,000 men and 80 percent of its equipment. By June 10th, when a cease-fire took hold, Israel had also captured the *Golan Heights*. It was a humiliation for Arab arms so deeply felt that only some future victory, of almost any kind, could salve the Arab world's wounds and open the way to peace. Another major consequence was the rise of *Palestinian* nationalism and consolidation of a leadership position for the *PLO*. From a longer term perspective, the war gave Israel, for the first time, tangible assets in the form of land that could be offered to the Arab states in exchange for permanent peace. In the meantime, Israel gained strategic depth, which would prove extremely important in the *Fourth Arab-Israeli War* and afterward. *See also land for peace; Resolution 242.*

Suggested Readings: Benny Morris, *Righteous Victims: A History of the Zionist–Arab Conflict, 1881–1999* (1999); Richard B. Parker, ed., *The Six-Day War* (1996).

Arab-Israeli War, Fourth (October 6–25, 1973). Called by Israelis the Yom Kippur War, by Arabs the Ramadan War, and by some the October War. On July 18, 1972, *Anwar Sadat* dramatically expelled 20,000 Soviet military and technical advisers from Egypt, but kept the military hardware they had supplied. On November 30, 1972, he made the decision for war. Sadat believed that *détente* between the *superpowers* meant that Egypt's window of opportunity to change the situation in the Middle East might be closing. He assumed (correctly) that the superpowers would prevent either side from achieving a total victory. Yet he thought he needed a partial victory to restore Egyptian pride and shake loose the *Suez Canal* from effective Israeli control: he intended to force Israel to the negotiating table by inflicting a shock to its sense of military invulnerability. This time, it was the turn of top Israelis to make impolitic remarks that aggravated tensions: *Dayan* spoke of how the old *Palestine* was "finished" and that those in the *refugee camps* should just settle in other Arab countries and give up thoughts of returning. That helped firm up an Arab front in favor of war, with the Saudis agreeing to lead *OPEC* in an *embargo* of *oil* to the West when fighting broke out. Syrian and Egyptian officers began meeting in secret to complete *war plans*, and Soviet ships and planes were preloaded to resupply the Arab armies. In the final hours before the attack, on October 6th, the Jewish Day of Atonement, Israeli officials finally realized an attack was coming and ordered *mobilization*.

It was too late to prevent breakthroughs, however, by the well-practiced Egyptians across the Suez Canal through weaker points in the *Bar-Lev Line*, and by some 1,400 Syrian tanks and support units in the *Golan Heights*. After ferocious fighting, the Israelis managed to stop (on October 10th) and then drive back the Syrians—who had by now been joined by token Iraqi and Jordanian units. In the *Sinai*, Israeli air and tank superiority was challenged by hand-fired SAM and anti-tank rockets deployed by dug-in Egyptian units. A huge tank-to-tank battle ensued, the largest since *World War II*. Israel began to push the Egyptians back, at a huge cost in lives for such a small nation, and an even greater cost in matériel. Israel's losses were made up by a massive U.S. airlift ordered by *Richard Nixon*. On October 16th the Israelis surprised Egypt by crossing the Canal, threatening to cut all Egyptian *lines of supply* and reinforcement to their army in Sinai. A joint Soviet-American *cease-fire* proposal was accepted for the 22nd, but there were violations on all sides, and Israeli forces continued encirclement of the Egyptian Third Army, trapped now on the east bank of the Canal. The situation then began to spin out of control. The Soviets went on military alert, loaded troop transports, and insisted on immediate military *intervention* by both superpowers. Nixon countered with a global alert (*DEFCON 3*) of U.S. strategic forces on the 24th as a *deterrent* threat aimed at Moscow. He and *Kissinger* simultaneously threatened not to resupply Israel's battlefield losses even after the war, unless Tel Aviv stopped the encirclement and spared the Egyptian Third Army. The next day, a United Nations *cease-fire* resolution was put into effect. On November 5th, Kissinger began his famous *shuttle diplomacy*, beginning the process that would end successfully, after his own time, in the *Camp David Accords*. A United Nations *peacekeeping* force was also put in place on the Golan Heights. *See also Resolution 338*.

Suggested Readings: Peter Allen, *The Yom Kippur War* (1982); Howard M. Sachar, *History of Israel* (1996).

Arabist. A scholar or analyst specializing in Arab social, political, and cultural affairs.

Arab League (League of Arab States). A regional organization formed in 1945 by Egypt, Iraq, Lebanon, Saudi Arabia, Syria, *Transjordan*, and Yemen. It was later joined by 12 more states: the *Gulf States*, Algeria, Djibouti, Libya, Morocco, Oman, Somalia, Sudan, Tunisia, as well as the *Palestine Liberation Organization*. It sent a force into Kuwait in the early 1960s to replace British troops defending against Iraqi plans for *annexation*. Otherwise, the Arab League has been mostly ineffective in resolving intra-Arab conflicts; for instance, it was unable to mediate the Yemeni civil wars of 1962 and 1994 or the *Lebanese Civil War*. Egypt was expelled from the League for its *separate peace* with Israel in 1979. It was readmitted in 1987, but the interim move of the League's headquarters from Cairo to Tunis was not reversed at that time. The Yemens merged in 1990 and thereafter shared a single membership. The League split over the *Gulf War*, with a majority voting in favor of multilateral action to *liberate* Kuwait. The League then moved its *Secretariat* back to Egypt.

Arab Legion. The Jordanian Army, commanded by a British officer, John B. Glubb, from 1921 to 1956. It held the *West Bank* for *Transjordan* during the *First Arab-Israeli War* in 1948. Its English officers were dismissed in 1956.

Arab nationalism. Anticolonial, anti-Turkish sentiments built among Arabs during the nineteenth century. During *World War I*, this movement was tapped into by the British, who encouraged and used the *Arab Revolt* against the *Ottoman Empire*, even while secretly betraying the cause of Arab independence in the *Sykes-Picot Agreement*. At the *Paris Peace Conference* (1919–1920), most Arab territories were assigned places within the *mandate* system. However, strenuous resistance to mandates in fairly short order led to independence for a number of the larger Ottoman provinces. Meanwhile, in *Palestine* Arab anger built toward a climax of armed hostility to *Zionism*, which had been enormously encouraged and facilitated by the *Balfour Declaration*. During the 1930s this led to protracted skirmishing between Arabs and Jews and a corresponding rise in *anti-Semitism* among Arab populations. After *World War II*, Arab nationalism took diverse paths. The *Ba'ath* movement at first sought *pan-Arab* ideals, then broke into national parties. For others, nationalism took the traditional form of attachment to an individual state, but this usually coexisted with some vague loyalty to the concept of a single Arab nation.

On the other hand, a movement contrary to the secular spirit of modern Arab nationalism was building, mainly among the rural population and the urban poor and less well-educated: the *Muslim Brotherhood* and other *fundamentalist* movements took aim at Arab nationalists, then later at the states and governments they controlled, seeking instead to define the Arab nation in unitary religious rather than worldly and national terms. Most political content was gutted by three key events: the *Iranian Revolution* of 1979 brought the realization to Arab states in the Gulf that Israel was not necessarily the most immediate threat to their interests; the collapse of the Soviet Union, 1989–1991, undercut any alternative to reliance on the United States for security against Iran and/or Iraq; and the *Gulf War* clearly demonstrated that some Arab states were far greater potential and actual threats to certain other Arab states and regimes than Israel ever was.

Suggested Readings: Youssef M. Choueiri, *Arab Nationalism, A History* (2000); Albert Hourani, *Arabic Thought in the Liberal Age, 1798–1939* (1983); Albert Hourani, *History of the Arab Peoples* (1997); Bassam Tibi, *Arab Nationalism: A Critical Enquiry*, 2nd ed. (trans. 1990).

Arab Revolt (1916–1918). The ultimately successful uprising by the *Bedouin* of Arabia, under *Ibn Ali Hussein* and others, against Turkey. The uprising was aided and abetted by the British under General Edmund Allenby (1861–1936). Its success gave birth to a new *Arab nationalism* and, though less importantly, to the legend of *T. E. Lawrence* of Arabia. Wartime British promises to the Arabs were undercut by the hard terms of the secret *Sykes-Picot Agreement* and subsequent division of the Arab lands of the *Ottoman Empire* into British and French *mandates*.

Suggested Reading: T. E. Lawrence, *Revolt in the Desert* (1927).

Arafat, Yassir (b. 1929). Founder of *Fatah* in 1959, and after 1969 the oft-challenged but long-surviving head of the *Palestine Liberation Organization* (PLO). During his career he escaped many *assassination* attempts, Israeli and Arab, and by enemies within the PLO. He kept the PLO intact and survived as leader despite its forcible, bloody expulsion from Jordan in 1971 and from Lebanon after the Israeli invasion in 1982. In 1974 the United States refused to *visé* Arafat so he could speak to the *United Nations General Assembly*, which then met instead in Geneva. Arafat spoke wearing a holstered pistol. That year, he called for a secular, "democratic" PLO state in Palestine. In 1988 he implied he would accept a two-state settlement. He made a major error in supporting Iraq during the *Gulf War*; that cost the PLO its Kuwaiti and Saudi financial support. Most Israeli leaders swore never to negotiate with him or the PLO. Yet, in private, they knew he was the key player on the Palestinian side during *peace talks*, which began in secret, to culminate in 1993 in an agreement among Arafat, *Shimon Peres*, and *Yitzhak Rabin* that sealed an accord for which all three were awarded the 1994 *Nobel Prize* for Peace. Arafat then headed the Palestinian Authority. He soon proved he had been a far more capable nationalist leader in exile than he was a governor of a proto-state. Old, sick, thoroughly corrupt, and in constant fear of assassination should he agree to a final peace with Israel, especially one that surrendered *Jerusalem*, in 2000 Arafat made his greatest mistake and showed conclusively that he lacked final vision. He rejected an offer from Prime Minister Barak of *land for peace*, which was remarkably generous, given past history and the PLO's weak political and military position. That led to a renewal of the *Intifada*, election of a far more hard-line government in Israel, and unraveling of years of incremental progress toward a real and lasting peace. *See also Gaza; West Bank.*

Suggested Readings: Diana Reische, *Arafat and the Palestine Liberation Organization* (1991); Barry Rubin, *The Transformation of Palestinian Politics* (1999).

Aral Sea. An inland sea in Kazakhstan, drained by the Soviets in the 1960s and 1970s to irrigate crops in a near-desert zone. That led to environmental and economic disaster: excessive irrigation caused it to dry and contract, and it may yet disappear entirely. An important fishing industry has been destroyed, with some ships dry-marooned more than 100 miles from shore. As a result, *Central Asia* was threatened with drought, civil conflict, and quarrels over a dwindling fresh *water* supply.

arbitrage. Purchasing *goods*, *services*, or *currency* in one foreign market and selling them quickly in another, to take advantage of varying prices or rates.

arbitration. Peaceful settlement of *disputes* between states by joint and voluntary submission of conflicting claims to binding judgment by a third party. *See also Alabama claims; arbitration clause; arbitration treaties; arbitrator; Beagle Channel dispute;* compromis; *conciliation;* exceptio rei judicatae; *good offices; Hague Conferences; international (public) law; League of Nations; mediation; Nobel Prize; pacifism; Permanent Court of Arbitration; Root Arbitration Treaties; Treaty of Washington (1871); Vatican.*

arbitration clause. Inclusion in a *treaty* of the stipulation that in cases of interpretive disagreement the states concerned will submit to *arbitration*.

arbitration treaties. A host of pre–*World War I* treaties between both major and minor powers, promising to submit *justiciable disputes* to binding *arbitration*. It was hoped that this would avert military clashes. *See also cooling off treaties; Permanent Court of Arbitration; Root Arbitration Treaties.*

arbitrator. A neutral, third party usually specified in the *arbitration clause* of a treaty. It can be another state, ad hoc court, the *Secretary-General*, or some mutually acceptable individual such as a former *head of state* or *government*. The pope has performed this function several times in Latin America. Retired or third-party justices may also act in this capacity.

archetype. An ideal model or pattern.

architecture. (1) A synonym for *grand strategy*. (2) A once fashionable metaphor referring to the *regimes*, structures, and institutions that support regional or *international security* and world order.

archive. The stored diaries, memoranda, military plans, *diplomatic notes*, *treaties*, and related material of a state's foreign policy. This resource is used by *foreign services* and leaders to ensure continuity, consistency of interpretation, and institutional and historical memory. In most Western countries, archives remain closed to scholars for at least 30 years. They were totally shut until 1992 in Russia, then partly opened. They remain entirely shut in many closed societies.

Arctic. The northern polar region. Unlike *Antarctica*, it is divided among the *Arctic nations* and has resident *indigenous peoples*. *See also territorial sea.*

Arctic Circle. The circumpolar line at 23° 28" south of the North Pole.

Arctic Ocean. The great circumpolar ocean of the northern hemisphere, itself subdivided into several seas. Its marine environment is particularly fragile.

Arctic states. Those states with territory and/or *sovereignty* claims above the *Arctic Circle*: Canada, Finland, Iceland, Kalaallit Nunaat (Greenland), Norway, Russia, Sweden, and the United States.

Ardennes Offensive (December 1944–January 1945). Battle of the Bulge. The Ardennes is a heavily wooded area of France, Belgium, and Luxembourg. It was thought by most French military strategists to be impenetrable by *armor*. That belief was played upon by German generals who, during the *Battle of France* in 1940, turned the flank of the *Maginot Line* and captured Paris. The last German offensive in *World War II* was also launched in the Ardennes on December 16, 1944. *Hitler* threw in almost all his *reserves* in a vain attempt to recapture the strategic port of Antwerp and thereby cut the Allied armies in two, dividing the British and Canadians from the American Army. An initial German breakthrough took the Allies by surprise and produced a bulge in the American line 100 miles deep. However, further German advances depended on capturing enemy fuel reserves—the *Panzers* started the offensive with only one-quarter of the minimum fuel necessary to reach their objectives. When this failed, and as the winter skies cleared, overwhelming Allied *air superiority* wasted the Panzer formations. Allied ground resistance also toughened, then held. This firming was accompanied by an extraordinary *flanking* maneuver by the Third Army under General *George Patton*. The battle exhausted Britain's supply of men, but hardly dented American reserves. German losses were so extensive (100,000 men, 800 tanks, and 1,000 combat aircraft) that it proved impossible to hold the Western Allies along the Rhine or contain the Soviets in the Carpathians and along the Vistula. The Ardennes Offensive thus was Hitler's last, great mistake of the war: it hastened the Nazi collapse—and hence his own death—by several months. One unforeseen consequence is that it thereby spared Germany the *atomic bombs*, which only became operational two months after the Nazi surrender and hence were instead used against Japan.

Suggested Reading: John S. Eisenhower, *The Bitter Woods* (1969).

area defense. An *active defense* of a *strategic* area.

Argentina. The Buenos Aires area was colonized by the Spanish in 1515 primarily to block further southward expansion by Portugal from bases in Brazil. In fact, at that time the Portuguese were barely ensconced in coastal Brazil, which they, too, were holding defensively. The presence of Europeans in short order led to the unintended decimation by *disease* of the sparse, nomadic Indian population, a process aggravated and worsened by subsequent Indian *tribute* and *slavery*, until most of the original natives had been wiped out or *assimilated*. Argentina was governed for 300 years by the Spanish, as part of its vast possessions in the *New World*. Buenos Aires was founded in the Río de la Plata and was for many decades a wild and semi-independent port with little contact or control over the nomadic Indians of the interior plains. It was the only port in South America that regularly welcomed *smuggling* (that is, trade) by Dutch and English captains and ships; it even dealt with *privateers*. This arose because, in an attempt to staunch the illegal flow of silver and maintain a closed *mercantilist* system, the *Spanish Monarchy* had forbidden Argentina to trade even with Peru or *New Spain*. An *audiencia* was established in Buenos Aires in 1661. This effort at extending royal rule and law failed, however, and the court was closed in 1672. Another audiencia was founded in 1783, barely in time to greet Argentine independence. Buenos Aires was also made the seat of a much larger administrative area (Viceroyalty) in 1776, also too late to preserve imperial ties. In 1806, and again in 1807, as an off-shoot of the *Napoleonic Wars* in Europe, Buenos Aires was attacked by an English naval and marine force.

A revolt began in Buenos Aires in January 1809 that aimed at overthrow of a liberalizing viceroy. In early 1810 Buenos Aires moved into open rebellion against local Spanish officials intent on liberalizing reforms, on the model of what was then happening in areas of Spain liberated from the French. From that point onward, de facto independence was never really challenged by Spain. Republicans among the population quickly capitalized on the rebellion and the main chance offered by the continuing *Peninsular War* in Europe, and attendant preoccupation and weakness of Spain, and moved the initial revolt toward a formal break. They garnered widening support because they were motivated in good measure not just by nationalist or republican sentiment but also by a desire to break free of Spanish *mercantilism* and embark upon a new policy of *free trade*. Argentine nationalists subsequently struck for outright independence, proclaiming it formally when they arrested the Spanish viceroy on May 25, 1810. They then secured independence militarily under the leadership of *José de San Martín* and Manuel Belgrano (1770–1821).

Peace and contentment did not follow. Instead, there was more than a decade of *civil war*, essentially over which territories would be governed from Buenos Aires and which might strike out on their own as independent states. When Bolivia was briefly federated with Peru, 1836–1839, under André de Santa Cruz (1792–1865), that new state appeared so threatening to the *balance of power* in South America that Chile and Argentina both declared war on the Confederation and broke it apart. Argentina was governed roughly, 1829–1852, by *Juan Manuel de Rosas* (1793–1877), essentially in the interests of himself and the cattle barons. Rosas employed *death squads*, which may have killed 2,000 persons—a huge number relative to the population at that time. He was overthrown by a tripartite invasion of Argentina (whose borders remained ill-defined) by forces from Brazil, Uruguay, and Entre Río. In 1853 a national convention drafted a new, *liberal* constitution. The new constitution did not solve everything either. It took another 20 years, into the 1870s, for Argentina to achieve political stability. It took even longer for a reasonable balance to develop between Buenos Aires and the several interior and northern provinces, where sheep interests now competed with the more established cattle barons and the influx of European migrants was changing the old class, social, and economic mix.

In the interim, Argentina became embroiled in the bloody *War of the Triple Alliance* (1864–1870) when Paraguayan troops crossed into its territory in pursuit of Brazilian forces in Uruguay. In the latter nineteenth century, Argentina opened to investment and immigration and emerged as a major international agricultural exporter; it was comparable in this, and other ways, to nineteenth-century Canada. From 1880 to 1916, Argentina was governed by a single party controlled by the 2,000 families of the ruling *oligarchy*. By *World War I* Argentina ranked among the leading nations in terms of *standard of living* and was thought to have a bright future. The Radical Party finally won in 1916, and the 1920s saw mild reforms. The cattle barons and landowners, backed by the army, retook power in 1930. Starting with the *Great Depression*, Argentina fell into decades of civil and political strife. In 1943 semi-*fascist* sympathizers in the military took over in a *coup*. In 1946 *Juan*

Perón sidled into power, with his charismatic and ambitious wife, Eva (Evita). Perón was reelected in 1952, then ousted in 1955. There followed a succession of nondescript military and civilian governments, with the military always in control behind the scenes. The Peronists won the 1973 elections and Perón returned from exile, but he died the next year. Another wife, Isabela, succeeded him but was deposed by another coup in 1976.

The late 1970s were marked by the *dirty war* against leftist guerrillas, in which many thousands of Argentines were "disappeared" (murdered) by death squads. The economy was also badly mismanaged by the generals. Desperate for a foreign distraction, the *junta* sought to stir nationalist sentiment first by confrontation with Chile over the *Beagle Channel*, then with an ill-conceived or executed *invasion* and occupation of the *Falkland (Malvinas) Islands*. After defeat in the *Falklands War*, a civilian government displaced the generals. The new government revealed and disavowed Argentina's secret *nuclear weapons* program and signed *nonproliferation* agreements with Brazil, which was also undergoing a transition to civilian rule, and with the *IAEA*. In 1983 Raúl Alfonsín (b. 1927) succeeded the generals. He initially prosecuted some officers for *human rights* violations. However, in 1986 Alfonsin passed a morally retrograde law making *superior orders* an acceptable defense for perpetrators of the dirty war. In 1989 and 1990, President Carlos Menem pardoned almost all officers who had conducted the dirty war, along with some former guerillas then in prison. Neither man agreed to a final settlement with Britain over the Falklands.

Hyperinflation threatened Argentina's newfound internal *stability* during the 1980s. By 1990 the inflation rate reached 20,000 percent per annum. Under another Peronist, Carlos Menem, Argentina shifted toward overall economic and political accommodation with the United States, restored relations with Britain (1990), and began an impressive economic recovery by *pegging* its currency to the U.S. dollar (1991)—thereby wrestling hyperinflation down to reasonable levels of normal inflation. Argentina was the only Latin American country to send troops to the *Gulf War*. It also joined United Nations *peacekeeping* in Croatia in 1991 and pressed for the OAS to intervene to restore democracy in Haiti. In 1993 *rapprochement* with Britain led to a visit by the U.K. defense minister. Even so, Argentina did not renounce its claim to the Malvinas. In the second half of the 1990s Argentina's economic miracle was strained by a deep recession, in turn greatly exacerbated by an unpayable load of external debt and by continuing the currency peg to the dollar past levels, which the relative strength of the dollar made imprudent. This led to overpriced Argentine exports and a gravely uncompetitive economy, and thus to deeper recession. At the end of 2001, a rise in unemployment led to bloody riots that toppled the government of Fernando de la Rua, who left office with the economy in ruins, the debt crisis unresolved, and a major currency *devaluation* looming.

Suggested Readings: Daniel K. Lewis, *The History of Argentina* (2001); James Scobie, *Argentina: A City and a Nation* (1964).

Arias, Oscar Sanchez (b. 1940). President of Costa Rica, 1986–1990. He won the *Nobel Prize* (for Peace) in 1987 for proposing a negotiated solution to the various conflicts then afflicting Central America. He enlisted the *Contadora group* in support of his efforts. His plan essentially called for withdrawal of all foreign powers from regional affairs, cessation of aid to antigovernment *guerrillas* in El Salvador and Nicaragua, and social reconstruction based on democratic principles and a compromise peace. Although this plan was not formally adopted, its main outlines later found expression in the settlements brokered by the United Nations and other international bodies in El Salvador (1990–1993) and Nicaragua (1989–1990).

aristocracy. (1) A hereditary leadership class enjoying great economic, political, and social privilege relative to others in a given society. These advantages may have been earned, at least by the first generations, through military service and/or an extended education and expectation of service in public life. Eventually, they are merely inherited and enjoyed by the late-born (some of whom will retain a sense of noblesse oblige), the lazy, and the mediocre without their carrying any substantial corresponding responsibilities. (2) A system of government in which a state is ruled by a hereditary elite. (3) Colloquial: rule by the most able persons in a given society. Aristocracies overall went into decline along with the rise of the modern nation-state: central monarchies tamed provincial and local power, professional armies replaced *feudal* military obligations, and *industrialization* raised new monied classes to power. The *levée en masse* finished aristocracy as a serious political alternative to *popular sovereignty*. Nonetheless, in Europe the aristocracy retained economic and military dominance to the sixteenth century, real political power well into the eighteenth century, and a lingering social ascendancy into the twenty-first. *See also caste system; Confucianism; elitism; French Revolution; new monarchies; Normans; revolution in military affairs.*

armaments. *See arms.*

armed conflict. A term introduced into the 1949 *Geneva Conventions* upon the insistence of the *International Committee of the Red Cross* in order to prevent future evasions of state legal and humanitarian obligations in times of war, such as arose in prior legal evasions by some states that claimed that earlier conventions did not apply to their actions because no *state of war*, in the classic *de jure* sense, existed in the absence of a formal *declaration of war*. Although one problem was solved by the less determinative phrase, another was raised as to whether the international *laws of war* would then have to be applied to "armed conflicts not of an international character."

armed hostilities. Actual combat, whether legal and declared, or illegal. *See also armed conflict; state of war; war; warfare.*

armed humanitarian intervention. On rare occasions, Great Powers—and even some smaller powers—have intervened militarily in what otherwise are generally, and were historically, considered the *internal affairs* of other states, in the name of an ostensible general interest in ending a humanitarian outrage or disaster that is rooted in political conflict. Although this phenomenon took on a new salience post–*Cold War*, in legal theory it has been supported for centuries as a permissible exception to the doctrines of *noninterference* and *nonintervention*: *Grotius* and *Vattel* both listed it among permissible exceptions to the principle of nonintervention. Among the more important examples are these: (1) The Great Powers intervened with the Ottomans during the *Greek War of Independence* (1821–1829), at least rhetorically in behalf of Greek rebels and Orthodox religious refugees. (2) The *Royal Navy* sought to enforce an international ban on the *slave trade* during the nineteenth century. (3) Russia intervened in Turkey in 1877, ostensibly in behalf of Bulgarian Christians repressed by the Muslim Ottomans; *Gladstone* lent support to Bulgarian independence on the ground of liberal principle. (4) The United States intervened in Cuba, ostensibly to right Spanish wrongs and misrule, in the *Spanish-American War* in 1898 and ended up repressing a nationalist rebellion in the Philippines. (5) Multinational intervention under United Nations auspices took place in the Congo in 1964. It was roundly condemned by a majority of African states but was contemporaneously praised by international legal scholars as a valid armed humanitarian intervention. (6) British troops intervened in East Africa in 1964, at the request of *Commonwealth* governments, to repress army mutinies in the newly independent states of Kenya, Tanganyika, and Uganda. (7) India intervened in Bangladesh in 1971, citing the huge burden brought on by the Bangladeshi refugee crisis, as well as charges of *genocide* by the Pakistani Army against East Pakistanis. (8) Tanzania invaded Uganda in 1980, in some part in response to the brutality of the regime of *Idi Amin*. (9) India intervened, by formal invitation, in the civil war in Sri Lanka from 1987 to 1990. (10) The United Nations intervened militarily during 1992–1993 to permit aid agencies to feed millions starving in Somalia. (11) Several West African states, led by Nigeria, intervened in Liberia and Sierra Leone in the mid-1990s, as civil wars led to massive human rights and refugee problems in those countries. Great Britain in 2000 also sent troops to Sierra Leone. (12) *NATO* intervened to impose an interim settlement of the war in Bosnia in 1995. (13) NATO intervened in *Kosovo* in 1999 in response to a campaign of *ethnic cleansing* there by the Serbs. *See also abatement; intervention; protectorate.*

armed neutrality. (1) The combined foreign policy of the *League of Armed Neutrality*. (2) *Woodrow Wilson's* policy of arming the U.S. *merchant marine* in 1917, announced within days of receipt of the *Zimmermann Telegram*. (3) A generic stance of *neutrality* backed by a large military establishment that serves as a *deterrent* to potential *aggressors*. The two most successful practitioners of this policy historically have been Sweden since 1814 and Switzerland since 1815.

Armée d'Afrique. The French colonial army based in Algeria, from the time of the French conquest. It was responsible for the conquest and policing of much of the *French Empire* in West Africa. It included units of Turcos, Algerian native infantry; Zouaves, who were European infantry but who dressed Berber-style in brightly colored native uniforms; and Spahis, or Arab-style light *cavalry*.

Armenia. Armenia has existed in some form since the ninth century B.C.E. The modern state occupies perhaps 1/10th of historical Armenia. In 300 C.E. most of its population converted to *Christianity*—a faith persevered in by Armenians despite subsequent conversion of most neighbors to *Islam* during and after the seventh century. Armenia was divided between the Roman and Persian Empires in 387 C.E. Located at a major geopolitical crossroads, Armenians suffered repeated invasion: Seljuk Turks, eleventh century; Mongols, thirteenth century; Turkmen tribes, fourteenth to fifteenth centuries; and *Tamerlane* and Persian Safafids. The resulting waves of emigration and population displacement constituted a prolonged *diaspora*. With failure of the *Crusades*, Armenia lost its independence in the fourteenth century to the *Ottomans*, who occupied a devastated and depopulated country. In 1828 northern (Persian) Armenia was ceded to Russia after the Persians were defeated in a short, sharp war. Russians ruled with a less heavy hand than did the Turks, who in 1894–1896 and again during *World War I* carried out the *Armenian genocide* in their portion of a divided nation. At *San Stefano*, Armenia briefly enjoyed Russian protection, but this was reversed at the *Congress of Berlin*. A rump Armenian republic was briefly de facto independent, 1918–1920. Armenia was to become formally independent under the *Treaty of Sèvres* (1920), but that agreement was never *ratified*. Instead, it was *partitioned* between Turkey and Soviet Russia in 1921. In 1922 Armenia was made part of the *Transcaucasian SFSR*. In 1936 *Stalin* split Armenia from Azerbaijan, leaving Armenians in the *enclave* of *Nagorno-Karabakh*, and Azeris in the *exclave* of *Nakhichevan*. This conflict was otherwise suffocated by the *Pax Sovietica* until the late 1980s.

In 1988 Armenians suffered from a great earthquake as well as *pogroms*, which forced several hundred thousand *refugees* out of Azerbaijan. Then war flared with Azerbaijan, which cut off all land routes to Armenia and blocked *oil*, *food*, and other deliveries. The Soviets were unable to sort out matters before both states became *sovereign* in 1991. Armenia declared independence after the failed *coup* in Moscow, but its independence was not widely *recog-*

nized until December 25, 1991. With the collapse of the Soviet Union the *Armenia-Azerbaijan War* intensified. By 1994 Armenia had significantly expanded, *de facto* not *de jure*, at the expense of Azerbaijan. In addition to its core population of four million, 1.5 million ethnic Armenians live in Azerbaijan, including Nagorno-Karabakh, as well as in Georgia, Russia, or Turkey. Desultory fighting continued in Nagorno-Karabakh through the 1990s. In October 1999, a foiled coup attempt and attack on the Armenian parliament killed the prime minister and many others. That same year, Azerbaijan's President Geidar Aliev and the newly elected Armenian President Robert Kocharian began direct talks over Nagorno-Karabakh, jointly mediated by the United States and the Soviet Union. They met more than a dozen times by 2001.

Suggested Readings: S. A. Adshead, *Central Asia in World History* (1994); Martha B. Olcott, *Central Asia's New States* (1996); G. Walker, *Armenia* (1980).

Armenia-Azerbaijan War (1988–1998). In February 1988, an old territorial dispute between these two Soviet republics over possession of *Nagorno-Karabakh* flared into open warfare. Soviet intervention in 1988, 1989, and 1990 failed to prevent an increase in the fighting. With independence for both *nations* at the end of 1991, the war took on new significance and lethality, despite being overtaken in news coverage and in public and policy awareness by the *Balkan* conflict, which flared with the breakup of *Yugoslavia*. In May 1992 Armenia cut a six-mile-wide corridor to the *enclave*, forming a land bridge. Fighting then spilled into *Nakhichevan*. In April 1993, Armenian gains led Turkey to warn that, unlike in *Bosnia*, it would not wait to intervene to stop dismemberment of Azerbaijan. In June Armenian forces consolidated their corridor to Nagorno-Karabakh, expelling most Azeris (900,000 were made *refugees* by the war) and precipitating a brief *civil war* within Azerbaijan. CIS and OSCE mediation efforts failed to end the fighting, which instead stuttered to a halt in 1998. The OSCE, the United States, and Russia jointly mediated direct talks between the warring sides, 1999–2001.

Armenian genocide. From 1894 through 1896, massacres of Armenians by the *Ottomans* occurred under the leadership of *Abdul Hamid II*. This had the effect of partly alienating several Western *Great Powers*, most notably Britain, which had long supported Turkey in the *Great Game* against perceived Russian *encroachment*. This was one of the first occasions when outside powers made *human rights* a direct concern in their foreign policy. There were also follow-up Cilician *pogroms* in 1909. From 1915 through 1917 a second and far greater genocide against Armenians by the Ottomans took place. This was mainly a response to Armenian volunteers enlisting in fair numbers in anti-Turkish units fighting in support of the tsar's armies, and to several massacres of Turks inside Russian-occupied Ottoman territory by an Armenian *provisional government* that had been proclaimed there in April 1915. The sultan's forces reacted with a genocide of some 700,000 Armenians from 1915 to 1917. That is a consensus estimate by regional specialists: the actual numbers remain hotly disputed by both communities, with Armenian sources usually asserting a death toll in the range of 1.5 million and some Turkish sources denying the events even occurred. Whatever the precise number, it was large and the attending civilian suffering was enormous. Some of the victims were simply murdered, but most died during forced marches or from gross neglect after being herded into *concentration camps* set up in the Syrian desert. For decades, Turkey officially denied the extent (and even the fact) of the carnage, causing deep contention with—and lasting bitterness among—Armenians. *See also war crimes trials.*

Suggested Reading: G. Walker, *Armenia* (1980).

armistice. A mutually agreed suspension of hostilities, with the expectation of proceeding to a formal peace, whether a compromise, negotiated settlement, or a *diktat*. The most famous is that of *World War I*, which took effect on the 11th hour, of the 11th day, of the 11th month, 1918, a moment still marked by silent reflection, and wearing of the poppy, on Armistice Day in the many nations once part of British Empire and Commonwealth and the French Empire and community, which lost men in the Great War. *See also cease-fire; peace treaty; truce.*

armor. (1) Metal plating or chain mail molded to fit the body and used to deflect projectiles or blades. It was in common use until the seventeenth century in Europe, and even later in Japan and China, but became effectively obsolete with the introduction of gunpowder weapons starting in the fifteenth century. By the seventeenth century it entirely disappeared from European battlefields. It made a minor comeback during the first months of *World War I* as all armies issued steel helmets. Kevlar vests and other devices to protect individuals were introduced later in the twentieth century. (2) A generic term for steel plated and reinforced military vehicles, but more often referring explicitly to tanks. Tanks were first used in combat by the British at the *Somme* (1916) and en masse at *Cambrai* (1917), but were never decisive in World War I. The *Reichswehr* had no tanks until 1918, other than some 170 captured vehicles.

During *World War II* the tank came into its own as a key instrument of both offense and defense, beginning with the stunning German *Blitzkriegs* into Poland in 1939, France and the Low Countries in 1940, and Operation *Barbarossa* against the Soviet Union in 1941. The largest armored battle ever fought was *Kursk* (1943), where twelve *Panzer* divisions encountered massed Soviet armor formations and thousands of antitank guns. The second largest armored battle was a two-week mêlée in France in 1944, around Falaise, where ten Panzer divisions faced ten *Allied* armored divisions on an 800-square-mile battlefield. Falaise showed an evolution in armored warfare in just four years from the explosive, war-winning impact of Blitzkrieg to a new tactic in which tanks became a blunt instrument of industrialized, mechanized *attrition*, as all armies learned how to defend against tanks with antitank guns and minefields, tank-busting aircraft, and armored counterattack.

During the *Cold War* both *NATO* and the *Warsaw Pact* built massive, heavily armored forces without ever fighting. The *Third Arab-Israeli War* witnessed huge tank battles, which were decided by highly effective advances in antitank warfare, both from missile-firing infantry and *air power*. In the *Gulf War*, Iraqi armor was so handily defeated by *Gulf coalition* air power, especially helicopter gunships, that questions were raised about whether the day of the tank was done, at least when put up against the air force of a first-rate military power. By 2000 the only NATO country with aircraft large enough to transport heavy tanks was the United States. Major powers began researching "smart armor," capable of deploying only when it came under fire, and laser weapons, against which no armor would be effective. *See also radiological weapons; revolution in military affairs.*

Suggested Reading: Martin van Creveld, *Technology and War From 2000 B.C. to the Present Day* (1989).

arms. A generic term for weapons of all types, with "small arms" referring to weapons that an individual may wield and "heavy armaments" used for weapons and ordnance that require whole crews (armor, artillery, air, or ship) to deploy.

arms buildup. Increasing levels of *armaments* and military preparedness, qualitatively or quantitatively. This does not necessarily occur in competition with any other state; for instance, it may reflect an overdue refit of old or technologically obsolete equipment, nor must it imply threat and foreboding, as is the case in an *arms race*. *See also economies of scale.*

arms control. Mutually agreed upon restraints on the research and manufacture, and/or the levels and locales of deployment, of troops and weapons systems. This frequently is, but should not be, confused with *disarmament*. Arms control does not imply the utter suffocation and dismantling of militaries, which is the ultimate aim of disarmament proposals. Instead, it argues that shared interests (mutually enhanced *security*, reduced costs, and perhaps lessened tensions) may be secured by selective limitations on arms research, procurement, and/or deployment. Most arms control is achieved by negotiation of highly specific *treaties*, but it is also possible to have *de facto*, tit-for-tat reductions tied to changes in political realities. There is much debate about the possession of armaments by states and the conduct of *arms races* as causes of war. Much of it amounts to a house of canards. Some advocates of arms control are moved primarily by belief in such a connection and see arms control as a principal path to peace. It seems more likely, however, that for the most part acquisition of armaments reflects rather than causes conflict among groups, peoples, and nations. In other words, states generally do not fight because they have arms, so much as have arms because they consider it necessary to fight, and at least critical to be armed in order to deter potential *aggression* or carry out an active defense.

That is why arms control agreements tend to follow or parallel reductions in interstate conflict rather than precede and cause lessened tensions, though they may do that as a secondary and reinforcing effect. In a sense, arms control thus becomes achievable only after it is no longer really needed. For instance, in 1990–1991 U.S. and Soviet negotiators scrambled to codify and clarify rapid reductions already taking place as a result of the end of the *Cold War* which had been unimaginable just five years earlier. Yet such agreements are still useful as they regularize, give legal sanction and authority to, and subject to *verification* a change in real-world relationships. *See also ABM Treaty; accidental war; Anglo-German Naval Agreement; Antarctic Treaty; arms build-up; Biological Warfare Treaty; Chemical Weapons Convention; Comprehensive Test Ban; conflict management; continuity of safeguards; Conventional Forces in Europe Treaty; crisis management; CSBMs; deterrence; Disarmament in Europe Accord; first-strike capability; Five Power Treaty; fixed satellite; Four Power Treaty; Geneva Protocol; Hague Conventions; IAEA; intelligence; Intermediate-Range Nuclear Forces Treaty; land mine; limited war; Moon Treaty; Mutual Force Reduction Treaty; National Technical Means of Verification; Nine Power Treaty; Nuclear Non-Proliferation Treaty; nuclear weapons free zone; Open Skies; Outer Space Treaty; Partial Test Ban Treaty; proliferation; revolution in military affairs; Rush-Bagot Treaty; SALT; satellites; SDI; sea mine; second-strike capability; security dilemma; START; Washington Conference; World Disarmament Conference.*

Suggested Readings: Hedley Bull, *The Control of the Arms Race* (1961); Jozef Goldblat, *Arms Control: A Guide to Negotiations and Agreements* (1994); Philip Towle, *Arms Control and East-West Relations* (1983).

arms exporting nations. Many countries are in the arms business. The top exporters in the second half of the twentieth century, in terms of gross volume of arms sales, were the United States, the Soviet Union (later, Russia), Britain, France, China, Germany, Slovakia, Israel, Sweden, Brazil, North Korea, and Canada. *See also economies of scale.*

arms importing nations. Among the leaders in terms of gross volume of arms imports in the second half of the twentieth century were Saudi Arabia, India, the United States, Japan, Indonesia, Iran, Vietnam, China, Malaysia, and South Korea.

arms limitation. A synonym for *arms control.*

arms race. Efforts by states to acquire numerical and/or qualitative (technological) superiority in troops and weaponry, accompanied by a sense of threat and fear of possible or impending military conflict. In times of *crisis* or prolonged tension, competitive procurement of arms may contribute to a spiral of deployment and make more likely *accidental war*. The commonly held belief that arms races lead to wars is demonstrably false. To cite just one major example, although the *Anglo-German naval arms race* clearly did contribute to tensions in the buildup to *World War* I, for nearly 50 years before that, from c.1855 (*ironclad* revolution) to c.1904 (just before the *Dreadnought* revolution), Britain, France, and Russia were also engaged in an expensive and fierce naval arms race without ever going to war, and indeed while drawing together in an informal alliance—the *Entente Cordiale*—that ended their protracted arms race.

Alternately, though this is not a widely recognized or popular observation, arms races may also contribute to peace by reinforcing *deterrence* because rearmament by a likely victim will raise the expected costs of war to a potential *aggressor*. That is the main assumption behind a policy of *armed neutrality* and all preparedness measures by genuinely peaceful powers. Arms races have been a constant feature in international history. Thus, adoption of the stirrup in the eighth century in Europe led to an arms race among *feudal* forces of mounted warriors. By the end of that arms race, armored knights formed lances that were the equivalent of twentieth-century tank formations, supported by hosts of retainers and infantry. And since c. 1500 and the modern *revolution in military affairs*, in a real sense the world's major powers have been in a perpetual arms race, which shows no sign whatever of abating. *See also arms buildup; arms control; Cold War; Dreadnought; ironclad; mobilization; nuclear weapons; security dilemma; war.*

Suggested Readings: Hedley Bull, *The Control of the Arms Race* (1961); Michael Howard, *The Causes of War and Other Essays* (1983).

army. *See military units.*

Arnold, Benedict (1741–1801). American traitor. He fought in the *French and Indian Wars* as a young volunteer in the colonial *militia*, experience that gained him an early commission as a general in the colonial army upon the outbreak of the *American Revolution*. Arnold was a much admired and decorated colonial officer, who might have risen to top command but for the fortunes of war and the judgment of his superiors. He led an early expedition into *Québec* in 1775, but failed to take that fortress city over the winter of 1775–1776. In the spring, he was forced to retreat to Lake Champlain. In 1777 Arnold defended Connecticut from British invasion. In the Saratoga campaign (July–October 1777), he contributed much to the final American victory at Saratoga (October 17, 1777). The next year Arnold was placed in charge of defending the capital at Philadelphia. There he was drawn into the swirl of congressional politics and also married into a *United Empire Loyalist* family. In 1779 Arnold was brought up on charges of insubordination. He was ultimately cleared of all but a few minor offenses. Still, this sharply curtailed his career within the colonial army. *George Washington*, who long had been a supporter of Arnold's, was compelled to formally reprimand him and henceforth had a jaundiced view of his subordinate. In 1780 Arnold was sent to upper New York to hold the strategic position of West Point, gateway to the Hudson and lower New York. He now made the decision that marked his place in history: Arnold conspired to surrender West Point to the British, for money and for a command in the British Army. He got both, even though the plot was uncovered and foiled before he could carry it off. In 1781 Arnold led British forces into Virginia and Connecticut. After the war he lived out his days in foreign *exile*, broadly despised—no one admires a traitor, not even those who receive the benefits of betrayal—on both sides of the Atlantic. *See also Pierre Laval; Vidkung Quisling; Wang Jingwei.*

Suggested Readings: David C. King, *Benedict Arnold and the American Revolution* (1999); James Kirby Martin, *Benedict Arnold, Revolutionary Hero* (1997).

Aroostook War (February–May 1839). A *border* war among private citizens that eventually drew in the governments of the United States and Great Britain. It was fought over where to draw the U.S.-Canadian border in the Aroostook River valley between Maine and New Brunswick. The "war" was not much more than a brawl between American settlers and Canadian lumberjacks. However, as it dragged on it threatened to escalate into a fully fledged conflict involving American troops, under the command of *Winfield Scott*, and British *regulars*. Scott and the British worked out an agreement, and both sides enforced this against local *filibusters* and would-be troublemakers. The boundary was then set in the *Webster-Ashburton Treaty* (1842).

Arras, Battle of (April–May 1917). The opening day of this battle (April 16th) saw the Canadian Corps capture *Vimy Ridge*, a strategic high point held by the Germans that had broken a French attack in 1915. The Germans were stunned and opened to a penetrating assault, but—as so often happened— the Allied offensive faltered as a result of communication and supply problems. *Attrition* soon set in, and by the end of May total casualties on all sides exceeded a quarter-million. Meanwhile, an assault launched by the French at *Chemin des Dames* to coincide with the attack on Vimy-Arras was an utter disaster and provoked the *French Army mutinies.*

Arrow War. *See Opium Wars.*

arsenal. (1) A storage place for arms, explosives and military supplies. (2) All weapons a state possesses.

Article 51 (of the United Nations Charter). This Article of the *United Nations Charter* permits the use of force in *"self-defense." See also aggression; Gulf War; Korean Conflict; nuclear reactor (Osiraq, Iraq), attack by Israel.*

artillery. Large-bore weapons—whether stationary in fixed *fortifications* or mobile on land or at sea—that fire solid shot or *case shot, canister, grapeshot,* or explosive projectiles, along with the skilled troops and science of warfare that accompany and operate the guns—originally, as many as forty horses pulled a single siege gun. Artillery was introduced to warfare in Europe as part of the *gunpowder revolution.* Its effective use by the kings of the centralizing *new monarchies* of Europe, established by c. 1500 in France and England, permitted literal bombardment of the old, fragmented *feudal* order into submission to centralized authority. That development partly reflected the great expense of artillery, which only the kings could sustain, but also its destructive power: cannon firing iron rather than stone balls enabled kings to reduce the stone castles of their recalcitrant barons and establish a real monopoly over the use of armed force on land. The same logic of expense and firepower then advantaged the *Great Powers* over the small and middling, producing a much greater differentiation among states. Artillery played a key role in warfare, and in political repression, ever after.

Artillery became standardized, with interchangeable parts, as well as lighter and more mobile, under the innovative guidance of *Gustavus Adolphus, Frederick the Great,* and then *Napoleon.* In 1688, at the siege of Philipsbourg, *Vauban* invented ricochet fire, wherein a reduced charge allowed an iron shot to ricochet in multiple directions, creating a lethal hazard to man and beast on any battlefield or inside a defending fortress. A further *revolution in military affairs* in artillery occurred from the 1870s, as French designers invented breech-loading guns, which vastly increased the rate of fire, and recoilless carriages, which made it unnecessary to resight the gun after each firing. By *World War I,* artillery was a major weapon, with ranges in some cases exceeding 50 miles. At the start of that war, and until 1918, its presence on the battlefield and ability to break up any mass attack was a major factor leading to *trench warfare.* During the Great War, artillery delivered not merely explosive ordnance, but also *poison gas* shells. By 1918 aerial reconnaissance and mathematically projected firing techniques (from map grids) made artillery an overwhelming weapon in the final *Allied and Associated Power* offensive in the west, as firepower finally displaced human flesh as the major instrument of victory in industrial warfare. *See also barrage; bombardment; cannon; combined arms; élan; howitzer; Napoleonic warfare; pike; terrae dominum finitur; turret.*

Suggested Readings: Jeremy Black, *War and the World* (1998); Martin van Creveld, *Technology and War From 2000 B.C. to the Present Day* (1989); Michael Howard, *War in European History* (1976).

Aruba. This *West Indies* island split from the *Netherlands Antilles* in 1986. It is an *overseas territory* of the Netherlands with the same status as the *Antilles*.

Arusha Declaration (1967). A set of loosely *socialist* and collectivist principles laid out by *Julius Nyerere*, touted by him and others as a model for developing a unique brand of *African socialism*. It was widely popular at first for its egalitarian rhetoric, but was deeply resented in the implementation because of its insistence on sometimes forced resettlement of peasants in Ujamaa villages (collectives), amounting to socialism by bayonet. Its manifest failure as an economic strategy led to abandonment of the program after 1987. *See also collectivization.*

Aryan. (1) In demographic studies: Ancient Indo-European, Sanskrit-speaking tribes that spilled out of the Caucasus and Central Asia around 2000 B.C.E. Their migration was multifaceted, fracturing into Greek, Germanic, Italic, Celtic, Iranian, Sanskritic, and Hindi peoples who moved in nearly every direction and remade the history of Europe, the Mediterranean, and India. The Aryan migration to India is usually dated c. 1500 B.C.E. There, Aryan *cavalry* conquered and subsequently intermingled with the *indigenous* population, becoming a ruling elite and absorbing much from the peoples they had mastered. It was long thought that the Aryans destroyed India's extant urban civilizations, but that thesis is now widely disputed, with ecological changes offered as a competing explanation. Aryan contribution to the rise of classical Indian civilization is moot, but present evidence suggests it is most likely that—contrary to the conclusions of earlier historical writing that saw Aryans as having civilized a primitive pre-Aryan India—the Aryans were semibarbarians, the *Mongols* of an earlier age, as compared to some of the more advanced cultures of Gangetic India, which they overran. On the other hand, they were singularly responsible for writing the *Vedas* (magical incantations and hymns with assumed scriptural form, reverence, and veneration) and developing Brahman *Hinduism*, a syncretic religion that combined indigenous cults of worship with the Aryan priesthood and traditions of sacrifice and elaborate ritual (Brahmanas means "manuals of ritual"). They also composed the *Upanishads*, texts of secret knowledge of the path to salvation. These deeply influenced extant systems of belief and contributed to the reformation of Hindu society and rigidification of the *caste system*. The Aryans also introduced Sanskrit, giving license to an efflorescence of much wider Indian literature, poetry, and spiritual speculation.

(2) In *Nazi* race theory and *ideology*: A non-Jewish, north European Caucasian; the "superior race" supposedly responsible for creating all higher civilization, including lost Atlantis. *Hitler* believed that the Dutch, English, French, Norwegians, Swedes, and other "Nordic peoples," along with some Italians, were of "Aryan stock." The speciousness of this claim was demonstrated late in *World War II* when the SS, desperate for new recruits, "dis-

covered" that Croatian fascists shared the "Aryan bloodline." *See also* Herrenvolk; *India; social Darwinism;* Untermenschen.

ascaris. African troops employed by European colonial armies. *See also* Tirailleurs Sénégalais.

ASEAN. *See Association of Southeast Asian Nations.*

ASEAN + 3. The *Association of Southeast Asian Nations,* plus China, Japan, and South Korea. They began meeting under this rubric from 1997, parallel to meetings of *APEC.* In addition to regular *summits,* finance ministers also meet and consult. The intention is to develop a regional association for Asia that mimics the role of the *Group of Seven.*

ASEAN Regional Forum (ARF). An *Asia-Pacific* forum founded in mid-1993. It includes the *ASEAN* states as well as other Pacific countries with security interests in the region, most notably China, Japan, Russia, and the United States. It is modeled on, and was inspired by the success (and cost-efficiency) of, the *CSCE.* Fundamentally driving its creation was a vacuum of power in Asia left by the ebbing of the *Pax Americana,* which characterized the *Cold War.* Like the CSCE, the ARF looked to initiate and implement CSBMs and aimed at cooperative, *preventive diplomacy.*

Ashanti. A West African *empire* that grew up inland from the *Gold Coast* at the end of the seventeenth century, drawing at first upon refugees from slave-raiding along the coast who had escaped into the forest belt and then using firearms acquired in the Atlantic trade to expand. The Ashanti broke free of Denkyira in a war of independence, 1698–1701, establishing their own state under the central leadership of a king based in Kumasi. Ashanti expanded north, forcing into *tributary* status several small savannah states such as Bono, which it conquered in 1724. Its further advance north was blocked by powerful savannah states. So it expanded south next: by 1745 it had pushed aside Akim and Akwamu so that its traders took the lion's share of the coastal trade in *gold* and *slaves* with the Dutch at Elmina. That same year Ashanti musketeers defeated an armored *cavalry* army from Dagomba, ending the ancient supremacy of savannah cavalry states over the forest peoples of West Africa. Ashanti pressure on the coastal states led to creation of a Fante coalition to oppose its further advance. In 1765 Ashanti invaded the deep south, and by 1807 the Fante states submitted. Ashanti also raided deep into Ewe and Aja lands, astride the *Slave Coast.* By the early nineteenth century, Ashanti was a territorially sated empire, larger than England.

Conflict continued, however, between Ashanti and the coastal Fante. That put Ashanti also into conflict with the British, who after 1807 opposed and increasingly acted against the *slave trade* and sold the Fante firearms to prop them up against the power of Ashanti. In 1823 an Ashanti army raided the British base at the Cape Coast. The next year the British sent a punitive expedition north under the governor of their main West African colony in Sierra Leone, Charles McCarthy. It was destroyed by the Ashanti, and McCarthy's head was carried off as a trophy—a fact that aggravated the British toward revenge for several generations. In a larger war with the British, 1873–1874, provoked by British acquisition of the Dutch coastal forts and closure of the coast to Ashanti trade, a deep British raid entered the Ashanti capital of Kumasi, razing it to the ground and severely punishing elements of the Ashanti Army, then numbering some 40,000 warriors, many of whom were unmotivated slaves. This led to annexation of the southern Ashanti provinces to the *Gold Coast* colony. During the later *scramble for Africa*, the British declared a *protectorate* in the north to insulate the area from French advances against *Samori Touré*. Britain invaded the heartland of Ashanti in 1896, using predominantly Nigerian *mercenaries*, and kidnapped the king. In 1900 Ashanti rose against the British; once again they were invaded by Nigerian and Central African troops under British command and at last succumbed. In the colonial period, "Ashanti" was used to refer to the British protectorate area in what is now northern Ghana, 1896–1935. It was later merged with the Gold Coast. The Ashanti remain the main *tribe* (or *ethnic group*) in northern Ghana.

Suggested Reading: Igor Wilks, *Ashante in the 19th Century* (1975).

Ashanti Wars. *See Ashanti.*

Asia. The world's largest, most populous continent, stretching from Japan to the *Middle East*, and by convention subdivided into *Central Asia*, *East Asia*, *Northeast Asia*, *South Asia*, *Southeast Asia*, and *West Asia*. *See also Asia-Pacific*; *Pacific Rim.*

Asia and Pacific Council (ASPCA). It was founded in 1966 to encourage regional economic and political cooperation among non-Communist Asian states.

"Asia for Asians." The slogan under which Japan pursued *hegemony* in *East Asia* before *World War II*. At first it touched a responsive chord in a region dominated by white foreigners. After the *conquests* and brutal *occupations* of 1931–1945, however, it was obvious to most that it really meant "Asia for the Japanese." *See also Hirohito.*

Asian Development Bank (ADB). Headquartered in Manila, it was founded in 1967 to finance regional *development* and *infrastructure* projects by extending *soft loans*. Since the 1980s it has, along with the *IBRD* and other *regional banks*, increased its lending for poverty alleviation programs. It had $40 billion in capital funds by 1994, and its capital funds continued to expand along with member economies into the twenty-first century. Extraregional members include Britain, Germany, the United States, and numerous smaller *OECD* countries. In the 1980s some Asian *NICs* (e.g., South Korea) were upgraded from the status of borrower to themselves becoming major providers of the bank's capital fund. The United States and Japan hold large shares, with Japan historically playing a leading role in managing bank affairs. As has the *African Development Bank*, the ADB established a distinct fund (the *Asian Development Fund*) to assist the poorest states in the *Asia-Pacific* region—the area of its charter mandate. In addition, in 1989 the ADB joined with various *private sector* lenders to set up the *Asian Finance and Investment Corporation*.

Asian Development Fund (ADF). Created under the auspices of the *Asian Development Bank*, this is a special fund that provides interest-free loans to the poorest states in the *Asia-Pacific* region. These loans can take up to 50 years for repayment of principal, with an initial 10-year grace period.

Asian Finance and Investment Corporation (AFIC). This partial subsidiary of the *Asian Development Bank* was established in 1989 in cooperation with various commercial banks. Its express purpose is to make capital available to *private sector* borrowers in order to stimulate creation of, and sustain, a wide economic base for national and regional *development*.

Asian financial crisis (1997–1998). A collapse of East Asian growth rates and an attendant loss of confidence in regional banks and the stability of Asian economies in the second half of 1997, continuing into 1998, partly as a result of a speculative assault on local currencies, but more as a result of underlying bad credit and speculative and investment excesses of previous years. It shook the *Asian Tigers* to the core and led to severe political instability and major *structural adjustment* reforms in several countries, especially Indonesia, where it had major political ramifications. *See also International Monetary Fund (IMF).*

Asian Tigers. Hong Kong, South Korea, Singapore, and Taiwan; so-called owing to ferocious *GNP* growth rates that ate into world market share in the 1970s and 1980s. Their prestige was much diminished by the *Asian financial crisis* of 1997.

Asia-Pacific. The huge region comprising *East Asia* plus *Oceania*. *See also Pacific Rim.*

Asia-Pacific Economic Co-operation (APEC). Founded in 1989, a general forum for discussion of *Pacific Rim* economic issues. It consists of all the major trading nations of the Pacific region, totaling 21 in 2000. Its 1993 summit in

Seattle was for the first time one of *heads of state* rather than finance ministers. It was also the first time the "three Chinas" met formally. Its *Secretariat* is in Singapore; it holds every second meeting in a Southeast Asian nation. In 1993 APEC warned the *EU* not to block agreement on the *Uruguay Round* of *GATT* and itself promised to form a vast *free trade area*. By 2000, that still seemed a distant prospect. Still, the two sets of *NAFTA* countries were keenly interested in not being excluded from any alternative, all-Asian *free trade* regime. The *Pacific Islands Forum* is an official observer at APEC meetings.

askaris. *See ascaris.*

Asoka (c. 269–232 B.C.E.). Mauryan Emperor of India. *See also India.*

Asquith, Herbert (1852–1928). British prime minister, 1908–1916. A successful domestic reformer, he was blocked thrice in his effort to introduce *Home Rule* for Ireland. Devious and widely disliked, but lacking dynamism or determination to pursue *World War I* all-out, he was held responsible by many for the disaster at *Gallipoli* and the *stalemate* on the *western front*. He then lost his Irish base by violently suppressing the *Easter Rising* (1916). He failed to oust *Lloyd George* during a war cabinet struggle in December and was instead outmaneuvered and resigned. He was replaced as prime minister by Lloyd George, who promised to pursue a more vigorous war policy. In the 1920s Asquith's bitter dispute with Lloyd George split the Liberal Party, which ceased to be the main opposition to *Tory* rule, giving way to *Labour*.

Assad, Hafez al (1928–2000). Dictator of Syria. He participated in a successful *coup* in 1963, becoming defense minister, from which position he presided over the loss of the *Golan Heights* to Israel in the 1967 *Third Arab-Israeli War*. He took full control of the country in 1970 in another coup, the 10th in Syria inside 10 years, and held onto power until his death. He was from the minority and secretive Alawi sect, a ninth-century off-shoot of *Islam* and a social group that had close ties to the French colonial system. His rural background at least led him to pay attention to basic service needs in Syria's villages. In general, Syria's economy at first improved under Assad, though starting from a low level. Later, as it clung to a failed *dirigiste* model of Soviet-style *socialist* development, it lagged behind other Middle Eastern states making more rapid readjustment and engagement with the wider world economy. Also, Assad was never able to overcome the antipathy most Syrian Muslims felt for his Alawi regime, which only led him to increased repression. In 1982 this tension culminated in his orders to ruthlessly put down a *sunni* rebellion in Hama, the third largest city in Syria. He had some 20,000 Syrians killed by their own air force and army in a full-scale repression of Muslim opposition. This pushed the opposition underground and ensured that Assad would have to always rule brutally, which was his instinct in any case.

In foreign policy, Assad made Syria a Soviet *client state*, was a hard-line opponent of Israel, and reputedly sponsored *state terrorism*. He lost the *Golan Heights* during the *Third Arab-Israeli War* and was unable to reclaim them during the *Fourth*. He intervened in the *Lebanese Civil War* and achieved lasting influence over Lebanese affairs. Assad supported Iran in the *Iran-Iraq War*. With collapse of the *Soviet Union* he lost his main source of arms and technical aid. Growing instantly more accommodating of Western concerns and interests, he joined the *Gulf coalition* against Iraq in 1990–1991, sending Syrian troops to fight other Arabs under an American commander. Assad then joined Mideast *peace talks* in 1992, offering a compromise peace with Israel—sincerely or not—on the condition of return to Syria of all the Golan Heights. In frail health for many of his final years and with his prestige declining internally and abroad, Assad clung to power through *terror* and *secret police* until his death. He was succeeded by his son, who began with the same oppressive policies he learned from his father.

assassin. A murderer of a prominent person for political reasons. The term remembers a secret sect of *Ismaili* fanatics known as hashshāshin ("hashish eaters"), or the Assassins to Westerners. They were originally headquartered in a mountain fastness at Alamut. They fought the *Crusaders* in Syria from the tenth to thirteenth centuries in a *jihad* that promised martyrdom to holy warriors high on Allah and hashish. They were displaced from Persia in 1256 by the invading *Mongols*, who massacred most of the Assassins they found. The Syrian Assassins were overwhelmed by the *Mamluks* of Egypt.
Suggested Reading: Bernard Lewis, *The Assassins* (1967).

assassination. The murder of a prominent public figure, especially for political reasons. Most assassinations are neither indiscriminate nor random, whereas acts of *terrorism* may be either. Even when a given assassin is deranged, the act itself is aimed at a particular individual or a member of a highly select group precisely because that individual or group is prominent. For this same reason (specificity of the target), political assassinations can be an effective instrument of policy by states, though they are seldom indulged in because of the logic of *reciprocity*. Assassinations are certainly more effective than the usual desultory or counterproductive consequences of most indiscriminate terrorist acts. *See also* coup d'etat; *wet affair*.

assimilation. (1) The widely experienced historical pattern of merger, natural or planned—or even forced—of different cultural, linguistic and racial groups into a dominant, national culture. (2) A French (and Portuguese) colonial policy of educating native elites who were then eligible for full citizenship and political participation. In practice, this was strictly limited and failed to satisfy either the few nationalist elites that it produced or the colonial governments they opposed. *See also* Aborigines; *Ainu; apartheid; colons; Creoles;*

cultural imperialism; ethnic cleansing; genocide; Inca; Indian Wars; mission civilisatrice; négritude; *Russification.*

associated state. A new type of *international personality* that has replaced the *protectorate* for certain statelets. Authority over foreign affairs is delegated to a *principal state,* but the associated state is otherwise treated as fully *sovereign* and *independent* under *international law.* Examples include *Cook Islands; Marianas; Marshall Islands; West Indies Associated States.*

Association of Southeast Asia (ASA). A subregional organization founded in 1961 by *Malaya,* the Philippines, and Thailand, since subsumed into *ASEAN.*

Association of Southeast Asian Nations (ASEAN). This regional body was established in 1967 by five non-Communist states (Indonesia, Malaysia, the Philippines, Singapore, and Thailand), mainly to insulate themselves from the *Vietnam War* and the *Cold War.* Thus, in 1971 ASEAN declared its subregion a *ZOPFAN.* The original five were later joined by Brunei (1984), Vietnam (1995), Laos (1997), Myanmar (1999), and Cambodia (1999). Papua New Guinea attends as an observer, upon Indonesia's invitation. ASEAN promotes limited economic cooperation and coordinated *diplomacy* toward regional issues that do not directly concern disputes among its members. For example, it took a unified position on the Vietnamese *invasion* and *occupation* of Cambodia but divided over the issue of Indonesia's occupation of *East Timor.* In 1976 it established a permanent *secretariat* in Jakarta. In 1980 it signed a trade cooperation agreement with the *European Community,* reflecting the fact that ASEAN members' trade is more extensive outside than inside the association. From the 1970s, friendly Western powers (Australia, Canada, the *European Union,* and the United States), as well as South Korea and Japan, met with ASEAN states in a postministerial conference, or PMC. Concerned by China's rising military power and new assertiveness, in 1992 ASEAN proposed *demilitarization* of the *Spratly Islands.* As a post–Cold War *balance of power* developed in the region, it edged into security areas with creation of the *ASEAN Regional Forum.* It also serves as a *caucus group* within APEC and in economic negotiations with major *OECD* economies. In 1992 it created the ASEAN Free Trade Area (AFTA), a regional common market. In 1995 ASEAN signed a *Nuclear Weapons Free Zone (NWFZ)* proclamation.

assured destruction. A *strategic doctrine* that relied on mutual assurance of massive destruction of enemy facilities, and indirectly of population, through launch of a *second strike* as the main guarantee of nuclear *deterrence.* It was converted by its critics into the pejorative (but not wholly inaccurate) MAD, or mutual assured destruction. This doctrine took hold once American-Soviet parity in *nuclear weapons* was reached, especially once *ICBMs* could be launched by undetectable *submarines*. It mostly reflected a desire to stabilize the *Cold War* relationship of the *superpowers* by avoiding a further *arms race* in defensive weapons systems, which would only encourage development of new offensive systems to overcome them. *See also ABM Treaty; BMD; flexible response; massive retaliation; SALT; SDI.*

Aswan Dam. (1) Low Dam: The first major effort to dam the Nile, it was completed by the British, then in control of Egypt, in 1902. It greatly reduced the annual flood and significantly improved irrigation and agricultural production. (2) High Dam: A 6,500-foot hydroelectric dam spanning the Nile. The West refused to finance the project, partly to resist Egyptian manipulation of the *Cold War*, in which *Nasser* tried to play Washington against Moscow, but also because *Eisenhower* and *Dulles* thought that financing the High Dam would greatly burden the Soviet economy. Nasser nationalized the *Suez Canal* Company to gain control of its revenues and to end Egypt's *servitude* to Britain, sparking the *Suez Crisis*. The High Dam was completed in 1971 with massive Soviet assistance and was heralded as an archetype of *Soviet bloc* aid to Third World countries. Both as a megaproject, which Nasser hoped would propel Egypt into the first rank of industrial nations, and as a Soviet bribe of Egyptian fealty in the *Cold War*, it failed.

asylum. (1) Diplomatic: granting refuge to a national of a host state under the domain of immunity of one's *embassy*. For example, Cardinal Mindszenty of the Hungarian *Catholic Church* was famously given asylum in the U.S. embassy in Budapest, 1956–1971. Similarly, several Russian Protestant families were given sanctuary in the U.S. embassy in Moscow, 1978–1983. For different reasons, Manuel Noriega received temporary sanctuary in the Papal Legation during the 1990 U.S. invasion of Panama. Japan is notable for its enduring policy of refusing to provide asylum for anyone deemed to have committed *political offenses*. (2) Territorial: granting protection to, and refusing to *extradite*, an individual for civil, humanitarian, or political reasons, especially in cases in which individuals or groups feel in need of international protection from the government of their own states. Countries of first asylum, that is, those in which political or civil *refugees* first physically arrive, are not necessarily countries of their final settlement, those which agree to give them more permanent shelter and protection. *See also dissident; political prisoner; prisoner of conscience.*

asymmetrical interdependence. When the effects of *interdependence* are felt extremely unequally, with one society experiencing much higher *vulnerability* than the other. It is social science *jargon* of the worst sort because it is actually a misleading way to avoid saying that one state is highly dependent on another.

asymmetrical threat/strategy. The idea that smaller powers facing the United States in a conflict might not wait for full U.S. deployment but instead *escalate* rapidly to the use of some *weapon of mass destruction* in order to deter or block United States penetration of the conflict.

Atatürk, né Mustapha Kemal (1881–1938). Turkish statesman. His adopted name meant "father of the Turks." As a young officer he helped found the Vatan, a secret society pledged to political revolution and basic, modernizing reform of the *Ottoman Empire*. He aligned with the *Young Turk* movement before *World War I*, which compelled Sultan *Abdul Hamid II* to restore the constitution of 1876, but Atatürk grew disillusioned with the movement over time. He strongly opposed the sultan's decision to align the Empire with the *Central Powers* upon the outbreak of World War I. Despite his reservations, at *Gallipoli* he threw back the British and ANZAC forces, a feat that propelled him to a new level of political prominence. He also stopped a Russian advance into Turkish territories in the *Caucasus* in 1916. He fought the British again, at Aleppo in 1918, but the war was lost. He was sent to Anatolia in 1919 to put down a rebellion against the new sultan. Instead, he better organized the revolt, setting up a *provisional government* and organizing a "national army" to sustain it. He called for a nationalist uprising to expel the foreign interests he saw controlling Turkey in the wake of its defeat. The enraged sultan declared a *jihad* against Atatürk, and he was sentenced to death in absentia. When the sultan signed the humiliating *Treaty of Sèvres*, the people turned massively to support Atatürk as he marched his new army on *Constantinople*.

The *Allied and Associated Powers* called upon the Greeks—who stood to gain much from enforcing the hated treaty—to stop Atatürk, but he defeated them in the *Greek-Turkish War* (1919–1922). Having also defeated and repressed the *Kurds* and subdued the sultan, he negated the *caliphate* and, in 1924, abolished the *sultanate*. Negotiating from strength, he secured the much more favorable *Treaty of Lausanne*, regaining for Turkey its provinces of Smyrna and eastern Thrace, some Aegean islands, and a resumption of control of the *Dardanelles*, which had been internationalized under Sèvres. He then founded the modern Turkish state, both *secularizing* and *modernizing* it, a change symbolized by his decision to move the capital from Constantinople to Ankara. He proclaimed guiding principles which came to be known as Kemalism: republicanism, populism, statism, reformism, and secularism. Mostly, these are now merely ritual incantations without governing reality. Atatürk's accomplishments were many and great, not least being the cultural transformation of Turkey into the world's most successful Muslim country— surely one of the twentieth century's larger historical ironies. That success led to emulation by other secular-minded leaders of Muslim populations, most notably in Iran under the *Pahlavis* and Egypt under *Nasser*. However, Atatürk also ruled the new Turkish republic as an uncompromising and repressive *autocrat*: like most national visionaries, he could never imagine or accept that his country's fate might be better placed in hands other than his own. His *cult of personality* lingered for decades after his death and had power to suppress new thinking about Turkey's historical path well into the twenty-first century. *See also Alexander II; Mehemet Ali; Oliver Cromwell; Peter I; Reza Pahlavi; Sun Yixian.*

Suggested Reading: Andre Mango, *Atatürk* (2000).

Atlantic, Battle of (1939–1945). The greatest naval contest in history. This *World War II* battle was waged for control of the Atlantic sea lanes supplying essential war matériel to Britain (and to a lesser extent, the Soviet Union) from the Americas. Over its chill course the Western Allies lost 2,452 merchant ships and 175 *warships*, whereas the Kriegsmarine lost 696 of 830 U-boats. Several German surface raiders were also sunk, including the Graf Spee and later the Bismarck. The main German effort was made by U-boats. By war's end, the casualty rate on the U-boats was 63 percent dead and another 12 percent captured (25,870 submariners killed of 40,900 crewmen), the highest death rate of any arm of any service in the war. Initially, Germany had the upper hand, in spite of wastefully pursuing construction of a surface navy until early 1943. When *Dönitz* took command of the Kriegsmarine he immediately redirected all construction and crews into U-boats, eventually building a fleet of more than 300 submarines. The Germans even landed units in the Canadian arctic to set up weather stations to serve their U-boat fleet. Into 1942 the *Royal Navy* was stretched thin, despite a remarkable expansion of the corvette and destroyer fleet of the Royal Canadian Navy (RCN), which escorted almost half of all *convoys*.

The U.S. Navy entered the battle even before the United States entered the war, acting as a *nonbelligerent* force to escort convoys that the British and Canadians could not protect and enforcing a hemispheric security zone clearly aimed at excluding Germany and assisting Britain. In July 1941, the United States extended the exclusion zone to include Iceland, to which it escorted convoys. On several occasions "neutral" U.S. destroyers attacked and sank German U-boats; two U.S. warships were also sunk by U-boats, with significant loss of life. With Germany's declaration of war on December 11, 1941, the United States made an all-out commitment to the battle. The Allies were thus eventually able to take the offensive, and finally turned the tide by mid-1943. Still, it was a desperate affair: the U-boats sank nearly 1,300 ships in 1941, and another 1,662 in 1942. By 1943, however, American shipyards were building more Liberty Ships (mass produced cargo carriers) than the U-boats could sink—construction averaged three months per ship and 1,500 per year at the height of production. U.S. shipyards also turned out 200 escort ships per year, which the Allies used to sink more U-boats than Germany could build or crew.

Intelligence breakthroughs (Ultra intercepts), improved radar, sonar, aircraft patrols from island bases, small *escort carriers* mass produced later in the war, and an effective convoy system supplemented by hunter-killer groups of tailing destroyers were critical components in the Allied victory. Together, they finished the U-boat as a strategic threat by 1943. Dönitz recalled all his boats that May because of unsustainable losses; his fleet was reduced to a minor threat to lives and shipping by the end of the year. The U-boat "wolf packs" returned to the Atlantic in September 1944, but by then the Allied advantage in ships and technology was so great that most German submariner crews never returned to their home ports. This great victory at sea permitted massive amounts of *Lend-Lease* to flow to Russia and Britain and allowed the safe passage of North American troops and supplies needed for invasions of North Africa (1942), Sicily and Italy (1943), and France (1944). For the same reason, the U-boats made a major contribution to the German war effort: they slowed the supply of war matériel to Britain and Russia, delayed the build-up necessary to launch a *second front*, and thereby significantly prolonged the war. *See also Jutland, Battle of; Leyte Gulf; Midway, Battle of; Trafalgar, Battle of.*

Atlantic Charter (1941). A statement of principles drafted by *Franklin Roosevelt* and *Winston Churchill* in August 1941, when they met aboard the cruiser Augusta off Newfoundland. After United States entry into the war, the Atlantic Charter was endorsed as a statement of *war aims* by the *United Nations alliance*. Its terms were liberal, even though many eventual signatories were not: (1) no territorial *aggrandizement*; (2) border changes only following upon popular consent; (3) *self-determination*; (4) *free trade* to replace the beggar-thy-neighbor policies of the 1930s; (5) economic cooperation on an international scale; (6) freedom from want (poverty) and fear (of *aggression*); (7) *freedom of the seas*; and (8) *disarmament* of the *Axis* states. Like the *Fourteen Points*, the Atlantic Charter stirred public enthusiasm and fed illusions that the peace would be a permanent and liberal one. Indian hopes were dashed sooner than most, when Churchill clarified that its terms did not apply to India, Burma, or other parts of the *British Empire*. It found postwar resonance in the *Charter of the United Nations* and the *Bretton Woods* system. *See also Four Freedoms.*

Atlantic Community. The liberal democratic nations of Europe and North America that share a political and cultural heritage and common economic and security interests. This broad notion has no institutional or organizational expression, yet is an influential idea in *NATO* relations, and more generally in relations among leading Western democracies.

Atlanticism. (1) The tendency to see transatlantic connections as the most important in world affairs. (2) The tendency in foreign policy to view the United States–Europe relationship as the main focus of *national security* and interests. *See also Eurocentrism.*

Atlantic Ocean. A vast ocean (31.5 million square miles) bounded by the east coast of the *Americas* and the west coasts of *Africa* and *Europe*. It has been the locale of great naval contests and massive *fisheries* and is a vital conduit of world trade.

Atlee, Clement (1883–1967). *Labour* prime minister of Britain, 1945–1951. He fought in 1915 at *Gallipoli*, where he suffered a grievous wound. He demanded *Chamberlain's* resignation as prime minister in 1940 and then joined *Churchill's* war cabinet, serving as deputy prime minister after 1942. He replaced Churchill as prime minister in the middle of the *Potsdam Conference*. Mainly interested in *Labour Party* reforms at home, he started the process of shedding Britain's empire by granting independence to Burma, India, and Pakistan in 1947. He also approved rapid withdrawal from (some might say abandonment of) the British *mandate* over *Palestine*. He was important in framing the British response in the early *Cold War*, taking the United Kingdom into the *Brussels Treaty* and NATO and joining with United Nations forces in Korea.

atmospheric testing. Detonating *nuclear weapons* above ground. The practice was common in the 1950s and continued by the French into the 1990s. It is forbidden to all states adhering to the *Partial Test Ban Treaty*.

atomic age. The present era, dating from test detonation of the first *atomic bomb* on July 17, 1945, and subsequent use of nuclear technology in scientific research and energy production and for military purposes.

atomic bomb. An explosive *fission* device, producing extraordinary destruction of lives and property primarily as a result of its *blast* and *radiation effects*. A *critical mass* of fissile material is forced together suddenly by a *conventional* explosion acting as a trigger, producing an uncontrolled chain reaction. The first Trinity test was made by the United States at Alamogordo, New Mexico, on July 17, 1945. That was two months after the surrender of *Nazi Germany*, against which the race to build the bomb was run. These weapons have been used in war only twice, at *Hiroshima* and *Nagasaki*, cities fatefully chosen from a final list of targets that included Kokura and Niigata. The bombings were not necessary to end the war (Japan was already beaten militarily, though it was not defeated and had not surrendered), but they ended it quickly and with the least overall suffering. Many hundreds of thousands of Japanese troops had yet to be faced and had not yet surrendered in the Pacific, southeast Asia, and China. The development and use of atomic weaponry stunned world opinion and frightened, and perhaps later restrained, leaders the world over. Atomics may thereby have helped to preserve the long peace of the *Cold War*. *See also fusion; hydrogen bomb; Los Alamos; Manhattan Project; Minatom; nuclear weapons; Peenemünde; plutonium.*

Suggested Readings: John Gaddis et al., eds., *Cold War Statesmen Confront the Bomb* (1999); Richard Rhodes, *Making of the Atomic Bomb* (1986).

atomic demolition mine (ADM). A low-yield, *tactical*, defensive *nuclear weapon* for use against advancing troops and *armor* formations.

atomistic economy. One in which many small producers compete in every industry.

Atoms for Peace. A 1953 United States proposal for cooperation on the development of peaceful uses for nuclear technology. It led to creation of the *IAEA* in 1957.

atrocity. Savage, cruel, murderous acts committed against defenseless civilians or *prisoners of war* by a military force or by a political power. Real atrocities, sometimes on a massive scale, are all too frequent and horrific occurrences. However, false atrocity stories are also an integral part of *propaganda* and *war*, used to stir up domestic or even international support for one's own cause and bring approbation down on one's enemies. *See also Akbar; Amritsar massacre; Armenian genocide; Aztec Empire; Bataan death march; Black Hole of Calcutta; Black 'n Tans; Boxer Rebellion; concentration camps; Congo;* conquistadores; *death camps; ethnic cleansing; genocide; Herero-Nama War; Holocaust; Indian Wars; Katyn massacre; Frederick Lugard; Lusitania Notes; My Lai massacre; Nanjing, rape of; Sharpeville massacre; St. Bartholomew's Day Massacre; torture; war crimes.*

attaché. Any specialist with a diplomatic mission representing and reporting on areas such as culture, trade, or military affairs. For a military attaché appointed to an unfriendly state, and nowadays also for a trade attaché assigned even to allies, this duty may amount to *espionage*. In *intelligence*, attaché positions are often preferred cover for a *legal agent*.

attrition. "Ermattungsstrategie." Wearing down an enemy by eroding its forces and morale. In the eighteenth century and earlier, this was often done by avoiding battle, which exhausted premodern treasuries and forced armies to live off the land. Since at least the eighteenth century and the development of modern mass armies, it has been accomplished by inflicting continuous damage and casualties, though usually while suffering heavy losses to one's own forces. In fact, the winning side often takes heavier casualties, which points to the psychological character of attrition as a strategy: its aim is to make the enemy decide that further fighting is not worth the cost. Classic examples of this effect—even if not planned as a strategy—include the final victory over the *Confederacy* by *Ulysses S. Grant* and the North Vietnamese victory over the United States in the *Vietnam War*, in both of which the winner took far heavier casualties than the loser both because it was prepared to do so and because it could afford to do so.

In wars between disproportionately powerful foes, even repeated *tactical* victories accompanied by psychologically high levels of attrition may erode the relative position of the weaker or less motivated power and thus lead to 'strategic' defeat. Once again, that effect was experienced by the United States in Vietnam. The Soviet Union also felt it during the *Afghan-Soviet War*. In a sense, to bring about that effect in the mind of the enemy is the basic purpose of all *guerrilla* armies. Among major and well-balanced adversaries, attrition has been a deliberate policy, as conceived and implemented (unsuccessfully) by the Germans at *Verdun*. More often, however, it results from the development of effective countermeasures to what had previously been seen as some war-winning weapon that both sides then scrambled to build en masse: *ironclads, machine guns*, the *submarine* and torpedo, the tank, and *strategic bomber* were all seen as—and for a time, in fact were—weapons of revolutionary offensive promise and destructive ability, only to be matched or overcome by defensive countermeasures, so that the new weapon and the new countermeasure combined to raise the overall rate of attrition of personnel and matériel. Similarly, *trench warfare* in several major wars resulted not from design but because huge flanking maneuvers devolved into stationary fronts that neither side had intended, and then attrition set in as one or the other army sought to overcome the trench system of the other side. *See also American Civil War; armor; Crimean War; decision, battle of; encounter, battle of; Iran-Iraq War; Vietnam War; World War I; World War II.*

audiencia. The main governing institutions of *Spanish America*, second in status only to the *Viceroyalties*. They were technically and at core high courts of law, but, in the absence of competing institutions in the founding days of *New Spain* and *Peru*, they quickly mutated into provincial governments with both legal and executive powers, as well as limited but over time increasingly influential representation of local interests in advisory committees. The first in the *New World* was created on Santo Domingo in 1511. The first on the mainland of the Americas was set up in New Spain (Mexico) in 1527. Subsequently, audiencia were established in various locales as the population grew or new economic interests developed within the Spanish overseas empire requiring legal and administrative attention. Audiencia were thus set up at Panama (1538), Lima (1543), Guatemala (1543), Guadalajara (1547), Bogotá (1547), La Plata (1549), Quito (1563), Concepción, Chile (1565–1575), Manila (1583), Buenos Aires (1661–1672 and 1783), Caracas (1786), and Cuzco (1787).

Most of them came under heavy *Creole* or other local influence over time, as Spain's imperial grip weakened during its losing European wars of the seventeenth and eighteenth centuries. There was an attempt to reverse this trend, 1751–1810, which had more than a little to do with spurring

Creoles into leadership roles in Latin America's drive for independence, 1810–1825.

Auerstädt, Battle of (October 14, 1806). *See Jena-Auerstädt, Battle of.*

Augsburg, Peace of (1555). This great settlement was occasioned by the defeat and abdication of *Charles V*, which gravely set back the cause of *Habsburg* dominion in Germany and Europe. It enunciated a principle of religious peace (or at least truce), which governed intra-German relations until the conflagration of the *Thirty Years' War* (1618–1648), namely, *cuius regio eius religio* or "whosoever controls the territory, decides the religion [of its inhabitants]." That permitted a truce of exhaustion between *Catholic* and most *Protestant* (*Lutheran*) powers in Germany. It excluded *Calvinists*, however. Augsburg's terms did not apply, and were not followed, outside the *Holy Roman Empire* (Germany). To the west, Charles' famous son, and Catholic king of Spain, *Philip II*, would later refuse a comparable request from his Burgundian subjects to permit the same tolerance of Protestantism and instead launch a zealous effort to repress Dutch religious liberties. He thereby provoked the Dutch Revolt, or *Eighty Years' War* (1566–1648). And in France, the *Wars of Religion* broke out almost immediately between Catholics and *Huguenots* (French Calvinists) and rent that country for thirty years.

In the short run, the Peace of Augsburg guaranteed peace in Germany, but at a price of delaying the final resolution of its great confessional conflicts until the next century, and at the additional cost of continuing political fragmentation as other major powers in Europe were beginning to construct powerful *new monarchies*. In the longer view, however, the Peace of Augsburg presaged a grand trend in international politics whereby civil and religious authority would ultimately discard universalist pretensions, at first to merge on a national basis in the absolute *sovereign*, but later giving way to notions of political *secularism* and ultimately to preservation and protection by a representative state of the beliefs and rights of individual subjects. *See also Counter-Reformation; Edict of Nantes; Peace of Westphalia; Protestant Reformation.*

August decrees (1789). *See French Revolution.*

Aum Shinrikyo. A Japanese millenarian *terrorist* cult that plotted the use of several different kinds of *weapons of mass destruction* against civilian targets. It was most notorious for carrying out a sarin gas attack on the Tokyo subway in 1995. *See also biological weapons; gas weapons.*

Aung San (1914–1947). Burmese nationalist. In 1941 he was part of a group called "the Thirty," which studied *guerrilla* tactics in Japan for use against the British. After fighting alongside the Japanese in *World War II* at the head of the Burma National Army, Aung San led a revolt against them in 1945 as it became clear that Japan would lose the war. His military experience propelled him to the political forefront as the war ended, and he briefly claimed the premiership during the struggle for power attendant on British withdrawal from Burma. Aung San would have been independent Burma's first prime minister, but he was assassinated six months before formal independence.

Aung San Suu Kyi (b. 1946). Daughter of *Aung San*. From the late 1980s the leading opposition figure in Burma (Myanmar), as well as a *Nobel Prize* (for Peace) winner. She was placed under house arrest in 1989, becoming a focus of international *human rights* concern and protest. From 1994, on-and-off the military *junta* held talks with her on the political situation in Burma, but the generals continued to restrict her political freedoms and those of her party and the country at large. In 2000 she was again arrested and confined to her home, and her contacts with domestic political allies and foreign journalists were heavily restricted.

Aurangzeb (1618–1707). Alamgir Emperor ("World Conqueror"). The most bloody and zealous of *Mughal* emperors. He reigned from 1658, after defeating his brother (Shuja) in a war of succession to Shah Jahan (1592–1666), whom he overthrew in 1658 and imprisoned. Aurangzeb ruled until his death in 1707. He ended the practice of tolerance of *Hindus* and *Sikhs*, enforced puritanical social and legal codes (the *sharia*), blocked construction of new Hindu or Sikh temples and restored a tax on temple pilgrims, reintroduced the hated *jizya* poll tax on all non-Muslims (dhimmîs), and squeezed ever more revenues out of a stagnant agrarian economy. Revolt was inevitable. It first broke out in the Punjab, where Sikhism took a newly martial, defensive form. In Maharashtra, led by Shivaji Bhonsle (1627–1680), Hindus rebelled in the 1660s–1670s, adopting highly effective *guerrilla* tactics, fortifying the *Deccan*, occasionally raiding Mughal cities, and in 1674 proclaiming the Maratha state. When Aurangzeb was tied down by war in Afghanistan, the *Rajputs* also rose against his rule. Finally, his son rebelled in 1680. Then Aurangzeb reasserted Mughal power: over the next quarter century his armies crushed the Punjab, overran Maharashtra and the Deccan, but never completely overcame Maratha resistance, and chased his son to exile in Persia. The cost in lives and treasure of this *imperial overreach* was enormous. A swollen capital moved with the emperor, stripping India of its surplus grain to feed his elephants, armies, and tens of thousands of camp followers. As Aurangzeb neared his nineties, famine and *black death* broke out to add to the overall misery of endless war. His death was followed by another succession struggle, which broke the back of Mughal power.

Auschwitz. The largest and most notorious of all *death camps* set up by the *Nazis*, it was located near a small Polish town from which it took its name.

Himmler took a direct interest in the camp's construction, as did *Eichmann* and *Heydrich*, once the *Wannsee conference* set in motion the full and "*final solution to the Jewish problem.*" The SS converted a small farmhouse into a makeshift gas chamber and began the killings on March 26, 1942. They added a second building in July as more trainloads of Jews arrived for "extermination." In March and June 1943, four crematoria and additional gas chambers were erected that raised the ability to slaughter human beings to an industrial scale and employed industrial methods. Auschwitz also became the site of obscene medical experimentation and the worst forms of sadism. Occasionally, there were also episodes of saintly self-sacrifice among the victims. A complex of satellite service and slave labor camps sprang up around Auschwitz. Some held Russian prisoners of war, others served as Jewish slave labor centers rented out to German industry by the SS. Just before Auschwitz's surviving inmates were liberated by the *Red Army*, its overseers were killing Jews—and smaller numbers of *Roma*, Poles, and Russians—at a rate of more than 20,000 per day in massive gas chambers that employed Zyclon B gas pellets manufactured by the German petrochemical industry. That was too many dead for even its massive crematoria to handle, so bodies were burned also in mountainous pyres. Probably some 1.5 million people died in this one camp—that toll is partly an estimate, but mainly it is based upon the insanely evil but meticulous record-keeping habits of the SS mass murderers themselves. *See also anti-Semitism; biological warfare; Holocaust; Warsaw Ghetto.*

Ausgleich. The compromise of 1867, converting the *Austrian Empire* into the *Dual Monarchy* of Austria-Hungary where each was *autonomous* domestically, but *foreign policy* was run from Vienna. It was prompted by Austria's defeat in the *Seven Weeks' War.*

Austerlitz, Battle of (December 2, 1805). The key battle in the *War of the Third Coalition.* A French army of some 70,000 under *Napoleon* defeated a larger but badly led Austrian and Russian force, knocking Austria out of the war, ensuring that Prussia remained neutral, and forcing a Russian strategic retreat. The allies lost more than 30,000 troops, some of whom drowned as ice broke beneath their horses and caissons while crossing a frozen lake. The victory made the legend of Napoleon's military genius and ostensible invincibility grow apace. In later life, Napoleon always remembered Austerlitz fondly, as his "favorite battle." *See also Alexander I; Napoleonic Wars.*

Australasia. Australia, New Zealand, Tasmania, and nearby scattered islands. *See also South Pacific.*

Australia. *Aborigines* arrived in Australia perhaps as long ago as 40,000 (or more) years, probably from Southeast Asia or Polynesia. They remained primarily hunter-gatherers into modern times, and thus were a stateless and widely scattered people when the first Europeans sighted the southern continent. The continent's coastline was first explored and mapped by *James Cook* (1729–1779) in 1770 and by later expeditions. Australia as a continent-nation began to take shape when a *penal settlement* was established by the British at Botany Bay in 1788. By the 1830s white settlement took hold in the four Australian colonies (New South Wales, Tasmania, South Australia, and Victoria) with Aborigines pushed onto reserves in the outback. In 1850 the "white colonies" were given self-government in domestic affairs, but Britain retained control of foreign policy. On January 1, 1901, they became independent as the Commonwealth of Australia.

Prime Minister Alfred Deakin (1856–1919) helped frame a whites-only immigration policy, which marked Australia psychologically for decades as a European outpost rather than an Asian country. Australians fought as part of the *British Empire* contingent in the *Boer War* and again in *World War I*, to which Australia sent 412,000 of its young men. The terrible casualties they suffered at *Gallipoli* in 1915, the same year that six Australian states were federated into one confederation, stimulated a raw *nationalism* and awareness of *national interest* distinct from the interests of the British Empire. After World War I, Australia regarded itself and was treated by London as virtually *independent*. It attended the *Paris Peace Conference* and joined the *League of Nations*, though Australia had little influence over either. Even so, Australia took formal control of its foreign policy only with passage of the *Statute of Westminster* in 1931.

During *World War II* the exigencies of its geography and the very real threat to its security from Imperial Japan led Australia into an independent decision for war. It declared war on Germany in September 1939 and fought as well against the other *Axis* powers as they entered the conflict. It joined the *United Nations alliance* upon its formation, greatly relieved at the entry of the United States into the Pacific War. Australia became a major support base for American and other Allied operations against the Japanese Empire after the fall of the Philippines. John Curtin (1885–1945), wartime prime minister, 1941–1945, worked well with the United States and embraced its security guarantees, even as he sought to preserve the Commonwealth link to Britain as a counterweight to Australia's new security dependence on America and for cultural reasons. After World War II, Australia pursued a more homegrown foreign policy, even as it also shifted under the U.S. security umbrella as British influence rapidly receded from Asia. Australia joined *ANZUS* in 1951, fought in the *Korean Conflict*, and sent troops to fight in the *Vietnam War*, not because it was a proxy of the United States but because—correctly or not—it saw its national interests at stake in those conflicts. From the 1970s Australia increasingly saw itself as a Pacific nation, rather than a European outpost under siege in Asia. Under John Frazer (b. 1930; prime minister, 1975–1983), Australia turned firmly toward the Asia-Pacific region in its foreign policy and began to open as well to Asian immigration and cultural influences. In 1993 it began a national debate over becoming a *republic*, though the initiative failed by a narrow margin in a later referendum.

In foreign policy, a 1987 defense white paper identified Australia's main security area as the southwest Pacific, and a 1989 parliamentary committee called for regional leadership of local island states. After World War I, Australia had been designated the *Mandate Power*, and after World War II, the *Trustee Power*, for Nauru and Papua New Guinea, both of which it eventually assisted to independence. At the start of the twenty-first century Australia no longer had *dependencies* but still oversaw in a mostly benign manner several tiny South Pacific island territories, including Norfolk, Coral Sea, Cocos, Kiritimati, and the Ashmore and Cartier Islands. Most Australian aid went to the region, notably to East Timor, where in 1999 Australia played the leading role in international intervention to secure independence from Indonesia and provide on-the-ground protection to East Timorese under assault from Indonesian militia and military-sponsored thugs. It also took a regular part in United Nations *peacekeeping* operations, including in Cambodia and Somalia in the 1990s. In 2001, it committed special forces to the U.S.-led war against *al Qaeda* and activated its alliance commitments under ANZUS (Australia, New Zealand, United States Treaty). Australia maintains claims in *Antarctica*, where it is one of the *Treaty Powers*.

Suggested Readings: Geoffrey Bolton, ed., *Oxford History of Australia*, 2nd ed. (1996); Neville Meany, *Search for Security in the Pacific* (1976); David Walker, *Anxious Nation* (1999).

Australia and New Zealand Army Corps (ANZAC). The joint forces of these nations in *World War I* and *World War II*, as well as in the *Vietnam War*. Two-thirds of all Australians who enlisted in World War I became casualties. *See also Gallipoli, Battle of.*

Australia, New Zealand, United States (ANZUS) Treaty (1951). A defensive military pact coordinating Australian and New Zealand defense policy with that of the United States. Originally aimed at placating fears of revived Japanese power, it also signaled displacement of Britain as the dominant *sea power* in the area. In 1985 New Zealand refused visitation to U.S. *warships* because of the U.S. "no confirm/no deny" policy regarding whether specific ships carried *nuclear weapons* and as a result of the use by some U.S. ships of nuclear power for propulsion. The United States renounced its obligations to New Zealand on August 11, 1986, since the latter no longer upheld the terms of the treaty. That effectively ended ANZUS, although formally there is no mechanism to expel a member and the treaty still operates. In 1987 New Zealand declared itself a *nuclear weapons free zone*. The United States responded by downgrading New Zealand's designation from ally to friendly country. Relations improved in 1994, but not enough to revive the full military *alliance*. The United States maintained close ties with Australia, which also grew disdainful of New Zealand's growing *isolationism* and which was in any case the much more important *regional power*. In 2001, Australia activated its alliance commitments under ANZUS in response to the U.S.-led war against *al Qaeda. See also Kiwi disease.*

Australian New Guinea. The *mandate/trusteeship* name for Papua New Guinea.

Austria. The First Republic (1918–1934), was proclaimed in Vienna in 1918 after Austria's catastrophic defeat in *World War I*. It thus was forced to build upon the detritus of the *Austrian Empire*. This rump republic was both sanctioned and proscribed by the *Treaty of St. Germain* (1919).

Politically unstable, Austria endured a brief *civil war* in 1934 between *Social Democrats* and Austrian *Nazis*. The Nazis murdered Chancellor *Englebert Dollfuss* in 1934 in a failed coup, then worked to facilitate *Hitler*'s takeover, which came on March 13, 1938, in Austria's *Anschluss* with the *Third Reich*. Fully incorporated as a province of Nazi Germany during *World War II*, Austria was invaded and occupied by the *Allies* in 1945. The controversy over whether to treat Austria as a willing collaborator of Nazi Germany, or Hitler's first victim was ultimately resolved with the emergence of the Second Republic after 1945. Like Germany, Austria was divided into four *occupation zones*. After Communist-led strikes, Austria was secretly rearmed by the West starting in 1950 with establishment of a B-Gendarmerie as the core of a future Austrian Army. Meanwhile, the Soviets nakedly exploited their occupation zone, so that only massive U.S. aid prevented deep political and economic destabilization. Unlike Germany, the Allies agreed to early withdrawal under the *Austrian State Treaty* (1955), by which the occupation was ended on terms of permanent Austrian *neutrality* and *disarmament*, and union (Anschluss) with Germany was forbidden. Austria was diplomatically shunned during the presidency of *Kurt Waldheim*, who was charged with being passively complicit in *war crimes* while an officer in the *Wehrmacht*. The end of the *Cold War* made neutrality archaic, as did Austria's acceptance into the European Union (EU) on January 1, 1995, after a *referendum* on the issue of membership. In 1999 the EU applied highly controversial diplomatic sanctions against Austria to protest the inclusion of the leader of a far-right, arguably even *neo-Nazi*, party in a coalition government in Vienna. Many saw this as unwarranted interference in the operations of a democratic state, however, and even some of the sponsors of the initial action came to regret it as imprudent and intimidating to other small states in Europe.

Suggested Readings: Evan Bukey, *Hitler's Austria, 1938–1945* (2000); Richard Rickett, *A Brief Survey of Austrian History*, 5th ed. (1975).

Austria-Hungary. The *Austrian Empire*, after the *Ausgleich* of 1867 until its demise in 1918. *See also Dual Monarchy.*

Austrian Empire. Austria was controlled by the *Habsburg dynasty* from c. 1300. For centuries it fought a hard, defensive campaign against the *Ottoman Empire*—Austria fought wars against the Turks in 1663–1664, 1683–1699, 1716–1718, 1737–1739, and 1788–1791. Austria's domination of Italy and central Germany (the *Holy Roman Empire*) under *Charles V* was challenged, mainly by France, during the *Thirty Years' War* (1618–1648).

Austria emerged from that titanic contest a much lessened power and at daggers drawn with France in a dynastic and interstate rivalry that lasted on-and-off to 1815. Things also looked grim in the east, where an ascendant Ottoman Empire was closing on Vienna itself. At the Battle of St. Gotthard (August 1664) in Hungary, a Habsburg army defeated the Turks and forced upon them a twenty-year truce, deflecting them for a time into Ukraine, Poland, and Russia. In 1683 the Turks were back, however, bombarding the walls of Vienna itself. In a final paroxysm of Christian unity against the Muslim invader, armies from Poland, Russia, and Venice (but not France, where *Louis XIV* would have welcomed the city's fall) lifted the siege and relieved the Habsburg capital. An allied counterattack against the Turks then lasted to 1699, pushing them far from Vienna. Indeed, in the wake of this war Austria went on to acquire vast new territories in the east and south to add to its hereditary home provinces and Balkan lands: it took firm control of Hungary, Transylvania, Croatia, and Slavonia. After that, the Ottomans found they had their hands full dealing with Russian aggression into Ukraine, Crimea, and Central Asia, and Vienna enjoyed a respite from Turkish wars and used it to consolidate its expanded empire.

Austria was still opposed in its ambitions, titles, and claims in Germany after the defeat of Louis XIV. During the eighteenth century a new player arrived to join the German game: *Prussia*. In 1740 Austria was stunned by the assault of *Frederick the Great*, who attacked in a naked *aggression* that began the *War of the Austrian Succession*, in which *Maria Theresa* and Austria lost *Silesia*. Austria and Prussia (and France, and England, and other powers) had at it again in the *Seven Years' War*, which confirmed Austria's loss of Silesia and further weakened Vienna's position within Germany. In the wake of these defeats, and with his mother finally passed from the scene, Emperor *Joseph II* began much needed domestic and military reforms. These were interrupted by the *French Revolution*, however, which changed every political calculation in Europe, both in domestic and foreign policy. Austria began as a champion of the monarchical principle, but was humiliated by French Revolutionary armies in 1793, and thereafter repeatedly by *Napoleon I* during the Wars of the First, Second and Third Coalitions (see *Napoleonic Wars*), and was forced into alliance with France. Austria rejoined the anti-French coalition in 1813, fighting to victory in the War of the Fourth Coalition. Under the able Count *Metternich* Austria took part in the *Congress of Vienna* and then anchored the *Concert* system. Austria also joined the *Holy Alliance*.

Until 1848 (the year it abolished *serfdom* internally) Austria exercised great influence but also took on commitments well beyond its *capabilities*. Austria staggered through the *revolutions of 1848*, mauled but intact, and in 1850 finally created a *customs union* among its many provinces. Despite Austria's weakness vis-à-vis Europe's other *Great Powers*, it managed solid economic growth and went on the offensive against Turkey during the nineteenth century and was a key player all through the *Eastern Question*. Austria turned against Russia diplomatically during the *Crimean War* and fought briefly with France in the *Franco-Austrian War* (1859). Defeat in the *Seven Weeks' War* (1866) ended its long effort to control Germany and focused Vienna on the problem of holding onto southeastern Europe. In 1867 Hungarians were given equal status with Germans in the *Ausgleich*, which created the *Dual Monarchy*. That awkward arrangement signaled the internal decay and weakness of the empire, symbolized for many by the decrepitude of Kaiser *Franz Joseph* and his regime's inability to accommodate modernizing demands from a rising bourgeoisie and assertive ethnic nationalisms. As one historian has put the central bargain at the core of the dual empire, "It was a simple enough construction: the Austrian Army might misuse Hungarian peasants, so long as Hungarian landlords could misuse Austrian towns. Heavy doses of Hungarian chauvinism could anesthetize at least the Hungarian victims of it all. The Czechs could be forgiven for concluding that, whatever Austria had achieved against the Turks, she had failed to save western civilization from the Hungarians." Austria-Hungary thereafter became intensely conscious of its faltering position and jealous of any slight to its imperial *prestige*.

Thus, Austria was prepared to strike hard at the Serbs, who foolhardily salted every imperial wound by sponsoring the assassination of the Austrian heir, Archduke *Francis Ferdinand*, in 1914. Relying on its alliance with Imperial Germany, Vienna declared war on Serbia, launching the *mobilization crisis* and opening the floodgates of *World War I*. Austria held off Russia only with massive German aid after 1915. It fought Italy to a standstill at *Isonzo* and humiliated the Italians at *Caporetto*, but itself succumbed to the *Allied and Associated Powers* in November 1918. In the end, with doubts growing about the *kaisertreu* reliability of non-Austrian units, not even the German alliance was enough. The Austrian Empire shattered on the battlefields of World War I into its several component nations, even before the war ended: on October 6th Yugoslavia was declared independent by the Serbs, Croats, and Slovenes; the next day Poland declared independence; on the 28th Czechoslovakia was founded; and Hungary declared a republic on November 1st. The war ended for Austria three days later. Austria was reduced to a small republic, which 20 years later, would be annexed by Nazi Germany.

Suggested Readings: David Good, *Economic Rise of the Habsburg Empire, 1750–1914* (1984); R. Kann, *History of the Habsburg Empire, 1526–1918* (1974); V. S. Matmatey, *Rise of the Habsburg Empire, 1526–1815* (1978); Robin Okey, *The Habsburg Monarchy* (2000); Norman Stone, *The Eastern Front, 1914–1917* (1976); A.J.P. Taylor, *The Habsburg Monarchy* (1948); Samuel

R. Williamson, *Austria-Hungary and the Origins of the First World War* (1991); A. Wheatcroft, *The Habsburgs* (1996).

Austrian Netherlands. At the end of the *War of the Spanish Succession* the Treaty of Rastadt (1714) gave the *Spanish Netherlands* to Austria (also see *Treaty of Utrecht*). In the wars of the eighteenth century it was always the case that these territories could not be retained by Austria whenever France moved to seize them. In 1789 they revolted and deposed *Joseph II*—not in the same cause as the radical *French Revolution* but against it, under the leadership of conservative Catholic nobles who objected to Joseph's "Imperial Edict of [Religious] Toleration." Order was restored by 1792, but the province was then invaded by French republican troops. The Austrian Netherlands were later outright annexed by *Napoleon*. At the *Congress of Vienna* (1815), they were united to the *Netherlands*. In 1830 they revolted against the Dutch, taking their independent place among the family of nations as *Belgium*, under the international guarantees of the *Treaty of London*.

Austrian State Treaty (May 15, 1955). An agreement among the four occupying powers (Britain, France, the Soviet Union, and the United States) to withdraw, on condition of creation of a *neutral, republican* Austria confined to its 1937 frontiers. It also banned another *Anschluss*.

Austro-Hungarian Empire. *See* Ausgleich; *Austrian Empire; Dual Monarchy.*

Austro-Prussian War (1866). *See Seven Weeks' War.*

autarchy. Absolute *sovereignty;* this should not be confused with *autarky. See also autocracy.*

autarky. In its most radical form, this is when a government tries to achieve total national *self-sufficiency* by imposing commercial, and usually political and cultural, isolation on an entire nation. States attempting this to some degree included Japan under the *Tokugawa shoguns*, before its forced opening in the nineteenth century; Russia under *Nicholas I*; the Soviet Union under *Stalin*, 1928–41, and indeed quite consistently throughout its entire 74 years of existence; *Nazi Germany* before and during *World War II*; Albania in its *Communist* period; South Africa in response to international sanctions brought on by *apartheid*; Burma (Myanmar) under a series of severe military regimes; Cambodia under *Pol Pot* and the *Khmers Rouges*; and China under *Mao*, especially during the *Great Leap Forward* and the *Cultural Revolution*. This policy always has enormously distorting effects on all aspects of a country's political and social life. *Hitler's* drive for absolute "Autarkie," which deemed it necessary to secure raw materials and agricultural land to the east to sustain an expanding population without dependence on foreign trade or sources of strategic materials, helped propel the Nazi state into war. During World War II, Germany adopted an imperial policy that insisted on barter agreements that exploited and tied Eastern Europe to its war economy. Conversely, in North Korea an extreme effort at absolute autarky over more than fifty years led to starvation and unenviable status as one of the world's poorest (and perhaps its worst governed) country. This extreme policy should not be confused with more modest, though similarly problematical, efforts at economic *self-reliance*, such as that pursued by India after its independence from British rule or by many Latin American states into the 1980s. *See also autarchy; comparative advantage; isolationism; post-imperialism; World Economic Conference (1933).*

authoritarianism. A style of government without tender regard for individual rights or representative principles and usually military or *secret police*–based. Authoritarian systems are usually without much ideological content beyond a high regard for public order. They may be savagely brutal and repressive, or only moderately so. Some political scientists make arcane distinctions among (*taxonomies* of) authoritarian regimes, to wit: bureaucratic-military, organic-statist, mobilizational, and so on. Others do a disservice to historical accuracy by imputing to the term an unvarying meaning of actively antidemocratic, when authoritarianism in practice is often more modest and even reasonable on issues of power and responsibility, depending on the degree of social or political disorder to which it may be a response. In this sense, *Konrad Adenauer* was essentially authoritarian.

A different distinction was made by the *Reagan* administration, which differentiated authoritarian from *totalitarian* regimes on the basis of the respective scope of their intervention in daily life. This was done to support the *Reagan Doctrine* and justify waivers of Congressional *human rights* conditions on aid to authoritarian allies, notably in Central America. It was argued that these systems were less damaging to human freedom because they could be more easily overthrown from within as they left large areas of social and economic life free of government control, in contrast to totalitarian regimes. The latter were portrayed as so pervasive in their control of private and public affairs that it was near impossible for reform to take place without severe outside pressure applied. The extent to which this theoretical distinction was confirmed, or not, by the collapse of the *Soviet bloc* in 1989–1991 remains moot. *See also autocracy; communism; corporatism; democracy; despotism; enlightened despotism; fascism; popular sovereignty.*

Suggested Readings: Samuel Huntington and Clement Moore, *Authoritarian Politics in Modern Society* (1970); Robert H. Jackson and Carl G. Rosberg, *Personal Rule in Black Africa* (1982).

authoritarian liberalism. A conceptually awkward term, but descriptively useful, employed mainly to portray a widespread nineteenth-century style of

Latin American development and government wherein doctrines of economic *liberalism* were deployed by *caudillos* and other *authoritarian* regimes, which presided over economically but not politically liberal patterns of development. It is sometimes rendered as "progressive authoritarianism." A twentieth-century variant was the development policy pursued by *Augusto Pinochet* in Chile, of *capitalism* without *democracy*. *See also positivism.*

authoritative interpretation. A method of resolving interpretive disputes in which a *treaty* is interpreted by reference to a related, but subsequent, treaty.

autocracy. The system of government and accompanying ideology supporting rule by an *autocrat*. The world's most successful autocracy was Imperial China, where autocrats ruled for nearly 3,000 years with the aid of a *Confucian* scholar-elite and gentry, which enabled central control over the economy, military, intellectual life, and most high culture. Successive autocracies were also a staple of India's political history. In European history the idea eventually evolved from *absolutism* into a modified, and fairly sophisticated, theory of government by benevolent dictatorship. *See also authoritarianism; communism; corporatism; democracy; despotism; enlightened despotism; fascism; popular sovereignty.*

autocrat. A ruler with (theoretically) unrestrained political power—the term literally means "self-sustaining power." An autocrat's claim to *legitimacy*, on the other hand, may rest on *dynastic* or religious traditions, but not on participatory or representative principles. An autocrat resides above the system he or she governs by decree, perhaps inhibited by personal morality or making of humbug genuflections in the direction of legal formalities, but never truly restrained by the rule of law. *See also Akbar; Alexander II; Aurangzeb; autocracy; Bourbon dynasty; Byzantine Empire; Julius Caesar; caliphate; Catherine the Great; Cixi; Frederick the Great; Habsburg dynasty; Hirohito; Hongwu emperor; Ivan the Terrible; Justinian I; Vladimir Lenin; Louis XIV; Manchus; Mao Zedong; mandate of heaven; Mongols; Napoleon I; Nicholas I; Nobunaga Oda; Peter the Great; Roman Empire; Josef Stalin; Tamerlane; Tokugawa Ieyasu; Toyotomi Hideyoshi; Wanli emperor.*

autointerpretation. Interpretation of *treaty* or other legal duties by the obligated *state* itself.

autonomous development. A close synonym for *autarky*, but less extreme in the application.

Autonomous Soviet Socialist Republic (ASSR). An administrative unit of the *Soviet Union*, of lesser stature than a full republic. The Russian republic contained 16 of these. Several proclaimed *independence* after 1991, but this was nowhere *recognized*.

autonomous variable. *See variable.*

autonomy. When a *dependency* or other weak state, or a province or region within a state, is effectively self-governing on most or all internal matters, but without a similar grant over foreign affairs. Sometimes, devolution of central powers to local authorities is an effective means of dampening ethnic conflict that otherwise threatens to tear apart an established state. *See also Canada; commonwealth status; finlandization; free association; Indonesia; sovereignty; United Kingdom.*

aut punire aut dedire. A maxim of the *Roman Empire*, used most often to demand satisfaction from neighboring states, which demanded that a foreign power must punish a known criminal itself or allow another power (Rome) to do so. It has modern application as a qualifier of *jurisdiction* over *war crimes*, which in the case of *grave breeches* may be tried and punished by an international tribunal or any *sovereign* state.

Auzou strip. A patch of desert along the Libya-Chad border. A part of Chad, it was long coveted by *Muammar Quadaffi* for its rich deposits of *uranium*. Libya's *occupation* (1973–1988) angered so many *OAU* member states that the 1982 *summit* in Tripoli was canceled. The Auzou strip was a main object of Libyan policy in the *Chad-Libya War*. In 1994 Libya withdrew its forces after the *International Court of Justice* affirmed Chad's *sovereignty* over the territory.

Avignon Captivity (of the papacy). *See Great Schism; Guelphs and Ghibellines; Holy Roman Empire; Papal States;* res publica Christiana.

Ávila, Camacho (1897–1955). Revolutionary leader and president of Mexico, 1940–1946. He instituted major domestic reforms in all walks of Mexican life, from peasant agriculture to industrial policy and education, though he left intact the *secularism* of the *Mexican Revolution* and the *one-party state* of the PRI. He improved relations with the United States in general, including cooperating in *Franklin Roosevelt's* plans for hemisphere defense. He took Mexico into *World War II*, declaring war on the *Axis* in 1942, though Mexico played only a minor role and contributed few forces.

avulsion. When a *border* river changes course suddenly but for natural reasons, the original *boundary* is left unaffected. *See also accretion; thalweg.*

Axis. A term that gained currency in reference to the coalition of mostly *fascist* states that fought and lost *World War II*. It originated in a typically bombastic rhetorical flourish by *Mussolini* in 1936, who intended it to describe how European—and even world—history would thereafter revolve around a Rome-Berlin axis. Formal alliance came in the *Pact of Steel* signed in May 1939. *Hitler* expanded the term to include Japan, seeing such an Axis alliance as a counterweight to Britain and France. Although Japan signed the *Anti-Comintern Pact* in 1936, Tokyo did not sign a formal alliance with Rome and Berlin until September 1940, when Hitler's victories over Britain, France, and the Netherlands opened the prospect of a Japanese assault on the exposed Asian holdings of those European empires. Minor states that also joined the Axis were Bulgaria, Hungary, Rumania, and the Nazi *puppet states* of Croatia and Slovakia. Spain was not an Axis power, though it sympathized with the cause. The term is not usually applied to Finland, even though—for reasons pertaining to the *Russo-Finnish War*—it fought beside Germany during World War II. Little cooperation between Japan and other Axis states took place: offensives were not coordinated, and (outside *uranium* shipments to Japan) there was little cooperation on military research. *See also United Nations.*

ayatollah. "The sign of God." A title of senior clerics within the *shi'ite* tradition of *Islam. See also caliph*; imam; *Iranian Revolution*; *Ruhollah Khomeini*; mahdi; *sultan.*

Ayub Khan, Muhammad (1907–1974). President of Pakistan, 1960–1969. He took effective control in 1954 as the minister of defense who imposed *martial law*, but he sought the presidency only in 1960. His constant repressions alienated the Bengalis of *East Pakistan.* He provoked the *Second Indo-Pakistani War* in 1965, but his loss of men and *prestige* in the fighting weakened his hold on power and he was finally forced from office in 1969.

Azaña, Manuel (1880–1940). President of Republican Spain, 1936–1939. A lawyer and professor at Madrid University before entering politics, the eloquent Azaña served successive Republican governments before the *Spanish Civil War.* Despite his democratic credentials, as president of a benighted Republic during the Civil War he was unable to persuade the West to significantly aid the Spanish Republic or his *Popular Front* government against the *fascist* onslaught. It may be doubted, however, whether anyone could have made that case successfully to the deaf ears in London and Paris, which were then attuned only to the policy of *appeasement.* Azaña fled to France upon Franco's victory.

Azerbaijan. This Central Asian, mainly *Shi'ite* land was part of the Safavid Empire, which captured it from ancient Persia. It was overrun by Turkic invaders in the eleventh century and later became a province in the *Ottoman*

Empire. It was divided among the Ottoman, Persian, and *Russian Empires* in the eighteenth century. It fell partly under Russian control in 1813 after a war with Persia. In 1828 the rest of Azerbaijan was wrested from Persia by Russia. The Baku oil fields remained Europe's main source of oil before *World War I*. They were later surpassed by the Rumanian fields at Ploesti, and then by the vast deposits discovered in the *Middle East*. Azerbaijan was briefly *independent* in 1917–1920, but was reincorporated into the *Russian Empire* at the end of the *Russian Civil War* after being invaded by the *Red Army*. Within the Soviet Union it formed part of the *Transcaucasian SFSR*, until separation and *partition* in 1936, when *Stalin* fenced tens of thousands of Armenians in the *enclave* of *Nagorno-Karabakh* and left Azeris in the *exclave* of *Nakhichevan* between Armenia and Turkey.

After 1988, violence flared with Armenia over control of Nagorno-Karabakh. In 1990, riots in Baku led to a massacre of Armenians, then intervention by Soviet troops, and further bloodshed. With *de jure* independence of Azerbaijan in December 1991, the *Armenia-Azerbaijan War* flared into a full-scale interstate conflict. In June 1993, a brief *civil war* broke out, bred of recrimination over looming defeat in the conflict with Armenia, the outpouring of one million Azeri refugees from Nagorno-Karabakh, and the wider ambitions of Azeri leaders from Nakhichevan. A cease-fire in the enclave was declared in 1994, leaving it (and additional Azeri territory) in Armenian hands. Low-level fighting continued through the 1990s. In 1999 Azerbaijan's President Geidar Aliev and Armenian President Robert Kocharian began direct peace talks over Nagorno-Karabakh, jointly mediated by the United States and Russia. They met many times in the next two years.

Suggested Readings: S. A. Adshead, *Central Asia in World History* (1994); Martha B. Olcott, *Central Asia's New States* (1996).

Azores. An uninhabited island group in the Atlantic that came under Portuguese control after being discovered in 1427 by ships sent out by *Henry "the Navigator."* Portuguese settlement followed from c. 1439, with heavier settlement in the 1460s. Unusually, *slavery* did not take much hold in the Azores because its climate was not conducive to plantation agriculture. *See also Canary Islands*.

Aztec Empire. The Mexica were a small, backward Nahuatl tribe that in the thirteenth century moved into the central Mexico valley, where they hired out as *mercenaries* to existing, far more advanced *city-states*. About 1320 they began construction of their own city, Tenochtitlan (where Mexico City later rose).

Throughout the fourteenth century they remained vassals/allies of Tepaneca, one of the more powerful cities in the Valley of Mexico system. In 1420 the Mexica performed a *reneversement des alliance* when they turned on Tepaneca in concert with two of its enemies, Tecacoco and Tlacopan, forming the Triple Alliance that lay at the heart of their future expansion. Over time, Tenochtitlan grew to dominate the alliance. The Aztec were driven by an imperial-religious ideology that demanded constant, ritual human sacrifice: in 1487 some 20,000 captives were ritually murdered to dedicate a new Aztec pyramid. The Aztec expanded via rapacious conquest—Aztec emperors were chosen for their abilities as *warlords*—followed by yet more conquest, terror, and attendant human sacrifice. Under Itzcoatl (r. 1428–1440), the Triple Alliance conquered the Valley of Mexico. Under Moctezuma I (r. 1440–1468) and four successors, it conquered cities and territory far outside the valley and grew to control a vast and complex *tributary* and theocratic empire stretching from central Mexico to Guatemala, wherein a highly privileged, military elite governed a great mass of peasants, artisans, and conquered tribes from whose ranks sacrificial victims were taken. Technologically, the Aztecs were centuries behind the Spanish, who arrived in 1519 when *Cortés* and his band of holy—and unholy—warriors, cut-throats, and brigands invaded. Aztec social and political structure was overly hierarchical and brittle, and most importantly, the Aztecs were hated by many recently conquered cities and tribes. The Aztecs were themselves thus conquered with astonishing ease between 1519 and 1521, not by a few hundred Spanish *conquistadores*, but by a vast Indian alliance comprised of tens of thousands of subject Indians who eagerly rallied to an alien and as yet unknown banner in order to overthrow a known, hated, and feared tyranny. In that sense, the Aztecs were not conquered by the Spanish but by a great uprising of their subject Indian population, triggered by the arrival of Cortés and his men. However, it was the Spanish who collected the spoils, and subsequently enslaved Aztec and rebel alike, driving all into the *encomienda system*.

Suggested Readings: Inga Clendinnen, *Aztecs* (1991); Geoffrey Conrad and Arthur Demarest, *Religion and Empire* (1984); Martin Lunenfeld, *1492: Discovery, Invasion, Encounter* (1991).

B

Baader-Meinhof gang (Red Army Faction). A West German *Marxist*-nihilist group that undertook a frenzied and internationally prominent *terrorist* campaign in 1970–1971, with small cells active after that. Over a thirty-year period they murdered some 30 people, attempted another 40 murders, committed dozens of armed robberies, and carried out more than 2,000 arsons and bomb attacks. Their campaign peaked in 1977 when they *hijacked* a Lufthansa plane to Mogadishu, Somalia. It was retaken by a German antiterrorist team. Ulrike Meinhof (1934–1976) committed suicide in prison; her lover, Andreas Baader (1943–1977), was also found dead in his cell. In April 1998, the gang's surviving members issued a press release announcing that they were dissolving because their cause had "become history."

Ba'ath (Arab Socialist Renaissance) Party. Founded during the heyday of the *pan-Arabism* movement in the 1930s, it merged *Marxist* analysis with *Arab nationalism* and *Islamic* revival. It promoted the *union* of various Arab states on the main assumption and proposition that a single Arab nation existed that had been falsely and perniciously fractured by past non-Arab *imperialisms* (notably, *Ottoman*, French, and British). In time, however, the movement split along national lines as Arab elites and populations showed every sign of preferring to retain the discrete states they had inherited upon independence. One branch took power in Syria in 1963; another, in Iraq in 1968. Personal dictatorship (*Hafez al-Assad* in Syria and *Saddam Hussein* in Iraq) rather than Ba'ath ideology became the order of the day in both countries. *See also caliph.*

Babur (1483–1530). King of Kabul and founder of the *Mughal dynasty* in India. *See also Afghanistan; India; Mughal Empire.*

back-channel negotiations. Secret contacts between governments, which for political or public relations reasons are unable to negotiate openly. They involve using journalists, academics, business leaders, or third-party governments as interlocutors to relay messages and arrange other contacts. They permit governments to bypass their own bureaucracies, public opinion, vested interest groups, and/or dissenting elements of the policy elite and thereby break negotiating or political logjams. They risk making policy in a vacuum, in the absence of expert advice, and that it may later fail to gain public support.

backwash effect. In *dependency theory*, the idea that an inflow of expensive *manufactured goods* to *developing nations* stimulates export of *raw materials* at the expense of domestic *industrialization*.

bacteriological weapons. *See biological warfare and weapons; Geneva Protocol.*

bad actors. Intelligence slang for *terrorists*.

Badoglio, Pietro (1871–1956). Italian general; governor of Libya, 1929–1933; conqueror of Ethiopia, 1936. He opposed the attack on France in 1940, but remained loyal to the regime into *World War II*. He succeeded *Mussolini* in 1943, and negotiated with the *Allies* to take Italy out of the *Axis* alliance. The *armistice* he arranged led instead to German occupation of northern Italy and to civil war. Badoglio was rejected by the Italian *resistance* and retired.

Baghdad Pact. A 1955 security alliance concluded by Iraq and Turkey at the instigation of the United States, and also joined by Britain, Iran, and Pakistan. The United States hesitated to join openly out of concern for adverse reaction among Arab states. Britain thus bore the brunt of criticism and of formal alliance commitments. In 1959, Iraq withdrew after a domestic revolution, and the alliance was renamed the Central Treaty Organization (CENTO). It was meant to reinforce *containment* by excluding the Soviets from the Middle East, but some critics charged that it encouraged Soviet attention to, and penetration of, that region. When Iran withdrew in 1979, CENTO was dissolved.

Bagirmi. A small, Central African state with its capital at Massenya. Around 1500 its governing class converted to *Islam*. This, along with the adoption of *cavalry* and firearms, spurred it to violently expand, mainly through slave-raiding, at the expense of technologically less-advanced, pagan peoples to its south in Cameroon and southern Chad. It also made war on *Bornu*. It was absorbed by the competing European *imperialisms* of the nineteenth century.

Bahamas. A chain of hundreds of small islands, with but a handful inhabited by the Lucayas Indians. To fill out the *encomienda system*, from 1509 the Lucayas were deported en masse by the Spanish to Hispaniola, where the local Indian population was already dying in droves from disease and mal-treatment. The Lucayas were subsequently and straightforwardly made slaves, bought and sold in island marketplaces. Within four years, there were no Lucayas left on the Bahamas. European settlement began in 1647. The main islands became a British colony in 1783. Autonomy was granted in 1964; independence, in 1973.

Bahrain. Coastal Bahrain was dominated by Portuguese traders from the early sixteenth century. The *Persian Empire* contested for control during the seventeenth and eighteenth centuries. In 1783 Persian forces were thrown out of Bahrain by an uprising led by the local Arab sheikh, who established the dynasty that thereafter reigned in Bahrain. It was made a British *protectorate* in 1861. *Oil* was discovered in 1932, giving this *microstate* sudden strategic importance. Independent by 1971, it participated in OPEC *embargoes* in 1973 and 1979. The *Iran-Iraq War* and *Gulf War* led it to align with Saudi Arabia and the West in search of protection against Iraq and/or Iran, the first of which threatened the regime militarily and the second ideologically and doctrinally. With much of its oil reserve depleted by the 1990s, Bahrain turned to earning *foreign exchange* by processing and refining oil from other states in the region.

Bakassi. A disputed coastal peninsula on the Cameroon/Nigeria border. An Anglo/German treaty gave it to *Kamerun* in 1913. As the *successor state*, modern Cameroon gained legal title. However, Nigeria activated a dormant claim in the 1990s and then occupied the area, probably because of its oil deposits. In 1994 France sent a token military force to Cameroon to deter additional Nigerian actions. Cameroon brought the issue of Nigeria's illegal *occupation* before the *Security Council*.

Baker, James (b. 1930). U.S. statesman. He held various posts in the *Ford, Reagan,* and *George H. Bush* administrations and authored the *Baker Plan* on debt restructuring in 1985. As secretary of state, 1989–1992, he oversaw several major *arms control* agreements with the Soviet Union and its *successor states*. He kept a low profile during the *Gulf War*, but was active in the subsequent drive to arrange comprehensive peace talks for the Middle East. He resigned to take charge of the unsuccessful elder Bush reelection bid in 1992. In 1998 he was asked by the United Nations to assist the referendum process in *Western Sahara*. In 2000 he was active on *George W. Bush*'s campaign and legal team.

Baker Plan. Proposed by *James Baker* to the *International Monetary Fund* (IMF) and *International Bank for Reconstruction and Development* (IBRD) in September 1985, its premise was that credit could be restored to *LDC* borrowers only through *growth*. It had three parts. (1) debtor nations must undertake market reforms to remove inefficiencies; (2) commercial banks should provide $20 billion in loans; (3) the IMF and IBRD should increase lending by $3 billion per year. The Baker Plan had mixed results: *structural adjustment* was unpopular, especially subsidy cuts, and *debt service* actually exceeded inflows from commercial banks.

baksheesh. In parts of India and the Middle East, a tip or bribe asked of foreign businesses before awarding a public contract. *See also* "dash"; guanxi; la mordida.

bakufu. The bureaucracy of the *Tokugawa shogunate*, centered in Edo (Tokyo) and opposed both to the Imperial Court at Kyoto and the regional *daimyo*. The lead bakufu council in charge of foreign policy and daimyo relations was the Rōjū. The bakufu wrote the Code for Military Houses, which established control over the daimyo, regulated commoners, enforced the ban on *Christianity* that aimed at ideological unity and control over the daimyo and *samurai*, and commanded its own (small) army of samurai. At the start of the nineteenth century the bakufu explored Western knowledge, but in 1825 it reiterated an expulsion order against all foreigners. Bakufu power slipped fatally after the arrival of *Matthew Perry* in 1853. For fifteen years, efforts the bakufu made to resist further foreign penetration were undone by antiforeign violence, which led Western powers to demand compensation or new concessions. Each new concession was then received with contempt and violence by radical xenophobes among the samurai and daimyo. The bakufu sought to restore Tokugawa authority in the 1860s even as they introduced reform, but their methods of bloody purge and repression of regional rebellion was an overreach. In the Boshin War (1868–1869), the bakufu was overthrown. With that, 700 years of warrior rule in Japan passed into history.

Bakunin, Mikhail (1814–1876). Russian *anarchist*, active in abortive *revolutions* in Germany (1848) and France (1870). He had wide influence, along with another anarchist *Proudhon*. Bakunin was seen as a personal and political bête noir by *Karl Marx*, who opposed him within the *First International*. Bakunin objected, in particular, to Marx's idea of a *dictatorship of the proletariat*, correctly prophesying that this would corrupt any social revolution into a political or party tyranny. He also rejected reformist politics, which meant that his views remained largely impractical and philosophically sentimentalist.

balance of payments. The annual tracking and measurement of all economic transfers of a nation with the rest of the world economy, including all exports and imports of *goods and services, investment,* and *reserve currency.* For accounting purposes the concept is often subdivided into *capital account, current account,* and *reserves.* If a balance of payments deficit reaches proportions that cause financial markets to lose confidence in the economy, it will become difficult to obtain additional foreign capital. States must then undertake reforms (*adjustment*) that restore investor and lender confidence. In addition to changes in price levels, international capital movements have long played a role in balance of payments adjustment. Indeed, in the confusion after collapse of the *Bretton Woods* system, *exchange rate* variation became a favored means of adjustment. When calculated globally, balance of payments surpluses and deficits equal zero. *See also devaluation; International Monetary Fund; macroeconomics; official financing; Opium Wars.*

balance of power. This term is subject to considerable abuse and often takes on multiple meanings other than the primary ones given here; for example, the declaration "we seek a favorable balance of power" nearly always masks a policy that in fact seeks advantage, or even *preponderance.* Still, the two main usages are: (1) a policy of supporting the weaker side in a *crisis* or ongoing conflict, to maintain an *equilibrium* and thereby, it is hoped, to deter *aggression* and prevent *war*; and (2) a condition in which the distribution of military and political forces among nations means no one state is sufficiently strong to dominate all the others. Balance of power may be global, regional, or local in scope. Forming a balance may be a conscious policy or occur reflexively, as one state attempts to overthrow the existing balance. If a *revisionist power* is also a *Great Power,* an attempt to overthrow the balance will almost certainly propel other Great Powers together in spite of their differences (e.g., the United States and Soviet Union in *World War II*).

Maintaining a balance of power may help preserve the independence of states, avoid war, and permit diplomats to seek peaceful resolution of disputes. However, the primary interest that the balance of power protects is not *peace*; it is the survival of the Great Powers, sometimes at the expense of smaller powers (e.g., the *partitions of Poland*) and often through the means of rebalancing wars. The balance of power is conservative in that it seeks to maintain the status quo, at least against violent change. The primary value the balance of power projects is international (Great Power) order, not necessarily social or political justice among nations. Just as peace may give way if war is necessary to preserve or reestablish a balanced system, concern for justice or principles such as *self-determination* may fall victim to anxiety about maintaining a viable international order.

Yet, the moral content of the balance of power should not be overlooked or underestimated. As the *classical school* of *Grotian* theory notes, and great political leaders have always understood, at its best the balance of power seeks not mere equilibrium, but also a just equilibrium and a peaceably evolving international order. Nor is it invariably opposed to *liberal-internationalist* conceptions of world order, as cruder *liberals* sometimes aver. Rather, it is both capable of underwriting and reinforcing a liberal-international order and indeed remains essential to that prospect. Without a modicum of national political justice, ethnic and other challenges arise that may overwhelm a given balance; but without practical attention to the balance of power, idealistic policies that aim to enhance international justice may instead lead to chaos, upon which even greater injustices are usually in close attendance. *See also balance of terror; balancer; bandwagoning; Otto von Bismarck; collective security; Concert of Europe; correlation of forces; Henry Kissinger; Louis XIV; Napoleon I; Napoleonic Wars; nationalism; new world order; peaceful coexistence; Renaissance.*

Suggested Readings: Inis Claude, *The Balance of Power* (1965); Edward Gulick, *Europe's Classical Balance of Power* (1955).

balance of terror. When moderate state behavior is exhibited because of shared, intense fear about the implications of a failure of *nuclear deterrence*. It is a far narrower notion than *balance of power*, focusing exclusively on one type of weapon and source of power and assuming virtually no freedom of maneuver. The phrase is usually attributed to *Winston Churchill*. *See also crisis stability.*

balance of trade. The difference between the values of *exports* and *imports*, described as favorable if the former exceed the latter. A surplus in the balance of trade was seen by *mercantilists* as a key to national economic health, and well into the *free trade* era many countries still enacted policies of limited *protectionism* in order to create a trade surplus. Yet, there is nothing inherently undesirable about a trade deficit—it might, for instance, reflect a faster domestic *growth* rate; and of course, protectionism is sure to generate retaliatory barriers to one's own exports.

balancer. A state that, like Britain at its peak, lends support to whatever is the weaker side in a sustained conflict in order to maintain a *balance of power*. Some critics contend that this violates the principle that states pursue only their own *national interests* as *vital interests*, by calling for a measure of altruism from the balancer. However, that mistakes apparent for real interests. Thus, Britain's concern for the balance of power was not merely to keep peace in Europe (an *Idealpolitik* motive), but primarily to keep other *Great Powers* at loggerheads while it expanded overseas, preserved from any threat posed by the rise of a triumphant *hegemon* on the continent (a *Realpolitik* motive). Still others view British policy in the nineteenth century as a drive for *hegemony*, rather than any balance. Even so, Britain did not seek domination over other

European Great Powers as had France, and as would Germany. Instead, it sought to expand and consolidate its supremacy outside Europe.

Baldwin, Stanley (1867–1947). British statesman. *Conservative* prime minister in 1923, 1924–1929, and 1936–1937. In 1922 he helped break the coalition that supported *Lloyd George*, bringing down the government. In the 1920s he faced constant economic dislocations stemming from *World War I*, from major industrial actions to *war debts* and *reparations*. In the 1930s he was mostly passive in foreign policy, despite having supported the *League of Nations* during his earlier turns as prime minister. He repeatedly responded without vigor to the key crises of the mid-1930s: the *Abyssinian War*, during which he approved the shameful *Hoare-Laval Pact*, the *Rhineland* crisis, and the start of the *Spanish Civil War*. However, he began British *rearmament* and sharply increased fighter production, which contributed importantly to victory in the *Battle of Britain*. On India, he responded to growing demands for *Home Rule* with the *India Act* of 1935. He was distracted from the important issues of the day by a constitutional crisis over the marriage of King Edward VIII to the divorced Wallis Simpson. Baldwin opposed the marriage and resolutely, but with considerable tact and skill, managed the affair through Edward's abdication (December 11, 1936) in favor of the king's younger brother, who ascended the throne as George VI (1895–1952; r. 1936–1952).

Balfour, Arthur (1848–1930). British statesman. *Conservative* prime minister, 1902–1906; first lord of the Admiralty, 1915; foreign secretary, 1916–1919. The nephew of Lord *Salisbury,* to whom as a young man, he acted as private secretary. Balfour first entered parliament in 1874. He opposed *Home Rule* for Ireland and used troops to violently suppress Irish dissent, even while reforming land laws. He oversaw the finale of the *Second Boer War* and supported arrangement of the *Entente Cordiale* with France in 1904. He was a key player in the coalition government formed to fight *World War I*, especially in maintaining close relations with the United States during its *neutrality*. He succeeded *Churchill* at the Admiralty after *Gallipoli*. As foreign secretary, he was engaged in negotiations with *Woodrow Wilson* over war loans and, later, American entry into the war. He is most famous for the 1917 wartime declaration, which took his name, that he issued calling for a Jewish homeland in *Palestine*. He was active at the *Paris Peace Conference*, was an enthusiastic supporter of the founding of the *League of Nations*, and participated later at the *Washington Conference*. He then served as chancellor of the University of Cambridge.

Balfour Declaration (November 2, 1917). *Arthur Balfour* wrote to Lord *Rothschild* that Britain favored a homeland for Jews located in *Palestine*. This declaration took on real meaning when the *Allied and Associated Powers* endorsed it at the *Paris Peace Conference* in 1919 and, later, when Britain inherited Palestine from Turkey and ran it as a *mandate territory*. It became the basis for *Zionist* claims on Britain, as the mandate power. Britain backed away from the commitment in 1939, and abandoned it and Palestine shortly after *World War II*. *See also Arab nationalism; Israel; Palestine Liberation Organization.*

balkanize. To divide a country or region into small, ineffective, and quarrelsome states, such as those in the *Balkans* or the *successor states* to former *French West Africa*. *See also Austrian Empire; Berlin Conference; Central America; Central Asia; Ottoman Empire; Soviet Union; Yugoslavia.*

Balkan League. The alliance of Bulgaria, Greece, and Serbia that fought against Turkey in the *First Balkan War*, but then broke apart and fell to fighting over division of the spoils.

Balkan Pacts. Three major attempts were made in the twentieth century to settle disputes over territory in the *Balkans*. (1) 1933: *Alexander of Yugoslavia* tried to arrange an accommodation with Bulgaria, Greece, Rumania, and Turkey. Bulgaria coveted too much of Macedonia to agree, but the others formed an *entente* that lasted to 1940. (2) 1954: Greece, Turkey, and Yugoslavia signed a pact that lasted until the next crisis broke out over Cyprus. (3) 1988: Albania, Bulgaria, Greece, Rumania, Turkey, and Yugoslavia met but failed to conclude an agreement; things then fell apart with the post-*Tito* disintegration of Yugoslavia.

Balkans. The largely alpine region located below the Danube, surrounded by the Adriatic, Aegean, Ionian, and Black Seas and containing the *Balkan States*. In terms of religion, it is further divided among *Catholics*, *Muslims*, and *Orthodox*. For several thousand years it formed a natural *boundary* region, with control shifting between various European and Asian empires. It is a strategically complex region, since it is a largely impenetrable land area that yet has a long coastline that abuts crucially important waterways. As late as the end of the twentieth century its poor roads, narrow mountain passes, and inclement weather proved severe obstacles both to the expansionist ambitions of local *warlords* and to effective intervention by the worlds' most advanced military powers. *See also Austrian Empire; balkanize; Balkan Wars; Eastern Question; Habsburg dynasty; Ottoman Empire; pan-Slavism; Straits Question; Venice.*
    Suggested Reading: Leften Stavrianos, *The Balkans Since 1453* (1958).

Balkan states. The states occupying the Balkan Peninsula of southern Europe. Albania, Bulgaria, Greece, Rumania, the European portion of Turkey, and Yugoslavia—which after 1991 broke into the *successor states* of Bosnia, Croatia, Macedonia, and Slovenia, with Serbia and Montenegro alone retaining the federal name "Yugoslavia." In 1999 *Kosovo* became a de facto *NATO protectorate*, but legally remained part of Serbia.

Balkan War, First (1912–1913). Under Russian prodding, Bulgaria and Serbia agreed to *partition* Macedonia, then an *Ottoman* province. They were joined by Greece and Montenegro (the Balkan League) in their attack on Turkey. The European *Great Powers* intervened to force Turkey to cede most of its remaining holdings in Europe (*Rumelia*), the lion's share of which went to Bulgaria in exchange for agreeing to creation of an independent Albania.

Balkan War, Second (1913). The creation of Albania frustrated Serbian and Montenegrin territorial ambitions. Bulgaria feared a secret deal between the other *regional powers* to exclude it from the *partition* of Macedonia. Within a few months of the settlement of the *First Balkan War*, Bulgaria launched an attack on Greece and Serbia, its recent allies. It was immediately attacked in its turn by Rumania and Turkey. That created the unusual situation of the Turks, Serbs, and Greeks being de facto allies against Bulgaria, in spite of being technically still in a *state of war* with each other. Bulgaria was defeated and forced to surrender its earlier gains. In the *Treaty of Bucharest* Serbia and Greece emerged with the most territory. Bulgaria was even forced to cede an eastern province to Rumania, held by Bulgaria before the Balkan Wars. Bulgaria would try to retrieve these lands during *World War I*. Turkey, too, was left a wounded, bitter, and reduced power. In contrast, Serbia was enlarged and unduly cocky, causing Austria to look with great alarm at this new *nationalist* threat to its multinational empire. All this fed into the *mobilization crisis* and outbreak of *World War I*.

Balkan War, Third (1991–1999). Serbia supported attacks by ethnic Serb *militia* on Slovenia within days of that state's declaration of independence from *Yugoslavia* on June 25, 1991. Fighting spread to Croatia, which declared independence, then failed to honor a security commitment to Slovenia. By December, 30 percent of Croatia was in Serb hands, and a so-called Serb Republic of Croatia was declared, but not *recognized*. In 1992–1993 the war spread to Bosnia, where Serb militia declared a Serb Republic of Bosnia and besieged Sarajevo and other Muslim and Croatian *enclaves* in defiance of United Nations *resolutions*. French President *Mitterand* flew to Sarajevo in June 1992 to arrange humanitarian relief; UN troops followed. In July the United Nations called off the airlift because of fighting near the airport. After a brief reopening, the airport closed again in September after an Italian Air Force relief plane was shot down. In August the *Security Council* called for a *cease-fire* and access to all detention centers, where it was suspected that *genocide* was taking place. The UN next *embargoed* military supplies to all sides, giving an unintended advantage to the Serbs, who drew upon the huge Yugoslav Army stockpiles in Serbia, particularly for *armor* and *artillery*. Croatia then entered the war, turning on its erstwhile Muslim allies under a secret agreement with the Serbs to partition Bosnia. By early 1993, 70 percent of Bosnia was under Serb control.

A United Nations (represented by Cyrus Vance) and European Community (represented by Lord Owen) Vance-Owen peace proposal was drafted in 1992. It aimed at a single Bosnian state divided into a *federation* of 12 ethnic subregions. Croat and Serb militia ignored the Vance-Owen plan and instead continued to pound Bosnia's Muslims in an effort to compel a two-way *partition*. The United Nations eventually passed tougher *sanctions*, while NATO threatened air strikes and to lift the arms embargo on purchases by the Muslims. That forced Serbia to the table, and to sign (but not to respect) the Vance-Owen plan. Serbia next declared it was closing its border with Bosnia, whose "Serb parliament" still rejected the United Nations/European Community plan. In August it was agreed to abandon the idea of a federal Bosnia and carve it into three ethnic states, with the Muslims reduced to a few enclaves. NATO again threatened air strikes, even while Britain and Canada openly discussed withdrawal of their *peacekeeping* forces and the Russian *Duma* warned of intervention against the Serbs. In the first half of 1994, Bosnian Muslims made some gains against Bosnian Croats, NATO forced an end to Serb sieges of Sarajevo and Goradze, and Muslims joined in a loose federation with ethnically related Croats. In 1995 the *Dayton Peace Accords* set up a NATO *protectorate* over Bosnia that internally aimed at suffocating the fighting, and thereby externally aimed at preserving NATO from possible breakup over its internal divisions, while publicly mouthing good intentions about preserving multiethnic democracy in the Balkans. Checked in Bosnia, Serbia's Milošević turned next to *ethnic cleansing* of *Kosovo*, 1998–1999. That led to a second NATO intervention and a second Balkan protectorate. Skirmishing continued in Kosovo and northern Macedonia, but the major fighting was over by 1999. *See also concentration camps; war crimes trials.*

ballistic missile. A missile that takes a parabolic, ballistic trajectory (one influenced principally by gravity and atmospheric conditions), flying without power beyond the initial thrust of takeoff. *See also cruise missile; guided missile.*

ballistic missile defense (BMD). Any complex of some or all of ABM systems, lasers, *charged particle beams*, projectiles, target acquisition systems, and tracking and fire-guidance radars for defense against *ballistic missiles*. Proponents of building BMD systems argue that they are needed by advanced countries because (1) *rogue states* or cornered dictators do not respect *arms control* agreements on *ballistic missiles*; (2) some militarily advanced states (China, North Korea, Russia) abetted *proliferation* of missile technology; and (3) smaller powers historically have not been *deterred* from the use of force by the nuclear arsenals of opponents (e.g., North Korea in 1950; Indonesia during the *Konfrontasi*; the DRV in the *Vietnam War*; Argentina during the *Falklands War*; Pakistan in *Kashmir*, prior to 1998). The end of the *Cold War* and the emergent threat of rogue states with ballistic missile and *nuclear weapons* (or other *weapons of mass destruction*) stimulated broad interest in BMD research and deployment—public disclaimers notwithstanding—among advanced industrial powers. Japan and the United States openly pursued advanced research into BMD from the 1990s. *See also Strategic Defense Initiative.*

balloons. *See air power; barrage balloon; Hague Conference; prohibited weapons; zeppelin.*

Baltic. The region of northern Europe bordering the Baltic Sea. *See also Baltic States; East Prussia; Hansa; Scandinavia.*

Baltic States. Estonia, Latvia, Lithuania, and sometimes (but not usually), Finland. Note: Even as late as the *Congress of Vienna, East Prussians* were considered a Baltic rather than a Germanic people by many. *See also CIS; Hansa; Russian Empire.*

Baluchistan. A mountainous region straddling southeast Iran and northwest Pakistan; the Baluchi people are similarly divided.

Bamboo Curtain. The policy of rigid secrecy and repression in China during the first decades of *Communist* power. The term played on *Winston Churchill's* famous phrase about an *Iron Curtain* descending across east and central Europe, drawn down by *Stalin.*

banana republic. (1) A disparaging reference to the states of Central America, whose agricultural economies depend largely on the export of tropical fruits, coffee, or some other single agricultural commodity whose world price fluctuates greatly and on whose sole income they depend. (2) A disparaging reference to any state dependent economically and politically on a larger power, especially if that power is the United States.

Bancroft Conventions. Named for U.S. statesman George Bancroft (1800–1891). These *naturalization* treaties reflected a rising respect for American power in world affairs occasioned by the *American Civil War* by resolving longstanding disputes over *expatriation* of foreign citizenship by naturalized Americans. The first was signed with the *North German Confederation* in 1868, followed by other German and Scandinavian states. Britain signed in 1870, ending a dispute over naturalization pertaining to a conflict between the principles of *jus soli* and *jus sanguinas*, which helped cause the *War of 1812*. The Conventions were a historic, but not a final or universal, victory for an international right of expatriation over the doctrine of *indefeasible allegiance*. Even so, disputes continued for decades between the United States and nonsignatory states, notably Russia, over continuing detention, imprisonment, and sometimes military *impressment* of naturalized Americans.

bandit suppression campaigns (1931–1934). A series of five military actions by the *Guomindang* to eradicate the *Communists* in the *Jiangxi Soviet*. The first four were savaged by *guerrilla* attacks. The fifth was successful and forced the Communists onto the *Long March. See also Chiang Kai-shek; Lin Biao; Mao Zedong.*

Bandung Conference (1955). A conference of twenty-nine African and Asian states that launched the main associations and themes of the *Nonaligned Movement*: anti*colonialism*, formal state opposition to *racism*, and *neutrality* in the *Cold War. Nehru* hoped to emerge from the conference as the lead spokesman for the *Third World*, but encountered competition from China, notably *Zhou Enlai.*

bandwagoning. A simple-minded, social science idea that rather than there being an automatic propensity for states to combine (to form a *balance of power*) against concentrations of hostile power, smaller states instead tend to "hop on the bandwagon" of a successful alliance in order to draw protection from it or to gain from its *aggression*. An oft-cited example is the accession of central and east European states to the *Axis* in its halcyon, expansionist days of 1939–1942. Given the variety of responses by the small nations of Europe to the rise of Nazi Germany, that association is better explained as the product of particular locale and leadership ambition. However, such absence of supporting evidence has never stopped some social scientists from asserting that they have discovered some general truth about international relations.

Bangladesh. Originally a Hindu area, *Bengal* province was conquered by Muslim invaders in the twelfth century. The British ruled it as East Bengal, an important province of the *Raj*, from the eighteenth century until their departure from the *subcontinent* in 1947. As a mostly Muslim area, it supported the *Muslim League* and became *East Pakistan* upon the *partition* of India. It was ruled as an effective colony by (and for) West Pakistanis from *Punjab*, from which it was separated by 1,000 miles of Indian territory. In March 1969 *Yahya Khan* imposed *martial law* and sent in troops to intimidate the population. Even so, the *separatist* Awami League gained control of the assembly by 1971. The Pakistani Army, largely West Pakistani in makeup, then savagely intervened. That provoked a declaration of *independence*, followed by a *civil war* that killed 1 million and created 10 million refugees, who mostly fled into India. In December 1971, the *Third Indo-Pakistani War* began, ultimately ensuring that Bangladesh achieved independence.

In the midst of this turmoil, in 1970 a cyclone took an estimated 500,000 lives, in perhaps the greatest natural disaster in human history. After independence, a series of coups and assassinations kept Bangladesh chronically unstable. Desperately poor and doomed to suffer devastating annual monsoons, Bangladesh also was the locale of extensive *human rights* violations. These took on a new, *fundamentalist* flavor after it was declared an Islamic republic in 1988 and included persistent mistreatment of tribal groups, notably the Chakmas of Chittagong. Another cyclone killed 125,000 in 1991, after which more realism took hold of its foreign policy. It accepted humanitarian assistance, even when delivered by foreign (including United States) troops, and agreed to a *stabilization program* designed by the *International Monetary Fund*. Given its basic economic weakness, it was most concerned with obtaining debt assistance and other aid from outside powers or agencies. Because of its geopolitical location, its foreign policy must be overwhelmingly concerned with relations with India, including the perennial issues of how to share the Ganges (centered on a struggle over the Farraka Barrage dam), offshore oil resources, and problems attendant on economic migrants and refugees.

Suggested Reading: Kathryn Jacques, *Bangladesh, India, and Pakistan* (2000).

Bank for International Settlements (BIS). Beginning with the great crisis of the 1930s, European *central banks* met regularly in Switzerland to discuss and coordinate policy. The United States remained aloof until the Federal Reserve joined the system in 1960. The central banks of most major economic powers now belong to, or tacitly coordinate with, this forum.

banking. Banking has performed a vital role in national economic development, trade, and war. Venetian and Florentine power rested heavily on banking expertise, which was mostly absent elsewhere in Europe before the *Renaissance*. The House of *Fugger* played a key role in financing the *Hapsburgs*, whereas the House of *Rothschild* was important in all Europe during the nineteenth and early twentieth centuries. Before the nineteenth century few countries had a sophisticated banking system. England was most advanced, followed by France. In both cases, war provided the initial stimulus. Swiss banks were relatively unimportant before *World War I* but, along with American houses such as J. P. Morgan, grew to prominence during and after that war. Russian financial weakness was revealed by the *Crimean War*, which led to the founding of the Russian State Bank in 1860. The Austrian and German banking systems developed only in the second half of the nineteenth century. Effective private banks in Japan were founded during the reforms of the *Meiji Restoration*, whereas China's banking system was still primitive before the *Chinese Revolution* (1911).

As in Medieval Europe, banking in the postcolonial *Islamic* world was initially hindered by usury laws forbidding collection of interest. Early banks in Islamic countries (e.g., Egypt, the *Ottoman Empire*, and *Persia* in the nineteenth century) were organized by Europeans interested in financing world trade; that was also true of early banks in China, India, Africa, and Latin America. The United States chartered its first national bank in 1791, but allowed the charter to expire in 1811. A second effort at national banking failed in 1836. However, the *American Civil War* prompted reform of the banking system. *See also central banks; Knights Templars.*

Suggested Readings: Rondo Cameron, ed., *Banking and Economic Development* (1972); Herbert Feis, *Europe: The World's Banker, 1870–1914* (1965).

banner system/troops. (1) A highly effective form of *Inner Asian* military organization introduced to the *Jürchen* and then to China by the *Manchu* leader *Nurgaci*, who arranged his army, 150,000 strong, into eight regiments, each beneath a colored banner (blue, red, yellow, white, and four more with borders).

These were used to coordinate tactical maneuvers and build unit solidarity and morale. During the *Qing* conquest of China, separate Chinese banners (eight by 1642) and *Mongol* banners were created; a number of former Russian captives also became soldiers with one or other banner. An elite drawn from the banners were located in different zones around Beijing, displacing the eunuchs who had guarded the *Forbidden City*. The *Qianlong* emperor later settled about 20,000 banner troops, along with their families, in military colonies on the far western frontier with Russia, where the only recently and hard conquered male Muslim population was excused from shaving their heads or growing the Manchu queue. Bannermen *plundered* during wartime and lived off state subsidies in times of peace. Qing emperors often drew top advisors from their ranks, bypassing the bureaucratic scholar-elite. The banner troops subsequently proved militarily unreliable, however, during the *White Lotus Rebellion* and especially during the *Taiping Rebellion*, after which they were supplemented by large formations of local militia and even regional armies. They were phased out and replaced by a professional army (New Army) beginning in 1901. (2) Under the *Tokugawa* in Japan, bannermen (hatamoto) served as shogunal retainers and guards of the main routes to Edo. *See also Yuan Shikai.*

Bantu. A subfamily of more than 400 languages spoken by most of the peoples living south of the equator in Africa, excluding speakers of Khosian languages, such as the Khoikhoi (known to the British and Boers as "Hottentots") and the San, or "Bushmen." Alternately, an ethnic designation of the speakers of Bantu languages. Many Bantu peoples formed small states, while some framed significant civilizations such as *Great Zimbabwe*. Others remained stateless through the seventeenth and eighteenth centuries, kept in this condition by chronic political, economic, and social instability born of marauding bands of militarized raiders such as the Yaka and Imbangala, slave raiders from the coast (Portuguese and *Swahili Arab*), the enormous turmoil of the *Mfecane* of *Shaka Zulu* in the early nineteenth century, and slave-raiding by *Tippu Tip* and others later in the nineteenth century.

Bantustans. Ten so-called homelands of blacks in South Africa were set up under *apartheid*. Four were ostensibly independent (Bophuthatswana, Ciskei, Transkei, and Venda), but none were recognized internationally. Individual chiefs at the head of each homeland responded differently, though most rejected the apartheid notion of "separate development." The majority of blacks continued to live outside the Bantustans, with no representation whatever.

Bao Dai, né Nguyen Vinh Thuy (b. 1913). Emperor of *Annam*, 1932–1945. He adjusted his sails to whatever political wind was blowing, *collaborating* with the French, Japanese, *Viêt Minh*, Americans, and South Vietnamese. He abdicated in 1945. In 1949 he was made *head of state* in South Vietnam by the French. When he was deposed in 1955, by *Diem*, South Vietnam was declared a republic (RVN).

Barbados. It was settled by England from 1627 (the Spanish had never bothered), both as a trading base with *New Spain* and a site to grow tobacco. When the tobacco failed, planters turned to sugar—and required *slaves*. Barbados developed a *slave*, plantation economy until *emancipation* came to the *British Empire* in 1833. *Independence* was granted in 1966. It sent a token force to the *invasion of Grenada*.

Barbarossa. The code name for the German invasion of the *Soviet Union* by four million men, the greatest single assault in history, on June 22, 1941. It was named by *Hitler* for Frederick I (1123–1190 C.E.), *Holy Roman Emperor*, who was also called Barbarossa ("the Red Beard").

Its immediate purpose was the rapid destruction of Soviet armies all along the frontier, an 1,800 mile front, in a vast *Blitzkrieg* that was to utilize massed *artillery* and *armor* (*Panzers*), air support, and total political and strategic surprise. Hitler was so confident of victory that he made little provision for delay, none for the possibility of defeat, and grossly underestimated the logistical problems to come. In the rear of the armor formations, 90 percent of German transport was still horse-drawn. In the bitter *Historikerstreit* of the 1980s, some German and Austrian historians argued that this was a justifiable assault, a *preemptive strike* made necessary because the Soviet Union was planning to attack Germany. Other historians have demonstrated conclusively the falsity of that view. In fact, *Stalin* was caught unprepared, materially and psychologically, in spite of receiving advance warnings from *Churchill* and *Roosevelt*, and far more detailed warnings and information from his own intelligence and border troops. Soviet troops were mostly engaged in preparing fixed border defenses along the expanded frontier of 1940, rather than in preparing for the war of movement that was coming. Stalin ignored all warnings, thinking them a British and American provocation to bring him to blows with Hitler—which, to a large degree, in fact they were. As to Soviet warnings, these might be the product of *counterrevolution* in the ranks of the *Red Army*, which he never trusted. Mostly, however, he relied upon his own prior judgment as expressed in the *Nazi-Soviet Pact*, which should have bought him time to rearm but for the unexpectedly sudden collapse of the Western Allies in the *Battle of France* in 1940. Stalin's ideology, but also his tsar-like view of Russia's geopolitical position and history, left him utterly convinced that Germany alone would never attack the Soviet Union. Hence, he refused any preparedness measures, as too provocative. The Soviets were therefore still supplying bulk raw materials to Germany (as agreed by Stalin in the Nazi-Soviet Pact) on the day Hitler's all-out attack began.

The initial assault was devastating, in part because of the damage done the Red Army by the prewar *Yezhovshchina*. The armored formations of the *Wehrmacht* and *Waffen SS* slashed deep into Russia, pushing the Soviets back on three huge fronts, destroying entire armies, and capturing several million Russian prisoners. Stalin was stunned and appears to have come close to a mental breakdown during the first two weeks of the crisis. From the first hour, the ferocity of the fighting and the scale and frequency of atrocity by both sides, but especially by the Germans, set a brutal tone that lasted for the rest of the Russo-German war. The Germans failed to complete their planned pincer encirclement of the Red Army, partly because Soviet resistance stiffened and partly because Hitler diverted troops from the central attack on Moscow (one of his generals noted that Hitler had an intuitive fear of retracing the invasion route taken by *Napoleon*) to support attacks on military formations farther south. The onset of the worst winter in Europe in 100 years quickly proved that the Germans were ill-prepared for a long campaign. By Christmas, German armies had taken Minsk and encircled another entire Russian army at Kiev, occupied the Crimea, begun a 900-day siege of Leningrad, and were within twenty miles of the spires of the Kremlin in Moscow. Finally, the Soviet lines held. For once making use of available intelligence—that the Japanese would strike the United States and not his Siberian frontier—one day before *Pearl Harbor* Stalin unleashed a reserve of forty Siberian divisions against utterly surprised and exhausted German formations. The ensuing Battle for Moscow was won by the Soviets, but for tens of millions the full horrors of race war and *genocide*, which added to the barbarization of the *eastern front*, were only just beginning. *See also Pripet Marshes*.

Suggested Reading: Gabriel Gorodetsky, *Grand Delusion. Stalin and the German Invasion of Russia* (1999).

Barbary pirates. Although some actual *pirates* infested the North African coast, most of the so-called Barbary pirates were navies of small Muslim states in the *Maghreb* that harassed and plundered Mediterranean commerce, especially after the end of the *Reconquista* in Spain. Regarded as pirates by Europeans, these corsairs were a thorn in the side of *Ferdinand* of Aragon, who fought them from 1490 to 1511 but became their tacit protector against the *Ottoman Empire*, with which Spain contested for power in the Mediterranean throughout the sixteenth century. *Charles V* also opposed them, and *Oliver Cromwell* sent an expedition against them in the 1650s. Other powers intermittently sought to repress them during the eighteenth and nineteenth centuries. The Barbary pirates continued to raid commerce in the western Mediterranean until after the *Congress of Vienna*. *See also Barbary States; Ifriqiya; Thomas Jefferson; Tripolitan War; Trucial Oman.*

Barbary States/Coast. Small Islamic states located along the western Mediterranean coast of Africa and home for several centuries to the so-called *Barbary pirates*. By the end of the sixteenth century *Tunis, Algiers,* and *Tripoli* were fully incorporated into the *Ottoman Empire*. *See also Ifriqiya; Morocco.*

Barents Sea. The North Atlantic between Spitsbergen and the European continent. In 1920 some 39 states signed the Svalbard Treaty regulating economic exploitation of the Svalbard archipelago and Barents Sea. Tensions subsided until a fisheries and *boundary* dispute between Norway and the Soviet Union, resolved by treaty in 1977. The Barents was the locale of shadow jousting by nuclear submarines during the *Cold War*, as it marked the outward passage for Soviet naval vessels based in Murmansk.

Bar-Lev Line. Israeli fortifications behind the *Suez Canal*, 1968–1973. The Egyptians crossed the canal and broke through the Bar-Lev Line in October 1973, stunning the defenders, who nonetheless later rallied.

barrage. From the French usage, during *World War I*: a curtain, barrier, or wall of artillery fire. In a creeping barrage the artillery instituted a slowly advancing wall of fire, behind which ground units advanced at a set and prearranged pace.

barrage balloon. A large gas balloon held by wires and deployed near military installations or cities during *World War I* and *World War II*. They were used to deter enemy aircraft from accurate low-flying bomb runs, for fear of hitting the cables.

barter agreements. Direct exchange of *goods and services*, such as plum jam for engine parts, without capital transfers. States short on *foreign exchange* or those in a forced *dependency* relationship use these to facilitate trade. For example, barter agreements became commonplace during the *Great Depression* and were also extensively used within the COMECON bloc.

Baruch Plan. Named for Bernard Baruch (1870–1965), U.S. financier and statesman. It was a half-serious effort to snuff out the nuclear *arms race* before it got started. The United States asked for control of all atomic energy and research to be given to an international authority with unlimited powers of inspection. Once this agency had control, the United States would agree to stop manufacturing *nuclear weapons* and destroy its stockpiles. The *Soviet Union* refused the plan, because the paranoia of *Stalin* and the Soviet system would not permit the international inspections it called for as a *verification* method, and more rationally, because the United States and Great Britain would have retained knowledge of how to construct nuclear weapons, and in all likelihood would have controlled the United Nations agency as well. Much intellectual energy has been wasted speculating about whether a little more sincerity on the American side might have encouraged a little more cooperation on the part of the Soviet Union. Everything that is now known about Soviet foreign policy after the war and about Stalin, however, belies the notion—insofar as it was ever more than wilder fantasy—that somehow a wholly harmonious "nuclear duopoly" might have been constructed that would have evaded all the conflict and confrontation of the *Cold War*.

baseline. The inside limit for measuring the *territorial sea*, drawn from the low-tide mark. Under *UNCLOS III*'s archipelagic regime, in an archipelago the baseline would be measured from the outer edge of the outermost *island*. *See also contiguous zone; EEZ; internal waters; line of death; straight baseline.*

basic needs. In *development*, proposals to shift plans (and indices used to measure national development) from *macroeconomic* ends such as *growth*, to progress in meeting basic human needs for the general population, such as primary and secondary education, housing, nutrition, sanitation, and elementary health care. This approach is sometimes referred to as "poverty alleviation." The idea is often coupled with *basic rights* and sometimes with political participation rights. *See also Human Development Index.*

basic rights. An approach to *human rights* stressing satisfaction of certain minimum physical needs (subsistence; housing; freedom from arbitrary arrest, detention, or *torture*) before pressing for more ambitious rights, such as equitable pay, political representation, and free speech and assembly. Not all liberals are comfortable with this approach. Some argue that prior guarantees of civil and political rights are the best way to ensure provision of subsistence rights, by setting up means for people to make effective, rights-based demands of their own societies. *See also basic needs.*

Basque. An *ethnic group* numbering some 700,000 persons, not closely related to either the Spanish or French, living on both sides of the border in the western Pyrenees. Most supported the Spanish republic during the *Spanish Civil War* in the hope of achieving local *autonomy*. They had backed the losing side and their desire for autonomy was subsequently ignored or repressed by *Franco*. Some autonomy was granted in 1980 after Spain's own transition to democracy following Franco's passing. A radical independence organization, the *Euzkadi Ta Askatasuna* (ETA), kept up low-level *terrorism*, mainly against other Basques who sought reconciliation with Spain. This prompted retaliation by the government in Madrid, including at times broad disrespect for Basque *human rights*. In 1997 the level of brutality prompted millions of Spaniards to demonstrate against the violence.

Bastille, fall of (July 14, 1789). *See French Revolution.*

Basutoland. The former name of Lesotho, when it was a *protectorate*.

Bataan death march. After the fall of the Philippines to Japan in 1942, American and Filipino soldiers were mercilessly marched to *prisoner of war* camps. Nearly 10,650 died or were murdered along the way, as wounded or stragglers were shot or bayoneted. Another 17,600 died within weeks of arrival. This cruel story hardened anti-Japanese sentiment in the United States and the Philippines, both during and after *World War II. See also Nagasaki, atomic bombing of.*

Batavia. The Dutch name for Jakarta, when they possessed it as a valuable colony.

Batistá, Fulgencio (1901–1973). Cuban military dictator, 1934–1940; president, 1940–1944, 1952–1959. His corrupt regime was overthrown by *Fidel Castro* during the *Cuban Revolution*, and he retired into comfortable exile.

battalion. *See military units.*

battle cruiser. A *capital warship* that almost possessed the firepower of a *battleship* (eight, or more, 12-inch guns), only clad in a lighter armor (closer to that of a *cruiser*) allowing it a faster speed than its heavy-plated cousin. It was the brainchild of *John Fisher,* who built a handful of battle cruisers at the expense of many more cruisers, which he thought they would replace, because he thought speed would be the best protection for his fleet. In 1916 Britain had ten battle cruisers to Germany's five. In battle, they proved unable to replace cruisers or withstand fire from battleships. *See also pocket battleship.*

battle fatigue. An American term from *World War II* (the British equivalent was "battle exhaustion") for *shell shock*, or what was later called *post-traumatic stress disorder*, brought on by direct and prolonged exposure to the horrors of combat.

battlefield nuclear weapons. *See tactical nuclear weapons.*

battleship. A *capital warship* designed to bring to bear maximum firepower (14- to 16-inch guns were common) and protected by heavy armor plating of the deck and hull. Speed was sacrificed to firepower and armor in these massive, floating *artillery* platforms. They were, in their day, the largest and most complex weapons systems yet devised, intended to project power to the four corners of the earth and to represent the full *power* and *prestige* of the *Great Powers*, which alone among the states were capable of building them in fleet quantity. Later, even smaller nations acquired battleships, while the United States, oddly among the Great Powers, lagged far behind until it felt the influence of the ideas of *Theodore Roosevelt* and *Alfred T. Mahan*. The first battleship was probably the HMS Mary Rose, a three-decker built by Henry VIII of England. *See also Anglo-German naval arms race; battle cruiser; Dreadnought; John Fisher; Five Power Naval Treaty; gunpowder revolution; Jutland, Battle of; Leyte Gulf; Pearl Harbor; pocket battleship; two-power naval standard; Washington Naval Conference.*

Bavaria. Long an independent duchy within the *Holy Roman Empire*, Bavaria was also a German Electorate from 1623. It became an independent kingdom in 1805, but was incorporated into *Bismarck's* Germany in 1871. In 1918 a *soviet* republic was proclaimed, but was crushed. Bavaria was the site of early *Nazi* efforts to gain power. After *World War II* it was an influential state in West Germany. Largely *Catholic*, it exerts a broadly conservative pressure on German foreign and domestic policy.

Bay of Pigs invasion (1961). Two weeks before *John Kennedy* took office, President *Dwight Eisenhower* cut relations with Cuba. After his swearing in, Kennedy immediately approved ongoing *CIA* training of Cuban exiles for an invasion to overthrow *Fidel Castro*. On April 17, 1961, some 1,400 anti-Castro Cubans landed at the Bay of Pigs, armed and transported by the CIA. They hoped for a rising of the population, which never materialized, and counted on U.S. air support, which Kennedy, at the last minute, decided not to provide. Within three days most were dead or captured. The fiasco lowered U.S. *prestige* in Latin America, and generally. It almost certainly pushed Castro closer to Moscow. It may also have encouraged the Soviets to place missiles in Cuba, as *extended deterrence* against another attempted invasion of its ally and/or because *Khrushchev* concluded that Kennedy had blinked during the Bay of Pigs operation and could be bluffed and bullied into accepting the presence of Soviet missiles.

Suggested Readings: Trumbull Higgins, *The Perfect Failure* (1987); Peter Wyden, *Bay of Pigs* (1979).

bayonet. A steel stabbing weapon attached by a ring to the end of a musket or rifle. It was *Vauban* who invented the socket bayonet (1687). Its introduction en masse near the end of the seventeenth century, during the wars of *Louis XIV*, greatly changed the European battlefield. It eliminated *pike men*, who had been used to defend musketeers against *cavalry*, by making it possible for *infantry* to both fire at charging cavalry or other infantry and to defend against cavalry with a stabbing weapon of their own.

BCCI bank scandal. An international financial scandal that became public in 1992. It involved corrupt favors to and from high officials and government agencies from many countries, including the *Vatican*, the *CIA*, and *PLO*. This Pakistani-based investment bank embezzled billions from depositors, which it used to finance *terrorism* and drug operations worldwide.

beachhead. A shoreline or transriverine area secured by a military force, which then awaits reinforcements capable of penetrating deeper into enemy territory.

Beagle Channel dispute. For more than 100 years Argentina and Chile quarreled over control of the Beagle Channel, which joins the Atlantic and Pacific Oceans at the southernmost point of South America. Of special concern was the fate of three small channel islands (Lennox, Nueva, and Pictón).

The dispute was placed in long abeyance by terms of a 1902 treaty, but arose again by the early 1970s. In 1972 Argentina withdrew from the treaty. A British-led *arbitration* awarded the islands to Chile in 1977. However, the *junta* in Argentina rejected the decision. During 1978 both countries stepped up military preparations. This crisis was defused by joint acceptance of an offer of *mediation* by Pope *John Paul II*. A settlement was reached in early 1984 by which the new civilian government in Argentina essentially accepted the terms of the 1977 arbitration that had awarded Chile the islands. In return, Chile foreswore title to Argentina's *Antarctic* claims and to *territorial waters* or an *EEZ* on the Atlantic side of the continent, beyond the normal *twelve-mile limit* surrounding the channel islands.

Beaufort Sea. The Arctic Ocean northeast of Alaska.

Bechuanaland. The former name of Botswana, while it was a *protectorate*.

Bedouin. Nomadic tribes of the Arabian desert and later also North Africa. Bedouin frequently came under the influence of *marabouts* and warred with the coastal *city-states* of North Africa. They also resisted European penetration of Tunisia, Tripoli, and Morocco. Many supported the *Arab Revolt* against the *Ottoman Empire* in *World War I*. Israel as well as several *Arab* countries later forced the Bedouins out of nomadism and into settlements. *See also Qatar; Saudi Arabia; Yemen.*

Beer Hall *Putsch* (November 9–10, 1923). *Hitler's* first attempt to take power, in Bavaria. He thought the *Reichswehr* would join the revolt, but it sat aside. He and about 600 *Nazi* supporters burst into a beer hall in Munich and seized the Bavarian State Commissioner, who was speaking there. They forced him to declare the overthrow of the Bavarian and national governments. He renounced the declaration as soon as the Nazis let him go. The next day, Hitler and his supporters were joined by *Ludendorff* in a march on the Town Hall. Bavarian police met the Putschists with a hail of bullets, killing sixteen. The man just beside Hitler was shot, pulling him to the ground, and safety, in his death spasm. Ludendorff was untouched, but was arrested. Hitler was sentenced to five years in prison for *treason*; he served nine months, using the time to write "Mein Kampf" ("My Struggle"). The *Putsch* brought him and his *revanchist* message to national prominence. As important, it decided him against openly illegal methods. Afterward, he sought the constitutional path to power, supplemented by street violence whenever that proved useful.

BEF. *See British Expeditionary Force.*

beggar-thy-neighbor. Foreign economic policies that look to maximize domestic interests through aggressive export strategies, ranging from import controls, *tariffs*, export *subsidies*, *quotas*, and other mechanisms that do not take due notice of the effect on the economies of trading partners. This often leads to mutual *retaliation*, which hurts the very interests one is trying to promote. *See also Smoot-Hawley Tariff.*

Begin, Menachem (1913–1992). Israeli prime minister. He migrated to *Palestine* from *Nazi*-occupied Poland in 1942, becoming head of *Irgun*. He was involved in *terrorist* operations against British forces, most infamously destruction of the King David Hotel in *Jerusalem*, an action that killed 91, including a number of Jews. He led *Likud* in government, 1977–1983. His greatest moment came in 1978 when he signed a peace agreement with *Anwar Sadat* of Egypt, for which they shared the *Nobel Prize* for Peace. In 1982 he approved an invasion of Lebanon and shelling of Beirut, which drove the *PLO* out of its bases all the way to Tunis, and set up an Israeli security zone in south Lebanon. The war severely damaged Israel's image and support within the United States and entangled Israel in Lebanon's ongoing civil war. Begin quit suddenly in 1983, reportedly grief-stricken over the death of his wife, but also despondent over criticism of his conduct of the Lebanese war.

behavioralism. A social science approach to studying international politics that regards only observed behavior as relevant and measurable phenomena. It stresses *quantification* of *variables* and the use of *causal modeling*. Its adherents tend to dismiss the role of *volition* and reject as putatively intuitive and unscientific—and therefore valueless—historical case studies, although these are more empirically sound and often more theoretically rigorous than most social science treatises, as well as nearly all philosophical or normative approaches other than, of course, the behavioralist practitioner's own and often unexamined biases, or *paradigm. See also postbehavioralism; traditionalism.*

Belarus. "White Russia." Formerly Byelorussia. What is now Belarus was from the ninth century an outer province of *Kievan Rus*, though quite loosely held, as was much of the territory of that ungainly early and *feudal* state. This condition ended with the internal chaos and then collapse of Kievan Rus and the invasion of all the Russias by the *Mongols* in the early thirteenth century. In the remainder of the Middle Ages, Belarus was fought over and disrupted by Poland-Lithuania and Russia (Muscovy). Ultimately, it fell to Poland and thereafter took a quiet place within the Polish-Lithuanian medieval empire. However, in the late eighteenth-century *partitions of Poland*, Belarus too came under the sway of the *tsars*. It was thereafter a province of the *Russian Empire*. It straddles the natural, northern invasion route into Russia from Europe (and vice versa). Its capital, Minsk, was burned during the *Napoleonic Wars*, as in 1812 *Napoleon* passed through Belarus, twice, first on his way into Russia and then during the *retreat from Moscow*. It was badly scoured by foragers and scarred by battle, and especially damaged by the *scorched earth* policy of its Russian defenders. During the nineteenth century, particularly under *Nicholas I*, its large Jewish population was severely persecuted, suffering many *pogroms*. After the assassination of *Alexander II*, for which Jews were unfairly blamed by Russian *anti-Semites*, many Jews made a fresh exodus, 1882–1911, primarily to the United States—the doors of most European countries, and of the *Ottoman Empire*, remaining closed to them.

Belarus was again a locale of *Great Power* warfare in *World War I*, during which the *eastern front* snaked through its territory. Much of Belarus was lost to Germany by the *Bolsheviks* in the *Treaty of Brest-Litovsk* (March 3, 1918), but returned to Russian control upon Germany's defeat by the Western *Allied and Associated Powers* in November 1918. It became an *autonomous republic* within the Soviet Union in 1922. Belarus was overrun and occupied by German troops again during *World War II*, a time when its people suffered all the terrors of Nazi occupation, but in which some also turned on their own and against the Jews, cooperating in the Nazi *Holocaust*. After the war its territory was much expanded at the expense of Poland. It held (nominally) one of the three seats in the *United Nations General Assembly* granted the Soviet Union in 1945 in *compensation* for the automatic majority then enjoyed by the United States.

Modern Belarus is ethnically and culturally closer to Russia than is even Ukraine and does not have a strong *nationalist* or *secessionist* movement. Yet, because the Soviet Union broke up along existing internal borders in 1991, according to the principle of *uti possidetis*—and somewhat to their own surprise—Belorussians became independent and found themselves in control of a large nuclear arsenal in the bargain. Belarus subsequently agreed to hand over all nuclear weapons to Moscow and to abide by the *START* agreements. It retied its economy to Russia's with a 1993 trade agreement and remained in the ruble zone. During the first five years of independence its unreformed economy stagnated, until it collapsed in 1994. In 1996 Belarus and Russia signed a *union of sovereign states* treaty in name only, because it did not seek to extinguish the *international personality* of Belarus, which continued a separate, *sovereign* existence. From 1994 Belarus was governed by former *Communists* and *apparatchiki*, under President Aleksandr Lukashenko. By 2001 it had made almost no progress toward economic reconstruction after seven decades of Soviet mismanagement and fell behind most other East European countries except similarly badly governed Ukraine.

Belgian Congo. Former name of the colony and, later, the Republic of the Congo. *See also Congo.*

Belgium. Belgium rests on a historic invasion plain. As a result, for more than 2,000 years it was the possession of various conquerors: Romans, Franks, Burgundians, Spaniards, Austrians, French, and Germans. Belgium emerged from medieval *Flanders* under *Habsburg* dominion. During the *Eighty Years' War* Belgium split from the Dutch Republic and became the core of the *Spanish Netherlands*. In 1714 Belgium was ceded to Austria and renamed the *Austrian Netherlands*. It was rejoined to the *Netherlands* as part of the general settlement of the *Congress of Vienna*. Belgium became the first region on the continent to *industrialize* along the new, English lines. It had abundant resources, a long tradition of industry, and was physically and politically close to Britain. Belgium revolted against Dutch rule in 1830, becoming an independent constitutional *monarchy* in 1831, guaranteed by the Great Powers in general and Great Britain in particular.

Belgium then developed as one of the most advanced industrial societies on the continent. It escaped the conflict that afflicted other European states during the *revolutions of 1848*. Domestically, Belgium must perpetually balance the interests of Flemish (Dutch-speaking) and Walloon (French-speaking) *ethnic groups*. An unusual international position as *buffer state* in the nineteenth century was sustained by a British guarantee of Belgian *neutrality* issued in the *Treaty of London* (1839), reaffirmed during the *Franco-Prussian War* (1870–1871). It was invoked by London in August 1914, when German troops invaded as part of the *Schlieffen Plan*, pillaging towns and massacring civilians. Belgium fought bravely and well during *World War I*. It again tried to cleave to neutrality in the *interwar years*, refusing cooperative defensive efforts such as extension of the *Maginot Line* along the Franco-Belgian border. Belgium was invaded by Germany anyway in 1940. Its surrender after just 18 days cut off Anglo-French armies and forced a mass evacuation from *Dunkirk*. It was occupied during most of *World War II*.

Liberated in 1944–1945, Belgium subsequently abandoned its historic neutrality. It joined the *BENELUX*, participated in the *European Recovery Program*, and ultimately joined NATO. It sent a small contingent to fight in the *Korean Conflict*. Belgium also participated in United Nations *peacekeeping* operations. Its colonial practices in the Belgian Congo (Zaire) ranked with the very worst when King *Leopold II* had personal control (1885–1908). Belgium abandoned the Congo in 1960, but intervened several times after that. It was the *mandate* power in *Rwanda* and *Burundi* (then *Ruanda-Urundi*) before their independence. From 1991 to 1994 Belgium supported the Hutu government in Rwanda, pulling out when massacres of Tutsi began. Despite such African distractions, the main lines of its foreign policy concern Europe, as defined by membership in NATO and the EU.

Suggested Readings: Paul W. Schroeder, *The Transformation of European Politics, 1763–1848* (1994); A.J.P. Taylor, *The Struggle for Mastery in Europe, 1848–1918* (1954; 1971).

Belize. Formerly British Honduras. This area was settled by *Maya*, but their cities had returned to the jungle by the time *Cortés* and his *conquistadores* surveyed the coast. It was not settled by Europeans until English *pirates* set up a base at Roatán Island in the Gulf of Honduras in 1642 to harass shipping along the *Spanish Main* and supply forest workers harvesting the rich jungle timbers of Belize. In the 1660s these foresters established a permanent mainland colony at the mouth of the Belize River. Spain acknowledged all English claims in the Caribbean, except for Belize, in 1670. The modern state was, before its independence, the last British *colony* on the American mainland. It secured independence in 1981, after which Britain kept a garrison in the sparsely populated country because Guatemala refused to *recognize* this new state and laid claim to nearly 5,000 square miles of Belize, which it insisted had been wrongly ceded to Great Britain in 1859; some Guatemalans maintained that all Belize should be annexed. In 1991, with an improved security climate in Central America in general, Guatemala finally extended full *recognition*. Britain announced it could not afford its garrison any longer and pulled out on January 1, 1994. Belize thereafter relied on the United States to deter its immediate neighbors from seizing its territory. In 2000, Guatemala and Belize agreed to take their border dispute before the *OAS*.

belligerency. (1) The actual or legal condition of being at *war*. (2) *Recognition* of a *state of war* within a society, which has the effect of giving international status to *insurgents*. This falls short of full recognition but still carries certain rights. For instance, the *Confederacy* was treated as a belligerent by Britain for purposes of trade, but was never formally recognized.

belligerent/belligerent community. In *international law*, any political community actually engaged in making *war*, whether a *sovereign* state or some subnational group. The term does not, however, cover strictly private armies or navies (or, since changes were made to the *Geneva Convention* of 1949 in a supplemental protocol, groups of *mercenaries*), whose activities the *community of nations* have declared to be illegal. *See also recognition.*

belligerent equality, doctrine of. In *international law*, the position that the protections and obligations of the *laws of war* apply equally to all *belligerents*, regardless of the underlying merits of the *casus belli* of any party to a given conflict. This approach assumes the moral equivalence of belligerents, for purposes of applying the law. It thus leaves issues of the rights and wrongs of starting a conflict to other aspects of the law (the *jus ad bellum*) or to moral argument and to history. Instead, it concentrates on the actual conduct of war (*jus in bello*) in an effort thereby to improve the chance of ameliorating its worst features. *See also aggression; armed conflict; just war tradition; state of war.*

belligerent rights. The legal rights accruing to a state that is formally at *war*. These include rights to *visit and search*; to seize *contraband* trade with the enemy; to attack and destroy (under the *laws of war*) the productive capabilities, military forces, and equipment of the enemy; and to have its soldiers treated in accordance with the *Geneva Conventions*. *See also angary; blockade; booty; capture;* levée en masse; *neutral rights; occupation; prize; requisition.*

bellum justum. *See just war tradition.*

Belorussia. *See Belarus.*

BENELUX. (1) Shorthand for Belgium, the Netherlands, and Luxembourg. (2) A *customs union* negotiated in 1944–1945, set up in 1948, and composed of those three states.

Beneš, Eduard (1884–1948). Czech statesman and twice president of Czechoslovakia. He spent *World War I* as a refugee in Paris, where he worked closely with *Tomáš Masaryk*. From 1918 to 1935 he served as foreign minister (also as premier, 1921–1922). He attended the *Paris Peace Conference* and supported formation of the *League of Nations*. He was instrumental in coordinating Czechoslovak policy within the *Little Entente*. From 1935 to 1938 he was president, resigning in disgust and bitter disappointment over the outcome of the *Munich Conference*. During *World War II* he headed the Czechoslovak *government-in-exile* in Paris, moving to London when Paris fell in 1940. He returned to Czechoslovakia in May 1945, after its liberation from the Germans. He served as president again, 1946–1948, but he was never trusted by, and could not sufficiently please, *Stalin*. Beneš resigned in June 1948 after a Soviet-sponsored *coup*.

Bengal. A large state in eastern India, occasionally independent during more fragmented periods of Indian history. A *famine* there in 1769–1770 took perhaps 10 million lives. Bengal broke free of central *Mughal* control as that empire collapsed, then it fended off *Maratha* raids. It ultimately fell to troops of the *East India Company*. It was divided by Lord *Curzon* in 1905, over fierce nationalist protest that gave impetus both to a *boycott* of British goods and creation of the *Muslim League*. Bengal was reunited in 1911. It was the main base of political support for *Subhas Bose* before and during *World War II*, when it also experienced a terrible famine that took some three million lives. It was divided in 1947 between India and *East Pakistan* (later *Bangladesh*).

Suggested Reading: P. J. Marshall, *Bengal—the British Bridgehead. Eastern India, 1740–1828* (1987).

Ben-Gurion, David, né Gruen (1886–1973). Israeli statesman. In 1906 he moved as a *Zionist* immigrant to *Palestine* from his native Poland. He was deported by the *Ottomans* to the *neutral* United States because of his pro-*Allied* sympathies during *World War I*. Later in the war he helped raise and joined the Jewish Legion to fight alongside the British against the Ottomans. In the 1930s he chaired the World Zionist Organization, headed the *Jewish Agency*, and was a key figure in Israel's armed, political, and diplomatic struggle for statehood. He became Israel's first premier, 1948–1953 and 1955–1963. He led the country during the first two *Arab-Israeli Wars* and aligned it closely with major Western powers, first France then the United States. He authorized the founding of *Mossad* in 1951. He died at an advanced age in retirement on a kibbutz.

Benin, Kingdom of. A West African *city-state* centered on the walled Edo city of Benin, not to be confused with the modern republic, located farther to the west. In the thirteenth century (the precise date is unknown), Benin adopted a dynasty from the prestigious and ancient *Yoruba* city of Ife, to fill the position of Oba, and settled into a stable, quiet period. In the mid-fifteenth century, however, it began to expand and to trade *slaves* to the Portuguese (who arrived in 1486) on *São Tomé and Principe*. From c. 1520 Benin chose a policy of *isolationism* from the European traders who offered goods along the coast in exchange for *slaves* and *gold*. It would remain isolated in this way for nearly 200 years. However, within Africa it maintained lively trade and political relationships with the *Yoruba* states, toward which it expanded. By the end of the sixteenth century Benin governed most Edo as well as some *Ibo* and Yoruba areas in the Niger delta. However, Benin could not withstand the larger historic forces that coursed through West Africa, and its territory was thus incorporated into the British *protectorate* of Nigeria after a British military expedition was launched to capture Benin City in

149

1897. Benin is widely known for the high quality of its art, especially sculptures and brasses, much of which was hauled away by the British.

Suggested Reading: Allan Ryder, *Benin and the Europeans, 1485–1897* (1969).

Benin, Republic of. This territory (under the name Dahomey) was colonized by France in the late nineteenth century and merged into *French West Africa* in 1904. It achieved *independence* in 1960, led by an elite with origins in the return of former *slaves* from Brazil. A *coup* in 1972 led to a *Marxist-Leninist* regime in 1974 and a name change to Benin in 1975. Under the coup leader, Ahmed Kérékou, Benin turned abruptly away from France, suffered economic collapse, and witnessed a sharp rise in *human rights* abuses. In 1989, as Kérékou's *Soviet bloc* allies collapsed, he renounced Marxism-Leninism and appealed for Western *aid*. In 1991 elections, he was defeated anyway, by Nicéphore Soglo. The remainder of the 1990s was spent in electoral jockeying between these two men, with Kérékou returning to the presidency in 1996 and Soglo's wife leading the parliamentary opposition to him from 1999. Armed banditry in the countryside emerged as a major problem, alongside endemic poverty, trafficking in child slaves, and chronic lack of development *infrastructure*, problems all left unresolved by the musical chairs of Benin's capital politics.

Bentham, Jeremy (1748–1832). English utilitarian philosopher. A child prodigy who entered the University of Oxford at age twelve to study law, his critical focus was on law-making in a democratic polity. He based his critique of law on the pleasure principle at the center of utilitarian moral reasoning: that the core function of public law is to distribute punishments and rewards in a balanced way, so as to secure the greatest moral and public good (the greatest happiness) for the greatest number in a given society. In the practice of too many utilitarian philosophers, however, this principle reduced to the moral crudity of rarified efforts to *quantify* human happiness. Bentham's impact on international relations was two-pronged and powerful, as he was the leading intellectual of the day in the greatest power of the Age, the *British Empire*. His was an indirect influence, stemming from passionate endorsement of *free trade* and economic (though not social) *laissez-faire*. That was the positive side. However, he also fomented a powerful opposition to creating formal international organizations among states, for which there was some movement under way on the Continent and already considerable need. He was also actively involved in early peace societies that focused on a singularly narrow, material, and market-driven solution to the problem of *war*. Bentham's fully dressed mummy resides at University College, London, which he founded, and where it is trundled out to sit as a dinner guest once per year.

Berber. The Hamitic peoples of North Africa living along the *Barbary Coast* and penetrating as well into the Sahara desert. Their peak of influence in world history came when, united under the Almohads ruling from Marrakesh from the twelfth century, they governed all the Maghreb and most of Spain. *See also caliph; Maghreb.*

Berchtesgaden. A Bavarian resort used as a southern headquarters by *Adolf Hitler*. The *Allies* feared it would be used for a last-ditch, suicidal defense by the *SS* and other *Nazi* fanatics. It was not.

Beria, Lavrenti Pavlovich (1899–1953). A longtime member of the CHEKA and *OGPU*, Beria headed the *NKVD* from 1938, overseeing with relish its use of *forced labor*, executions, *show trials*, and *purges*. He was notorious for using his police powers to satisfy gross sexual perversions, and was greatly feared by other Soviet leaders. After *Stalin's* death (March 5, 1953) he briefly joined a ruling troika with *Malenkov* and *Molotov*. He contemplated various radical departures from *Stalinism*, including restricting the role of the *Communist Party*, partially dismantling the terror system he had devised and managed, and permitting greater cultural and administrative autonomy to the subject nationalities of the Soviet Union. His most radical idea concerned the two Germanies, which he proposed to permit to unite into a single, but *neutral*, state. Unrest under *Ulbricht* persuaded Beria that the Soviet Union would be better off with a neutral, united Germany than a sullen and unstable satellite. His ambitions and proposals alarmed his colleagues and he was arrested and shot, but only after being made subject of a *treason* trial and absurd charge that he was a British spy, of a kind whose techniques he had himself pioneered and perfected.

Suggested Reading: Pavel Sudoplatov et al., *Special Tasks* (1994).

Bering Sea. The north Pacific Ocean, next to the *Aleutians*.

Bering Strait. The passage between the Pacific and Arctic Oceans that separates *Alaska* from *Siberia*.

Berlin. The Prussian, and later German imperial, capital. Berlin was raised to international political, though not yet cultural, prominence by *Frederick the Great*. After the French victory over Prussia at *Jena* in 1806, Berlin was razed to the ground by *Napoleon*. During the *revolutions of 1848* it experienced potato riots and political unrest. It was the main scene of the failed *Spartacist* revolt in 1918. On the international cultural scene, in the 1920s Berlin earned a reputation for decadence and avant-garde artistry. *Hitler* planned to rebuild it as an imperial capital, but ended up destroying most of it instead. Berlin was occupied by Allied armies from May 8, 1945 to September 8, 1994. It was made the German capital again in 1999, displacing the temporary West

German capital at Bonn. *See also Berlin, division of; Berlin airlift; Berlin Wall; East Berlin; West Berlin.*

Suggested Reading: David Large, *Berlin* (2000).

Berlin airlift (1948–1949). The Soviet Union *blockaded* the road and rail links to the western half of the city, from June 1948 to May 1949, trying to force the Western powers to vacate their *occupation zones*. In the first great *crisis* and test of the *Cold War*, the city's inhabitants were kept alive, warm, fed, and free, by a daunting display of *air power* and an impressive demonstration of American and Western resolve. *See also Lucius Clay; George Marshall; Harry S Truman.*

Berlin-Baghdad railway. The British feared that this project, chartered by a German company in 1899, represented a strategic German push and military threat to the *Middle East* that aimed at confirming Turkey's dependence on Germany—it was to pass through *Constantinople*. At the worst, some British feared it ultimately aimed at their position in India. More cynical observers saw it as an opportunity to ease strains on Britain and France by entangling Russia, which also opposed German involvement in a middle eastern railway, with Germany.

Berlin, Battle of (1945). The last major battle in the European *theater of war* during *World War II*. On one side was the assembled might of the *Red Army*, driving toward final victory against the once-feared but by 1945 only hated and despised *Nazi* enemy. The defenders of Berlin were made up of fanatic *Waffen SS*, scattered *Wehrmacht* units, and a hodge-podge of conscripted veterans of *World War I*, including old men of the home guard and 12-year-old boys of the Hitler Youth, alongside units of Baltic, French, Dutch, and other *fascist* volunteers. The Soviets had massive superiority in *air power, artillery, armor,* and troops, by a ratio of at least 10 to 1. Nevertheless, German and fascist resistance was ferocious, and the Soviets paid a bloody price for the honor of delivering *Hitler's* capital to *Stalin.* Taking the city from its defenders cost the Red Army more than 300,000 casualties, among them 100,000 dead, including casualties among Soviet all-women regiments. As the Soviets advanced, there was much rape and killing of German civilians. Through it all, Hitler brooded in his Führer bunker deep beneath the rubble, ordering mirage armies to counterattack this street or district, or break out from some Baltic envelopment and fight their way through to Berlin. Lastly, he ordered the total demolition of Germany itself—of all *infrastructure* and facilities—as the German nation, he said, had proven "unworthy" of his greatness. This order was countermanded, at long last, though still secretly, by his architect and minister for armaments and munitions, *Albert Speer.* Trapped underground, Hitler married his lover, Eva Braun (1912–1945). Then he and she, along with several top Nazis, committed suicide—*Goebbels* and his wife poisoned their six children first, even as Hitler killed his favorite dog. The conquest of eastern Germany, which culminated in the Battle of Berlin, was accompanied by mass rapes and murder of civilians by Soviet troops on a scale so vast that some historians argue the burning memory of it was a contributing factor in subsequently cementing the West German public to *NATO*.

Suggested Reading: Georgi K. Zhukov, *Memoirs of Marshal Zhukov* (1969).

Berlin, Conference of (1884–1885). It was hosted by *Bismarck* and attended by thirteen European powers, with the United States present as an observer. It drew and confirmed a number of borders in Africa, including that of the Belgian Congo; *internationalized* the Niger and Congo Rivers, checking British monopoly control of interior trade on both; and issued a pious—and only partly humbug—resolution calling for an end to *slavery* and the *slave trade* within Africa. It broke up Lower Guinea into *Dahomey* (France), *Togo* (Germany), and *Kamerun* (Germany); gave Gabon to France and Congo to Leopold II of Belgium; confirmed German claims to *Tanganyika* and *German Southwest Africa* (Namibia); affirmed British control of Egypt; and in general both curtailed British ambitions and forced London to assert direct colonial control in several areas where before it had governed with detachment. Its great accomplishment, from Europe's perspective, was to resolve simmering colonial disputes short of *Great Power* war by requiring formal notification and "effective occupation" of any new claims to establish *protectorates* or *colonies* in Africa. However, few Africans were invited, present, or represented, and among those who were, Zanzibar's claim to the eastern Congo was rejected in favor of a personal claim by Belgium's Leopold II. The Conference thus may be justly criticized for its arbitrary character and gross indifference to local conditions, especially ethnic divisions that straddled the borders defined in Berlin. Even so, most of the borders set at Berlin remain in place, accepted as legitimate *boundaries* in the Charter of the *Organization of African Unity* out of fear that to reopen the issue would *balkanize* the continent even further and lead to untold bloodshed in multiple wars of *secession*. On the ground it is an entirely different matter, as many formal political divisions in Africa are rejected by the peoples who live astride them. *See also Henry Morton Stanley; scramble for Africa; Tippu Tip.*

Suggested Readings: J. D. Fage, *A History of Africa* (1995); Roland Oliver, *The African Experience* (1991).

Berlin, Congress of (1878). A meeting of the European *Great Powers* called by *Bismarck* to revise the *Treaty of San Stefano* and address the regional *balance of power* in southern Europe, which had been unsettled by the accelerating decline of the *Ottoman Empire* and rebellion of several of its Christian provinces. An *autonomous* Bulgarian principality was created but cut back drastically in size from the ambitions of Bulgarian nationalists; Macedonia was returned to Turkey; *independence* of Serbia, Montenegro, and Rumania was formally *recognized*; and Russian control of the *Caucasus* was confirmed. Britain gained bases in Cyprus, and Austria received *Bosnia-Herzegovina* as *compensation* for Russian gains. Although stability returned for several decades after this settlement, final resolution of the *Eastern Question* was postponed to the aftermath of Ottoman defeat in *World War I*. Rewarding Austria and Britain for a victory over Turkey won with Russian blood caused deep resentment in Russia and worsened its relations with Germany and Austria.

Berlin, division of. At the end of *World War II* it was decided to divide the German capital into three *occupation zones*, American, British, and Soviet, in tandem with the larger division of Germany agreed at *Yalta*. A French zone was later carved out of the American and British zones. By 1949 the three western zones were united to form *West Berlin*, but the West German capital was moved to Bonn. The Soviet zone became *East Berlin*, and capital of *East Germany*. The failure to resolve the legal status of Berlin led to several crises: the *Berlin airlift* in 1948–1949; deadly rioting in 1953; Soviet denunciation of the occupation agreements in 1958; and building of the *Berlin Wall* in 1961. This latter event occasioned one of the most serious crises of the entire *Cold War*. Khrushchev once said of the exposed nature of West Berlin: "Berlin is the testes of the West. Every time I want to make the West scream, I squeeze on Berlin." Tension over the city's anomalous four-power status was eased in the early 1970s by agreements reached through West German *Ostpolitik* and under *détente*. Formal *recognition* of the two Germanies and agreement within the CSCE process to permit visitations and facilitate *family reunification* further eased tension. With the fall of the Berlin Wall in November 1989, the city—as well as Germany—was made whole again. In 1991 the Bundestag voted to move the German capital from Bonn back to Berlin, but this did not take place until 1999.

Berlin Wall. It was known cynically by its builders as the "antifascist defense barrier." The *East German* regime planned to build a wall between itself and *West Berlin* (and *West Germany*) as early as 1952, but *Khrushchev* opposed this. By mid-1961, however, the refugee outflow from *East Germany* had become a deluge: nearly 3.5 million left after 1949, or nearly one-sixth of the population; more than 200,000 fled west in the first six months of 1961 alone, mainly through West Berlin. On August 13, 1961, East Germany began constructing a fortified wall dividing the city of Berlin and reinforced its existing fortifications all along the intra-German border running from the Baltic to Czechoslovakia. The Wall that arose in time was a several-layers-deep barrier of concrete, barbed wire, watch towers, dogs, hidden mines, tripwire machine guns, and guards ordered to shoot to kill. Its main purpose was to stop the hemorrhage of East Germany's population to the West. At one point, Soviet and American tanks faced off at Checkpoint Charlie in the American zone, and war was a real possibility. However, the Western powers chose not to challenge this clear violation of four-power control out of fear the crisis might escalate to a full *NATO* versus *Warsaw Pact* confrontation. *Kennedy* later went to Berlin and declared that he and all free people everywhere were spiritual Berliners ("Ich bin ein Berliner").

The Wall succeeded in its immediate purpose of stanching the outflow of population, but at the cost of open concession that the East German regime had no real *legitimacy* among its people. Through a variety of ingenious methods, several thousand managed to escape in the years that followed; several hundred more were killed in the attempt. In time, the Wall achieved an impressive height and apparent permanence. It served for many in the West as a symbol of what was at stake in the *Cold War. Ronald Reagan* went to Berlin in 1987 to challenge *Mikhail Gorbachev* to tear down the Wall and end the era of Cold War confrontation. It was a decisive moment in the late Cold War. Even so, it was a colossal shock when the Wall and the regime that built it collapsed—peacefully—starting on November 9, 1989, after the Communist government announced it was opening the intra-German border. That day, newly made gates were opened, but within 24 hours the Wall was breached in hundreds of places by hundreds of thousands, from both sides, most of whom ignored the gates, with the more energetic dancing atop the broken Wall. In the days that followed many miles of Wall were torn down, by hand and by machine. Germany donated a large piece to the United States in symbolic gratitude for its long-term support for Berlin during the Cold War. It stands on display at Westminster College in Fulton, Missouri, site of *Winston Churchill's* famous *Iron Curtain* speech.

Bermuda. A quiet British *colony* in the Atlantic, off the coast of the Carolinas. During *World War II*, the United Kingdom leased a naval and air base in Bermuda to the United States.

Bernadotte, (Count) Folke (1895–1948). Swedish statesman. He tried to *mediate* peace in *World War I* and again during *World War II*. In 1944 in Berlin he met *Himmler*, who was supported by *Ribbentrop*, but who did not inform *Hitler* of the negotiations. They discussed the possible transfer of prisoners in the *concentration camps* to *Red Cross* authority, but failed to reach agreement. In a second meeting, held with the *Battle of Berlin* raging, Bernadotte affirmed to Himmler that the *Allies* would accept nothing less than *unconditional surrender.* Hitler was enraged when he heard of their meeting, and ordered Himmler shot for *treason.* Bernadotte was later appointed by the United Nations to mediate the *partition* of *Palestine.* He was assassinated by Jewish zealots (the *Stern Gang*) in September 1948, in the midst of the *First Arab-Israeli War.*

Bernadotte, Jean-Baptiste Jules (1763–1844). King of Sweden, 1818–1844. Although born a noble, he supported the *French Revolution*, serving loyally in its army. He rose to become one of *Napoleon I*'s marshals. He fought well at *Austerlitz* (1805) but not so well at *Jena* (1806). And he failed at Wagram (1809). He was elected heir apparent to the Swedish throne (1810), with Napoleon's approval. He took his new loyalties seriously, and arranged Sweden's entry into the war against France in 1813, in exchange for acquisition of Norway from Denmark (a French ally) and to regain Swedish Pomerania. He led a Swedish army against his erstwhile commander, seeing action at *Leipzig* (1813). He was made king (Charles XIV) in 1818, founding the dynasty of Ponte Corvo.

Bernstein, Eduard (1850–1932). German *Marxist* considered by many to have founded Marxist *revisionism*, which both developed and fed into the major streams of European *social democracy*. Before 1901 he lived for many years in the United Kingdom, where he was influenced by Fabian reformers. He rejected *revolution* in favor of reform and was elected to the *Reichstag* several times after 1902. He opposed Germany's *declarations of war* in 1914.

Bessarabia. Long a possession of the *Ottoman Empire*, this disputed province was ceded to Russia in the Treaty of Bucharest, which ended the *Russo-Turkish War of 1806–1812* (May 28, 1812).

Parts of Bessarabia changed hands between Rumania and Russia several times between the *Crimean War* and 1920, during moments of Russian weakness that followed defeats in wars with other *Great Powers*. It was retaken by Russia, along with *Bukovina*, by *Stalin* in 1940, while *Hitler* was busy fighting Britain and France in the west. It was returned to Rumania during *World War II* after being overrun by *Axis* armies, was retaken by Russia in 1944, and was incorporated into the Soviet Moldavian Republic after the war, with portions added to Ukraine. When this republic became independent as Moldova upon the *extinction* of the *Soviet Union* in 1991, fighting broke out in Bessarabia, with some Russian rogue units supporting ethnic Russians from *Trans-Dniestra* against ethnic Rumanians.

Bethmann-Hollweg, Theobald von (1856–1921). German chancellor, 1909–1917. Although he pursued a romantic, prewar *Weltpolitik* and urged Austrian toughness during the *mobilization crisis*, he was startled and angered that Britain *declared war* in 1914 over German violation of the guarantee of Belgian *neutrality* of the *Treaty of London* (1839). He said: "Just for a word, 'neutrality,' a word which in wartime has so often been disregarded, just for a scrap of paper, Great Britain is going to make war." He was wrong. Britain made war for a host of reasons, including to prevent Germany's *hegemony* and to preserve the *balance of power*—preserving Belgian neutrality served those purposes but was not of itself Britain's main *war aim*. It was fear of Russia, not Britain, that drove his fateful decisions and pushed him down the war path, whose unforeseeable consequences he feared only slightly less than he feared Germany being surpassed by Russia. Resisting fierce pressure from *Tirpitz*, for two years Bethmann-Hollweg argued against a naval policy of *unrestricted submarine warfare*, out of fear that it would bring the United States into *World War I* and hence lose the war for Germany. He was pushed aside by the military in July 1917. They sensed victory coming in Russia and wanted to break the stalemate on the *western front* by launching a full-scale *U-boat* campaign and then a spring offensive. Within a year his fears about the deadly U.S. impact on the war were confirmed. *See also William Jennings Bryan; Edward Grey; Lusitania notes.*

Bevin, Ernest (1881–1951). British foreign secretary, 1945–1951. After serving in *Winston Churchill's* wartime cabinet, he became foreign secretary in the postwar Labour government. He oversaw the peace treaties signed after *World War II* with the minor members of the *Axis* coalition (Bulgaria, Hungary, and Rumania) and with Italy. He coordinated closely with the United States over occupation policy in Germany and in the decision to rebuild and rearm West Germany and form *NATO*. He was responsible for coordinating mutual assistance under the *Marshall Plan*. He approved independence for India and Pakistan, setting the *British Empire* on the road to rapid *decolonization*. He helped initiate the *Colombo Plan*, but clung to the illusion that Britain had special *Commonwealth* ties, and so was more cautious than the United States, France, or Germany about the prospect of European federalism and political *integration*. He handed the issue of the British *mandate* in *Palestine* over to the *United Nations*, rather than devising a British solution or taking responsibility for *partition*.

bey. Turkish. "beg" (lord). (1) A title of later *Mamluk*, and other, provincial governors in the *Ottoman Empire*. (2) An honorific title of Tunisian and other Muslim rulers in the *Maghreb*. In Tunis, the bey was technically subordinate to the *dey*. The latter office was abolished early in the eighteenth century, when a powerful bey decided he should rule in name as well as fact. Almost the opposite occurred in Algiers, where the dey overthrew the bey.

BfV (*Bundesamt für Verfassungsschutz*). The (West) German security service charged with *counterintelligence*. During the *Cold War* it was often penetrated by the East German *HvA*. For instance, in 1954 the head of the BfV, Otto John, defected to East Germany. After the Cold War, one of BfV's major concerns was to intercept smuggled *plutonium* coming from Russia for sale in the *Middle East* and elsewhere. *See also BND.*

Bhopal disaster (December 3, 1983). The worst non-nuclear industrial accident in history occurred when toxic gas leaked from a chemical refinery in this Indian city, killing 3,500, seriously injuring 50,000, and affecting the

157

health of several hundred thousand more. Compensation from Union Carbide took a number of years to arrange. *See also Chernobyl.*

Bhutan. This small, mountain kingdom was ruled from Tibet in the sixteenth century. Under *Buddhist* rule, it followed a policy of strict *isolationism* for centuries. It came under British influence during the nineteenth century and was made a *protectorate* in 1910, three years after a monarchy had been established, displacing the Buddhist theocracy. After British withdrawal from the subcontinent, Bhutan was given its independence in 1949. It quickly became dependent on India, around which it continues to orbit today. The 1980s witnessed a revival of isolationist tendencies, starting with cultural policy and expulsion of Indian laborers. Bhutan is home to many refugees from Tibet and has as well its own Tibetan and Hindu minorities.

Bhutto, Benazir (b. 1953). Prime minister of Pakistan, 1988–1990, 1993–1996; daughter of *Zulfikar Ali Bhutto.* In 1986 she returned from exile to lead the opposition to dictator *Muhammad Zia ul-Haq.* In elections after Zia's death, she became a rare thing in international history—a woman *head of government* in an *Islamic* country. Her brief tenure was marked by a flood of three million refugees from Afghanistan. She tried to patch relations with India and generally adopted a moderate foreign policy line. Dismissed in 1990 under charges of abuse of power and corruption, she was an influential leader of the opposition until her return to power as prime minister after elections in 1993. In 1996 she was again overthrown, this time on charges of corruption and conspiring to murder her own brother, from whom she was alienated and who was a political rival. She and her husband were convicted of corruption charges in absentia in 1999. It is difficult to know if the verdict was just or not.

Bhutto, Zulfikar Ali (1928–1979). Pakistani foreign minister, 1958–1966; president, 1971–1973; prime minister, 1973–1977. He improved relations with China and the United States, but resigned over the government's provocative policy on *Kashmir.* He personally encouraged the mass slaughter of Bengalis in *East Pakistan* that began on March 26, 1971 and led to the loss of half of Pakistan. When *Bangladesh* became independent, he became president of West Pakistan. He withdrew Pakistan from the *Commonwealth* when Britain *recognized* Bangladesh. He moderated postwar tensions with India in the Simla Agreement of 1972, which set a de facto Kashmir *boundary.* Subsequent economic failure and rampant corruption led to riots, a grossly rigged election victory, and an anti-Bhutto *coup* in 1977. He was tried and hanged by the *junta,* which replaced him—on charges of complicity in political murders of opposition leaders—despite vigorous international efforts to have his sentence commuted. *See also Zia ul-Haq.*

Biafra. *See Nigerian Civil War.*

bicycle theory. A trite metaphor employed by political scientists rather than a *theory* of any substance or rigor. It suggests that international *negotiations* are like riding a bicycle, in that, when forward momentum slows, talks become unsteady and may collapse.

Bidault, Georges (1899–1982). *Resistance* leader; French statesman; founder of the MRP; prime minister in 1946 and again 1949–1950; foreign minister 1944, 1947, and 1953–1954. During his frequent visits to high office he was a supporter of European cooperation and *integration.* He strongly opposed in-dependence for Algeria, however, even after settler *terrorist* attacks in France. Charged with *treason,* he fled into exile, 1965–1968. Upon his return, he did not face trial.

bigemony. Social science *jargon,* journalistic slang, for the foolish idea, com-mon in the 1980s, that the preeminence and *integration* of the American and Japanese economies necessitated joint management of the world economy. Others referred to this notion by the even more awkward "Amerippon." *See also hegemony.*

Big Five. Immediately after *World War II:* the United States, the Soviet Union, Britain, France, and China.

Big Four. (1) In *World War I* and at the *Paris Peace Conference:* *Vittorio Orlando, Lloyd George, Georges Clemenceau,* and *Woodrow Wilson.* (2) In *World War II:* Britain, China, the Soviet Union, and the United States. Al-ternately, *Winston Churchill, Chiang Kai-shek, Joseph Stalin,* and *Franklin Roo-sevelt.* Churchill thought the inclusion of China in that grouping, in the rhetoric usually and too casually employed by Roosevelt, was "an absolute farce."

Big Three. (1) During *World War II,* the United States, the Soviet Union, and Britain. (2) *Franklin Roosevelt, Joseph Stalin,* and *Winston Churchill.*

Bikini Atoll. Part of the *Marshall Islands* chain. It was the site of U.S. *at-mospheric testing* of *nuclear weapons,* 1946–1958. The tests left a great deal of fallout, and almost left no Bikini at all.

bilateral. Any arrangement, *dispute,* interaction, or *treaty* between just two states. *See also multilateral.*

billets. Living quarters for troops in the field.

billiard ball model. A crude, social science image of world politics as analogous to a game of surreal billiards, in which collisions occur among balls (*states*) of varying weight and momentum (*power*), leading to outcomes decided by forces of *action and reaction*, rather than internal events or conscious decision-making. It is sometimes critically held up by political scientists as an image (caricature, really) of the so-called state-centric approach to world affairs, in which states are seen as unitary *rational actors* and little or no account is taken of other factors that determine outcomes.

binary weapons. A type of *chemical weapon* in which agents not in themselves lethal, but highly toxic when mixed, are stored in separate compartments in a warhead (or bomb or shell) and mixed upon firing or detonation. They are considered less hazardous to store and transport than premixed weapons.

binding resolution (of the Security Council). *See resolution; Security Council.*

bin Laden, Usama (b. 1957). *Terrorist* and *Islamist* agitator; co-founder of *al Qaeda*. He was born into exceptional privilege in Saudi Arabia, one of 52 children of a Yemeni billionaire contractor. His family was closely connected to the House of Saud, making its fortune from oil money funneled into building *infrastructure* needed to service the expanding *haj* to *Mecca* and Medina. Like most Saudis, bin Laden was raised within the extreme puritanical interpretation of *Islam* purveyed by the *Wahhabi* sect, which sustained political and religious authority in Saudi Arabia since the founding of that state. Nonetheless, also like many a wealthy Saudi, as a young man he reportedly often visited the nightclubs and brothels of Beirut. Bin Laden lost his political virginity at age 22, while raising money for the Afghan *mujahadeen* fighting Soviet invaders during the *Afghan-Soviet War*. In 1984 he moved to Peshawar, Pakistan, where he formed an organization (Makhtab al Khadimat) to recruit Arabs to fight in Afghanistan. In 1986 bin Laden set up his first independent training camp, called al Masadah ("The Lion's Den"). In 1988 he merged his expanding organization—which he financed largely through criminal activity, skimming donations made to Islamic charities, and from his large inheritance—with Ayman al-Zawahiri's *Egyptian Islamic Jihad*, to form al Qaeda.

His early anger over the Soviet Union's invasion of Afghanistan was later exceeded by hatred for the United States owing to its deployment of troops—including women and Jews, both of whom he despised—to Saudi Arabia during the *Gulf War*. The fact that the United States and its *Gulf coalition* allies (also including female and Jewish soldiers) thereby saved his homeland from likely invasion and dominance by the vicious, murderous, and wholly secular regime of *Saddam Hussein* of Iraq, which had in fact attacked Saudi Arabia with Scud missiles, was utterly lost on him and his *fanatic* followers. Bin Laden moved to Sudan in 1991, where a fundamentalist regime that had taken power in the north provided protection in return for payoffs and technical advice. While there, he directed the first al Qaeda attacks against American targets: his operatives helped kill eighteen U.S. Rangers in Somalia, whose mission was to bring humanitarian relief to millions of starving and ill-governed Muslims; and possibly also in New York, where it is thought he helped to plan the first World Trade Center bombing in 1993. In 1994 Saudi Arabia revoked his citizenship and many members of his family publicly renounced him. In 1996 the *Clinton* administration declined Sudanese offers to extradite bin Laden, while encouraging Sudan to expel him. He returned to Afghanistan, where the *Taliban* had just taken power. There, he formed a symbiotic relationship with the despotic Taliban regime, itself formed of young men raised in the Wahhabi creed, trained with Saudi-funded madrassa (Koranic schools) in Pakistan. In 1998 bin Laden organized same day (August 7th) car-bombings of two U.S. embassies, in Nairobi, Kenya and Dar es Salaam, Tanzania. Some 244 were killed, most of whom were African bystanders (twelve Americans died); many hundreds more were injured, some quite severely. Clinton responded to this attack on sovereign U.S. interests with a handful of cruise missiles fecklessly and ineffectually fired into a pharmaceutical plant in Khartoum, Sudan, which he said was making chemical weapons for bin Laden (this was never proven), and into mostly empty al Qaeda training camps in rural Afghanistan. (That he did so on the same day that Ms. Monica Lewinsky was to testify in an ongoing investigation of charges against him of perjury and obstruction of justice severely undermined his credibility and that of the U.S. response.) Bin Laden was subsequently indicted for the embassy attacks along with 22 others, but no military effort was ever mounted to seize him from his Afghan cave fastness.

On October 12, 2000, bin Laden sponsored a motor launch attack against the *destroyer* U.S.S. Cole, carried out by a suicide squad in Yemen; seventeen U.S. sailors died. In public, Clinton again declared unbending resolve to find and punish the perpetrators. In private, he even signed several *findings* authorizing lethal force against bin Laden and other al Qaeda leaders. However, he repeatedly declined to put boots on the ground, as advised by the military. No overt or effective covert action was taken against al Qaeda during the remainder of his administration. This lack of response to the killing of American diplomatic and military personnel apparently deepened the image of America, in al Qaeda eyes as a paper tiger, which might be driven from the region by additional terrorist attacks and casualties—as it had once been driven from Lebanon during the *Reagan* administration. Trained as a civil engineer, bin Laden carefully planned the extraordinarily bold, as well as historically callous and destructive, attack of *September 11, 2001*, against the United States itself. However, he miscalculated the response of a new administration, of the American people, and indeed of the whole civilized world. Every nation in the world, with the exception of Saddam Hussein's Iraq, publicly condemned the deed, many lent direct military assistance, and dozens more provided financial, and other intelligence and cooperation. By the end of 2001, under President *George W. Bush*, the United States had responded with a carefully crafted and calibrated, and thoroughly successful, military destruction of the Taliban and all al Qaeda bases in Afghanistan; beginning a worldwide hunt for al Qaeda operatives and supporters. Nor had any uprising of support for al Qaeda shaken the Muslim world, as bin Laden hoped and expected. To the contrary, most Muslim states also cooperated with the United States in suppressing al Qaeda.

Suggested Reading: Peter Bergen, *Holy War, Inc.* (2001).

biological diversity. What is retained, genetically, through conservation of many species. Motives for seeking this range from commercial interests to scientific prudence to sheer romanticism. *See also Amazon Basin; Earth Summit; Global Environmental Facility.*

biological warfare and weapons. Bacteria, viruses, or toxins have long been used to kill or disable people, livestock, or crops for political purposes and in war. Contemporary biological (or germ) warfare agents include anthrax, black rust, blight, foot-and-mouth disease, plague, rice blast, and many others. Biological warfare is not new. Rome and other classical empires used dead animals to infect wells or streams servicing besieged towns; in Medieval Europe, plague rats and infected bodies were catapulted into walled towns. Before the *American Revolution*, the British commander on the Appalachian *frontier* considered sending the Indian tribes blankets infected with smallpox, though this plan was not carried out.

Starting in the early 1930s and continuing all through *World War II*, Japan used biological weapons against civilian and military concentrations throughout its occupied territories, working outward from biological warfare factories set up in 1932 in *Manchuria* by the ultranationalist surgeon, Shiro Ishii. He also set up and performed biological experiments on *prisoners of war* (POWs), at the infamous Unit 731. The documentation of these horrors is only partially public. The United States captured the Japanese archives at the close of World War II, but they were returned in 1958. Ever since, Japan has repressed the files. Based on what was microfilmed before their return, what is known is this. Japan conducted widespread germ warfare throughout China and Southeast Asia, including in Indonesia (Dutch East Indies), Burma, and Singapore, and also in several Russian communities on the Manchurian border around Harbin. The majority of casualties, probably on the order of several hundred thousand, were Chinese. Attacks were made with germ bombs containing anthrax, typhoid, and various other pathogens. Food supplies were deliberately contaminated, including candy used to infect children, and there was deliberate targeting of jungle tribes for complete extermination.

Chinese, Australian, British, and American POWs were deliberately infected so that Japanese "doctors" could examine the effects of various diseases. Many were then vivisected (dissected alive), their organs removed while their hearts were still pumping. At least 10,000 POWs were experimented on, perhaps ten times the number of people whom Josef Mengele and other *Nazi* "scientists" killed in comparably sadistic medical experiments at *Auschwitz*. The Japanese hoped to use their biological weapons to attack the United States. They had begun experimenting with incendiary high-altitude balloon bombs, which if successful they planned to subsequently use to carry germ bombs across the Pacific. Some 2,000 incendiary balloon bombs were released, and about 200 reached North America. One exploded in Bly, Oregon, killing five children. When the war ended, Ishii and his men murdered the last 400 Chinese witnesses and burned down Unit 731. Instead of also killing the lab rats that had been infected with bubonic plague, Ishii and his men callously released these, causing an epidemic of plague estimated to have needlessly taken another 30,000 lives around Harbin in 1947 after a period of incubation. No Japanese national faced final justice for these utterly barbaric *war crimes*. In fact, in 1948 Ishii traded translations of his documents and copies of his research to the United States in exchange for a written guarantee of not being prosecuted. Justice for U.S. POWs had taken second place to the burgeoning fears of the *Cold War* and the express interest of some American scientists keen to obtain Unit 731's data on human test results to advance their own work. Ishii died of natural causes in 1959, unpunished and with his crimes not even fully documented.

By the end of World War II seven countries were researching biological weapons. Britain, Canada, France, Germany, Japan, the Soviet Union, and the United States. Many more later did research in the postwar era. During the *Korean Conflict* the United States was strenuously accused by China and the Soviet Union of using germ and chemical weapons. This provoked anti-American demonstrations in Western Europe and elsewhere. In fact, as Soviet documents released after the Cold War demonstrated, this was a calculated *disinformation* campaign crafted by the *Communist* side. Extreme measures were taken by North Korean and Chinese officials to fabricate false evidence to substantiate the charges, including infecting their own men awaiting execution (for desertion or other offenses) with plague and cholera. The campaign was approved at the highest levels, by *Stalin, Mao,* and *Zhou Enlai.*

In 1973 the Soviet agency *Minatom* set up an illegal—under the 1972 *Biological Warfare Treaty*—biological weapons research center at Biopreparet. In 1979 dozens of civilians at nearby Sverdlovsk (Yekaterinberg) were killed by an accidental release of anthrax. In 1998 it was revealed that the spores released in 1979 were a blend of four anthrax bacilli designed to overwhelm any vaccine. Soviet work on this and even more virulent plagues continued all the time *Gorbachev* was in power. The program was ordered ended by *Yeltsin,* following the breakup of the Soviet Union. Massive stockpiles of anthrax, plague, typhus, smallpox, and other diseases were buried on Vozrozhdeniye Island, the erstwhile Soviet weapons test site in the *Aral Sea.* After 1991 jurisdiction over the island, around which the Aral Sea continued to contract, was shared by Uzbekistan and Kazakhstan. Iraq was suspected of using biological weapons in the 1980s against Iran, and *Saddam Hussein* is thought to have repeated some of Unit 731's experiments on his own people and on Iranian prisoners of war. In 1995 Hussein's son-in-law defected and identified sites where the Iraqi dictator still had 8,500 tons of anthrax, nearly 20,000 liters of botulinum toxin, and over 2,000 liters of aflatoxin, along with large quantities of VX nerve gas (for his efforts, the son-in-law was killed, after he foolishly returned to Iraq). In 1991 Russian intelligence reported that North Korea had field-tested a broad range of biological weapons. Members of the apocalyptic Japanese cult *Aum Shinrikyo* failed in nine attempts to release anthrax into the Tokyo subway system in 1995. Therefore, they released sarin gas instead, killing 12 people, harming thousands, and causing mass panic. Immediately following the *September 11, 2001, terrorist attack on the United States* anthrax spores were delivered via regular mail to a number of locations in the United States, including the White House and Congress. These deadly letters killed several, infected others, caused widespread—yet only temporary—panic, and tied up and slowed down mail services. In addition, U.S. and allied forces located extensive biological weapons labs in Afghanistan upon liberating that country from the *Taliban* and *al Qaeda* in December, 2001. *See also Carthaginian peace; chemical and biological warfare; Geneva Protocol.*

Suggested Readings: Sheldon H. Harris, *Factories of Death* (1994); Joshua Lederberg, ed., *Biological Weapons* (1999).

Biological Warfare Treaty (1972). It ostensibly prohibits research, production, and stockpiling of *biological weapons*, but contains so large a loophole (except "for defensive purposes") that it actually prevents nothing at all. It was boosted in the *ratification* process in 1969 when *Richard Nixon* announced that the United States would unilaterally renounce all biological weapons as well as *first use* of *chemical agents and weapons*. It was initially signed by 111 nations, with more adhering since. *Verification* of *compliance* is in any case extremely difficult, given major advances in genetic engineering that postdated the treaty. *See also Geneva Protocol.*

bipartisanship. In U.S. foreign policy, when the two major parties agree on a common diplomatic position, such as *containment*, with the idea that partisan domestic politics and bickering is supposed to end "at the water's edge."

bipolarity. (1) Roughly, the *structure* of the international system during the *Cold War*, c. 1947–1990. (2) From reading far too much into #1, a theoretical alignment in which states cluster around two poles of power, said by polarity theorists to be the most stable of all possible *balance of power* systems. *See also tripolarity; multipolarity; unipolarity.*

bipolycentrism. *Jargon*, of the most tortured type, purporting to describe the late *Cold War* when the United States and Soviet Union were still in military balance but others (Germany, Japan, China) were gaining in political and economic influence.

Birobizhan. The Jewish Autonomous Region in a desolate area along the Chinese-Soviet frontier, set aside by the *Bolsheviks* as a homeland for Russia's millions of Jews. Only about 100,000 Jews migrated there. It was established in the 1920s by *Josef Stalin*, then Commissar for Nationalities. Its main purpose was to undercut the attraction of *Zionism* for Soviet Jews, as well as to treat them as just one among the many minority nationalities of the empire. In fact, *anti-Semitism* remained just as pronounced and pernicious in the *Soviet Union* as in *Tsarist Russia*.

Bishop, Maurice (1945–1983). Prime minister of Grenada, 1979–1983. His *socialist* government came to power in a *coup*, announced its *nonalignment*, and edged politically closer to Cuba. He was murdered during a second coup by a still more radical faction of his own New Jewel movement. That precipitated a United States and Caribbean invasion.

Bismarck, Otto von (1815–1898). "The Iron Chancellor." Prussian statesman. Minister (ambassador) to Russia 1859 and to France 1862; chancellor of Germany, 1871–1890. He was recalled in 1862 to head the Prussian cabinet. From that point forward, the key to his power was compliance by the king (and later, *Kaiser*), Wilhelm I. Otto von Bismarck used the *Zollverein* to cement the north German states to Prussia and build the industrial infrastructure upon which Prussia's later military success partly rested. He reorganized the army and bureaucracy and led Prussia into a brief, successful war with Denmark over the *Schleswig-Holstein* question. After securing his eastern border with friendly ties to Russia, this *Junker* statesman moved to eliminate Austria as a rival in Germany. "The great questions of the time are not decided by speeches and majority decisions," he said, "but by iron and blood." A dispute over division of the spoils from the Danish war provided the pretext for the astonishing victory over Austria in the *Seven Weeks' War* (1866). That confirmed Prussian mastery of Germany. In 1870 Bismarck deliberately provoked the *Franco-Prussian War* with the *Ems Telegram*. France was humiliated, *Louis-Napoleon* toppled, and *Alsace-Lorraine* annexed. Bismarck then proclaimed formation of the Second German Empire (*Reich*) in 1871, with himself as chancellor. The historian A.J.P. Taylor later wrote of his policy: "Bismarck fought 'necessary wars' and killed thousands; the idealists of the 20th century [fought] 'just wars' and kill[ed] millions."

With victory, Bismarck transformed his policy from *aggrandizement* to preservation of Germany's central place on the continent through a series of secret alliances designed to isolate France: the *Dreikaiserbund*, with Austria and Russia; the *Triple Alliance*, with Austria and Italy. His guiding light was to ensure that Germany was "one of the three in an unstable system of five Great Powers." In 1879, in response to the *world depression* then underway, he converted to *protectionism*. That provoked retaliation by other European powers, including Britain, and undermined the international *free trade* system. Bismarck presided over the *Congress of Berlin* on the *Eastern Question* and sparked the *Conference of Berlin* on Africa by suddenly reversing course, 1883–1885, in proclaiming four German *protectorates*—Togo, German Southwest Africa, Kamerun, and German East Africa. On the whole, Bismarck thought the *scramble for Africa* foolish but useful to Germany if it kept France and Britain distracted from European affairs and out of an anti-German alliance. Yet, historians still argue over why he adopted a colonial policy for Germany. Back in Europe, he secretly encouraged the *Mediterranean Agreement* of 1887, while that same year signing the *Reinsurance Treaty* with Russia. At home, he strengthened first the Prussian state then Imperial Germany, attempting a conservative *revolution from above*. Failing to win the *Kulturkampf* against German Catholics, he sought compromise with the middle classes. He also failed to reconcile the growing working class to the new Germany, despite social welfare reforms. In foreign affairs, he was well satisfied. "We Germans fear God," he boasted to the *Reichstag* in 1888, "but nothing else in the world." Yet he foresaw that *Wilhelm II* would be impetuous and dangerously *adventurist*. He resigned in 1890, rather than be dismissed. Much of what he had achieved for Germany was later gambled away by an unstable kaiser and the military class that upheld him, whose power Bismarck had done so much to build and sustain. *See also Machtpolitik; politics; Realpolitik.*

Suggested Readings: Theodore S. Hamerow, *Otto von Bismarck and Imperial Germany* (1994); Otto Pflanze, *Bismarck and the Development of Germany* (1963); J. E. Rose, *Bismarck* (1987); Fritz Stern, *Gold and Iron* (1977); A.J.P. Taylor, *Bismarck* (1955; 1987).

Black Death. Repeated epidemics of what was likely bubonic plague that devastated much of Asia and Europe starting in the fourteenth century. The disease probably originated in Asia. It did its worst work in towns and cities that straddled the main *trade routes*, especially the *Silk Road*, spreading westward along with merchants and *Mongol* invaders. It ravaged India and China before reaching Central Asia and Persia. It then jumped to Europe, where one-third of the population (some 25 million people) died in the first outbreak, 1347–1350. It arrived in Europe by many routes, including on Genoese galleys fleeing infection and Crimean Tartars in 1246. Plague ships arriving in Genoa two years later were driven away by clouds of flaming arrows fired by terrified residents. The Black Death recurred in frequent but less virulent waves for another century, until resistance built up among the surviving population. Overnight, the plague made land—the coinage of the European medieval economy—more plentiful while curtailing the supply of labor. This raised wages and prices, greatly contributing to a sharp economic decline, which added to other fourteenth century torments such as the *Hundred Years' War*. The plague underlay abortive revolutions, peasant uprisings, civil wars, and economic, social, and religious dislocation—it encouraged excesses of piety and hedonism alike—experienced from Ireland to *Byzantium* and from Italy to Scandinavia. Although the plague freed land and peasants by raising wages in Western Europe, it had the opposite effect in the east. There, it contributed to re-enserfment of the peasantry in Russia and other Slavic lands. It continued to occasionally sweep over Europe into the seventeenth century. In China and India, during times of war, famine, and weakened resistance, outbreaks occurred as late as the 1890s. *See also Aurangzeb; serfdom.*

Suggested Reading: Philip Ziegler, *The Black Death* (1969).

Black Hand. "Union or Death." A secret Serbian society formed by young zealots in the *officer corps* in 1911 and operating under command of the *intelligence* section of the Serbian General Staff. It promoted *irredentism* toward Serb lands in Austria and the *Ottoman Empire* and was behind the assassination of *Francis Ferdinand*.

"Black Hole of Calcutta" (June 20, 1756). A small British force surrendered to a *nawab* in Calcutta and was incarcerated in a dungeon. Several dozen died from heat and suffocation during the night. The tale, exaggerated in the telling but bad enough in reality, was used by British propagandists for empire to portray their Indian opponents as utter savages. Hence, *Clive* was sent back to India partly to avenge the Black Hole tragedy, though mostly to continue his campaign of conquest.

"black legend." A long debate has occurred among Latin American historians as to the character of Spanish colonial rule. The "black legend" refers to Spain's reputation among those (mainly classical liberals) who first condemned its record as especially oppressive, backward, and obscurantist, even by the standards of *colonialism* elsewhere. This picture was often attended by portrayals of precolonial Indian life as pacific and idyllic, which was far from the truth when considering, among others, the *Inca* and *Aztec*. Its converse was a "white legend," which stressed the so-called *Pax Hispanica* and supposed mildness of conditions of *slavery* in New Spain, as compared with that in the United States.

black market. One where *goods and services* are sold and purchased illegally to avoid government *price controls*, *rationing*, or taxes. Some analysts regard black markets as the real markets, where nearly pure relations of supply and demand set prices. Black markets are particularly prevalent in *soft currency* countries.

Black 'n Tans. An auxiliary military force of *World War I* veterans sent to Ireland during the *Irish War of Independence* (1918–1921), so-called for the motley admixture that made up their uniforms. They are still bitterly remembered by Catholic (nationalist) Irish for their often rough justice, and rougher injustice and occasional *atrocities*.

Black Sea. It lies between Europe and Asia, nestled among Bulgaria, the *Caucasus*, Ukraine, Rumania, and Turkey. Although landlocked, it is legally part of the *high seas*. *See also Black Sea Fleet; Crimean War; Exclusive Economic Zone.*

Black Sea Fleet. The main Russian (later, Soviet) battle fleet. It was initially built by *Potemkin*, 1784–1787 and was always based at the *warm water port* of *Sebastopol*, except during the brief *demilitarization* of the Black Sea that followed the *Crimean War*. With the breakup of the *Soviet Union* it became the subject of a bitter ownership dispute between Ukraine and Russia. In 1992 it was decided to divide the fleet, then comprising 21 *submarines*, 35 *capital warships*, and 250 frontline aircraft, but many crew refused to serve with Ukraine. In 1993 the *Duma* claimed Sebastopol as Russian territory, thereby also claiming the fleet, but *Boris Yeltsin* disavowed this move. It was agreed to place the fleet under joint command for five years. A later settlement gave most of the ships to Russia, which leased port facilities from Ukraine. *See also Straits Question.*

Black September. A Palestinian *terrorist* organization that carried out a massacre of Israeli athletes at the Munich *Olympic Games* in 1972. Participants were later identified by Israeli intelligence (*Mossad*). It was publicly reported that all were killed by secret Mossad execution squads, with the last expiring in 1993.

blackshirt. "Squadristi." (1) A member of the *fascist* Italian *paramilitary* organization before *World War II*; (2) Italian fascist divisions, including those that fought in Spain, 1936–1939; (3) any fascist street thug. Fascists in other countries also wore monochrome shirts, modeled on the Italian example: *brownshirts* were worn in Germany; Spain and China had *blueshirts*, and so forth. *See also blue division; march on Rome; Mussolini; SA; SS.*

Black Tuesday (October 29, 1929). The day the Wall Street stock market crashed, setting off widespread investor panic and precipitating a chain of financial collapses and international loan calls that built toward, and then exacerbated (but did not cause, for it was already underway), the *Great Depression*. It followed Black Thursday (October 24, 1929), which saw the first wave of panic selling. All this selling came on the heels of a multiyear speculative boom and before installation of more modern protections on limiting margin debt and automatic trading halts during any real or potential panic.

Blair, Tony (b. 1953). British prime minister (1997–). He first joined the *Labour Party* shadow cabinet in 1988. He was elected leader of the party in July of 1994, on the promise to introduce radical reform aimed at moving the party toward the political center and away from its long dalliance with radical leftism and militant trade unionism. Ultimately, he was able to eliminate from Labour's platform its doctrinaire, official adherence to *Marxist* interpretations of social and economic policy, and instead embed a commitment to *market economics*. This reorientation was dubbed "New Labour." In 1997 he led the Labour Party to a sweeping majority victory, becoming the youngest prime minister in over 200 years, since *William Pitt* (the younger) first took office. Domestically, Blair concentrated on reform of education and welfare policies. But perhaps his most far-reaching reform was to embrace *devolution* for Scotland and Wales. He also successfully oversaw peace talks that led to a historic breakthrough in Northern Ireland. In foreign policy, Blair maintained Labour's traditional focus on the *European Union*, accepting *monetary union*, and adoption of the Euro. He was also keen to use force to intervene in *Kosovo*. He emerged as an undisputed world leader in the wake of the unprovoked *September 11, 2001, terrorist attack on the United States*. His was by far the strongest European voice in support of a forceful U.S. response to the threat of *terrorism*, and he never hesitated in committing the British military to the forefront of the fight. Upon the defeat of the *Taliban* and *al Qaeda* in Afghanistan at the end of 2001, Blair committed Great Britain to lead the United Nations military force dedicated to securing peace and stability in that benighted nation, and to long-term efforts at reconstruction of Afghanistan's broken infrastructure and rehabilitation of its shattered, *warlord* politics.

"blank check." The guarantee of German support to Austria, given by Kaiser *Wilhelm II* on July 5, 1914, in the event Austria should attack Serbia and in turn be attacked by Russia. *See also mobilization crisis.*

blast effects. The immediate destruction caused by the concussive force of a *nuclear* bomb, as distinct from the lingering lethality of *radiation effects.*

Blenheim, Battle of (August 13, 1704). A decisive battle in the *War of the Spanish Succession*. It took place in southwest Germany, where a British army under *Marlborough* defeated a combined Bavarian-French force. Blenheim was the first truly strategic defeat of the French Army in half a century. Some 108,000 soldiers took part in the battle, on all sides, of whom 30,000 were casualties. The victory saved Vienna from capture by the French and Bavarians, kept Austria in the war, and preserved the grand alliance of Great Britain, the Netherlands, and Austria. Bavaria was forced to terms, and France was driven onto the defensive. *Marlborough* and Prince Eugene, the great allied commanders, were showered with accolades. Blenheim was one of several major setbacks these commanders together, and severally, gave the hegemonic ambitions of *Louis XIV.*

blister agents. *See chemical weapons; mustard gas.*

blitz. Slang for the German bombing campaign against London and other British cities, September 1940–May 1941. Derived from *Blitzkrieg.*

Blitzkrieg. "Lightning war." A *Nazi* term for the style of rapid attack and *infiltration tactics* that disregarded the safety of flanks in favor of stunning advances and tactical breakthroughs. The aim was to punch a hole in an enemy's defensive line, then exploit confusion and opportunities in the enemy's rear. This was inflicted on Poland, Norway, Denmark, the *Low Countries*, and France, 1939–1940, and the Soviet Union in 1941. It involved a lightening *armored* breakthrough, supported by tactical *air power*, followed by quick exploitation of the local advantages created and encirclement of enemy armies on either flank of the breakthrough point. This required fully mechanized forces (including the infantry), constant movement in a series of rapid flanking maneuvers, and a revolutionary coordination of command and control of ground and air units. It grew out of new technologies of armored transport and the tank and tactical bomber, which were all designed to avoid a descent into *trench warfare* comparable to 1914–1918, after the initial movement phase of *World War I.* It drew from experience of the closing days of that war, in which movement had been reestablished by specialized shock troops and armored formations, first by the Germans, and then by the advancing *Allies* during the final German collapse. Its main tactic involved an armored spearhead joined to an infantry shaft, instead of an assault on a broad front. This was highly effective early in the *Battle of France*, although Colonel *Charles de Gaulle* found its weakness during the Battle of the Meuse in 1940: strike at the junction of armor point and infantry shaft with an armored counterattack, and break the spear. A critical component of blitzkrieg was the key element of political and strategic surprise, which attended all *Hitler's* early attacks. By 1943 better defenses against armor, principally by armored divisions used as defensive formations, and a hard-learned sense of bitter realism about Nazi Germany blunted the effectiveness of blitzkrieg and stiffened anti-German resistance everywhere. In a highly modified sense only, in 1944 the *Red Army* turned these tactics back against German formations, as did *Patton* in the south of France. *See also Napoleonic warfare.*

bloc. An informal coalition or *alliance* (though it may also incorporate formal ties); some uses imply high rigidity in both diplomacy and military doctrine. *See also caucus group; G-7; G-77; Nonaligned Movement; Soviet bloc.*

blockade. In *international law*, effective (not just declared) isolation of a port or coast and interception of all ships and goods in transit from that port or coast. In 1909 an international convention on blockade was drafted, but not ratified. Blockade is the favored policy of *sea powers*, as it makes for *total war* effects against an enemy while limiting these effects for the blockading state. Since *Trafalgar*, and certainly in the course of the twentieth century, fights among surface navies grew more rare and were even more rarely the final determinant of warfare at sea. Instead, choking off an enemy's trade became the major use of sea power. The law of blockade became accordingly more important. It was also relatively stable until 1914. Classically, there are several types of blockade. (1) Pacific blockade: one applied in peacetime as a form of *reprisal* or in support of *sanctions* and affecting mainly ships of the target country. Pacific blockades were enforced under United Nations authority against Iraq (1990–), Serbia (1992–2000), and Haiti (1993–1994). (2) Paper blockade: a declared blockade that lacks effectiveness and thus may be legally ignored by third parties. (3) Long-distance blockade: the rule that the distance of the blockading force from the coast is irrelevant for purposes of law, as long as the action is effective. (4) Close blockade: one so effective within the close limits of the *cannon-shot rule* or daylight visibility (in an era before night-vision technologies) that *neutral rights* were effectively suspended and neutrals traded at their own risk. (5) Land blockade: interception of commerce on land. There is no such thing as an aerial blockade in law, but the 1990s concept of *no-fly zone* may represent an evolution in that direction. In warfare and in applying sanctions, blockades are used to cripple an enemy's economy. Britain used this weapon against *Napoleon*, who counterblockaded; against Germany in *World War I* (continued for negotiating purposes long after the *Armistice* was signed), and again in *World War II*, with Germany counterblockading each time with *U-boats*. The *Union* blockade of the *Confederacy* was a major factor deciding the *American Civil War*, though it was at first misapplied. *See also Balkan War, Third; Battle of the Atlantic; Berlin airlift; Continental System; contraband; Cuban Missile Crisis; embargo; free ships make free goods; Gulf War; infection; League of Armed Neutrality; Lincoln; quarantine; ultimate destination; unrestricted submarine warfare; War of 1812.*

blood agents. *See chemical weapons.*

Bloody Sunday (January 9, 1905). A massacre of more than one hundred (and wounding of another 1,000) peaceful, common petitioners for improved working conditions. It took place in the great square outside Tsar *Nicholas II*'s Winter Palace in *St. Petersburg*. It proved the spark that set off the *Russian*

Revolution of 1905. The term has been used since to refer to other massacres, of lesser scale, which also occurred on Sundays. *See also Ulster.*

blowback. Slang for any unintended consequences of foreign policy decisions, and especially of *covert operations.*

BLS states. Botswana, Lesotho, and Swaziland, collectively considered.

Blücher, Gebhart Leberecht von (1742–1819). Prussian field marshal. He fought in the *Seven Years' War,* against Prussia as an officer in the Swedish *cavalry.* Captured and made a *prisoner of war,* he changed to the Prussian side to finish the war. After thirteen years in rural retirement, he was recalled in 1787 and served throughout the *Wars of the French Revolution.* He was captured in 1806 at *Jena,* but was later exchanged for a French officer. At first he fought with the Prussian Army, but he offered his services to the state of Brunswick when it remained in the war against France after Prussia withdrew, defeated. Blücher became military governor of Pomerania in 1807, but was maneuvered out of that position by *Napoleon* in 1811. In his seventies, Blücher returned to Prussian service and helped win a major victory over Napoleon at the *Battle of Leipzig* (1813). He invaded France on January 1, 1814, entering Paris alongside *Alexander I* and other allies, after Napoleon's forced abdication. He again retired to his farm, but was recalled to command in Belgium upon the start of Napoleon's *Hundred Days.* He is best remembered for his late-in-the-day, yet dogged and decisive, attack that crumbled Napoleon's flank and decided the *Battle of Waterloo.*

Blue Division. Spanish *fascist* volunteers, mainly *blueshirts,* fighting for the *Nazis* on the *eastern front* in *World War II.*

blueshirts. *Fascist* street organizations that engaged in political thuggery and murder of opponents. (1) China: In the 1930s Whampoa Military Academy cadets and graduates were organized as leaders of *death squads* and political intimidation units by that academy's erstwhile first commandant, *Chiang Kai-shek,* in direct emulation of *Mussolini's* fascist *blackshirts.* Many later served Chiang's regime as *secret police.* (2) Spain: Before, during, and after the *Spanish Civil War,* Spanish fascists organized in blueshirt clubs and street formations to better intimidate their political enemies. Some later fought, and died, for the fascist cause as volunteers in the *Blue Division. See also blackshirts; brown-shirts.*

blue water navy. One whose large and powerful *warships* are capable of operating far from coastal waters, in the deep blue waters of the major oceans. *See also brown water navy; sea power.*

Blum, Léon (1872–1950). French socialist. He was an early supporter of *Dreyfus*. In 1921 he rejected *Lenin's* hard line in the *Comintern*, splitting French socialists from the Communists. He also opposed occupation of the *Ruhr*. In 1936 he led a *Popular Front* government, becoming the first socialist prime minister of France. However, he was unable to garner support for strong opposition to *Hitler* because (1) a deep mood of *defeatism* gripped national life; (2) the *Spanish Civil War* badly divided French public opinion, making it difficult to form an anti*fascist* front in foreign policy; and (3) the democratic right in France failed to understand that the real danger to national liberty was not internal but external—not the French socialists, but German and Italian armies, made more threatening by *fifth columnists* and potential collaborators among domestic fascists. In 1938 Blum was again premier, but could marshal almost no support for a policy of active resistance to Nazi Germany's growing *aggression*. Despising his socialist politics and his Jewish faith, the extreme right in France embraced the defeatist slogan, "Better Hitler than Blum." He condemned the *appeasement* policy of the *Munich Conference*, and after the *Battle of France*, defeat, and surrender, he opposed *Vichy*. He was imprisoned at *Dachau* during *World War II*. Tried by Vichy, he masterfully turned the proceedings into a judgment on the regime's *collaboration*, which led to the embarrassed cancellation of the trial. Liberated from Dachau, he headed a caretaker government in 1946. He soon resigned, unable to overcome the constitutional chaos of the Fourth Republic, which continued the moral and political paralysis of the Third.

BMD. *See ABM Treaty; Ballistic Missile Defense; Strategic Defense Initiative.*

BND (*Bundesnachrichtendienst*). The (West) German foreign *intelligence service*. During the *Cold War* it was deeply penetrated by the East German *HvA*. For instance, its head of section for Soviet *counterintelligence*, Heinz Felfe, was for years a Communist *mole* who fed *disinformation* to Western intelligence services.

boat people. *Refugees* who take to the seas, often in unsafe boats or homemade rafts, or just inner tubes, in the hope of finding sanctuary in a neighboring country. Participation is not always voluntary, and there have been many thousands of uncounted deaths of boat people. The most extensive outflows were of ethnic Chinese (Hoa) from Vietnam with the end of the *Vietnam War* (1975–1979), Cuba (*Mariel boat lift*, 1980), and Albania, Cuba (again), and Haiti in the 1990s. In 1979 Vietnam pledged to the *UNHCR* to limit this dangerous exodus, and several *OECD* countries agreed to accept 250,000 boat people. Most Asian countries refused to allow more than a handful to resettle. In all, some 800,000 boat people left Vietnam between 1975 and 2000. Most transited through Hong Kong to the United States and Canada, but 100,000 were forcibly deported from Hong Kong back to Vietnam. After

1989 the outflow abated, but it rose again by 2000. *See also humane deterrence; piracy.*

Boers. *See Afrikaner; Boer Wars.*

Boer War, First (1881). This war was a short clash between the British and the *Afrikaners* (Boers), who sought to renege on the surrender of their independence to Britain in 1877 that had been the price of British protection against the *Zulus*, and who were impressed by the Zulu victory over a British column at *Isandlwana* (1879). The Boers rose against the British and inflicted a sharp defeat at Majuba. Rather than be drawn into a protracted war, in the Convention of Pretoria (1881) Britain conceded *autonomy* to the Boers in the *Transvaal*, with the proviso that Great Britain retained a right of review of Transvaal's foreign relations. Most other limitations on effective self-government were lifted by 1884.

Boer War, Second (1899–1902). Great Boer War. Preceded and in part precipitated by the *Jamieson Raid* organized by *Cecil Rhodes*, this final conflict in South Africa was deliberately provoked by the British high commissioner in a bid to end *Afrikaner* (Boer) independence and consolidate British colonial possessions in the southern cone. Properly provoked, Boers from *Transvaal*, led by *Paulus Kruger*, attacked British units in Southern Africa in a bid to restore their full political independence, which had been reluctantly surrendered to Britain during the *Zulu Wars*. The *Orange Free State* joined its sister republic in its fight against the "uitlanders." After early Boer victories against small garrisons, a counterattack by British reinforcements forced the Boers into *guerrilla* tactics. The Boers were finally defeated by *Kitchener*, who employed *scorched earth* and set up *concentration camps* to collect Afrikaner civilians, with many suffering and dying from a typhoid epidemic while under British guard. In face of this, Boer "bittereinders" fought on, in an already lost cause, conducting an ultimately ineffectual harassing campaign of guerrilla warfare. That policy and tragedy was never forgotten, or forgiven, in the historical memory of the Boers.

The South African War formally ended with the Treaty of Vereeniging negotiated by *Jan Smuts* in behalf of the Boers. Vereeniging completed the British conquest of southern Africa by incorporating the Transvaal and Orange Free State into the *British Empire*, while expressly limiting the franchise to whites and giving to the Boers an effective veto over black political participation. In addition to its local impact, the Second Boer War had far-flung international consequences. It worsened London's relations with Berlin and for a moment raised the possibility of a British war with Germany arising out of Kaiserine support for the Boers. That left London in a weakened international position by revealing its diplomatic isolation, but also exposed the kaiser and Germany as reckless. Britain was so in need of United States *neutrality*, if not overt support, it bowed to American demands over a bitter Venezuelan *boundary* and customs dispute (where the United States strongly backed Venezuela), most issues pertaining to the *Panama Canal*, and a long-standing dispute over the final boundary dividing the Alaskan panhandle from British Columbia. *Theodore Roosevelt* converted this *rapprochement* into a near de facto Anglo-American alliance. In 1908 Britain was so confident of U.S. support that it abandoned its Caribbean naval stations, which it had held for more than three centuries, leaving but a few gunboats behind in what had become an American lake. For all the death and suffering, Rhodes had after all overstretched the British Empire, which within the decade gave back to the Boers at the conference table what had been taken away on the battlefield and in the concentration camps and burned-out farms: their political independence.

Suggested Readings: J. S. Marais, *The Fall of Kruger's Republic* (1961); Bill Nasson, *The South African War* (1999); Thomas Pakenham, *The Boer War* (1979).

Bohemia. This historic region was formerly an Austrian and *Habsburg* province and an electorate in the *Holy Roman Empire*. After the *Congress of Vienna* it was part of the *German Confederation*. From 1920 it formed the core of *Czechoslovakia*. With the breakup of that state after the *Cold War*, most of historic Bohemia remained in the *Czech Republic*. *See also Battle of White Mountain; Count Johan Tilly; Thirty Years' War.*

Bohemia-Moravia. A *protectorate* set up by the *Nazis* during the German *occupation* in *World War II*, 1939–1945. This territory reverted to *Czechoslovakia* after the war.

Bokassa, Jean-Bedel (1921–1996). Dictator of Central African Republic (Empire), 1965–1979. He served for many years in the French Army, in *World War II*, Indochina, and Algeria. He took power in a *coup* in 1965. He proclaimed himself emperor in 1976 in a *Napoleonic* coronation that consumed a quarter of the *GNP* in one of the world's poorest countries. He was a ruthless and corrupt tyrant whose *human rights* abuses were infamous. Despite this, he had French support for years. In 1979 he ordered a massacre of schoolchildren protesting that their uniforms had to be purchased from one of his factories. That finally precipitated a French-supported coup against him, and he was forced into exile. French President *Valery Giscard d'Estaing* admitted accepting a gift of diamonds from Bokassa, which contributed to the French president's defeat by *Francois Mitterrand* in the 1981 presidential election. Apparently mad, and a reputed cannibal, Bokassa returned home in 1986 despite having been condemned to death *in absentia*. His sentence was commuted to prison time; he was later released and died quietly in 1996.

Bolívar, Simón (1783–1830). South American revolutionary. Bolívar was born into a family of landed wealth in Caracas. As a young man he spent time in Europe, where he absorbed the republican ideals of the *French Revolution* along with older notions of civic virtue. He returned to Caracas in 1807. When Venezuela rebelled against Spain, it sent Bolívar to England to seek aid. His mission failed. He returned to help write the Venezuelan declaration of independence, issued on July 5, 1811. Bolívar was named to head the national army, but he was betrayed by royalists. He fled to the Colombian portion of *New Granada* (August 12, 1811) to raise a new, republican army. While there, he issued the Cartagena Manifesto calling for Latin Americans to unite to form a republic and fight Spain. In 1813 he invaded Venezuela and in a series of six bloody engagements defeated the Spanish. He entered Caracas on August 6, 1813 and ruled as military dictator. The victory was followed by a *civil war*, which lasted until 1814. On June 15, 1814, Bolívar was badly defeated at la Puerta and had to abandon Caracas for New Granada, where he was given command of republican troops and used them to force Bogotá into federation with New Granada. After suffering defeat at the hands of another Spanish army in 1815, he fled to Jamaica and Haiti, where he wrote an eloquent defense of Latin liberties (Jamaica Letter).

Bolívar returned to Venezuela on December 28, 1816, to embark on several more years of fighting that this time would prove successful. In 1817 he established a firm base in eastern Venezuela, at Angostura, where he built a new army. In 1819, with his army augmented by British and Irish *mercenaries*, veterans of the *Napoleonic Wars*, Bolívar began the liberation of New Granada. In a heroic march, he led several thousand men across wild lands and through the Andes to achieve complete surprise over Spanish forces occupying Bogotá, winning a key victory at Boyacá (August 7, 1819). Having led the region out from under Spanish rule, he tried to create a great Latin republic, *Gran Colombia*, modeled on the United States federal structure. This federal state had considerably less concern for states' rights or for civil and constitutional liberties, however. At first, it comprised Colombia (then including Panama) and Venezuela, following his key victory at Carabobo (June 24, 1821). On September 7, 1821 Bolívar became president of Gran Colombia, which he hoped to lead into alliance with Great Britain in defiance of threats of the *Holy Alliance* to intervene in Latin America in behalf of the Spanish monarchy. On July 23, 1822, Quito (Ecuador) was added to this already unwieldy state after a victory at Pichincha (May 24th) by one of his lieutenants. On July 27th he met secretly at Guayaquil with *José de San Martín*, who had liberated Chile and was Protector of Peru. For reasons that remain unclear, after the meeting San Martin retired from the fight, leaving the liberation of southern Peru to Bolívar.

Accordingly, in March 1823, Bolívar launched an invasion of southern Peru, where he was not entirely welcome among the Creole community of Lima. Nonetheless, he was the man of the hour, and on February 10, 1824,

Bolívar was made dictator of Peru. On August 6th, he defeated a Spanish army at Junín in the Andes; and on December 9th his lieutenant defeated another Spanish force at Ayachcho, ending Spain's rule in Peru. On August 6, 1825, the northern part of Peru was separated and renamed Bolivia in appreciation of Bolívar's efforts during the *revolution*. He was elected president of Gran Colombia on April 30, 1826. Bolívar invited leading nationalists to a congress in Panama in 1826 to discuss his grand vision for a highly centralized South American confederacy, including a proposed position that only he might have filled—president for life. Things quickly fell apart, owing to his dictatorial tendencies and to the vastness and near ungovernability of the South American empire he envisioned. Unthinkable just a few years before, in 1828 several Latin American patriots tried to assassinate him, justifying the act as an attempt at *tyrannicide*. Bolivia rejected Colombian troops, and in 1829 Venezuela severed its ties as well. The vision of a single Latin commonwealth died with Bolívar, who was just 47. He said of his lifetime efforts and his final failure: "Those who have served the cause of the revolution have plowed the sea." *See also Francisco Miranda; Giuseppe Garibaldi; Lajos Kossuth; Marquis de Lafayette; Napoleon; revolution on horseback.*

Suggested Readings: John J. Johnson, *Simón Bolívar and Spanish American Independence, 1783–1830* (1968); John Lynch, *The Spanish American Revolutions, 1808–1826* (1986); Gerhard Masur, *Simón Bolívar* (1966).

Bolívarian states. Bolivia, Colombia, Ecuador, Peru, and Venezuela.

Bolivia. Spanish conquest of the *Incas* occurred in the 1530s, with the largely Indian population subsequently suffering a fall into political repression and economic exploitation under the *encomienda*. An *audiencia* was established at La Plata (Charcas) in 1559. In its peak years, 1579–1635, the great silver mine at Potosí pumped massive new wealth into Europe, underwriting Spain's many, and mostly losing, wars. *Creoles* evolved as the local ruling class, but one in tension with Spanish viceroys and corregidors. *Túpac Amaru* led a bloody *jacquerie* in the high Andes, 1780–1781. And in northern Bolivia another Indian rising, by the Aymará, lasted from 1780 to 1782, before being put down. During this time Bolivia formed part of the original Spanish *Viceroyalty of Peru*. In 1809 Bolivia, a *mestizo* leader, Pedro Domingo Murullo, seized temporary control of La Paz and declared independence from Spain. Although the uprising was overwhelmed by Spanish garrison troops from neighboring Peru in January 1810, Bolivia thus became the first part of the Spanish Empire in America to proclaim independence. Under the leadership of *Simon Bolívar*, after whom the new country was named, independence was effectively secured in January 1825. Bolivia immediately fell under the control of *caudillos*, as did several other newly independent Latin American states.

Bolivia was briefly federated with Peru, 1836–1839, under Andrés de Santa Cruz (1792–1865). Santa Cruz was a mestizo caudillo who governed reasonably well until that effort at federation, which appeared so threatening to the *balance of power* in the southernmost region of the continent, caused Chile and Argentina both to declare war on the Confederation and break it apart. In the *War of the Pacific* (1879–1884), Bolivia lost its last coastal territory to Chile and thus became completely landlocked. In the *Chaco War* (1932–1935) it lost another rich area to Paraguay and other areas to Brazil. In total it forfeited half its territory in a 50-year period and ended up as a landlocked state. Usually under military rule (it had 189 *coups d'etat* in its first 168 years) and riven with unrest and poverty, Bolivia had no international influence until *World War II*, when its tin was important to the Allied war effort. In the 1950s the United States began to assist in Bolivian *development*. Relations subsequently waxed and waned with changes in government in both countries. In the 1980s Bolivia became closely associated with United States–backed, paramilitary antidrug efforts, as it was a major locale of the global cocaine industry. In 1993 it began an experiment in democracy, after a rare period of sustained *growth*. Among its eight million people, 60 percent are of indigenous Indian extraction; 30 percent are Indian-European.

Suggested Readings: J. Valerie Fifer, *Bolivia. Land, Location, and Politics Since 1825* (1972); Scarlett O'Phelen Godoy, *Rebellions and Revolts in 18th Century Peru and Upper Peru* (1985); Harold Osborne, *Bolivia. A Land Divided* (1985).

Bolshevik Revolution. The *coup d'etat* in Russia in November 1917 that brought the *Bolsheviks* to power and precipitated the *Russian Civil War*. *See also Bolshevik; Bolshevism; Vladimir Lenin; Old Bolsheviks; Russian Revolution, November (October) 1917; Josef Stalin; Leon Trotsky.*

Bolshevik Russia. This was never an official term, but was nonetheless widely used in the West once Russia fell under rule by the *Bolsheviks*, just as in later decades Communist China became a common form used for China after 1949.

Bolsheviks. "Majority." (1) The radical wing of the Russian *Social Democratic Party*; they split with the *Mensheviks* in 1903. Under *Lenin*, the Bolsheviks at first remained an obscure group of exiled radical dissidents. They played almost no role in the *Russian Revolution of 1905* and formed a discrete political party only in 1912. Had it not been for the calamity of *World War I*, they would not have had the opportunity—which they made the most of—to seize power in a *coup d'etat*, known as the second *Russian Revolution*, or November Revolution, in 1917. They thereupon consolidated their power by brute and cruel force during the *Russian Civil War*. The Bolsheviks eventually reconstituted as the *Communist Party* of the Soviet Union in the 1920s. During the 1930s most *Old Bolsheviks* were *liquidated* by *Stalin*. (2) Loosely, and most often used as a derogatory in the West, anyone who sympathized with *Bolshevism*. *See also Brest-Litovsk, Treaty of; collectivization; Marxism-Leninism; Stalinism; Leon Trotsky.*

Suggested Readings: Vladimir N. Brovkin, ed., *The Bolsheviks in Russian Society. The Revolution and the Civil War* (1997); Richard Pipes, *Russia Under the Bolshevik Regime* (1994); Adam B. Ulam, *Bolsheviks* (1998).

Bolshevism. The *ideology* and practices of the *Bolsheviks*, to wit: *Expropriation* of private property, *collectivization* of agriculture, *war communism*, a *one-party state*, suspension of civil and political liberties, *liquidation* of state and party enemies, support for *subversion* of foreign powers and societies, *Red Terror*, tactical shiftiness, and veneration of *Marxism-Leninism* as a catchall economic, political, and social doctrine. *See also cultural revolution*; Historikerstreit; *Vladimir Lenin; permanent revolution; socialism in one country; show trials; Josef Stalin; totalitarianism; Leon Trotsky*; Yezhovshchina.

bomb. *Ordnance* dropped from an aircraft. Until the 1970s, most were crudely aimed and gravity directed. High-technology smart bombs are guided to target by inboard TV cameras and/or lasers or electronic signals. *See also air power; carpet bombing; indiscriminate bombing.*

bombardment. Sustained shelling by *artillery* or the *navy*. In its day and in *just war* terms, bombardment of fortified towns or other positions raised the same questions of *civilian* versus *combatant* and *collateral damage* as later *strategic bombing*.

bomber. An aircraft whose primary function is to deliver *ordnance* to enemy targets rather than destroy other aircraft, as does a *fighter*. By convention, bombers are divided into heavy, medium, and light classes, according to payload and range.

Bonaparte. *See Napoleon I (Bonaparte).*

Bonapartism. Rule by a charismatic military leader, à la *Napoleon I* or *III*, who purports to rise above class and sectoral interests to embody the spirit and interests of the nation as a whole. It had a long history as a political possibility, centered on Napoleon's descendants, and a sometime reality in France. During the *Fifth Republic*, some feared *Charles de Gaulle* might retailor lingering Bonapartist sentiment to support a personal dictatorship; he did not. The term was also used about *Third World* nations plagued by military dictators, whether charismatic or not, who made comparable claims. *See also Saddam Hussein; Juan Perón; Muammar Quadaffi; Achmed Sukarno.*

Bonin Islands. A small island chain in the North Pacific. Japan retained residual *sovereignty* over this chain under terms of the *Japanese Peace Treaty*. The United States occupied the Bonins until full sovereignty over them was returned to Japan in 1968. The adjacent Volcano Islands, including battle-scarred Iwo Jima, were returned that year as well.

booby trap. *See prohibited weapons.*

boom. Slang for rapid economic *growth.*

boomer. Common navy slang for a nuclear missile–bearing *submarine. See also hunter-killer.*

booty. Any moveable enemy property that may be claimed as part of the *spoils of war. See also laws of war.*

Borah, William Edgar (1865–1940). U.S. senator (R-Idaho), 1907–1940; chairman of the *Foreign Relations Committee,* 1924–1940. He led the *isolationists* in the Senate who opposed the *Versailles Treaty* because it committed the United States to join the *League of Nations.* He also opposed *Republican* presidents in the 1920s who sought to have the United States join the *World Court* and played a decisive role in reshaping the *Kellogg-Briand Pact* from a proposed French alliance into an innocuous statement of general principle. In the 1930s he advocated *disarmament,* even in face of the *rearmament* programs of the *Axis.*

Borden, Robert (1854–1937). Prime minister of Canada, 1911–1920. He governed Canada during *World War I,* riding out a hugely divisive national crisis over *conscription.* He was able to parlay Canada's wartime contribution into a new status and quasi-independent voice within *British Empire* affairs. He attended the *Paris Peace Conference,* where along with *Jan Smuts* he won agreement to let the *Dominions* sign separately from Britain and join the *League of Nations* as individual states.

border. In premodern times, borders had only vague meaning and definition. With the rise of *nation-states,* borders became clear lines marking the limit of *jurisdiction* between two distinct *territories,* whether *states, colonies, dependencies, protectorates,* or any of the above and *territorium nullius.* Most borders were set by *conquest* and *diktat,* or *negotiation,* resulted de facto from *stalemate,* emerged naturally from clear *topography,* or were decided by a combination of methods. Numerous borders remain disputed by two or more states. *See also boundary; frontier; maritime frontier;* uti possidetis.

border states. The *slave states* lying between the *Union* and the *Confederacy* that sought compromise rather than *secession.* Delaware, Maryland, Kentucky, and Missouri. Like several other states, their populations had divided loyalties between North and South when the *American Civil War* finally came.

Bormann, Martin (1900–1945). *Nazi Party* official. Bormann served in *World War I* and subsequently joined a *Freikorps* unit, before joining the Nazi *SA*. Thereafter, he rose in the party bureaucracy, overseeing its and *Hitler*'s personal finances. He kept close to Hitler, but avoided a public role. When *Rudolf Hess* flew to Britain in an abortive effort to negotiate a *separate peace*, Bormann moved into a commanding position in national party headquarters. He gained enormous power by controlling access to Hitler, even by other top Nazis. Later in the war, he became commander of the Volksstrum (People's Army), but his main interest was always in Hitler's staff and party bureaucracy. During Hitler's final days Bormann continued his byzantine maneuvering for power, including secretly encouraging efforts by *Himmler* to obtain a *separate peace* with the Western Allies. When *Göring* independently tried the same thing, Bormann persuaded Hitler to have him arrested and argued for his execution. It was Bormann who oversaw the disposal of Hitler's body after his suicide and who ordered survivors to attempt a mass breakout from Berlin, as it fell to the Soviets. He was tried in absentia at *Nuremberg*, found guilty as a major *war criminal*, and sentenced to death. The sentence was never carried out, however, because Bormann was not located by the Allies after the war. In 1972 a skeleton was unintentionally unearthed by an excavation crew in Berlin. It was identified through forensic evidence as Bormann's, but as is common in such cases, for some the facts were not permitted to overcome belief that he had somehow escaped to South America after the war.

Borneo. A large island in the Malay Archipelago, subdivided into *Sabah*, *Sarawak*, *Brunei*, and *Kalimantan*, which are in turn divided among Brunei, Indonesia, and Malaysia.

Bornu. An independent West African *emirate*, under the Saifawa dynasty, located near Lake Chad during the African middle ages. It traded with *Kanem* and the *Hausa* states and was a terminus of the trans-Saharan *trade route* that led to *Tripoli*. It later migrated south of the lake, both to evade pressure from Kanem—which was itself collapsing and migrating to the southwest—and to conduct slave raids in the southern *sudan* to feed the ancient trade with North Africa. Its armored knights resisted a Kanem migration in the sixteenth century. They repeatedly raided deep into Hausa lands to the south and warred with the *Tuareg* to the north. After the fall of *Songhay*, Bornu was the largest state in sub-Saharan Africa. It faced pressure from Bulala, which had occupied much of old Kanem in the fifteenth and sixteenth centuries, and later also from *Bagirmi*, another *cavalry* power of central sudan. Bornu reconquered much of old Kanem from the Bulala in the late sixteenth century, forcing the Bulala to accept *tributary* status. Bornu passed its peak by the close of the seventeenth century, falling well behind the Hausa states. In the early nineteenth century it faced conquest by the *Fulbe*, who launched a jihad against Bornu after their victory over the Hausa. A Muslim *warlord* from what had been Kanem, Amin al-Kameni, helped Bornu fend off the Fulbe. In 1837 his death led to political disintegration.

Borodino, Battle of (September 7, 1812). The Russians under *Kutuzov* and the French (and their allies) under *Napoleon I* fought this savage battle 75 miles outside Moscow. Nearly 250,000 troops engaged in heavy fighting, with massive casualties on both sides. Napoleon did not show his old verve and maneuver: he attacked crudely and frontally all day. Although the Russian Army was driven back and withdrew under cover of dark, and was forced to abandon the capital, it was not eliminated as a fighting force and it badly mauled Napoleon's legions. During the French stay in Moscow, the Russians gathered new strength while Napoleon's regiments bled men, discipline, and fighting cohesion. The failure to win at Borodino and the subsequent disaster in the snows—when the French were harassed, humbled, and then routed during the *retreat from Moscow*—destroyed Napoleon's army, fatally damaged his reputation for invincibility, and thus roused his many enemies to concerted action. *Talleyrand* foresaw all this, saying contemporaneously and accurately of Borodino: "It is the beginning of the end."

Bose, Subhas Chandra (1897–1945). "Netaji" (Leader). Indian nationalist. After the *Amritsar massacre* he questioned the policy of nonviolence upheld by the *Congress Party*. He became party president in 1938 but broke with *Mohandas Gandhi* (he had never accepted Gandhi's insistence on nonviolent resistance) before the war, calling openly for armed *insurrection*. An admirer of *Hitler* and *fascism* in general, in early 1941 he fled in disguise to Afghanistan, from there to Moscow, and thence to Berlin. In 1943 a German *U-boat* carried him on a three-month voyage around Africa (*Suez* was of course closed) to Singapore, to attend the only conference held to plan Japan's *Greater East Asia Co-prosperity Sphere*. During 1944–1945 he led the *Indian National Army* alongside Japanese forces against British and Indian troops in Burma, setting up a provisional capital in Rangoon and briefly invading northeast India in March 1944. He also declared war on the United States. The INA surrendered in 1945. Bose died in Taiwanese exile that August.

Boshin War (1868–1869). *See* bakufu; *Japan*; samurai.

Bosnia. This mountainous province was ruled by Catholic Croatians in the Middle Ages (twelfth through fifteenth centuries), and then was briefly an independent duchy before falling under Turkish sway and becoming a province of the *Ottoman Empire*, 1463–1878. In 1878 the *Congress of Berlin* gave Austria the right to administer the area as a *protectorate*. Austria formally annexed Bosnia in 1908, precipitating the *Bosnian Crisis*. Bosnia remained part of the *Austro-Hungarian Empire* until 1918. It was incorporated into *Yugoslavia* the next year. During *World War II* it was annexed by the Nazi *puppet* *regime* in Croatia and was the scene of vicious *guerrilla warfare* and ethnic massacres. After the war it was again dominated by Serbia, within the remade *Communist* Yugoslavia. In 1991 Bosnia's parliament declared independence, after an earlier declaration by Croatia. In April 1992, this was *recognized* by the *European Community* and the United States. War followed, in which well-armed Bosnian Serbs pursued a policy of *ethnic cleansing* aimed at joining the lion's share of Bosnian territory to Serbia. At the end of 1992 Croatia too attacked to carve out Croat sections of Bosnian land, leaving *enclaves* of Muslims cut off, starving, and at the mercy of Serb and Croat *militia*. EC and United Nations mediators proposed *partition* into a patchwork of ethnically defined territories in a loose federation. UN troops were helpless to prevent fighting or deliver humanitarian aid, in the face of Serb militia refusal to permit access to the Muslim enclaves. In February 1993, the United States began to airdrop relief supplies. Six months later the UN still would not intervene with force, and all three *ethnic groups* engaged in intensified *ethnic cleansing* to secure as much land as possible before the expected partition. The *Vance-Owen peace plan* was then abandoned in favor of a three-way partition reflecting the reality of Croat and Serb gains. The Muslims objected, but the *Security Council* refused to lift the arms *embargo*. NATO intervened in 1995 to set up a de facto *protectorate* ostensibly dedicated to building a multiethnic Bosnia, but really just freezing in place the three-way conflict, without hope of resolving it. *See also Third Balkan War.*

Suggested Reading: Noel Malcolm, *Bosnia. A Short History* (1994).

Bosnia-Herzegovina. *See Austrian Empire; Bosnia.*

Bosnian Crisis (1908–1909). Austria claimed Bosnia at the *Berlin Congress* of 1878, but the province remained nominally part of the *Ottoman* domains. Fearing a revival of Turkish influence, Austria formally *annexed* Bosnia in October 1908. That precipitated a *crisis* with Serbia and Russia, which demanded *compensation*. Germany threatened *intervention* in behalf of Austria in January 1909, while Britain was reluctant to see Russian warships in the *Straits*. This combination forced Russia to back down, humiliating it and forcing it closer to the *Entente Cordiale*. The memory lingered, to stiffen Russian resolve during the *mobilization crisis* of 1914. The affair also angered Serbia and generally raised tensions in the region where two *Balkan Wars* would soon follow and *World War I* would begin. *See also Eastern Question.*

Bosporus. The narrow channel passing under the walls of Istanbul (*Constantinople*), linking the Black Sea with the Sea of Marmora, and through the *Dardanelles*, the Mediterranean as well. Its *strategic* importance to Russia and Britain made it the central issue in the *Straits Question*. *See also Nelidov Project.*

Botha, Louis (1862–1919). South African general and statesman. A relative moderate, he was elected to the Volksraad (Parliament) of the *Transvaal Republic* in 1898. He voted against war with Great Britain, but joined the Transvaal Army when war came anyway. He was commander-in-chief of all Boer forces during the *Second Boer War*, conducting the siege of Ladysmith but suffering defeat at Bergendal in August 1900. He then recognized that the Boers could not defeat the British in a *conventional* campaign, so he converted his farmers' army into a *guerrilla* force. Botha invaded *Natal* in September, while *Jan Smuts* invaded *Cape Colony*. Botha and his men fought for two more years before accepting defeat. Botha attended the peace conference at Vereeniging and signed the peace treaty named for that town, which ended the Boer War. In 1907 Botha became premier of the Transvaal, which he represented at the Imperial Conferences in London in 1907 and 1911. Along with Smuts, he worked for moderation and reconciliation between Boers and the British in Cape Colony. In 1910 he became the first premier of the Union of South Africa, bringing those two peoples together. In 1914–1915, he suppressed a Boer rebellion. During *World War I* he again cooperated with his old enemy, working with Britain to conquer German Southwest Africa (Namibia); he would maneuver to make it a South African *mandate* at the *Paris Peace Conference*, which he attended.

Botha, Pieter Willem (b. 1916). Defense minister of South Africa, 1966–1978; prime minister, 1978–1984; president, 1984–1989. He was *hard line* and highly repressive in support of *apartheid* at home and supported aggressive *intervention* and *sabotage* by South African forces of neighboring African nations, regardless of the consequences for negative world opinion about South Africa. His retirement opened the way to overdue reform. In 1998 he was found guilty of contempt for refusing to testify before the *Truth and Reconciliation Commission*. *See also Nelson Mandela.*

Botswana. Formerly Bechuanaland (to 1966). The Sotho moved into Botswana to escape the *Mfecane* of *Shaka* and the *Zulu*, in turn disturbing the Tswana peoples already established there. A British *protectorate* was proclaimed in 1885 in response to the German annexation of *Namibia*. From 1886 Botswana was used as a defensive base against *Boer* and German *encroachments* on territories in East Africa such as *Rhodesia* and Kenya, which Britain considered more important. Botswana became a base for offensive operations against German *colonies* in southern Africa during *World War I*. Upon independence as Botswana in 1966, it adopted a pragmatic approach toward *apartheid* in South Africa—reflecting an overall economic and military vulnerability to its large, powerful neighbor. From the 1970s it enjoyed high rates of *growth*, significant *foreign direct investment*, and an excellent return on its diamonds.

Bougainville insurgency (1989–1997). In 1989–1990 a *secessionist* movement sprang up among landowners on this Solomon Island that belongs to Papua New Guinea. New Zealand and the Solomons hosted talks in 1990–1991 that led to lifting of a *state of emergency* declared earlier. Talks broke off, but resumed in 1993. After nine years of fighting, the drive for secession was defeated in 1997. The struggle may have claimed 20,000 lives.

boundary. A line of *de jure* (though sometimes just *de facto*) demarcation separating two territories. Boundaries often follow *natural frontiers* such as coastlines or rivers or water basins; others follow lines of longitude or latitude. Many simply mark the line of control reached by one side's military forces in the last decisive war. Some social scientists committed to *critical theory* appear so confused by these basic facts that one incomprehensibly suggested that we should treat real borders "without reference to political boundaries, and indeed, without any reference to physical boundaries." He might try crossing without a *passport. See also accretion; avulsion; border; frontier; maritime frontier; thalweg.*

Bourbon dynasty. The dynasty that ruled France upon the accession to the throne in 1589 of *Henri IV* of Navarre and held it until declaration of the First Republic in 1792, during the *French Revolution.* It resumed power briefly in 1814, and then again in 1815 after the *Hundred Days,* with the restoration of *Louis XVIII.* The Bourbons were overthrown in 1830 in favor of the *July Monarchy.* Bourbons also ruled in Naples, 1735–1806, and again, 1815–1860; and in Spain, 1700–1931. The Bourbons were noted for rigid conservatism in political and social affairs. *Talleyrand* famously said of the French branch of the family: "They have learned nothing, and forgotten nothing." *See also Armand Richelieu; Carlists; Habsburg dynasty; Louis XIV; Louis XVI; Romanov dynasty.*

bourgeoisie. (1) The middle class. (2) In *Marxism,* the class that developed the capitalist *mode of production* and opposes the interests of the *proletariat.*

Boutros-Ghali, Boutros (b. 1916). Egyptian and world statesman. As foreign minister of Egypt he participated in the *Camp David Accords.* He became *Secretary General* of the *United Nations* at the beginning of 1992. He was exceptionally active and unusually (some would say, refreshingly) blunt as he publicly lectured states large and small on their financial and other obligations to the UN. He proposed an ambitious agenda of moving from *peacekeeping* to *peacemaking* and was strongly supportive of UN intervention and humanitarian efforts in Angola, Bosnia, Cambodia, Haiti, Somalia, and elsewhere. However, he came under severe U.S. criticism for mismanagement of UNO finances, and, though supported by the African *bloc,* the *Clinton* administration blocked his reelection and he served only one term.

Boxer Protocol (1901). A humiliating agreement forced upon China and the *Qing* dynasty after the defeat of the *Boxer Uprising*. It forbade importation of modern arms for two years; allowed foreign garrisons on Chinese soil to guard all legations and concession areas; required China to pay massive *reparations* over 40 years; and expanded *extraterritorial* economic, political, and legal privileges of foreigners resident in China. In 1908 the United States remitted its portion of the Boxer reparations. In 1919 the *Bolsheviks* renounced any additional payments to Russia. *See also Marco Polo Bridge incident.*

Boxer Uprising/Rebellion (1898–1901). A violent, antiforeigner uprising led by the Society of Harmonious Fists (or Boxers United in Righteousness), with roots in the drought-stricken, poor north of China—in 1898 their main base was in *Shandong*. The Boxers were mainly poor peasants loosely organized in self-defense (martial arts) secret societies, many of which were anti*missionary* and anti*Christian*. Under the *unequal treaties* forced on China by foreign powers, Christians enjoyed special legal protections; this was doubly resented by the xenophobic Boxers. Most were men, but there were also segregated female regiments such as the Red Lanterns Shining. Many were illiterate, mystical fanatics who believed that they were invulnerable to bullets. Insofar as they had any coherent political aim, it was to expel all "foreign devils" from China and to save the *Qing dynasty*, to which ends they killed Christian missionaries and Chinese converts in a series of vicious atrocities, and indiscriminately attacked foreign nationals. Antiforeign sentiment was aggravated after 1898 by the practice of *concession diplomacy*.

By early 1900, the Boxers had moved from the countryside into Beijing and other major cities. On June 17th, the *Great Powers* (Austria-Hungary, France, Great Britain, Italy, Japan, and Russia) seized the Dagu (Taku) forts, near Tientsin, to land troops in the expectation of war with the Qing, who were sympathetic to Boxer aims. A relief column of 2,000 foreign troops (the "Seymour Expedition") was mauled by Boxers and retreated to Tientsin. Dowager Empress *Cixi* wavered about openly supporting the Boxers until the German consul was killed, thousands more Christians were massacred, and the foreign legations in Beijing—housing some 900 diplomats, missionaries, soldiers, and scholars, as well as 3,000 Chinese Christian refugees–came under a Boxer siege, which would last 55 days. On June 21st Cixi formally *declared war* on the foreign powers. However, most provincial commanders abandoned the Qing, withholding the regular Chinese Army from the fighting. On August 14th a column of 20,000 American, British, French, German, Japanese, and Russian troops relieved the foreign legations. Fighting continued for another year, as German troops led by General Lothar von Trotha—who would later conduct a *genocide* in *German Southwest Africa* during the *Herero-Nama War*—engaged in massacres and bloody reprisal in Shandong, while Russians carried out mass killings in the Amur-Ussuri region. China agreed to the peace treaty, the *Boxer Protocol*, in September 1901. Its humiliating terms fatally weakened the hold of the *Manchus* while strengthening *nationalists* led by *Sun Yixian*, even though Sun's attempt to take direct advantage of the rebellion was defeated by Qing troops.

boyar. A Russian noble service class, below the rank of prince, especially those residing in and around Moscow. The boyars perennially contested the power of the early tsars, until tamed by *Peter I* (1698). Thereafter, they remained a drag on Russian *modernization* through the nineteenth century. *See also* strel'sty.

boycott. In international relations, when nationals of one state refuse to buy goods or services from another. The term stems from the ostracism (social and economic excommunication) by Irish peasants in County Mayo of an especially hard English land agent, Captain Charles Boycott, following a recommendation by *Parnell* during the Irish Land War (1879–1882).

Other examples are when Chinese nationalists boycotted American goods after 1905 to protest anti-Asian immigration laws in the United States; Chinese boycotted Japanese goods as part of the *May 4th Movement*; many Indians refused to buy British goods after 1905 to protest the partition of Bengal, and, later led by *Gandhi*, Indian consumers kept up a sustained and highly damaging boycott of British textiles; the *Arab League* boycotted Israeli goods, 1948–1993; the United States boycotted Cuban trade after 1960; an international boycott of South Africa lasted from 1965 to 1992. Although boycotts supposedly imply voluntary action taken by private international actors for public policy reasons, and therefore lie outside the purview of *international law*, very often they are backed by governments as an extension of their foreign policy, making the term nearly interchangeable with a full trade *embargo*. *See also sanctions.*

Boyne, Battle of (July 12, 1690). In 1690 the Dutch Protestant king *William III* (of Orange) defeated the *Jacobite* forces of the deposed Catholic, James II (1633–1701), in this critical battle in *Ulster* that ended the Catholic threat to England. For centuries thereafter, Protestants in Northern Ireland celebrated the triumph of their ancestors with deliberately provocative annual parades through Catholic neighborhoods, sparking bouts of intercommunal violence. *See also Marlborough, John Churchill, Duke of.*

Bradley, Omar (1893–1981). U.S. general in *World War II*, affectionately known by his troops as the "G.I.'s General," both for his solicitude and his concern for minimizing casualties. He commanded under *Patton* in North Africa and Sicily. On the *western front* he fought under *Eisenhower*. He oversaw the formation of *NATO* as head of the Joint Chiefs of Staff, 1948–1953. Although he supported the war effort in Korea, he was deeply distrustful of the motives of *Douglas MacArthur*.

Brahman. The priestly class and elite caste of classical *Hinduism*. The Brahman caste probably originated in *Aryan* culture; it was chiefly responsible for commentary on sacred texts (the *Vedas*) and for sustaining the more rigorous aspects of the *caste system* in subsequent centuries.

brain drain. An outflow of highly educated or skilled persons from one country to another as a result of greater economic opportunity abroad or a wish to escape government repression at home. Before *World War II* the United States became a major beneficiary of brilliant scientists (often Jewish) fleeing *fascist* persecution in Europe. After WWII the United States was able to attract large numbers of foreign scientists, engineers, and doctors to its high salaries and advanced facilities. The loss of trained personnel to other countries can be a major problem, as the costs of education are largely or wholly borne by the general public in the losing country, but the gains made may be merely private for the individual who emigrates.

Brandenburg-Prussia. *See Prussia.*

Brandt Commission. A United Nations ad hoc commission, headed by *Willy Brandt*, which reported in 1980 on *North-South issues*. It recommended a set of broadly *social democratic*, *multilateral* solutions to issues of *development, famine*, and North-South trade. These proposals were much applauded within the *UN General Assembly*, especially by the *Third World* states, but, given a historic turn toward market solutions to development problems then just beginning, few were ever enacted.

Brandt, Willy, né Karl Herbert Frahm (1913–1992). German statesman. Mayor of West Berlin, 1957–1966; foreign minister, 1966–1969; chancellor, 1969–1974. A life-long *Social Democrat* (SPD), he left Germany for Norway in 1933 upon the *Nazi* seizure of power. He took out Norwegian citizenship and changed his name, but remained active in German Social Democratic circles. Upon the invasion of Norway by Germany in 1940, he moved to neutral Sweden, where he remained active in the anti-Nazi *resistance* during *World War II*. After the war he returned to Germany and renewed his citizenship. He served in the Bundestag, 1949–1957, and was elected mayor of the divided city of *Berlin*. He rose to international prominence as an anti-Communist during the *Berlin Wall* crisis in 1961. He was a driving force behind *Ostpolitik* and *détente* in the late 1960s and early 1970s, for which he won the 1971 *Nobel Prize* for Peace. He was forced to resign after it was learned that a member of his personal staff was an East German *agent of influence*. Much admired among Social Democrats generally, he later chaired a United Nations commission on issues of economic *development* that popularly bore his name.

Braun, Werner von (1912–1977). German rocket scientist. Braun was fascinated by rocketry from his boyhood. In 1930 he founded the Society for Space Travel and established an experimental rocket base outside Berlin. He moved to *Peenemünde* in 1936 to direct rocket research for *Hitler*. He headed the team that built the *V-1 and V-2 rockets*, as well as the world's first jet fighters. Braun's main frustration before and during *World War II* was that Hitler did not appreciate the potential of the weapons he was designing. He was briefly imprisoned on espionage charges in 1944, for refusing to cooperate with an effort by *Himmler* to transfer the V-2 project to *SS* control. He was released on the personal order of Hitler and returned to Peenemünde. He was captured, along with his research team, by the U.S. Army as the war ended. His subsequent career is a testament to the cold pragmatism of international relations. Driven by *Cold War* imperatives, his past service to the Nazis was overlooked in favor of his future service to the United States: he was made a U.S. citizen in 1955 and later headed the U.S. Ballistic Missile Agency. He was singularly responsible for the development and success of America's early *ICBM* force. He oversaw the launch of the first U.S. satellite, Explorer I, in 1958, and headed the Marshall Space Flight Center, 1960–1970. There, he guided the Mercury, Gemini, and Apollo programs. His Saturn V rocket carried the Apollo astronauts to the moon.

Brazil. Brazil fell into the Portuguese *sphere of influence* after 1500, when it was discovered by Pedro Cabral, as it fell under amended terms of the *line of demarcation*. At first, sparse Portuguese settlements cleaved to the coast and were mostly planted there to support ships protecting the fleets returning from India and Asia, around Africa, from raids by French *corsairs*. This naval contest with French *privateers* continued to the end of the sixteenth century. In 1532 Lisbon determined on promoting settlement to forestall freelance French encroachment. The native, coastal population (mainly Tupí-speaking Indians) was politically divided and heavily engaged in intertribal warfare. The various Tupí peoples were slowly killed by disease, sometimes exterminated deliberately, and in general conquered or pushed back into the interior and the *Amazon basin*—though this process took more than 200 years. African slaves were first imported c. 1538, but by the 1540s the Portuguese population was still only about 2,000 persons. In 1549 a central government was established by royal decree, at Salvador, which became the capital. In 1570 the devout Catholic King Sebastião of Portugal decreed all Indians to be free (vast numbers were already dead from imported infectious *diseases*), but making exceptions for cannibals and rebels that provided excuses to keep many Indians in *slavery* nonetheless. Yet, there were not enough Indians left to fill the forced labor needs of a now-growing colony. Immediately, therefore, white settlers started to import African slaves in larger numbers to work on plantations growing a newly imported crop (from the Spanish Caribbean), which would drive the economy and determine much of Brazil's social and racial composition for 300 years: plantation sugar. As a result, modern Brazil has the second largest black population in the world, virtually all descended from slaves. It also developed a distinct, interracial population—Portuguese rule and culture was more tolerant of miscegenation than was Imperial Spain's.

During Portugal's "Spanish Captivity" (1580–1640) under *Philip II*, Brazil was a target of anti-*Habsburg* assaults by the Dutch and English. In 1624 Dutch marines first invaded Brazil, but were repulsed. The Dutch returned in force to capture, after a bloody battle, and hold Recife in 1630. They remained in Brazil, skirmishing constantly and at one point controlling nearly 2,000 miles of coast. From 1640, when Portugal overthrew Spanish rule, Lisbon and Amsterdam were allied; this abated the fighting in Brazil, but did not end it. The Dutch were finally defeated and driven into Surinam in 1654—mainly by Brazilian settlers, rather than the Portuguese military. In the interior, "bandeiras" (mostly, thieves and slavers akin to the kind of men who ran Portugal's slave markets in Angola and Mozambique) pressed against the missions, which sought to protect the remaining Indians who had fled the coastal settlements as well as newly encountered Amazonian tribes. This led to small wars between small armies of bandeiras and Indians armed and trained by the *Jesuits*, as well as settler rebellions against the Jesuits (who were making progress in Lisbon convincing the monarchy to place all Indians under protection of their Order) in 1661, and again in 1680. In the latter sixteenth century the sugar industry faced severe competition from the West Indies. *Gold* was discovered in Minas Geras in 1690, leading to the first settlement in the interior, from whence many Indians had already disappeared as a result of slave-raiding and disease. In the 1720s, diamonds were also found there. The Jesuits, long-standing defenders of the remaining interior Indians, were expelled in 1759. In 1763 the capital was moved from Salvador to Rio de Janeiro. From c. 1750–1800 cotton production made inroads in world markets. In a closed, *mercantilist* system, Brazil's ports were closed to all but Portuguese trade, with a modest exception for British ships sailing between Portugal and Brazil that dated to the Anglo-Portuguese alliance of 1654.

In 1807 the Portuguese monarch, Dom Joao VI (John VI), had temporarily moved to Brazil, after Lisbon was taken by *Napoleon*. British troops came to Portugal's aid, however, and the court (minus the monarch) returned to Portugal in 1808. An appetite for monarchy was thus established in Brazil, and a taste for Brazil whetted in the monarchy. The *Peninsular War* also opened Brazil's trade to all comers after 1808, as Britain exacted trade rights as the price of independence for Portugal from Spain, which thereby remained outside the *Continental System*. In 1815 Brazil ceased to be a legal colony when it was made a kingdom, and the constitutional equal of Portugal. In 1817 the "Republic of Pernambuco" was briefly proclaimed in the north, but the rebellion was put down by Portuguese troops. The French had been driven out of Portugal in 1811, yet still King John had not returned from Brazil. Instead, in 1815 he elevated Brazil to equal status with Portugal, as a kingdom. In

1819 a *mutiny* in the Portuguese Army overthrew the king's regents in Lisbon. The new Cortes (parliament) in 1821 ordered King John to return. He did (March 7, 1821), but with great reluctance. The Cortes next revoked Brazil's trade privileges, attempting to reimpose a *mercantilist* regime, and otherwise demonstrated that it intended to once again treat Brazil as a colony and not an equal. When the Cortes tried to force the prince regent, Dom Pedro (1798–1834, r. 1822–1831), also to return to Portugal (September 7, 1822), he replied "fico" ("I remain") and was crowned as the first emperor of Brazil the next month. Mopping-up operations, mostly by British *mercenary* sailors and marines, were then conducted against Portuguese forces located mainly in northern Brazil. Brazilian independence was thus accompanied by significant popular unrest but little serious violence.

Dom Pedro I abdicated in 1831 in favor of his five-year-old son, Dom Pedro II (1825–1891, r. 1831–1889), and returned to Portugal. The new emperor thus reigned under a regency, 1831–1840, and then on his own to 1889. Brazil won the Paraguayan War, better known as the *War of the Triple Alliance* (1864–1870), in which Brazil and Argentina formed an alliance with the Colorados in Uruguay against the aggressive dictator of Paraguay, Francisco Solano López, who had supported the losing Blancos in the long Uruguayan civil war. The *slave trade* was banned for Brazilians in 1850. Brazil had fought the War of the Triple Alliance with slave soldiers. Their performance led to partial abolition of slavery in 1871 ("free womb law") and full abolition of slavery in 1888. Dom Pedro II, identified with slave-owning interests, and after a damaging quarrel with the *Catholic Church*, was deposed (forced to abdicate) by an army revolt in 1889. A republic was proclaimed under the name United States of Brazil; this was changed to the Federative Republic of Brazil in 1967. Into the 1960s Brazil remained essentially agrarian, but the end of slavery led to a sudden rise in immigration (as substitute labor), a decline in the relative importance of sugar, and a rise in the role of coffee, rubber, cocoa, and cotton in the national economy. Brazil was ruled by its military after another revolt in 1930, during a world slump in commodity prices. Under the dictator Getúlio Vargas (1930–1945) it was run as a *corporatist* state. Vargas bent to American pressure to *declare war* on the *Axis* in 1942 (his personal sympathies may have leaned the other way) and sent troops to fight in Italy in 1944. He was ousted in 1945 and Brazil experimented with democracy, 1945–1964, and also became a charter member of the *Rio Pact*.

As its economy grew, Brazil sought to exert regional leadership, surpassing its old rival Argentina. In 1960 its capital was moved to the planned interior city of Brasilia. Vargas returned to power in 1950, but mounting failure and opposition led him to commit suicide in 1954. In 1964 the generals seized power and instituted a harsh regime widely criticized for *torture* and other *human rights* abuses. Brazil's economy experienced rapid *growth*, and by the 1980s it was a significant arms manufacturer and exporter and a rising industrial power. However, Brazil was also a major *debtor nation* in constant conflict with foreign creditors. With the generals thus discredited even on the economic front, Brazil returned to democracy in 1985. It also adopted a *neoliberal* economic program. Still, its inability to meet its foreign *debt service* led to acceptance in the 1990s of a *stabilization program* designed and approved by the *International Monetary Fund*. Brazil still faced international criticism of its *development* policies concerning the environment and *indigenous peoples*. In response, Brazil announced an *Amazon* environmental initiative in 1989 and hosted the *Earth Summit* in 1992, while resisting efforts to treat the Amazon basin as a global, rather than a national, resource. Other important decisions were held up by a simultaneous political crisis, which ended only when President Fernando Collor was impeached and replaced by Itmar Franco. In 1998 Brazil mediated a border dispute between Peru and Ecuador and began to shift its armed forces toward a more regional and *peacekeeping* orientation.

Suggested Readings: Roderick Barman, *Brazil. The Forging of a Nation, 1798–1852* (1988); Burns E. Bradford, *A History of Brazil* (1970); John Hemming, *Red Gold. The Conquest of the Brazilian Indians* (1978); A.J.R Russell-Wood, ed., *From Colony to Nation* (1975).

Brazzaville bloc. A regional association formed in 1960 by the new states in Africa, superseded by the *OAU* in 1963.

breeder reactor. A nuclear reactor built to produce *plutonium* for bomb construction or plutonium reactors by various enrichments of its uranium fuel.

Brenner Pass. A strategic Alpine pass between Austria and Italy. Its access and control was a major objective of both during *World War I*, leading to repeated futile mountain battles at *Isonzo* that cost hundreds of thousands of lives.

Brest-Litovsk, Treaty of (March 3, 1918). A separate *Carthaginian peace* signed by the *Bolsheviks* with the *Central Powers*. Negotiations began on December 3, 1917, among Russian, German, Austrian, Ottoman, and Bulgarian delegations. When the Bolsheviks resisted the full terms, Germany invaded Russia on February 17, 1918, meeting no resistance. The Bolsheviks signed. The deal pulled Russia formally out of *World War I* (fighting had mostly stopped four months earlier) and gave Germany possession or control of nearly one-third of Russia's territory (the Baltic States, Caucasus, Finland, Poland, and Ukraine) and one quarter of its population. Germany also took Russia's gold reserves and extorted massive *reparations*. The Bolsheviks agreed because the Army had melted away and in order to concentrate on consolidating power as they entered the *Russian Civil War*. The Germans wanted the full spoils of victory and to transfer 50 divisions to the *western front* to reinforce a last, great offensive before the arrival of U.S. troops could deny them victory. The treaty thus caused great bitterness against Russia among the *Allied and Associated Powers*. Britain and France intervened against the

Bolsheviks in an effort to keep Russia in the war and secondarily to prevent establishment of a Communist regime. The United States was at most a reluctant and minor participant in the interventions and the first to pull out. Germany's avarice at Brest-Litovsk set a moral precedent for what might have been a still harsher *diktat* on reparations at the *Paris Peace Conference*. *See also Vladimir Len; Erich Ludendorffin.*

Bretton Woods system. A conference held in Bretton Woods, New Hampshire, in July 1944, laid the ground for creation of the *International Bank for Reconstruction and Development* (IBRD) and the *International Monetary Fund* (IMF).

The long-term purposes of these talks, the most elaborate and ambitious economic conference ever held, were to set up a cooperative system to monitor *exchange rates*, maintain *liquidity*, and prevent *balance of payment* problems. The immediate aims were to assist in postwar *reconstruction*, ease the transition back to a *market economy* from wartime government administration and heavy rationing and regulation, and encourage *integration* of the world's major trading economies along liberal lines and away from renewal of the tariff wars of the 1930s. It worked extremely well. The Bretton Woods arrangements rebuilt the postwar monetary system on dollar convertibility to gold, which created an international *regime of fixed currencies* that orbited the U.S. dollar standard. Because Britain was weaker than first thought, and owing to the size of the U.S. economy and American control over *European Recovery Program* funds, the system evolved from an early plan for limited international management to dependence on primary U.S. management. Yet, it was greatly successful in aiding quick and sustained recovery among *OECD* nations. It lasted until 1971, when *Nixon* took the United States off the *gold standard*. It has been replaced by a system of floating *exchange rates* and loose collective management. One Bretton Woods initiative, a proposed *International Trade Organization*, failed to get off the ground; it was partly replaced by the *GATT* and then belatedly realized in the *World Trade Organization*. *See also John Maynard Keynes; Nixon shocks.*
   Suggested Reading: Alfred Eckes, *A Search for Solvency* (1975).

brevet promotion. British: "brevit." When a soldier or sailor is promoted temporarily, on the battlefield, as a result of casualties among officers or for conspicuous bravery or demonstrated leadership ability in combat or command situations. It does not usually confer the full powers (or full pay) normally associated with the new rank.

Brezhnev Doctrine (1968). Advanced a month after the invasion of *Czechoslovakia*, it declared a Soviet right to *intervene* where Moscow deemed *socialism* and the leading role of the *Communist Party* was threatened by *counter-revolutionary* forces. In short, Moscow viewed the *status quo post bellum* as irreversible concerning *Communist* states, while supporting *wars of national liberation* and proclaiming *peaceful coexistence* with the West elsewhere. The Brezhnev Doctrine was tacitly repudiated by the Soviet Union in 1989, and almost immediately the *Berlin Wall* and the *Soviet bloc* alike came tumbling down. *See also Afghan-Soviet War; East Germany; Wojciech Jaruzelski; Prague Spring; Reagan Doctrine; Sinatra Doctrine; Soviet legal thought; Tito.*

Brezhnev, Leonid Ilyich (1906–1982). First secretary of the CPSU, 1964–1982. He helped oust *Khrushchev* from power. Thereafter, his reputation within Russia became that of a stultifying bureaucrat who delayed domestic reform for a whole generation. That view underestimates the degree to which his foreign policy was one of *adventurism:* he threatened China with a *pre-emptive strike* in 1969; supplied regimes in the *Middle East* with advanced weaponry; intervened with military aid and Cuban proxies in the Horn of Africa and Arabia; and most disastrously, approved the invasion of Afghanistan in 1979. While opportunistic, his main purpose still seems to have been to consolidate rather than extend the gains made after *World War II:* he promoted the *Warsaw Pact* invasion of Czechoslovakia in 1968 to forestall reforms that might unravel Soviet control of Eastern Europe; he cooperated with *Richard Nixon* and *Willy Brandt* in designing *détente* in the early 1970s; and he pushed for the *CSCE* talks, hoping they would lead to formal *recognition* of Soviet postwar gains, as well as divide the United States from Western Europe. *See also Brezhnev Doctrine.*

Briand, Aristide (1862–1932). French statesman. Eleven times premier; foreign minister, 1925–1932. He was the first to propose an attack on *Gallipoli* during *World War I.* He shared the 1926 *Nobel Prize* for Peace with Weimar statesman *Gustav Stresemann* for their joint work on Franco-German *rapprochement* in the aftermath of World War I, and specifically for their success at *Locarno.* He reluctantly coauthored the *Kellogg-Briand Pact*, which sought to outlaw war when what he really wanted was a security guarantee from the United States. He provided as much support to the *League of Nations* as French *public opinion* permitted.

bridgehead. A tactical position gained on the enemy's side of a river, preparatory to bringing over more troops.

brig. A military (especially naval) prison.

brigade. *See military units.*

brigantine. A two-masted *warship* of the age of sail, square-rigged on the foremast.

brinkmanship. Manipulating a crisis to the brink of war to frighten an opponent into backing down or making concessions in the dispute at issue. This dangerous style of statecraft, including threatening to use *nuclear weapons*, was attributed to the conduct of U.S. foreign policy by *John Foster Dulles* in the 1950s, but it can be ascribed to many leaders and crises. It was a favored tactic of *Adolf Hitler*, for instance. Perhaps the most inept would-be practitioner, ever, was *Saddam Hussein*.

Britain. *See Great Britain; United Kingdom.*

Britain, Battle of (July 11–September 17, 1940). This prolonged air battle between the *Luftwaffe* and the Royal Air Force (RAF) was just barely won by the RAF. The battle was the key to Hitler's planned invasion of Britain (Operation Sea Lion) and thus a major turning point in *World War II*. Only if the RAF was eliminated and German *air superiority* established would the Kriegsmarine be able to escort an invasion force across the *English Channel* with any chance of success against the *Royal Navy*. After initial skirmishes, the battle began in earnest on what the Germans code named Adlertag (Eagle Day), August 8, 1940. There were several keys to the battle's outcome: (1) Britain was able to significantly outproduce fighter aircraft, and thus replace its equipment losses. (2) The battle took place over England, which meant the British could recover many of their downed pilots, whereas the Germans lost both aircraft and crews—nearly 1,400 aircraft, all told. (3) Britain was aided by a series of bad decisions born of *Nazi* arrogance. The most fateful of these was Hitler's choice—provoked by rage over two small British raids against Berlin—to switch bomber targeting from RAF airfields to raids on British cities, which caused many civilian deaths but allowed the RAF to continue the fight. When Luftwaffe losses became intolerable, Hitler called off the battle and invasion and turned instead to planning *Barbarossa*, his great attack on Russia set for 1941. For some time he continued to harbor the delusion that Britain was not Nazi Germany's natural enemy and to hope for a *separate peace*. That left Britain time to rearm and recover. It then served as a giant airfield for the deadly, punishing Anglo-American air raids of 1942–1945 and as the main supply base and jump-off point for the Allied invasions of southern Europe and then Germany, 1943–1945. *Winston Churchill* aptly said of the British nation: "This was their finest hour," and of the British, Commonwealth, and Allied pilots who won the battle and thus helped save civilization itself from Nazi barbarism: "Never in the field of human conflict was so much owed by so many to so few."
Suggested Reading: Richard J. Overy, *The Battle* (2000).

British Antarctic Territory. A South Atlantic colony comprising several small and desolate island chains, near the much larger *Falkland Islands*.

British Cameroons. Part of this colony joined with the *French Cameroons* to form modern Cameroon in 1960; the other part joined Nigeria in 1961.

British Commonwealth. *See Commonwealth.*

British East Africa. In disuse. It once referred to *Kenya, Uganda, Tanganyika,* and *Zanzibar.*

British Empire. The vast territories brought under the authority of the British Crown by adventurous explorers and merchants, settlers, early industrial and commercial advantage, and the cannons, soldiers, and marines of the *East India Company* and the *Royal Navy*. It once comprised a quarter of the world's population and stretched so far afield it was said—romantically by some, bitterly by others—that "upon its shores the sun never sets." It was likely some Irish wag, though it might as easily have been a Punjabi or Nigerian, who added: "because not even God would trust the British in the dark."

The British Empire did not come into formal, centrally managed existence until the start of the eighteenth century. Before that, from the sixteenth century, English overseas *imperialism* had been fairly haphazard and somewhat idiosyncratic. It was marked by sharp commercial rivalry with the Dutch Republic and dominated by the far-flung activities of the East India Company, the *Hudson Bay Company*, and similar charter monopolies. The state became increasingly concerned with the welfare and protection of these overseas enterprises during a prolonged war with Imperial Spain, which brought England into alliance with the Netherlands. As long as England was a relatively small power, threats nearer to home commanded most of its attention and resources. Still, it kept up a minor interest in active colonization and began to accumulate some overseas colonies and possessions, but outside North America these remained for many decades mainly coastal *entrepôts*. As a more formal imperial policy began to take shape, Britain aimed at displacing the Dutch, Portuguese, and especially the French from control of the *spice trade* and the *slave trade*. The main body of England's first empire (not counting Ireland, Scotland, and Wales) took shape slowly in North America and the Caribbean in the seventeenth century during the *French and Indian Wars*, firming with defeat of France in the *Seven Years' War* (1756–1763). In short order, the lion's share and most valuable parts of this American empire were lost in the *American Revolution*. The loss of its American colonies reduced British interest in slaving, and further opened the door to the influence of *William Wilberforce*. By the early nineteenth century, Britain was committed to playing a singular role in ending the international slave trade.

Australasia early on was used as a dumping ground for criminals and political dissidents, and only much later was economically developed, settled and vigorously developed, and exploited. Vast wealthy India became the central focus of imperial policy by 1778, replacing almost simultaneously the lost empire in America, but Britain's grasp extended into China and Southeast Asia as well, to *Hong Kong* and *Singapore*. Geography largely determined that Britain would acquire other colonies along the African and, later, also Mediterranean and Persian Gulf routes to India and China. In many of these acquired territories the British preferred *indirect rule* to outright conquest and occupation. Even in India, *direct rule* (by the government, as opposed to "John Company") was delayed until the mid-nineteenth century. The heyday of the Empire came with a magnificent quarter century effort sustained to final victory in the *Napoleonic Wars*. This triumph was followed by domestic *industrialization*, growing dominance of the global economy, international economic leadership on the issue of *free trade*, dominance of sterling as the world monetary standard, and the related *Pax Britannica* of the nineteenth century, a rather misnamed epoch considering it also saw Britain fight the *Afghan Wars*, the *Crimean War*, the *Zulu Wars*, the *Indian Mutiny*, the *Opium Wars*, two *Boer Wars*, several *Burma Wars*, the *Ashanti Wars*, and the *Mahdi*, all while playing the *Great Game* in Central Asia and Tibet. Between 1874 and 1902, nearly five million square miles (and more than 100 million people) were added to the already huge expanse of the British Empire.

However, just as it peaked in power, expanse, and prestige, a near-fatal blow was dealt to the Empire by *World War I*. That contest so tested and drained Britain and its Empire that British financial leadership of the world economy was brought to an end (1917), its own finances cracked and threatened to break, and massive casualties sapped its will to hold onto the Empire by force of arms. The first clear sign of this new weakness came with acceptance of separate seating for the *Dominions*, and remarkably also for India, at the *Paris Peace Conference*. That was quickly followed by acquiescence in de facto independence for most of Ireland, in the form of the *Irish Free State*, after the *Irish War of Independence* (1918–1921). Meanwhile, in India the *Amritsar massacre* (1919) led *Mohandas Gandhi* and the *Congress Party* to shift from calls for *Home Rule* to demands for outright independence. At first strenuously resisted, very soon Britain agreed to discuss this at the *Round Table Conferences*. By 1931 the Dominions were effectively *sovereign* under terms of the *Statute of Westminster*, and, although India was no longer under the lash, it too was straining hard at the imperial leash.

The Empire rallied to Britain one last, but crucial, time to meet the twinned threats of Nazi Germany and Imperial Japan in *World War II*. That constituted not just Britain's, but also the Empire's "finest hour." It was also its last, for World War II finished what democratization of Britain itself had begun and the Great War had advanced: the unraveling of imperial ties in the name of *self-determination* and *democracy*, from Singapore and Hong Kong in the Far East to India and the Horn of Africa, from bases in Egypt and throughout the Middle East to the Cape and Caribbean. The subcontinent departed first, from 1947. Then the *Suez Crisis* (1956) finished Britain in the Middle East. After that, why hold onto Africa? "Empire Day" became "Commonwealth Day" in 1958. *Decolonization* of West, then East, Africa accelerated into the late 1960s, until by the end of that decade only a few scattered, mostly Caribbean and Pacific Island, remnants of the old realm remained under the Union flag. For additional detail on this vast commercial, political, and military enterprise, which spanned several centuries and continents, *see also Act of Union; Aden; American Revolution; Anthony Eden; Atlantic Charter; Australia; Belize; Bengal; Benjamin Disraeli; Bevin; Burma; Canada; Cape Colony; Cecil Rhodes; Clive; colonialism; Commonwealth; Cyprus; Douglas Haig; Durham Report; Eastern Question; Falkland Islands; Fashoda crisis; Fenians; Frederick Lugard; George III; George Rodney; Ghana; Gibraltar; gold standard; Gurkhas; Horatio Nelson; Imperial Conferences; Imperial Tariff; India; India Acts; Indian Army; James Dalhousie; John Fisher; Kenya; Kitchener; King George's War; King William's War; Louis Mountbatten; Malta; Maori Wars; New France; Nepal; Newfoundland; Nigeria; Opium Wars; penal settlements; Princely States; racism; Rāj; Rhodesia and Nyasaland; sea power; Sikh Wars; South Africa; Sudan; Suez Canal; Sykes-Picot agreement; Tibet; UDI; unequal treaties; United Kingdom; Victoria; War of 1812; War of the Austrian Succession; War of the Grand Alliance; War of the Spanish Succession; War of Jenkins's Ear; Wellington; Whig history; White Man's Burden; William Gladstone; William Pitt (1708–1778); William Pitt (1759–1806); Winston Churchill; Zambia; and other specific colonies.*

Suggested Readings: *Cambridge History of the British Empire*, 2nd ed. (1963); Muriel E. Chamberlain, *Pax Britannica? British Foreign Policy, 1789–1914* (1988); R. Hyam, *Britain's Imperial Century, 1815–1914* (1975); Lawrence James, *Raj. The Making and Unmaking of British India* (1998); Lawrence James, *Rise and Fall of the British Empire* (1996; 1985). Wm. Roger Lewis, ed., *Oxford History of the British Empire*, 2 vols. (1998); Richard Shannon, *Gladstone*, 2 vols. (1984; 1999); Richard Shannon, *The Age of Disraeli, 1868–1881* (1992); Richard Shannon, *The Crisis of Imperialism, 1865–1915* (1976).

British Expeditionary Force (BEF). The British Army fighting in France during *World War I* and again early in *World War II*. A small professional force in 1914, it was hugely reinforced by New Army volunteers and conscripts—expanding from just seven to more than seventy divisions—as well as by Australian, Canadian, and Indian divisions and corps. *See also Dunkirk, Treaty of; Frontiers, Battle of; Douglas Haig; Maginot Line; Marne, Battle of; Somme, Battle of; Ypres Salient, Battles of.*

British Guiana. The colonial era name of Guyana.

British Honduras. The colonial era name of Belize.

British India. Those parts of the subcontinent that before 1947 were subject to British law and governance, including most of modern Bangladesh, India, and Pakistan, but excluding some of the *Princely States.*

British Indian Ocean Territory (BIOT). The Chagos Archipelago, south of the Maldives in the Indian Ocean. The only remaining British possession in the region. One island, *Diego Garcia*, was leased to the United States in 1965 for use as a naval base and satellite relay station. To make room, the Chagos Islanders were forcibly deported to Mauritius. The whole Chagos group is claimed by Mauritius.

British Isles. From the British point of view, the islands of Great Britain, Ireland, the Orkneys, Isle of Man, and all small adjacent islands. However, this is not a universally accepted term. There is, in fact, no widely accepted political term for this important archipelago off the Atlantic coast of Europe.

British Malaya. The British colonial possessions located on the Malay peninsula and archipelago that later became part of *Malaya*, and later still part of the Malaysian Federation. *See also Sabah; Sarawak.*

British North America. (1) Pre-1776: All seventeen British *colonies* in North America (including the Caribbean in some usages); (2) 1783–1867: The colonial territories now comprising Canada, to which *Newfoundland* was later joined.

British North America Act (1867). The founding legislation that established Canada as a self-governing *dominion*. It united Ontario, Québec, Nova Scotia, and New Brunswick into a single *confederation*. *See also Commonwealth.*

British North Borneo. The colonial era name of *Sabah*.

British Rāj. *See* Rāj.

British Somaliland. A British *protectorate* in the Horn of Africa from the late nineteenth century. In the 1890s the British faced *guerrilla* resistance from the "Mad Mullah," Muhammad Hassan (1864–1920), and heavy fighting continued into the 1920s. It became independent in 1960, but shortly thereafter voluntarily joined *Italian Somaliland* to the south to form Somalia. In 1991 the population of some two million in this northwestern portion of Somalia declared its *secession* from the 1960 union. It avoided the worst fighting before, during, and after the *United Nations intervention in Somalia*, but its claim to *sovereignty* was not *recognized* by other states.

British Togoland. A small possession, it was joined to the *Gold Coast* (Ghana) in 1957.

British West Africa. A disused term that once collectively referred to *British Cameroons, Gambia, Gold Coast, Nigeria* (Lagos, *Oil Rivers Protectorate*, northern Nigeria), *Sierra Leone,* and *Togo.*

British West Indies. A general reference to former British colonial possessions in the Caribbean: Bahamas, Barbados, Jamaica, Trinidad, Tobago, and the Leeward and Windward Islands.

brownshirt. (1) A member of the Nazi *SA* (*Sturmabteilung*); (2) any *fascist* street thug. *See also blackshirt;* Freikorps; *Night of the Long Knives.*

brown water navy. One limited to small, fast, coast-hugging warships that operate mainly in the brackish, littoral waters off major coastlines. *See also blue water navy.*

Broderbund. "Band of brothers." A secret, elite *Afrikaans* organization formed in 1918 to promote Afrikaner nationalist interests, including racial separation and language rights, within the Union of South Africa. It was opposed by *Jan Smuts,* but steadily gathered influence. It was a principal supporter of *apartheid* after 1948.

Brumaire, 19th (November 10, 1789). The *coup* that brought *Napoleon I* to power in France, ending the *Directory* and instituting the *Consulate.*

Brunei (Brunei Darussalam). "Place of Peace." This small territory on the island of *Borneo* was the site of an independent *Sultanate* that controlled all Borneo from the sixteenth century until colonial times. Pressed in by expanding European powers, in much shrunken form Brunei was finally made a British *protectorate* in 1888. It gained independence in 1984, much later than most other British *colonies* and protectorates. It has huge and rich deposits of *oil.* As one result, to protect itself from invasion by less wealthy but far more powerful regional neighbors, Brunei followed an entirely pro-Western line upon independence. For example, in the 1980s it gave funds to the Nicaraguan *Contras* at the request of the *Reagan* administration, which had been blocked by the U.S. Congress from directly aiding the anti-*Sandinista* cause. Malaysia rejects Brunei's claim to a full *Exclusive Economic Zone* and disputes its claim to the rights of any *coastal state* to the resources of the adjacent *continental shelf.* Malaysia also disputes one land border it shares with Brunei. Long-term Indonesian intentions and attitudes toward Brunei's independence remain a matter of deep concern to its government. Domestically, the sultanate is protected by an elite guard, which includes tough *Gurkha* regiments, and internationally by its membership in *ASEAN* and close ties to the United States.

Brüning, Heinrich (1885–1970). Chancellor of *Weimar Germany*, 1930–1932. Leader of the Catholic Center Party, 1929–1934. As the world financial crisis deepened, his efforts at moderate reform came to naught. Unable to form a parliamentary majority, he chose to govern by decree, which was permitted under an emergency provision of the Weimar constitution, dismissing the Reichstag in 1930. That departure from parliamentary practice in favor of centralized decision-making further weakened Weimar's shaky democratic credentials. The *Nazi Party* and the *Communist Party* both increased their popular support and their representation in the ensuing election. Even with additional powers, which he also used to try to ban the various *paramilitary* gangs that plagued Weimar Germany, including the *SA* and *Freikorps*, he was unable to forestall collapse of the economy. He was abruptly forced out by *Hindenburg*, after failing to convince him that any hope for restoration of the *Hohenzollern* dynasty required skipping over the exiled *Kaiser Wilhelm II*. Brüning fled to the United States in 1934, where he became a professor of government at Harvard. He returned to Germany, 1951–1954, to teach politics at Cologne University.

Bruntland Commission (1987). Named for *Gro Harlem Bruntland*, this 1987 international commission called for, and thereby gave prominence to, the idea of *sustainable development*.

Bruntland, Gro Harlem (b. 1940). Director-general of the *World Health Organization* (WHO), 1998– ; prime minister of Norway, 1977–1981, 1986–1989, and 1990–1996. Trained as a physician in Oslo and at Harvard, she became Norway's first female prime minister at age 41. She was also the first woman to head WHO, taking charge during the worst crisis in that organization's history. She was narrowly elected, mainly by Western donor countries, though opposed by Japan. This *bloc* of nations sought basic reform of an international agency that had sunk into disrepute and was misdirected and corrupt under her two-term predecessor, Hiroshi Nakajima. Bruntland was often at the center of controversy. In 1987 she chaired the Bruntland Commission, which gave international prominence to the idea of *sustainable development*. She also championed a liberal view of women's rights, including unfettered access to abortion, a position she staked out against loud *Vatican* and *Islamic* opposition, particularly at the *United Nations Conference on Population* in Cairo in 1994.

Brusilov Offensive (June 4–August 10, 1916). Under the command of General Alexsei Brusilov, the tsar's armies launched an offensive on the *eastern front*. In June, they broke through Austrian lines before Lutsk, to advance 40 miles and capture large numbers of prisoners. In July they attacked into the *Pripet Marshes*, but were turned back by German divisions. The Austrians were savaged, losing nearly one million total casualties, including 400,000 *prisoners of war.* Germany lost another 350,000, but Russia lost nearly a million, too. Without ready reserves, Brusilov could not follow up his territorial gains—the greatest by any army to that point in the war. *See also Erich Falkenhayn; Paul Hindenburg; Kerensky Offensive; Rumania.*

Brussels, Treaty of (March 17, 1948). This defense pact among Britain, France, and the *BENELUX* nations was the precursor to *NATO*. Initially, it came about as much from fear of Germany as from apprehension about the Soviet Union.

Bryan, William Jennings (1860–1925). Thrice-defeated (1896, 1900, and 1908) Christian *fundamentalist* and *Democratic Party* candidate for president. He ran on a class warfare platform, for a return to an agrarian economy, against monied interests and the *gold standard*; he also opposed *annexation* of the Philippines. He served as secretary of state to *Woodrow Wilson*, 1913–1915. A passionate *pacifist*, he resigned over the second *Lusitania note* sent to Germany, which might have led to war had *Bethmann-Hollweg* not persuaded the High Command to back down on the question of *unrestricted submarine warfare*. *See also cooling-off treaties; monetary standard; Open Door.*

Brzezinski, Zbigniew (b. 1924). U.S. national security adviser, 1977–1981. He was the constant opponent of Secretary of State Cyrus Vance within the *Carter* administration. He consistently argued for a *hard line* toward the Soviets, viewed *human rights* policy mainly as an instrument of *Cold War* ideological contest with Moscow, and over time won a prolonged, behind-the-scenes struggle for control of U.S. foreign policy, in particular toward the *Soviet bloc.* He finally got his chance to set policy in 1980, when Vance resigned, ostensibly over a failed military rescue mission of U.S. diplomats in Iran during the *hostage crisis*, but really over the policy quarrel with Brzezinski. The latter persuaded Carter to institute a tougher line in relations with Moscow, but it was too late to have any real effect, as Carter shortly thereafter lost the presidency to *Ronald Reagan.* Out of office, Brzezinski saw his influence grow, as he was consistently more accurate than most other analysts about the root causes (nationalism among the captive nations of the Soviet empire) of ever more clear cracks in the Soviet bloc. He published a timely book on the horrors of *communism* in the twentieth century in early 1989, "The Grand Failure," and was a widely respected elder statesman during the 1990s.

Suggested Readings: Zbigniew Brzezinski, *The Grand Chessboard* (1997); *Power and Principle* (1983).

buccaneers. "Boucaniers." French *pirates.* Initially, they raided Spanish and Portuguese shipping in the Caribbean and partly down the Atlantic coast of South America from bases nestled in Honduras and elsewhere in Central

America. Raids by boucaniers (or buccaneers, as they were later known to the English sailors who faced them) caused the Spanish to evacuate all settlements on the north coast of Hispaniola (Haiti) in 1603. These pirates then settled there themselves during the early- to mid-1700s. During the eighteenth century they concentrated more on English shipping in the Caribbean. They enjoyed passive support from several island governments, which benefited from the economic boom caused by pirates spending booty in local ports, but that also suffered from a loss of legitimate trade. In times of war between England and France—which constituted most of the eighteenth century—buccaneer vessels and captains were often commissioned as *privateers* by the French monarchy.

Buchanan, James (1791–1868). U.S. president, 1857–1861. As minister (ambassador) to Russia, he negotiated a *commercial treaty* that had eluded U.S. diplomats for over 30 years. He also was a rank apologist for tsarism, including bloody repression of a rebellion in Poland in 1831. He defended *serfdom* in terms akin to his strong support for slavery in the American South. He served as secretary of state to *James Polk* and helped settle the *Oregon Question*. As president, he watched with inept and tragic befuddlement as the great crisis unfolded that led to dissolution of the United States and to the awful carnage of the *American Civil War*.

Bucharest, Treaty of (1913). This treaty ended the *Balkan Wars*, which preceded *World War I*. Although its specific territorial adjustments would be overturned in that greater conflagration, it had two lasting effects: (1) it pushed Turkey out of its European holdings, except a small area around *Constantinople*; and (2) it created a weak Albania and set it tremorously in the midst of the unsatisfied territorial ambitions of the other *Balkan states*.

Buddhism. Founded by the Nepalese aristocrat Prince Siddhartha ("The Buddha," or "Enlightened One," 563[?]–480[?] B.C.E.).

Buddhism is a distinctively Indian faith in origin, but that in modern times is hardly found in India, where after gaining millions of adherents it ultimately entered a long decline. This was brought about partly by disruptive invasions, partly by the co-option of the Buddha in north India into a revived *Hinduism* (as an Avatar in the cult of Vishnu worship), and in part by violent repression in south India by a new devotional cult of Shiva worshipers (bhakti), who also slaughtered *Jains* by the tens of thousands, wiping out that faith in the south. The Asoka emperor in India (269–232 B.C.E.) was more kindly disposed and sent out Buddhist *missionaries* to Sri Lanka and west Asia. Buddhism spread historically from north India throughout Asia, notably to Bhutan, Burma, China, Indochina, Japan, Sri Lanka, Thailand, and Tibet. It reached Southeast Asia probably in the first century C.E. Buddhism was introduced to

China in the *Han dynasty* and enjoyed a golden age there from the fifth to the ninth centuries C.E., until harshly repressed by the *Tang* in 845.

Classical Buddhism was rooted in the mystical traditions of ancient Hinduism, but was founded also as a reaction against *Aryan* ritual and rigidity. The Buddha rejected *Brahman* claims to simply inherit piety. Instead, he posited that suffering could be eliminated through self-perfection and through "prajna," or enlightenment, in which an end to earthly woes came from the extinction of desire via the "eightfold path" (right conduct, effort, meditation, memory, occupation, resolve, speech, and views) of right living on the "middle way" between extremes of radical asceticism and hedonism. Classical Buddhism thus stressed a tolerant, moderate, and personal discipline and self-correction leading via a cycle of reincarnations to nirvana (in the Mahayana tradition, a condition of holiness, purity, and release from all desires and travails of earthly life—an end to suffering rather than a mystical paradise). One may halt the cycle of births and deaths only with full enlightenment and merger with the Buddha, the first being to achieve nirvana. This later led to development of the doctrine of "bodhisattvas," or enlightened souls, of which the Buddha was the first, who might intercede for the salvation of the still unenlightened. Along with elevation of Buddha to godhead came development of a monastic movement dedicated to preservation of the original doctrine—in short, Buddhism progressively became both more anthropomorphic and doctrinaire. A highly meditative version of Buddhism developed in China known as Chan (in Japan, Zen).

Socially, Buddhism tended to promote fatalistic resignation by the masses, but encouraged charity and good works and gave rise to a hugely influential and widespread monastic movement. Buddhist monasteries played an important role in the accumulation of wealth and dissemination of learning and culture in Asia, directly comparable to the great Cistercian and other monastic movements in European history. Politically, Buddhism was historically associated with traditional kingship systems. In Japan, Buddhism thrived for many centuries before its monasteries and sectarian armies were crushed in the sixteenth century by *Nobunaga Oda*. Under the *Tokugawa shoguns*, Buddhism was co-opted to serve the *bakufu* state, though in Satsuma a local sect was persecuted into the nineteenth century. State Buddhism lost favor in the early *Meiji Restoration*, but resumed a central place in Japanese life by the end of the nineteenth century. In the twentieth century, Buddhism informed nationalist movements in Thailand, Burma, and Sri Lanka. In the Republic of Vietnam (RVN), Buddhist monks opposed the minority Catholic regime of *Ngo Diem*. Buddhists were harshly persecuted in *Mao's* China and in Tibet. They were massacred in Cambodia, along with everyone else, by the *Khmers Rouges*. In the nineteenth and twentieth centuries Buddhism began to make minor inroads in North America and Europe.

Suggested Readings: William T. de Bary, ed., *The Buddhist Tradition in India, China, and Japan* (1972); R. H. Robinson, *The Buddhist Religion*, 3rd ed. (1982).

buffer state. A small, *neutral* state separating two *Great Powers*, such as Afghanistan during the *Great Game* or Italy from the *Renaissance* to its *Risorgimento*, said to provide a cushion to absorb their potential hostility. In fact, such states may just as easily be a temptation to mutual *aggrandizement*, as the historical experience of Belgium and Poland well illustrate. The term does not apply to weak, but clearly *aligned*, states trapped by their geography between larger powers, such as those of Eastern Europe during the *Cold War*. *See also balance of power*; *buffer zone*; cordon sanitaire; *forward defense*; *Hundred Days*; *neutral zone*.

buffer stock. Reserves of commodities held by states or under *International Commodity Agreements*, purchased or released for sale from time to time as a means of evening out price fluctuations.

buffer zone. A *neutralized* and often *demilitarized zone* of territory separating hostile powers. These may be created by agreement or by one power unilaterally, in order to insulate itself from attack by pushing back the *frontier*. Examples include: *Heligoland*, the *Rhineland*, 1919–1936, Israel's self-proclaimed security zone in southern Lebanon after 1982, and *NATO's* 1999 creation of small buffer zones between Kosovo and Macedonia, and Kosovo and Serbia. *See also buffer state*; *neutral zone*.

Buganda. *See Uganda.*

Bukhara. An independent *emirate* from the collapse of the Timurids (c. 1500) to its conquest by Russia in 1865–1868. It was linked by trade to Russia and *Siberia* and to the several peoples of *Inner Asia*. From 1864 to 1868 it fought a losing *jihad* against the Russians. It was a Russian *protectorate* until 1917. *See also Central Asia*; *Great Game*.

Bukovina. Long an *Ottoman* province, it was ceded to Austria in 1775. Its Rumanian half was extorted from Rumania, along with *Bessarabia*, and added to the *Soviet Union* by *Stalin* in 1940 while *Hitler* was occupied fighting in the west. After *World War II* a portion was added by the Soviet Union to Ukraine. With the end of the *Cold War,* its southern portion remained part of Rumania. The remainder stayed with Ukraine.

Bulganin, Nikolai Alexandrovich (1895–1975). One-time mayor of Moscow, he was active in the Soviet Military Council during *World War II*. He was Soviet defense minister in 1946, vice premier after *Stalin's* death in 1953, and a figurehead premier, 1955–1958.

Bulgaria. In the first millennium C.E., Bulgaria was settled by an amalgam of *Slavic* peoples and the Bulgars, who migrated from Central Asia in the seventh century and made constant *frontier* war on the *Byzantine Empire*. In the ninth century, however, Bulgaria was converted to *Christianity* (*Orthodox Church*) and made a rough peace with *Constantinople*. This state of affairs was upset by the "Bogomil heresy," which began in Bulgaria and was most deeply rooted there. It split its adherents from communion with the larger body of Orthodox believers. Heavily persecuted, it nonetheless lasted for several centuries in remoter areas. Bulgaria was conquered by the *Ottomans* in 1396 and remained under Turkish rule for the next 500 years. In 1870 the Turks allowed the establishment of a separate branch of the Orthodox Church for their Bulgarian subjects (the Exarchate).

This body led a nationalist revival, encouraged by Russia. The Turks sought to crush the movement in 1875–1876 with tactics so brutal they attracted international attention, particularly from *Gladstone* and among *pan-Slavists* in Russia, as the "Bulgarian atrocities." The rebellion and reactionary state *terror* drew the Ottomans into yet another war with Russia, which led to forced acceptance of Bulgarian *autonomy* in the *Treaty of San Stefano* (1878), amended by the *Congress of Berlin* later that year. In 1885, in defiance of the treaty interests of the *Great Powers*, Bulgaria expanded into eastern *Rumelia*, inflicted a defeat on Serbia, and emerged as the largest of the new Slav states in the Balkans. That provoked a grave European crisis that nearly led to general war and brought an end to the *Dreikaiserbund*.

Bulgaria was gravely dissatisfied with the territorial outcome of the *Balkan Wars*. The Ottomans had held off British, French, and ANZAC forces at *Gallipoli*, inflicting terrible damage on the Australians, in particular. That encouraged Bulgaria to join the *Central Powers* in October 1915. Things had been quiet on the Balkan front until then, but now Serbia was overrun by armies from Germany, Austria, and Bulgaria, sending the rump of the Serb Army over the mountains to Albania and thence by ship to Corfu. An Anglo-French expedition to aid Serbia was imposed on neutral Greece, too late to help Serbia; but the Allies stayed in Salonika anyway. Bulgaria's fate was now tied to that of the Central Powers, and its army was engaged in a war far beyond its abilities. The Bulgarian Army was badly beaten at Salonika in 1918, and Bulgaria asked for terms. While its nationalists gained no satisfaction at the *Paris Peace Conference*, Bulgaria did obtain less onerous terms than other Central Powers in the *Treaty of Neuilly*, as a result of *Allied and Associate Power* fear of creating a newly unstable situation in the Balkans and possibly war such as preceded *World War I*. Bulgaria lost minor territories to Greece, Rumania, and Serbia; had to pay some *reparations*; and was limited to a *self-defense* force.

Boris III (1894–1943) was the last king of Bulgaria, 1918–1943. In *World War II* he allied with *Hitler*, whom some believe later had him poisoned. Bulgaria joined with Germany to invade Yugoslavia in 1941, the same year it declared war on Great Britain and fought in Greece. It stayed out of the German war with the Soviet Union. In 1944 it was invaded by the *Red Army* anyway. Bulgaria then renounced the Tripartite Pact and switched sides in the war. The Soviets soon set up a *Communist* state, melding Bulgaria to the *Soviet bloc*. It joined the *Warsaw Pact* in 1955 and traded through COMECON. From Moscow's point of view, Bulgaria was the most stable and reliable of the Soviet *satellite states* of Eastern Europe; its Communists willingly participated in the Warsaw Pact invasions of Hungary (1956) and Czechoslovakia (1968). Suspicion lingers that the Bulgarian KGB was behind an attempt to assassinate Pope *John Paul II*. Domestically, it was highly repressive of Muslim and Turkish minorities and political *dissidents*. Several dissidents were assassinated overseas, one with a poisoned umbrella tip on a London street. In 1984–1985 ethnic Turks (numbering one million) were forced to change their names to Bulgarian ones, and speaking Turkish was forbidden. In 1989 more than 300,000 ethnic Turks were forced from their homes and herded to Turkey. In November 1989, *Todor Zhivkov*, Communist dictator for 35 years, was forced to resign by popular unrest. In January 1990, the National Assembly dismantled the Communist state. As elsewhere in Eastern Europe, in subsequent elections old-style communists newly decked out in nationalist clothing sometimes did well.

Suggested Reading: R. J. Crampton, *A Short History of Modern Bulgaria* (1989).

Bulge, Battle of (1944–1945). *See Ardennes Offensive.*

bullionism. A crude, *mercantilist* economic practice in which *sovereigns* desperate to maintain the full *war chests* thought necessary for military strength totally restricted the export of monetary metals. The practice arose from the quite literal need for bullion and coin to finance a nation's wars and from a basic misunderstanding of the nature of the underlying value of monetary metals.

Bülow, Prince Bernhard von (1849–1929). German foreign secretary, 1897–1900; chancellor, 1900–1909. He was at the center of Imperial German policy-making during many of the critical years before *World War I*, mostly supporting Kaiser *Wilhelm II*'s rash policy of *Weltpolitik*. However, he was often overruled or simply left uninformed by the Kaiser and High Command and thus was only partially responsible for the overall aggressive and *adventurist* course of Imperial German foreign policy. On the other hand, he played a key, aggressive role in the *First Moroccan crisis* and the *Bosnian crisis*. His mentality was that of the Age, as well captured by his description of Germany's acquisition of minor South Pacific islands. These were, he said, "milestones along the road . . . to *Weltpolitik*."

Bunche, Ralph (1904–1971). U.S. and United Nations diplomat. After stints in the *State Department* and with the *Joint Chiefs of Staff*, he joined the UN, where he was responsible for *trusteeship* and for overseeing early UN involvement in *peacekeeping*. In 1949 he negotiated discrete *armistice* agreements between Israel and several Arab states. He was the first American black awarded the *Nobel Prize* for Peace (1950).

Bund. *See German Confederation.*

Bundesbank. The highly independent *central bank* of Germany, charged above all else with holding down Germany's rate of *inflation*. That policy was rooted in memory of the devastation of the economy, and German politics and society, wrought by *hyperinflation* under *Weimar*.

Bundestag. (1) The Federal Diet in Prussia 1815–1866. (2) Since 1949, the lower house in the bicameral German legislature.

Bundeswehr. The rearmed and renamed (after *World War II*) German armed forces. This term replaced *Wehrmacht*, which had too many *Nazi* connotations for democratic or Allied comfort, and *Reichswehr*, which retained Imperial significance. The Bundeswehr was fully integrated into *NATO* in 1955. It first deployed outside Germany during the *Gulf War*, when it sent a squadron of fighters to Turkey. It next deployed outside NATO's normal area of operations and saw its first post–World War II combat in 1995 as part of a NATO *peacekeeping* force in Bosnia. It again saw combat duty during NATO's intervention in *Kosovo* in 1999.

bureaucratic authoritarianism. A *political science* term used mainly about Latin American regimes run by *technocratic* and military *elites*. It suggests that *dirigisme* and elite disdain for *popular sovereignty*, rather than any given *ideology*, were the main motive forces behind government policy and practice in many Latin American states, c. 1960–1985. *See also authoritarianism; corporatism; junta; positivism.*

bureaucratic politics. A political science *model* positing that for most modern states foreign policy often is not the result of *rational decision-making* by leaders, or of any kind of clear individual leadership at all. Instead, it is said to result principally from competitive bargaining among different parts of the bureaucracy. This causes grave policy distortions, in formulation and implementation, as outcomes of bureaucratic struggles are not rationally intended. Instead, they often have most to do with budgets and internal turf wars (over policy jurisdiction) and negotiated internal compromises, than with devising rational or optimal solutions to foreign policy problems, let alone pursuing any objective *national interest*. Thus, no matter how well or in what detail decision makers formulate policy guidelines and principles, they will lose control to the bureaucracy during the implementation phase. Yet, critics cogently point out that bureaucrats take their policy lead from decision makers, rather than from where they sit in a civil service hierarchy: powerful and self-confident leaders frequently circumvent the bureaucracy, and indeed usually do so during a *crisis*. Also, the model fails to properly account for the effects of objective, external (international) events and *actors* as formative influences on foreign policy. Lastly, it is unlikely that the model has much application for those less developed states where charismatic rulers or traditional political systems are decisive, rather than modern bureaucracies. *See also organizational process model*.

Suggested Readings: Graham Allison, *Essence of Decision* (1971); David Beetham, *Bureaucracy*, 2nd ed. (1996).

Burgenland. This small territory was part of Hungary under the *Dual Monarchy*. Ethnically German, it was transferred to Austria at the *Paris Peace Conference*. It was the only land transferred between defeated states, to accord with the *Wilsonian* notion of *self-determination* of peoples.

Burkina Faso. Formerly Upper Volta. This area was host to several small states (the Mossi states) from about the eleventh century. Like other desert and *Sahel* states, they relied primarily on armored *cavalry* and conducted *slave* raids into the lands of their neighbors. The Mossi states (Ouagadougou, Tengkodogo, and Yatenga) held off the more powerful *Mali* and *Songhay* empires into the sixteenth century. Over the next several centuries the area was buffeted by larger imperial clashes, pertaining to the *slave trade*, the arrival of the *gunpowder revolution* in West Africa, and a *fundamentalist* revival of *Islam*, which saw several *jihads* sweep over the region. Then came the Europeans directly. The French established control, 1896–1897, and governed it as a colony until independence was granted in 1960. The first government was toppled in a *coup* in 1966, followed by another coup in 1980. A radical military clique took power in a third coup in 1982. The most radical, *Marxist-Leninist* faction within the military launched yet another coup in 1983. This group changed the country's name to Burkina Faso in 1984. This *junta*, too, split into contending factions. A bloodier coup took place in 1987. Meanwhile, the regime revived an old dispute with Mali over the Agache border region. Among the world's poorest states, and subject to severe drought, its inhabitants depend largely on foreign aid or repatriated earnings of family members working in Côte d'Ivoire, Ghana, or Nigeria. In response to *donor country* pressure, a civilian constitution was adopted in mid-1991 under which elections were held later that year, and subsequently, but without inspiring confidence in the fairness of the results. *See also Samori Touré*.

Burma. The site of several ancient kingdoms, it was also ruled at times as a Chinese province. In the eleventh century C.E., a long Burman struggle entered a new phase with conquest of an ancient rival state, the Mons, a *Buddhist* kingdom to the south. The enlarged Burman empire survived until overrun by the *Mongols* (under Kublai Khan) in 1287. When the Mongols departed, control of what is now Burma (Myanmar) was again contested between Burman and Mons states. In the sixteenth century the Toungoo dynasty (Burman) was ascendant. In the eighteenth century a Mons revival led to a major war, culminating in Burman victory in 1758. A unified Burma then briefly expanded into north India and clashed also with *Siam*.

Burma fell under British control in three successive Anglo-Burmese Wars. (1) 1824–1826: Burma was expanding toward Bengal, a territory also coveted by the *East India Company*. In a sharp war, Burma lost Arakan and Tenasserim to company troops, along with Assam and the *Princely State* of Manipur. The Burmese inflicted serious damage on several company expeditions. (2) 1852: *Dalhousie* struck against Burma, annexing Rangoon and Irrawaddy and making most of Burma an effective British *protectorate*. (3) 1885: The British decided to take full control of Burma after the French conquest of *Tonkin* the year before. In a brief campaign (under two weeks), the British moved into northern Burma in order to deny it to the French, who threatened their own conquest from Indochina. Resistance to the British continued for about five years, and was often fierce and bloody, but ultimately was overcome.

Britain governed Burma as part of its larger empire in India, but never persuaded the Burmese to accept direct rule from London. From 1931 to 1933 Burmese peasants actively resisted British rule and, in particular, British land policy. In 1937 it was administratively separated from India. During *World War II*, Burma was overrun by the Japanese Army, sending its large Indian population on a via dolorosa back to India. It was retaken by British and *Indian Army* troops in vicious jungle fighting. Some Burmese, led by *Aung San*, fought alongside the Japanese only to revolt against them in 1945. *Independence* was achieved by peaceful negotiation in 1948, though Burma declined to join the *Commonwealth*. Early agreements to respect the rights of Burma's multiple ethnic minorities were largely tossed aside in the 1950s, as Burma turned increasingly inward and overtly encouraged Burman *nationalism*. That led to decades of *guerrilla warfare* with several ethnic groups, including the Arakanese, Kachins, *Karen*, Mon, Shans, and Wa, in revolt against central government and ethnic exclusivity. A low-level Communist *insurgency* also smoldered in the north, hampered by internal divisions but dangerous nonetheless. In turn, the government used these insurgencies to justify broad repression of civil and political rights even to the majority population.

In 1962 *Ne Win* led a coup that established an *autarkic* regime, which ruled until 1988. It openly discriminated against ethnic Chinese and Indians, thereby undermining both the economy and the civil service. In foreign policy, Burma remained strictly *neutral*—for instance, it did not join *ASEAN* or *SEATO*—until the 1990s, when it moved closer to China and opened discussions about leasing military bases and other forms of military cooperation. It also inched toward a *rapprochement* with Thailand. Burma was traditionally a strong supporter of the United Nations, to which it lent *U Thant*. It later bristled under international criticism of its *human rights* practices, as it descended under a series of misfit rulers and ill-conceived four-year plans from one of the wealthiest new nations at independence to one of the poorest in Asia. In 1988 Burma was placed under *martial law* and renamed Myanmar. Elections in 1990 were voided by the military when the opposition won. Japan and most western countries responded by canceling aid and *embargoing* arms, and the *International Monetary Fund* (IMF) and *International Bank for Reconstruction and Development* (IBRD) spurned loan requests. Opposition leader and *Nobel Prize* (for Peace) winner, *Aung San Suu Kyi*, daughter of Aung San, was placed under house arrest, raising more international protest. The *junta* opened *peace talks* with Karen rebels in January 1994. It showed no leniency toward *dissidents* and entrenched a permanent political role for itself in a new constitution. Also in 1994, Myanmar attended an ASEAN foreign minister *summit* for the first time. In 1999 it joined ASEAN as a full member.

Suggested Reading: U Htin Aung, *A History of Burma* (1967).

Burma Road. The *supply line* to China (Yunnan) used by the *Allies* to support *Chiang Kai-shek* from December 1938 and throughout *World War II*. Built with conscripted labor, it ran more than 700 miles through dense jungle and high mountains. It was closed for several months in 1940 when *Churchill* was compelled to bow to Japanese pressure after the *Battle of France*. It was closed again in 1942 when the Japanese defeated the British in, and pushed them out of, Burma. That seriously threatened Chiang's forces by cutting their only overland supply route. To compensate, the Allies flew supplies "over the Hump," as pilots called the Himalayas. When the Burma Road was reopened in 1944, it again became a vital link in the war against Japan in China. *See also Second Sino-Japanese War.*

Burmese Spring. A brief outburst of public demonstrations from March to September 1988, brutally crushed by Burma's military.

Burundi. A small, densely populated, land-locked state that was peopled by peasant-farmer Hutus (or Bahutu) before the sixteenth century. Pastoralist, cattle-herding Tutsi (or Batutsi, or Watusi) migrated to Burundi, where they slowly established a *tribute* state in which Tutsi kings ruled alongside Hutu chieftains in a precolonial system in which caste had at least as much importance as *tribe*. By the end of the seventeenth century, Burundi was a Tutsi-dominated state. The area was taken over by Germany in 1899, but was captured by Belgian forces during *World War I*. Belgium ran Burundi as part of a large *mandate* (*Ruanda-Urundi*) under the *League of Nations* and then as a United Nations *trusteeship territory*. The Belgians abolished the traditional chieftains, ruling through Tutsi kings alone and thereby reinforcing Tutsi dominance of the Hutu.

Unlike in Rwanda, in Burundi the Tutsi monarchy survived into independence, which came in 1962. At first Burundi was free of overt ethnic trouble. A failed Hutu coup in 1965 led to bloody Tutsi reprisals and progressively mounting tension and bloodshed. The monarchy was overthrown and it became a republic in 1966, but it was still dominated by the Tutsi minority, through the military. Burundi suffered multiple coups (1965, 1976, 1987, and 1996) and repeated tribal massacres, mainly of peasant Hutu by the dominant Tutsi: 150,000 were butchered after an abortive rising in 1965, a greater slaughter took place in 1972–1973 (10,000 Tutsi and from 100,000 to 300,000 Hutu died), and yet another massacre of Hutu occurred in 1988. A rare, peaceful election in 1993 brought the first civilian to power in 30 years: Melchior Ndadaye, a Hutu. He was overthrown and killed in a *coup* less than three months later, as Tutsi officers moved to prevent reforms aimed at bringing Hutu into the army and bureaucracy. Some 800,000 (mostly Hutu) refugees fled Burundi, about half fleeing to then Hutu-run *Rwanda*. Upon sharp international protest, the coup faltered. Nonetheless, tribal killings in the villages continued for months; estimates of the dead range from 25,000 to 150,000.

With Tutsi military engaged in *hot pursuit* of Burundi Hutus across the frontier with Rwanda, interstate war threatened. In April 1994 the Rwanda and Burundi presidents, both Hutus, were killed in a still unexplained air crash. That, and an ongoing civil war with Tutsi guerrillas in Rwanda, sparked the great genocide of 1994, which took 800,000 Tutsi lives, while the United Nations and the world watched and did nothing. After a month, Belgium and France sent troops into Rwanda and Zaire before the UN finally acted, while a half-million Tutsi refugees fled into Burundi from Rwanda. Burundi's internal conflict appeared to have almost no impact on affairs beyond its borders, except for neighboring Rwanda, and certainly outside influences did not much penetrate the deeply unjust ethnic politics that characterized its society. In fact, the Tutsi-Hutu conflict that simmered and exploded from time to time between 1962 and 1994 underlay the larger regional conflict that engulfed most states in Africa's *Great Lakes* region after 1997, even though the main battlefields lay in the Congo.

Suggested Readings: David Birmingham and Phyllis M. Martin, *History of Central Africa* (1983); René Lemarchand, *Burundi. Conflict and Genocide* (1996); Wm. Roger Louis, *Ruanda-Urundi, 1881–1919* (1979).

bus. Common military slang for Post-Boost Vehicle (PBV). It is the part of a *missile* left after the booster rockets fall away. It carries the guidance packages and the re-entry vehicle(s), which convey the *warhead(s)* to target. The bus is critical to the operation of *MIRVs*, as it contains the mechanisms that allow for independent targeting and sequential release of the warheads.

Bush Doctrine (2001). The *September 11, 2001, terrorist attack of the United States* provoked *George W. Bush* to adopt a proactive, anti-terrorist stance of hunting down and destroying terrorist organizations and threats with "global reach"—wherever they appeared, anywhere in the world. First enunciated in his September 20th speech to a joint session of Congress, and reiterated before the United Nations General Assembly on November 10th, the Bush Doctrine also defined all regimes and states that harbor terrorists as enemies of the United States, subject to its full wrath and potentially targetable by the full range of instruments of power (economic, diplomatic, and military) available to Washington. Thus broadly defined, this doctrine potentially had sweeping implications for U.S. foreign policy, and hence to some degree, for that of all other states, on matters of economics, finance, intelligence, weapons procurement, diplomacy, alliance formation and maintenance, and covert activity.

Bush, George H. (b. 1924). *Republican* president of the United States, 1989–1993. He had more experience in foreign policy before becoming president than anyone before him, though his reputation was somewhat tarnished by doubts about his role in *Iran-Contra*. He was ambassador to the United Nations (1971), ambassador to China (1974), director of the *CIA* (1976) and vice president for eight years (1981–1989). Elected as the hinge of history turned from the *Cold War*, he oversaw a transformation in U.S.-Soviet relations, including breakthroughs on nuclear and conventional *arms control*. Closer to home, he authorized the use of force against *Panama* (1989), helped wind down the long civil war in *El Salvador*, and overall improved relations with Central and Latin America. He contributed to a shift toward *Great Power* cooperation in the UN on matters of peace and security, culminating in leadership of a grand coalition of states during the *Gulf War*. He approved a UN request for U.S. troops in *famine* relief operations in *Somalia* in December 1992, but declined to enter the war beginning in *Bosnia*. In 1991–1992 he withheld $10 billion in loans to aid resettlement of Russian Jews in Israel, in order to stop new settlements and put Mideast peace talks on track after a decade of neglect since *Camp David*. He signed *NAFTA* with Canada and Mexico and generally favored *free trade*, even launching the idea of a hemispheric free trade agreement. He did not fare as well in U.S.-Japanese economic relations. He was defeated by *Clinton* in 1992 in an election that rarely touched on foreign policy, with which Bush was most comfortable. From 90 percent favorable in the polls during the Gulf War, his ratings fell precipitously. He was widely viewed by the electorate as a foreign policy president. That, added to a mild recession, a three-way electoral contest, and national exhaustion with Cold War and other foreign policy problems, contributed to his popular free fall and electoral defeat. Clinton later fired *cruise missiles* into Iraq to punish *Saddam Hussein* for apparent complicity in an assassination plot against Bush after he left the presidency and was visiting Kuwait.

Suggested Reading: George H. Bush and Brent Scowcroft, *A World Transformed* (1998).

Bush, George W. (b. 1946). *Republican* president of the United States, 2001– . Son of President *George H. Bush*; governor of Texas, 1994–2000. He won a bitterly contested electoral college victory by the narrowest margin in U.S. history, even while equally narrowly losing the popular vote. He thus defeated sitting *Democratic Party* vice president, Al Gore. The election came down to the results in Florida, which were not known for weeks as recount after recount was started, and stopped, by state officials or courts. The issue was decided when the U.S. Supreme Court made a ruling favorable to Bush (a 5–4 split decision that barred further recounts of already twice-counted ballots). Like most governors elected president, Bush was inexperienced in foreign policy. His first year was dominated by Asian-Pacific affairs, including: a quarrel with China over a U.S. surveillance aircraft that crash-landed on Hainan Island after being damaged in flight by an errant Chinese fighter pilot; a reversal of *Clinton* administration efforts to *appease* North Korea with grants and energy assistance; and revived rhetorical and *arms export* commitments to *Taiwan*. Other key foreign policy issues were: stepped-up efforts to build a national and even international consensus on revising or abandoning the *ABM Treaty* (1972), in order to permit testing of a national *ballistic missile defense*; a Pentagon review aimed at reconfiguring U.S. military procurement toward an even greater high-technology orientation, and reconsideration of the extant post–*Cold War* policy of maintaining sufficient reserve and lift capacity to fight two *Gulf War*–sized conflicts simultaneously (see *two-front war*); a badly bungled non-election of the United States to the *United Nations Human Rights Commission (UNHRC)*; retraction of consent to the *Kyoto Treaty* (which the Senate had already voted against 95–0); strong emphasis on better relations with Mexico and within the Western Hemisphere; the usual fare of G-8 summitry; stroking of Moscow's abiding interest in issues of *prestige* while significantly improving relations and developing an affinity for *Putin*; and resolving inter-allied squabbles within NATO.

Following the *September 11, 2001, terrorist attack on the United States*, Bush emerged as a principal world leader in a manner remarkably similar to that by which *Harry Truman* rose to the innovative demands of an exquisite moment of historical confluence, to reset the parameters of American foreign policy for a generation. All presidents respond to crises with whatever inner resources of character were already present before a given crisis began. So, too, with George W. Bush, whose deep strength of inner character was quickly revealed and widely applauded. Similarly, the attack of September 11th united the American people to an extent not witnessed since *Pearl Harbor*. In his demeanor and even his homespun rhetoric, Bush captured this renewed spirit of confident moral authority and deep geopolitical and national resolve. In less than a month, he marshaled and channeled America's power on multiple fronts, and its enemies in the *Taliban* and *al Qaeda* felt the first lashes of what was intended to become a mortal beating. He laid out a new strategic doctrine—the *Bush Doctrine*—on making war against terrorist organizations with "global reach" and on all state sponsorship of *terrorism*. Even as the military campaign against *Usama bin Laden*'s fanatic followers was underway in Afghanistan and elsewhere, Bush called for reinstallment of UN weapons inspectors by Iraq. At the end of 2001 his administration was openly mooting the possibility of toppling *Saddam Hussein*'s regime as part of its declared war on terrorism.

business cycle. Recurring fluctuations in a nation's overall economic activity, marking out periods of *growth* or *recession*. The study of economic statistics appears to show the reoccurrence of regular patterns of cyclical rise and fall in demand, which have historically appeared as financial crises, *recessions*, or *depressions*. These may be mild (sometimes called inventory cycles) or severe. Efforts have also been made to limit or control these cycles through *fiscal policy* or *monetary policy*, taxes, spending, and so forth. Much longer statistical patterns are usually referred to as *secular trends*. *See also Kondratieff cycles*.
  Suggested Reading: A. W. Mullineux, *Business Cycles and Financial Crises* (1990).

Buthelezi, Gatsha Mangosuthu (b. 1928). Leader of KwaZulu and *Inkatha*. He was expelled from the ANC in 1950. After 1986 his followers engaged in an increasingly violent political struggle with the ANC and other black groups in South Africa. He accepted secret funds for Inkatha from the *apartheid* government. In 1993 he allied with right-wing whites who, for reasons of their own, shared his fear of one-person/one-vote politics. He joined *Mandela*'s reconciliation government in 1994.

buyers' market. One where the prices of *goods and services* are low. The antonym is, of course, *sellers' market*.

Byelorussia. "White Russia." *See also Belarus*.

Byrnes, James Francis (1879–1972). U.S. secretary of state, 1945–1947. He supported *Truman*'s policies on quick restoration of Germany as a bulwark against the Soviet Union and agreed on the usefulness of the *United Nations*. He parted company with his president over the *Truman Doctrine*. He was replaced by *George C. Marshall*.

Byzantine Empire. Originally, the eastern half of the *Roman Empire*, with its great capital at *Constantinople*, built on the site of the ancient Greek city, Byzantium, by *Constantine the Great* in 330 C.E. It developed as a distinct and highly successful civilization after the breakup of the old Roman Empire (395 C.E.) into discrete halves, and outlasted the Western Roman Empire by more than 1,000 years. It was centered in Greece and Asia Minor, but for centuries also had important holdings in North Africa, the Levant, the Balkans, and for a while in Italy and Spain. The entire Roman Empire, including its eastern half, was officially converted to *Christianity* by Constantine, though large communities of Christians were already present and active before that, especially in Asia Minor and North Africa. Over time, the forms of Christianity extant in the Byzantine Empire evolved into the *Orthodox Church*, distinct from the Latin or *Catholic Church* of Western *Christendom*. The two branches divided progressively from the eighth *Ecumenical Council*, after which Catholics and Orthodox moved into *schism* over the issue of conciliar versus papal authority and the question of which formed infallible (guided by God away from error) church teaching.

The Patriarchs of the Orthodox Church at times exercised real power in secular affairs, just as the Byzantine emperors had a major say—at times, definitive—in Church governance. Orthodoxy was also challenged by the many Christian doctrines that fermented quickly in the Balkans and Middle East. Unlike the Latin West, where popes and emperors waged unholy war with one another for several centuries, ultimately fatally weakening both, the response of church and state in the Byzantine east was to unite, with both acting to repress "heresy." The East was in intellectual and cultural ferment, and heresy was thus a chronic problem. It took its major—but not its sole—form in doctrinal differences between Nestorians and Monophysites, as well as the latter tradition and more mainstream Orthodoxy, which sought to maintain imperial as well as doctrinal unity. Although Orthodoxy was an ideological pillar supporting the Byzantine emperors, and Greek language and Hellenistic values were the Empire's main cultural motif, straddling the major east-west *trade routes* as it did, Byzantium was not just rich materially and culturally, it also and always was greatly ethnically and religiously diverse.

From the fifth to the eleventh century, Byzantium faced wave upon wave of powerful barbarian invaders, including (but not limited to): Visigoths, Huns (under Attila, 406–453), and Avars; a great Vandal invasion to the south, which wrenched away most North African possessions; various migrating tribes collectively known as *Slavs*; and from the ninth century also Bulgars in the Balkans. In addition, Constantinople faced the chronic Greek problem of a struggle for regional mastery with the (then Sassanian) Persian Empire. The degree of this pressure may be measured by the fact that the Western Roman Empire fell (476) to other barbarian peoples invading mostly through Germany and Gaul, into Italy, Spain, and Africa: Ostrogoths, Franks, Visigoths again, and various Germanic tribes who had long pressured the northern *frontier* before it collapsed. Byzantium enjoyed a major revival under Emperor *Justinian I* (r. 527–565), the great codifier of Byzantine law, whose reforms included a doctrine of caesaropapism (supremacy of Caesar over the Orthodox Church). Justinian's generals pushed back the Persians, but in 532 internal quarrels (between "Blue" and "Green" factions) led to election of a rival emperor and civil war. Justinian emerged from a great slaughter secure, and his generals were dispatched to defeat the Vandal kingdom in North Africa, which they did. Under Justinian the Empire was constantly at war, and although for a time it actually managed to reestablish imperial claims to north Italy, while heavily *fortifying* a defensive line against Persia, this effort to reunite the broken halves of the old Empire was ultimately defeated by the Lombards, who drove the Byzantines from northern Italy in 569. South Italy and Sicily would later be lost to *Arabs*, and then to the *Normans*, barbarian invaders originally from far-off Scandinavia. The Byzantine Empire held on to Italian lands for some time, but it would never again go on the offensive in the west or be able to restore "the glory that had been Rome."

Instead, in the early seventh century Persian armies once again loomed just across the Straits, eager to breech the gates of Constantinople, while armies and raiding parties of Avars pressed hard along the northern border. Both were beaten back, but at great cost. Then came a wholly new and greatly dynamic force intent on *holy war*. The explosion of *Islam* out of Arabia brought fanatic Arab armies north, keen on *jihad*, all out for plunder and conversion by the sword. This new, Muslim enemy quickly overran ancient Byzantine provinces in Egypt and North Africa, the Levant and Syria, and took Sicily as well, and they continued westward, beyond the reach of Byzantium to also overrun all North Africa and Iberia. They were finally turned back from the southern border of Latin Christendom by Charles Martel, grandfather of *Charlemagne*, who stopped the Muslim, or Saracen, invasion of southern Gaul in 732. The Muslim tide first seriously threatened Constantinople itself in the late seventh century. The Empire now turned inward, toward Hellenization of its culture and ideals, a natural enough reaction, perhaps, to a growing sense, as well as reality, of hostile siege and encirclement. In the eighth century a Byzantine counterattack recovered Asia Minor. In 812, in exchange for holdings in Italy, including *Venice*, Charlemagne's title as "Emperor of the West" was recognized by Constantinople, thereby overcoming jurisdictional disputes with the Catholic Church partly in order to secure at least one friendly border, to the west.

From the ninth century through the eleventh, the Byzantine Empire enjoyed a succession of mostly strong emperors and respite from imminent danger of being overrun, although it did face attacks by the Normans, who rounded Iberia by longship from their Atlantic strongholds in northern France and England to rip southern Italy from Constantinople's grasp and raid the Adriatic coast. Also, Byzantium's final doctrinal break with the *res publica Christiana* in the West came during the eleventh century. The year 1054 saw formal confirmation of the deep Orthodox-Catholic schism, which had been brewing, literally for centuries, through evolving debates of earlier Ecumenical Councils and then in competing bulls, claims, decrees, and false histories issued by the Patriarchate in Constantinople and the Papacy in Rome. Venice now emerged as a competitor with Byzantium for the Mediterranean carriage trade, but also an important trading partner carrying Byzantine goods farther west. As always, when the Empire enjoyed relative peace, its depths of talent in law, art, philosophy, architecture, and high culture enjoyed a renaissance, proving it one of the great world civilizations of the Age.

The Byzantines could never rest secure for long, however, before again facing grave external threat. In the eleventh century the danger came from the east, in form of the Seljuk Turks, a nomadic warrior people from Central Asia then constructing an empire of their own on top of prior Arabicized peoples and caliphates. They captured Asia Minor from Byzantium upon defeating a Byzantine army at Manzikert in 1071. Greatly endangered, Constantinople turned for help to its co-religionists in the Latin Christian states and to the popes. The result was the fanatically exuberant Latin response known as the *Crusades*, a 200-year prolonged intervention and engagement of Latin Christendom in the affairs and wars of the eastern Mediterranean. This gained relief for the Byzantine Empire during the twelfth century, but ended in disaster when the cruder knights and retainers of the Fourth Crusade *sacked* Constantinople instead of attacking Muslim armies in the *Holy Land*, displaced the Greek Empire from its capital, and established there the "Latin Empire of Constantinople" in 1204.

All this occurred just as yet another scourge from *Inner Asia* arrived in the Middle East and Levant: the *Mongols*. Remarkably, the Byzantine Empire was not entirely finished. Its Hellenic peoples persisted and resisted, preserving essential institutions and the line of Byzantine succession intact in Nicaean and other exile, until they were able to expel the faux-emperors of the Latin Empire and restore the Byzantine Emperors to Constantinople in 1261. They did so just in time to face a final, and this time also fatal, assault from the rising power of the Muslim world: The *Ottoman Empire*. The Ottomans were a Turkic people who succeeded the Seljuks in Asia Minor. They now pressed home a sustained siege of Byzantium, cutting off Constantinople from its historic Balkan and Middle Eastern *hinterlands*, one province after another, until it was hemmed into the Peloponnese. Other vultures circled as well: *corsairs* from North Africa, armed merchant ships from Venice, and rebellious Slavs and Bulgars in the northern mountains. The Empire was reduced to the confines of Constantinople and a small hinterland by the middle of the fifteenth century. Under *Muhammad II* the Ottomans crossed the Straits with an army that battered down the walls of Constantinople with *artillery*, while their navy hammered it from the sea. In 1453 the city fell, extinguishing Byzantium. That was an event of world historical importance that sent shock waves—and subsequently, the explorers, adventurers, misfits, and conquerors of the *Age of Exploration*—around the world.

Bitterness over the great betrayal by other Christians in the sack of Constantinople in 1204 is felt deeply still, in former Byzantine and presently Orthodox lands. And well it should. Later Western historians (notably Henri Pirenne, father of the Pirenne thesis, as laid out in his 1925 classic work, *Medieval Cities*) noted that the Byzantine Empire served for centuries as a great bulwark of the whole Christian world against an ascendant Islam under the Arabs, held back the *Mongol* hordes as well, and then resisted the Ottoman Turks, and that behind this defensive perimeter the great civilization of the Latin and Atlantic states slowly took shape until it could stand on its own. The Byzantine Empire's great success as a civilization and longevity as a political entity was accomplished in a region that occupied the crossroads of several world civilizations, and was constantly under threat from warlike societies in Arabia and North Africa and nomadic invaders from Central Asia and even northern Europe (the Normans). With the Fourth Crusade, it also faced an unexpected invasion from Western Europe. To survive all that for more than a thousand years was a remarkable achievement, attributable principally to flexible Byzantine diplomacy, sustained wealth and military power, and an advanced culture and highly skilled administration. "Byzantine" later became a synonym for excessive adornment and bureaucracy, including great corruption and license, but in fact it describes the advanced creation of a powerful, centralized state akin to that of Imperial China, and many centuries ahead of later large states and empires in the Muslim world and the Latin West.

Suggested Readings: Michael Angold, *The Byzantine Empire, 1025–1204* (1997); Robert Browning, *The Byzantine Empire* (1992); Michael Grant, *From Rome to Byzantium* (1998); John Haldon, *Byzantium* (2000).

C

C³I. Command, control, communication, and *intelligence*; with computers added in the 1990s, this became "C⁴I." These are the principal means by which a commander plans, directs, and controls field combat operations. For most of recorded history this amounted to shouted orders amplified by trumpet and drum signals, and the use of colored flags. A *revolution in military affairs* in C³I began during the *French Revolution*, when a semaphore telegraph first connected Paris to the frontier garrisons. It has continued ever since. *See also flag; sigint.*

Cabinda. A former Portuguese *colony* on the southwestern African coast; currently an Angolan *exclave.*

cabinet. A council of ministers that advises the *sovereign*, president, or prime minister, according to the given form of government in a particular country. In states with cabinet government the cabinet is a tight, decision-making body that is (sometimes only nominally) answerable to the legislature. In presidential systems it tends to be more administrative. *See also Chancellor of the Exchequer; finance minister; foreign minister; national security adviser.*

cabinet noir. "Black chamber." A secret installation for intercepting and decrypting foreign diplomatic or *intelligence* correspondence. The term dates to the nineteenth century, when such *sigint* techniques were pioneered by the tsarist *Okhrana.*

Cable Network News (CNN). An all-news service that rose to global prominence in the 1980s because of its live coverage of unfolding international events. During the *Gulf War* it was widely watched not just by the public, but also by civilian and military leaders of combatant states. The so-called CNN effect—arousal of *public opinion* by same-day or instant news coverage (by CNN, the BBC, or whomever)—actually dates to the *Crimean War*, the first conflict covered by journalists with access to telegraph offices, in turn, connected by cable to the major world capitals. That increased domestic pressures, shaped public opinion, permitted civilian leaders to intervene in even tactical military decisions, and thereby partly drove key decisions and events. The late twentieth century advent of global media merely amplified this effect in later wars, famines, and other conflicts. *See also Radio Free Europe; Voice of America.*

cabotage. In *international law*, a right of carriage of goods between ports of the same state.

Cadmean victory. One costing the winner nearly as much as the loser. *See also defeat; victory.*

cadres. Originally, experienced military or *Communist Party* members who organized and trained fresh recruits. Later in Communist history it came to mean full-time party officials and the management class that ran state-owned farms or firms.

Caesar, Gaius Julius (c. 100–44 B.C.E.). Roman dictator. He began his career in the politics of the *Roman Empire* as a "democrat," working in 70 to overthrow the constitution imposed by Sulla (138–78 B.C.E.) before his death. He then spent a year in Spain. In 61 he was elevated to consul. He helped reconcile Crassus (115–53 B.C.E.) and Pompey (106–48 B.C.E.) and then joined them in a Triumvirate to govern Rome (60 B.C.E.). He became governor of Cisalpine Gaul. For nine years, from 58 to 49, he conducted the conquest of Gaul, pushed Germanic tribes back across the Rhine, and in 55 invaded Britain. In 54 he compelled the south of (what would later be) England to submit. He completed the conquest of Gaul at the Battle of Alesia (52 B.C.E.), where he crushed and scattered the combined armies of all the Gallic chieftains. Meanwhile, in Rome the aristocratic party had taken charge as Crassus died while campaigning in Asia in 53 B.C.E. and Pompey had switched his allegiance to the aristocrats, breaking the Triumvirate. Pompey compelled the Senate to issue orders *decommissioning* Caesar, removing him from command in Gaul, disbanding his army, and ordering him to return to Rome—where he would face almost certain death, with or without trial.

With his legions intact and in full defiance of Pompey and the Senate, Caesar crossed the Rubicon (49 B.C.E.), a minor stream that constituted the border between Roman Italy and Cisalpine Gaul, to begin a great Roman civil war. This changed Rome's history forever, not least from its original character as an imperial republic to a new form of what ultimately would be called "Caesarean" dictatorship and empire. Pompey's forces were too scattered across the Mediterranean to deal with this assault by well-led, highly keen, and loyal—to Caesar—legionnaires. Pompey fled Rome for Greece. Caesar put down Pompey's legions in Spain and was elevated to dictator within three months. Then he turned to face new armies that Pompey raised in Greece, Asia Minor, and Egypt. Caesar was first defeated in a naval battle in the Adriatic and forced to fall back. However, at Pharsalia (August 9, 48 B.C.E.) Caesar utterly crushed Pompey's (and the Senate's) army. Pompey fled to exile in Egypt, where he was later murdered; the Senate buckled, and Julius Caesar was master of all Rome.

Caesar went next to Egypt. There, he had an affair with Queen Cleopatra and fought the "Alexandrine War." He crushed the last of Pompey's loyalist generals, at Thapsus in North Africa (April 6, 46 B.C.E.), as well as a rebellion in Spain led by Pompey's sons. Back in Rome, he was made "imperator" by the cowed Senate, as well as consul and dictator for life, and for good measure was also proclaimed to be divine. Time itself was changed to account for Caesar: the Roman month "Quintilis" was changed to "Julius" and is remembered still in successor nations, cultures, and languages as "July." As dictator, he started well: he planned and commissioned major public works and improvements. But his tenure was cut short on March 15 (the Ides of March), 44 B.C.E. by sixty republican assassins in the Senate, including his young friend Marcus Junius Brutus (85–42 B.C.E.). The stated reason for the murder was fear that Caesar planned to overthrow the Republic and found a hereditary monarchy.

Suggested Readings: Julius Caesar, *The Conquest of Gaul*; Michael Grant, *Julius Caesar* (1969; 1975).

Caesarism. *Absolutism* as the style of government disguised by a facade of republican constitutionalism, in combination with unmitigated *imperialism* as a foreign policy. *See also Julius Caesar; Napoleon I.*

Cairo Conferences. (1) *Franklin Roosevelt* met with *Winston Churchill* and *Chiang Kai-shek* from November 22 to 26, 1943, en route to *Tehran* to meet *Stalin*. Their discussions dealt mainly with issues of the war against Japan. They issued the joint Cairo Declaration, which stated four common positions on the postwar settlement in Asia: Japan would lose all islands in the Pacific it acquired since 1914, including the old German *mandates*; all lands taken from China were to be returned (including *Taiwan*, *Manchuria*, and the *Pescadores*); Japan was to be expelled from additional lands, including *Sakhalin* and the *Kurils*; and *Korea* was to become independent "in due course." (2) Roosevelt and Churchill met again in Cairo from December 3 to 7, 1943, to discuss the invasion of Europe, set for spring 1944. *See also Potsdam Declaration.*

California. Russia laid claim to northern California early in the nineteenth century, as part of *Russian America*, but did not press this claim after 1825. The southern half passed from Spain to Mexico, but remained largely unsettled even as its superb natural harbors attracted Americans interested in the Asia trade. In 1845 a mere captain of the Army Topographical Corps, John C. Frémont (1813–1890), proclaimed California independent. His brief-lived "Bear Flag Republic" was soon *annexed* by the United States: on July 7, 1846, elements of the U.S. Navy took Monterey and claimed California. Northern "Californios" (California residents of Mexican origin, who had themselves earlier rebelled against Mexico) tended to accept U.S. annexation; southern Californios resisted, leading to armed conflict. Acquisition of California's ports was the secret objective of President *James Polk* in the *Mexican-American War*. The territory was cut off from military relief from Mexico by American forces under the command of *Zachary Taylor*. Under the *Treaty of Guadalupe Hidalgo* (1848), California was formally ceded to the United States by Mexico. This acquisition gave the United States *vital interests* in the Pacific, and earned it many decades of *revanchist* hostility from Mexico. California achieved additional prominence with the *gold rush* of 1849, as over 100,000 "Forty-Niners" poured into the territory from the rest of the United States and even from Europe, overwhelming its prior Spanish-American character. The question of admission of California to the union as a *free soil* state, also starting in 1849, was the first stroke in the great political rift, which led ultimately to the *American Civil War*. California made only a minor contribution to the *Union* effort in the Civil War, even though its population and importance had swelled with the gold rush. After 1900 it pressed for *Oriental exclusion laws* (as did British Columbia in Canada), hurting relations with Japan. During the *Cold War* it was a center for *strategic* industries. If independent, at the start of the 21st century it would have ranked among the leading dozen or so *OECD* economies.

caliph. A spiritual and temporal leader claiming succession from the prophet Muhammad in his political function, and thus the right to rule all Muslims. The main split in *Islam*, between the majority *sunni* and minority *shi'ite* traditions, began with a dispute over the proper succession to the caliphate. The first four caliphs were all related to Muhammad and chosen by the "Companions" of the Prophet, and on their *legitimacy* there was no disagreement of consequence. These were the "Orthodox Caliphs," who together ruled from 632 to 661 C.E. Abu Bakr was first (573–634). He was succeeded by Umar (c. 581–644), Uthman (c. 574–656), and Ali (c. 598–661). However, the third caliph Uthman (Usman) was murdered by mutineers, a fact that severely troubled the early and intensely devout community of the faithful. Uthman was succeeded by Ali (656), the first convert to Islam made by Muhammad, and his son-in-law by marriage to Fatima, Muhammad's daughter. Ali, too, was assassinated (661). His successor, Mu'awiya, who founded the Umayyad Caliphate (661–750), was accepted by sunnis as legitimate, but rejected by shi'ites, who proclaimed only the descendants of Ali as the rightful successors to Muhammad. These shi'ite claimants became known as "Alid" candidates.

The sunni Umayyads ruled the Islamic world from Damascus. They were overthrown and succeeded by a shi'ite dynasty, the Abbasids, who asserted descent from Muhammad's uncle. The Abbasids moved the caliphate to Baghdad and reigned—more in the imperial Persian than the tribal Arab style—as the Abbasid Caliphate, 750–1258, becoming less overtly shi'ite and more orthodox sunni, as were most of their subjects, over time. The Abbasids were not recognized in Spain, however, where a branch of the Umayyads survived and ruled from 780 to 1031. Nor after a time were they accepted in Egypt or the *Maghreb*, where a rival shi'ite dynasty, the Fatamids, who were rooted in a Berber resurrection, claimed the caliphate based on direct descent from Fatima. The Berber Fatamids thereby essentially reversed the prior Arab conquest of North Africa. The Fatamids ruled in Egypt, 909–1171. Long before they lost control in Egypt in 1171, they had already lost most of the Maghreb to rival Berber dynasts (notably, the Almohad Caliphate, based in Marrakesh) and were thrown out of *Jerusalem* and *Palestine* by the *Crusaders* (1099). The main line of sunni caliphs in Baghdad was overthrown by the *Mongols* in the thirteenth century; Baghdad itself fell to the Mongols in 1258, and the Abbasids retreated to Egypt, now bereft of the Fatamids, taking with them their shadow of a claim to the caliphate. There, *Mamluk* sultans held off the Mongols in 1260.

The title was assumed by the *Ottoman* emperors in 1517, when they conquered Egypt from the Mamluks. Their assertion was clearly political rather than theological: it was intended to reinforce imperial control over the Arab and Muslim populations of the Turkish empire. The Ottoman emperors therefore did not earn respect or full acceptance as caliphs by all Muslims within their empire, let alone the many millions in far off Africa, India, and Indonesia. Regional Muslim potentates sometimes adopted the title, though without asserting that they stood in direct line to Muhammad or claiming the right to rule all Muslims. All Ottoman *sultans* asserted a full claim to the title until it was formally renounced by *Atatürk* in behalf of the secularized Turkish republic in 1924. The cause of the caliphate became a major international issue after *World War I*. A movement to sustain the caliphate (kalifah) won adherents as far afield as India, where it was endorsed by the *Muslim League*. There has been no universally recognized claimant to the title since 1924. *See also ayatollah; imam; mahdi; mullah; sultan.*

Suggested Readings: Marshall Hodgson, *The Classical Age of Islam* (1974); Marshall Hodgson, *The Expansion of Islam* (1974); Hugh Kennedy, *The Prophet and the Age of the Caliphates* (1986).

caliphate. The jurisdiction of a *caliph*. Theoretically, this extends to all Muslims. Historically, since the split between *sunni* and *shi'ite* Islam and the later rise of non-Arab, Muslim empires, the authority of caliphs was often disputed or ignored in more distant provinces or rival empires.

Calvinism. The stern and originally deeply intolerant religion founded by John Calvin (1509–1564), emphasizing doctrines of predestination, the literal truth of the *Christian* Bible, and the sanctifying role of grace. It spread quickly through north Germany and Switzerland. Its early militancy contributed to the *Wars of Religion* in France and Germany, the English Civil Wars and the rise of *Cromwell*, the *Eighty Years' War* in the Netherlands, the *Thirty Years' War* in Germany, and religious rebellion and national and dynastic conflict in England and Scotland. It was the predominant religion of the Boers, some of whom drew upon Calvinist interpretations of scripture to define and defend *apartheid. See also Augsburg, Peace of; Protestant Reformation; Jean-Jacques Rousseau.*

Calvo clause. A legal doctrine written into contracts with *aliens* (investors, contractors, and others), and upheld by most Latin American countries as a principle of regional *international law*, since c. 1900. It maintains that a *host nation* retains *jurisdiction* over any dispute arising from transactions with foreign corporations or persons, such as over *compensation* for *nationalization.* That denies *parent countries* a right to intervene on behalf of their nationals, and hence the clause has been widely rejected outside Latin America. *See also Drago Doctrine; Monroe Doctrine; remedy; responsibility.*

Cambodia. The *Khmer Empire* from the ninth to thirteenth centuries stretched from modern Thailand (Siam) across much of Indochina, reaching a peak of syncretic *Hindu* and *Buddhist* culture, though also espousing a claim to divinity by *Khmer* monarchs that was alien to Indian culture. This was expressed in the unique architectural heritage of the *Khmer* capital at Angkor and the extraordinary religious edifice of Angkor Wat. The *Khmer* empire was frequently at war with *Annam, Tonkin,* and *Champa.* As it declined, it fell increasingly under Siamese domination. In 1623 the Khmer requested Vietnamese (Annamese and Tonkinese) intervention against *Siam* (Thailand).

A second intervention occurred in 1658, and in 1660 Cambodia became a *tributary* of Vietnam. A secessionist struggle and civil war led to another intervention in 1714–1716, a Siamese invasion in 1717, and a switch of allegiance from Vietnam to Siam. In 1739 a Khmer army tried to dislodge the Vietnamese from formerly Khmer territory in the Mekong delta. By 1749 the Cambodians had lost the war and further territory in the east. In 1755–

1760 Vietnamese control extended deeper into Cambodia. Siam, at war with Burma, was unable to intervene. From 1769 to 1773 Vietnamese and Siamese fought again, with Siam retaining most of Cambodia. Yet another Vietnamese-Siamese war was fought over control of Cambodia, 1831–1845. Then the French arrived in Indochina.

As Annam and Tonkin themselves came under rising French pressure, Cambodia appealed for French assistance (1854) and was made a French *protectorate* in 1863, while retaining its monarchy and limited internal autonomy. With French aid it regained three provinces from Siam in 1907. In 1941 *Vichy* signed these provinces back to Thailand, but they were returned to *French Indochina* in 1945. Cambodia was occupied by Japan during *World War II*. The French returned in October 1945 in the wake of Japan's defeat and surrender. Independence came in 1953, followed by rigged elections flowing from the *Geneva Accords* (1955). Prince *Norodom Sihanouk* ruled conservatively under the French and Japanese (and French again) masters, 1941–1954. He became an effective dictator in 1955 and head of state in 1960. Cambodia tried to escape the escalating wars elsewhere in Indochina by proclaiming its *neutrality*. Out of practical necessity, it tilted toward China and turned a blind eye to *Viêt Cong* (NLF) incursions and bases along the *Hô Chí Minh Trail*, which paralleled its border with Vietnam. Even that effort at *appeasement* did not prevent a bloody Communist *insurgency* by the *Khmers Rouges*, who were backed by China and Vietnam. In 1970, with U.S. support, *Lon Nol* overthrew Sihanouk and abolished the monarchy. Sihanouk then set up a *government-in-exile* in China. Some 30,000 U.S. and 50,000 Army of the Republic of Vietnam (ARVN) forces then secretly moved 60 kilometers into Cambodia to cut the Hô Chí Minh Trail; the United States pulled out by June 30, but ARVN units stayed into 1971. This incursion and attendant secret bombing provoked a public outcry in the United States, though in terms of *international law*, the United States and Republic of Vietnam were within their legal rights in attacking an enemy on territory whose government had effectively ceased to sustain a claim to *neutrality*. From 1973 to 1975 Khmer Armed National Forces (FANK) held back the Khmers Rouges. With U.S. aid severely cut back, and People's Army of Vietnam (PAVN) overrunning South Vietnam, the Khmers Rouges launched a new offensive. Lon Nol fled on April 1, 1975. On April 17th, Khmer Rouge fighters walked into Phnom Penh.

Under *Pol Pot's* orders, the Khmers Rouges immediately set about deurbanization and deindustrialization of the country and began the *Cambodian genocide*. The Khmer Rouge regime was dislodged during the *Cambodia-Vietnam War* (1977–1991). Despite the ghastly revelations that followed about Pol Pot's misrule, Vietnam faced sustained international opposition to its installation of a *puppet regime* under Khmer Rouge defector Heng Samrin, and continuing insurgency from the Khmers Rouges and other *guerrilla* groups. Sihanouk, with his usual guile, formed a new opposition coalition-in-exile, including some Khmer Rouge leaders, in 1982. With Vietnam's economy in shambles, Hanoi pulled out its forces starting in 1988. Pol Pot's regime was finally expelled from Cambodia's seat in the *United Nations General Assembly* in 1990. UN-supervised elections were held in 1993. Voter participation was high despite murders of UN personnel and other efforts at intimidation by the Khmers Rouges, as the country returned to constitutional monarchy.

However, the *one-party state* run by the Vietnamese-sponsored Cambodian People's Party (CPP), 1979–1991, survived intact, and now a new dictator emerged from its ranks: Hun Sen. He refused to accept electoral defeat and instead forced acceptance of a two–prime minister partnership in which he shared power with the real winner, Prince Norodom Ranariddh. With renewed fighting among various Cambodian factions by 1994, it became clear that the specter of Cambodia's long, national nightmare had not been exorcized. In 1997 a Hun Sen *putsch* forced the opposition into exile. Massacres followed, with a consolidation of CPP power under a renewed regime of fear and oppression.

Suggested Readings: David Chandler, *A History of Cambodia* (1983, 2000); Stephen Heder, *Propaganda, Politics, and Violence in Cambodia* (1996).

Cambodian genocide (1975–1978). *Khmers Rouges*, led by the megalomaniacal butcher *Pol Pot*, emptied Cambodia's cities after April 1975 ("Year Zero") in an utterly mad scheme of forced *collectivization* and deliberate deindustrialization and refeudalization. Nearly the entire population was herded into the countryside and put into *forced labor* on the farms. The Khmers Rouges also *liquidated* all those identified as "class enemies" of the party and peasantry. That included persons who spoke foreign languages, had higher education, or even wore glasses, and thus were presumed to be educated. Over the next three years, in the "killing fields" of Cambodia (briefly renamed, with sick irony, "Democratic Kampuchea"), at least two million died. There was no international intervention, and the killings came to an end only with an invasion (for unrelated reasons) by Vietnam during the *Cambodia-Vietnam War*. In retreat, the Khmers Rouges herded many thousands of captive civilians into *refugee camps* along the Thai border, where they were kept under Khmers Rouges control, and away from international humanitarian observation, into the 1990s.

Suggested Readings: David Chandler, *Voices From S-21* (2000); Ben Kiernan, *The Pol Pot Regime* (1996).

Cambodia-Vietnam War (1977–1991). At root, this was but one more battle in a long contest for *hegemony* between Cambodians and Vietnamese in Indochina. At another level, it represented a challenge by Vietnam to Chinese hegemony in the region. At yet a third level, it represented a *proxy war* in the *Sino-Soviet split* and battle for dominion between the giants of the Communist world. The only thing that clearly did *not* play a role in the decision was any Vietnamese concern over what *Pol Pot* and his men were doing in the "killing fields" of Cambodia. After all, Vietnam had assisted the *Khmers Rouges* into power and even kept news of Cambodian massacres of Vietnamese from its own people. Border skirmishes broke out in 1977, escalating to an ill-conceived attack by the anti-Vietnamese Khmers Rouges (from which all ethnic Vietnamese had been *purged* and killed in 1973) into Vietnam in September. The motivations for the Cambodian attacks are not decipherable and may only be described as irrational. In December, Vietnam sent 60,000 troops across the border in a retaliation raid. The Khmers Rouges bloodily *purged* their eastern military units, killing perhaps 100,000 Cambodians held "responsible" for the Vietnamese attack. Many others fled into Vietnam, where they were organized into an anti–Khmers Rouges army under Heng Samrin, a former Khmers Rouges commander who was in fact responsible for killing ethnic Vietnamese at Tay Ninh in September 1977. China sent pilots and other military aid to the Khmers Rouges while the Soviet Union backed Vietnam. Heavy fighting erupted again in June 1978. On December 25, 1978, Vietnam crossed the border in force, driving the Khmers Rouges from power and into refugee camps and military bases along the Thai border. A long *guerrilla* war followed, as well as a major clash between Vietnam and China in early 1979 (*Sino-Vietnamese War*) and battles with Thai border troops in 1985. Hanoi's forces were withdrawn starting in 1988. A United Nations–supervised settlement followed after 1992.

Suggested Reading: Stephen J. Morris, *Why Vietnam Invaded Cambodia: Political Culture and the Causes of War* (1999).

Cambrai, Battle of (November 20–30, 1917). This *World War I* battle on the *western front* witnessed the first massed use of tanks, by Britain, in an effort by *Haig* to overcome with machine warfare his failures with *infantry* at the *Somme* and *Third Ypres*. Some 325 tanks led the attack, followed by infantry and supported by *artillery*. Both flanks successfully advanced, but the center met witheringly effective defensive fire. The Germans then counterattacked with their usual success.

Cameroon. A locale of the *slave trade* from the fifteenth century to the nineteenth, *Bismarck* declared it a German possession (*Kamerun*) in 1884. It was captured from Germany in 1916, during *World War I*. After the war it was divided by France and Britain into approved *mandates*; and after *World War II*, into *trust territories*. In 1956 a civil war broke out between Communist and nationalist groups. The French portion became independent as Cameroon in 1960. The British section split in 1961: one part joined Nigeria after a *plebiscite*; the other part merged with the former French Cameroon. The resulting linguistic and cultural division of the national elites overlies patchwork ethnic divisions common to African states, as well as a north-south religious divide (*Islam* and *Christianity*) typical of West Africa. Ahmadou Ahidjo (1924–1989) was president, 1960–1982. In his time Cameroon was relatively stable and prosperous, avoiding entanglement in major wars in neighboring Chad and Nigeria, though suffering chronic civil and *human rights* abuses at home. It maintains close ties to France. Regionally, its most serious disputes are with Nigeria. In 1994 Cameroon openly disputed an oil field (Bakassi), which straddles its *frontier* with Nigeria, even accepting in-country deployment of French paratroopers as a *deterrent* to possible Nigerian military action. In 2001 it began work on a Cameroon-Chad oil pipeline funded by the *International Monetary Fund*.

Suggested Readings: J. F. A. Ajayi and Michael Crowder, eds., *History of West Africa*, 2 vols. (1974).

camouflage. The art of concealing troops and equipment from the enemy, historically by using foliage or painted patterns or similar basic concealment. Despite its obvious utility, camouflage was not widely adopted by modern militaries until the twentieth century. American rangers and other backwoods fighters had adopted it from the Indians, but most European armies eschewed camouflage in favor of the brightly colored uniforms necessary to minimize casualties from *friendly fire* on the compact, smoke-filled battlefields of Europe. Other armies, in more traditional societies, had different concepts of war— as displays of conspicuous bravery, often with little accompanying killing— which made using camouflage inconceivable. The *Boer War* taught the British, the hard way, to abandon scarlet tunics for khaki. Yet, by *World War I* only Germany and Russia had followed suit, adopting monochrome feld grau and brown. French, Austrian, and other troops still marched or charged to their deaths in the summer of 1914 wearing combinations of sky blues and greens, yellows and bright reds. Some Austrian and Italian alpine troops even sported plumage. Such ostentation did not survive the rigors of *trench warfare* and industrialized mass killing. Camouflage was universally adopted in *World War II*, including for all equipment. A modern camouflager must contend with infrared scopes and other night vision technologies, supersensitive listening devices, radar, and satellite surveillance. *See also cavalry*; *stealth technology*.

campaign. A military operation with specific objectives, as in the Manchurian campaign of the Japanese Army, or, over a season, as in a spring campaign.

Campaign for Nuclear Disarmament (CND). An anti-nuclear weapons organization that advocated unilateral *disarmament* for Britain. In the 1960s and again in the early 1980s, it generated significant public protests.

Camp David talks/accords (September 17, 1978). Camp David is a rural retreat near Washington, DC, sometimes used by presidents to conduct personal diplomacy. Two agreements between Israel and Egypt were signed there after 13 days of tense negotiations (*Boutros Ghali*, the Egyptian foreign minister, resigned, and the Egyptian and Israeli leaders both threatened to leave the talks at different points) overseen by President *Jimmy Carter*. Signing were *Menachem Begin* and *Anwar Sadat*, in behalf of Israel and Egypt, respectively. The first agreement promised full *diplomatic relations*, Israeli withdrawal and removal of settlements from *Sinai*, and a *peace treaty*, which followed on March 26, 1979. A second, "Framework Agreement" designated *Resolution 242* as the basis for a more comprehensive peace and promised to resolve the Palestinian problem through negotiations on the future status of *Gaza* and the *West Bank*. The thorniest question, concerning the final status of *Jerusalem*, was deferred.

Campo-Formio, Treaty of (October 17, 1797). A temporary peace between Austria and France, arranged by *Napoleon* after his greatly successful Italian campaign. It transferred much of Belgium to France, established the fleeting Cisalpine Republic in Italy, and brought *Venice* into the Austrian *sphere of influence*. As a general settlement, it did not survive renewal of the struggle between France and Austria in the *War of the Second Coalition*.

Canada. The world's second largest country at 3,851,788 square miles (approximately 10 million square kilometers), but sparsely and unevenly populated and developed. The Genoese explorer John Cabot (1474–1557) landed in what is now Atlantic Canada in 1497. Yet, it was mainly the French who settled there in the sixteenth and seventeenth centuries—in small numbers compared to the English colonies to the south. Jacques Cartier landed in 1534 and proceeded up the *St. Lawrence River* valley. Full colonization began about 1600. Québec City, one of the oldest settlements in North America, was founded in 1608 by *Samuel de Champlain*. Early colonial Canada was divided into small, separately governed colonies: the English in *Newfoundland* and in *Upper Canada*; the French in *Acadia* and *Lower Canada*—the remnants of the once vast territory of *New France*. By 1660 there were still only 2,500 French in Canada, as compared with many more than that in the West Indies and 100,000 English colonists in North America. The English captured Québec City in 1759, during the *Seven Years' War*, and all *Québec* was ceded to England in the *Treaty of Paris* in 1763. These British North American colonies did not favor secession from the *British Empire* or join in the *American Revolution*, much preferring to remain under British rule or, in the case of Québec, not having any choice. That war swelled the population of the Canadas through an influx of *United Empire Loyalists*, the first of several waves of migration of political dissenters from the United States. (Smaller numbers of American dissidents would arrive during *McCarthyism* and the *Vietnam War*, adding to an extant impulse toward soft anti-Americanism, which sometimes characterizes Canada's popular culture, but especially its chattering classes.)

The Canada Act of 1791 established limited local self-government. Canadians played a minor role, mostly as militia, in the *War of 1812*. Afterward, they relocated the capital from York (Toronto), which had been burnt by an invading American army, to Ottawa. The peaceful future to come was foretold by the border settlement and *demilitarization* of the Great Lakes in the *Rush-Bagot Agreement* (1818). The rest of the eastern border was resolved in the *Webster-Ashburton Treaty* (1842) after the near-run *Aroostook War*; the far western frontier, or the *Oregon Question*, was addressed peacefully by 1846, leaving only minor Pacific coast issues unresolved until 1902. Domestically, in 1837 the *Mackenzie-Papineau Rebellions* in Upper and Lower Canada revealed a rising need for political reform and a growing demand for *autonomy* and convinced Britain to unite the provinces. This took place in 1840 after issuance of the *Durham Report*. In another sense, however, modern Canada took shape in response to the *American Civil War*: the British, the French, the Russians, and other North American powers recognized the emergence of a new colossus in the Western Hemisphere, and moved to settle their outstanding differences with Washington. In Britain's case, the *Treaty of Washington* put an end to a decades' long dispute about the lie of the Canada–U.S. border in the west, as well as most other outstanding disputes. Simultaneously, modern Canada took shape in 1867 under the leadership of Prime Minister Sir John A. Macdonald (1815–1891) and through passage by London of the British North America (BNA) Act, which set up a *confederation* of four former British colonies: New Brunswick, Nova Scotia, Ontario, and Québec. These were later joined by six more provinces. British Columbia joined Canada in 1871, upon completion of a national railroad linking it to Ontario and Québec; three more western provinces were added in the latter nineteenth and early twentieth centuries, carved out of vast but still sparsely populated western territories. The last province to join was Newfoundland, in 1949. Canada also has three huge Arctic territories that are not provinces (Nunavut, Yukon, North West Territories), but that enjoy broad self-government. Other than the Yukon, which has significant white settlements dating to the Klondike *gold rush*, they are sparsely populated by native (Inuit) peoples.

Canada began the twentieth century committed to the imperial tie. It fought as part of the Empire contingent in the *Boer War*. In 1911 a Liberal government was defeated over a proposal for *free trade* with the United States, an issue that would beset Canadian politics for the rest of the century. Because it remained constitutionally part of the British Empire, Canada found itself automatically at war with Germany and Austria in August 1914 upon Britain's *declaration of war*. It sent over 630,000 of its young men to fight in Europe, where they earned a reputation for toughness and for taking ground where other troops did not. However, *conscription* was bitterly opposed in Québec and badly divided the country. Heavy casualties, at hellish places such as *Ypres*, the *Somme*, and *Passchendaele*, stirred nationalist emotions and thoughts of independent foreign policy, though not yet of full separation from the Empire. Given Canada's contribution to the war, London agreed. Canada, along with other dominions (and India) therefore attended the *Paris Peace*

Conference on their own accord, and later sat separately from Britain in the *League of Nations*. Even so, Canada's foreign policy remained Britain's constitutional responsibility until the *Statute of Westminster* was passed in 1931. In the interwar years under *Mackenzie King*, Canada shared the *isolationist*, "fortress North America" outlook of its southern neighbor. Yet when Britain *declared war* on Germany in 1939, Canada immediately followed suit, after a decorous delay of a single week to display symbolic independence. Perhaps the greatest impact of *World War II* on Canadian national life was the impetus it gave to economic *integration* with the United States. Politically, however, rather than uniting in a common cause and shared sacrifice, conscription again split the nation. Canada fought until 1944 with an all-volunteer force, which consequently was undermanned and took heavy casualties (as late as 1945, all its combat troops were volunteers). Its main military contribution came in the *Battle of the Atlantic*, but it was importantly represented on D-Day and in the *Normandy campaign*. The First Canadian Army carried out the liberation of Holland and fought well in Germany. After the war, Canadians believed that their military efforts had earned them a greater voice and profile in world affairs, especially at the new *United Nations*, which they eagerly embraced. They were gravely disappointed to discover that, other than Britain, the *Great Powers* had hardly noticed. Even so, the postwar years were ones of considerable diplomatic activism and high levels of engagement in world affairs and have justly gone down in Canadian foreign policy lore as a golden age of global responsibility and creative statecraft.

Canada embraced the Western view of the early *Cold War*, participating in the *Berlin airlift*, joining *NATO*, and fighting in the *Korean Conflict*. During the *Suez Crisis*, Prime Minister *Lester Pearson* helped initiate United Nations peacekeeping operations, and Canada was a mainstay of such efforts ever after. The *Vietnam War* opened a rift with the United States, which widened in the 1970s with introduction of a *protectionist* economic and energy (*oil*) policy and a narrow redefinition of the *national interest* by Prime Minister *Pierre Trudeau*. Repeated efforts to diversify trade and political connections were unable to overcome the tug of economic integration with the United States. A *separatist* ("sovereigntist") movement in Québec then focused attention on domestic unity. Election of a secessionist government in that province in 1976 led to a (defeated) *referendum* on "sovereignty-association" in 1980. Pierre Trudeau then "repatriated" the BNA Act, giving Canada full constitutional independence from Britain: it retains the monarch as its *head of state*, but this is of purely symbolic significance. However, Québec refused to adhere to the new constitution, and the idea it might yet leave the Canadian union reverberates powerfully in national politics. In 1992 a referendum on an inclusive constitution was rejected by nearly every region, not just Québec. In 1988 real economic interests momentarily overcame symbolic politics, as Canada took a decisive continental turn by signing the *Canada–United States Free Trade Agreement* and subsequently joined *NAFTA*. Canada sent a small contingent to the *Gulf War*. With the end of the Cold War it withdrew its already reduced NATO force from Europe, converted part of its military to a UN standby force, and warned that it would no longer carry the same peacekeeping burden. In 1993 it announced that fiscal restraint and political frustration meant a pullout after 29 years of peacekeeping duty in Cyprus. Even so, it continued to participate in many UN and NATO operations, including those in Bosnia and Kosovo. It supported the UN *blockade* of Haiti, sending destroyers to help enforce it, but refused to participate in an invasion. In general, it maintains broader international associations than most states of comparable weight, a fact which reflects its bicultural heritage and multicultural character as a nation of immigrants. In addition, this approach to world affairs expresses the *liberal-internationalist* conviction of its foreign policy elite that the interests of Canada are best served by providing a moral example of support for *international organization* and respect for *international law*.

Suggested Readings: D. G. Creighton, *The Story of Canada* (1971); W. J. Eccles, *The French in North America, 1500–1783* (1998); R. T. Naylor, *Canada in the European Age, 1453–1919* (1988); Peter C. Newman, *Empire of the Bay* (1998).

Canada–United States Free Trade Agreement. Signed in 1988 and implemented in 1989, it established a *free trade area* between the United States and Canada. Full *tariff* elimination was completed by January 1, 1999. This bilateral treaty was reinforced by, but remained legally distinct from, the *NAFTA* agreement signed by Canada, Mexico, and the United States.

canals. *See Canal Zone(s); Grand Canal; international waterways; Panama Canal; Suez Canal.*

Canal Zone(s). (1) Panama: The ten-mile-wide area straddling the *Panama Canal*, controlled by the United States from 1904 to 2000. The original 1904 treaty was revised in 1979 to permit abolishing the zone in 2000. Panama also received control of ports at either end. (2) Suez: The zone around the *Suez Canal* occupied by the British under treaty, 1936–1956, and contested by Israel, 1967–1979. It was returned to Egyptian control after signature of the *peace treaty* with Israel.

Canaris, Wilhelm Franz (1887–1945). German admiral. He enlisted in the Imperial Navy in 1905. As a young officer he was aboard one of four German *cruisers* sunk during, or scuttled after, the *Battle of the Falklands* against the British in 1914. He found his way back to Germany and into the *Abwehr*, or German military *intelligence*. From the beginning, he rejected *Hitler* and Nazism. Nonetheless, he rose through the ranks to become a full admiral and head of the Abwehr during *World War II*. In operational terms, the Abwehr had little success against the Allies. Canaris is remembered for using his position to protect anti-Nazis, especially among the *Junker* class, and for his sympathy for several failed plots to assassinate Hitler. He lost control of the

Abwehr when Hitler transferred it to *Himmler* in 1944. Canaris does not appear to have been directly involved in the *July Plot*, but his loyalty was openly suspect by mid-1944; Hitler therefore had him arrested, tried, and hanged. His torture and execution were slow and particularly cruel.

Canary Islands. Located in the Atlantic off West Africa, they were discovered c. 1350 by Spanish and Portuguese explorers, both of whom later returned to take *slaves* among the native (Guanches) population. In 1393 a Castilian expedition took the first Canary slaves. Portugal and *Castile* laid claim to the islands, but European settlement was delayed by strong native resistance. Another Castilian invasion captured several small islands in 1402. Portugal invaded Grand Canary in 1425. The Guanches were ultimately overcome by this twin assault. The Canaries went to Castile (Spain) by treaty in 1479 in exchange for Portuguese title to the Azores, Madeira, and Cape Verde, in a preview of the later Iberian treaty on a *line of demarcation*. Today the Canaries are an overseas province of Spain.

canister. An early and primitive form of *case shot*. Unlike the more sophisticated *grapeshot*, canister shot was simply a metal can full of nails or bits of jagged metal or balls. It burst when fired to scatter shrapnel at close range.

Canning, George (1770–1827). British foreign secretary, 1807–1809; 1822–1827. An early *Whig*, he supported *Pitt* during the *French Revolution* and on the issue of *Catholic emancipation*. In 1798 he spoke eloquently in the House against the *slave trade* and for war with the *Directory* in France. He was Prime Minister William Pitt's choice to run the *Royal Navy*, 1804–1806. As foreign secretary he assisted Secretary of War *Castlereagh* in destroying the Danish fleet at the *Battle of Copenhagen* (1807) and in launching the *Peninsular War*. He and Castlereagh quarreled and foolishly dueled in 1809—Canning was slightly wounded in the thigh, on the second shot—after which both men were forced to resign. Canning's stubbornness and detestation of Castlereagh kept him out of high public office for a decade. During this time he spoke strongly in favor of Catholic emancipation, as an MP for Liverpool. He was briefly ambassador to Lisbon (1814) and governor general of India (1822). He became foreign secretary for the second time in 1822 (as MP for Harwich), when Castlereagh committed suicide. He quickly moved to limit Britain's involvement with the *Congress system*, which had formed the centerpiece of Castlereagh's diplomacy, and to strengthen its overt opposition to the *Holy Alliance*. Canning thus supported the Latin American colonies in their rebellions against Spain and Portugal and prodded the United States into taking a more assertive position in issuing the *Monroe Doctrine*. He also began to whittle away at *protectionist* measures, moving Great Britain toward the freer trade that would culminate in repeal of the Corn Laws. In 1826 he *recognized* the new Greek state, during the *Greek War of Independence*. He served as prime minister for just five months before his death in August 1827.

cannon. Any mounted weapon that fires heavy ordnance, such as a howitzer or mortar.

cannon fodder. (1) Infantry, fed to the enemy's cannons in the course of combat. (2) Any wasteful dissipation of military personnel.

cannon shot rule. *See artillery;* terrae dominum; *three-mile limit; twelve-mile limit.*

Canton trade system. *See Guangzhou (Canton) trade system.*

CANZ Group. Canada, Australia, and New Zealand. A compact, informal, small power *caucus group.*

capabilities. (1) In *power* analysis: The material or tangible components of power: *industrial* capacity, military might, *natural resources, population,* advanced *technology, territory, topography,* and national wealth. (2) In military terms: Specific hard assets required to complete mission goals.

Cape Colony. Located on the Cape of Good Hope at the southern tip of Africa, it was first settled by the Dutch in 1652. For 150 years it was a service port for ships plying the Indian Ocean trade, importing Javanese slaves at first, then buying slaves from the Portuguese in Mozambique and Angola. Over time, miscegenation led to a distinct (though minority) community of so-called Cape Colored. Dutch farmers (trekboers) slowly migrated inland, displacing, killing, or enslaving scattered Khoi and San pastoralists they encountered. To administratively catch up with this migration, Stellenbosch was added to the colony in 1685 and Swellendam in 1745. Still, by the end of the eighteenth century only about 16,000 whites lived in Cape Colony. It was captured and held by the British, 1795–1803, during the *Napoleonic Wars*. It was restored to the Batavian Republic (Netherlands) in 1803. It was retaken, permanently, by British forces in 1806, a fact legally confirmed in 1814 at the *Congress of Vienna*. In the nineteenth century it became the main British base in southern Africa, but one about which London was increasingly ambivalent as the geopolitical importance of the Cape diminished with the end of the French wars and, later, construction of the *Suez Canal*. As in the rest of the *British Empire*, the Cape saw abolition of *slavery* in 1833. That started the *Boers* on their *Great Trek* into the interior, away from such British laws. The British followed, expanding into *Natal* in 1843. The colony received a constitution in 1853 and full self-government in 1872. The British *recognized* the independence of the Boer's *Orange Free State* in 1854, but rescinded it (and annexed that republic) during the *First Boer War*. Cape Colony also proved key to British success in the *Zulu Wars*. *Cecil Rhodes* was premier, 1890–1896. In 1912 Cape Colony joined the Union of South Africa. Under *apartheid*, the still mainly English population of Cape Town was less supportive of white minority rule than were most Boers.

Capetian dynasty. The great *dynasty* that ruled much of France directly from its founding by Hugh Capet in 987, until 1328, and through its *Valois* and *Bourbons* branches until 1848, interrupted during the *French Revolution* and *Napoleonic Wars*, 1792–1814, and briefly in 1815. Capetian monarchs began to steadily centralize political and economic power in France during the reign of Louis XI (r. 1461–1483), after the *Hundred Years' War*. The process accelerated under *Henri IV*, *Richelieu*, *Mazarin*, and especially *Louis XIV*.

Cape Verde. The islands were discovered in 1444 by Portuguese ships sent out by *Henry the Navigator*. They were uninhabited and were first settled by Portuguese in 1460. *Slaves* were then brought from Africa, and over time these populations comingled into a single people. Poverty and occasional famine dotted Cape Verdean history, but little more of note occurred until *independence* was proclaimed in 1975 after a *revolution* in Portugal. Although some thought was given to union with Guinea-Bissau, which had for years been administratively joined to Cape Verde, nothing came of this project. Run as a *one-party state* until 1990, free elections were held in 1991. For most of the 1990s Cape Verde's economy declined as markets and produce both dried up as a consequence of drought. It maintains close ties to Portugal and with an *emigré community* in the United States. *See also Canary Islands; line of demarcation*.

capital. (1) Wealth, whether in money, *capital goods* used to produce other goods, "human capital," or financial capital. Capital is thus one of the *factor endowments* of an economy. Financial capital contrasts with income received during a given period (revenue).

(2) An alternate term in *Marxism* for capitalists (the owners of physical capital) as a class, as distinct from labor (*proletarians*). It is always used pejoratively, as in "the interests of monopoly capital." (3) A city hosting a country's seat of government. *See also foreign direct investment; infrastructure; investment; patient capital; profit; social overhead capital; venture capital*.

capital account. A subset of the *balance of payments* system of measuring a country's financial transactions; it is all public and private investment that flows in and out of a given economy, as well as an accounting of all long- and short-term capital exchanges with the world economy made through borrowing.

capital controls. Government restrictions on the export of financial *capital*. These aim at maintaining currency, interest rate, and *exchange rate* stability.

capital flight. When capital moves in large volumes from a country whose economy is weakening or whose political situation has become unstable. In a usage peculiar to some in the *Third World*, it may also refer to transfers of *foreign exchange* by national elites or corrupt governments into *hard currency* accounts abroad, as insurance against risk of economic collapse or loss of political power.

capital formation. The increase in the *capital* stock of a national economy. Net capital formation subtracts *depreciation* and the cost of repair and replacement from the gross figure.

capital goods. Physical capital. Machines, tools, and other such primary goods used to produce secondary goods for sale; not for final use themselves. *See also consumer goods.*

capital intensive. Economic activity with high *capital* costs, relative to *labor*. *See also comparative advantage.*

capital investment. The total of all funds invested in a firm or national economy.

capitalism. There is no consensus definition of this term. Nonetheless, it is generally taken to mean an economic system where wealth, investment, *profit*, exchanges, distribution, and ownership of property are mainly in private hands, there is a basic reliance on market forces, and there exists broad social encouragement and legal protection of property ownership and for free movement of both *labor* and *capital*. Capitalism developed slowly in Western Europe well before the eighteenth century but expanded rapidly after that, its inherent *cosmopolitanism* and urban impatience breaking down *feudal* structures, rewriting contractual laws, altering social and class relations, and greatly enriching and *modernizing* those societies where it first took deep root (Holland, Britain, Germany, France, and America).

In the nineteenth century, capitalism accelerated *industrialization* in several *Great Powers*, taking on a *dirigiste* form in some. Its expansion of *production* contributed to a rise in *population*, urbanization, and in many cases also a *crisis of rising expectations*. Around mid-century, *liberal* reform movements led to increased regulation of emerging capitalist economies that attenuated the worst abuses of labor, which had become extensive in the early decades of modern capitalism as *laissez-faire* economic ideas were misappropriated to the realm of social welfare, excusing and even appearing to justify coarse neglect of the suffering and destitution of one's countryfolk. This reform process was subsequently attended and reinforced by a rapid growth in trade unionism and *democratic socialist* movements among industrial workers in the major economies. The nineteenth century thus witnessed parliamentary reform in several countries, and the rise of mass political parties critical (from the point of view of both the new urban left and the old agrarian right) of the "alienation" from family and community said to flow from capitalism. The largest working-class party rose in *Bismarck's* Germany; the most significant trade union movement was in Britain.

By the early twentieth century several major economies began extensive reforms, which overlay the original laissez-faire system. If, at the end of the nineteenth century, capitalism was closely misidentified in many minds as necessarily leading to *imperialism* and *colonialism*, phenomena that had discrete causes and that primarily attached to the Great Powers, it was in fact more clearly developing a close association with the advance of *democracy*—at least in the major *metropolitan* countries. The greatest crisis faced by capitalism came with the *Great Depression*, 1929–1939, the most severe in a series of cyclical downturns or *world depressions*. During this cataclysm, old-style capitalism was rejected by tens of millions, who turned instead to the radical socioeconomic solutions proffered by *fascism* and *communism*. Fascism lost the war that followed, but competition with Communist ideas and states continued through the *Cold War*. For four decades after *World War II* there was significant regulation of private economic activity, and in some countries even *nationalization* of key industries, as the welfare state developed in advanced capitalist societies. This trend was largely reversed during the 1980s with a move back to less choking regulation and to *privatization*. In the 1990s former Communist regimes turned to capitalism at varying rates of speed and success. In many *developing countries* there was a broad, *elite* antagonism to capitalism as an economic model immediately after independence. However, even several former *Marxist-Leninist* regimes in Africa and elsewhere in the *Third World* proclaimed an economic epiphany in 1991 and started the conversion (in both senses of the word) to *market economics*. Not all such attempts were successful or happy, however.

It is worth noting that capitalism, like communism, was never monolithic. Instead, capitalism assumed different forms according to locale and culture. For instance, Japanese capitalism emphasized producer interests and industrial efficiency, whereas the American version accented free markets and consumer gratification. *See also autarky; banking; GATT; International Bank for Reconstruction and Development; International Monetary Fund; Keynesian economics; liberalism; Marxism; mercantilism; mode of production; monetarism; physiocrats; profit; reform liberalism; regional banks; self-reliance; self-sufficiency; Adam Smith; socialism; state capitalism; supply side; sustainable growth; Max Weber.*

Suggested Readings: William Ashworth, *A Short History of the World Economy* (1987); Jan De Vries and Ad Van Der Woude, *The First Modern Economy* (1997); J. Foreman-Peck, *History of the World Economy* (1983); Robert L. Heilbroner and Lester Thurow, *Economics Explained* (rev. ed. 1998); Kenneth Pomeranz, *The Great Divergence: Europe, China, and the Making of the Modern World Economy* (2000); Paul Samuelson and W. Nordhaus, *Economics* (16th ed. 1997); S. Viljoen, *Economic Systems in World History* (1974).

capitalist. A person with financial *capital* available for investment, who accepts risk of losses in exchange for the opportunity to earn *profits*, as distinct from wages or rents, usually through investment, management, and/or other participation in the expansion of productive economic activities in a *market economy*.

capitalize. To supply (a firm, market, or national economy) with *capital*.

capital markets. Banks, insurance companies, trust societies, and *stock exchanges* from whose holdings investment capital is transferred to commercial enterprises and manufacturers. *See also money market.*

capital mobility. The ability of financial and investment *capital* to move across national boundaries, from economy to economy, to take advantage of shifts in interest rates or investment opportunities, or to avoid onerous regulation.

capital warship. The largest *warships*, including: *aircraft carriers, battleships, battle cruisers,* and heavy *cruisers,* and since *World War II* also nuclear *submarines.*

capitulations. (1) A rule by which Westerners (and later Japanese) were made exempt from local laws and *jurisdiction* in China. (2) Any similar rule, imposed by a strong state on a weaker state. *See also extraterritoriality; servitude.*

Caporetto, Battle of (October 24–November 12, 1917). Using a plan drawn up by *von Ludendorff*, Austrian and German units cut off and trapped the advancing Italian Army, which had fought repeated battles on the *Isonzo* front since 1915. The Italians were routed and surrendered en masse: of Italy's nearly 300,000 casualties, 275,000 were taken prisoner. By the 11th day, the *Central Powers* were near Venice, but had overrun their lines of supply and the advance petered out. This humbling defeat would likely have knocked Italy out of *World War I* had France and Britain not rushed in reinforcements, thereby weakening the *western front* before the German spring offensives of 1918. Caporetto cost Italy any hope for territorial gains it might have made at the *Paris Peace Conference*, where it received far less than its leaders and people thought their sacrifice in war had earned. That national humiliation fueled later *fascist* propaganda. Italian arms were partly redeemed by a victory at Vittorio Venito (October 24–November 3, 1918). *See also mutilated victory.*
    Suggested Reading: Ernest Hemingway, *A Farewell to Arms* (1958).

capture. The legal right whereby a state takes ownership of enemy property seized at sea during a war. *See also prize.*

caravel. A fast, shallow-draft vessel with both square sails and triangular, lateen sails, developed in Iberia and ideal for long voyages of discovery. They played a key role in the *Age of Exploration*. *Columbus* took two on his first voyage to America.

Caribbean. From "Carib," the European name for the dominant native Indian population of the region, located mainly in the Lesser Antilles—Arawak Indians dominated the Greater Antilles. (1) That part of the Atlantic Ocean contained by *Central America*, *South America*, and the *West Indies*. (2) The region comprising the *nations* and *dependencies* of the West Indies.
    Suggested Readings: Peter Hulme, *Colonial Encounters: Europe and the Caribbean, 1492–1797* (1986); David Watts, *The West Indies: Patterns of Development, Culture and Environmental Change Since 1492* (1987).

Caribbean Basin Initiative (1984). Announced in 1982 and in effect from 1984 to 1996, it gave participating states *preferential tariff* treatment on certain goods in the U.S. market.

Caribbean Community and Common Market (CARICOM). It was established on July 4, 1973 (by the Treaty of Chaguaramas) as the effective successor to *CARIFTA*. It aims at economic, social, and technical cooperation, eventual creation of a full *customs union*, and coordination of foreign economic policy. In 2001 its full members were: Antigua, Bahamas, Barbados, Belize, Dominica, Grenada, Guyana, Jamaica, Montserrat, St. Kitts (St. Christopher and Nevis), St. Lucia, St. Vincent, and Trinidad and Tobago. Associate members were: British Virgin Islands, Anguilla, and the Turks and Caicos Islands. Members with observer status were: Dominican Republic, Haiti, and Suriname.

Caribbean Free Trade Association (CARIFTA). The predecessor of *CARICOM*, it was formed in 1968 to work toward a *free trade area* among former British colonies. It shares a *Secretariat* and much the same membership with CARICOM.

Carlists. Supporters of the line of Don Carlos (1788–1855), who claimed the Spanish throne in an inter-*Bourbon* succession struggle that led to civil wars in Spain, 1834–1837, and again, 1870–1876, each of which the Carlists lost. This quarrel kept Spain out of the larger political currents in Europe, thus avoiding the plunge into the *Revolutions of 1848*, but also held it back from faster *modernization* and *liberal* reform after that date. Carlism enjoyed a revival in the early twentieth century, contributed to the instability of the Spanish

Republic, and supported *Franco* during the *Spanish Civil War*. In 1937 Franco forced the Carlists to merge with the *Falange*.

Carlsson, Bernt (1938–1988). Swedish diplomat. He headed the *Socialist International*, 1970–1976. As United Nations Commissioner for *Namibia* 1987–1988, he helped negotiate the regional settlement that led to Cuban and South African withdrawal and Namibian independence in 1990. He was killed in a *terrorist* bombing of a Pan Am plane over Scotland.

Carnegie, Andrew (1835–1918). American billionaire and philanthropist who made his billions in *oil*, iron, and steel. He founded numerous endowments, including those dedicated to studying international conflict, *ethics*, and *peace*.

Caroline Affair (1837). *See William Lyon Mackenzie.*

Caroline Islands. Some 500 small islands off the Philippines, settled by Spain, then sold to Germany in 1899. In *World War I* they were seized by Japan, and in 1921 made a *mandate territory*. During *World War II* the Japanese had a naval base on Truk. After 1947 they were made part of the *Trust Territory of the Pacific Islands. See also Federated States of Micronesia.*

Carpatho-Ukraine. An alternate name for *Ruthenia*, ceded by *Czechoslovakia* to the *Soviet Union* in 1945 and now part of Ukraine.

carpetbagger. A derogatory term for Northerners who went South after the *American Civil War* to join *Republican Party* administrations during the period of *Reconstruction*. Some were genuine reformers, others were opportunist scoundrels; all were hated by white Southerners, who identified the carpetbaggers as the worst symbol of their *defeat* and "*occupation.*"

carpet bombing. When fleets of bombers drop their ordnance in wide, destructive patterns (lay a carpet of bombs) rather than aim with precision (precision bombing) at specific targets. The British called this "area bombing." They were the first to develop a doctrine to support it, which they applied with vigor against German cities in *World War II*. The United States carpet-bombed the DRV (North Vietnam) for many years without winning a strategic victory. *See also air power; indiscriminate bombing; strategic bombing; thousand bomber raids; total war.*

Carranza, Venustiano (1859–1920). Mexican revolutionary and president, 1915–1920, a period of continuous civil war and repeated U.S. *intervention*. He was opposed by *Pancho Villa* and especially by *Emiliano Zapata* after it became clear his dedication to *agrarian reform* was fairly shallow. He alienated

Woodrow Wilson by his (entirely defensible) refusal to take Mexico into *World War I*. He introduced a fairly radical constitution in 1917, severely and clearly separating church and state, breaking up and redistributing some larger land-holdings, and granting some workers' rights. He was taken by the military and assassinated, or committed suicide, in 1920.

Cartagena Group. "Permanent Mechanism of Consultation and Political Co-ordination." Also known as the Group of Eight. It was formed in the 1980s to discuss matters of common regional and foreign policy interest at top levels of government, including that of *foreign ministers* and *heads of state* and of government, as a means of consolidating *democratization* in the region, after several decades of military rule. Its membership included the larger countries and economies of Latin America: Argentina, Brazil, Colombia, Ecuador, Mexico, Peru, Uruguay, and Venezuela.

cartel. A producers' organization that limits competition and sets high prices by creating artificial shortages through low production quotas. It may also seek to control the market through stockpiling (hoarding) and setting marketing quotas (dividing markets). Cartels may be vertical (member firms control all stages of production) or horizontal (member firms control all production of the same product). Cartels are inherently unstable: there develops a great temptation to defect from the quota system to take advantage of the high prices it helped create. Such defection results in falling prices for all members of the cartel, including those who stick to the quotas, and hence causes discord among members, which leads to breakdown in the cooperation needed to sustain the cartel. Also, if prices rise or technology advances, artificial substitutes may undermine cartel pricing power. Sometimes this is so apparent even cartel members agree and end their attempts at coordination. That is what happened, for instance, to the International Natural Rubber Association: its members dissolved it in 1999. *See also Central Selling Organization (CSO); chaebol; drug cartels; international commodity agreement (ICA); OPEC; zaibatsu.*

Carter Doctrine. A proclamation issued in the wake of the 1979 Soviet invasion and occupation of Afghanistan, stating that the United States would regard as a threat to its *vital interests* any Soviet *aggression* toward the Persian Gulf. It led to establishment of important U.S. bases in the region and to the *Rapid Deployment Force*. It reaffirmed the earlier *Truman* and *Eisenhower Doctrines*, and partly repudiated the *Nixon Doctrine*.

Carter, James Earl (b. 1924). *Democratic* president of the United States, 1977–1981. Carter's foreign policy suffered from his chronic inability to decide between the ultimately incompatible courses suggested by two key advisers, Cyrus Vance and *Zbigniew Brzezinski*. Its main motif was *human rights*, which by Carter's own later admission was an insufficiently examined electoral promise that cut across too many policies and interests to be applied consistently. By 1978 it had largely subsided to rhetoric. Carter also proclaimed that U.S. policy was too absorbed with relations with the *Soviet Union* and that it should look more to problems of world order, such as *population* growth or issues of *distributive justice*. His successes were negotiating the *Panama Canal* agreement, facilitating the *Camp David Accords*, finishing the full restoration of relations with China begun by *Richard Nixon*, and continuing the process begun with the *Helsinki Accords*. However, Carter's handling of U.S.-Soviet relations was weak, even inept. He was unable to gain Senate consent to *SALT II*, was stunned by the invasion of Afghanistan, and hobbled himself with ineffective but politically damaging *sanctions* introduced in response.

Carter was then weighed down by the *hostage crisis* in Iran, which dogged his final year and made him appear indecisive and uncertain. In addition, he faced a prolonged recession, historically high interest rates, and world inflation that followed upon the *OPEC* oil price shock of 1979 and was also a legacy of spending on the *Vietnam War*. Probably his greatest accomplishment as president is one of which he was not proud at the time, nor particularly pleased about: the decision made with the *NATO* allies in 1979 to carry out a deployment of intermediate-range nuclear missiles in Europe. When later implemented by the *Reagan* administration, this decision forced the Soviet leadership to reconsider the real-world effects of their bloated and offensive nuclear force structure, and eventually also their entire political and economic relationship with the West. Out of office, he enjoyed public respect for his many good works, election observation, and human rights monitoring, though he was criticized by some for interfering in U.S. diplomacy toward North Korea and Haiti during the *Clinton* years. His extraofficial work recovered a personal reputation badly damaged by his job performance when president, even if he sometimes wore his humility perhaps too proudly.

Suggested Readings: Zbigniew Brzezinski, *Power and Principle* (1983); James Carter, *Keeping Faith* (1982); Cathal J. Nolan, *Principled Diplomacy* (1993); Gaddis Smith, *Morality, Reason, and Power* (1986); Cyrus Vance, *Hard Choices* (1983).

Carthaginian peace. A brutal peace, or *diktat*, imposed upon the vanquished by the victor: "Where they make a desert, they call it peace." Calgacus said this as a warning to the ancient Britons, about the *Roman Empire's* desolation of Carthage in the *Punic Wars*.

Casablanca bloc. *See Organization of African Unity.*

Casablanca Conference (January 14–24, 1943). *Franklin Roosevelt* and *Winston Churchill* met in Casablanca to discuss Allied policy; *Stalin* declined to attend. The main decisions taken were: (1) agreement to demand *uncondi-*

tional surrender from the *Axis* powers; (2) agreement on an invasion of Sicily and Italy, to precede the main invasion of Europe (the Sicilian invasion was the last time Britain prevailed in Allied counsels on a major strategic decision); (3) launch of a sustained *strategic bombing* offensive against Germany; and (4) approval of the U.S. Navy plan to advance on Japan via the central Pacific, through the Caroline and Marshall Islands and, most importantly, the Philippines. It signaled the beginning of the great island-hopping campaign in the Pacific, a campaign that greatly shortened that war. The most important decision concerned the invasion of Sicily. Churchill pressed for it, in part with the intention of deflecting the Americans from their determination to open a *second front* in France in 1943, which he feared could not be opened until 1944 without sustaining severe Allied casualties.

Casement, Roger (1864–1916). Irish nationalist. As a British consular officer he was responsible for issuing a report on the Congo that exposed atrocities and misrule under Leopold II (1835–1909) of Belgium. This brought international attention to bear and forced the Belgian government to take over administration of the Congo colony from Leopold. In 1913 Casement joined the Irish Volunteers, a nationalist militia and forerunner to the *Irish Republican Army* (IRA). He spent much of *World War I* trying to recruit Irish *POWs* from the British Army to join an Irish Brigade in the German Army. Just before the *Easter Rising* he landed in Ireland from a German *U-boat*, hoping to deliver arms to the IRA. He was captured and "exposed" by the British as a homosexual; he then converted to Catholicism, was convicted of *treason*, and hanged.

case shot. There were two forms of this short-range *artillery* ammunition: *canister shot* and *grapeshot*. All case shot were short-range projectiles made of nails or metal fragments, or encased iron balls, fired from a cannon. It could mow down an assaulting force of *infantry* or *cavalry*. Its antonym was "solid shot," which had a much longer range and worked (when the ground was not rain-sodden and soft) by bouncing and ricocheting among enemy ranks, tearing off heads and limbs.

case study. (1) A history. (2) An in-depth examination of a given phenomenon (*crisis*, *war*, *negotiation*, *trade* system, etc.) or institution. (3) A method in *political science* that seeks to illustrate or discover causal connections by tracing them through a series of illustrative cases, which are then compared.

Casey, William (1913–1987). Director of Central Intelligence (DCI), 1981–1987. He revived *covert action* by the CIA, in disuse after the 1970s. That move was heavily criticized by those who saw Casey as a key, though shadowy, figure in the *Reagan* administration, who was charged with circumventing the will of Congress, and perhaps the law too, by using the CIA and other channels to send secret aid to the *Contras*. More importantly, during his years as DCI, the agency failed to correctly assess the decaying economic situation within the *Soviet Union* and was slow to foretell the collapse of that empire.

"cash and carry." *See Neutrality Acts.*

cash crops. Those crops (for example, coffee, cocoa, cotton, jute) grown principally for sale abroad in order to procure *hard currency*, as opposed to agricultural production of food crops for personal consumption or domestic sale. *See also depressions, world; subsistence economy.*

Caspian Sea. The largest inland, salt sea in the world, located between southeastern Europe and southwestern Asia.

caste system. Originally, an idealized Vedic class division of *Hindus* by *Aryans* according to skin color ("varna") and social status. The four broadest varnas (color categories, or castes) were brahman, kshatriya, vaishya, and shudra, each ranked morally and socially by the degree of "pollution" that attached to its members at birth. The class of Untouchables ("harijan") developed later, as a lower ranking fifth caste, or outcaste ("panchamas"), for those shudra (or "dasas") in the most menial occupations, who were considered wholly "unclean" by all the higher castes. The caste system thus arose not just from socioeconomic forms and conquest, though both played a role, but also from Hindu-Aryan ritual and ideas of religious and racial taboo. Thus, an even older, pre-Aryan "jati" (birth group) system, which determined one's occupation, worked to subdivide each varna class into many hundreds of subcastes. This complex socioeconomic and political arrangement, sustained in religious guise and with ritual sanction, varied additionally in India's diverse regions. Although there was some social mobility among castes, overall the caste system—both historically and into the modern period—hobbled economic *development* in Hindu areas by decreasing incentive and erecting barriers to upward mobility based upon occupation. This kept a large portion of India's population restricted to subsistence agriculture and other forms of menial, unproductive labor. In turn, that limited their purchasing power as consumers and retarded development of a merchant/middle class and service sector. Those problems were only compounded by a deeply rooted misogyny in Indian society, Hindu and Muslim.

Suggested Readings: A. L. Basham, *The Origins and Development of Classical Hinduism* (1989); Susan Bayly, *Caste, Society and Politics in India from the 18th Century to the Modern Age* (1999); Burton Stein, *A History of India* (1998).

Castile. "Country of castles," named for the *feudal* military structures that dominated its landscape and national life into the fifteenth century. This one-time independent, wealthy, powerful, Christian kingdom led the campaign to expel the Moors from Iberia and comprised the core of Imperial Spain. *See also Ferdinand and Isabella; Philip II; Reconquista; Spain.*

Castlereagh, Robert Stewart (1769–1822). Viscount. Secretary for Ireland, 1797–1801; secretary for war and the colonies, 1805–1809; foreign secretary, 1812–1822. Born to an Ulsterman, he sat in the Irish Parliament as a *Whig* from 1790. He crossed over to the *Tories* in 1795, but as secretary for Ireland strongly supported *Pitt's* drive for *Catholic emancipation*. He helped suppress the Irish insurrection of 1798 ("The Year of the French") and then worked for full constitutional union of Britain and Ireland in the *Act of Union* (1800). He resigned as secretary for Ireland along with Pitt when they met stiff opposition to Catholic emancipation, especially from King George III. As secretary for war, Castlereagh ordered destruction of the Danish fleet at the *Battle of Copenhagen*, launched the *Peninsular War* and selected Wellesley (*Wellington*) to lead it, and was largely responsible for gathering and sustaining the coalition that defeated *Napoleon*. Not all his plans worked out though. Failure of the Walcheren Expedition, for which he was blamed by colleagues, led (on September 21, 1809) to a duel with *George Canning*. That was a remarkably foolish act that cost two enormously talented men high office. Castlereagh made it back to the top first, as *Liverpool's* foreign secretary. In making the peace, Castlereagh emerged as Britain's greatest-ever foreign secretary, driving home to victory over France, 1812–1815, and then envisioning a reasonably just *balance of power* in Europe, and working to this end with *Metternich* at the *Congress of Vienna* and, later, within the *Congress system*. Castlereagh succeeded in both rehabilitating France and securing all major British war aims, including neutrality of the *English Channel* ports and buffer states surrounding France in the north, in Germany, and in Italy; and acquisition of important naval bases in South Africa and Ceylon. He grew increasingly disillusioned with the reactionary policies of the continental powers, keeping Britain in the Congress system but distancing it from the so-called *Holy Alliance*. He took his own life, with a penknife, in 1822, just before he was to depart for the *Congress of Verona. See also Metternich.*

Suggested Readings: Henry Kissinger, *A World Restored* (1957); Paul Schroeder, *The Transformation of European Politics, 1763–1848* (1994); C. Webster, *Foreign Policy of Castlereagh* (1931).

Castro, Fidel (b. 1927). "Maximum Leader." Cuban dictator. Prime minister of Cuba, 1959–1976; president, 1976– . Castro (or Fidel, as he liked to be called) was arrested in 1953 after a failed attempt to foment *revolution*. In 1957 he organized and led a minor rebellion against the corrupt *Batista* regime that turned into the *Cuban Revolution* after two years of fighting. Dynamic and charismatic, Castro also exhibited a deep and corrupting megalomania— his prolix nature is infamous, including six- to eight-hour harangues of sun-baked crowds, interviewers, or diplomats. He appears to have been ideologically neutral as a young man, but moved left as he graduated from student politics to street fighting, and then *guerrilla warfare*. He embraced *Marxism-Leninism* openly only after taking power, partly because it helped justify his dictatorship. His ascendant characteristic was a lust for personal power. To get it and keep it, he showed himself willing to use mass violence, terror, and repression on a scale limited only by the isolation of Cuba, rather than by any apparent internal or moral restraint.

Castro tacked Cuba against a hostile U.S. gale for more than 30 years, steering always to the *radical* (and dictatorial) left. To his chagrin, he played little role in the *Cuban Missile Crisis*. In the 1970s he found a new outlet for his personal and ideological ambitions, which at last exceeded the shores of Cuba: he intervened in Angola largely on his own accord, dragging the Soviet Union behind him into that war, and then supported Communist *revolutions* in Angola, Mozambique, and Ethiopia (the latter was a particularly vicious regime) at levels of commitment well beyond Cuba's ability to sustain. In 1980 he cynically permitted the *Mariel boat lift*, to relieve pressure on his regime by those he saw as troublemakers and malcontents. In 1983 his own daughter, Alina, fled Cuba. In 1989 he publicly lamented the fall of the *Berlin Wall* and bitterly criticized *Gorbachev* for *glasnost* and *perestroika*. As his Soviet *subsidies* disappeared, he grew more, not less, defiant of *world public opinion*, taking extra repressive measures to quell dissent. Three things sustained him in power into the 21st century: (1) his military and *secret police*; (2) the unpopularity among Cuba's poor of exiles in Florida who threatened to return to reclaim their expropriated property; and (3) the U.S. *embargo*, which exacerbated the structural weaknesses of Cuba's *planned economy* but also provided an external enemy upon which Castro could fasten blame for all internal failings.

Suggested Readings: Thomas G. Patterson, *Contesting Castro* (1994); Robert Quirk, *Fidel Castro* (1993).

casus belli. A justification or an event that occasions, or one that merely serves as a pretext for, a declaration or an *act of war*.

casus foederis. When binding legal obligations previously entered into under terms of an *alliance* must be honored. This principle governs when a *state* is obliged to become an active participant in the ongoing *war* of a power to which it is allied.

casus non praesatur. When unintentional failure to fulfill international legal obligations does not lead to liability for the state concerned.

Catherine II, of Russia, née Sophia Frederika (1729–1796). "The Great." This Prussian princess from Anhalt-Zerbst became tsarina by *dynastic marriage*, changing her name to Catherine Alexievna upon her obligatory conversion to Orthodoxy and marriage in 1745, at age 16, to Peter (1728–1762), grandson of *Peter I* and heir to the Russian throne. She was famous for her infidelities even before she became empress of Russia in 1762. Her coronation preceded by days the murder of her deposed (and estranged) husband, Tsar Peter III, an act in which she probably played no small part. She genuflected toward the *Orthodox Church* but fancied herself a child of the *Enlightenment* because she corresponded with *Voltaire* and other philosophes. A mass of contradictions, as were the times in which she lived, she kept black *slaves* at her side at court and reissued Peter's famous edicts on beards and western dress. She took several of her advisers as lovers (or was it lovers as her advisers?). When nativist unrest at these Prussian presumptions arose, she had the young prince Ivan, around whom the opposition was rallying, murdered. The most important of Catherine's lover-advisers was *Potemkin*, a veteran of the *Russo-Turkish Wars*. She ordered her generals to ruthlessly repress the *Pugachev rebellion*, 1773–1775. During her reign, Russia greatly expanded its territorial holdings and somewhat expanded and modernized its economy, but not sufficiently to truly compete with the Western powers. In 1780, in an overly ambitious compact, she secretly agreed with Emperor *Joseph* of Austria to divide Turkey; three years later she unilaterally annexed the *Crimea*. She oversaw the three eighteenth-century *partitions of Poland*, annexation of *Courland*, and fought expansionist wars against the *Ottoman Empire* (1774 and 1792), and Sweden (1790). In all, she added perhaps 200,000 square miles to the Russian Empire. She loathed the *French Revolution* and intervened against it, but without success before her death in 1796. Domestically, she presided over a worsening of the condition of the serfs, but also a modest expansion of the liberties of the gentry. In some of her political attitudes and in her cultural reforms, she was a clear *Westernizer*; but on social and economic policy—most notably concerning serfdom—she was content to see rough and raw exploitation of the vast majority of her subjects continue, and even deepen. *See also Alexander I; Alexander II; Nicholas I; Nicholas II; Peter I.*

Suggested Readings: John Alexander, *Catherine the Great* (1988); I. de Madariaga, *Russia in the Age of Catherine the Great* (1981); I. de Madariaga, *Catherine the Great* (1990).

Catholic Church. Catholicism is among the oldest, and is the largest, of *Christian* denominations, with followers numbering more than one billion people by 2000. It was carried to the Americas and parts of Africa and Asia by the *Jesuits* and other *missionaries*, taking root along with European *imperialism* after 1500. That made it the largest Christian denomination; before that, the *Orthodox Church*, the great historic rival of the Catholic Church since the *schism* of 1054, was more populous. By the twenty-first century, most Catholics lived outside the historic homeland of the faith in the Middle East and Europe, and increasing numbers paid only nominal allegiance in their daily lives to Church authority on matters of morals and conscience—although new Church histories, which delve into the attitudes of the mass of the faithful, rather than merely recount clerical successions and doctrinal quarrels, reveal that is not a wholly new development. Doctrinally, the Catholic Church holds to the apostolic succession of bishops, including the doctrine of the primacy of the pope on matters of faith and doctrine, first promulgated in 1870, and maintains a vast scheme of moral and philosophical doctrine. It also retains vast institutional wealth, much of it acquired from centuries of bequests and landownership, and residual political influence in many lands with large Catholic populations. The Catholic Church was once a significant secular power in all of Europe and then later in central Italy, but since the *Renaissance* the temporal mandate of the Church was progressively confined, until by the twentieth century it was reduced to the few hectares of the *Vatican*.

Controversies of international significance involving the Catholic Church are legion, and from the fifth century (fall of the *Roman Empire* in the West) through the sixteenth century (to the *Protestant Reformation* and Catholic *Counter Reformation*) were also formative in European history, and indeed in many aspects of world history. Thereafter, the secular influence of the church waned dramatically, though it still importantly struggled with various states (notably Austria, then in the nineteenth century also Italy and Germany) over internal issues of religious and social policy and the question of the relation of the Church to the modern state. More recent examples of Church involvement in political controversies include: the role of the *Solidarity* movement in Poland; *John Paul II* and other recent popes in social policy debates in predominantly Catholic countries; the development of a Marxist strain of Catholicism in Latin America known as *liberation theology*; conflict between the Vatican and Israel over the Church's role in the *Holocaust* and control of the Holy Places in *Jerusalem*; Catholic opposition to birth control at international conferences on *population*; Church opposition to Chinese state interference in private worship and continuing interest in a proselytizing mission; and potential or actual schisms between Rome and several national churches in Africa. *See also Charlemagne; concordat; Counter Reformation; Crusades; Ecumenical Councils; Great Schism; Guelphs and Ghibellines; Holy Roman Empire; Index; Inquisition; John XXIII; just war tradition; Kulturkampf; Lateran Treaties; Old Catholics; Papal States; Pius IX; Pius XI; Pius XII; prohibited weapons; real patronato; res publica Christiana; Roman Question; two swords; Unitate Churches; Vatican Councils.*

Suggested Readings: Owen Chadwick, ed., *Pelican History of the Church*, six vols. (1970–); Owen Chadwick, *The Popes and European Revolution* (1981); Eric Hanson, *The Catholic Church in World Politics* (1987).

Catholic emancipation. An emancipation issue that dogged English-Irish relations from first passage of the Penal Laws against Nonconformist *Protestants* and *Catholics* in the sixteenth century, and especially from 1673, when a Test Act (requiring an oath on Anglican sacraments and doctrine) was passed that excluded Catholics, Jews, and Nonconformist Protestants from sitting in Parliament. Legal and economic restrictions on English Catholics began to ease progressively from 1778, though not without arousing deep and at times violent opposition. Pending a loyalty oath, *William Pitt* passed legislation in 1793 that permitted Catholics to serve in the armed forces, attend universities, and sit in the Irish (but not British) Parliament. Political divisions deepened, and Pitt's government fell over the issue—despite Britain then being at war with France—when millions of Catholic subjects were brought into political union without a corresponding religious (and civil) emancipation in the *Act of Union* with Ireland (1800).

George III forced the crisis when he refused Pitt's efforts at Catholic emancipation, which he viewed as a contradiction of his coronation oath, which made him defender of the Anglican faith as head of the Church of England. Civil war seemed possible when the Irish Catholic reformer *Daniel O'Connell* was elected, but was then refused permission to take his seat in the House of Commons. To resolve the crisis, *Wellington* moved to repeal the Test Act in 1828, and full emancipation (excepting that no Catholic may reign as British monarch) passed the next year. The issue split the *Tories*, allowing the *Whigs* to take power in Westminster. *See also Irish Question.*

Catholic Reformation. *See Counter Reformation.*

Caucasus (Caucasia). The region between the Black and Caspian Seas, split by the Caucasus Mountains into *Ciscaucasia* in Europe and *Transcaucasia* in Asia. For centuries this was a frontier battleground among the *Ottoman, Persian,* and *Russian Empires*, with most of the area falling under Russian control in the nineteenth century: Georgia was annexed to Russia in 1801; Baku and other parts of Azerbaijan were annexed in 1813; and Persian Armenia and the rump of Azerbaijan were both absorbed into the Russian Empire in 1828. Russian expansion then continued into the western Caucasus, at Turkish expense. From 1834 to 1864 a fierce *jihad* by local tribes was waged in the Caucasus Mountains against Russian forces. Except for a brief period of independence after the collapse of the Russian state during *World War I* and the *Russian Civil War*, the Caucasus remained under imperial Russian sway until the end of the Soviet Union in 1991. Their complex ethnic makeup was further muddied by *Stalin*, who deported several Caucasian groups to *Siberia* during *World War II*. When these divers peoples returned after the old tyrant's death, ancient quarrels over land were aggravated by more recent redistributions. The region's main subdivisions are *Abkhazia, Ajaria, Armenia, Azerbaijan, Georgia, Kurdistan, Nagorno-Karabakh, Nakhichevan,* and North and South *Ossetia*. Still within post-Soviet Russia are North Ossetia and ethnic *enclaves* such as Adygei, *Chechnya*, Dagestan, Ingushetia, Kabardino-Balkaria and Karachevo-Cherkes. *See also Balkans.*

caucus groups. Voting blocs in the United Nations, and other *multilateral* forums, which meet to plot common procedural strategy and map out arguments and positions. They may be regional (African, Asian, Latin American, Nordic, *WEOG*) or interest oriented (Arab, *CANZ, nonaligned, Group of 77*).

caudillo. "Little head." (1) In Latin America, any military dictator or regional boss, especially in the nineteenth century after the wars of independence, 1810–1825. Those conflicts gave many their start and a veneer of popular *legitimacy*. Generally, whether on the left or the right, they ruled behind a facade of republicanism. (2) In Spain, only *Franco* used the title—and he surely showed no love of the Spanish Republic. *See also Juan Manuel Rosas; Antonia Santa Anna; warlord.*

causal modeling. The use of simulations or diagrams to illustrate the presumed relations among different proposed *causes.*

causation. A cause is any agent (instrumentality) that produces an effect; an effect is any consequence (result, outcome) that proceeds from any cause. Causation is the direct and indirect relation of causes to effects. In normal discourse (that is, explanation uninfected by *scientism* or the terminological fetishism of *variables*), the following terms are employed: (1) a necessary cause is one without which an effect will not occur, but not in itself enough to bring about the full effect; (2) a sufficient cause is one that in and of itself may be said to produce a given effect; (3) an efficient cause triggers an effect; whereas (4) a permissive cause underlies an effect, allows it to occur, but does not actively bring it to pass. Thus, it might be said that "*anarchy* is a permissive cause of war, but clashing *national interests* and other conflicts usually provide the necessary causes, while key decisions, individual personalities, ambitions and vanities may be the efficient causes. It cannot be fairly said that any one force or thing is a sufficient cause of all wars, though it may be identified as a cause of a given war." Another way of differentiating causality is to look for (5) a primary cause, or the key agency producing an effect; for (6) secondary causes, or agencies that reinforce the primary cause, but are less influential in and of themselves; and for (7) tertiary causes, which help to produce the effect but that are clearly not of the first or second order of influence. An important and abiding controversy in all historical argument revolves around the relative importance of *agent* and *structure* in any given explanation. There is also a never-ending argument about whether historical explanation is tidal and linear, in which case the explanations of major events are located in prior events, or whether history is more riverine, diverted by this or that happenstance and obstacle wherein relatively minor events may have hugely disproportionate consequences, as in the case of the assassination in 1914 of Archduke *Franz Ferdinand*, the heir to the Austrian throne. As the great Cold War historian John L. Gaddis has put it: "History is always the product of determined *and* contingent events: it is up to historians to find the proper balance between them." Of course, that also holds true for political scientists. *See also agent-structure problem; determinism; game theory; falsification; historicism; paradigm;* post hoc ergo propter hoc; *rational choice theory; reductionism; relativism;* sine qua non; *volition.*

cause and effect. *See causation; variable.*

cavalry. (1) Historically: Horse-borne soldiers who fight as a coordinated unit not, as in Medieval chivalric warfare, as a collage of knights each charging and fighting by himself. Cavalry, and the use of horses as draught animals, dominated much of warfare for 1,000 years. Where Alexander the Great, Rome, or Imperial China constructed great *infantry* empires, the *Mongols* were a wholly cavalry power that overran almost all infantry armies they encountered. The *Fulbe* of West Africa were also a cavalry empire, as was *Songhay*. Such cavalry empires dominated West Africa until they met their match in *Ashanti* and in other coastal or forest peoples armed with modern European firearms. Medieval Europe was constructed socially as well as militarily around the mounted warrior. Such also formed the core of *Crusader* armies. That state of affairs lasted until England invaded Scotland and the English heavy cavalry was defeated by *William Wallace* at Stirling Bridge (September 11, 1297) and Robert the Bruce at Bannockburn (June 24, 1314).

In these battles heavily armored men and horses, of a type that had dominated *Norman* and European warfare for two centuries, were met effectively by *pike* men and archers and defeated. The same thing happened on the continent, where Swiss infantry formed into pike squares smashed the Burgundian cavalry at Laupen (1339).

The English learned from their Scottish wars, however, and during the *Hundred Years' War* (1337–1453) English and Welsh archers standing off with their longbows destroyed the heavy cavalry of the French at Crécy (1346) and again at Agincourt (1415). The *gunpowder revolution* greatly increased infantry firepower at the expense of cavalry, while *siege warfare* hampered cavalry's effectiveness. Thereafter, cavalry remained an important though lesser arm, even when *Cromwell* or *Frederick the Great* or *Napoleon* used it in brilliant and effective new ways. Dragoons (musket-bearing cavalry, or mounted infantry) were used for their mobile firepower; heavy cavalry delivered blunt shock force; and light cavalry (a *Habsburg* innovation) provided reconnaissance and skirmishers. In defense, infantry were protected by pike men until 1687, when *Vauban* invented the socket *bayonet*. By the *Crimean War* and the *American Civil War*, cavalry was useful mainly for scouting, skirmishing, and harassing of enemy supply lines: it had lost its shock value because it simply could not sustain a direct charge into enemy rifle fire or cannonade—as the Light Brigade discovered, at great cost, in the Crimea.

Still, cavalry retained a romantic (and class) appeal and thus remained in use well into the twentieth century. In 1914 the Russian Army had more than one million horses, organized into thirty-seven cavalry divisions. It was these divisions that led the unexpected Russian advance into eastern Germany that August. Similarly, the *Reichswehr* deployed 750,000 horses in 1914, and even the tiny *British Expeditionary Force* brought nearly 200,000 horses with it to France. The largest cavalry force ever assembled in a single battle, eight full German divisions, fought near Lille during the *race to the sea*. French cavalry rode to their slaughter in Alsace and Lorraine that summer still wearing brass helmets topped by plumes, in scarlet trousers and sky-blue tunics soon stained scarlet too. Such "elegant anachronism," as Michael Howard has termed it, was an essential part of the cavalry myth and appeal. On the *western front*, horses were quickly converted into pack or draught animals rather than mounts, however, as *trench warfare* developed and barbed wire and shell holes proved insurmountable by horse, and largely also by men.

The fact that the day of cavalry was over was not universally realized, even then. Poland actually used cavalry in the opening battles of *World War II* in the east, when mindlessly heroic—or were they merely fatalistic?—charges were smashed bloody by *Panzers* and Stuka dive bombers. Even after that, cavalry still appeared in warfare: under the winter conditions of the *eastern front* during World War II, Russian *Cossacks* sometimes were used to overrun frozen and immobile German guns or outflank trenches; and in 1942 the last-ever Italian cavalry charge was made into the guns of a Soviet infantry division. Cavalry also played a significant role in the *Second Sino-Japanese War* and in the *Chinese Civil War*, but ultimately the horse was replaced even in scouting by the motorized armored car. (2) From the mid-20th century: Mechanized or airborne infantry. After World War II, some armies also designated light armored units as "cavalry," and some helicopter units as "air cavalry." *See also artillery; Boer Wars; Mamluks; Murat; Napoleonic warfare; Normans; retreat from Moscow.*

Suggested Readings: Martin van Creveld, *Technology and War From 2000 B.C. to the Present Day* (1989); Michael Howard, *War in European History* (1976).

Cavour, Camillo Benso di (1810–1861).

Italian statesman. An active entrepreneur involved in railways and trade as well as landowning, he was liberal prime minister of *Piedmont*, 1852–1861. He sought unification of all Italy, under Piedmont's king, as his main foreign policy goal, but he was opposed to social revolution. He took Piedmont into the *Crimean War* in order to gain a place at the conference table, but otherwise secured little. He next allied Piedmont with *Sardinia* and France, under *Napoleon III*, in a short but successful war against Austria in 1859; Piedmont gained Lombardy for its effort. He disliked and distrusted *Mazzini*, who criticized the French alliance. In 1860 he arranged French acceptance of Piedmont's *annexation* of Modena, Parma, and Tuscany. He rushed Piedmontese troops into Rome before the city fell to *Garibaldi*, partly to forestall the latter from proclaiming a separate southern republic after he had conquered Sicily and Naples. Great Britain backed Piedmont diplomatically against France. A series of rapid *plebiscites* then allowed Piedmont to annex Naples, the *Papal States*, and Sicily. The unification of Italy was complete, with the notable exceptions of Rome (which contained the pope and the *Vatican*, then under French protection) and Venice. This compromise avoided antagonizing Catholic opinion in Italy and Europe. Cavour proclaimed the unified Kingdom of Italy on March 17, 1861, with himself as prime minister. He died a few months later. His vision of Italy as a future *sea power* dominating the Mediterranean and Adriatic was never realized.

Cayman Islands. These small West Indies islands are *dependencies* of Jamaica. In the second half of the twentieth century they developed as an off-shore (of the United States) banking center.

cease-fire. A form of *truce*, or temporary halt in fighting. It may be a prelude to a *peace treaty*, or merely an agreed pause during which wounded are removed and resupply takes place. Unilateral cease-fires are sometimes proclaimed to obtain propaganda advantage or to test the willingness of an opponent to continue fighting. *See also armistice; war termination.*

Ceauşescu, Nicolae (1918–1989). Rumanian dictator, 1967–1989. He was courted by the West because he took a somewhat independent line from Moscow in foreign policy, including keeping ties to China after the *Sino-Soviet split* and to Israel, and because he denounced the 1968 invasion of Czechoslovakia and crushing of the *Prague Spring* by the *Warsaw Pact*, from which he withheld Rumanian troops. At home he was brutal, corrupt, and inept and suffered from escalating megalomania. He and his similarly corrupt and vicious wife, Elena, were barely literate but still styled themselves the "Great Builder and Hunter" and the "Great Scientist." Together, they demanded the title "Beloved Comrades of the People." Ceauşescu's regime left bitter divisions between ethnic Rumanians and Hungarians, as well as tens of thousands of orphans born of a perverse and idiosyncratic ban on contraception. In 1989 Ceauşescu was astonished at the appearance of public discontent and dissent, which erupted in jeers halfway through a speech he then failed to finish. After a foiled attempt to flee and a summary trial, he and Elena were taken out and shot—much to their surprise—on Christmas Day, 1989.

censure. To express disapproval, as in a vote criticizing a state for *human rights* abuses, *aggression*, or disregard of United Nations *resolutions*. It is a large step from censure to *sanctions*.

Center (Moscow). The command headquarters of the Soviet *secret service*. *See also KGB.*

Central African Federation. An alternate name of the former *Federation of Rhodesia and Nyasaland*, 1953–1963. It broke into the component parts of Malawi, Zambia, and Rhodesia (Zimbabwe).

Central African Republic. Formerly Ubangi-Shari, it was a French colony from the end of the nineteenth century until independence in 1960. Those *tribes* or *ethnic groups* that first encountered the French tended to be concentrated along river routes into the interior of the country, and hence are known as Riverines. Early association of these groups with French education and administration led to their dominance of the Central African Republic after independence. Under President David Dako, Chinese influence grew until a break in relations in 1965, when Dako's cousin, *Jean-Bedel Bokassa*, seized power in a *coup*. In 1976 Bokassa proclaimed himself emperor and renamed the country Central African Empire. He was ousted (with French help) in 1979, and Dako resumed the presidency. The economy was badly damaged by Bokassa's depredations. In 1981 another coup ousted Dako and set up a military regime. Into the twenty-first century, the Central African Republic remained one of the world's poorest and least well-run countries.

Central America. The narrow isthmus portion of North America that joins it to South America and comprises Belize, Costa Rica, El Salvador, Guatemala, Honduras, Nicaragua, and Panama. In Spanish colonial times the region was known as the Captaincy-General of Guatemala. This was a subdivision of the *Viceroyalty* of *New Spain* (Mexico), which included Chiapas and Soconusco, which are today provinces in southern Mexico, but excluded Panama (which was part of Colombia to 1903) and Belize (which was a British colony until 1981).

The Captaincy-General of Guatemala became independent from Spain in 1821, coincidentally with the independence of New Spain. Costa Rica, El Salvador, Guatemala, Honduras, and Nicaragua broke from Mexico to form the short-lived *Central American Union*, 1824–1838. They became separate *republics* thereafter.

Suggested Reading: Miles Wortman, *Government and Society in Central America, 1680–1840* (1982).

Central American Common Market (CACM). It was founded in 1960 by Costa Rica, El Salvador, Guatemala, Honduras, and Nicaragua to create a *customs union*, with a parallel scheme to "rationalize" industrial development in the region. After early success into the 1970s, in spite of the *Football War*, efforts at economic *integration* were blocked in the 1980s by several crises: *revolution* in Nicaragua, *civil war* in El Salvador, and *guerrilla* conflicts in Honduras and Guatemala. In 1993–1994, CACM was relaunched and joined by Panama.

Central American Union (1824–1838). "United States of Central America." The *Captaincy-General of Guatemala* gained independence in 1821, coincidentally with the independence of *New Spain* (Mexico). Its five constituent republics then broke from Mexico to join a short-lived federal experiment called the Central American Union, 1824–1838. This was an attempt at *federation* of the former Spanish Central American states (excluding Panama, which was still part of Colombia), more or less along the old administrative lines of the Captaincy-General. It was formed by Costa Rica, Guatemala, Honduras, Nicaragua, and El Salvador, partly to mutually forestall absorption by Mexico. It broke down within a generation, after endless quarrels and a civil war. Subsequent efforts to revive the Union, in the 1840s, 1880s, 1890s, and 1920s, met with sharp resistance from the various republics, acting severally or jointly.
Suggested Reading: T. L. Karnes, *The Failure of Union: Central America, 1824–1960* (1961).

Central Asia. The region lying between the Arabian Sea and the southern border of Russia, defined at its broadest to include the *Caucasus*, to wit: Afghanistan, Armenia, Azerbaijan, Georgia, Iran, Kazakhstan, Kirghizstan, Pakistan, Tajikistan, Turkmenistan, and Uzbekistan. Warrior cultures thrived in Central Asia, a region whose conflicts frequently spilled into the surrounding, more urban and settled regions of China, India, Russia, and the Middle East. In the early nineteenth century (c. 1820) much of Central Asia fell under the Russian Empire. In 1864–1868 Russia invaded and conquered the emirate of *Bukhara* and the independent Khanates of *Khiva* and *Kokand*, establishing *protectorates* that lasted to 1917, except for Kokand, which it annexed in 1873. Absorbed into the Russian and Soviet empires for most of the twentieth century, Central Asia returned to *balkanized* independence in 1991. *See also Turkestan.*
Suggested Readings: S. Adshead, *Central Asia in World History* (1993); Luc Kwanten, *Imperial Nomads: A History of Central Asia, 500–1500* (1979).

central banks. Government chartered and run national banks. They do not lend money to individuals as do other banks. Instead, they issue currency, lend to governments and private banks, and oversee and manage national monetary systems, paying special attention to the money supply, *interest rates*, and the relative value of currencies. Central banks developed along with the state, initially as a consequence of the need to organize royal finances to prosecute wars, then as an aid to centralized national planning and economic development. The Bank of England, for instance, was founded in 1694 as a wartime expedient to address the national debt arising from *Elizabeth I*'s war with Spain; *Napoleon I* founded the Bank of France in 1800, and so on. *Alexander Hamilton* founded the first American national bank in 1791 to assist industrial and commercial development, but it did not survive past 1811. The United States did not establish its present Federal Reserve System until 1913. The *European Union* set up its central bank, the *ECB*, in the late 1990s. By the end of the twentieth century the major, agreed role of central banks was to maintain price stability against the twin threats of *inflation* and *deflation*. *See also* banking; *Bank of International Settlements*; *Bundesbank*; *Eurosystem*.

Central Committee. In the Soviet Union and China, as well as other Soviet-style *Communist parties*, the Central Committee was the main coordinating body for policy and ideology and for maintaining party control. From its broader membership were drawn more compact and important executive bodies, such as the *Politburo* and its even tighter decision-making circle, the Standing Committee. *See also Mao; Stalin.*

Central Europe. A political and cultural rather than geographical concept of shifting meaning. Depending on one's location and point of view, it has on occasion also been called *Eastern Europe*, as during the *Cold War* when it included the core countries of *Czechoslovakia* (now Czech Republic and Slovakia), Hungary, and Poland. Historically, it also comprised large parts of Germany (*East Prussia, Silesia*). *See also* Mitteleuropa.

Central Intelligence Agency (CIA). "The Agency." The main civilian, and not the largest, of the American *intelligence agencies*. The CIA serves as the main clearing-house for information gathered by other U.S. agencies and conducts independent intelligence gathering and *covert operations*. It was set up in 1947 to adapt to peacetime the work of the wartime *Office of Strategic Services* (OSS), primarily to undertake analysis and provide covert political support for U.S. *containment* of the Soviet Union. Initially, it reported directly to the president through the *National Security Council* (NSC). The Director of Central Intelligence (DCI) is the key person in the CIA, with direct access to the president through provision of intelligence briefings. Some presidents asked for these daily; others less frequently, but always during a *crisis*. *Alan Dulles* was DCI, 1953–1961. Richard Helms was DCI, 1966–1973. William Colby served in that position during the most turbulent years in the agency's history, 1973–1976. As DCI from 1981 to 1987, *William Casey* worked closely with *Ronald Reagan*. In the wake of revelations in the early 1970s of earlier CIA bungling and sometimes also illegal activities ("the family jewels"), starting in the mid-1970s Congress began regular oversight of the CIA through various committees and subcommittees.

The CIA is best known to the public for covert operations that failed, such as the *Bay of Pigs* and *pacification* in Vietnam (the latter a qualified success, perhaps, in a larger failed war). It is better known to specialists for operationally successful interventions in the *internal affairs* of several nations, including: postwar elections in Italy, where it helped keep the Italian *Communist Party* from taking power; support to the Shah of Iran against *Mossadegh*; the overthrow of Jacobo Arbenz in Guatemala (the full records of this activity have yet to be released); and aiding destabilization of the democratically elected *Marxist* government of *Salvador Allende Gossens* in Chile in 1973. Less well known, since 1969 the CIA has played a key role in monitoring various *arms control* treaties and peace agreements, including *verification* of Soviet compliance with the several *SALT* and *START* treaties, Israeli and Egyptian troop withdrawal and other disengagement agreements following the *Fourth Arab-Israeli War*, and later the *Camp David Accords* and *peace treaty*. In 1990, technical assistance was offered to India and Pakistan, in which CIA would monitor violations along the common border, with information to be provided to both sides. And in 2001, top CIA officials were directly and openly involved in (mostly unsuccessful) efforts to negotiate and monitor a *cease-fire* agreement on the *West Bank*.

The CIA's covert successes may well be numerous, but they remain mostly unknown, by definition. The most public success was so-called *overt-covert* aid to the *mujahadeen* during the *Afghan-Soviet War*. Another major success was made public in 1997: ten years earlier, a CIA *mole* in the Taiwanese military stole vital documents that prevented Taiwan from completing its development of *nuclear weapons*. That probably stopped a major war in Asia. Yet, to concentrate on covert actions is largely to miss the main point about the CIA, whose main task is not *secret diplomacy* but analysis of all types of economic, social, and political information. Thus, the CIA was most strongly criticized in official circles for apparently failing in its main role during the *Cold War*: to gather and accurately analyze information about the capabilities and intentions of the Soviet Union and other hostile states. For example, in June 1950, the CIA advised the *Truman* administration that North Korea would not attack the South. CIA calculations of battle damage and the political will of the DRV (North Vietnam) to fight on in face of American bombing also was deeply erroneous. Estimates of the Soviet economy and military spending appear to have been consistently, even grossly, wrong into the late 1980s. In 1981 *Ronald Reagan* gave the CIA a supporting function to the main Federal Bureau of Investigation role in domestic counterespionage. With the end of the Cold War, the CIA faced significant budget cuts and therefore sought an expanded role in countering *terrorism*, conducting *economic espionage*, tracking *proliferation*, and monitoring the rise of religious *fundamentalism*, as well as providing intelligence training to newly allied or friendly states among former Soviet and/or *Warsaw Pact* republics. And the CIA paid much more attention to China from the 1990s. The CIA budget remains secret ("black"), but was revealed in the mid-1990s to be several billion dollars annually, at a minimum.

After revelations in the 1970s of illegal and unsavory covert activity, the CIA was forbidden from carrying out *assassinations* and its covert operatives were generally harnessed. The CIA was also torn apart from within during the 1970s by *counterespionage* suspicions and "mole hunts" on the part of James Jesus Angleton, head of counterintelligence. Despite the disruptive internal hunts and all the damage to morale, while failing to turn up the suspected moles, it was later discovered that the CIA in fact was penetrated to its very core by the *KGB*. Most spectacularly, one of Angleton's successors at the head of counterintelligence was revealed to have been a longtime Soviet *double-agent* working for the KGB (subsequently, the *FSB*). The full truth about the CIA's rate of success or failure is, of course, not publicly known—and not even widely known to most of its own agents. Therefore, overall judgments must remain shaky and conditional, at best. For example, after 1989 the agency was severely criticized (including by this author) for failing to predict the collapse of the Soviet bloc, but documents released in 1999 showed that, in fact, the CIA had given progressively more urgent warnings that the days of communism and *Gorbachev* were numbered. A more grave failing occurred after the Cold War, as a combination of CIA intelligence and presidential policy failure toward Middle Eastern terrorist and other attacks on U.S. personnel and interests on the part of the *Reagan* administration (in Lebanon), *George H. Bush* administration (at the end of the *Gulf War*), and the especially feckless *Clinton* administration (toward Iraq, and attacks against American interests and personnel in Somalia, Yemen, Sudan, and Afghanistan). This contributed significantly to failure to foresee or deter the disaster of the *September 11, 2001, terrorist attack on the United States*. In the wake of that catastrophe the agency received vastly increased funding, re-emphasized the need for *humint*, and came to enjoy a popular approval by the general public not seen since before the Vietnam War. It was revealed during the campaign against *al Qaeda* in Afghanistan that the CIA had developed a paramilitary capability during the 1990s, known as the Special Activities Division, which included unmanned surveillance as well as armed Predator aircraft used to strike at highly specific targets, and political intelligence assets used to maximize the benefits derived from providing humanitarian assistance. *See also Air America; Iran-Contra; National Security Agency.*

Suggested Readings: *Jane's Intelligence Review* (1991–); Stephen Knott, *Secret and Sanctioned* (1996); John Ranelagh, *The Agency* (1986).

Central Powers. (1) An alternate term for the *Triple Alliance* of Austria, Germany, and Italy, 1882–1914. (2) Austria-Hungary, Germany, the Ottoman Empire, and Bulgaria in *World War I*. Italy declined to fight in 1914, enticed by secret promises into joining the *Entente* in 1915. *See also Constantinople Agreement; Treaty of London* (1915).

Central Selling Organization (CSO). A producers' *cartel* that runs the world's diamond market. Its most important members come from Botswana, Israel, Russia, and South Africa.

central strategic systems. In U.S. strategy during the *Cold War*, those systems considered essential to maintaining the nuclear *balance of power*.

Central Treaty Organization (CENTO). *See Baghdad Pact.*

cession. Transfer of territory by mutual agreement. *See also Crimea; Louisiana Purchase.*

Cetewayo (1825?–1884). Also known as Cetshwayo. King of the *Zulu* nation. He secured his throne in 1856 by killing his half-brother, his major rival, during one of many Zulu *civil wars*. He spent the next 16 years consolidating his rule. By 1872 he was undisputed ruler of the Zulu nation and was recognized by Britain as king. However, his kingdom stood in the way of expansion of the British and Boer colonists in South Africa. In 1878–1879 he went to war with Britain. His regiments ("impi") wiped out a British column at *Isandlwana* (1879) in the first *Zulu War*. British reinforcements quickly overwhelmed the Zulu. Cetewayo was captured and held prisoner in *Cape Colony*, 1879–1882, while the British partitioned his kingdom into thirteen separate chiefdoms, in a classic application of the strategy of "divide and rule." Cetewayo was released and sailed for England in 1882 to plead his case before Queen *Victoria*. She intervened to have him reinstated as monarch of the Zulus, but this was resisted by the new chiefs when he returned to South Africa. Another Zulu civil war ensued in 1884, during which Cetewayo was killed—it is thought that he was poisoned. His erstwhile kingdom was annexed by the British in 1887.

cetirus paribus. "All other things being equal." A common qualifier in international legal judgments.

Ceuta. This coastal *enclave* was occupied by Portugal in 1415, as part of their effort to bypass North African agents and gain direct access to the gold of *Guinea.* Prince *Henry* "the Navigator," who was present at the capture, launched further coastal explorations from Ceuta. It remains a Spanish enclave surrounded by Morocco. Its future is tied to Spain's efforts to reclaim *Gibraltar* from Britain. *See also Melilla; Morocco.*

Ceylon. A large island in the Indian Ocean, off the tip of the Indian subcontinent. It was also the former name of *Sri Lanka*.

Chaco region. A harsh, barely arable region located in northwest Paraguay, peopled in pre-Columbian times by the Chané. Its ownership was the main issue in the *Chaco War*.

Chaco War (1932–1935). A bitter war fought between impoverished Bolivia and Paraguay for control of the *Chaco region* on their common border. Paraguay won and was able to keep most of the territory, an outcome mediated and ratified by a commission of the United States and five Latin American states in 1938. The outcome left Bolivia landlocked, denying it access to the Atlantic and reconfirming its prior loss of an outlet to the Pacific, which it surrendered after losing the *War of the Pacific* (1879–1884). Some 100,000 died, on all sides.

Chad. Lying along the historic trans-Sahara salt and Arab *slave trade* routes, Chad was made a French colony around 1900. However, northern Muslims violently resisted the French and were not repressed until 1930. Chad was given independence in 1960, with most power going to the Sara of the south. It remained a desperately poor, *Sahel* nation. By 1966 there was steady fighting between northern Muslims, supported by Libya, and southern Christians and animists, supported by France. A coup in 1975 gave Muslims brief control of centralized power. The civil war resumed, 1979–1982, ending when guerrilla forces under Hissène Habré took control of the capital in 1982. The 1980s saw severe drought, the effects of which were aggravated by continuing low-level internal fighting in the north and the overlap of the *Chad-Libya War*, waged on and off until 1987 over possession of the *Auzou strip*. An OAU military force tried to police the peace after 1988, but Chad remained too ethnically and religiously divided, north versus south. Heavy fighting resumed in 1991, partly because Habré's Western backers were preoccupied with the *Gulf War*. He was deposed and fled into exile in Senegal. Idriss Deby took power with French support, and for the next decade rebellion was isolated to the country's northern, desert fringe.
    Suggested Reading: J. F. A. Ajayi and Michael Crowder, eds., *History of West Africa*, 2 vols. (1974).

Chad-Libya War (1973–1988). In 1973 Libya took advantage of the civil war in Chad to invade and occupy the *Auzou strip*. In 1980, seeking to protect this claim, Libya arranged an "invitation" to send troops into Chad from one faction in the still ongoing civil war. When it was announced that the two countries would form a *union*, international opposition increased: in addition to France, Chad was supported by anti-Libyan Arab states such as Egypt and Saudi Arabia and by the United States. The key was the effort of Libya's

Quadaffi to obtain *uranium* for his *nuclear weapons* program from the Auzou strip and create a *client state* in Chad. His effort was aided by the near-disintegration of Chad as a result of three decades of civil war. Protests over the proposed union from surrounding African states and the dispatch of French troops forced the Libyans to pull back in 1981. In June 1982, southern rebels under Hissène Habré took the capital, ending the civil war but launching a new phase of the conflict with Libya. With French support, including air cover and several thousand troops, Habré took the offensive in 1983. France and Libya agreed to withdraw in 1984, but Libyan troops stayed in the Auzou strip, which Quadaffi said was annexed to Libya. In 1987 Chadian forces inflicted a decisive defeat on the Libyans, who fled, leaving behind thousands of dead and over $1 billion in military equipment.

chaebol. Industrial conglomerates formed after *World War II* as the backbone of South Korea's early *industrialization*. During the 1990s, many collapsed under a weight of bad debt, laying off workers who had expected life-time employment with their companies and thus contributing to popular demands for political and economic reform. *See also* zaibatsu.

Chamberlain, Arthur Neville (1869–1940). British *Conservative* statesman. Son of *Joseph Chamberlain* and half-brother of *Austen Chamberlain*. As *chancellor of the exchequer*, in 1932 he helped implement his father's scheme for a preferential *imperial tariff*. As prime minister, 1937–1940, Chamberlain took complete—and often inflexible—control of British foreign policy. Although inexperienced in diplomacy, he was convinced he could avoid war by face-to-face negotiations with *Hitler*. Instead, Chamberlain will be forever remembered as the main dupe of the *Munich Conference* (1938), where in essence he betrayed Czechoslovakia to Hitler by agreeing to hand the *Sudetenland* to Germany. He appears to have genuinely believed that Germany had legitimate grievances arising from the *Treaty of Versailles* and that territorial concessions at the expense of the Czechs would satisfy Hitler, but mostly Chamberlain could not face the prospect of his country again suffering the carnage it had seen on the *Somme* or at *Ypres*, or a dozen other battles on the *western front* in *World War I*, and the damage to its empire and civilization, which he believed another war would complete. Back in London, as he stepped out of the plane and into the newsreel footage and history, he self-consciously echoed the words of *Disraeli* after the *Congress of Berlin* fifty years earlier, announcing that he had achieved "peace with honor; it is peace for our time." He then advised the British nation: "Go home, and get a nice, quiet sleep."

Chamberlain's animosity for the *Soviet Union* always prevented him from seeing the utility and the necessity of an alliance with that state, which was the one continental *Great Power* with the raw capabilities to oppose and possibly (though this is not likely, as long as Hitler remained in power) even deter Germany, and which, before the Munich Conference, had actively sought a compact with the West. Britain's policy of *appeasement* actually predated Chamberlain's prime ministership and was an honorable and effective tradition in the diplomacy of the *British Empire*. However, it was so discredited by subsequent events after 1938 that statesmen have completely ceased to use the term out of fear of damaging association with Chamberlain and the betrayal at the Munich Conference. Chamberlain abandoned appeasement, reluctantly, when Hitler occupied the rump of Czechoslovakia in 1939. He belatedly offered—now much less valuable—security guarantees to Greece, Poland, and Rumania and accelerated rearmament of Britain itself. With deep aversion for any real fighting, Chamberlain cautiously led Britain into *World War II* when Germany attacked Poland in September 1939. His heart was not in the fight, and he appeared weak and indecisive during the period derisively known in the press as the *Phony War*. He resigned in May 1940, as Germany launched its *Blitzkrieg* against the western powers. He was replaced as prime minister by his longtime political nemesis, *Winston Churchill*. Chamberlain died shortly after stepping aside. Whatever his failings of vision and leadership, there can be no doubt that his motives were the highest: to preserve a peaceful and great democracy from the barbarization and carnage that war with Germany would surely bring. He was wrong, but he was not insincere.

Suggested Readings: Robert Caputi, *Neville Chamberlain and Appeasement* (2000); Robert Shay, *British Rearmament in the Thirties* (1977).

Chamberlain, Houston Stewart (1855–1927). An English, racist philosopher who was raised mainly on the continent and who became rabidly anti-English. He took out German *citizenship* in 1916, in the middle of *World War I*. His rambling theories about race were picked up by the *Nazis*, then in search of intellectual cover for their own specious race claims. Chamberlain developed a "Theory of Race," which he claimed explained all major historical developments and placed the German people at the apex of civilization. Chamberlain had a significant influence on the thinking of *Adolf Hitler*. They admired each other greatly, had meshed views about race and the Jews, and shared a fascination for the person and work of the composer Richard Wagner (1813–1883), whose daughter Chamberlain married.

Chamberlain, Joseph (1836–1914). British statesman. Chamberlain was a fierce opponent of *Home Rule* for Ireland, resigning in protest from his position as head of the Board of Trade—where he had attempted serious social reforms—and thereby helping to split the Liberal Party. From 1891 he was leader of the Liberal Unionists. In 1895 he became secretary for the colonies. He worked for an imperial federation of British colonies in Africa, including organizing the West African Frontier Force, which conquered Nigeria with significant bloodshed and ruthlessness. It was intended as a direct military challenge and counter to France, which had long since abandoned ideas of *informal empire* in West Africa and since the early 1880s had been conquering new lands from the Senegal to the great bend of the Niger, with every intention of cutting off the British in Ghana and Nigeria; and to Germany, which had annexed Togo and Kamerun in the mid-1880s. Chamberlain largely provoked the confrontation with the *Boers* that led to the *Second Boer War*. He then argued for a powerful colonial policy that drew the Boer republics into the folds of the Empire, so that the great riches of the *Rand* might help sustain Britain's "civilizing mission" in the wilder parts of the world. He once declared: "The day of small nations has long passed away. The day of Empires has come." There was more than a whiff of *racism* and *social Darwinism* in this rhetoric and in Chamberlain's policies. Blinded to larger strategic threats to real British interests by a rawly global imperial ambition, Chamberlain mistakenly viewed France as the main enemy of Britain's *vital interests* and repeatedly tried to influence policy toward an alliance with Germany. He resigned from his colonial duties in 1903 in order to promote his idea for an *imperial tariff* system. Chamberlain was knocked from public life by a stroke in 1906. His tariff scheme was implemented, in a more modest form than he proposed, by his two accomplished but also controversial sons, *J. Austen Chamberlain* and *Neville Chamberlain*. *See also Frederick Lugard; Cecil Rhodes; scramble for Africa.*

Chamberlain, J. Austen (1863–1937). British *Conservative* statesman, son of Joseph Chamberlain; half-brother to *Neville Chamberlain*. He was first elected as a Liberal-Unionist, but served most of his life as a Conservative Member of Parliament. He was secretary for India, 1915–1917, and a member of the War Cabinet during *World War I*. Chamberlain was committed to European solutions to diplomatic problems, rather than always taking a strictly imperial view of matters. He supported *Lloyd George*, which cost him among Tories, but still served as foreign secretary, 1924–1929, and first lord of the admiralty, 1931. He is most closely associated with *Locarno* in 1925. Chamberlain was awarded the 1925 *Nobel Prize* for Peace (in 1926) for his role in crafting the *Dawes Plan*, jointly with Charles Dawes (1865–1951).

chambers of the Court. When justices numbering fewer than the full complement of the *International Court of Justice* gather to hear a *dispute*. This permits the states concerned a voice in the composition of the adjudicating panel. It was first used in 1981 by Canada and the United States to resolve a fisheries-boundary matter. *See also application.*

Champagne, Battles of. This region formed the southern shoulder of the German salient along the *western front* during *World War I*. (1) First Champagne (December 20, 1914–March 17, 1915): This "Winter Battle" saw heavy casualties but failed to dent the German lines. (2) Second Champagne (September 25–October 31, 1915): Launched in coordination with the British attack at *Loos*, and also using chlorine *gas* to start the assault, twenty French divisions attacked along a 20-mile front. While the German front line was overcome, the second line of trenches held. Nearly 145,000 casualties over a month of fighting gained little ground for France.

Champa, Kingdom of. Founded in 192 C.E., this Indo-Viet kingdom was located in central Indochina. It was a seafaring state, sometimes trading with, but at other times raiding, its northern (*Tonkin*) and western (*Khmer*) neighbors. In 1069 a Vietnamese army captured the Champa capital and king, forcing annexation of three Champa provinces. A Champa fleet sacked the Khmer Empire's capital at Angkor in 1177. Overall, Champa was slowly eaten by the Vietnamese, bite by bite from the twelfth through the seventeenth centuries, a process which accelerated after a major Vietnamese victory in 1471. A nominal Champa king survived under Vietnamese control until 1822.

Champlain, Samuel de (1567–1635). French explorer and soldier who set the early pattern of France's colonization of North America. His first voyage to the *New World* was in service of the Spanish, in the Caribbean, 1599–1601. He sailed for Canada on a fur expedition in 1603, exploring the *St. Lawrence River* valley. He returned to chart the coasts of Nova Scotia and New England, 1604–1607. In 1608 he founded Québec City, as a military outpost and fur-trading center. He forged an alliance with the Huron, and led several French-Indian expeditions against the empire of the powerful *Iroquois League* in 1608–1609. In 1611 he pushed farther up the St. Lawrence River valley and established another city and fortified outpost, Montréal. He went to Paris in 1612 to obtain royal approval of his monopoly over the lucrative fur trade and returned to *New France* as its governor. In 1615 he led another expedition against the Iroquois. He was active in the Anglo-French War of 1626–1630 and was forced to surrender Québec to English troops in 1629. When the city was restored as part of a general settlement in 1632, he resumed his governorship of the colony. As governor, he continued to promote French exploration and expansion into the interior of North America. His close alliance with the Huron set the stage for a century of French-Indian wars with the British and their North American colonists.

Chanak crisis (1922). Britain and Turkey almost went to war over *Atatürk*'s opposition to Britain's presence in Chanak, the eastern shore of the *Dardanelles*. The crisis was resolved by giving Turkey territory in exchange for *internationalization* of the Dardanelles and the *Bosporus*, a deal confirmed in the *Treaty of Lausanne* in 1923.

Chancellor of the Exchequer. The grandiose, but historic, title of the U.K. finance minister.

Channel Islands. British possessions in the *English Channel* near France: Alderney, Guernsey, Jersey, and several smaller islands. They were the only part of the United Kingdom occupied by Germany during *World War II*. The Nazis governed these islands as they governed Europe: with military force, political terror, and imported slave labor. They foolishly expended huge sums to fortify them. The islands were bypassed by the Western Allies during the invasion of France: the fanatic German garrison in the Channel Islands actually launched a commando raid against the American rear in Normandy in March 1945. The islands were liberated upon the *surrender* of Germany in May 1945.

Channel Tunnel. The Channel Tunnel Treaty was signed on February 12, 1986, by France and Great Britain. It authorized a 55-year lease to a private venture to build a two-tunnel connector (with a smaller, linking tunnel between them) under the *English Channel*. The project had been first proposed in the late 1870s, but it was long opposed by Britain for *strategic* and *security*, as well as for cultural, reasons. Construction of the main rail line of the "Chunnel," 50 kilometers in length, was completed in late 1993. Passenger service began in 1994.

Charcas. *See Upper Peru.*

chargé d'affaires (ad interim). (1) A lower-ranking *diplomat* placed in temporary charge of a mission in the absence of the accredited *ambassador*. (2) A diplomatic *envoy* sent to a posting where there is no ambassador.

chargé d'affaires (en titre). The fourth rank of *diplomats*, accredited by and to *foreign ministers*, not to *heads of state*.

charged particle beam. An experimental weapons system, researched under *SDI*, which uses channeled, concentrated beams of subatomic particles, produced by nuclear explosions, to destroy targets. *See also Edward Teller.*

Charlemagne (742?–814). "Carlos Magnus," or "Charles the Great." King of the Franks, 768–814; "Emperor of the West," 800–814; grandson of Charles Martel, who had stopped the Muslim (Saracen) invasion of southern Gaul in 732. Charlemagne began to build out his kingdom by disinheriting his nephews, who fled to Lombardy, adding their lands to his. In alliance with Pope Adrian, Charlemagne next conquered Lombardy. In 778 he invaded Iberia, intervening in a civil war among the Muslims; but he was defeated at the Battle of Zaragoza. He fought the Iberian Muslims on-and-off for two more decades, but his main struggle was with the Saxons and other Germanic peoples to the east, and these wars did not end until 804. The great markers of his reign were successful expansion of the Frankish Empire, religious reform, and his imperial coronation. He fought over and conquered new lands in

Saxony, Italy, Spain, and Bavaria, which he annexed in 788, setting his eastern *frontier* on the Danube. He was an improvisational leader in a conservative age, forever experimenting in domestic and foreign policy.

Charlemagne was a patron of learning and of law, and his court was a beacon of some light in an otherwise darkening time of secular economic decline, constant warfare, and repeated, destructive invasions of Western Europe by warrior cultures from the south (Saracen *Arabs*), north (*Vikings*), and east (various Germanic tribes). He inculcated education for the clergy, importing Irish clerics to assist in this task, and took a direct hand in church governance and doctrinal affairs. He administered his vast domains directly— via appointed representatives who traveled often and widely and wielded his delegated powers. And he promoted trade and commerce. Even so, within his realm, forced conversions to *Christianity* of conquered pagans were commonplace, as were cruel slaughters and displacement of those pagans who still resisted. In 799 he went to Rome to aid Pope Leo III, who faced unrest among, and possible deposition by, his subjects. In return, Charlemagne was crowned by Leo, on Christmas Day in 800, as "Emperor of the West." In 812, in exchange for holdings in Italy, including *Venice*, his title was recognized by the *Byzantine Empire*. His last years were spent fending off Viking invaders. After his death, the Carolingian Empire ceased to expand, settling into a defensive posture against the new nomadic threat from the north and continuing invasions from the east. Thereafter, it broke apart into factional states. Yet, a new pattern had been set, one from which Western Europe (*res publica Christiana*) would slowly emerge, centered not on the Mediterranean but further to the north and west. *See also Holy Roman Empire; Napoleon I.*

Suggested Readings: D. Bullough, *The Age of Charlemagne* (1966); Roger Collins, *Charlemagne* (1998); Henri Pirenne, *Muhammad and Charlemagne* (1939).

Charles I (Karl I), of Austria (1887–1922). Emperor, 1916–1918, and king of Hungary. He secretly attempted to negotiate a *separate peace* for Austria with the British and French during the latter part of *World War I*. The effort led to tighter German control of Austrian policy, and even of its field operations. After the war he abdicated. He twice tried to reclaim the title of king of Hungary, but failed. He died in exile, deeply embittered at the end of the empire and of his twin thrones.

Charles IV, of Spain (1784–1819). His reign was dominated by the politics of the *French Revolution* and the *Peninsular War*. His fleet was destroyed along with the French fleet at *Trafalgar*, and in 1808 he was forced to abdicate by *Napoleon I*. That weakening of Spanish power during his rule opened the door for the independence movement in Latin America.

Charles V, of the House of Habsburg (1500–1558). When Charles succeeded to the throne of the *Holy Roman Empire* in 1519 he was already duke of Burgundy and king of Spain—which meant the united crowns of Castile and Aragon, along with Naples, Sardinia, and Sicily, and the immense lands of New Spain in the Americas. He would later add the crowns of Hungary (1526), Bohemia, Lombardy, and Rome. The *Protestant Reformation* (Lutheran) had begun in Germany two years before, in 1517, and Charles soon found many of his German subjects in open revolt against his empire and Catholic faith. He determined to hold the empire together and to defend the Faith, as he understood it. In 1521 he personally presided over the Diet of Worms, in which the *Catholic Church* effectively declared war on *Lutheranism*. The first actual wars he fought were in Italy, against France, with brief peaceful respites in 1526, 1529, 1538, and 1544. Financed with loans from the *Fuggers*, in 1535 Charles defeated the Ottomans and captured *Tunis*. Then it was back to Germany to fight rebellious princes. By the late 1540s he was at war again with the Ottomans and with France—in 1542 a combined Franco-Ottoman fleet raided Habsburg territory—which felt threatened by Habsburg encirclement, as well as with an alliance of rebellious Protestant princes in Germany. Charles won a major victory at Mühlberg (1547) over the Schmalkaldic League, but then overreached in his efforts to restore absolute imperial and Catholic authority, alienating even his Catholic subjects. By 1552 Charles was losing to the rebels and the French in Germany and to other foreign armies on nearly all fronts. He therefore agreed to the great compromise of the *Peace of Augsburg* (1555), which granted legal recognition to Protestantism. Recognizing that the vast Habsburg *domains* were too diverse and scattered to be ruled from one center, he abdicated in two installments: first, as Holy Roman Emperor in 1555 in favor of his brother Ferdinand (whom he failed to convince to renounce his claim to the throne, in a bitter family quarrel); and then in 1556 when he resigned as king of Spain in favor of his son *Philip II*. Charles thereupon retired to a Spanish monastery in Estramadura.

Habsburg power had peaked with Charles, though for a time it looked as though the son would succeed where the father failed. Afterward, the vast Habsburg domains evolved as increasingly separate western and eastern halves, and then as distinct Spanish and Austrian empires. He also left his son a "political testament" that called for defense of the Catholic faith even above empire and for alliance with his uncle Ferdinand, head of the Holy Roman Empire. Charles also cautioned Philip to permit more rights to the conquered Indians of the *New World* and to refuse to permit the Netherlands to break free of Spanish control, for fear this would lead to disintegration of the whole empire. The empire Charles had built was too large, had too many distant borders and far-flung enemies, and was too unwieldy to be properly defended with the technology and transportation systems of his day. Mostly, however, Charles had failed because he sought to preserve two ideas that over the course of his life and reign became increasingly anachronistic: a sole, unifying faith for all *Christendom* and a single empire for the same. Tragically, his son, grandson, and great-grandson would continue to pursue the first from their base in Spain in another 100 years of bloody and destructive confessional warfare. *See also* encomienda; *Venezuela*.

Suggested Readings: Martyn Rady, *The Emperor Charles V* (1988, 1995); Royall Tyler, *The Emperor Charles the Fifth* (1956).

Charles X, of France (1757–1836). *See Bourbons; July Monarchy.*

Charles XII, of Sweden (1682–1718). King at age 15, a fact that provoked Sweden's enemies to underestimate it and him, just three years later he led the superb Swedish Army against a combined Danish, Polish, and Russian attack that launched the *Great Northern War* (1700–1721). He defeated the Danes in 1700, humbled the Russians at *Narva* (November 30, 1700), and thereafter deposed the Polish king. Yet, as good as the Swedish Army was, this was a youthful monarch who loved war too much for a state with an economy and population base unable to sustain conflict for long. In 1708 he invaded Russia, nearly capturing *Peter I*. Charles then marched all the way to Ukraine, to be beaten utterly at *Poltava* (July 8, 1709), where he lost his army and was forced to flee for "protection" into an enforced exile in Turkey. There, he was effectively imprisoned at times and was forced to remain for several years while Peter and his other enemies picked apart the Swedish Empire in the north. Finally escaping, he returned to Sweden in 1715, raised a new army and attacked into rebellious Norway in 1716. His ambitions were undimmed and went so far as a scheme to displace the Stuarts from the Scottish throne. He was killed in battle against the Danes, in Norway, on December 11, 1718. His wars and especially his ill-advised invasion of Russia crippled Sweden and confirmed its fall from the ranks of the *Great Powers*.

Charles XIV. *See Jean-Baptiste Jules Bernadotte.*

charter. (1) A simple nonbinding *declaration* of principles, such as the *Atlantic Charter*; (2) a binding *treaty* setting out the constitution of an *international organization*, such as the *Charter of the United Nations*.

charter colony. A colonial settlement founded by grant of a royal charter, or license, for example, Virginia. This loose legal connection allowed exploration and exploitation of new colonies by private interests within a framework that formally recognized the authority and indirect rule of a *metropolitan* sovereign. *See also crown colony.*

charter company. Private, for-profit commercial enterprises granted governmental powers over colonial territories by imperial governments that did not themselves wish to take on the commitment or expense of *direct rule*. The most spectacular examples were the British *East India Company* and the *Hud-*

son's *Bay Company*, which both came to govern territories larger than Western Europe. There were many other examples, however, including the Royal Niger Company in West Africa, the Imperial British East Africa Company, the British South Africa Company, the German Southwest and Southeast Africa Companies, the Dutch East and West Indies Companies, the Portuguese Niassa Company in Mozambique, and French and Belgian *concessionaire companies* in West Africa and the Congo, among others.

Charter of Paris (1990). *See Paris, Charter of (1990).*

Charter '77. Seven hundred Czechoslovak *human rights* campaigners founded this *Helsinki watch group* in 1977. All were eventually arrested and some, especially *Václav Havel*, became celebrated *political prisoners*. In 1989 they led the *Velvet Revolution*, which overthrew the *Communist* system in *Czechoslovakia*.

chauvinism. Assertive, even belligerent *nationalism*; the term derives from the behavior of one Nicolas Chauvin, a loud and zealous fan of *Napoleon I. See also jingoism; patriotism.*

Chechnya. This Muslim, *Caucasian* land fiercely resisted progressive Russian acquisition of the Caucasus from the *Ottoman Empire* over the course of the eighteenth and nineteenth centuries. With the *Russian Revolutions* (1917) it briefly broke free, with many Chechen supporting the *White Army* of Anton I. Denikin (1872–1947) during the *Russian Civil War* (1918–1921).

In 1921 the *Red Army* occupied Chechnya and forced most Chechens back into the Russian Empire, later reconstituted as the *Soviet Union* by the *Bolsheviks*. A Chechen Autonomous Region was created by *Stalin*, then commissar for nationalities, in 1922. In 1936 Chechnya was administratively enlarged by the addition of Ingush territories and became a "republic" within the Soviet federation. None of this really meant anything, however, as the reality of Soviet *totalitarianism* was pervasive and obliterated local administrative differences. Chechnya's population was deported en masse to *Siberia* by Stalin during *World War II*, along with Crimean *Tartars* and "Volga Germans," for supposed *collaboration* with the *Nazi* invaders (they later migrated back).

In 1991 Chechnya declared independence, but neither Russia nor any other state *recognized* this. After the *extinction* of the Soviet Union on December 25, 1991, Chechnya constituted an ethnic *enclave* within the Russian-dominated Caucasus. In 1992 Russia separated the Ingush into a separate "republic" of Ingushetia. War broke out in 1994, as *Yeltsin* moved massive Russian military formations into Chechnya to curb its assertion of independence and contain the violent local feuding, kidnapping, and killing among competing clans, which had become ubiquitous. The Chechen capital of

Grozny was leveled by indiscriminate Russian *artillery* and air attacks, but Chechen fighters then withdrew to the surrounding mountains, emerging only to assault Russian *convoys* and encampments. Russia, too, took many casualties and received sharp international criticism for the way it was conducting the war—there were brutal atrocities on both sides. Russia pulled out in 1996, leaving Chechnya smoldering but essentially undefeated. Fighting subsequently spilled over into Dagestan and other ethnic enclaves in the Caucasus, and in 1999 Russia again attacked Chechnya in force. In 2000 *Putin* came to power in Moscow on the strength of economic decline, but also of sharp criticism of Yeltsin's handling of the Chechen war and a promise of quick victory. He stepped up air and ground attacks and in general delivered a great deal of physical punishment to Chechnya, but still without winning the war. There were about 1 million Chechen in 2001, including many living in the neighboring enclave of Dagestan and in a *Cossack*-dominated province of Stavropol.

CHEKA (*Chrezychainaya Kommissiya*). The full title was "All Russian Extraordinary Commission for the Suppression of *Counter-Revolution* and *Sabotage*." This was the *Bolshevik* secret and political police. It spread terror under this name, 1917–1922, executing many hundreds of sailors, for instance, after the *Kronstadt mutiny*. Its name was changed to the *OGPU* (1923), *NKVD* (1934), and *KGB* (1954). It conducted the *Red Terror* and confiscations of food, seed, and fuel, which contributed to privation, and then mass starvation, in the Soviet countryside, 1919–1923. In *Lenin's* time, and continuing under *Felix Dzerzhinsky*, it executed at least 200,000; that compared with 14,000 people executed in *tsarist Russia*, for all reasons, in the preceding 50 years. Under *Stalin*, the scale of killing and iron persecution conducted by the successor organizations to the CHEKA was unparalleled in history. *See also* GULAG.
   Suggested Reading: G. Leggett, *The Cheka* (1981).

chemical agents and weapons. Instruments of *war* or *terror* employing chemical compounds to asphyxiate, poison, corrode, or burn the lungs or flesh, or poison the blood. Choking agents (asphyxiates) are also known as pulmonary agents and include chlorine and phosgene weapons. Chemical blister agents corrode the skin upon contact, and additionally blind and destroy any mucous membrane or lung tissue they encounter. They include *mustard gas*, lewisite, and phosgene oxime. Chemical blood agents are essentially poisons carried to the vital organs by the blood system, where they starve these organs of oxygen. They include cyanide, hydrogen cyanide, and cyanogen chloride. Ancient and medieval peoples sometimes poisoned the water supply of cities they besieged, and frequently used various poisons to sour the blades or weapon-tips with which they made war. The use of chemicals and gases as *weapons of mass destruction* really arrived with the mass production capabilities of *industrialization*, in particular the invention of industrial dyes, which co-incidentally produced large amounts of poisonous chlorine gas as a by-product. The 1899 *Hague Convention* pledged 25 states to abstain from using such weapons in the event of war. To no avail: chemical weapons were in fact used extensively during *World War I*. Heavier-than-air chlorine and related gas weapons, which caused accumulation of fluid in the lungs leading to death by drowning in one's own excess bodily fluids, rained down in the form of gas artillery shells. When opposing troops took simple *countermeasures*, such as wearing gas masks, adamsite was added to the mix to induce vomiting and force mask removal and inhalation of the deadly agents. Phosgene gas was heavily used in that war due to its relative ease of production and ready availability. Mustard gas was a particular favorite. Blood agents were tried, but their usage fell off sharply as it proved technically difficult to saturate a targeted area with sufficient poisons to be militarily effective. Germany was the first to break the Hague taboo on chemical weapons, but the *Allies* soon followed suit and chlorine, phosgene and mustard gases became the most hated weapons among soldiers fighting in the trenches, on all sides. And with good reason: the type of deaths and injuries these weapons caused was often intensely painful and excruciatingly prolonged and disfiguring, even by the brutal standards of *total war* and *trench warfare* which had taken hold by 1915. Chemical weapons were not used in *World War II* (though some use was made by Japan in China), not due to moral restraint but because (a) most tacticians deemed them to be militarily ineffective and (b) massive stockpiles on all sides proved a real and mutual *deterrent*. Nonlethal types of chemical weapons were used by the United States in the *Vietnam War*, including psychedelic "BZ," tear gas, and Agent Orange defoliant. (Note: A 1998 charge by CNN and Time magazine stating that the United States had used sarin gas in Laos was proven false and retracted.) Lethal gases were used by the Soviet Union in Afghanistan and by Iraq against Iran in the *Iran-Iraq War* and against its own *Kurdish* population. The *terrorist* organization *al Qaeda* researched use of chemical weapons. *See also binary weapons; chemical and biological warfare; gas weapons; incendiary weapons; nerve weapons.*

chemical and biological (CB) warfare. Waging war with *chemical weapons* or *biological weapons*. These include blister *agents*, which blister and erupt the skin or lungs ("odorless dust" and *mustard gas*); blood agents, which asphyxiate by inhibiting the blood's ability to convey oxygen (hydrogen cyanide); choking gases (phosgene); diseases (anthrax, cholera, plague, hoof and mouth); incapacitators (psychedelic agents); *nerve agents*; and toxins (various fungi extracts).

Chemical Weapons Convention (CWC). In August 1992, after 24 years of negotiations, this treaty banning *chemical agents and weapons* was agreed upon at the United Nations Disarmament Conference in Geneva. It superseded the

1925 *Geneva Protocol*. Signatories were required to declare stockpiles and destroy them within 10 years, with a possible 5-year extension. It has strong enforcement provisions: an organization was created to oversee implementation, states are able to call for "challenge inspections" of suspected cheaters, and nonsignatories may be subjected to *embargo* on chemical exports. The treaty identified 29 chemicals and 14 chemical families subject to international supervision. It entered into effect in 1995.

Chemin des Dames, Battle of (April 16–19, 1917). This offensive on the Aisne front was launched by the French Army in conjunction with an Anglo-Canadian assault on *Vimy-Arras*, also on April 16, 1917. The French, under Neville, hoped to rupture the German lines, partly by their first use of tanks (small, ineffective Renaults). Unbeknown to them, however, the main German strength was in reserve units in deep bunkers 10,000 yards to the rear. The Germans broke up the attack with well-timed and accurate *artillery*, firing partly on the basis of a captured copy of the French battle plan. By the end of the third day the French had lost 130,000 men. As French reinforcements were brought up by truck, they bleated ironically, lambs to the slaughter who knew their fate. Then, they refused to go. The stupidity and carnage of one more failed attack thus provoked the *French Army mutinies*.

Chen Yi (1901–1972). Chinese Communist general. He was a leading figure in the war against Japan and in the *Chinese Civil War*. He was defense minister, 1958–1966, but was stripped of power and humiliated during the *Great Proletarian Cultural Revolution*.

Chernenko, Konstantin Ustinovich (1911–1985). General secretary of the CPSU, February 1984–March 1985. His brief and ineffective tenure merely delayed an improvement in U.S.-Soviet relations and the succession from *Andropov* to *Gorbachev*.

Chernobyl nuclear accident (April 26, 1986). A partial core meltdown and explosion at this Soviet facility near Kiev had multiple effects: (1) it produced a radioactive cloud that traveled over several countries; (2) it further delegitimized the Soviet system at home when it emerged that official secrecy had exposed tens, perhaps hundreds, of thousands to radiation for several days longer than necessary; (3) it brought severe international criticism over the delay in reporting (Sweden, not the Soviet Union, announced detection of the cloud); and (4) it led to agreement on environmental notification procedures within the *United Nations Environmental Program* and heightened the profile of the *IAEA*. On April 6, 1993, a smaller explosion occurred at Tomsk. It was promptly reported, even though it occurred at a hitherto secret *Minatom* installation. *See also Bhopal.*

Chetniks. (1) Serbian radical nationalists who fought the *Ottomans* before 1918. (2) Led by General Draza Mihailovic (1893–1946), Chetnik units fought the Italians, Germans, and the Yugoslav Communists during *World War II*. At first they were actively supported by the British. As Mihailovic became more interested in prosecuting an ongoing *civil war* with Communist *partisans* led by *Tito* and made local truces with the Italians, which enabled him to solidify a base in western Serbia, the British switched their support to the Communists. Mihailovic may have wanted to spare the civilian population from German reprisals, something Tito showed little concern for, and to preserve his force for a critical point later in the war. Withdrawal of British support pushed the Chetniks further toward accommodation with the Germans. Many thousands were *liquidated* by Tito after the war. Mihailovic was captured in 1946, tried, and shot.

Chiang Kai-shek (Jiang Jieshi, 1887–1975). Chinese dictator. As a youth, he studied in both Chinese and Japanese military academies and in the Japanese Army. While in Japan, he joined the *Revolutionary Alliance*. He deserted in 1911 to return to China, then deep in the throes of *revolution*. In 1913 he took part in an unsuccessful revolt and afterward fled to Japan. He returned to China in 1915 to join the Third Revolution, which preserved the Chinese Republic from an imperial restoration under *Yuan Shikai*. Chiang's corruption showed early: he was involved with the infamous Green Gang underworld in Shanghai and involved in manipulating China's currency markets. From 1918 to 1923 he rose through the ranks of the *Guomindang* and consolidated its and his power in southern China. *Sun Yixian* sent him to Russia for several months in 1923 to study *Leninism* in practice and for military training, after which Chiang returned to become the first head of the Whampoa Military Academy. From that influential position, where he also received considerable military aid from the Soviet Union, Chiang built up a base of personally loyal supporters in the new officer corps.

After Sun died in 1925 the morally cunning and nimble Chiang showed he had learned much from *Bolshevism*: he set out to unify China by military means, also emulating Lenin in his tight, dictatorial control of the Guomindang. He led the *Northern Expedition,* which defeated some 34 *warlords* and unified most of China under his dictatorship by 1928. He also bloodily purged the Guomindang and the cities of members of the Chinese *Communist Party* (CCP) in the *Shanghai massacre*. He then expelled Soviet advisors from his army and marched against Communist strongholds holding out in *soviets* in the countryside. Also in 1927, he married an American-educated Christian Chinese woman who, as "Madam Chiang," helped secure U.S. diplomatic and military support. From 1930 to 1934 Chiang conducted five *bandit suppression campaigns* against the Communists, driving *Mao* and *Zhu De* and their followers onto the *Long March*. Chiang led the Guomindang throughout the long *Chinese Civil War* and the *Great Depression*. During the 1930s he began to introduce faintly *fascist* overtones to state propaganda and Guomindang ideology, but mostly he was a *militarist*. In 1931 a more immediate threat had appeared: after the *Mukden incident*, Japan invaded *Manchuria* and thereafter intermittently pressed against the border, deeper into China proper. Pragmatic and crafty, Chiang walked a tightrope between his domestic and foreign enemies, but usually leaned in the primary direction of pressing the fight against the Communists even at the expense of defense against the Japanese. Nationalist and Manchurian troops were unhappy that Chiang insisted on pursuing this vigorous war against the Communists, instead of concentrating on expelling the foreign enemy. A Manchurian unit detained him at the end of 1936 and held him for nearly two weeks in what is known as the *Xi'an incident* (December 1936). While detained, he met and argued with *Zhou Enlai* and the local commander, who both sought to persuade him to sign an agreement for a common anti-Japanese front. He finally agreed—verbally only—to join forces with the Communists.

This tenuous and coerced contract was adhered to for the first years of the *Second Sino-Japanese War*, but collapsed after January 1941 when Chiang ordered an ambush of Communist troops (some 3,000 were killed), which became known as the New Fourth Army Incident. The Sino-Japanese War blended with *World War II* after the Japanese attacks on *Pearl Harbor*, *Hong Kong*, *Singapore*, and other Pacific territories. Already, from 1937 Chiang and the Guomindang had been forced to retreat into the southern interior, abandoning China's coast and fertile plains, and hence also most of its cities and population, to the Japanese. Now Chiang received American aid to supplement British supplies that came to his holdout area in the south over the *Burma Road*. Chiang attended the *Cairo Conference* and, in *Roosevelt*'s eyes at least, was seen and depicted during the war as one of the *Big Four*. On the other hand, he quarreled often with the American theater commander, "Vinegar" Joseph Stilwell (1883–1946), who did not regard him at all highly. Chiang's postwar regime received strong initial U.S. support, but it was so corrupt that its renewed war effort against the Communists was badly weakened and often ineffectual. American support for Chiang waned as he proved incapable of working toward national reconciliation, managing the economy, or conducting successful military operations once the Civil War resumed on an enlarged scale.

Chiang's forces were defeated during 1949 in the renewed civil war. He then led some two million Nationalists (including about one million troops) into armed exile on Taiwan. There, he formed a *government-in-exile*, which asserted it was the sole legitimate government of all China and vainly sought to continue the fight to "recover" the mainland. In time, this posture became merely rhetorical, as Taiwan turned strictly toward its own defense. Chiang and his wife remained favorites of hard-line anti-Communists in the United States, and elsewhere, throughout the *Cold War*. He also remained president of the Republic of China (Taiwan) from 1950 until his death in 1975. He was succeeded by his son.

Suggested Readings: Lloyd Eastman, *The Nationalist Era in China* (1991); Lloyd Eastman, *Seeds of Destruction* (1984); Paul Sih, ed., *Nationalist China During the Sino-Japanese War, 1937–45* (1977).

Chiapas. *See Mexico.*

Children's Vaccine Initiative (CVI). A major program aimed at developing new, more robust vaccines and possibly a combined antigen that would reduce transportation risks and administrative costs while targeting multiple diseases. It was begun in 1990 with funding from diverse private and public sources, ranging from the Rockefeller Foundation to the *World Bank*. The WHO agreed in 1993 to merge the resources of its Expanded Program on Immunization with the CVI.

Chile. The southernmost tip of Chile was peopled in pre-Columbian times by small tribes of nautical migrants known as "sea nomads." To their north, after 1440, there stretched the great *Inca Empire*. The Spanish conquest of the Incas took only from 1536 to 1540 in the north, but resistance by the Araucanian Indians continued in the remoter south into the late nineteenth century. From 1541–1664 the fighting was particularly heavy and bloody, with the Araucanians compelling the Spanish to keep their settlements to the north side of the River Bío Bío. After the Spanish conquest of the north, however, the bulk of the native population there toiled under the *encomienda system*, supplemented by enslavement of *prisoners of war* taken in the protracted southern war. This system of indentured Indian labor lasted in Chile through much of the colonial period. An *audiencia* was established at Concepción (1565–1575).

As with most of Spain's American colonies, Chile's war of independence was sparked by the *Peninsular War* in Europe, and fought from 1810 to 1818. It began on September 18, 1810, when a *junta* of leading citizens, mainly *Creoles*, was formed in Santiago and proclaimed for the deposed Ferdinand VII. This nominal loyalty to the Spanish king then captive in France was really a de facto assertion of independence from Madrid. The war was marked by bitter rivalry among the rebellion's leaders, but also the remarkable Andes-crossing expedition of *José de San Martín* and decisive victory over the Spanish defenders of Santiago at the Battle of Maipú (April 5, 1817), with independence secured by February 1818. When Bolivia was briefly federated with Peru, 1836–1839, under Andrés de Santa Cruz (1792–1865), the new state appeared so threatening to the *balance of power* in South America that Chile and Argentina both declared war on the "Confederation" and broke it apart.

Chile won again in the *War of the Pacific*, 1879–1884, enlarging itself by a third. While superficially evolving as a stable democracy, 1833–1927, in fact Chile was controlled by an oligarchy of just twelve leading families whose old wealth was land-based, supplemented by nineteenth-century additions of newly rich who made their fortunes in nitrates taken from the annexed Bolivian territory, and other export commodities during the great post-1850 economic boom. In the 1880s, under José Manuel Balmaceda (d. 1891), Chile attempted to *nationalize* British nitrate and mining concerns, but ran into stiff domestic and British opposition. It fought a brief civil war in 1891—between Congress and the Navy on one side, and supporters of presidential authority on the other—over the issue of distribution of the nitrate income. Congress won and established a new dominance over national politics. A brief period of military rule, 1927–1931, ended with a return to constitutional government, 1932–1973.

However, by the 1950s, class and ideological differences were openly and badly dividing Chilean society. Montalva Eduardo Frei (1911–1982), president, 1964–1970, was a severe critic of the *Alliance for Progress*. In 1970 *Salvador Allende* won the presidency with a plurality (36 percent) of the votes. He was killed in a *coup* that installed a repressive *junta* led by *Augusto Pinochet* (1973–1990). Over the next months and years this cruel dictatorship arrested more than 100,000 persons, tortured many, and killed several thousand *desaparecidos*. There was also a period of high tension with Argentina, 1978–1980, over the *Beagle Channel*. Yet, the junta's *neoliberal* economic policies gave Chile one of the region's fastest growing economies. Whatever Pinochet's economic success, the human rights abuses of his regime were unforgivable in the eyes of many Chileans who, in a *plebiscite* in 1988, emphatically rejected his bid to be installed as president-for-life. In 1989 elections, Pinochet was beaten by Patricio Aylwin Azócar, who served as president until 1994. This return to democracy enhanced Chile's reputation in regional *development*, as throughout the 1990s its inflation rate stayed low and its *growth* rate high. In 1994 Eduardo Frei, a Christian Democrat, was elected president and continued Chile's policies of high growth and welcome of *foreign direct investment*. Pinochet retired from his post as head of the army in 1998, but remained in the Chilean Senate and thus was immune from any prosecution. However, while in London for medical treatment he was indicted by a Spanish court. A prolonged international dispute ensued, in which Chile argued that Pinochet must not be extradited to Spain. It won that point, but when Pinochet returned to his own country, Chilean courts stripped away his immunity and he was charged with crimes committed while dictator. In 2000, Chile, now a fully restored and increasingly self-confident democracy, elected its first socialist government since Allende.

Suggested Reading: Simon Collier and William F. Sater, *A History of Chile, 1808–1994* (1996).

China. China has the longest recorded history of any human society, dating back at least 4,500 years. The central themes of this ancient history—which sent strong echoes into the modern period—were agrarian self-sufficiency based upon an intense exploitation of the land, but marred by frequent *famines* and attendant banditry or even rural rebellion; centralized rule and relative cultural homogeneity maintained through a vast bureaucracy that was guided for more than 2,000 years by a quasi-theocratic official ideology (*Confucianism*); constant frontier pressure and repeated invasion and conquest by far less civilized, but militarily more efficient, warrior-nomads from *Inner Asia*; and deep, self-imposed isolation from, and dangerously insular attitudes toward, more distant foreign (especially maritime) influences and powers. China's history was also influenced by its large population: by 500 C.E. the population was about 50 million, only half that of the *Roman Empire* at its height but already at a level Western Europe would not reach until 1200 C.E., by which time China had more than 100 million. Plague, war, and the *Mongols* cut China's population to about 80 million in 1400. It rose to 150 million in 1600, declined to 120 million, but returned to 150 million by 1750. It then exploded, reaching 430 million by 1850, declining by 60 million during the disastrous years of multiple rebellion, famine, and foreign war in the 1850s and 1860s, and then exploding again to put enormous pressure on the country's agricultural economy and social system. Despite tens of millions more deaths in the twentieth century, China's population was 650 million by 1949 and reached 1.2 billion in 2000.

(1) Pre-Imperial China: Archaeological finds and advanced research showed that the once-thought merely legendary "Three Dynasties" of China's Bronze Age actually existed. They were: Xia (c. 2200–1750 B.C.E.), Shang (c. 1750–1040 B.C.E.), and Zhou (c. 1040–256 B.C.E.). Of these, only Xia had not been archeologically confirmed by 2000, though some scholars argued that it should be located with China's earliest known Bronze Age culture, at Erlitou. The Zhou are also problematic. Their precise origins remain unclear. However, many scholars agree that they were for a long time frontier vassals of the Shang, but overthrew them and came to rule more than 50 vassal states of their own in what is considered the first unification of China. In 771 B.C.E. they moved their capital east to Luoyang as the result of invasion by the Rong, beginning the "Spring" and "Autumn" period of the *Eastern Zhou* (771–256 B.C.E.). This is often further divided to account for the breakdown of central Zhou authority during the *Warring States* period (403–221 B.C.E.), at the end of which began the classical Imperial period.

(2) Imperial China: The imperial history of China is some 2,200 years old, progressing through multiple ethnic Chinese and Inner Asian dynasties whose rise and fall are used to periodize the history of Chinese civilization, thus: *Qin* (221–206 B.C.E.); Early *Han Empire* (206 B.C.E.–8 C.E.); Late Han Empire (25–220 C.E.); *North-South Disunion* (220–589); *Sui* (589–618); *Tang* (618–907); *Song* (960–1279); *Yuan*, or Mongol (1279–1368); *Ming* (1368–1644);

and *Qing* (1644–1912). In 1211 part of northern China was overrun by the Mongols, with the remainder conquered between 1217 and 1223. The Southern Song were defeated by Mongol armies in 1279. However, the Mongol emperors continually looked beyond China to new conquests and their vast empire to the west; they also never achieved full acceptance under the *mandate of heaven*. The Ming ousted them in 1368. The first Ming emperor, *Hongwu*, remade China by harkening to pre-Mongol imperial traditions while retaining Mongol military innovations. Ming China also experienced a surge in economic growth and overseas expansion, but then deliberately turned inward to fearful defense of the northwest frontier and into radical *isolationism*. In the fifteenth century China was still a world leader in many areas of technology, having enjoyed an advanced level of economic development for many centuries before the West. However, after 1500 it suffered from recurring ossification of the central government and scholar-elite into both endemic corruption and a rigid Confucianism that ultimately was unable to adapt the rural economy to the expanding population. This crisis was symbolized and aggravated by, and personified in, the progressive isolation and irresponsibility of the *Wanli emperor* (r. 1572–1620). Nor was conservative China able to adjust its foreign policy to fend off the growing threat to its internal political, economic, and social structures posed by modern international commerce or outright foreign imperialism. In 1600, China was among the most populous (120 million), richest, and successful civilizations in human history, an equal to ancient Rome. It was about to be left far behind by revolutionary developments in the West, however, in what some economic historians call the *Great Divergence*.

Despite the brilliance of its scholar-elite and imperial civilization, Ming China collapsed into *warlordism* and civil war and was overthrown by the Qing (*Manchus*) in 1644, led by the son of *Nurgaci*. The first significant contacts between China and the modern West thus came under the Manchus. The Qing produced several remarkable emperors, notably *Kangxi* and *Qianlong*. They also suffered extraordinary internal convulsions and peasant uprisings, including the massively destructive rebellions of the *White Lotus* (1796–1804), *Nian* (1851–1868), and *Taiping* (1850–1864), which left millions dead and Qing China near-fatally weakened and exceptionally vulnerable to external threats and pressures. Before the twentieth century, China failed to achieve the key technological and organizational breakthroughs of market formation and integration that spurred the *industrial revolution* and vaulted even several small Western powers ahead of China in their advanced social and economic organization, and military prowess, and which led to startling advances in navigation, military innovation, and economic productivity. During the early nineteenth century, China felt the effect of its social and bureaucratic rigidity and self-inflicted educational backwardness. The conflict erupted over the *opium trade*, leading to the *Opium Wars* (1839–1842; 1856–1860) with Great Britain, after which China's humiliation and weakness was made manifest in the debilitating terms of the *Treaty of Nanjing*. This was followed by other *unequal treaties* with other foreign powers, as France, Germany, Russia, and the United States forced open its trade, its borders, and ultimately displaced Qing law and influence from parts of its coastal cities (*treaty ports*). China was also pulled into the *Tonkin Wars* with France. *Cixi* and others sought to resist the *treaty system* and reform the dynasty through partial *Sinification* and "self-strengthening." It did not succeed. Japan joined the imperial scramble for *spheres of influence* and exclusive trade rights in China during the *First Sino-Japanese War* (1895), as a result of which China lost control of Korea, Taiwan, and Manchuria. It then began a final descent into republican *revolution*, social and political chaos, and prolonged, vast and bloody national and human tragedy, the likes of which few nations have ever suffered.

(3) Republican China: After the failed *Boxer Rebellion*, the *Chinese Revolution* of 1911, led by *Sun Yixian* and the *Guomindang* (Nationalists), turned out the Manchus. A republic was established in 1912, but it was quickly distorted into a personal military dictatorship under *Yuan Shikai*, who even so could not handle the many provincial warlords who broke away from the center. During *World War I*, Japan struck again, expelling Germany from *Shandong* to itself emerge as the main threat to China's unity, security, and independence. Tokyo's ambition to dominate, and indeed colonize, large parts of China was exposed in the *Twenty-one Demands* of 1915. The United States moved into the vacuum left by European preoccupation with World War I to defend its perceived interest in the *Open Door* and to uphold the Asian *balance of power*. However, China was not really supportable, as a result of its internal fragmentation and instability: the radical decentralization and militarization of the countryside, which began with the White Lotus and Taiping Rebellions, culminated in a division of China among competing warlords after the death of Yuan Shikai in 1916. Hundreds of warlords clashed in, ruled over, and devastated the countryside. In addition, the *May 4th movement*, which developed from 1919, left the intellectual classes in ferment and deeply divided over whether or not China should adopt a *Marxist* path to *modernization*, but unified in their rejection of foreign influences. At first, Communist and Nationalist armed forces worked jointly to defeat the southern warlords, but in 1927 the *Shanghai massacres* signaled the start of the protracted *Chinese Civil War*. The Guomindang did not reestablish central authority over northern China until the defeat of most of the northern warlords by 1928, then it turned its attention to crushing the Communists who had taken refuge in the countryside.

Radical officers in Japan began direct and increasing military pressure on China from their takeover of Manchuria in 1931. Even nationalists were dismayed at the decision by the Guomindang, and *Chiang Kai-shek* in particular, to *appease* the Japanese so as to keep his army free to pursue the Communists, whom he drove onto the *Long March* from their base in the *Jiangxi*

Soviet after the fifth *bandit suppression campaign* in 1934. Japan took full advantage of the continuing Chinese Civil War to move against China proper in 1937, starting the *Second Sino-Japanese War*. Their brutal occupation and disregard for Chinese lives was realized, and later symbolized, by the *rape of Nanjing*. That huge conflict merged with the even wider conflict of *World War II*, from the attack on *Pearl Harbor* on December 7, 1941, though, even before that, informal American military aid had been sent to China. Communists and Nationalists nominally put aside their differences in order to fight parallel wars against the Japanese after the *Xi'an incident* (December 1937). Despite continuing animosity among the various Chinese forces, during World War II China engaged and held down the great bulk of the Japanese Army, albeit with significant logistical and air support from the United States and lesser aid from Britain.

There was extensive *collaboration* along the seaboard, but on the whole the Chinese response to the Japanese occupation was revulsion and resistance. During the war, Chiang Kai-shek was treated as one of the *Big Four*, consulting at several of the major wartime conferences. With the defeat of Japan in 1945, the civil war in China flared into the open once more. The war years had greatly drained Guomindang morale and personnel, however, while the Communists had learned new skills of *guerrilla warfare*, which they now used to effect against compatriots. The Civil War was won by the Communists by early 1949, and *Mao Zedong* proclaimed the establishment of the People's Republic of China (PRC). There followed an orgy of executions of political and class enemies during the consolidation phase of the *Chinese Revolution* of 1949, which took several million—perhaps as many as ten million—lives. With the rump of the Nationalist movement exiled to Taiwan, even while proclaiming its intention to rearm and return in force, it looked as though the civil war was still unfinished business. In fact, it was over.

(4) The People's Republic: Almost immediately the Communist regime in China found itself at war with the United States: Mao entered the *Korean Conflict* when American and United Nations forces failed to heed Chinese warnings and a major troop buildup and approached China's border with North Korea in November 1950, in pursuit of the remnants of the North Korean Army, which had invaded South Korea earlier that year. China fought these U.S. and UN forces to a standstill, though it took extremely heavy casualties. Despite sharing Communist *ideology*—almost immediately, Mao moved to initiate Soviet-style *industrialization* under a series of *five-year-plans*, along with a *terror* state and regular *purges* that sought to crush all political dissent—relations with the Soviet Union worsened steadily after *Stalin's* death in 1953. By the late 1950s the *Sino-Soviet split* was apparent and increasingly dangerous. It flared openly in 1966 and again in 1969, when Chinese and Soviet forces clashed bloodily at several points along their lengthy but disputed common border. China made some effort to challenge the Soviets for leadership among more radical *Third World* countries, but it did not

have the same resources to commit or appear quite as serious about projecting power beyond its immediate neighborhood. However, it did achieve an independent nuclear capability, which made the conflict with Russia dangerous in the extreme. Domestically, China lurched from one radical experiment to the next. Forced *collectivization* marked the early 1950s, the *Hundred Flowers campaign* and an anti-rightist purge was underway (1956–1957), and anti-*revisionist* campaigns became routine. When even all that suffering and coercion failed to achieve the great economic advance Mao expected, he launched the so-called *Great Leap Forward* (1958–1961).

That colossal effort, too, failed to advance China's *industrialization* or progress toward modernity. Instead, its utterly fanatic, fantastic, and brutal effort to coerce the peasantry into joining even larger Peoples' Communes and then expropriate the crops they produced, leaving them at bare subsistence or below, met fierce resistance and led to a famine that took at least 25 million lives (and may have taken as many as 40 million) through mass persecution, executions, and especially massive starvation in the Chinese countryside. Barely pausing, and still not recovered from the earlier disasters, China entered yet another period of Maoist-inspired internal chaos: the *Great Proletarian Cultural Revolution* (1966–1976), in which neither prior service to the *Communist Party* (CCP) or the *People's Liberation Army* (PLA) spared cadres from being purged, or even killed, by vicious teenage thugs organized into units of *Red Guards*. The antics of the Red Guards spread to China's Foreign Ministry and foreign embassies, leading to severed relations with several countries and an ever deeper split with Russia. As the violence unleashed approached the level of civil war, Mao felt compelled to call in the PLA to rescue the CCP from the Red Guards, who were then purged in their turn. This greatly enhanced the role played by the PLA in Chinese national politics, though not in the way *Lin Biao* had intended. In all, some 16 million young Chinese were sent down to the country, a "lost generation" both to China and themselves. Not all were sent as punishment: covertly, the CCP used the program to control the swelling population of the major cities.

In foreign policy, during the 1960s China aided the DRV (North Vietnam) against the RVN (South Vietnam) and the United States in the *Vietnam War*. Elsewhere in Indochina it armed the *Khmers Rouges* in their *insurgency* in Cambodia and the *Pathet Lao* in Laos. In 1971 the majority in the UN finally ousted Taiwan from the China seat in the *United Nations General Assembly* and *Security Council*, and the People's Republic emerged as a major diplomatic player. In a stunning *rapprochement* in 1972, *Richard Nixon* visited China. Formal U.S. *recognition* came in 1978. Relations with Vietnam deteriorated after the Vietnam War ended, and they became openly hostile during the *Cambodia-Vietnam War* (1978–1991). China attacked Vietnam in 1979 (*Sino-Vietnamese War*), to "punish" Vietnam for toppling *Pol Pot*. It was the PLA that was bloodied, however. China invaded *Tibet* in 1951, and thereafter methodically and ruthlessly crushed Tibetan *nationalism* and repressed *Buddhist* practices there. It won the sharp *Indo-Chinese War* (1962) and allied with Pakistan to counterbalance India, which in turn allied with the Soviet Union against China. From the end of the Korean Conflict to the early 1990s, China closely supported the quixotic regime of *Kim Il Sung* in North Korea, but Beijing dropped special trade privileges for that regime as it moved toward membership in the *World Trade Organization*. Beijing also continued in a state of suspended hostility with Taiwan. It had an uneasy, but also at times coolly cordial, relationship with Japan. On the whole, however, China remained deep into isolationism as long as Mao lived. This was exemplified by China's refusal of all foreign offers of humanitarian assistance when the city of Tangshan was destroyed by an earthquake on July 28, 1976, killing perhaps 650,000 and injuring another 800,000 people, with many more left destitute.

An intense succession struggle began even before Mao's death, starting with the *Tiananmen Square incident* (April 4–5, 1976) and closing symbolically with purging from the CCP of the *Gang of Four* and their spectacular *show trials* in 1980. Already by 1978, however, China's new leadership—which closed ranks around the twice-purged and twice-"rehabilitated" *Deng Xiaoping*— moved to reform the state, economy, scientific research, and armed forces (the *Four Modernizations*), proclaiming that they would build "socialism with Chinese characteristics." The disastrous policies of the Great Leap Forward and the Cultural Revolution were partly disavowed—full disavowal would have threatened the *legitimacy* of the CCP itself, and that could not be tolerated—but China remained a closed and highly repressive society. In 1982 China reached the population mark of one billion people. By 1988 its economy was booming, but internal political and social tensions were also building again as economic reform and progress was not accompanied by comparable cultural openness or any easing of the CCP's political dictatorship, which ensured that pervasive corruption diverted much of China's new wealth into those hands with well-placed contacts, or "*guanxi*." A student movement for democracy, which incorporated public outrage at staggering levels of corruption, spontaneously occupied *Tiananmen Square* in Beijing. It was then crushed by PLA tanks and troops in several June days of internationally televised brutality and repression.

In foreign policy, the collapse of the Soviet Union in 1991 led to improved relations with Russia. China also developed *rapprochements* with Japan and India. Relations with the United States improved, despite Tiananmen, but deteriorated after 1994 over *human rights* questions. By that year, parts of China were effectively decommunized by market reforms: guanxi was more important than ideology, for foreign investors and Chinese themselves. After 1990, China's defense spending increased significantly. Combined with the collapse of Russian power, that gave it the world's numerically largest military. Elements of the PLA spoke ominously of enforcing China's claim to all islands of the South China Sea, including the *Spratlys* and even the Malacca Straits, and began to acquire a *blue water navy*. China also signed an agreement with

Vietnam renouncing the use of force over border disputes, and made important inroads into increased influence over the newly independent, formerly Soviet states of Central Asia. This geopolitical thrust aimed principally at advancing China's age-old problem of pacifying Tibet and Xianjiang, including by crushing *Uighur* resistance. Beijing dropped special trade privileges for North Korea as it moved toward membership in the *World Trade Organization*, which it finally joined in 2001. That year, relations with the United States again were troubled by human rights issues (especially by growing persecution of the quasi-Buddhist religious sect, the Falun Gong); by a minor military incident near Hainan Island involving a mid-air collision of a U.S. reconnaissance plane and a Chinese fighter; and by continuing U.S. support for, and escalating Chinese attempts to intimidate, Taiwan. That would-be island nation remained as the cork in the bottle of China's regional aspirations into the new century. All that foreign policy movement after 1990 reflected a far greater underlying geopolitical tension produced by the fact that it was China's long-term goal, and perceived national interest, to displace the United States (and Japan and Russia) as the predominant power in Northeast Asia. The United States was almost certainly prepared to adjust to that change with reasonable and relative ease, but it remained equally unlikely to cease resisting Beijing's new assertiveness and welcome it as a strategic partner in global governance until China showed clear signs of genuinely embracing the idea of the rule of law, internally as well as internationally. Not yet a democracy and no longer Communist in any sense but in name, China at the start of the new century was nevertheless once again a large, united and powerful nation. The ever-evolving Sino-American relationship thus was already among the most important of all bilateral relationships at the start of the twenty-first century, even as it remained closely tied to the unanswered question of whether China could find a new principle of legitimacy to displace atavistic communism and outdated territorial nationalism, and thus lend moral support to what otherwise appeared as merely bullying regional claims born of its sheer size. *See also agricultural revolution; banner system; Canton trade system; Cixi; compradors; culturalism; foot binding; Forbidden City; isolationism; overseas Chinese.*

Suggested Readings: John K. Fairbank, *China* (1992); Charles Hucker, *China's Imperial Past* (1975); Ann Paludan, *Chronicle of the Chinese Emperors* (1998); T. Robinson and D. Shambaugh, *Chinese Foreign Policy* (1994); G. Segal, *Defending China* (1985); Jonathan Spence, *The Search for Modern China* (1990).

China Incident (1937). *See Marco Polo Bridge incident.*

China-Japan Peace and Friendship Treaty (1978). This agreement represented the beginning of a slow *rapprochement* in Sino-Japanese political relations, and a new trading relationship, after the death of *Mao Zedong*. It represented an effort at historic reversal of relations that were deeply hostile since the *First Sino-Japanese War* in 1895.

China lobby. A vocal political grouping in the United States, primarily though not exclusively in the *Republican Party*, which long argued for strong American support for the defense of *Taiwan* against what it viewed as *aggression* and potential invasion of that island republic by the People's Republic of China (PRC).

China, Republic of. *See Taiwan.*

China War. The term preferred by Japanese for their country's conquest of *Manchuria* after 1931 and the war with China that followed. The Chinese officially call the conflict the "Chinese People's War of Resistance Against Japanese Aggression." In most English-language histories, this conflict is known as the *Second Sino-Japanese War* (1937–1945). *See also Pacific War.*

Chinese Civil War (1927–1949). China was mostly reunified after defeat of northern *warlords* by the *Guomindang* (Nationalists) under *Chiang Kai-shek*. In the middle of this campaign the *Communist Party* (CCP) was turned on by Chiang, in the *Shanghai massacres*. Surviving Communists fled the cities; those led by *Mao Zedong* set up the *Jiangxi Soviet*. By 1934, Nationalist attacks forced the Communists onto the *Long March* to the northwest. During that harsh trial, Mao consolidated his hold as the leading political boss on the Communist side, while his partner *Zhu De* emerged as their most able field commander. Chiang pressed the fight, insisting on eliminating domestic enemies before fully engaging Japan, which had invaded *Manchuria* in 1931. At the end of 1936 Chiang was forced, in the *Xi'an incident*, to join forces with the Communists. When the Japanese attacked China in 1937, after the *Marco Polo Bridge incident*, Communists and Nationalists combined to resist the invader, or rather, ceased fighting each other to better fight the Japanese in parallel campaigns. This fragile truce among Chinese factions broke down, actually but unofficially, when Nationalist troops ambushed Communist troops in the "New Fourth Army Incident" in January 1941.

The fighting in China merged with *World War II* after the Japanese attacks on *Pearl Harbor*, *Singapore*, and other Pacific territories at the end of 1941. The Japanese war had two critically important consequences for China's internal divisions and the outcome of its civil war. First, the Japanese drove the Nationalists far inland from their main coastal bases and then cut them off from resupply by invading Burma and cutting the *Burma Road*. Then, in the summer of 1944, the Japanese offensive in the south, the "Ichigo ('No. 1') Offensive," which aimed at taking out Allied air bases in the Nationalist zones of control, greatly relieved pressure on the Communists in the north by drawing off Japanese troops and further decimated the Nationalist armies. Therefore, the Communists were able to move out from enforced isolation into central China, pick up additional support among the peasantry by instituting ever more radical land reform programs, and increase the size of the CCP and the *People's Liberation Army* tenfold in eight years, to more than 900,000 troops. With the defeat of Japan, the United States sent marines to hold Beijing and Tientsin and airlifted Nationalist troops from their southern bases to secure the northern cities and accept the Japanese *surrender*, but at first Washington still called for a coalition government to be formed with the Communists and for an effort at genuine democratic reconstruction of war-torn China. On the other side, *Stalin* backed Mao from the beginning, including supplying captured Japanese war matériel. That did not prevent him, however, from militarily occupying former tsarist territories in Manchuria under cover of expelling the Japanese—the Soviet Union had declared war on Japan on August 8, 1945, and attacked the Japanese Army all across northern China and Mongolia. Outright civil war resumed as Chiang moved to reconsolidate his erstwhile military dictatorship and attacked Communist formations in November, but the fight was now engaged on far more equal terms militarily than before the Japanese invasion in 1937.

As Chiang grew more desperate, so did his *secret police* engage in repression, assassination, and terror, further corroding his already tarnished legitimacy in China. In the end, the civil war was as much lost by the Nationalists as won by the Communists: Chiang and other Nationalist leaders proved incompetent; there was massive corruption, a debilitating inflation, and much plain stupidity, all of which dogged the Guomindang effort. The Nationalists stayed in the cities, where they were besieged and garrison after garrison isolated and forced to surrender, and they overstayed and thus were badly overextended in Manchuria—contrary to U.S. military advice to consolidate on the other side of the *Great Wall*. The war shifted character in 1948, as confident and well-equipped Communist armies moved to fully conventional operations against the demoralized garrisons of the Nationalists. In the fall, *Lin Biao* destroyed a garrison force of some 400,000 Nationalist troops in Manchuria. In another huge and protracted conventional battle, *Zhu De* committed upwards of 600,000 troops and inflicted serious damage on Nationalist divisions. The war climaxed as these several battles overlapped in early 1949. The Huai-Hai campaign (November 1948–January 1949) was the decisive action during the end game of the war. Beijing fell on January 31, 1949, as in successive engagements the Guomindang lost nearly half a million troops, killed or captured, and its will and physical ability to resist further was fatally diminished. Communist troops advanced north to south, following the ancient path taken before them by the *Manchus*, and even earlier conquerors of China: Nanjing fell on April 23rd. On October 1st, Mao declared the founding of the People's Republic of China (PRC). The defeat forced remaining Nationalist forces to retreat to *Taiwan* (Formosa), where they maintained the Republic of China (ROC). There they regrouped and sought to rearm, in the hope of carrying on the fight until one day they could return to the mainland. However, they received only enough American support to survive on *Formosa*, but never to seriously threaten to restart the war.

Suggested Readings: Stephen Levine, *Anvil of Victory* (1987); Suzanne Pepper, *Civil War in China* (1978).

Chinese Revolution (1911). At its end, the *Qing dynasty* was fairly easily overthrown by a combination of once-rival factions of revolutionaries, principally led by General *Yuan Shikai* and Dr. *Sun Yixian*. On October 14, 1908, the *Guangxu* emperor died; the next day *Cixi*, the *Dowager Empress*, also died, raising the child emperor *Pu Yi* to the throne. In 1909, provincial assemblies long promised but much delayed by Cixi finally met, and in 1910 the first National Assembly convened. On October 10, 1911, rebellion broke out in Wuhan as units of the New Army *mutinied*. The rebellion spread, until most of China's provinces declared and asserted independence from the Qing state. Desperate, the Qing permitted Yuan Shikai to return from retirement. Instead of helping the *Manchus* put down the rising, on November 11th he accepted election by the rebel National Assembly as premier of China, subsequently concurred in by the Qing court, and then counseled the Qing on, and arranged for the abdication of, Pu Yi.

On January 1, 1912, Sun Yixian—who had been in the United States— became China's provisional president in Nanjing. On February 12, 1912, the court acting for Pu Yi accepted his abdication, in exchange for his right to remain in the *Forbidden City* and a large annual stipend. Sun Yixian also stepped down, and on February 13th Yuan Shikai became president, in Beijing, of the first Chinese Republic in more than 2,500 years. The Nanjing Constitution of that year was supposed to establish China also as a democracy. However, real power lay in the hands of Yuan Shikai, who assumed dictatorial powers in 1913 and thereafter led the revolution and the republic to disaster. Also threatening peace and security was a breakdown of central authority and widespread revival of *warlordism*, which overwhelmed the national government by 1916. Many powerful warlords remained untamed until 1928, when *Chiang Kai-shek* finally brought most to heal; some even survived into the 1930s. Traditional, *Confucian* China seemed dead, though, in fact, much Confucian thought and tradition survived in revised or hidden form. Imperial China certainly was gone. Ahead lay decades of bloody political unrest, *civil war*, Japanese *aggression*, more civil war, *famine*, and then *Maoist* dictatorship, purges, disastrous social and economic policies, mass terror campaigns, and erection of a vast, Communist dictatorship and bureaucratic state.

Suggested Reading: Shinkichi Eto and Harold Schiffrin, eds., *The 1911 Revolution* (1984).

Chinese Revolution (1949). The *Chinese Revolution* of 1911 had overthrown the *Manchus* and established a republic. It had also further divided and decentralized China and weakened its ability to resist foreign demands for *capitulations* and substantial *servitudes*. Ultimately, by opening the way to *warlordism* and then the *Chinese Civil War* between the *Guomindang* and the *Communist Party* (CCP), it had gravely weakened China and thereby encouraged the 1937 invasion by Japan—precisely the opposite of what its progenitors had hoped, which had been above all to strengthen China's ability to resist foreign aggression. And it was that invasion more than any other factor that permitted Communist victory when the Civil War resumed at the end of *World War II*. Japanese intervention had likely saved the Communists from defeat and *liquidation* in the late 1930s. It also severely weakened the Nationalists by cutting them off from their seaboard city bases for eight years, while allowing the Communists to organize in the countryside so that they emerged in 1945 with a much larger and better equipped army and a more secure political and financial base in the northern interior—and with the Soviet Union at their back, supporting them with captured Japanese equipment and supplies of surplus Soviet arms.

The Communists also used cynical but highly effective *mass line* techniques to manipulate peasant grievances, as so many others had done before them in China's history, and use peasant support as their springboard to power. Peasants also were encouraged to attend mass meetings and to denounce—and sometimes also to kill—the wealthier among them, not just larger landowners, and then to confiscate and redistribute their possessions. That was a recipe for "land reform" guaranteed to lead to grave injustices and loss of innocent life, to remove more skilled peasant farmers from the land on charges of being exploiters, but also to attach to the CCP the poorest in the countryside and those who most directly benefited from confiscations. But then, much of this was modeled on *Mao Zedong*'s admiration for what had been done in the Soviet Union, where in the 1930s *Stalin* mercilessly squeezed *"surplus value"* from the *kulaks* and other peasants to force the pace of heavy *industrialization*. The Nationalists also share blame for peasant suffering, however, as when their armies recovered former Communist-held areas, expropriated landlords followed in their wake and ordered armed thugs to murder, often by fiendishly cruel means, peasants identified as having led the land reforms. Mao had wanted class warfare, and he got it. The peasants were just the cannon fodder, for both sides.

Once firmly in power, Communist concerns shifted to control of the cities; to ending all remaining foreign servitudes, the last of which were Soviet, imposed by Stalin as the price for aid against Japan in 1945; and to rapid *modernization* of the Chinese economy and nation—by which was meant full-scale industrialization based on *nationalization* of all extant industrial plant and state control of all new enterprises, and squeezing "surplus value" from the peasants to provide the necessary capital for industrialization. In its political character the 1949 Communist Revolution is often depicted as a great peasant uprising against exploitation by the cities and the old agrarian order.

Insofar as that is true, then the later forced *collectivization* of the countryside imposed by Mao and the Communists, which led to widespread *famine* and tens of millions of deaths, was an utter betrayal of the Chinese peasantry. From 1949 to 1954 the revolution in the countryside was made at a cost of one million landlord and "rich peasant" lives, but from 1954 to 1958 China's peasants (80 percent of the population) forfeited their early, hard-won gains and were forced into tens of thousands of collective farms and communes. There they stayed until 1978, exploited to service a hard state monopoly over food prices and markets designed to squeeze capital from the countryside to modernize industry and the cities.

Also in 1954, the legal order was remade with a *Stalinist* constitution, and thereafter Mao's *cult of personality*—along with his own psychological corruption—deepened and spread. Next came Soviet-style industrialization, with accompanying *five-year plans*, emphasis on heavy industry over consumer goods, massive production bottlenecks, gross inefficiencies, and phony overfilled quotas. The Communist Revolution thus set out to remake China in the image of two of the worst ideas of the twentieth century: collectivized agriculture and state-run industrialization. From 1958 to 1961, perhaps 30 million Chinese starved to death, victims this time not of frenzied class warfare campaigns but of grossly mismanaged *agrarian reform*. Hundreds of millions more suffered through the subsequent disasters of the *Great Leap Forward* and the *Great Proletarian Cultural Revolution*.

Suggested Readings: Thomas Kampen, *Mao Zedong, Zhou Enlai and the Evolution of the Chinese Communist Leadership* (2000); Maurice Meisner, *Marxism, Maoism, and Utopianism* (1982); Jonathan Spence, *Mao Zedong* (1999).

Chinggis Khan (1162–1227). Also known as Jenghiz Khan or Genghis Khan. *See also Mongols; Song dynasty; Yuan dynasty.*

Chou En-lai. *See Zhou Enlai.*

Christendom. *See* res publica Christiana.

Christian Democracy. Moderate *Catholic* political parties, formed in many countries in Europe and Latin America in the twentieth century. Their main tenets were acceptance of *democracy; capitalism,* of a reform variety that sought to implement the "social gospel"; and Catholic and *conservative* social values.

Christian Democratic Union (CDU). The main center-right party of the Federal Republic of Germany since 1949. Founded by *Konrad Adenauer,* during the *Cold War* it cleaved to a pro-American position on *NATO* and relations with the *Soviet bloc* and strongly supported European *integration.* It guided the extraordinary German recovery from *World War II* and was the governing party for most of the period since 1949. Under *Helmut Kohl,* it oversaw the reunification of the two Germanies in 1989–1990. It took the lead on more activist foreign policy in the post–Cold War period, especially toward the breakup of *Yugoslavia* and the *Maastricht Treaty*. After decades in power it was defeated in the late 1990s amidst financial scandal.

Christianity. Originating among the Jewish subjects and the *slave* populations of the eastern *Roman Empire*, upon the conversion of the Roman Saul (Paul) this new, apocalyptic religious movement was spread by proselytizers through the Near East (Anatolia and the Caucasus) and down the Nile into East Africa during the first three centuries of the Common Era. Christianity's early, Middle Eastern form drew upon the philosophical traditions of the Greco-Roman world, but was most deeply influenced by *Judaism*, to which it was intimately related and from which it directly sprang. It was later, though to a lesser extent, influenced by *Islam*, which Christianity—especially its Nestorian and Byzantine branches—in turn also greatly influenced. Christianity was a persecuted religion from the second century under the *Roman Empire*, but was granted toleration in 313 after the conversion of *Constantine I* (274–337) in 312. In 324 it was made the state religion, though paganism and other faiths were tolerated.

After the fall of Rome, as *Christendom* was besieged by additional waves of barbarian invasion, Christianity evolved as a warrior culture that sustained *Byzantine* emperors in the eastern Empire, while among the Latin Kingdoms of the West it warred against pagans as it expanded deep into Western and, later, North Europe. Its original base in the Middle East and North Africa was overrun by the explosion of that other great warrior culture, Islam, in the eighth century. By 1000 C.E. it was the dominant faith in Western Europe, where there formed a strong sense of a *res publica Christiana*, and from whence came the Christian counterattack: the successful *Reconquista* in Iberia and the failed *Crusades* to retake the Holy Lands of the Middle East. Christianity remained the dominant religion in the Nile Valley south of Egypt until the fourteenth century, when several ancient Christian kingdoms (*Nubia* and parts of *Ethiopia*) were finally overrun or severely truncated by rising Islamic powers. It spread beyond Europe and the Middle East, crossing whole oceans in the company of European *imperialism* and *colonization* after 1500. Originally winning converts partly by promising to slaves spiritual equality, Christianity increasingly became a religion of slave owners and slave societies, especially with its expansion into the *New World*, but also in Africa, Central Asia, and the Slav lands of Eastern Europe. Christianity also formed hybrids with traditional religious belief systems, whether African, *Mayan*, *Incan*, *Buddhist*, or *Hindu*, or merely some local cult. It thus became a rich and complex phenomenon, spanning entire continents and diverse cultures, always showing a core adaptability that helped it survive for two millennia and to become a world religion.

Christianity's tenets vary greatly with historical era and sectarian doctrinal emphasis, but its central beliefs almost always include the following: mono-theism; messianism (specifically, the divinity and sanctifying life example of Jesus of Nazareth, the Christ, or "anointed one," who lived c. 4 B.C.E.–29 C.E.); the role in history and direct, divine inspiration of biblical prophesy, with special emphasis on the New Testament gospels composed by the fol-lowers of Jesus after his execution by the Romans and codified by episcopal authority in the third century C.E.; and various conceptions of social justice springing from the genuinely radical notion—bespeaking slave origins—of the equality of all believers in the eyes of God. Christianity eventually split into three major camps, after two great *schisms*: *Catholics* (Latin, or Roman rite) split with the *Orthodox* in 1054; the Latin church then divided into Catholics and *Protestants* during the *Reformation* and *Counter Reformation*. Protestants continued subdividing ever after, over this or that finer point of doctrine, until they formed numerous denominations and sects with a wide variety of beliefs. Catholics and Orthodox remain more internally cohesive groups than most Protestant denominations, but both these larger sects also face constant schismatic tendencies: the Catholic Church faced a schism in France after *Vatican II*, and others in East Africa also in the late twentieth century. Until the seventeenth century the Orthodox were the most numerous among Chris-tian sects. Beginning in the late fifteenth century, Catholics (and soon after, also Protestants) expanded to the Americas, into West and Southern Africa, and throughout Asia, so that Latin Christianity became a world faith by the nineteenth century while Orthodoxy remained geographically limited. By the twenty-first century the Christian world comprised nearly a billion Catholics, hundreds of millions of Protestants and Orthodox, and many local blends of off-shoot and hybrid belief systems. *See also Calvinism; clash of civilizations; Coptic Church; Ecumenical Councils; Japan; Hideyoshi; Tokugawa; Inquisition; Renaissance; Taiping Rebellion; two swords; Uniate Church.*

Suggested Readings: David Chidester, *Christianity* (2000); John McManners, ed., *Oxford History of Christianity* (1994).

Chue Teh. *See Zhu De.*

Churchill, Winston Spencer (1874–1965). British statesman. First lord of the admiralty, 1911–1915, 1939–1940; minister of munitions, 1917; secretary for war, 1918–1921; chancellor of the exchequer, 1924–1929; minister of defense and prime minister, 1940–1945 and 1951–1955. The son of an aris-tocratic English father (*see Marlborough*) and an American mother, Churchill could be personally abrasive, was frequently emotional, even weepy, and very often drunk. He was also a talented artist, an extraordinary orator, a gifted amateur historian, and a first-rate political opportunist: he switched parties twice to stay near the centers of power. Churchill was, most of all, the out-standing statesmen of the twentieth century. A poor student, he struck out early to make his own mark in and on the world. He attended Sandhurst rather than Oxford or Cambridge, and took a junior commission. He was briefly a war correspondent in Cuba in 1895, but rejoined his regiment in time to see service in India, on the Northwest Frontier, in 1897. The next year Churchill was part of *Kitchener's* expedition to the Sudan and saw action at the *Battle of Omdurman*. He resigned his commission to bid for a seat in Parliament, but lost. He went to South Africa as a war correspondent during the *Second Boer War*, was captured by the Boers, and dramatically escaped.

Propelled by this feat to celebrity status, Churchill was elected as a Conservative member of Parliament in 1900. In 1904 he joined the Liberals and was made undersecretary for the colonies. In 1910 he became home secretary. In 1911 he became first lord of the admiralty, a post he used to modernize the *Royal Navy* and that he still occupied at the start of *World War I*. Churchill was compelled to resign in 1915 over the fiasco at the *Dardanelles* and *Gallipoli*, a failed campaign he had urged in support of Russia and to flank the *western front*, and with which he became identified for the rest of his life. Churchill returned to the War Cabinet in 1917, but in a much diminished role as minister of munitions. He was minister for war and air, 1918–1921, then returned to his role in charge of the colonies. In this office he oversaw the consolidation of British imperial gains in Africa and the Middle East that resulted from the *Treaty of Versailles* and *Sèvres*. He played a key role in negotiating an end to the *Irish War of Independence* in 1921. During the *Russian Civil War* Churchill argued unsuccessfully for intervention to strangle the *Bolshevik* infant in its revolutionary nursery. He lost his seat in the massive defeat of *Lloyd George's* Liberals in 1922, but returned to Parliament as a Conservative in 1924. Churchill was chancellor of the exchequer, 1924–1929, during which he tried to return Great Britain to the *gold standard*. He also responded harshly to a bitter *general strike* in 1926.

In the interwar years Churchill voiced a number of unpopular opinions that helped keep him out of high office. The two most controversial were: (1) his refusal to support concessions to India on *home rule*; and (2) his repeated warnings against taking *Hitler* lightly, his calls for stepped-up military preparations for what many feared would be another *Great War*, and his insistence that the Western states embrace *collective security*. He was a bitter and vocal critic of *Neville Chamberlain* and *appeasement*, calling the *Munich Conference* a "total and unmitigated defeat." Churchill was finally recalled to the cabinet—after ten years "in the wilderness"—to take charge of the Royal Navy in the early days of the *Battle of the Atlantic*. With Hitler's attack on France and the Low Countries in May 1940, and victory in the *Battle of France*, the nation turned to Churchill and he became prime minister. In this role he fully embraced what he privately believed was his destiny to be a great national leader in wartime, even though he publicly warned the nation: "I have nothing to offer but blood, toil, tears and sweat." His most memorable turn of phrase about the *national character* of the British applied as well to his own: the country's "finest hour" during the *Battle of Britain* was also his. There can be no doubt about the value of Churchill's leadership when Britain stood alone, with its *Commonwealth* and Empire, against Hitler's legions in the summer and fall of 1940, or about his contribution to the survival of civilization itself in keeping alive armed resistance to *Nazism* until the Soviet Union and the United States entered the war, to ensure victory over Hitler.

A life-long anti-Bolshevik, Churchill surprised many with the alacrity with which he greeted the advent of alliance with *Stalin*. In a *Realpolitik* explanation of breathtaking simplicity, he remarked on the night he heard of Operation *Barbarossa*: "If Hitler were to launch an attack on Hell itself, I would contrive to make at least a favorable reference to the Devil in the House of Commons." His role was not so honorable or effective when it came to the loss of *Singapore*, however. Upon hearing the news about *Pearl Harbor*, Churchill rejoiced in private, because he understood that with the addition of America's overwhelming power the *British Empire* would survive to defeat Hitler. He made full use of an exceptionally close personal relationship with *Franklin Roosevelt* to advance his own strategic plans and ideas, including a repeat attempt to confirm his long-held conviction that the Mediterranean was the "soft underbelly of Europe," through which a body blow might be struck at the Nazi empire. By 1943 Churchill was deeply frustrated by the decline of Britain's relative power among the *Big Three*. He realized that his own influence over Allied strategy and policy was fading, just as the opportunity to begin shaping the postwar period began to appear over the horizon of war. He thought he understood better than the genial, but also naïve, American president the nature of Stalin's regime and ambitions—and almost certainly, he did. Churchill accomplished what he could during key conferences at *Cairo*, *Casablanca*, *Tehran*, and *Yalta*. He was unable to persuade Roosevelt or *Eisenhower* to drive straight on to Berlin, in order to deny that great political prize to the Soviets and ensure that Germany fell into the Western *sphere of influence* in the coming confrontation with Stalin, which he foresaw. He was dismissed by the electorate at the moment of triumph in 1945, while at *Potsdam*.

Thereafter, Churchill was most popular and influential in America, where his powerful anti-Soviet voice was important in persuading the public to endorse a tougher policy toward Moscow in the early *Cold War*. That was his second great act of service to humanity and the cause of civilization: to ring the clarion warning about the Soviet Union. On the other hand, Churchill's narrow dedication to imperialism, even after two world wars had changed the geopolitical map of the world forever, led to his major foreign policy failure: an inability to recognize or accept that the British Empire had entered terminal decline and to adjust policy to that reality, especially with regard to India and the far-flung military commitments in the Middle East and Africa necessary to sustain British control of the subcontinent. Nevertheless, Churchill was reelected prime minister, 1951–1955. In 1953 he was awarded the *Nobel Prize* for Literature. His personal motto: "In war: resolution. In defeat:

defiance. In victory: magnanimity. In peace: goodwill." *See also Atlantic Charter; balance of terror; Bamboo Curtain; Declaration on Liberated Europe; Dodecanese; Dresden; El Alamein; English Channel; Halifax; Iron Curtain; Munich Conference; national interest; nuclear weapons; Round Table Conference; Russia; second front; unconditional surrender; Warsaw Rising.*

Suggested Readings: Winston S. Churchill, *The Second World War*, 6 Vols. (1953); Martin Gilbert, *Winston Churchill* (1991).

CIA. *See Central Intelligence Agency.*

Ciano, Galeazzo (1903–1944). Son-in-law to *Benito Mussolini* from 1930; Italian minister of *propaganda*, 1935; foreign minister, 1936–1943. Early on, he opposed the *Axis* alliance with Germany, even trying to block the *Pact of Steel*. He helped keep Italy neutral through 1939 and into 1940, but massive German victories proved just too tempting to his father-in-law, who attacked France in mid-1940 so as not to "miss the bus" on conquest. Once Italy was in the war, however, Ciano—a raw opportunist—actively endorsed an *expansionist* policy for Italy in Africa, *annexation* of Albania, and *aggression* against Greece. His diary recorded growing disillusionment with Mussolini, whom he voted to overthrow in 1943. As things fell apart, he fled, only to be dragged from hiding by more loyal *fascists* and summarily tried and shot. He wrote in his diary, which became a prime source on Italy's role in *World War II*, a self-consciously Roman and self-pitying imperial lament: "Victory finds a hundred fathers, but defeat is an orphan."

cipher. An encoded message. Some diplomatic, most military, and virtually all *intelligence* messages are sent in cipher. A common technique, before invention of unbreakable computer logarithms, was the "one-time pad," or cipher book (pad), specific to a given mission that did not depend on a preset or general (and therefore crackable) master code.

cipher clerk. An *embassy* or *intelligence* officer whose function is to encrypt and decode *ciphers*.

CIS. *See Commonwealth of Independent States.*

Ciscaucasia. The European portion of the *Caucasus*, lying north of the Caucasus Mountain range.

citizen. A native born or *naturalized* person who theoretically has legal rights against, but also duties to, a state. Duties may include military service in time of war. The antonym is *alien*. *See also* jus sanguinis; jus soli; *statelessness*.

citizenship. The legal status of being a citizen (*subject*) of a state, delimiting all rights and obligations of individuals vis-à-vis that state. In modern form it dates to the Italian *Renaissance*; but it evolved significantly as a result of the *Enlightenment* and was universalized and radicalized during the *French Revolution*. *See also Bancroft Conventions; deportation; exile; expatriation*; jus sanguinis; jus soli; *nationality; naturalization; stateless person.*

city-state. A small state that does not extend much beyond the confines of a single city and its supporting, agricultural hinterland. When the *Eastern Zhou* disintegrated, China was divided among a host of such minor states in the *Warring States* period. In ancient Greece (Athens, Corinth, Sparta), Italy, Phoenicia (Carthage, Sidon, Tyre), and throughout Mesopotamia and much of the ancient Mediterranean world before the *Roman Empire*, city-states were a principal form of political organization. The *Maya* were organized into city-states. In West Africa, the Edo of *Benin*, the *Hausa*, and the *Yoruba* all developed advanced city-state systems. After Rome fell, city-states—and *free cities*—revived in Europe. During the Middle Ages, around the Baltic, *Hansa* cities dominated politics and trade for more than 200 years. In Italy in 1035 Milan became independent, and in 1176 a league of Lombard city-states successfully fended off the forces of Emperor Frederic Barbarossa (c. 1123–1190). City-states were the key political entity in Italy during the *Renaissance*, and others existed in north and central Europe. They remained independent longest in divided, decentralized Germany. Over time, smaller cities were absorbed by large ones, which were then taken over by the *nation-states* that emerged all over Europe after c. 1500. That pattern, of city-states eventually succumbing to some larger, imperial power, was repeated in most places: Macedonia overran the Peloponnese; the *Aztec* and *Inca* conquered the city-states of central Mexico and the Andes, respectively; the king of *Qin*, the victor of the city-state wars, became China's first emperor, and so on. The closest approximation in modern times are *Singapore* and the *Vatican*. *See also city-state system; microstate.*

city-state system. A political subsystem in which the main players are *city-states*, protected by geography, or luck, from outside powers. In classical Greece, Athens and Sparta contended for dominance over less powerful city-states, mostly isolated from the larger conflict of the Persian Empire and Indian *subcontinent*. The *Maya* lived in a complex, war-prone city-state system from the fourth through the ninth centuries C.E. For one hundred years, *Renaissance* Italy was shielded from the great contest between the *Habsburgs* of Spain and their great rival, the *Valois* of France. Hence, Italy hosted a sustained struggle among five main Italian states (*Venice*, Florence, Milan, Naples, and the *Papal States*), the survivors from among, and conquerors of, dozens of smaller cities and towns. The *Machiavellian* intrigues of the peninsula later found resonance in *Great Power* statecraft, carried forth by Italian ambassadors, the first moderns to bear that title and perform that office on a permanent basis. Venice was the greatest of the Italian cities, but no matter: after defeating Spain, French armies poured into the peninsula, ending the era of the Italian city-states but setting off generations of Great Power and sectarian warfare that lasted until the *Peace of Westphalia* in 1648.

civil defense. All measures to protect the civilian population in wartime. Although still feasible in *conventional* conflicts, it is no longer attempted because it is hopeless regarding most nuclear scenarios.

civilian. (1) All nonmilitary aspects of a nation's life and economy. (2) Under the *laws of war* (and in the *just war tradition*), any person not a soldier, who therefore may not be deliberately killed or targeted. *See also collateral damage.*

civilian primacy. The Anglo-American, and also broadly democratic, tradition whereby the military is subordinate to constitutional civilian authority.

civilized states. A classical legal term for states that seek to maintain minimal moral and legal rules and standards based on the core principles of *consent, reciprocity*, and compliance with *international law*, rather than reliance on unilateral force. *See also community of nations; nonintervention; outlaw state; pariah state; Treaty of Paris (1856); world community.*

civilizing mission. *See British Empire;* mission civilisatrice; *mission, sense of; white man's burden.*

civil war. Armed conflict within a single state, usually over control of the apparatus of government or in behalf of a given region's desire to secede to form a new state. Civil wars frequently attract *intervention* by outside powers, which can be decisive to the outcome. *See also rebellion; Taiping Rebellion; and other specific conflicts, by country.*

Cixi (T'su Hsi, 1835–1908). "The Dowager Empress." She was concubine to Emperor Xianfeng (d. 1861), upon whose death she became co-regent with her son, Emperor Tongzhi, who died at age eighteen in 1875, and then maneuvered to have her pregnant daughter-in-law commit suicide while she became regent to her three-year-old nephew, Emperor *Guangxu*. She thus selected and controlled two minor emperors, as well as confining the latter to palace arrest, 1898–1908. She thereby was de facto ruler of China for nearly half a century, possibly even killing her own son to retain full powers. Deeply conservative and *xenophobic*, after the catastrophic defeat of the *First Sino-Japanese War* (1894–1895), she opposed all serious reform, moving to stop the *Hundred Days of Reform* with a *palace coup* and bloody *purge*. She sought to preserve everything traditional in China and personally and bitterly hated foreigners. She wavered over, then openly supported, the *Boxer Rebellion*, finally declaring war on the Western powers, with dire long-term results for the *Qing dynasty*. She was forced to flee Beijing in 1900, having declared war on the foreign powers without gaining support from her own provincial officials and officers, returning only in 1902 with the departure of foreign troops from the *Forbidden City*. She made a half-hearted effort at constitutional reform from 1905. Her high-handed, reactionary rule kept China backward relative to foreign powers, especially Japan, which chose a far different response to the Western threat (see *Meiji Restoration*). Her policies deeply alienated the Qing dynasty from the Chinese people and helped cost it the *mandate of heaven*.

clash of civilizations. In the immediate post–*Cold War* period some scholars suggested that the historic tension between modernizing *secularism* and reactionary *fundamentalism*, along with older religious/cultural divisions among *Confucianism*, *Christianity*, *Islam*, *Hinduism*, and other great religious/cultural traditions, would henceforth dominate world politics through a clash of civilizations that identified the major fault lines of world affairs. Those scholars proposed that, instead of a continuation of the contemporary international state system, the world was evolving toward a community of civilizations in which smaller states would group together for common purposes on a regional, or "civilizational," basis. Crudely and ahistorically conflating Christianity with *Westernization* and *modernization*, and overly impressed by the parochial and still only partial *integration* of European states, they argued that the ebb tide of Christianization of the non-European world, which attended Europe's twentieth century retreat from empire, meant that the dominance of Western ideas and organizational principles in world affairs had also ended. Indeed, in the extreme they argued that to profess belief in universal ideas with roots in the history of the West (*human rights*, *sovereignty*, political liberty, market economics) was simultaneously false, immoral, and dangerous.

Even if all that were true to some degree, the claims of this "theory" remained specious and shallow. Fundamentally, "civilizational" divisions in the modern world are at best of secondary, or even tertiary, importance as compared with ethnic, national, and territorial (state) divisions when it comes to *causation* in matters of war, peace, and international intercourse. Moreover, major religious faiths and the civilizations they historically underpinned are not just deeply divided from each other. They are also much less internally cohesive than often thought, are subject to frequent and debilitating *schism* the more widespread they become, and—in their political and social aspects—remain on the defensive against an intense assault, especially in deeply traditional societies, by the cumulative effects of mass literacy, mass communications, modern consumerism, *globalization*, and other secular forces to which states appear to adapt more readily. Finally, in the political and even in the economic realm, nations and states still command far more intense and violent loyalties than civilizations, continue to identify and organize most collective interests, and still define most conflicts. "Civilizational" differences are thus highly unlikely to lead directly to global conflict. Despite several decades of Cassandra-like warnings from social scientists about the looming demise of the state system, states look to remain the dominant international players for a very long time. *See also end of history.*

Suggested Readings: Samuel P. Huntington, *The Clash of Civilizations and the Remaking of World Order* (1996); Salim Rashid, ed., *The Clash of Civilizations? Asian Responses* (1997).

class. (1) A social group sharing certain attributes, attitudes, and usually also economic interests, as in landowning class, entrepreneurial class, or working classes. (2) In *Marxism*, a group identified by its relationship to prevailing *modes of production*, such as the *bourgeoisie* or *proletariat*. (3) In media parlance and much sociology, the various strata into which people divide according to their level of income, education, occupation, or some other eclectic criteria.

classical. (1) Any idea or thing that has stood the tests of time and circumstance. (2) Previously widely accepted.

classical school (of economic liberalism). These influential theorists argued that the best economic and governmental systems are those that are the least intrusive into private lives and the private sphere. They anticipated that a "*harmony of interests*" would result that was beneficial to the public good as a natural by-product of the pursuit of enlightened self-interest by individuals. For discussion of their core doctrines *see free trade; gold standard;* laissez-faire; *mercantilism; neomercantilism; reform liberalism; Adam Smith.*

Suggested Readings: A. W. Coats, *The Classical Economists and Economic Policy* (1971); D. P. O'Brien, *The Classical Economists* (1975).

classical school (of international relations). A distinct body of thinking and literature about international relations *theory*, rooted in the works of *Grotius* and *Kant*, but incorporating as well the insights and historical-philosophical approach of twentieth century *realism* and *liberal internationalism*, which it does not see as in essential conflict. The classical school is methodologically traditional. It is dismissive and even contemptuous, therefore, of what it sees as the crude *scientism* of positivist social science and theories of *structural realism* and *rational choice theory*. It is similarly dismissive, for different reasons, of the moral *relativism*, ahistoricism, and penchant for "scholarly activism" over scholarship of deconstructionism, *critical theory*, and *postmodernism*. A recent variant, sometimes called the "English School," originated in the London School of Economics, Oxford, and other English universities during the 1960s and later, but was contributed to importantly by several non-British writers. It contrasted sharply and consciously with the crude *positivism* that dominated American social science after c. 1960. Among its most important thinkers were Martin Wight, R. J. Vincent, Hedley Bull, James Mayall, and Robert H. Jackson. The central shared concept of these thinkers is that, in contrast to crude *neorealist* abstractions such as the notion of international *anarchy* or the *security dilemma*, there in fact exists a rudimentary *international society* (or at least an *anarchical society*) in which normative considerations and rules of self-restraint play an essential role, and raw power does not rule every day or on every question. *See also community of nations; international law; international organization; world community; world governance.*

Suggested Readings: Hedley Bull, *The Anarchical Society* (1975); Hedley Bull, *International Theory* (1996); Robert Jackson, *The Global Covenant* (2000); Martin Wight, *Power Politics* (1946).

classified information. Knowledge deemed key to *national security* and therefore kept hidden by a government under its prevailing system of secret classification. Even among the top ranks of officialdom, in all states, access to information is restricted by degrees of classification. *See also archive.*

class struggle. In *Marxism*, the (putatively) mortal struggle carried on between antagonistic social classes for control of the *means of production*, which must culminate in the triumphal establishment of *communism* (the final *mode of production*) by the *proletariat*.

Clausewitz, Karl Maria von (1780–1831). Prussian military theorist. He joined the Prussian Army in 1792 at the age of twelve and saw combat in the *Rhineland*. He spent three years in military school in Berlin, 1801–1804, graduating first in his class. Serving as a junior officer, he was captured by the French at *Jena-Aüerstädt* in 1806 and was a *prisoner of war* (though under conditions of honorable self-confinement, rather than in a French prison camp) for nearly a year. Upon his release he rose to hold a position on the *General Staff*. From 1807 to 1811 he helped modernize and reconstruct the badly defeated Prussian Army. He then resigned his commission in protest over Prussian political subservience to *Napoleon I* and offered instead to serve Tsar *Alexander I*. He traveled—but was denied commission—with the Prussian Army during the campaign of 1813. After Napoleon abdicated in 1814, Clausewitz was reaccepted into the army as chief of staff to one of *Gebhard von Blücher's* corp commanders (he also served as chief of staff to *von Gneisenau*) and saw action during the *Hundred Days*. He served with the Prussian army of occupation in the *Rhineland*, 1815–1817, before returning to teach at the War College in Berlin in 1918.

The next year Clausewitz started work on his famous treatise, the single greatest work on *war* yet written: "Vom Kriege" (On War). His clear thinking influenced all subsequent work on the topic and launched what later became the subfield of strategic studies. Clausewitz sought to systematically understand armed conflict and its relation to politics, rather than to limit war, as had been the case in the *just war tradition*, or purport to teach how to wage war more effectively in the field. His exceptional concentration on the underlying nature of war partly spoke to his experience of defeat at the hands of Revolutionary France, whose superior morale and mass organization had clearly advantaged it over Prussia. In this regard, his approach differed greatly from the *scientistic* pose and pretensions of his Swiss contemporary, *Jomini*, whose theories of war often were little more than abstract peons to the Napoleonic style of "l'audace" and direct observation of the effectiveness of *combined arms* by his heroes, *Frederick the Great* and *Napoleon*. Clausewitz also attempted to reduce the understanding of war to its bare essentials in theory, but he never forgot how complex it was in fact. He argued that war consists of three elements (his famous trinity), none of which were overtly normative: violence associated with popular passions; chance and probability, which affect command decisions; and a rational effort to achieve political goals. The third point was key: it unified his view of war by lending it rational purpose. It was, however, heavily qualified by the second, which recognized the importance of creative, intuitive individuality in command and of unpredictable circumstance (the *fog of war*). In that he departed from *Machiavelli*, who also had a rationalist view of war, though nowhere near the extreme rationalism of Jomini. Moreover, Clausewitz appreciated that war was deeply affected by externalities, including the nature of the states and societies waging it and the more general historical circumstances of each epoch. Again, this departed from the scientism of Jomini (or later, of *Mahan*), who wrote about timeless principles of war and disregarded the *revolution in military affairs* that marked his own Age.

On the other hand, not even Clausewitz foresaw the astonishing rational futility of future conflicts such as *World War I*, in which *trench warfare* was shaped more by the physical means available with which it was therefore waged, than by any clear political purposes toward which it was ostensibly intended. Some later writers, notably the great Capt. Basil Liddell-Hart, attributed the bloody-mindedness of many World War I generals to Clausewitz's influence, especially his tactical emphasis on the "big battle" as always preferable in war to a series of small encounters. Clausewitz's most important contribution was, nonetheless, to convincingly demonstrate that war is part of a continuum of social and political conflict, that it is fundamentally an extension of prior political struggle by alternate (violent) methods, rather than an utter break with peacetime politics among nations. "War," he famously wrote, "is not merely a political act, but also a political instrument, a continuation of political relations, a carrying out of the same by other means." He put the point more directly in an explanatory note: "war is nothing but the continuation of policy with other means." Following from that key insight, and despite his central search for general strategic principles, he noted that war as actually practiced is heavily influenced by nonmilitary factors such as *national morale*, the political goals of elites, and the internal character of the societies engaged. From this, he argued for civilian primacy, to best maintain the political (rational) focus that was the central purpose of making war, and by extension also to determine the means and scope of violence to be employed and the objectives that made such violence purposeful. He also systematically laid out several central concepts of all subsequent war studies, including the notions of *friction*, the idea of *total war* ("absolute war"), and "armed observation" (*wars of observation*). He died in 1831, ingloriously, from cholera. *See also Helmuth von Moltke; new military history; Schlieffen Plan.*

Suggested Readings: Raymond Aron, *Clausewitz: Philosopher of War* (1985); Stephen J. Cimbala, *Clausewitz and Chaos: Friction in War and Military Policy* (2000); Karl von Clausewitz, *On War* (1818); Michael Howard, *Clausewitz* (1983); Peter Paret, ed., *The Makers of Modern Strategy* (1986).

clausula rebus sic stantibus. A legal doctrine that a *treaty* remains binding only so long as no vital changes occur to conditions that all parties had assumed when signing it. The claim that such changes have occurred may be genuine or invoked to cover a desire to discard a treaty commitment for other reasons. *See also Helmuth von Moltke;* pacta sunt servanda; *validity.*

Clay, Lucius D. (1898–1978). Clay was an engineer by training and an administrator rather than combat soldier by inclination and talent. During *World War II* he was in charge of the massive procurement program that kept the U.S. war effort going and fed *Lend-Lease* aid to Britain, the *Soviet Union*, and other allies. His most public role came as military governor in Germany, 1945–1949. He worked consistently but unsuccessfully for German unity. Getting along well personally with Soviet military counterparts, he found it difficult to understand why his superiors could not achieve the same easy relations with *Stalin.* Yet, once the irrevocable break came he adjusted masterfully. He was in charge in western Germany during the most tense days of *occupation* and the *Berlin airlift,* which he both inspired and oversaw. As military governor he had virtually unlimited powers (he once reportedly joked to his secretary, "take a law"). Under his stern but not unkind guidance, Germans laid the basis for the later renaissance of *West Germany* into a prosperous *capitalist* democracy. On that project he worked closely with *Konrad Adenauer.* Clay retired from the army after 1949. He played *éminence grise* to *Eisenhower,* 1952–1961. Clay was a nonpartisan and trusted professional, so *Kennedy* turned to him in the wake of the *Berlin Wall crisis* and sent him as his personal representative in Berlin, 1961–1962.

Suggested Readings: Lucius D. Clay, *Decision in Germany* (1950); Jean Smith, *Lucius D. Clay* (1990).

clean bomb. A *nuclear weapon* with minimal *radiation effects. See also dirty weapon; neutron bomb.*

Clemenceau, Georges (1841–1929). French premier, 1906–1909, 1917–1920. His caustic tongue and penchant for dueling earned him the sobriquet "The Tiger." He opposed *colonialism* as a fatal distraction from the need to recover *Alsace-Lorraine* for France. His political fortunes waxed and waned over several decades. The *Dreyfus Affair* returned him to national stature after a period in the political wilderness. His rough, strike-busting tactics as premier alienated workers and undercut his parliamentary support. Yet, the nation turned to him to reverse a turn toward *defeatism* in 1917, when *mutiny* swept the trenches, *victory* seemed unattainable, and *defeat* was a real possibility. Something of a *Jacobin* in temperament, he used heavy-handed methods, as usual. He executed traitors, spies (such as Mata Hari), and some mutineers. When asked his policy, he said: "Home policy? I make war! Foreign policy? I make war! All the time, I make war!" In fact, he quietly accepted that the French Army was incapable of launching any new offensive until bolstered in 1918 by the arrival of fresh American troops. His major influence came at the *Paris Peace Conference*, where he was often *Woodrow Wilson's* foil and always his personal bête noir. He worked for a punitive peace, pressing for separation of the *Rhineland* from Germany and high *reparations*, an issue on which he was essentially tricked and betrayed by *Lloyd George*. Like *Churchill*, he wanted Allied intervention in the *Russian Civil War*, but he could not convince Wilson of the need. Despite his stern performance at Paris, the French public judged him too soft on Germany, and he was ousted in 1920. *John Maynard Keynes* said of Clemenceau: "He had one illusion, France; and one disillusion, Mankind, including Frenchmen." *See also* cordon sanitaire; *Fourteen Points.*

Suggested Readings: Georges Clemenceau, *Grandeur and Misery of Victory* (1930); David Watson, *Clemenceau* (1974).

Cleveland, Grover (1837–1908). *Democratic* president of the United States, 1884–1888, 1892–1896. In a quiet foreign policy era, he opposed a rising tide of *imperialist* sentiment in the United States, as in refusing to annex *Hawaii.* Yet, he also invoked the *Monroe Doctrine* against Britain when it disputed a *boundary* between *British Guiana* and *Venezuela.* London was astonished at this pugnacious twist in what had been improving relations since the end of the *American Civil War.* Britain conceded, restoring good relations.

client state. A smaller power beholding to a larger power for aid, military supplies, or diplomatic support. It gives diplomatic support in return; for example, the many small states *Napoleon* at first set up in north Italy and the *Rhineland*, Cuba's relations with the Soviet Union after 1958, or *South Vietnam*'s with the United States. *See also satellite state.*

Clifford, Clark (1906–1998). Washington lawyer and political insider. He was one of the so-called *Wise Men* who made up the Washington establishment and advised successive U.S. presidents. He was personally approached for advice on various issues of domestic and foreign policy by Presidents *Truman, Kennedy, Johnson* and *Carter*. He started as a naval aide to Truman, then became special council to the president. From that position he wrote much of the legislation supporting the *European Recovery Program* and establishment of the *CIA*, helped to articulate the *Truman Doctrine*, and was involved in setting up *NATO*. He opposed *George Marshall* on the issue of *recognition* of Israel, persuading Truman to an early decision. He succeeded *McNamara* as secretary of defense in 1968. After a full review of Vietnam policy, he helped change the course of the *Vietnam War* by convincing Johnson to end troop escalation, denying *Westmoreland's* request for more troops to "finish the job" after the victory over the *Viet Cong* during and shortly after the *Tet Offensive*. Clifford later helped stop the bombing campaign and brought in the other Wise Men to counsel Johnson to end the war. In 1992 his reputation suffered from suggestions he was implicated in an international bank scandal. In 1998 he settled with the Federal Reserve Board for $5 million, and other charges were set aside due to his failing health.

Suggested Readings: Clark Clifford, *Council to the President* (1991); Walter Isaacson and Evan Thomas, *The Wise Men: Six Friends and the World They Made* (1986).

climate. An underlying factor affecting national *power*, such as by limiting *food* supply, but about which nothing can be done on a national basis. Some suggest climate as the main reason why most *Great Powers* historically were temperate-zone countries, with more extreme locales of either heat and cold limited in the development of civilization and technology and less conducive to diversified agriculture. In the late twentieth century, *global warming*, perhaps due to atmospheric pollution and in any case with potential adverse effects on agricultural production and on delta states such as Egypt, became a topic of *multilateral* negotiation. A toothless but nonetheless much-ballyhooed convention on climate was agreed to at the *United Nations Conference on the Environment and Development*.

Clinton, William Jefferson, né Blythe (b. 1946). *Democratic* president of the United States, 1993–2001. As the first president of the post–*Cold War* period took office, the question that concerned serious people was: would he aid transition to a more orderly and democratic world order or delay it through neglect? Clinton was a compulsive adventurer and risk-taker; even close political allies admitted that he was habitually mendacious in both private and public affairs. Senator Bob Kerry (D-Neb.) called him "an unusually good liar." Clinton's presidency was sustained—and saved—by an economic boom that began months before he took office and tailed off just as he departed. This expansion was driven by new technologies, the *peace dividend*, deregulation, and expanding international markets. The economy was further helped by budget deals Clinton made with congressional Republicans, who captured the House of Representatives in 1994, for the first time in 40 years. He was thus compelled to balance the federal budget. He also made solid appointments to the Federal Reserve and Treasury. Clinton was uncomfortable with foreign policy and ignored it throughout his first term. He turned to it only after failing to achieve a significant domestic legislative record. Even before the debacle of impeachment, his administration—among the most corrupt in American history—was marked by intense and prolonged financial and political scandals, some rooted in his earlier activities while governor of Arkansas, others related to new actions while president, or to actions of his wife, several cabinet officers, or political operatives. The cumulative effect was serious erosion of his governing authority and real damage to the powers and prestige of the presidency.

A cautious pragmatist, with an eye always on the electoral ramifications of any position, he established no clear or consistent foreign policy except in *free trade*, an issue on which he genuinely led both his party and the country forward. Enervating scandal was exacerbated by three other broad characteristics: (1) lack of strategic vision, resulting in inconstant foreign policy purpose and resort to mere rhetorical flourishes and photo opportunity interventions; (2) poll-driven stands, taken without real daring or leadership, that squandered years of opportunity to reform the rules and institutions of *world governance* in a *liberal-internationalist* direction; (3) excessive and ill-considered threats of force that were not carried out, which led to further transgressions by the threatened parties that eventually required a major U.S. military commitment. Specifically, Clinton cut U.S. *NATO* forces in Europe to 100,000 and cut defense spending, including for *SDI*. At the *Earth Summit* and on Angola he took new positions. In finalizing *NAFTA* and the *Uruguay Round* of the *General Agreement on Tariffs and Trade* and agreeing to China's membership in the *World Trade Organization*, he advanced the long-standing free trade agenda of the United States. His intervention in peace negotiations in Northern Ireland had mixed results; his efforts in the Middle East were tardy, ineffectual, and possibly counterproductive. In 1994 Clinton ended a 20–year trade *embargo* against Vietnam, but left in place a more politically risky—but no less irrational—embargo against Cuba. In the 1992 campaign he had criticized *George H. Bush* for being "soft" on *human rights* abuses in China; in office he approved sales of missile and other *dual use technology* to Beijing and visited *Tiananmen Square*. He gave North Korea aid and technical (including nuclear) assistance tied to foregoing nuclear *proliferation*, but failed to obtain effective *verification* agreements or prevent destabilizing missile tests. Therefore, at the end of his term, he belatedly resumed funding of research on *ballistic missile defense*.

Clinton typically spoke of *multilateralism* more as an end than a means of diplomacy. This allowed him to cite United Nations or NATO reluctance as cover for his own inaction toward war in Bosnia until 1995. When *genocide* began in Rwanda he was singularly responsible for premature withdrawal of

UN forces already in-country and for blocking authorization of *armed humanitarian intervention*. That sprang from his experience of Somalia, where American lives were lost after he expanded the original mission inherited from Bush. Neither of those moral and political disasters, nor the later collapse of Congo into anarchy and a regional war, prevented his later touring the continent and speciously proclaiming that an "African Renaissance" was underway. That had no relation to reality, but played well electorally in Harlem, which was the sole point. Despite the multilateral rhetoric, he showed a penchant for unilateralism, including a casual and even feckless use of force, especially if *air power* could be detached from casualties on the ground. Most serious foreign problems were left to slip from attention until they reached crisis point. Clinton would then issue ultimata and threats of force. In Iraq, Bosnia, and Kosovo, he was eventually compelled to carry out his threats, using force more often and against more countries than any peacetime president since the pre–*World War I* years of *Woodrow Wilson*. Over eight years he regularly bombed Iraq, but still allowed it to unilaterally end weapons inspections and recommence its search for *weapons of mass destruction*. He committed naval forces to *blockades* of, or deployed ground and/or air forces to Serbia, Haiti, and Iraq, and sent *cruise missiles* into Iraq, Serbia, Sudan (where they destroyed the country's only pharmaceutical plant), and Afghanistan, ostensibly as the first strikes in a war against *al Qaeda* terrorism that saw no follow through action. This irresolute use of force raised false expectations of the utility of air power even as it eroded America's reputation for resolve and the effectiveness of its *coercive diplomacy*. The culmination of this ad hoc style was Kosovo, where failed diplomacy led to a cautious bombing campaign that permitted Serbia to *rape* and kill, then *ethnically cleanse* hundreds of thousands of Kosovars. This was followed by an open-ended American and international occupation—to a *protectorate*—that tried to freeze a *status quo ante bellum* no longer acceptable to either side.

If Clinton's foreign policy had overall coherence, and this is doubtful, it was this: a view of the *national interest* that saw a revitalized economy as a prerequisite to diplomatic strength; pragmatic (though sometimes also personal) rather than doctrinal assessment of when to intervene militarily; and a weak effort to replace *containment* of the Soviet Union with a new strategic concept of "enlargement" of the community of democratic, market societies. Clinton's presidency ended in personal and political disgrace: he was impeached by the House in 1998, though acquitted by the Senate. He was later found in contempt by a Federal judge for perjury and obstructing justice. On his penultimate day in office, his license to practice law was suspended and he signed a public admission that he had indeed lied under oath. Corrupt and vulgar to the end, on his final day he issued pardons to political contributors that even close allies thought suspect. "If you act recklessly you will pay a heavy price," Clinton said on December 16, 1998. *See also apology; Armenia-*

Azerbaijan War; Usama bin Laden; Land Mine Treaty; Salman Rushdie; Margaret Thatcher.

Suggested Readings: David Halberstam, *War in a Time of Peace* (2001); Richard Posner, *Affair of State* (1999).

Clive, Robert (1725–1774). English adventurer and empire builder. An employee of the *East India Company* who once failed to commit suicide when his pistol misfired, Clive was the first of the English *nabobs* in India. He was taken prisoner by the French at Madras in 1746. In 1751 he made a daring forced march to capture Arcot from the local *nawab*, whose army was away fighting a rival; he then held Arcot for 50 days against a vastly superior Indian force. With his core of British regulars, more numerous regiments of *sepoys*, and local nawab alliances, he became a dominant power. By 1752, at age 27, he was able to make and unmake hitherto powerful nawabs. After three years in England he was sent back to avenge the *Black Hole of Calcutta*. At Plassey (June 23, 1757), Clive's 800 British regulars and 2,400 sepoys overmatched 50,000 Indian troops (of the nawab of Bengal) and several dozen French gunners. The battle was lost to France by internal betrayal and to superior British discipline and tactics. The victory made the 32-year-old Clive de facto ruler of Bengal and brought him a fabulous personal fortune. In 1760 he returned to England and entered Parliament. He returned to Calcutta, 1765–1767, as governor of Bengal. He left again for England, where he died of opium use and a severe depression that led to a second, but this time successful, suicide effort.

close air support. When aircraft attack in a *tactical* support role, close in to the advance line of friendly troops. *See also interdiction.*

closed economic system. See *collectivization*; COMECON; *five-year plans; market economy; planned economy.*

clothing. See *textiles.*

Club of Rome. A once influential group of economists making analyses and predictions about future world trends and problems. From time to time, it was accused by critics of spreading *neo-Malthusian* fears about *growth.*

coalition. An *alliance* of more than two *states*, made to perform some joint action or fight a specific enemy. Coalitions may be ad hoc and include highly disparate states or they may be *treaty*-based. They may be fragile and temporary or bind states closely against a common and present danger. *See also Anti-Comintern Pact; Axis alliance; Central Powers; CENTO; Gulf coalition; Napoleonic Wars; NATO; SEATO; Triple Entente; United Nations alliance; Warsaw Pact.*

coastal states. Those with ocean coastlines, and hence claims to *territorial sea/ waters* and *Exclusive Economic Zones. See also landlocked states; UNCLOS III.*

co-belligerency. Relations between *combatants* on the same side, but not joined in a formal *alliance*; for example, the United States was an "Associated Power" in *World War I.*

Cochin China. (1) A Western term for Vietnam that may have derived from a Portuguese mispronunciation of a Chinese place name, Giao Chi. (2) A French term for southern Vietnam, governed as a colony within *French Indochina.* It was used after *World War II* partly to perpetuate the French propaganda assertion that there were two distinct Vietnams. Cambodia historically claimed much of the Mekong Delta region of Cochin China, which has a significant Khmer minority. *See also Annam; French-Indochina War; Tonkin.*

codification. Systematic enumeration, in written form, of international rules and/or principles.

Cod Wars. (1) 1750s: An undeclared codfish war was fought between the navies of England and France off the Grand Banks of *Newfoundland.* The contemptuous term was coined by *Frederick the Great*, who thought the stakes not worthy of the costs. (2) 1958–1961: A *fishing* rights dispute between Britain and Iceland, prompted by the latter's then novel claim of a *twelve-mile limit*, led to clashes in which naval vessels of these two *NATO* allies sometimes escorted fishing boats, leading to dangerous maneuvers, warning shots, and the odd ramming-incident. Ultimately, Britain accepted the new limit. (3) 1972–1976: The old dispute broke out again in the 1970s when Iceland asserted first a 50-mile *Exclusive Economic Zone*, then in 1975 extended that claim to 200 miles. It was settled by a compromise that favored Iceland, whose claims later found general favor in *UNCLOS III.* (4) 1995: Canada and Spain threatened to use naval force in a dispute about quotas and regulatory control of cod stocks off the Grand Banks of Newfoundland, with each ordering warships to move (very slowly) toward the area. Before they arrived, a negotiated settlement was reached. (In 1998 a so-called tuna war broke out among Japan, New Zealand, and Australia over quotas of southern bluefin tuna, with the latter countries closing their ports to all Japanese fishing vessels to compel Japan to adhere to a quota agreement.)

coercion. The use or threat of force to obtain another state's compliance with a desired objective.

coercive diplomacy. Intimidation or threat of punishment to force an adversary to undo an action already taken. This term (which is mainly confined to academic usage) is contrasted with *deterrence*, where the threat made is to undertake powerful retaliation for some future action that might be taken by an adversary. Advocates portray coercive diplomacy as defensive, and as distinct from bullying or blackmail. *See also compellence; gunboat diplomacy; Iraq; Kosovo.*

cognitive dissonance. Cognition is the act of knowing as well as the various processes of perception. Cognitive dissonance is a psychological theory about perception that maintains that individuals tend not to believe, accept, or even perceive information that is contrary to their preformed notions of how the world or an opponent operates. Instead, they become cognitively rigid, unconsciously screening out such information or actively reinterpreting it so that it does not contradict their preferred and preexisting beliefs. In this form, the idea has been applied as a model of foreign policy *decision making* by some theorists to suggest that interstate conflicts often are exaggerated because of *misperception*, by one or both sides, of an opponent's intentions and the offensive or defensive meaning of certain actions.

cohabitation. A term coined by the French (who else?) for periods of ideologically mixed or coalition government. *See also National Front; Popular Front.*

Cohong. A Chinese merchant house established as a monopoly in 1720 to act as agent between the *Qing* emperors and western merchants. From 1760 to 1842 they were the sole agents permitted to conduct business or negotiate with westerners, and all western trade was similarly limited to Guangzhou (Canton). This permitted the Qing to maintain the fiction of all foreign trade being part of the *tribute system.* This arrangement ended with the *Treaty of Nanjing* and establishment of the *treaty port system. See also East India Company; Qianlong emperor.*

coimperium. Joint control of a territory by two powers, with neither claiming it as their exclusive, *sovereign* possession. *See also condominium.*

Colbert, Jean-Baptiste (1619–1683). As *Louis XIV*'s key minister, Colbert was to restore France's tattered finances, which he did in part simply by renouncing one-third of the royal debt. He saw commerce as the servant and instrument of state power, in line with *mercantilist* thinking. He sought creation of a vast overseas empire and set up joint-stock companies to compete with the Dutch and English *East India Companies*, along with similar trading houses for the West Indies, Africa, and the Americas. He was among the first to attempt a complete, centralized regulation of industry. In 1664 Colbert set up comprehensive *protective tariff* barriers. He raised these in 1667, leading to Dutch retaliatory tariffs and contributing to the war that broke out in 1672. The revocation of the *Edict of Nantes* and the launching of several new and increasingly protracted wars by Louis XIV came soon after Colbert's death, and undid his fiscal policies by denuding France of many members of its trading class (who were *Huguenots*) and squandering much of its national treasure. On the other hand, the logic of Colbert's policies were to prepare France for war; the fact that war resulted from and then ruined his policies resides in the region of irony, not tragedy. *See also Continental System; physiocrats; Adam Smith.*

cold launch. A launch-safety system that uses an external power supply to eject a missile from its silo before igniting inboard thrusters. *See also hot launch.*

cold war. Intense rivalry and conflict between or among nations that falls just short of active, armed hostilities. It may or may not lead to *war* at some point. Thus, the long cold war between England under *Elizabeth I* and Spain under *Philip II* did end in war, including dispatch of the *Spanish Armada* and an attempted invasion of England in 1588 (and later).

However, the *Great Game* between Russia and the *British Empire* in Central Asia, Tibet, and Persia never led to war, though it might have on several occasions. The modern usage, to refer to the period of protracted American-Soviet conflict, c. 1947–1990, is usually attributed in origin to Bernard Baruch (1870–1965). *See also concert; hot war.*

Cold War (1947–1990). The period in post–*World War II* world affairs marked by deep *ideological*, economic, and political hostility and competition mainly between the United States and the *Soviet Union*, but which drew in as well all other *Great Powers* and numerous smaller powers at various levels of conflict and involvement. During the Cold War, interpretive disputes over its origins and fundamental character were legion. Some saw it as the primary product of Soviet ideology, or of Russian territorial *expansionism* and geopolitical *opportunism* concealed behind the championing of "international *socialism*." Others, notably scholars influenced by the *Wisconsin School*, saw it as the offspring of American *imperialism* and drive for *postwar* economic *hegemony*. Still others saw it as a basic contest of incompatible ideologies and economic and social systems, and thus as much broader and deeper structurally than direct American-Soviet competition. And some viewed it as a fairly traditional clash of Great Power interests set off by a vast disturbance of the *balance of power* caused by the vacuum left by the defeat of Germany and Japan in World War II, further fueled by the perennial dictates of *power politics*, and thus as merely overlain and thinly veiled by ideological differences among the victors. A smaller, and less coherent, group of more theoretical analysts argue it was largely a great misunderstanding, caused by a series of *misperceptions* by each side of the other's real interests and positions, reinforced by a climate of fear arising from an *arms race* produced by what they called the *security dilemma*.

The most persuasive general explanation of the origins of the Cold War remains the simplest, not least because it is the interpretation best borne out by evidence extracted from Soviet and East European archives that became available after the Cold War formally ended with the *Charter of Paris* in 1990. This evidence appears to confirm that the Cold War sprang most directly from the paranoid *authoritarianism* and romantic aggressiveness of Soviet foreign policy, which had deep roots in Russian history, but more immediately in a *Leninist* ideology, which spoke to the entrenched interests of the Soviet *nomenklatura*. This fundamental ideological hostility to the Western powers on the part of the Soviet leadership found particular expression in the character (fears, ambitions, and psychological perversions) of *Joseph Stalin*, in a crude causal mix that first befuddled and then greatly alarmed the United States and Western Europe. Those powers were not without later responsibility for misunderstandings and deliberate exaggerations of the degree of the threat posed to world order by the Soviet Union, but at its beginning they were more rather than less willing to accommodate legitimate Soviet *national security* fears and *reparations* needs. In short, *Communist* ideology was the root cause of the conflict, and *Stalinism* its fullest expression. This argument for a central, Soviet origin of the Cold War seems confirmed—at least to this author—by the fact that, at its end, every state that bordered the Soviet Union had *aligned* against it, either formally or de facto, out of abiding fear of its military capabilities and reckless habits of opportunistic expansion and internal meddling. (A joke common in Russia at the time, noting that even Moscow's own *satellites* and Communist-governed China greatly feared it, put it this way: "the Soviet Union is the only state completely surrounded by hostile Communist powers.") Finally, the late Soviet Union's most articulate and honest leaders, most notably *Eduard Shevardnadze*, both privately and publicly agreed that the foreign policy pursued by the Soviet Union was counterproductive to international peace and security and that its domestic policies had grossly distorted their country's development.

The course of the Cold War began at *Yalta* and *Potsdam* when the Western powers acquiesced in de facto Soviet occupation of Eastern Europe, which they could not prevent in any case, agreeing that Russia had a right to "*friendly states*" astride its western borders. At first the conflict centered on Soviet disregard for certain Yalta accords and an interpretation of others to mean its intent to impose Communist regimes and *satellite states* on Eastern Europe should not be opposed. It was; and this led to sharp conflict over Soviet behavior in Poland and Rumania in 1945, and later its sponsorship of a Communist *coup* in *Czechoslovakia*. However, the heart of the Cold War struggle in Europe always concerned what to do about Germany. Specifically at contest was Germany's place in the balance of power: each side feared that a unified Germany might ally with the other side, or more distantly, that it might be able to maneuver between them and one day rearm and regain its full independence. Issues of forcible *repatriation*, both of *prisoners of war* and civilian refugees, gravely complicated matters as a four-power occupation and administration was imposed on Germany after its surrender on May 8, 1945, while a separate four-power division also took hold in Austria. Arguments about reparations and joint governance (currency union, barter exchanges) broke out immediately, though they were handled reasonably well by *Lucius Clay* and *Georgii Zhukov*. In March 1946, *Winston Churchill* publicly warned that an *"Iron Curtain"* was descending across Europe. This fear appeared fully warranted as the Soviets imposed *Stalinist* regimes wherever the *Red Army* still resided, probed into northern Iran, and backed the Communist side in the Greek Civil War (1947–1949). When the Soviets blockaded *Berlin*, 1948–1949, they forced the Western powers into a massive display of military capability and geopolitical will: the *Berlin airlift*.

As reflected in *George Kennan's* famous *X article* and *Long Telegram*, the *Truman* administration's policy response of *containment*—the unifying theme of American foreign policy for the next four decades—arose from two basic sources: first and primarily, it arose from fear of Soviet opportunistic expansionism into any abutting territories where political instability existed or direct and indirect subversion opened the door to a Communist takeover; but secondly, it arose from the belief that Western Europe and Japan could not recover from World War II economically or politically without massive U.S. aid and provision of security assistance and political stability. That meant it was necessary to oppose Moscow's demands for vast reparations from the occupied zones of Germany, while at the same time pumping *liquidity* into Europe through the *European Recovery Program* (Marshall Plan), as well as into Japan. The outcome, not really intended by either side, was to lock the division of Germany into place by 1949, just as in Asia the division of the Korean peninsula was also locked into place by events, rather than prior intentions. This de facto partition was reinforced by mutually exclusive *recognition* of *West Germany* by the West and *East Germany* by the *Soviet bloc*, then by creation of opposing military alliances (*NATO* in 1949; the *Warsaw Pact* in 1955), into which each half of Germany fit by the mid-1950s.

Meanwhile, the conflict had already spread to other continents. In 1947 *MacArthur* was instructed by Kennan, acting for *George Marshall*, to commence the *reverse course* of deconstruction of the *zaibatsu* and other erstwhile imperial structures in Japan, and instead build up that defeated nation as a bulwark against the Soviets in northeast Asia. The *Truman Doctrine* and, later, and even more so, *NSC-68* universalized America's commitment to anti-Communism just as it appeared that "international communism" was gaining the upper hand outside Europe. The first major episode was the fall of China to the Chinese Communists, under *Mao* and *Zhou Enlai*, and its subsequent radicalization during the *Chinese Revolution* (1949). The impact of that shift in power in Asia was aggravated by Soviet detonation of its first *atomic bomb*, also in 1949, quickly followed by the start of the *Korean Conflict* in early 1950. Those events spurred the rise of *McCarthyism* in the United States.

More importantly, despite a brief thaw after the *secret speech* by *Khrushchev* and partial *destalinization* of the Soviet Union, the Cold War several times nearly went "hot" between the superpowers during successive sharp crises, including: ongoing tension over the *division of Berlin*, peaking with erection of the *Berlin Wall* (1961); two 1950s crises with China over *Quemoy and Matsu*; the *Hungarian Uprising* (1956); the *Cuban Missile Crisis* (1962); and the *Fourth Arab-Israeli War* (1973). Ad hoc events often deflected the Cold War contest into peripheral areas of the Third World, but ideology played a role as well. Under Khrushchev, the Soviet Union embraced *peaceful coexistence* with the West in potential nuclear crises but still supported wars of *national liberation* and generally was *adventurist* in its foreign policy. For its part, the United States repeatedly intervened against local Communists, or just perceived Communists, in its own hemisphere. It fiercely opposed the *Cuban Revolution*, even sponsoring a failed invasion by Cuban exiles at the *Bay of Pigs*.

Under *Kennedy* and *Johnson*, the U.S. containment effort became bogged down in faraway wars against local Indochinese Communists, all of which were of minimal strategic significance, in *Laos* and *Cambodia* indirectly, and in the *Vietnam War* directly, massively, confusedly, and with tragic consequences. With the United States thus preoccupied and overcommitted to a peripheral area, the Soviets paid little to no price for crushing the *Prague Spring* in 1968 with a Warsaw Pact invasion, after which they asserted an international right to intervention in any socialist state (the *Brezhnev Doctrine*). At the end of the 1960s, China, the third major player in the Cold War game, switched sides for the second time. The shift had its roots in the *Sino-Soviet split*, fierce ideological antagonism, competition for leadership of the *Nonaligned Movement*, and long-standing Chinese grievances about Russian territorial claims along their historic northern *frontier*. The actual trigger for Sino-American *rapprochement* was a small Soviet-Chinese border war along the Ussuri River, and a broader Soviet threat to attack China, in 1969. Upon assuming office, also in 1969, *Richard Nixon* moved quickly to negotiate *détente* with Moscow and reestablish formal *diplomatic relations* with China, then deep into the *Cultural Revolution*.

The 1970s were, in retrospect, deeply illusory for both sides. The United States sank into *Watergate* and post-Vietnam malaise, and even a brief neo-*isolationism*, and appeared to many to have lost its will and ability to lead: Nixon resigned; *Ford* was hamstrung from the start; and, although *Carter* was effective on hemispheric or regional issues, such as the *Panama Canal* or the *Camp David Accords*, he was inept on the larger conflict of the Cold War with Moscow. The Soviet Union, on the other hand, looked ascendant—both to itself and to those in the West who still deeply feared and loathed it. It continued a massive buildup of both nuclear and conventional forces, and for the first time it intervened in ongoing wars in Africa, directly with military aid and advisers (*Somalia* and *Ethiopia*), and indirectly with *proxy*

Cuban troops (*Angola* and *Mozambique*). The *Helsinki Accords*, signed in 1975, were already seriously subverting Soviet *legitimacy* from within, a fact of enormous significance that became clear only some years later. And then the Soviet leadership made a disastrous decision: they invaded Afghanistan in late 1979, only to become bogged down in an expensive and bloody Third World War they could not win (the *Afghan-Soviet War*). That reawakened many in the West: American rearmament began in Carter's last year and continued during the first *Reagan* term. Of vital importance, NATO agreed to deployment of new *ballistic missile* systems in Europe, shattering Moscow's hopes that the Western alliance would crack under the strain of antinuclear protests. Meanwhile, *Deng Xiaoping* shook the Maoists from China's back and began an economic restructuring that promised (or threatened, from Moscow's point of view) to lead China past the Soviet Union, something Russians had already watched Germans and Japanese accomplish after c. 1965.

In a real sense, the Cold War had already been won by the United States and other Western powers by the mid-1960s. That was not apparent at the time because the internal inertia of the Soviet Union under *Brezhnev* and several successors delayed final resolution of the underlying political and ideological conflict, from which public and much elite attention was then diverted into noncentral—and essentially apolitical—technical issues of *arms control*. More important, because it was fundamentally subversive of *totalitarianism* and therefore of legitimacy in the Soviet Union, the West renewed emphasis on *human rights* through the Helsinki process as well as bilaterally in the 1970s and 1980s. That issue had been at the heart of the Cold War in the beginning, defining the sides and the stakes, but was set aside by the West during the late-1950s and through the 1960s because of fear that confrontation over such core values was just too dangerous between nuclear-armed adversaries. Now, the failure of the Soviet idea on all fronts—international and domestic, technological and political, moral and economic—was apparent to all, even its own leaders. Therefore, effective *surrender* of the Soviet Union was negotiated by *Gorbachev*, at the behest of Shevardnadze and others, who conceded everything on the central geopolitical issue at stake: not only would Moscow at last permit German reunification, but a unified and democratic Germany would take its place within NATO to play there a leading role as a member of the Western community of nations. That was a fundamental shift in the balance of power that Moscow could no longer prevent by the end of the 1980s, but also one that its system could not long survive.

And so, after the *revolutions of 1989*, which stripped away its outer empire, the Soviet Union itself began to collapse, shedding republics as it did so in a reverse *domino effect*, until it went *extinct* on December 25, 1991. Contrary to politically correct arguments arising from assumptions of *moral equivalence*, in fact the Cold War *was* won, and decisively so on virtually all fronts, by the Western powers. Such a conclusion may not be dismissed as triumphalism, for it was explicitly stated and recognized in the *Charter of Paris* (1990) itself. In that terminal document of the Cold War, NATO and the Warsaw Pact (just months before the latter dismantled itself) accepted a "common security framework" for their future relations based upon unfettered interactions among free ideas, free markets, and free peoples. It is impossible to construct a moral, political, and ideological surrender that could be made more complete. *See also Acheson; Adenauer; Andropov; Bevin; George H. Bush; Carter Doctrine; Castro; CIA; Chernenko; De Gaulle; Dobrynin; double containment; Eisenhower Doctrine; flexible response; France; Germany; Grenada; KGB; liberal-internationalism; linkage; massive retaliation; Nitze; Nixon Doctrine; nuclear weapons; revisionism; Reagan Doctrine; SALT; Schmidt; Sinatra Doctrine; Soviet Union; space race; SPUTNIK; START; Taiwan; Truman Doctrine; two-plus-four talks; United Kingdom; United States; Yeltsin;* and various national leaders and concerned countries.

Suggested Readings: David Armstrong and Erik Goldstein, eds., *The End of the Cold War* (1991); S. J. Ball, *The Cold War* (1998); John Gaddis, *We Now Know* (1997); Akira Iriye, ed., *Origins of the Cold War in Asia* (1977); Melvyn Leffler, *Preponderance of Power* (1992); Hugh Thomas, *Armed Truce* (1986); Vladimir Zubok and Constantine Pleshakov, *Inside the Kremlin's Cold War* (1996).

collaboration. Voluntary cooperation with the officials of an *occupation* power, usually taken as implying sheer opportunism on the part of collaborators. Real, or just accused, collaborators are often subjected to rough justice after *liberation*. *See also fraternize.*

collateral damage. The unintentional destruction of people or property caused by weapons not directly aimed at them, but at nearby targets. In the *just war tradition*, inflicting collateral damage may be permissible under certain constrained circumstances, such as unavoidability as a result of the enemy locating legitimate targets too close to civilians. In actual warfare, this happens all the time. *See also friendly fire.*

collective goods theory. Analysis of payment for and allocation of *public goods* or goods that are jointly provided and from which it is difficult or impossible to screen out noncontributors; internationally, some IR theorists define these as the *balance of power, liquidity,* and so forth. *See also free rider problem.*

collective security. A theory that aims at preservation of peace through shared *deterrence* of *aggression*. It offers an advance guarantee that overwhelming diplomatic opposition, *sanctions,* and ultimately, force will be brought to bear against the aggressor. Its proponents frequently contrast it with the *balance of power.* It was the central *security doctrine* promoted by Woodrow Wilson and embedded in the Covenant of the *League of Nations.* However, that organization never met the key precondition of participation by all the *Great Powers*, suffered from a lack of will among the Western powers, and was faced with several powerful aggressors all at once: Japan (1931), Italy (1935), Germany (1939), and the Soviet Union (1940). The *United Nations Charter* contains modified collective security provisions. *See also Abyssinian War; Bosnia; Gulf War; Korean Conflict; Kosovo.*

collective self-defense. Assistance given by other states to a state acting in self-defense, under *Article 51 of the United Nations Charter*. Note: This should not be confused with *collective security*.

collectivization. Under *communism* and some variants of *socialism*, moving from private to collective (which most often meant state) ownership of property and the *means of production* and compelling the adoption of new social, work, and even living arrangements by all those collectivized. At the extreme, it meant forcible elimination of all private ownership. At the least, it involved heavy government regulation of economic activity, usually including setting of prices and wages. Its most destructive applications came in peasant *agriculture* in the 1930s in the Soviet Union, where it was wedded to *Stalin's* brutal campaign against the *kulaks* and Ukrainian *nationalism*. This exemplar ought to have been enough for the world to learn the cost of forced socialization of agriculture. Instead, this doctrinaire idea again killed many millions in the 1950s in *Mao's* China. Having murdered more than one million landlords in 1949 and 1950, in the mid-1950s the Communist state became the ultimate landlord and exploiter of the Chinese peasantry. Some 26,000 peasant communes were set up, comprising virtually every peasant household in China. The *Communist Party* (CCP) thereby reversed its earlier land reforms—which it no longer needed to retain peasant loyalty, since the *Chinese Civil War* was won—and introduced instead the raw coercive idea of "primitive accumulation," wherein peasants were reduced to a bare subsistence level so that the state could buy the grains grown with their labor and sweat at forced low prices. This also suppressed wages in the cities, where deliberate nonproduction of consumer goods further supported state capital accumulation, which was then plowed into Soviet-style heavy *industrialization* based upon *five-year-plans*. All this left the peasantry at such precarious margins of subsistence that, when the disaster of the *Great Leap Forward* set in, some 25 million starved to death. And yet, the idea killed by the million again in the 1970s in Cambodia under the *Khmers Rouges*. In the 1980s, in *Marxist* Ethiopia, it brought terror and ruin to the countryside in support of a truly vicious and narrow regime. All told, the idea of socialized agriculture led to tens of millions of thoughtless, futile deaths in collectivization campaigns—conducted by callous and driven ideologues—all of which were later abandoned as failures. Lesser efforts took place under non-Communist, but still socialist, governments, with lesser harm but still extensive coercion, as in Tanzania in the 1960s and 1970s. Some killing occurred there too, but nowhere near the levels of the campaigns in China, Russia, or Ethiopia. All of these societies ultimately retreated from the abysmal failure of collectivized agriculture, but at varying rates. In China, partial decollectivization took place after 1979. In Russia, *Yeltsin* ordered the collectives broken up starting in 1991, an effort supported by aid from the *International Finance Corporation*. *See also expropriation; individualism; liquidation; nationalization; privatize.*

Suggested Reading: Robert Conquest, *Harvest of Sorrow* (1986).

Collins, Michael (1890–1922). "The Big Fella." Irish nationalist and *guerrilla* leader. Collins first fought in the *Easter Rising*, a failed uprising that nonetheless was critically important in modern Irish history. Arrested along with other *Irish Republican Brotherhood* fighters, he was briefly imprisoned. He was elected as a *Sinn Féin* member of parliament in 1918, joining those who formed the *Dáil* (Irish Parliament) in Dublin rather than taking their seats in Westminster. He was commander-in-chief of the *Irish Republican Army* (IRA) throughout the *Irish War of Independence* (1918–1921), during which he used terror tactics to provoke British counterterror, which in turn rallied nationalist opinion behind the IRA. He penetrated British Intelligence's headquarters in Dublin Castle, and his "twelve apostles" executed numerous British agents and Irish informers. Along with Arthur Griffith (1872–1922), in 1921 Collins undertook the thankless task of negotiating the *Anglo-Irish Treaty*, which partitioned Ireland between a rump *Ulster* and the *Irish Free State*. Collins understood that the IRA was buckling and that control of the 26 southern counties of the Free State was all that nationalists could reasonably expect to obtain at that time. He defended the treaty against IRA irreconcilables, winning a *referendum* in its favor but failing to convince a minority of his old comrades-in-arms. He headed the Free State Army in the *Irish Civil War*. He was killed in a country ambush in August 1922. His funeral occasioned a spectacular demonstration of devotion and respect, including on the part of some former enemies. *See also Eamon de Valera.*

Suggested Reading: James Mackay, *Michael Collins: A Life* (1996).

Colombia. In pre-Columbian times this region contained only small states, such as Tairona, Cenu, and Chibcha, along with many more local Indian tribes. A Spanish expedition to coastal Colombia in 1509 led to years of fierce Indian resistance. In 1519 Panama was founded by the *conquistadores*. From that base, the vast territory of Colombia, or *New Granada* (comprising the modern states of Colombia, Ecuador, Panama, and Venezuela) was conquered by Spain in the 1530s. An *audiencia* was established there in 1547. It was ruled nominally by the Spanish Monarchy for 300 years, though *Creoles* soon emerged as a local ruling class that did not always share Imperial Spain's views or implement its policies. A peasant rebellion was put down from 1780 to 1783. On June 14, 1810, a rebellion began in Cartagena, spread to Bogotá by July 20th, and led to deposition of the *viceroy*. Colombia gained actual independence in August 1819 after the Battle of Boyacá and as part of the wave of successful Latin American rebellions and wars of independence against Spain, 1810–1825. At first, Colombia was part of *Simón Bolívar's* dream of a much larger state of *Gran Colombia*. Ecuador and Venezuela broke away in 1829–1830, however, forming separate states. Colombia—then still incorporating modern Panama—from 1830 to 1886 changed its name to the Republic of New Granada. With some U.S. connivance, but largely on its own accord, Panama broke away from Colombia in 1903.

Sometimes numbered among Latin America's more successful democracies, Colombia actually suffered long periods of violent upheaval and civil conflict. The worst episode was from 1948 to 1958, when the carnage was so great (as many as 200,000 died) that the period is simply remembered as "la violencia." The chaos ended in military government and a power-sharing arrangement (*national front*) between the dominant Liberal and Conservative parties, which in turn were dominated by an oligarchy of leading families. In 1964 a Communist guerrilla movement, FARC, was founded; the next year, a pro-Cuban group, the ELN, began jungle operations. From the 1970s Colombia also contended with *drug cartels* and *narco-terrorists*, whose huge profits corrupted the legal and political system, distorted the normal economy, and led to formation of private armies. In 1989 the drug baron Pablo Escobar, head of the so-called Medellín cartel, ordered the assassination of a presidential candidate and launched a terror bombing campaign to intimidate the judiciary and country into abandoning its anti-cocaine policies. Caesar Trujillo, who also opposed the drug cartels, was elected anyway. In 1993 his government hunted down and killed Escobar. In 1994 Colombia signed a *free trade* agreement with Mexico and Venezuela. Oil production reached significant levels beginning in 1995, but overall development was retarded by escalating violence as right-wing *paramilitaries* began a new assault on drug-financed cadres of the two main, left-wing insurgencies, the ELN and FARC. Intermittent peace negotiations began in 1998. Although FARC received an effectively autonomous zone from which the government withdrew, Colombia increased cooperation with the U.S. military to combat the guerrillas and the cocaine trade. At the end of the twentieth century, Colombia remained a deeply divided society, with enormous differences among living standards and social and economic opportunities open to its varied social classes, as well as between its urban elite and depressed and immiserated rural population.

Suggested Readings: Jesús María Henao and Gerardo Arrubla, *History of Colombia*, 2 vols. (1938; trans. 1972); Anthony McFarlane, *Colombia Before Independence* (1993).

Colombo Plan. A model for early foreign aid, focusing on the Pacific region, first developed by the *Commonwealth* in 1950. Japan, the United States, and other states joined later. Japan later became the major donor.

colonialism. Extending one's *sovereign* authority over new *territory*, by conquest if populated, or by settlement if not. Colonialism by European states was the most extensive and recent in history, but should be seen as another example of *imperialism*, a general historical and political phenomenon that has involved nearly all peoples on all populated continents in every recorded epoch. Indeed, it was a key feature of state-creation all over the world and, arguably, in many places also of the spread of higher civilization—as in intermittent Chinese expansion into, and governance of, *Inner Asia*—though this was largely unintended, in its initial phases at least, and was nearly always a bloody and brutal affair attended by mass injustice and suffering. All that said, it is largely the most recent, overseas, European colonialism that dominates modern academic imagination and political memory, especially in those exploitative aspects that were indeed pervasive and profound, notably during the era of the *slave trade* in Africa and the *encomienda* forced labor system in Latin America. This tendency to speak only to the negative results of colonialism was reinforced by *Third World* and other political opposition to continuing colonialism by some European states that prevailed in the *United Nations General Assembly*, c. 1955–1975. Thereafter, with the collapse of the Portuguese Empire, the issue faded into habitual rhetoric as most colonies (outside the *Soviet bloc*) were independent, though echoes may still be heard in demands for political and historical *apologies* and for *reparations*. However, history is more complex than the political needs of a given regime or *caucus group* and of a particular historical moment, and thus more needs to be said. For while the practice of colonialism is most often and loudly—and sometimes also accurately—blamed for *underdevelopment* of former colonies, it must in fairness also be said that colonialism had long-term positive and integrative effects as well. Sometimes these were the result of deliberate policies. At other times they were simply structural, flowing unintentionally from the administrative needs of a distant monarch or metropolitan government, and often from a base desire to centralize economic exploitation.

Whatever the motivation, whether exploitative, missionary, paternalistic, or in latter days also *liberal*, colonialism in fact had the following positive effects: (1) It helped diffuse new technologies globally, including the very military technologies that helped some colonized peoples seize back their independence in the twentieth century. (2) It promoted centralization and rationalization of national authorities (state-creation) in hitherto near-anarchic areas, such as much of Central Africa and the interior of South America, which had hosted stateless peoples. (3) In many regions having first aggravated *slavery* by attaching it to overseas markets, it later set out to, and in fact did, end even older systems of indigenous *slavery*, along with heinous local practices such as *sati* or human sacrifice; of course, in other areas the absence of preexisting systems of wage labor led colonial administrations to rely on forced and tribute labor for decades. (4) In Latin America for more than 300 years, and in its later phase in parts of Africa during much of the twentieth century, colonialism provided previously and endemically war-torn regions with internal order and peace essential to economic development and began the process of integrating these regions with world markets, including building ports, roads, railways, and other *infrastructure*. (5) Some late colonial administrations genuinely looked to expand local self-government; others unwittingly imparted modern ideas of *self-determination* and representative government to new populations, or at least to local *elites*. (6) Colonialism began the process, albeit seldom equitably, of transformation of subsistence economies to modern agricultural production and at least partial industrial development. This was very much a mixed blessing, as it produced many economic losers and in some areas also *famine* among dislocated subsistence farmers. Yet, it is hard to make a serious argument that in the longer term whole populations are better off living perpetually with the threat of famine, which was the natural condition of subsistence farming for thousands of years. (7) After its initial horrific decimations caused by *disease* and conquest, colonialism improved average life-spans globally by transplanting key food crops (maize, cocoa, and cassava to Africa, the potato to Europe, among others) and draft and other domesticated animals (horse and oxen to the Americas, where few draft animals were in use), which sustained expanded population growth for whole continents and over several centuries. (8) In some colonies, latter-day colonialism initiated primary education and expanded literacy, which again diffused liberal ideas and ideals to new populations and led to evermore insistent demands for independence. (9) Colonialism helped bring access to modern medical benefits to hundreds of millions of people. Of course, much of that might have been achieved by different, more peaceful, more just, and less murderous and coercive means. *See also Asia for Asians; Bandung Conference; Berlin Conference; Black Legend; British Empire; concessionaire companies; Eastern Question; East India Company; Indian Wars; indigenous peoples; mandate system; manifest destiny;* mission civilisatrice; *mission, sense of; Mongols; neocolonialism; scramble for Africa; Siberia; tribe;* territorium nullius; *trusteeship system; unequal treaties;* uti possidetis; *white man's burden.*

Suggested Reading: L. H. Grann and Peter Duignan, eds., *Colonialism in Africa*, 5 vols. (1969–1975).

colons. French (and other white) settlers in France's overseas *colonies* or possessions. The most famous and troublesome were the one million who settled in Algeria; Morocco received some 200,000; and other colonies, proportionately fewer. The colons often settled on land that had been forcibly expropriated from the local population, and although they enjoyed full political representation in Paris, the native population did not. Many were fierce about holding onto overseas empire because they came from very poor European backgrounds—almost half the colons in Algeria in the 1880s were from Spain, southern Italy, or Malta; most of the rest were poor French—and nothing to return to should a local nationalist movement win its *war of national liberation*. *See also Algerian War of Independence*; Organization de l'armée secrèt.

colony. (1) A group of settlers in a detached territory who are subjects of a distant, parent state. (2) Any territory ruled by a distant power, whether owing to *conquest* or *settlement*.

Columbus, Christopher (1451–1506). Cristóbal Colón, or Cristoforo Colombo. Genoese explorer. He was at sea from age fourteen. Once shipwrecked, he survived by clinging to *flotsam* until he reached Portuguese shores. He stayed in Portugal to marry and to sail with Portuguese fleets. In 1477 he made his first significant voyage of discovery, sailing as far west as Iceland. He sailed to Cape Verde and along coastal West Africa in 1482–1483. He applied to the kings of Portugal, France, and England to sponsor a voyage of exploration for a westward route to India and Cathay (China), but was refused. After seven years of supplication, and only after the fall of *Granada* to Castilian armies to close out the *Reconquista* in January 1492, he finally found a royal patron: *Isabella* of Castile. Contrary to legend, the faculty of the University of Salamanca did not argue with him that the world was flat. Instead, they disagreed with his assessment of the width of the Atlantic Ocean, saying it was much farther across than Columbus believed; they were right, and he was lucky. In August 1492, he sailed with three small ships (the slow Santa Maria and two fast *caravels*, the Pinta and Niña) and just 120 crew. He discovered the *New World* on October 12th (to his death he believed he had reached the coast of Asia), most likely landing at Watling's Island in the Bahamas. He next discovered (from Europe's point-of-view) Cuba and *Hispaniola*. He returned to Spain in March 1493, having lost the Santa Maria on a West Indian reef. He sailed again that fall with 1,200 men and 20 ships, on a deeply troubled second voyage. Convinced he was an instrument of divine will, a conceit that the religious coincidence of his name reinforced, upon his arrival he introduced Indian *slavery* and launched the *encomienda system*. He returned to Spain in 1496, sick and dejected, having proven a disastrous colonial governor. His third trip lasted from 1498 to 1500, during which he mapped the northern coastline of South America. He offended the new royal governor (partly by being a non-Spaniard) and was sent home in leg irons, along with his brother. He was restored to favor by Isabella and made a final voyage from 1502 to 1504, charting the Gulf Coast of Mexico. *See also Age of Exploration; Americas; Hernando Cortés; Henry "the Navigator."*

Suggested Readings: Miles H. Davidson, *Columbus Then and Now* (1997); Felipe Fernández-Armesto, *Columbus* (1991); Martin Lunenfeld, *1492: Discovery, Invasion, Encounter* (1991); William Phillips and Carla Rahn, *The Worlds of Christopher Columbus* (1992).

combatant. (1) A state (or other identifiable political group or *belligerent*) at *war*; not a *neutral* party. (2) In *international law* and in the *just war tradition*, persons enlisted for or actively engaged in warfare, as distinct from *civilians*.

combat area. That part of the *high seas* designated by a *belligerent* as forbidden to *neutrals* under the law of *blockade*.

combat fatigue. *See battle fatigue.*

combined arms. Maneuvering and utilization of all the major elements of armed force on a battlefield (traditionally, this meant *cavalry*, *infantry* and *artillery*, but since the early twentieth century it has included *air power*) in combination, rather than severally, to maximize firepower and provide offensive shock. *See also* Blitzkrieg; C³I; *Clausewitz*; *Jomini*; *Gustavus Adolphus*; levée en masse; *Napoleonic warfare*; *trench warfare*.

"comfort women." "Ianpu." During *World War II*, hundreds of thousands of Korean women; many thousands more from the Philippines, Vietnam, and China; and some Dutch, British, and Australian women as well were forced into Japanese Army brothels. There, they were sexually enslaved and repeatedly raped by Japanese troops. Thousands died or committed suicide under conditions of brutal mistreatment and sustained physical and emotional duress. After the war, Japanese acknowledgment of the plight of former comfort women was begrudging at best. Lack of a full and formal *apology* and of appropriate *restitution* harmed Japan's reputation in Asia for decades. *See also crimes against humanity; rape; white slavery.*

Comintern. *See Internationals, Third (Communist).*

comity of nations (*courteoisie*). Practices of reciprocal courtesy among nations, such as not publishing each other's *diplomatic correspondence*, formally signaling respect when warships under different *flags* pass on the *high seas*, and adhering to accepted *protocol* when dealing with an *ambassador* or receiving a visit by a foreign *head of state* or *head of government*. These practices have no binding character: violations may be seen as an *unfriendly act*, but are not a *casus belli* and will not sustain claims for *damages*.

command economy. A synonym is *planned economy*. (1) Emergency regulations in wartime, whereby the government institutes *rationing* of consumption and heavily intervenes in the economy in order to steer production toward meeting wartime needs. (2) A peacetime, national economy in which key decisions about production and distribution of *goods and services* are made by centralized government authorities, the major *factors of production* are in state hands, and most economic activity is heavily regulated. The underlying idea is that state planners can be more rational and fair than markets. However, the record of planners and command economies, as in the *Soviet bloc* or China under *Mao*, was most unimpressive. The large bureaucracies they generated tended to gross inefficiency, *labor* was underutilized even as it was coerced via state *terror* or simply conscripted and forced, resources were wasted on a massive scale, wages and rural income were artificially suppressed in order to extract *surplus value*, environmental damage was more extensive than under any other economic system to date, and the *standard of living* even of the elite classes was unenviable and noncompetitive by world standards. Only a handful of command economies (Cuba, North Korea, Vietnam) staggered out of the 1990s essentially unreformed. The rest had either totally collapsed (Soviet bloc) or had a major face-lift in an effort to save *face* for the Communist Party (China). *See also capitalism; five-year plans; Great Leap Forward; market economy.*

commando. A military unit trained to conduct lightning raids, such as against coastal installations or *terrorist* camps. *See also Dieppe raid; Entebbe raid.*

command responsibility. (1) The practical obligation of officers for the disposition, discipline, protection, and use of troops and weapons in war. (2) The moral and legal obligation of officers to ensure that troops under their command perform their tasks while engaged in warfare according to humanitarian principles and the *laws of war*. *See also superior orders; Yamashita Tomoyuki.*

commerce. The interchange of *goods and services*. This is distinct from manufacturing industry. *See also depressions, world; Age of Exploration; GATT; mercantilism; Adam Smith; trade; trade routes; World Trade Organization.*

commerce raiding. *See Alabama claims; Battle of the Atlantic; buccaneers; cruiser warfare; pirates; privateers; submarines; war crimes.*

commercial treaty. A treaty governing *trade*, usually intended to lower mutual *tariff* and other barriers to freer exchange of *goods and services*. *See also free trade; General Agreement on Tariffs and Trade; World Trade Organization.*

commissioned officer. One holding command by virtue of a commission (a certificate of royal, presidential, or other formal state authority).

Committee of Permanent Representatives (COREPER). A committee of the *European Council*. Once it emerged from the *Luxembourg Compromise*, most major decisions, proposals, and initiatives on *integration* in the *European Community/European Union* came from this committee.

Committee of Public Safety (1793–1795). The revolutionary government of France that under *Danton* and *Robespierre* instituted *The Terror*, executed the king (and queen and thousands of nobles and citizens), and declared war not just on the states of Europe but against its several crowns and the principle of monarchy itself. It was overthrown by *Thermidor*, which led to the *Directory*.

Committee on Disarmament (CD). An international *arms control* body that comprises acknowledged *nuclear states* as well as several dozen interested, non-nuclear states. It meets in Geneva to discuss issues of *proliferation* and *nonproliferation*.

commodity. Any *goods* available for *trade* or sale. *See also factor endowments.*

commodity agreement. *See International Commodity Agreement (ICA).*

Common Agricultural Policy (CAP). Agreed upon by the *EEC* in 1968 as a *protectionist* system for farmers, for years its heavy *subsidies* stimulated overproduction and harmed consumers with its exaggerated prices, as it absorbed up to two-thirds of the *European Union* budget. Reforms were introduced in 1992, and the CAP was again modified by the *Uruguay Round* of GATT. However, as late as 2001 it still accounted for 46 percent of the EU budget, still overcharged Europe's consumers, and still blocked most Third World and other producer access to the huge EU market.

common heritage principle. By analogy to the *feudal* practice of common grazing lands, this is the idea that certain resources should fall outside the *domain* of *sovereignty* and thus belong instead to humanity as a whole. The idea has application to *multilateral* approaches to global problems, such as marine pollution or *global warming*. It has been put forward assertively by *LDCs* as a vehicle for claims for *distributive justice* and greater economic aid. *See also Antarctic Treaty; Exclusive Economic Zone; landlocked states; Moon Treaty; New International Economic Order; Outer Space Treaty;* res communis; *Seabed Treaty; UNCLOS III.*

common market. This goes beyond a *customs union*, but not as far as pooled economic *sovereignty*, in that, besides internal *free trade* and common external *tariffs*, it seeks to harmonize financial policy.

Commonwealth. An association of most of the former territories of the *British Empire*. The British monarch is its titular head. *Heads of state* or *government* meet once per year. Its finance ministers also meet, and it maintains a *secretariat* in London. The evolution from empire to commonwealth began with the *British North America Act* (1867) and subsequent acts, especially the *Stat-*

ute of *Westminster* and the latter *India Acts*, which devolved power from the British Privy Council to local governments in the *dominions*. The process was completed after *World War II*, with Britain's slow but sure withdrawal from overseas empire. The Commonwealth divided badly over *apartheid* (South Africa withdrew, 1961–1994).

Because it makes decisions by consensus, in the 1960s the Commonwealth nearly split again over the question of *sanctions* against Rhodesia over *UDI*. In 1976 it was granted separate *observer status* by the United Nations General Assembly. In 2000 it had more than 50 *sovereign* members, as well as several small *dependencies*, *protectorates*, and *associated states*.

Commonwealth of Independent States (CIS). Headquartered in Minsk, Belarus, it tried to replace some functions of the *Soviet Union* upon that state's *extinction* in 1991, with 11 of the 15 former Soviet republics joining the CIS. Those abstaining were the *Baltic States* and Georgia. The CIS sought to coordinate policy, in particular on currency and trade, via *heads of government* meetings. By 1994 six members signed defense *pacts* with Russia (the Central Asian states plus Armenia), not all entirely voluntarily. It was crisis-riven from the start: Moldova threatened to leave over Russian aid to *secessionists*; Georgia made a desperate offer to join only because it wanted to stave off Russian aid to rebels in its secessionist province of *Abkhazia*; the dispute between Armenia and Azerbaijan over *Nagorno-Karabakh* erupted into open war; Russia savagely pounded *Chechnya* in two wars in the latter 1990s; and Russian *agents provocateur* and armed forces continued to operate on the national territory of several members with or without permission. *See also near abroad; Newly Independent States.*

commonwealth status. The constitutional association of a *microstate* with a former colonial or *trusteeship* power. There is internal *autonomy* but little or no control of foreign policy and direct inclusion in the larger economy. *See also free association; Marianas Islands.*

communal conflict. A struggle for power (or rights) between ethnic or religious communities within a single society or state. The struggle may remain peaceful and political or may turn gruesomely violent (as in India during the partition, or in Rwanda and Burundi, or in Ulster, Cyprus, Spain, or Indonesia), but does not arise to the level of armed combat known as *civil war* (as it did in Sri Lanka).

Communauté Financière Africaine (CFA). "African Financial Community." Founded in 1948, it connects France to its former African colonies by linking a common currency (the CFA franc) to the French franc. The rate was unchanging at 50:1 from 1948 to 1994, when the CFA was devalued by 50 percent. *Devaluation* was a response to *International Monetary Fund* (IMF) and *International Bank for Reconstruction and Development* pressure, and economies floundering under overpriced exports. In exchange for the devaluation, France wrote off all bilateral debt from the 14 countries in the CFA zone, and the IMF extended new credit lines.

Commune. *See Paris Commune.*

communism. (1) A nineteenth-century theory of moral and social organization that argued for collective ownership of the *means of production*, an ultimately classless society, and a more rational and, it was hoped, equitable redistribution of goods, services, power, and wealth in industrial societies. (2) Actual, twentieth-century systems of social and political organization in which all productive property was seized by exceptionally centralized, *totalitarian* states and enjoyed and run (usually into the ground) in the name of the *proletariat* by highly privileged, ideological, and managerial elites. (3) Whatever a ruling *Communist Party* said it was at any given point in time to suit its own shifting elite and tactical interests. Among more pithy definitions are these: In 1920 *Lenin*, glibly and unintentionally exposing the truth of #3 above, said: "Communism equals Soviet power ["vlast"] plus electrification of the whole country." He meant that a certain level of modernization under the guiding hand of the *Bolsheviks*, the *vanguard* party of *Marxist-Leninist* theory and practice, was in and of itself sufficient for communism to come into existence. Until the late 1980s that slogan was emblazoned in huge neon letters across the Moscow River. In later decades, as it became increasingly difficult to reconcile Russia's dingy historical experience and material realities with *Marxism's* sparkling theoretical elegance, Soviet leaders amended Lenin's claim to say only that they were working toward communism. Under *Brezhnev*, as Western states clearly pulled far in front of the Soviet Union in material development and the general contentedness of most of their citizenry, the claim was made that the Soviet Union had achieved "real socialism," in contradistinction to the *Social Democracy* practiced in much of Western Europe. The Soviets did not take down the neon sign, however, or remove the relics of their Bolshevik saint, Lenin, from his Red Square mausoleum. Adlai Stevenson hit the more general mark: "Communism is the corruption of a dream of justice."

Before the *Bolshevik Revolution* and establishment of the *Comintern*, little daily distinction was made, by anyone, between *democratic socialism* and communism. The switch in nomenclature was demanded by Lenin to distance his ruthless vanguard party of dedicated revolutionaries from (i) orthodox *Marxists*, in particular the *Mensheviks*, who were loyally awaiting the turn of history to bring first the *bourgeoisie* and only then the proletariat to power; and (ii) democratic socialists in the West, such as *Bernstein* and *Jaurès*, who supported trade unionism over revolutionary action and believed parliamentary and other democratic participation was a viable path to reform and ultimate political power for workers. As an ideal and an *ideology*, communism promised everything. In practice, it mostly delivered personal and political repression, mass suffering, social chaos, mass starvation, state-sanctioned sadistic cruelty, a perpetual siege mentality, xenophobia, war, economic backwardness, and vast spiritual and moral destitution.

During the twentieth century, Communist states conducted permanent class warfare among the peoples they ruled, deployed an exterminationist ideology that eliminated whole social categories in the name of defending the revolution, and by their external *subversion* caused grave and permanent tension with non-Communist societies on their borders. Suppression of even the most basic *human rights* by Communist regimes was unmatched, except by *fascist* states, with which Communist societies had much in common. Between 85 million and 100 million people, mostly peasants, died as victims of various Communist regimes, from *forced labor*, firing squads, *secret police* brutality and *torture*, *summary execution*, class extermination campaigns, and several deliberately engineered *famines* and others that developed as a consequence of ill-conceived efforts to *collectivize* peasant agriculture. Ultimately, most Communist regimes reduced to criminal gangs ruling vast exploitative, even slave, enterprises on the scale of nation-states and empires. *See also Albania; anarchism; Angola; Berlin Wall; Bolshevism; Leonid Brezhnev; Cambodia; Cambodian genocide; Fidel Castro; Nicolae Ceauşescu; China; Chinese Civil War; Chinese Revolution (1949); Cold War; counterrevolution; Cuba; Cuban Revolution; cultural revolution; Deng Xiaoping; dictatorship of the proletariat; East Germany; end of history; Engels; Ethiopia; Eurocommunism; fascism; five-year plans; Mikhail Gorbachev; Great Leap Forward; Guinea; GULAG; Hoxha; individualism; International(s); KGB; Khmers Rouges; Nikita Khrushchev; Kim Il Sung; Laos; Leninism; liberalism; Maoism; Mao Zedong; Karl Marx; Mozambique; North Korea; PKI; Poland; purges; Red Terror; Rumania; show trials; Solidarity; soviet; Soviet Union; Stalin; state capitalism; Tito; Leon Trotsky; Trotskyism; Vietnam; Vietnam War; Warsaw Pact; World War II; Yemen; Yezhovshchina; Yugoslavia.*

Suggested Readings: Stéphane Courtois et al., *Black Book of Communism* (1997, 1999); François Furet, *The Passing of an Illusion* (1999); Karl Marx and Friedrich Engels, *The Communist Manifesto* (1848); Adam Ulam, *The Communists* (1992).

Communist Information Bureau (COMINFORM). It was established by nine European *Communist parties* ostensibly to coordinate information and policy, but really to permit *Stalin* to extend his political influence into Western Europe. It lasted from 1947 to 1956.

Communist Manifesto. A long, impassioned pamphlet written by *Karl Marx* and *Friedrich Engels* in 1848, sparked by the upheavals of that year and exhorting Europe's *proletariat* ("workers of the world") to unite and overthrow the *ancien régime*. It was no more than a statement of general principles and aspirations, intended as a call to arms. Marx's major analytical work, "Das Kapital," was not published for several decades more. Even so, many of the *Communist Manifesto*'s phrases and ideas resonated in the history of class conflict in later decades, however false or oversimplified they eventually proved. Among the most famous words to echo ironically through sterile and soul-crushing factory towns, brutal *five-year plans*, forced *collectivization*, and the sprawling *Gulags* of Marxist regimes in too many nations, were these: "A specter is haunting Europe—the specter of *communism*. . . . The history of all hitherto existing society is the history of *class struggle*. . . . The theory of the Communists may be summed up in the single sentence: Abolition of private property. . . . The ruling ideas of each age have ever been the ideas of its ruling class. . . . The workers have nothing to lose but their chains. They have a world to win. Workers of the world, unite!"

Communist parties. Those advocating theories of *communism*, and especially of *Marxism-Leninism*, but including variants, such as *Maoism*, that reflect the ideology of specific leaders. The term was not widely used until after the *Bolsheviks* split from the Russian *Social Democratic Party* (SPD) and the *Comintern* was founded.

(1) Communist Party of China (CCP): It was founded in 1920–1921, aided by Soviet advisers working through the Comintern. It thus split with Chinese *anarchists* and *democratic socialists* to follow the *Bolshevik* (Leninist) path of secrecy, conspiracy, and class warfare. At first it cooperated with the *Guomindang*, but mainly in order to infiltrate it. In 1922, the CCP had only about 200 members in China, with a few dozen more overseas. It was forcibly split from the Nationalists in 1927 after the *Shanghai massacre* of its urban *cadres* and supporters. It was marginal until it dropped its ideological concentration on the *proletariat* in favor of the Chinese peasantry and land reform. It fought the *Sino-Japanese War* (1937–1945) and then resumed the *Chinese Civil War*. That effort made the Party: it expanded from perhaps 40,000 in 1937 to more than 800,000 by 1940 and 1.2 million by the end of the war. With victory over the Nationalists, it took power in 1949 and proceeded to implement the goals of the leadership of the *Chinese Revolution* of 1949. It had three million members by 1947, about 4.5 in 1949, some six million by 1953, and nearly 13 million by 1957, or four times the size of the *People's Liberation Army*. That was a good size at which to initiate a *purge*, or so the leadership seemed to think. The CCP initially carried out historic land reforms, at the price of the slaughter of about one million landlords and "rich peasants" from 1949 to 1954. Then it reversed individual peasant gains through *collectivization* of all *agriculture*. It also subsequently was responsible for the disastrous *Great Leap Forward* and for unleashing the murderous devastation and cultural destructiveness of the *Great Proletarian Cultural Revolution*. After 1978 the CCP moved briskly toward market economics ("socialism with Chinese character-

istics"), but continued to repress all political dissent. *See also cultural revolution; Deng Xiaoping; five-year plans; Jiangxi Soviet; Mao Zedong; one-party state; opium trade; population; Shanghai massacres; totalitarianism; Wang Jingwei; Zhou Enlai; Zhu De.*

(2) Communist Party of the Soviet Union (CPSU): The ruling party from 1920 to 1991, though the name was changed to CPSU only in 1952. It conducted forced *collectivization*, *purges*, and *five-year plans*, led the country through *World War II*, and waged the *Cold War*. It also created an extraordinary legacy in Russia of unrequited anger, entrepreneurial lethargy and backwardness, and deepened national and ethnic divisions. It was left without an empire to rule with the *extinction* of the Soviet Union. Some of its most prominent surviving members were charged with crimes—economic, political, and humanitarian—but few were convicted. It was banned for a short time in Russia in 1993 and in several other former Soviet republics. Its cohorts continued to wield considerable power within the bureaucracy and in outlying regions, and by 2000, Communists were again a significant political force in Russia. *See also Andropov; anti-Semitism; Beria; Brezhnev; Central Committee; CHEKA; Chernenko; cultural revolution; democratic centralism; Dzerzhinsky; Gorbachev; GULAG; Katyn massacre; KGB; Khrushchev; Lenin; Molotov; Nazi-Soviet Pact; NKVD; nomenklatura; OGPU; Politburo; totalitarianism; Trotsky; Stalin; Zhukov.*

(3) German Communist Party (KPD): It was the largest and most important Communist Party outside the Soviet Union until crushed by *Hitler* after the *Nazi* seizure of power in 1933. It aided in its own defeat by adopting Moscow's *party line* that the Nazis were not true revolutionaries (which they were), but simply part of the ruling *bourgeoisie*. Based upon that mistaken ideological prejudice, Red Commando *paramilitary* units actually collaborated with Nazi *brownshirts* in violent attacks upon German *democratic socialists* in the SPD. It was a fatal strategic error repeated all across Europe during the 1930s, worsening among fanatic believers in Moscow's leadership with the stunning announcement of the *Nazi-Soviet Pact*, though ending for others on the same day, and for the same reason. In France, slavish Communist devotion to the party line contributed to an overall national attitude of *defeatism*, though this was reversed when Hitler attacked the Soviet Union and sent Europe's Communists, too, to his *death camps*, and others into the *resistance*. *See also East Germany; Erich Honecker; Spartacists.*

(4) Other: After 1945, Communist parties (though not all used that name formally) were put into power by the Soviet Union's occupying forces in Bulgaria, Czechoslovakia, East Germany, Hungary, Mongolia, Poland, and Rumania. Communists came to power more or less independently of Moscow in Albania, Angola, Cambodia, China, Cuba, Ethiopia, Laos, Mozambique, Vietnam, Yemen, and Yugoslavia. Communist parties were large and highly influential for decades in France, Italy, India, Indonesia (before 1965), and

Spain (before the *Spanish Civil War*). *See also Eurocommunism; fellow traveler; Partai Kommunis Indonesia (PKI); Pathet Lao; Spartacists; Viêt Minh.*

Communist Revolution, China (1949). *See Chinese Revolution (1949).*

Communist Revolution, Russia (1917). *See Russian Revolution, November (October), 1917.*

community of nations. In *international law* the community of nations, also known as *civilized states*, is comprised of those states that accept binding legal obligations with each other. It is generally taken to have originated with the *Peace of Westphalia* (1648), but for 200 years applied only to the "Christian states" of Europe and then the Americas (the United States and the Latin *republics*).

The formal admission of the *Ottoman Empire*, in the *Treaty of Paris* (1856), was a turning point. It was followed by quick expansion to the *Balkans* and Asia (China, Japan, Persia, and Siam). By the end of *World War I* the term was taken to include all fully *sovereign* states. After *World War II* another rapid expansion occurred, with admission of the new states born of *decolonization*. A similar augmentation took place from 1989 to 1993, with admission of a wave of *successor states* from the breakup of *Czechoslovakia, Yugoslavia,* and the *Soviet Union.* Membership in the community of nations requires *recognition* by existing members of the *international personality* of a new applicant (state). By the end of the twentieth century the community of nations included all fully independent and recognized states, all *unions*, and all *neutralized states.* With important qualifications, it also included divided states where sovereignty had been in dispute, such as North and South Vietnam, and East Germany and West Germany before German unification in 1990, or remain in dispute, such as North and South Korea. Cyprus and Taiwan were special cases of disputed sovereignty, although in the case of Cyprus only one state (Turkey) challenged its claim to the whole island. With respect to Taiwan, the vast majority of states recognized it *de facto* but not *de jure*, leaving it in a legal limbo all its own. The community of nations also included, with minor qualifications, the *Vatican* and various *microstates* that, despite their size and arguable lack of real viability, were recognized as members. Entities not considered members of the community of nations, though still with rights and duties under international law, included: *associated states, condominiums, trusteeship territories,* unrecognized *belligerents, international organizations* (not even those with a degree of *international personality,* such as, preeminently, the United Nations), or *tribes. See also* jus cogens; *state obligations; world community.*

Comoros. This island nation was ruled by independent Muslim *sultans* before being made a French *protectorate* in the late nineteenth century. One island,

Mayotte, is predominantly Catholic. A *referendum* in 1976 confirmed its preference to stay attached to France rather than the Muslim Comoros, which declared independence in 1975. A leftist clique ruled from 1975 to 1978, when it was deposed in a *coup* that had support from France. A *mercenary* regime took control briefly in 1989, but was overthrown by direct French military intervention. In December 2001, the smallest of its three islands (Moheli) was attacked by a small force of white mercenaries. After a brief fire fight, five of the invaders were killed and the rest were driven off.

compact. A binding contract between or among nations. A synonym for *treaty*.

comparative advantage. In "Principles of Political Economy" (1819), David Ricardo (1772–1823) argued that an economy most benefits from trade where it has a relative advantage in the *efficiency* with which it produces a service or goods. Ricardo advised specialization in such areas to maximize one's comparative advantage. It would enhance the benefits to all trading partners, he added, if they exchanged goods from which each enjoyed a comparative advantage. This theory is the underlying assumption of *free trade*: each country in a pure free trade system will use its comparative advantages to provide goods for which it is the most efficient producer. Countries with plentiful, cheap *labor* will focus on labor-intensive goods, whereas high technology economies will maximize that advantage, and so on. Of course, in practice even free trade nations seek to protect those sectors where the comparative advantage of others threatens domestic production, job creation, and perhaps a government's political base. *See also competitive advantage; import substitution; mercantilism; neoliberalism.*

compellence. The use of threat, intimidation, and ultimately force to compel an adversary to do, or undo, something. It is little more than social science *jargon*, born of a fetishism for typology, which tries to incorporate notions of *coercive diplomacy* with cruder ideas of bullying and blackmail.

compensation. (1) In *diplomacy*: Territorial, financial, or other inducements given by one state to another to gain acquiescence in an act of *aggrandizement* or to maintain the *balance of power*, as in *partitions of Poland* and at the *Congress of Vienna*. It arose from the essentially dynastic nature of early modern wars: in a system where the principle of *legitimacy* was dynastic succession, territory was the personal property of the *sovereign* and might be exchanged without regard for the wishes of its population, expressed or implied. When to that principle was added the dictates of the balance of power, in which a gain for one was seen as a loss for another, compensation was essential if war was to be avoided every time a minor ruler died childless or some sickly son or incapable brother inherited and proved inept or unstable. (2) In *interna-*

tional law: Funds paid by *belligerents* to *neutrals* under the right of *angary,* for property that has been *requisitioned* for wartime use. (3) In *economics:* Monies paid to a firm (foreign or domestic) whose assets have been *nationalized. See also damages; expropriation; indemnity; reparations.*

compensatory financing. Stop-gap loans or grants to *LDCs* made on highly advantageous terms to compensate for shortfalls in export earnings that result from "acts of God" (nature), such as floods or drought, or from a global recession. The *International Monetary Fund* began a scheme in 1963. COM-PEX and STABEX are run by the *European Union.*

competitive advantage. The idea that global market forces and new technologies mean that the classical measures of *comparative advantage* (e.g., *labor* costs or skills) are no longer adequate. Instead, it is recommended that nations develop grand strategies (national industrial plans) to develop competitive superiority in selected industries. Some critics of the idea argue that pragmatism and overall adjustment to market forces are more important than preset, market-distorting national strategies.

competitiveness. A measure of the *efficiency* of an enterprise or national economy when compared with its competitors. This measure looks at overall national economic performance, such as levels of productivity, *standards of living,* and *export-import* ratios.

COMPEX. A *compensatory financing* scheme set up under the *European Community* and maintained by the *European Union* for those *LDCs* not party to the *Lomé Conventions.* It operates like *STABEX,* but is smaller.

complex interdependence. Political science *jargon* for a situation in which countries have multiple networks of contacts and a wide range of transactions, including government and private economic exchanges and all types of social and cultural activity. Under these conditions, such as exist between Canada and the United States or among members of the *European Union,* each society is highly *sensitive* to events and policies in the other country. Therefore, it is said that *power* must be measured differently than in "normal" international relations: *low politics* not *high politics* will tend to dominate, small is not the same as weak, and the crude *realist* idea that force ultimately decides political outcomes does not apply. That may all be true, but the term itself is merely pretentious social science jargon to describe the obvious. *See also theory.*

composite international person. Any political entity comprised of more than one *state,* such as a regional *federation* or a *union of sovereign states. See also European Union.*

331

composite state. *See union of sovereign states.*

compradors. (1) In China: Hereditary merchant families chosen by the emperors to act as agents in trade and other dealings with westerners. They proliferated in and around the *treaty ports* and formed the nucleus of a rising Chinese bourgeoisie by the late nineteenth century. Their potential to help China modernize was cut short by *warlordism, civil war,* and the *Chinese Revolutions* of 1911 and 1949. (2) In *dependency theory:* Any elite in the *periphery* that owes its privileges and even its derivative social manners to cooperation with *capitalist* elites in the *core,* which it helps to more thoroughly exploit local resources and labor. They are depicted in dependency theory and other variants of *Marxist* analysis as a social product of the *world capitalist system. See also Cohong system.*

comprehensive security. (1) An OSCE doctrine holding that threats to security may arise from a multitude of sources. (2) A doctrine developed in the 1980s suggesting that Japan's security required a regional presence via cultural, diplomatic, and economic initiatives, but with military activity still restricted to defense of the *home islands. See also Kuranari Doctrine.*

Comprehensive Test Ban (CTB) Treaty. A proposal to extend provisions of the *Partial Test Ban Treaty* to underground testing. It aimed to snuff out *vertical proliferation* in *nuclear weapons.* It was opposed by the *George H. Bush* administration, but championed by the *Clinton* administration. In 1999 the U.S. Senate rejected the Comprehensive Test Ban Treaty, in a major foreign policy rebuff to President Clinton.

compromis. Agreement to submit a *dispute* to *arbitration,* which sets terms and conditions of the resolution process and appoints the arbitration court, often on an ad hoc basis.

Comte, Auguste (1798–1857). *See positivism.*

compulsory jurisdiction. A misleading but widely used term referring to the *Optional Clause of the Statute of the International Court of Justice* (Article 36), granting advance jurisdiction without requiring specific agreement. It applies only in cases where both states have accepted the clause. Some states later retracted their prior *consent.* In short, giving the court compulsory jurisdiction is actually voluntary. *See also limited jurisdiction.*

compulsory rules. Those applying irrespective of formal *consent. See also* jus cogens.

concentration camp. (1) In general: A detention center used to concentrate a civilian population under military control. Its purpose is to deny political and material support to *guerrillas* by forcibly depopulating the territory in which they operate, and from which they draw sustenance, recruits (or *conscripts*), and *intelligence*. The *Qing* used such camps to isolate rebels during the *White Lotus Rebellion*. Concentration camps were used by the Spanish in Cuba in the 1860s, and again in the 1890s. *Kitchener* coined the modern term, employing forced concentrations of civilians to break *Afrikaner* resistance during the *Second Boer War*. They were subsequently used by most armies fighting guerrillas or *partisans*, including the Italians in Libya after 1922. Indeed, the barbed wire (a late nineteenth century invention of American cattle ranchers) and guard towers typical of such camps became a visual metaphor for the multiple horrors and moral collapse of the twentieth century. (2) Under the *Nazis*: Political concentration camps were set up by the Nazi Party immediately upon taking power in Germany in 1933; within a year, almost 100,000 Germans (mainly socialists or Communists) were imprisoned in makeshift camps. By 1936 these camps had been expanded to house the many victims of a growing *police state*. A special category of Nazi concentration camp, the *death camp*, was set up during *World War II* to exploit *slave labor* and exterminate Jews, *Roma*, people with disabilities, homosexuals, and others disdained by *Hitler* and his henchmen. *See also Armenian genocide; Auschwitz; Bernadotte; Dachau; ethnic cleansing; final solution to the Jewish problem; Gestapo; Holocaust; SS; Ustaše.*

concert. (1) A common plan or accord among several *states*. (2) Harmony among states. *See also Cold War.*

Concert of Europe (1815–1853). The informal system of consultation set up by the *Great Powers* (Austria, Britain, France, Prussia, and Russia) to manage the *balance of power* at the end of the *Congress system*. It confirmed their *condominium* over the smaller powers on matters of international significance, but helped keep the peace for decades. Most historians date it from the *Congress of Vienna* in 1815, though some prefer 1822, when Britain pulled out of the Congress system. It ended with the breakdown of Great Power consensus in the *Crimean War*. Twentieth-century *realists* admired its high level of Great Power cooperation and unconcern with *ideology*. Most liberals found its abjuring of principled abstractions morally repugnant and thought it also practically dangerous. Insofar as it worked, and other factors besides the Concert prevented war during this period, such as generational and financial exhaustion of the Great Powers, it did so because all Great Powers accepted the principle of the balance of power as a defensive and mutually agreeable arrangement. They also agreed that any gain by one of their number must be by consensus and be accompanied by *compensation* to the rest. Sometimes this compensation was had at the expense of hapless smaller powers, caught between the driving hammer of one Great Power's ambition and the anvil of another's resistance. More often, it was had outside Europe, in the form of colonial swaps and/or *de jure* acceptance of each others' *de facto* territorial conquests. *See also Holy Alliance; Quadruple Alliance; Quintuple Alliance.*

concessionaire companies. Colonial companies given concessions of monopoly economic and territorial rights, first in central and southern Africa, later in West Africa, in return for building *infrastructure* such as railways or ports or sponsoring *cash crop* development. They frequently employed *forced labor* and were responsible for awful atrocities on the rubber plantations of King Leopold's *Congo*. Several deployed private armies and conducted punitive raids and outright wars with precolonial African states. *See also Cecil Rhodes.*

concession area. *See concession diplomacy.*

concession diplomacy. The enforced extraction of territorial and legal concessions from China after the *First Sino-Japanese War* (1894–1895), the *Treaty of Shimonoseki*, and the *Triple Intervention*. In 1898 France extracted concessions in south China, Germany acquired *Shandong*, Russia took the *Liaodong peninsula*, and Britain added *Kowloon* to *Hong Kong*. This slicing off of pieces of China helped provoke the *Boxer Rebellion*. *See also extraterritoriality; opium trade; spheres of influence.*

conciliation. When a commission makes nonbinding recommendations on settling a *dispute*, restores communication, or restarts face-to-face negotiation. It may or may not go on to offer *mediation*.

concordat. A treaty between any state and the *Vatican* (previously, the pope) concerning church affairs. Most grant legal rights to the hierarchy of the *Catholic Church* over matters such as taxation of church property and education of the faithful. Some, such as that agreed with *Napoleon* by Pius VII, elevated Catholicism to the status of state religion; others had a narrower compass. Major concordats were signed with France (1801), Spain (1851), Colombia (1887), Fascist Italy (1929), Nazi Germany (1933), and Poland (1993).

The concordats agreed with *Mussolini's* Italy and with *Hitler's* Germany remain the most controversial. They were both negotiated by Cardinal Pacelli (later, *Pius XII*), in an effort to gut social and political Catholicism of its growing, national independence of the papacy. This worked: in Italy and Germany, Catholic political parties were swept aside without papal objection, while the Vatican became the sole recognized voice of Catholic authority. In return, the faithful were tacitly assured that it was morally permissible for them to serve reprehensible dictatorships. Many top Nazis, such as *Bormann* and *Himmler*, were fanatic opponents of organized religion. Hitler was mostly bored by the subject. Nevertheless, in part to retain traditional Church privileges within Germany in face of Nazi paganism and revolution, and partly flowing from an ongoing papal campaign against what was seen as the greater threat—official atheism and anti-religious *pogroms* within the Soviet Union—the Vatican signed a concordat with the Nazis ordering German priests to refrain from involvement in politics. In return, the Church was guaranteed special legal status, retained its property, and was allowed to operate parochial schools. In 1937, dissatisfaction with Hitler's serious violation of the terms of the concordat led to a papal encyclical on the question. The next year, Pope Pius XI (1857–1939) publicly condemned the *Nuremberg laws* and drafted a major statement of papal opinion denouncing *anti-Semitism*, then reaching a crescendo within Germany. He died the next year and his successor, Pius XII (Pacelli), declined to publish the pastoral letter. *See also Lateran Treaties; Vatican Councils.*

conditionality. When qualifications (conditions) with respect to fiscal policy—such as limits to consumer *subsidies* and on internal lending (credit), controls on expansion and the size and wages of the public sector work force, currency *devaluation*, and other restrictive national economic policies—are required by a lending agency, especially a *multilateral* agency such as the *International Monetary Fund* (IMF) or *International Bank for Reconstruction and Development* (IBRD). Such conditions applied by the IMF to its lending has stirred much bitter criticism among *developing country* borrowers. *See also First Tranche; stabilization program.*

condominium. (1) The idea that the *Great Powers* should act together to impose orderly solutions to questions of international peace and security, as in the *Concert of Europe.* (2) The exercise of joint governance and shared *sovereignty* over a territory by two or more extraterritorial states, as in the Anglo-Egyptian Sudan (1899–1955) or the *Île des Faisans* since the seventeenth century. Other examples of note are: Samoa (1889–1900), Tangier (1923–1956), and the *Saar* (1919–1935). Note: This is different, legally, from *occupation.*

Condor Legion. German air force "volunteers" fighting for *Franco* in the *Spanish Civil War* from November 1936 to May 1938. It numbered about 6,500 men, several squadrons of bombers and fighters, and two tank brigades. *See also Guernica.*

Condor program. *See Operation Condor.*

condottieri. *See Niccolò Machiavelli; mercenaries.*

confederacy. (1) A (mostly) archaic term for *alliance.* (2) The *Confederate States of America*, 1861–1865.

Confederate States of America (CSA). A *confederation* of eleven southern *slave states* that seceded from the *United States of America* from 1860 to 1865, rather than accept the presidency of *Abraham Lincoln*, which they believed would lead to limitation on the expansion of the "peculiar institution," *slavery*. The first to secede was South Carolina, on December 20, 1860. It was followed out early in 1861 by Mississippi (January 9th), Florida (January 10th), Alabama (January 11th), Georgia (January 19th), Louisiana (January 26th), and Texas (February 1st). Representatives of these seven states gathered in Montgomery, Alabama. There they enacted a constitution (which, as it happened, did not permit secession), declared an independent southern republic on February 8th, and set up a *provisional government*. Confederate hot-heads—unknowingly obliging Lincoln's desire not to have the Federal side fire the first shot—laid siege to a Federal garrison in Charleston harbor, Fort Sumter, in early April. That gave Lincoln maneuvering room to call for and raise an army to suppress secession. In turn, the call to arms in the North provoked four more Southern states to secede: Virginia (April 17th), Arkansas (May 6th), North Carolina (May 20th), and Tennessee (June 8th). Many, but by no means all, southerners saw themselves as a distinct *nation* and viewed the *American Civil War* that followed as a fight for national independence, and even as an anticolonial war. A few remained loyal to the Union, while most just hunkered down to make the best of a terrible situation they could not control, one of *conscription, inflation,* and "*invasion.*"

The Confederacy failed to obtain international *recognition* of its independence, partly because of a foolish and long-lingering belief in *King Cotton diplomacy*. Just nine million southerners—including three million slaves—opposed 22 million northerners. The Union also had nearly ten times the South's industrial capacity. Thus, four years of war slowly but surely saw early southern victories, earned by élan and luck, turn into grinding, bloody, bitter *attrition* and *defeat*. In its last days the severely truncated South resorted to desperate measures, including offering to recognize the French puppet regime in Mexico, enlisting slaves as garrison troops in the Confederate Army, and finally emancipating all its slaves. The main Confederate Army (of Northern Virginia) was defeated in April 1865; the last Southern troops surrendered in Texas, in the Trans-Mississippi region, five weeks later. In one sense only, the Confederacy "died of too much democracy": its war effort was hamstrung by the issue of *states' rights*, which impeded prosecution of a centralized war effort and undermined a sense of southern nationalism necessary if it was to succeed. Yet, the larger truth remains that a rural slave society and economy could not successfully, or alone, wage a *total war* to ultimate victory against a larger, determined, and also free and democratic, industrial power. *See also Gettysburg; Ulysses Grant; Robert E. Lee; William Sherman.*

confederation. *See union of sovereign states.*

Confederation of the Rhine (1806–1813). Created by *Napoleon I* after he abolished the *Holy Roman Empire*, this new constitutional arrangement for western (and later central and eastern) Germany was an effort to make permanent French *hegemony* in central Europe. Austria and Prussia were forced to *recognize* the Confederation after *defeat* in 1805 and 1806, respectively. Russia recognized it in the *Treaties of Tilsit*. However, once it was no longer sustained by French power, the Confederation fell apart in 1813, as French stragglers and deserters slunk or hurried across it during the *retreat from Moscow* and several allied armies approached its borders.

conference diplomacy. Multilateral negotiation, usually in open sessions. The first major conference of the modern era was the *Peace of Westphalia* in 1648. Conferences were held after most major *Great Power* wars in the seventeenth and eighteenth centuries, almost always excluding all but the Great Powers. The great, breakthrough achievement of nineteenth-century diplomacy was the *Congress System* and *Concert of Europe*. Less widely admired for their consequences were the *Congress of Berlin* (1878) and the *Berlin Conference* (1884–1885).

A new, public twist and an equally radical move to universal membership was given to conferences in the twentieth century. This arose from several sources: (1) the misplaced hopes of the *Hague Conferences*; (2) the personal influence of *Woodrow Wilson* at the *Paris Peace Conference*; (3) the views of Quakers, international lawyers, and *liberal-internationalists* who also demanded "*open covenants of peace, openly arrived at*"; and (4) most deeply, democratic pressures within several of the *Great Powers*, but especially the United States, further encouraged in 1919 by the widespread belief that *secret treaties* had helped precipitate and prolong *World War I*. Conferencing among states became permanent with the *League of Nations* and its successor, the *United Nations*. After that, it spread to *functional agencies* and regional associations such as *APEC*, the *OAS*, *OAU*, *OSCE*, and many others. *See also caucus group; Commonwealth; European Union;* la francophonie; *union of sovereign states.*

Conference on Security and Cooperation in Europe (CSCE). *See Organization of Security and Cooperation in Europe.*

Confidence and Security Building Measures (CSBMs). Practical steps taken to reduce levels of tension in a hostile relationship where there is no apparent or immediate solution to the basic conflict. They include exchanging military observers, giving advance warning of military *maneuvers*, and avoiding maneuvers in frontier areas to lessen the risk of *accidental war*. They may be virtually any other political or even social measure seen as a building block of trust necessary to eventual resolution of the underlying issues. They are most developed within the CSCE, but other countries have adopted them because of their practical utility. For example, in 1993 India and Pakistan agreed to advance notification of maneuvers, local *hot-line* communication between commanders, and other measures, concerning *Kashmir*.

conflict. Any given instance of the endemic antagonism in political life between various interests and/or principles. It may be ameliorated by respect for *international law*, through *diplomacy* and *negotiation*, or it may terminate in *war* or *cold war*.

conflict management. The idea that management of conflicts that defy resolution, rather than *grand strategy*, is the most practical contribution to the maintenance of peace. Academic students of conflict management mainly examine structures of *decision making*, *negotiation*, and *crises*, looking for techniques that are conducive to peaceful outcomes. Statesmen more often turn to *arbitration*, *mediation*, *containment*, CSBMs, *diplomacy*, *deterrence*, and/or the multiple possibilities of *international law*. *See also crisis management.*

conflict of laws. When different municipal laws, specific to the nations concerned in a claim, apply to the same case. *See also international law (private).*

Confucianism. A philosophical system founded by Confucius (Kongfuzi, or K'ung Fu-tse; 551–479 B.C.E.), amended by his major disciple Mencius (372–289 B.C.E.), and enormously important in shaping the worldview and histories of China, Japan, Korea, and Vietnam. Some argue that Confucianism is an ethical system existing in the absence of religion because, in spite of historical association with religious rites in various countries and eras, classical Confucianism did not insist upon piety or adoration of a deity. Its main texts are comprised of Confucius' known writings and compendiums of his teachings arranged by disciples into two compilations: (1) the Four Books, or the "Analects" of Confucius (dialogues with rulers and students) and "Mencius," along with parts of the "Book of Rites" or "Great Learning" thought to have been written by Confucius, and the "Doctrine of the Mean"; and (2) the Five Classics, or the "Book of Changes" ("I-ching"), "Book of Documents," "Book of Songs," "Book of Rites," and a collection of other antiquarian writings ascribed to the Shang and Zhou periods. These nine works were the core curriculum of the famous Chinese examination system. For 2,500 years Chinese civilization to a remarkable degree aspired to implement the ethical constructs of Confucius. During the *Song dynasty* renaissance, official neo-Confucian ideas added a sternly hierarchical thrust, through an emphasis on virtue rooted in contributing to harmonious family, social, and political relations or the "Three Bonds" of minister to prince, children to parents, and wives to husbands. Confucian family and political ideas were thus broadly similar and mutually reinforcing, amounting to a call for familial and social unity under a single authority.

Classical Confucians believed in moral perfectibility through education, a tradition that marked Chinese culture and government for two millennia. From 136 B.C.E. to 1911, China's imperial system upheld blended versions of Imperial Confucianism (also known as Legalism or Neo-Confucianism) as a state philosophy, and most dynasties based crucial scholar-elite (roughly, civil service) exams on its main texts. However, Confucian scholars tended to denigrate the callings of merchants and warriors, and state Confucianism repeatedly ossified into rigid *conservatism*. This held China apart from the extraordinary scientific and mercantile progress of the West after 1500 and made it slow to adapt to the new pressures it faced from Western powers from the eighteenth century onward. Some Chinese blamed the whole tradition for the fall of the *Ming dynasty*. However, many scholars turned instead to seeking a purified canon, convinced its corruption over time had led to China's decline. They did close textual analysis of compositions and records dating to the *Han dynasty*, which was closest to Confucius in time, sometimes exposing forgeries in the classical canon. Other scholars looked at later periods, generally elevating the Song at the expense of the Ming. Still others smuggled Western and other more modern Chinese ideas into gaps thus opened in the classical canon ("New Text Movement"). Once China succumbed to humiliating *servitudes* to foreign powers in the late nineteenth century, many nationalists rejected Confucianism outright, accusing the tradition of contributing to the country's weakness and comparative backwardness. *Mao* later tried to replace it with his own quixotic version of Sinified *Marxist* ideology. Yet, his thinking too reflected the abiding influence of Confucianism on all Chinese thought. A muted Confucian revival began in China in the 1980s; its importance and influence it is not yet possible to gauge. *See also Daoism; mandate of heaven; Maoism; rites controversy; Sinification; Taiping Rebellion.*

Suggested Readings: William T. de Bary, *The Trouble With Confucianism* (1991); Irene Eber, *Confucianism* (1986).

Congo. At independence the country was called the Republic of the Congo. The name was changed to Zaire in 1971, and to Democratic Republic of the Congo in 1997. In 1400, Kongo, a *tributary* empire spanning the great Congo River, was the largest state in Central Africa. In 1482 the first Portuguese ships reached the mouth of the Congo; on their return to Portugal, they carried Kongo emissaries to Lisbon. In 1491 these Kongolese, who were baptized while in Portugal, returned along with Portuguese *Jesuits* and converted Kongo's king. Portuguese *mercenaries*, and guns, helped Kongo fight its border wars, from which Portuguese ships carted away captives into *slavery*. This partnership, and state patronage of *Christianity*, lasted to 1543, until the death of Alfonso I. By that time, Portugal had shifted its trading interests southward into Angola, where it also began direct colonization by importing settlers from the home country from the 1570s. In 1556 a Kongo army was defeated by Ngola enemies, supplied with firearms by Portugal. Kongo thereafter went into a long decline, passed over by the main currents of the *slave trade*, and itself raided by Ngola and Yaka (stateless armed marauders, comparable to the Mane of West Africa or the mercenary bands in France during the *Hundred Years' War*) to supply the *São Tomé and Principe* slave markets. In 1569 the eastern half of the kingdom was overrun by Yaka and many Kongolese were sold to São Tomé and Principe. An appeal to Lisbon secured Portuguese military intervention, 1571–1574, in behalf of Kongo's Christian monarchy, but also a permanent Portuguese presence in Angola that eventually led to slaving wars, which helped break up the Kongo Kingdom. In 1665, at Ambuila, a large Kongo army was destroyed by the Portuguese and their African allies, and Kongo broke into provincial factions and rival dynasts. Kongo enjoyed a brief revival under the seventeenth-century restorer, Pedro IV (1694–1718).

By the end of the eighteenth century, Kongo had disintegrated as a result of its own *imperial overreach* and the long-term shift in Portuguese slaving interests south to Angola. It thereafter collapsed into ever smaller statelets and chieftaincies. In the east, these were overrun in the nineteenth century by *Swahili Arabs*. From 1879 to 1884 the Belgians penetrated up the Congo River into the *Great Lakes* region of Africa. This military and economic penetration followed the mapping expedition of the British explorer *Henry Stanley*, financed by King Leopold II (1835–1909) of Belgium. Leopold subsequently appointed *Tippu Tip* governor and established a trading company to exploit the region abutting the Congo River. This helped set off the *scramble for Africa*. At the *Conference of Berlin* Leopold was made the personal *sovereign* of the Congo Free State. In 1893 his forces defeated the Swahili Arabs of eastern Congo. His malign neglect and coarse exploitation (millions died in a little-known holocaust, 1885–1914) led to widespread disturbances, 1903–1905, and to an international campaign to relieve him of the Congo. In 1908 Congo was annexed directly to Belgium. The worst abuses eventually ceased, but the Belgian government did little better than Leopold over the next 50 years in allowing political expression or providing education and social amenities to the Congolese.

Then, in 1960, in a move widely criticized as precipitate and irresponsible, Belgium suddenly withdrew and gave Congo its independence. That provoked the *Congo crisis*. Fighting continued until 1965, when the head of the army, Mobutu Sese Seko (1930–1997), took power in a *coup*. He thereafter ran the country as a personal fiefdom, relying on patronage of the military to stay in power. The level of corruption under his regime was staggering: his personal wealth, stored in foreign accounts, eventually totaled billions of dollars. In 1967 Mobutu barely survived a *mercenary* revolt and attempted invasion by Congolese exiles, attacking from bases in Rwanda. In 1977 and again in 1978, *Katanga* (*Shaba*) province was invaded by mercenaries, who were defeated in part by French and Belgian intervention. For three decades, Mobutu presided mostly undisturbed over the most corrupt and inept government in sub-Saharan Africa. In spite of enormous natural mineral and other wealth Congo was misgoverned into pervasive poverty, persistent social unrest, and endemic political instability. Mobutu's hold on power grew increasingly tenuous after 1990, when other African nations were converting from *one-party* dictatorships to incipient multiparty democracies.

The Congolese economy finally reached total collapse, and *anarchy* took hold in parts of the countryside. In 1993 the annual inflation rate reached 7,000 percent and the *International Monetary Fund* (IMF) withdrew from any further involvement. Belgium finally abandoned Mobutu in 1993, but France lent support as *Mitterand* met Mobuto at the annual *summit* of *la francophonie*. In 1994 French and Belgian paratroops intervened to rescue European nationals endangered by Congolese garrison troops who were rioting over the inflation rate and Mobutu's failure to pay them. In the confusion, the French ambassador was killed while peering out his window at the rioters. The United States *embargoed* arms sales to Mobutu's regime and, along with France and Belgium, denied entry visas to his officials: with the *Cold War* over, the West had finally decided to let his government collapse. In May 1997, the regime fell, undermined by Mobutu's terminal illness (he died in exile in Morocco), regional dislocations caused by the *Rwandan genocide* of 1994, and the collapse of the Federal Army from indiscipline and in the face of advancing guerrilla forces loyal to Laurent Kabila, a Luba from Katanga and one-time *Marxist* guerrilla. A second rebellion, and then a wider regional war, broke out within a year. Five states—Angola, Chad, Namibia, Sudan, and Zimbabwe—backed Kabila against a rebel force sponsored by Rwanda and Uganda, which had originally sponsored Kabila until he turned against the refugee Tutsi minority from Rwanda resident in eastern Congo. In 2001 Kabila was assassinated, and succeeded by his son, as Congo's deadly dance with tragedy-cum-farce continued.

Suggested Readings: Roger Anstey, *King Leopold's Legacy: The Congo Under Belgian Rule, 1908–1960* (1966); Ann Hilton, *The Kingdom of the Kongo, 1641–1718* (1983); Adam Hochschild, *King Leopold's Ghost* (1998); J. K. Thornton, *The Kingdom of the Kongo* (1983); Jan Vansina, *Kingdoms of the Savannah* (1966).

Congo-Brazzaville (Republic of Congo). France colonized this Central African territory in 1885, granting independence in 1960. A *coup* in 1963 set up a *Marxist-Leninist* regime that invited assistance from both the Soviet Union and China. France remained the dominant influence on Congo's economic and social life, as it continued to provide aid and was the major trade partner. In 1990 Congo's leftist regime underwent an economic epiphany, renouncing Marxism-Leninism and moving toward a multiparty system. In 1997 a civil war broke out between Cocoye and Ninja militias, which left much of Brazzaville in ruins. In 1998 Congo-Brazzaville was drawn into the larger war in Congo, when ex-*Mobutu* generals used its territory as a base camp. Note: This much smaller state should not be confused with the Belgian Congo, which later became Zaire and was renamed Congo in 1997.

Congo crisis (1960–1965). Belgium abruptly left its Congo colony in 1960, with just six months' warning and preparation for independence. Six days after independence celebrations the army *mutinied*, Belgium soon intervened militarily, and intertribal and civil war broke out. Within weeks the resource-rich *Katanga* province seceded under *Tshombe*. The national government was led by the Federal prime minister, *Patrice Lumumba*, who called for United Nations assistance. The UN sent in *peacekeeping* troops, but they could not prevent Congo from splintering into several more parts. The situation became a *Cold War* crisis when Lumumba turned to the Soviet Union for military assistance. That provoked Western intervention. Meanwhile, Lumumba was ousted in a coup led by *Mobutu Sese Seko*, and Soviet advisors hurriedly left the Congo. In 1961 Tshombe's troops captured and murdered Lumumba. UN forces came under heavy attack and took serious casualties. Then UN secretary-general *Dag Hammarskjöld* was killed in a still-unexplained plane crash on his way to meet Tshombe to mediate a settlement. The UN prevailed by mid-1963, but only after heavy fighting against Katanga's largely white, *mercenary* army. Katanga was then rejoined to Congo. Intermittent fighting continued until 1965, when Mobutu took personal power in another coup.

Congo Free State (1886–1908). *See Congo.*

Congress. (1) A formal meeting of international envoys, usually senior *diplomats*, *foreign ministers*, or *heads of state* or *government*, especially during the nineteenth century. Some private groups also tended to call their international meetings congresses. (2) The bicameral, legislative branch of the U.S. federal government, comprising the Senate and House of Representatives. It is constitutionally co-equal with the judicial and executive branches. Its many committees, periodically assertive leadership, and the Senate's constitutional role in the treaty *ratification* process often cause U.S. foreign policy to appear—and to be—erratic, unpredictable, and even self-contradictory. *See also Congress system; human rights; Jackson-Vanik amendment; most-favored nation; Versailles Treaty; Watergate; white slavery.*

Congress of Vienna. *See Vienna, Congress of.*

Congress Party (of India). Founded in 1885, until 1947 it was called Indian National Congress. It was led for most of its very early years by Gopal K. Gokhale (1866–1915). Although it aspired to represent all Indians, from the start it was overwhelmingly *Hindu*. Even so, it was the key nationalist party before independence, opposing British expenditure of Indian tax revenues on imperial wars of *conquest* and *aggrandizement,* such as against Afghanistan and Burma. Still, it remained mostly an elite group that remained loyal to the British crown until about 1905. Then anger over *Curzon's* partition of Bengal, without reference to Indian opinion or interests, encouraged some to talk about demanding *home rule* and led Congress to support a *boycott* of British imports. Meanwhile, political repression after 1907 encouraged more radical nationalists to turn to *terrorism.* In 1910 Congress participated in the first-ever elections of Indians to the British Legislative Council. It supported the British war effort during *World War I,* but after the *Amritsar massacre,* under the unchallenged leadership of *Mohandas Gandhi,* it rejected the British *Rāj* and called for outright *independence.*

From the 1920s to the start of *World War II* it was dominated by the personality and policies of Gandhi. His organizational reforms, undertaken in 1920, made Congress a mass party by persuading higher-*caste* Hindus to accept membership for *harijans,* and allowed it to genuinely appeal to substantial numbers of Muslims and lower castes for the first time. After failure of the *Round Table Conferences* (1930–1932), Congress was banned while Britain experimented with a unilateral reform that carved India into sectarian electorates. This spurred violent protest, a fast-to-the-death by Gandhi, and an archetypical Gandhian pact with harijan leaders on proportional representation. In 1937, with the ban lifted, Congress won an impressively nationwide victory in provincial legislatures set up under the *India Act* of 1935. In 1938 Congress split badly between radicals under *Subhas Bose* and moderate nationalists led by Gandhi, until Bose was forced out. In 1939 Congress ordered noncooperation with Britain in its effort in *World War II,* and all its leaders resigned office. After the war, Congress presided over India's independence, which began badly with the awful *partition* of the subcontinent.

For nearly two decades after that, Congress was led by *Nehru.* In 1954 it declared *socialism* as its main goal for India, and for several decades it stressed forms of economic and national *self-reliance* that led to some advances but in general seriously hampered India's *modernization* and *industrialization.* Under Nehru's daughter, *Indira Gandhi,* Congress remained the governing party through the mid-1970s. In 1969 factional disputes led to a major split in the party. In 1977 it lost its hold on the national government for the first time in 30 years, and in 1978 it again divided along factional lines. One faction (Congress-I) returned to power under Indira Gandhi in 1980. Some Congress-I leaders may well have been complicit in the Delhi Massacre of *Sikhs* that followed the attack on the Golden Temple in June 1984, which also provoked Indira Gandhi's assassination. She was succeeded by her son and Nehru's grandson, *Rajiv Gandhi.* The nonsectarian, secular agenda of Congress remained attractive to most of India's religious minorities, even though it had been challenged by Indira's assault on Sikhism, especially once a Hindu revival movement took political form, and then political power, under the

Bharatiya Janata (BJP) in the 1990s. On the other hand, Congress atrophied by clinging to utterly stale economic policies of self-reliance long after international market forces made this impracticable. It thus floundered in opposition for more than a decade, ever searching for another charismatic leader—preferably from the Nehru family dynasty—to return it to power. In 1998 it turned to Sonia Gandhi, the Italian-born widow of Rajiv, to lead it out of the political wilderness back to power.

Suggested Readings: Sar Desai, *Legacy of Nehru* (1992); D. Low, *Congress and the Raj* (1977).

Congress system (1815–1822). The practice of *diplomacy* by regular *congress* (or conference), by the four *Great Powers* that defeated *Napoleon*: Austria, Britain, Prussia, and Russia, who were joined by France under its restored king. Five congresses were held: *Vienna*, 1814–1815; *Aix-la-Chapelle*, 1818; *Troppau*, 1820; *Laibach*, 1821; and *Verona*, 1822. France used these gatherings to return to international good graces, especially with the three *conservative* monarchies. Britain attended only as an observer from Troppau on and left the system at Verona. Austria, Prussia, and Russia met again in St. Petersburg in 1825, but the congress system had already been abandoned in favor of the much looser *Concert of Europe*, which included Britain. The postwar periods that followed *World War I* and *World War II* were far less successful in managing Great Power relations and the *balance of power*, even though they installed a system of permanent conferencing in the form of the *League of Nations* and the *United Nations Organization*.

conquest. Military *occupation* of territory of another *tribe*, society, or *state*. It may precede *annexation* or *subjugation*.

conquistadores. Principally, a term used for the Spanish adventurer-soldiers who conquered the *Americas*. Secondarily, it is used about similar Portuguese *slavers* and raiders who operated in the African interior from coastal bases. These were truly ruthless warriors, literally soldiers of fortune who disdained literacy, manual labor, and commerce, in favor of moving in *mercenary* companies—like flocks of raptors—whose members shared in the spoils of war and conquest. In their lifestyle they resembled the many nomad warrior tribes who invaded Western Europe after the fifth century. Their methods had been learned in, and their hearts steeled to cruelty and *plunder* by, generations of "*holy war*" against Muslim states during the Iberian *Reconquista*. In the *New World*, they first conquered the Caribbean islands. From there, *Cortés* led an expedition to conquer the *Aztec Empire* in the central Mexico Valley (1519–1521), and *Pizarro* led the remarkably similar conquest of the *Inca Empire*. From these two centers of power and wealth, smaller conquistadores expeditions fanned out in all directions. They overran southern Mexico and Central America in the 1520s and 1530s, though did not complete the conquest of the inland peoples of northern Mexico until c. 1600. From Cuzco in Peru, in the 1530s and 1540s they moved north into Panama, south to the Río de la Plata, and thence north again to Paraguay. Other expeditions sought to penetrate the Amazon Basin, with less luck. There was little honor, however, among cutthroats and thieves: within a generation of the conquest of the New World, with no sizeable concentrations of Indian enemies left to conquer, many conquistadores in Peru turned against Spain's attempt to assert its imperial governing authority and made war also on each other. Some conquistadores however, Cortés most famously among them, returned home to Iberia engorged with gold and silver to buy huge landed estates and accept noble titles. *See also* encomienda; *Peru*; requerimiento.

Suggested Reading: Michael Wood, *Conquistadors* (2001).

Conrad von Hötzendorf, Franz Graf (1852–1925). *Austro-Hungarian* field marshal. Conrad was the Austrian Army's chief of staff for most of the period 1906–1917. He was principally responsible for Imperial prewar procurement and strategic planning. He played a key role in exacerbating the conflict between Austria-Hungary and Serbia, which sparked the *mobilization crisis* of July 1914. At the last minute, as a *two-front war* with Russia and Serbia loomed, he changed the mobilization timetable. This delayed and enormously complicated Austro-Hungarian mobilization by sending an entire army to uselessly cool its heels in the *rear echelon* in Serbia before being transshipped to the Carpathian front to face the already assembled Russian Army. Conrad subsequently commanded badly in the initial campaigns of the war on the *eastern front*, pressing for ambitious offensives his forces could not sustain, and refusing to admit defeat in time to extricate armies that might fight again another day. By the spring of 1915 this combination of imprudence and vanity cost Austria-Hungary nearly two million men. That brought to a head the long-anticipated Austro-Hungarian emergency in which only Germany's intervention might save its weaker ally. Conrad was dismissed in 1917 by the new Emperor Karl I, but he retained a field command on the baleful Italian front.

Suggested Reading: Norman Stone, *The Eastern Front, 1914–1917* (1976).

conscientious objection (to military service). Ethical obligation, arising from religious conviction, deep-seated *pacifism*, or other ethical objection to *war* in general or to some specific armed conflict, which causes individuals to refuse to serve in the military even when *conscripted*. Most democracies have in recent decades permitted individuals who raised such objections to serve in noncombat roles, as with a medical unit. Some more radical objectors refused even that duty, however, and were jailed as a result. *Totalitarian* societies do not respect conscientious objection to military (or any state) service, and objectors sometimes have been executed. *Insurgencies* also seldom respect matters of individual conscience and treat moral objectors roughly, thereby confirming the observations of *Hobbes* and others about the *state of nature* and the preferability of life inside a *state*, even a tyrannical one. *See also Gandhi.*

conscientious objector. Someone who declines to fulfill national military obligations for moral, philosophical, or religious reasons. *See also pacifism.*

conscript. A drafted soldier; not a volunteer.

conscription. Compulsory military service, rare before the *French Revolution* and the *levée en masse*, but used extensively ever since. A popular American synonym is "the draft." Among the *Great Powers* universal conscription was introduced first in those nations that suffered great defeats: in Prussia (1814) and Austria-Hungary (1867).

Russia was a special case: the gentry served as officers under a system of near-*feudal* obligation. In 1699 (reformed in 1715) conscription was introduced by *Peter I*, ultimately on the basis of one draftee for every 75 serf households (the ratio applied as well to state peasants), with conscripts serving for 25 years in exchange for their freedom, should they survive. Russian recruits were branded with a cross sign, which some *Old Believers* interpreted as yet another indication that Peter was the Anti-Christ. In cases of apprehended deserters, men drew lots and one-in-three was hanged; the other two were flogged, had their nostrils slit, and were deported to *Siberia* to do hard labor. This Petrine military system survived until the *Crimean War* demonstrated that conscription of mass armies based on servitude and brutal treatment could no longer make up for Russia's continuing technical and organizational backwardness.

Prussia was another special case. Its radical 1814 law introduced conscription for all classes. Elsewhere, only the poor were conscripted: the sons of nobles or rich merchants could purchase commissions, as in the British Army, until well past the Crimean War, or buy replacements from among the unconscripted poor to serve in their stead. This was the practice, for example, even in the democratic *Union* during the *American Civil War*. After the *Revolutions of 1848* and the wars of *Bismarck* and German unification, conscription in free societies in Western Europe became more problematic. France reintroduced it in 1872 after its humiliating defeat in the *Franco-Prussian War* (1870–1871). In 1889 France increased its service requirement to three years, as its population was declining relative to Germany's, and turned as well to the doctrine of *élan*. Even in wartime, democracies tend to avoid conscription for as long as feasible. During most of the *American Civil War* the *Confederacy* (a quasi-democracy) relied on volunteers, but by 1865 was conscripting less enthusiastic whites and even some slaves—used mainly in garrison duty to free white troops for combat. The *Union* also began with volunteers, under varying enlistment periods, and when it introduced conscription it still permitted the wealthy to purchase replacements for themselves or their sons. After 1863, however, its massive conscript armies overwhelmed the less populous South.

The *Ottoman Empire* conscripted Muslims from 1844, and non-Muslims from 1909. Britain introduced civilian conscription only after taking immense losses on the *Somme* in 1916. It abandoned conscription in 1957 after acquiring *nuclear weapons*. During the *Second Sino-Japanese War* (1937–1945), the Nationalists in China employed savage conscription methods that led to a death and desertion rate of near 45 percent *before* conscripts reached the frontline units. Many starving and ill peasants were taken to the front roped together—hardly a prescription for turning out a motivated fighter, and a good part of the explanation for the Nationalists' relatively poor showing against the Japanese, who also could be remarkably brutal to their conscripts but had much higher overall morale. Canada fought all *World War II* without any conscription for overseas service, taking greater casualties as a result but forestalling the usual wartime political crisis in *Québec*. The United States employed conscription during World War II, the *Korean Conflict*, and most of the *Vietnam War*, but abandoned the draft as civilian opinion divided over whether to continue that war. At the end of the twentieth century most major military powers moved toward professional (volunteer) armed forces. *See also* impressment.

consent. A cardinal principle of *international law* by which changes in *rules* require consent by the parties concerned in order to be legally binding. Some legal theorists suggest that consensus among the states, rather than consent by every state, may become the standard by which a rule is considered binding and an obligation incurred. *See also* liberum veto; *unanimity rule*.

conservatism. In the broadest terms, conservatism is an outlook on political and social life that is skeptical about the perfectibility of the human condition and prefers conservation of traditional values, customary ways of life, and established habits of mind because it sees these as already constituting the historical wisdom of a given society about how best to adapt to its local environment and specific circumstances. Temperamentally, modern conservatives harbor deep suspicions that within each *utopian* project put forward by some eager reformer there lurks the real likelihood of an unforeseen, dystopian disaster—and they readily point to several actual *revolutions* of world significance from the eighteenth through the twentieth centuries as evidence in support of this fear.

In the usual journalistic and social science caricatures, conservatives are frequently portrayed as totally resistant to change. Indeed, in weaker analyses, resistance to change becomes the litmus test used to define conservatism, just as *liberalism* is similarly falsely and facilely associated with a desire for change of almost any kind. In this way, and only in such a fashion, may one arrive easily at what are otherwise historical non sequiturs such as pointing to the most doctrinaire *Marxists* and rigid revolutionaries among the *Communist* old guard in the Soviet Union or the People's Republic of China (PRC) as the "conservative wing" of the respective *Communist parties* in those states, under challenge by a "progressive" and "liberal wing" demanding change and reform. In the least accurate and most polemical versions of this common error, conservatives usually emerge as also indifferent to the suffering of the poor and generally hostile to social progress (as defined by the journalist or academic).

It is more accurate, however, to say that conservatism implies a cautious, moderate attitude toward change rather than an eager embrace of each possibility produced by the pell-mell pace of modern *technology* and philosophical speculation. As a mass political movement, conservatism dates to the *French Revolution* and *industrialization*, against both of which early modern conservatives upheld the putatively superior virtues of agrarian economics and of the *ancien régime* in politics and established religion. Conservative political parties to this day tend to be more solicitous of rural interests than are more leftist parties, but they have also developed strong bases of support among the middle classes. Conservatism thus ought not to be mistaken for *reaction*, in which all change is resisted, and certainly not for *fascism*, which is a revolutionary doctrine that democratic conservatives find as morally repugnant and dangerous as do adherents of *liberalism*, on top of which they see it as yet another radical effort to recast human nature in forms that ill-fit it.

In addition, many conservatives have been energetic state-builders and creative reformers (*Alexander Hamilton, Alexander II, Otto von Bismarck, Konrad Adenauer*, among others). The historical malleability of the term should already be apparent from this author's own convolutions in the preceding passage. In addition, it is reflected in the fact that by the close of the twentieth century most conservatives in Western countries were closely identified with what had been *classical liberal* policies a century prior, including *free trade, privatization*, and a libertarian approach to political rights and social values. *See also John Adams; aristocracy; Catholic Church; Winston Churchill; Confucianism; Conservative Party; Charles De Gaulle; Benjamin Disraeli; fundamentalism; Islam; radical; Ronald Reagan; Republican Party; socialism; Margaret Thatcher; Tory.*

Suggested Readings: Isaiah Berlin, *Against the Current: Essays in the History of Ideas* (1980); Isaiah Berlin, *Crooked Timber of Humanity* (1992); Edmund Burke, *Reflections on the Revolution in France* (1792); Michael Oakeshott, *Rationalism in Politics* (1962); Noel O'Sullivan, *Conservatism* (1976); Pekka Suvanto, *Conservatism From the French Revolution to the 1990s* (1997).

Conservative Party, of Britain (Tories). In 1832 the Conservative Party emerged as the successor to the *Tories*. It long considered itself the "natural governing party of Britain," and with good reason: surpassing even the *Democratic Party* in the United States, the Conservative Party is the most successful electoral machine in history. It ruled Britain sternly for large portions of the nineteenth century, under Peel and *Disraeli*, and from the moderate center during most of the twentieth. It split over the Irish *famine* and Corn Laws in the 1840s, which were fiercely opposed by Disraeli, and the party remained mostly out of power, 1846–1874. Under Disraeli, 1874–1880, it regained favor and power. When *Gladstone's* Liberals split in 1886 over *Home Rule* for Ireland, it again took charge. It was then joined by some former Liberal-Unionists, most notably *Joseph Chamberlain*. The Conservative Party pursued a policy of vigorous imperial expansion and consolidation, including managing the *Boer Wars*. It lost to the Liberals in 1905, but joined a wartime coalition in 1915. It dominated British politics and foreign policy, 1918–1840, under Baldwin and then *Neville Chamberlain*. His successor, *Winston Churchill*, led the party during the mid-1940s, lost to *Labour* in 1945, but then regained office in the 1950s. It was a strong supporter of anti-Soviet policies all through the *Cold War*. Under *Margaret Thatcher*, in the 1980s the party grew ever more leery of European *integration* and turned harder right in domestic policy. In the 1990s it split internally between those who wished to move toward the center and be more accepting of Britain's place in Europe and those who rejected the European idea. In foreign policy, Conservatives continued to hope for and sometimes to act as though a special relationship with the United States still existed, when in fact it was already a decreasing reality for Americans after the *Suez Crisis*. *See also British Empire; Heath; Roundtable Conference*.

Constantine I, né Flavius Valerius Aurelius Constantine (274–337 C.E.). "The Great." Emperor of *Rome*. He gained early military experience in expeditions to Egypt (296) and Persia. In 305 his father, Constantius Chlorus, was elevated to coemperor in the Western Empire, with Galerius ruling in the East. Constantine accompanied his father on an expedition against the Picts in Britain during which he was proclaimed as successor just before his father died at York. Galerius subsequently granted Constantine the lesser title "Caesar," but not the grand title "Augustus." The succession was contested, especially once Galerius died in 310 (at one point, Rome had six claimant emperors). Constantine, too, took up arms to assert and defend his claim. Before a major battle at the Milvian Bridge (312) Constantine claimed to have had a vision of a burning crucifix in the sky before him and to have converted to *Christianity*, though he was not baptized until just before he died at Rome, by Pope Sylvester. Henceforth, he took the Christian cross as his symbol and proclaimed the motto of his vision: "In hoc signo vinces" ("In this sign you shall conquer"). He combined, thereby, the imperial authority of Rome—with its own tradition of emperor-divines and personal cults—with the universalist and apocalyptic claims of Christianity, which was fast spreading throughout the Roman Empire in any case, with consequences that echo through history still. The next year, he issued the Edict of Milan granting full civil and religious rights to Christians within the Empire. In 314 he overcame the last claimant in the East (Licinius) and compelled him to surrender many eastern lands, including Greece. For most of the next decade he focused on reform of the law, reduction of corruption, and further campaigns against the barbarians at the *frontier*. In 323 war again broke out with Licinius. This time, Constantine had him put to death and became the sole emperor of Rome. In 324 he declared Christianity the state religion, though paganism and other faiths were tolerated. The next year he called the Council of Nicaea, the first of the great *Ecumenical Councils*, to deal with the "Arian heresy." In 330 he moved his capital to the ancient Greek city of Byzantium, which was built anew astride the strategic *Dardanelles* and *Bosporus* and renamed *Constantinople* ("City of Constantine"). His last years were not happy, politically or personally: he had his son (326) and wife (327) both executed for *treason*. In an act of final foolhardiness, he divided the empire among his remaining three sons, who then fought a civil war over the succession upon his death (May 22, 337).

Suggested Readings: Michael Grant, *Constantine the Great* (1994); John Holland Smith, *Constantine the Great* (1971).

Constantinople. The Greeks founded a city called Byzantium on this *strategic* site in c. 660 B.C.E. It was later captured by the Romans. The name was changed to Constantinople by *Constantine the Great* (274–337 C.E.) and served for a millennium as the great capital and center of power and learning of the *Byzantine Empire*. It was sacked by the Fourth *Crusade* in 1204. It finally fell to the Turks, under *Muhammad II*, in 1453, an event that sent shock waves—and European explorers—around the world. For centuries more it was the capital of the *Ottoman Empire*. The Greek Quarter was known as "Phanar," and housed the *Orthodox* Patriarchate of Constantinople. The city lost the status of capital in 1923, when the seat of Turkish government was moved to Ankara by *Atatürk* to signal a break from the religious and imperial pretensions of the Ottomans, and not least also to escape the reach of the *Royal Navy* and marines. Its name was changed to Istanbul in 1930. *See also Third Rome.*

Constantinople Agreement (1915). A secret treaty wherein France and Britain promised Russia the city of *Constantinople* and its *hinterland* should Russia stay in *World War I*. It was a mark of the frustration of the stalemate on the *western front*, and of the importance of Russia to the Allied cause, that France and Britain thus quit their traditional policy on the *Eastern Question*. It was among the secret pacts published by the *Bolsheviks* in 1918, along with the *Treaty of London* (1915), to the great embarrassment of the *Allied and Associated Powers*.

constructive engagement. A policy of continued contact, trade, and so forth, coupled with *quiet diplomacy* toward a country one is trying to influence to reform its *human rights* practices; for example, the United States and the United Kingdom toward South Africa in the 1980s or toward China in the 1990s or *ASEAN*'s policy toward Burma (Myanmar) in the mid-1990s.

consul. A nondiplomatic, official representative who still may enjoy *diplomatic immunity.* Posted to *consulates*, they see to *trade, immigration*, assistance to citizens traveling or residing abroad, and other mundane matters. *See also representation; Vienna Convention.*

consulate. The diplomatic premises occupied by a *consul*, usually in cities other than the capital and mostly to deal with nonpolitical matters such as trade, assisting nationals, and processing *immigration* applications. *See also embassy; legation.*

Consulate (1789–1804). The initial system of government employed by *Napoleon*, who ruled as First Consul after the coup of *Brumaire* (1799). It ended when he crowned himself emperor on December 2, 1804. During the Consulate, Napoleon introduced most of his major domestic reforms, making the period among the most important in French domestic history.

consul general. The senior diplomatic officer in a *consulate.*

consumer goods. Final *goods* ready for use, or consumption, and not for use in any further production. *See also capital goods.*

consumer price index (CPI). A composite statistic measuring prices over a range of consumer *goods and services*. It is used by firms and unions in planning investment or negotiating wages and by governments to help set *macroeconomic* policy. Some criticize it for overestimating the true rate of inflation, for instance, by not adjusting fully for improvements in the quality of goods and services.

Contadora Group. An ad hoc association formed in 1983 by Colombia, Mexico, Panama, and Venezuela to mediate the conflicts in Central America. In 1987 it backed a peace plan framed by President *Oscar Arias* of Costa Rica, which called for political amnesty for the guerrillas, internationally supervised and genuinely democratic elections, and a commission to investigate and report on wartime *human rights* abuses. The *Reagan* administration did not welcome the outside initiative, which it saw as needlessly complicating the process. Nevertheless, the group played a role—mostly positive—in negotiating an end to the wars in Nicaragua and El Salvador between 1989 and 1992.

containment. Any long-term foreign policy that aims at preventing expansion of an *imperialist* or otherwise *aggressive* adversary by supporting its weaker neighbors and blocking its military, political, economic, or ideological opportunities for *aggrandizement*. Its basic assumption is that the expansionist power cannot be reasoned with (compromises remain out of reach), but only contained and constrained from accomplishing goals that would fundamentally upset the *balance of power* or otherwise threaten international peace and security. A salient example from the seventeenth and eighteenth centuries was consistent Dutch opposition to the expansion of French power under *Louis XIV*. In the eighteenth and nineteenth centuries, England pursued containment of France, especially during the *French Revolution* and under *Napoleon I*. This idea was also an important part of the great settlement at the *Congress of Vienna*. Later, British containment efforts switched to thwarting Russian ambitions to acquire the outer provinces of the *Ottoman Empire* in Central Asia, penetrate the Balkans, and (or so London believed) move through Afghanistan into northern India. To that end, the British propped up the Ottoman sultans, supported the Persian Empire, justified several wars in Afghanistan—which in fact sought to extend Britain's presence there—and played the *Great Game* on the chessboard of Central Asia. In the twentieth century, France worked to contain Germany in the 1920s by direct occupation of the *Rhineland* and the *Ruhr* and by ringing it with such alliances as the *Little Entente*. France and Britain sought, but only intermittently and half-heartedly, to contain *Bolshevism* in the immediate aftermath of the *Bolshevik Revolution*. The United States tried to contain Japanese expansion in Asia from c. 1915 to 1941. Containment was never tried against *Nazi Germany*; its antonym, *appeasement*, was pursued instead.

The term applies most famously to the policy pursued by the United States toward the Soviet Union, c. 1947–1990. The premise of this *grand strategy* was that denying the Soviet Union opportunities to expand its political influence would force it to abandon territorial and ideological imperialism and address its own severe, internal contradictions. It was designed to both induce and compel the Soviets to choose between change and war, but then to foreclose the option of war. Before the Soviets finally agreed to change their behavior, containment required a half-century of sustained effort and cost several trillion dollars in military and related expenditure. It utilized the combined military forces of many nations in several alliances as a *deterrent* to the instrument of war, but also contributed to several episodes of actual warfare against Soviet proxies. Its main instrument was the *Marshall Plan* to aid recovery of Germany and Europe, bilateral aid to Japan, and U.S. leadership of a global economy that excluded the *Soviet bloc*, as it was built around free markets, *free trade*, and liberal democracy. Rapid recovery of the former enemy states of *World War II* and the *reverse course* of their quick incorporation into an American led trading and financial system addressed U.S. interests in expanding trade even as it denied Moscow influence over poor, hungry, and therefore potentially radicalized postwar populations. *NATO* then reinforced this core of political and economic containment by serving as a form of prudential military insurance against the—privately, considered highly unlikely—outside possibility that Moscow might try a direct military assault on Western Europe. In short, NATO was used to counterbalance Soviet military advantages in Europe, so as to enable the United States to play its true trump card—a vastly more efficient economy—through rapid reconstruction of Western Europe and Japan and incorporation of these centers of latent, and soon actual, industrial power into a community of free, market societies.

However, the *Truman Doctrine* began a movement of containment policy down a different and much more thorny path by globalizing American security commitments to areas that would prove of mere marginal relevance to the world balance of power. This error was huge, but understandable in light of apparent and dramatic advances of *communism*—which then not only appeared monolithic, but in many respects actually was, as *Stalin* and *Mao* fairly closely coordinated policy and cooperated militarily throughout north Asia, during the *Chinese Civil War* and toward Japan and Taiwan, and concerning Korea. The *Chinese Revolution* (1949) and then the first desperate months of the *Korean Conflict* importantly contributed to this perception and thus to the *militarization* of containment after 1950. Containment now shifted toward reliance on military means and perception of threats as nearly global (Africa and Latin America were still largely excepted), despite its original conception suggesting neither global reach nor primary reliance on military means. This trend was further reinforced by, and then itself became reinforcing of, the extreme militarization of the Soviet Union, which had never disarmed after World War II. The 1950s thus saw the start of an expensive *arms race* and extension of containment efforts to areas included in the United States' newly expanded definition of its *vital interests*. Ultimately, this allowed the Soviet Union to indulge in fairly low-cost troublemaking by providing aid and advisers to minor *belligerents* against whom the United States made unwise, and unnecessary, major commitments.

This new pattern was most tragically and bloodily evident in U.S. opposition to local, and sometimes merely perceived, Communist threats in areas peripheral to the main Cold War contest, and that could not possibly affect its overall outcome, such as Latin and Central America, most of sub-Saharan Africa, but especially the peasant societies of *Indochina*. Mistaken exaggeration of where and when the Soviet Union needed to be contained was epitomized in *John F. Kennedy's* inaugural commitment to "pay any price, bear any burden, meet any hardship, support any friend, oppose any foe to assure the survival and the success of liberty." Nearly 60,000 American GIs and more than two million Indochinese would pay the ultimate price, and bear the truly terrible burden, of that impolitic promise, reiterated by several of Kennedy's successors into the mid-1970s. Such tragic mistakes notwithstanding, sustained American commitment to containment contributed mightily to the extraordinary spectacle of the collapse and peaceful surrender of the Soviet bloc between 1989 and 1991. And that, after all, freed hundreds of millions of people from one of the worst systems of misgovernance and personal bondage yet devised in human history. Post–Cold War examples of containment include U.S. (and in some cases, also United Nations) policy toward Iran after 1979, Iraq after 1990, and Serbia after 1992. *See also collective security; détente; domino theory; double containment; flexible response; George Kennan; massive retaliation; NSC-68; Paul Nitze; peaceful coexistence; Reagan Doctrine; X article.*

Suggested Readings: S. J. Ball, *The Cold War* (1998); John Gaddis, *We Now Know* (1998); John Gaddis, *Strategies of Containment* (1982); Akira Iriye, ed., *Origins of the Cold War in Asia* (1977); Vojtech Mastny, *The Cold War and Soviet Insecurity* (1996); Ernest May, *American Cold War Strategy* (1993); Thomas G. Patterson, *Meeting the Communist Threat* (1988); Adam Ulam, *Understanding the Cold War* (2000); Vladimir Zubok and Constantine Pleshakov, *Inside the Kremlin's Cold War* (1996).

contiguity. Claims to neighboring *territory* or *territorial seas* based upon physical connection to one's own. *See also propinquity.*

contiguous zone. Formerly 12 nautical miles from the *baseline*, it was extended by *UNCLOS III* to 24 nautical miles. Within this zone, of what are otherwise the *high seas*, states claim limited *jurisdiction* for specific purposes, such as interception of illegal *immigration* or *smuggling*. *See also hot pursuit; territorial sea.*

continental shelf. The part of any continent or *island* contiguous with a coast and submerged in shallow water (up to 200m). A prime source of *fish* and sometimes *oil*, rights to this region were a major concern of the *UNCLOS III* talks. When it extends beyond the *Exclusive Economic Zone* (EEZ), the effective rights of an EEZ state are "prolonged" to the edge of the shelf. *See also islet.*

Continental System. An economic *blockade* of Great Britain and a corresponding effort to establish French economic and trade hegemony over Europe (as in *Colbert's* earlier mercantile war on English trade) instituted by *Napoleon I* with his Berlin Decree in November 1806 and reinforced by the Fontainebleau and Milan Decrees of 1807. Napoleon aimed to close Europe's ports to British commerce to compel London to negotiate or, better, to force it to its knees. Russia was added briefly to the system at *Tilsit* in 1807, and the *Iberian* and Italian ports were closed in 1808. The British responded with Orders in Council commanding all *neutral* ships to stop in England for *search and seizure* of *contraband* and to permit loading of English goods to run the French blockade. That led to a serious and protracted conflict with the United States over *neutral rights*, which culminated in the *War of 1812*. The British pounded Copenhagen in 1807 to punish the Danes but also teach the whole

Baltic region the reach of its *sea power* and the real cost of collaboration with the French. Napoleon's closed trading system was resisted throughout Europe for economic reasons as well: cheap British goods were in high demand. Napoleon was required to loosen his grip in 1809, when even the French proved adept smugglers of English wares. The hardships caused by the blockade led to *Luddite* riots in England in 1810–1811, but in the end the Continental System failed both economically and militarily, as the expanding, newly industrialized British economy proved stronger than anticipated and Continental consumer demand and Europe's coastline too difficult to patrol.

continuity of safeguards. A concept related to *nonproliferation*, in particular the *Nuclear Non-Proliferation Treaty*, and more generally to *arms control* agreements. It refers to acceptance of the principle of continuous, and even surprise, inspections as a means of *verification*, rather than permitting occasional or *pro forma* inspections, which might serve as a cover for violations. It was greatly expanded after the *Gulf War* showed that Iraq had succeeded in evading the old verification regime. *See also IAEA.*

continuity of states. Maintaining the legal identity of *international personalities* after a *revolution*, *territorial* change, or military *occupation*.

continuous voyage. *See ultimate destination.*

contraband. (1) *Smuggled* or illegal goods. (2) Goods supporting one country's war effort that another country declares contraband, especially under the law of *blockade*. During the *American Civil War* the principle was stretched to include freed slaves of Confederate (but not Union) owners, before the Emancipation Proclamation of 1862. During the twentieth century the definition stretched internationally with concomitant expansion of accepted legitimate targets, until it came to mean virtually anything, including *food* and excluding only medicines. *See also "free ships make free goods"; infection; neutral rights; noncontraband; total war.*

contra proferentum. By this rule, in cases of ambiguity a *treaty* is interpreted against the party that drafted it and that might have been more precise. *See also* obscuritas pacti.

Contras. The anti-*Sandinista* force that fought a harassing *guerrilla war* in Nicaragua in the 1980s, backed by the *Reagan* administration. *See also Nicaragua.*

control experiment. *See quantitative analysis; variable.*

controlled response. The attempt to limit one's military reply when attacked, in the hope of preventing *escalation* to all-out war by giving one's adversary time to reconsider and withdraw. *See also deterrence; escalation control.*

control test. A wartime legal test used to establish the status of a firm or property by assessing which state exercises preponderant influence over it.

control, test of. *See nationality.*

convention. (1) A synonym for any *treaty*. (2) A multilateral agreement (treaty) that is concerned with a specific problem or issue. Topics are as diverse as civil aviation, epidemic diseases, postal services, or *genocide*.

Convention (1792–1795). The governing body in France during the middle period of the *French Revolution*, from the abolition of the monarchy in 1792, through the full radicalization of the Revolution, to the establishment of the *Directory*. During this period the terms "left wing" and "right wing" entered the lexicon of political discourse, respectively denoting a *radical* versus more *conservative* attitude. They arose from the observed tendency of radical deputies (the Montagnards, led by the *Jacobins*) to sit en masse on the left side of the National Convention, whereas more conservative deputies (the *Girondins* and others) seated themselves to the right. *See also Committee of Public Safety; George Danton; Maximilien Robespierre; "The Terror"; Vendée rebellion.*

Conventional Forces in Europe, Treaty (1990). This agreement set out reduction targets in *conventional weapons* and troop levels and called for phased and equal reductions over four years. It was signed by the *NATO* countries and six *Warsaw Pact* states. Its obligations passed down, proportionately, to the 15 *successor states* of the Soviet Union.

conventional war. (1) Any war waged with *conventional weapons*. (2) War against *regular*, conventional forces, that is, not against *terrorists* or *guerrillas*. *See also counterinsurgency warfare; guerrilla war; nuclear war.*

conventional weapons. All weapons except *weapons of mass destruction*; to wit: *biological, chemical, gas, nerve,* and *nuclear weapons*.

convergence. (1) In classical *Marxism*, the notion that all historical development will ultimately converge in the achievement of *communism*. (2) The idea that historically vastly different societies are growing more alike out of a common, functional response to the conditions and circumstances of *modernization* and *industrialization*. This thesis de-emphasizes the roles played by *ideology*, national history, or distinctive religion or culture as shapers of modern life, positing instead the long-term homogenizing force of industrial *development* and *globalization*. A once fashionable (among academics) variant posited that *capitalist* and *Communist* societies were evolving toward a median position of state regulation of the economy and centralized wealth redistribution. That more precise notion did not survive the events of 1989–1991, which witnessed the defeat and formal surrender (in the *Charter of Paris*) of the Communist idea. The larger thesis remains moot. *See also end of history; liberalism; stages of growth; world system theory.*

conversations. A diplomatic term referring to exchanges of views and information between governments. Less formal and more tentative than *negotiations*, conversations do not necessarily aim at a *treaty*. *See also Military Conversations.*

convertibility. When one *currency* is freely exchanged for another according to market *exchange rates*.

convictio juris sive necessitatis. The conviction that a legal duty exists to obey a (specific) *rule*. Note: Only if this applies can a rule be said to derive from *international customary law*.

convoy. Merchant ships traveling in groups, under armed escort whenever possible. Venetian merchants, whose ships were preyed upon by *pirates*, for centuries traveled the Mediterranean in convoy. After 1500, Spain organized all merchant ships sailing to the *Spanish Main* into mandatory convoys—the "*flota*" and the "*galeones*" (*galleon*).

Protected by warship escorts, they were sent out twice annually (once each) from Seville. All ships would then return as a single treasure fleet, on average numbering 80–100 vessels, in the spring. This system mostly succeeded: during the *Eighty Years' War*, Dutch "beggars" captured the entire bullion fleet only once, in 1628. The English captured it just twice, in 1656 and 1657. On each occasion, the loss of the treasure fleet led to a major fiscal crisis in Spain, where American silver was needed to pay for imperial troops and to pay off *Fugger* loans. An additional purpose of the fleets—which were required to disembark at Veracruz (flota) or Panama (galeones) in the Americas, and only at Seville in Spain (until 1717)—was to concentrate royal control over trade, and especially over the supply of monetary metals, within the empire. This was in fact a fairly leaky *mercantilist* system, with much conniving at smuggling of silver in particular on both ends and via the Pacific route, also to Manila and thence to China. During the *Napoleonic Wars*, the British and French employed convoys to protect their Atlantic trade while raiding each others' fleets. The convoy system was controversial among the *Allies* in *World War I*, until the resumption by Germany of *unrestricted submarine warfare* in 1917. Then it proved invaluable. In *World War II* it was accepted from the beginning as the best defense against *submarines* and used by all seafaring *belligerents*. Convoys increase security by lowering the probability that an enemy surface raider (or submarine) will spot a merchant ship: 100 ships sailing individually along a known *trade route* present 100 possible instances of an enemy making contact with his target; 100 ships sailing together present only one such opportunity. The Kriegsmarine countered this tactic in World War II by developing the *wolf pack*. The Allies then took such countermeasures as deploying additional destroyers, designing long-range hunter aircraft, and building numerous *escort carriers* to actively seek out and kill German *U-boats*. *See also Battle of the Atlantic.*

Cook, James (1728–1779). English explorer. He joined the *Royal Navy* in 1755, apprenticing in the Baltic; he became a master in 1759. For eight years he surveyed the *St. Lawrence*, and then *Newfoundland* and Labrador (1763–1767). From 1768 to 1771, aboard The Endeavour he circumnavigated the globe. Along the way he charted the coasts of New Zealand (which he also circumnavigated) and eastern Australia, which he claimed for Britain, before returning via Java and the Cape of Good Hope. In another great voyage (1772–1775) into the South Pacific, he explored the Antarctic, Tahiti, the New Hebrides, and New Caledonia. On his final voyage, from 1776 to 1778, he sailed around the Cape, Tasmania, and New Zealand and then named and charted the Sandwich Islands (Hawaii). He failed in his principle aim, to return to England via discovery of the Pacific entry into the Northwest Passage. He instead charted parts of the Pacific northwest coast of North America and then returned to Hawaii, where he was killed by native Hawaiians. *See also Maori Wars.*
Suggested Reading: L. Withey, *Voyages of Discovery* (1989).

Cook Islands. This island group was discovered by *James Cook* in 1770. It was made a British *protectorate* in 1888 and a *dependency* of New Zealand after 1901. In 1965 it became self-governing in *free association* with New Zealand, which is responsible for its defense. It is not a United Nations or *Commonwealth* member; nor is it *recognized* by Japan as an independent *state*. Yet, it has *diplomatic relations* with a dozen countries and belongs to several *IGOs*.

Coolidge, Calvin (1872–1933). *Republican* president of the United States, 1923–1928. He succeeded to the presidency when *Warren Harding* died in office; then he was elected in 1924. He was a passive administrator in both domestic and foreign affairs. The most significant diplomatic developments came from subordinates: (1) *Frank B. Kellogg*, who signed the *Kellogg-Briand Pact*; and (2) Charles Dawes (1865–1951), who developed the *Dawes Plan*. The Coolidge administration decreased U.S. intervention in the Western Hemisphere and managed to keep out of *civil wars* in three areas where some Americans wanted armed action: China, Mexico, and Nicaragua. Opposed to the *League of Nations*, Coolidge nonetheless approved U.S. application to the *World Court*. However, conditions on adherence imposed by Congress proved unacceptable to other states. He called for *disarmament* and sponsored a naval conference in Geneva in 1927, but there was no agreement with Britain on *cruiser* limits. Relations with Japan deteriorated when Congress overrode him and continued *Oriental exclusion laws*. He was singularly immune to reason on the issue of *war debts*, opining of the Allies: "They hired the money, didn't they?" That attitude and policy contributed to deepening of the *Great Depression*.

cooling-off treaties. This was the popular name for some 30 bilateral Treaties for the Advancement of Peace negotiated by the United States with other nations, Germany being the major exception, during the first term of the *Wilson* administration. Wilson embraced the idea, but even he could not outdo for enthusiasm his ebullient secretary of state, *William Jennings Bryan*. The first was signed with El Salvador in August 1913. They committed signatories to almost nothing: they affirmed that in disputes involving "national honor," or otherwise not immediately solvable, the case would be referred to an ad hoc international commission whose recommendation would be nonbinding. During a one-year period of investigation neither party was to use force to resolve the dispute. *See also Root Arbitration Treaties.*

Coordinating Committee on Multilateral Export Controls (COCOM). Set up in 1949 under American pressure, it coordinated Western *embargoes* of goods with strategic value to the *Soviet bloc* and other *Communist* states. This action was intended to stall the Soviet Union's military advance, cripple it economically, and further isolate it politically. COCOM dissolved in 1994, without immediate agreement on replacing it with a new organization, in order to include post-Soviet Russia as a member. *See also containment; dual use technology.*

Copenhagen, Battles of. (1) April 2, 1801: A *Royal Navy* fleet destroyed the Danish fleet in Copenhagen harbor, ending the threat that *Napoleon* might revive the *League of Armed Neutrality* to break the British *blockade*. (2) September 5–7, 1807: The British bombarded the rebuilt Danish fleet over three days, again denying it to Napoleon but also confirming Denmark as a bitter, enemy power until 1815. *See also Continental System.*

Coptic Church. This is the indigenous *Christian* church in Egypt, some 1,700 years old and with ancient links to Ethiopia. It is comprised of Egyptian Christians who retained their faith after the arrival of *Islam* in Egypt in the eighth century. It has a distinctive rite, Monophysite, dating to its early association with the *Orthodox Church* in *Constantinople*: It was thus distanced from mainstream Christianity—both Latin and Orthodox—by the decision taken against the Monophysite view of the nature of Christ by the *Ecumenical Council* of Chalcedon in 451. It has a discrete hierarchy and until 1961 maintained a close and guiding relationship with its sister church in Ethiopia, to which for many centuries it sent bishops and other higher clerics. Copts constitute about one-seventh of the modern Egyptian population. They have sometimes been persecuted: in 1952 many Coptic churches were seized by the state, but these were returned in the 1990s, and Copts have sometimes been targeted for attack by *fundamentalists* of the *Muslim Brotherhood*.

Coral Sea. That part of the Pacific Ocean lying between Australia, New Guinea, and the Solomon Islands.

Coral Sea, Battle of (May 7–8, 1942). This naval victory over Japan was one of the first for the Americans in *World War II*. The rapidly rebuilt U.S. fleet, commanded by *Chester Nimitz*, used key breakthroughs in naval intelligence to great advantage in winning this engagement. The victory blocked the momentum of the Japanese advance in the Pacific. Coral Sea came just months after *Pearl Harbor*, and one month before the decisive American victory at *Midway*. It thus reasserted U.S. naval power in the Pacific and confirmed that the Japanese gamble on war with America had been high risk indeed.

cordon sanitaire. A buffer of small states between two larger, hostile powers or camps. *Clemenceau* proposed that Eastern Europe serve this purpose concerning the Soviet Union, in a metaphor likening *Bolshevism* to a communicable disease, requiring *quarantine*. In 1993 Russia's policy toward *Central Asia* and the *Caucasus* suggested it sought a cordon sanitaire along its southern border to contain Islamic *fundamentalism*. Calling for a cordon sanitaire is almost always a futile gesture. It is also often a de facto acceptance of weakness, masquerading as a policy of strength. *See also Hundred Days.*

core. In *dependency theory*, the center of the *world capitalist system* whose ruling elites are said to benefit from exploitative organization of the global economy. It is sometimes used as a synonym for those elites.

Corfu incident (August 27, 1923). After several Italian officers were shot while on an *observer mission*, Italy occupied the island of Corfu. Greece took the issue to the *League of Nations*, which successfully pressed for Italian withdrawal.

Corfu, Pact of (July 20, 1917). An agreement among exile leaders of the south *Slavs* that Croatia, Montenegro, Serbia, and Slovenia should unite against Austrian rule, under the Serbian king. It led to the founding of *Yugoslavia*.

Cornwallis, Charles (Marquis) (1738–1805). *See East India Company; Yorktown.*

Coromandel coast. The southeastern coast of the Indian subcontinent.

corporatism. (1) The vague ideology of Italian *fascism* that viewed society as an organic whole with mutually reinforcing functional parts called syndicates or corporates. It had roots in *Catholic* social doctrine, and hence also was experimented with in Portugal under *Salazar* and in Spain under *Franco*. In practice, it served to reinforce *Mussolini's* personal dictatorship and the endemic corruption of his regime. (2) In political science and in Latin American studies in the 1950s–1970s, the idea that all significant interest groups were created and controlled by the state. The term was also and often used, with little discrimination, as a descriptive-cum-pejorative adjective about societies or economic and political models (or personal opponents) of which a given commentator disapproved. (3) In literature on U.S. diplomatic history, an effort to achieve interpretive synthesis by combining economic, social, political, and ideological influences with changes in political structures and interactions between public and private entities to explain the overall thrust of American foreign policy.

corps. *See military units.*

Corregidor, Battle of (1942). A fortress island in the mouth of Manila Bay, near the *Bataan* peninsula, Corregidor was the locale of fierce fighting early in *World War II*, as its shore batteries held off the Japanese Navy and its American and Filipino garrison held out against the Japanese Army for several months. It was commanded by Lt. Gen. Jonathan Wainwright, who held out for another month after *MacArthur* was ordered to leave the Philippines. Its garrison suffered terrible abuse while *prisoners of war* in Japanese hands until the survivors were liberated in March 1945. An emaciated Wainwright was at MacArthur's side during the Japanese surrender ceremony aboard the USS Missouri in Tokyo Bay in September 1945.

corregidores. "Co-rulers." A Castilian title for regional officeholders that, after 1782, also became the title of provincial governors in *New Spain*.

correlation analysis. *See variable.*

correlation of forces. A Soviet concept akin to, but wider than, the *balance of power*. It included the role of political, social, economic, and morale factors in calculations of relative *power* and did not rely just on estimates of military balance.

corsair. "To chase." Arab and Berber merchants who governed Algiers and whose *galleys*, rowed by *Christian* slaves, engaged in trade and *piracy* on the Mediterranean for several centuries. *See also Barbary States.*

Corsica. A large island in the Mediterranean comprising an offshore province of France. Long autonomous as a result of its remoteness and mountainous terrain, this sleepy island (populated mainly by sheep herders and fishers) was a target of Genoese and other regional imperialisms for years. Under the patriot Pasquale de Paoli (1725–1807), the Corsicans fought off a Genoese invasion. France secured Corsica from Genoa by treaty and invaded with an overwhelming force of nearly 25,000 men in 1769. The next year, *Napoleon* was born into a family of minor Corsican nobility—his father was a *collaborator* with the French occupation. In 1789 the *French Revolutionary* assembly annexed Corsica to France. A *nationalist*, and often violent, movement for independence persisted into the twenty-first century.

Cortés, Hernando (1485–1547). *Conquistador* and conqueror of Mexico. Cortés first fought in the *New World* as part of a conquering army in Cuba in 1511. There, he witnessed a mindless slaughter of Indians, a policy that he determined to avoid when he invaded Mexico a decade later. Instead, his preference was to enslave most Indians within the *encomienda system*. He left Cuba on February 18, 1519, to invade the *Aztec Empire* in Mexico, with eleven ships, 550 men, 16 horses, some war dogs, and ten brass cannon. They fought briefly at Tabasco on the Yucatan peninsula, where Cortés took a local woman (Marina, or La Malinche) to be his interpreter and lover. He moved further up shore and then paused for four months to reconnoiter the Aztec position, found the town of Veracruz, and gather intelligence as well as allies from among local Indian tribes fiercely opposed to Aztec rule. These were legion, and Cortés soon counted many Indians among his growing *infantry*. Before moving inland he beached (not burned) his ships to show there was no going back. He next fought, overcame, and then forged an alliance with the Tlaxcalans, old enemies of the Aztecs. Thus reinforced, he marched on the Aztec capital at Tenochtitlan (later, Mexico City), reaching it on November 8, 1519. The Emperor *Moctezuma* (Montezuma) II and the Aztec military offered no real resistance, possibly in the misguided belief that Cortés was the incarnation of a feared Aztec deity (Quetzalcoatl), whose return had been foretold. In the end, this psychological factor was critical: both sides believed God or the gods were with them; for one side, this faith was cracked when their leader was killed and battles were lost; for the other, victories affirmed the justice of the "cause." One honest conquistador, Bernal Días del Castillo, who accompanied Cortés to *plunder* the great Aztec temples, sites of awful human sacrifice in the midst of the most glorious gold artifacts, put it this way: "We came here to serve God and the king, and also to get rich."

The conquistadores imprisoned Moctezuma in their own quarters and commenced their pillage of the city, still protected and fed by the Aztecs. Meanwhile, Cortés led a contingent to the coast to defeat a larger (900-man) rival Spanish force that sought to join in the plunder; he attacked his compatriots with surprise, and then with bribes and bravery easily persuaded the survivors to join his small army. So cruel was the occupation and so extensive was murder and massacre by the Spanish that the Aztecs finally rebelled in mid-1520. They let Cortés enter the city, then they cut the causeways and trapped his men with their gold in the central temple complex. After several attempts to break out, the Spaniards finally did so. As Cortés pulled out from Tenochtitlan, he left it burning behind him and without Moctezuma, who was killed during the Spanish withdrawal. The Spanish retreated to Tlaxcalan, fighting now enraged Aztec warriors en route. Cortés now gathered an anti-Aztec alliance from the surrounding cities, which had long seethed under the bloody tyranny of the Aztecs. Also, the smallpox that arrived with the Spaniards began to decimate the Aztec ranks. Cortés advanced toward Tenochtitlan in May 1521, reinforced with a few new Spanish arrivals but mainly supported by a vast Indian host determined to overthrow the Aztec Empire. Cortés broke the aqueducts that supplied Tenochtitlan, and he laid siege. Three months later, on August 13, 1521, the last Aztec leader, Cuauhtémoc, surrendered the city. Cortés later had him murdered too, during an expedition to conquer Honduras in 1524.

Cortés subsequently became governor of the conquered Aztec lands, and the richest man of the age. He ruled cruelly, in accordance with his nature: he was an unimaginative, brutal kleptocrat with no regard for the welfare of the Indian population, except for an instrumental concern with Indian welfare such that the encomienda system was sustainable. The natives—weakened by new infectious diseases and still politically divided—were nonetheless enslaved by the Spanish settlers who hurried to Mexico after the conquest and who demonstrated even less of a conscience than did Cortés. The Aztec economy was destroyed, its riches plundered and exported to buy estates or pay royal taxes in Spain. Central Mexico would take several centuries to recover from this decimation of its economy and population. Cortés led several more expeditions in Spanish America, including to Central America in 1524 and to Baja California in 1536. In 1528 he returned to Spain to defend his governorship of Mexico, which had been taken from him by a royal appointee; he was unsuccessful, but did receive a captaincy and a noble title that came with a huge land grant in Mexico and tens of thousands of encomienda Indians. Ever the conquistador, he also served in Africa, joining an assault on Algiers in 1541. He died of dysentery, amidst his riches in Spain.

Suggested Reading: Hugh Thomas, *Conquest* (1993).

cosmopolitan values. Global or universal principles; those belonging to the *community of nations* ("cosmopolis"), not a specific culture or state. *See also cultural relativism; human rights; Immanuel Kant; nationalism; secularism; war.*

Cossack. Turkish: "kazak," or "outlaw." (1) A member of a Turkic and Slavic people from south Russia who descended from runaway serfs, nomadic invaders, and local tribes originally beyond the reach of the tsars and who were particularly adept horse riders. The Don Cossacks rebelled against the tsars in 1670–1671, under *Stenka Razin*. In the seventeenth and eighteenth centuries hetmans of the Little Russian Cossack Host in Ukraine were repeatedly torn between accepting the protection of the Russian tsars or making profitable alliances with anti-Russian armies of Poles and Turks. *Peter I* made extensive use of the "Little Russian" Cossacks as his main *cavalry*, but they were capricious troops and could be bought by other sovereigns too, as when a secret deal was made between the Little Russian Cossack hetman and an invading Swedish army under *Charles XII* in the months before *Poltava* (July 8, 1709).

The Don Cossacks rebelled again, 1707–1708, under ataman Kondratay Bulavin (c. 1660–1708), also under the stimulation of the slow-motion Swedish invasion of the Russias, north to south. The greatest Cossack rising came under *Catherine II*: the *Pugachev rebellion*. After incorporation of the Ukraine and Crimea into the Russian Empire, the Little Russian and Don Cossacks alike formed core units of the tsarist cavalry and became a mainstay of the old regime. During the *retreat from Moscow*, Cossack units cut the French apart. The Cossacks remained loyal until the *Russian Revolution* (1917). In the *Russian Civil War*, the Cossacks regained some of their former freedom and formed independent units. They played a role also in the *Polish-Soviet War* (1920). During *World War II* many Cossacks fought against the Germans on the *eastern front*, where their horses could maneuver around frozen guns and vehicles; but some 50,000 Cossacks joined an anti-Soviet army set up by the Germans from Soviet *prisoners of war*, under ex-Soviet General Vlasov. The Allies later deported these men to Russia, where *Stalin* had them all shot. (2) A generic derogatory term meaning "uncouth barbarian."

Costa Rica. First surveyed by the Spanish in 1502, its native population was not fully subdued until the 1560s. It remained a primitive coastal settlement with little access to or exploitation of the interior until the eighteenth century. It was part of the *Captaincy-General of Guatemala* until that larger region gained independence in 1821, coincidentally with the independence of *New Spain* (Mexico).

It then broke from Mexico to join a short-lived federal experiment called the *Central American Union*, 1824–1838, but left that troubled association upon its breakup in 1838. Starting in the late nineteenth century it developed—rare for its region—a stable, reasonably democratic system of government and rule of law. It suffered through a brief coup in 1917, but otherwise remained stable until after *World War II*. Then it suffered a brief civil war, 1948–1949, after which it disbanded its armed forces. It thereafter maintained only armed police and some *militia*. It managed to escape the violence that troubled nearly all its neighbors and to sustain a peaceful democracy through the second half of the twentieth century, partly because it maintains no permanent military and therefore poses no threat to its neighbors, and partly because it relies on the United States (and perhaps OAS) intervention for defense in the event of *aggression* by some external power. Its economy suffered a major downturn in the 1980s. In 1987 President *Oscar Arias* won the *Nobel Prize* (for Peace) for a peace plan he promoted for Central America that was supported by the *Contadora Group*.

cost-benefit analysis. Any systematic, not necessarily *quantitative*, evaluation of the losses and gains to be had from a given economic or foreign policy.

Côte d'Ivoire. Formerly "Ivory Coast," the name change in all languages was insisted upon by Côte d'Ivoire after 1985. The area was penetrated by Portuguese traders in the sixteenth century. It became a French *protectorate* in 1842 and a *colony* in 1893. It was briefly joined to *Upper Volta* and part of *French West Africa*, but gained separate independence in 1960. It retained close ties with France under the paternalistic leadership and *one-party state* of *Félix Houphouët-Boigny* (1905–1994).

It was superficially among the most prosperous and peaceful of post-colonial African states and one of the most pro-Western. That led it to be seen by some as a model of how Europe might better have *decolonized* Africa. Structural economic problems (especially massive external debt) and sharply unequal distribution of the nation's wealth persisted, however, and were greatly aggravated by the *oil shocks* of the 1970s. In 1990 civil unrest broke out, contributing to a turn to multiparty democracy. By 1994 the Ivorian economy was failing and the value of the CFA (*Communauté Financière Africaine*) was halved, but the links to France remained strong. A *coup* in late 1999 led to a *state of emergency* in 2000. In 2001 the military tried to fix an election, but was driven from power by massive popular unrest. *See also Samori Touré.*

Council for Mutual Economic Assistance (COMECON). It was set up in 1949, ostensibly to increase trade within the *Soviet bloc* as a substitute for the *Marshall Plan* aid, which Moscow forced its east European *satellites* to forgo. Its long-term purpose was to cement the dependent relationship of those states within the Soviet empire. It did not foster integration of these economies with each other. Instead, it tied them all to Soviet needs and central plans, with the long-term effect of retarding *growth, modernization,* and *efficiency*. A handful of other states later became associated with COMECON, Soviet clients all: Albania, Cuba, Iraq, Laos, Mongolia, Nicaragua, Vietnam, and the special cases of Finland and Yugoslavia. Albania was expelled in 1961. COMECON collapsed in 1990 as member states looked to the West for aid, trade, and credits. It was formally dissolved in 1991.

Council of Europe. An interstate association begun in 1949 and comprising at its core the member states of the *European Union* (EU) and *EFTA*, but including as well non-EU states such as Cyprus, Malta, Turkey, and a number of former *Soviet bloc* nations at varying levels of association, for a total of 41 members at the close of the twentieth century. It is headquartered in Strasbourg. Despite its overlapping membership, it has no formal relation to the EU. Its agenda is mainly social policy and promotion of liberal-democratic values. Its most notable accomplishment to date was creation of the *European Court of Human Rights* and attendant *human rights* treaties. *See also European Council.*

Council of Ministers. The organ of the national governments of the *European Community*, established in 1958 by the *Treaty of Rome* and connected to the *European Commission* by a consultative committee. In 1965 France boycotted its meetings for seven months over the CAP and the degree of *supranational* control and *integration* within the European Community. The main instrument of the Council is COREPER. With the *Luxembourg Compromise*, the Council began to act more like a real executive, overtaking the Commission. In 1993 it restyled itself an organ of the *European Union*.

Council of the Indies. The Council of the Indies was established in 1524 to administer and make law for Spain's *New World* possessions. It comprised the sovereign and advisors, commanded viceroys and captains-general, regulated trade, and was the final court of appeal of any decision taken in the *audiencia* of the various colonies. From 1782 to 1790 this body was replaced by an intendant system, in the style of *Bourbon* France, and rule by "corregidores." *See also New Spain.*

Council of Trent (1545–1563). *See Counter Reformation.*

council of war. (1) A meeting of the highest ranking military officers and civilian leadership, if in a civilian-governed state, to make *war plans* or discuss logistical, strategic, or other problems. (2) A meeting held to concert military operations and attended by the top military and civilian leadership in any alliance.

counterattack. As the word suggests, an attack made (usually covering the same ground) in reply to a prior attack. The ability to counterattack is crucial; it aims at blunting the enemy attack and, if possible, at throwing him off schedule and balance and possibly overrunning his *lines of supply* if these were overextended in the original attack.

counterbalance. Supporting the weaker side in a disturbed *balance of power* in order to reestablish *equilibrium*. *See also balancer.*

counterespionage. *See counterintelligence.*

counterfactual. Historical argument that attempts to elucidate causal relationships by speculating on alternate outcomes to the factual outcomes of *history*, by analytically substituting key decisions or events for actual ones. It is a practice disdained by many historians. However, when counterfactual argument is handled deftly, and its insights and conclusions are treated with moderation, it can be highly useful. Not least, it helps to make the point that not all major events flow necessarily from major causes, which is an important and often necessary corrective to a general tendency among historians (and indeed, all passive observers) toward *determinism*. Similarly, second-order counterfactuals—wherein speculated changes clearly would not have significantly affected the main outcomes—may better (more persuasively) illustrate an argument upholding that, regardless of alternate circumstance or decision, things would have turned out more or less the same. *See also agent-structure problem; causation.*

counterfeiting (of currency or postage). *See state obligations.*

counterforce targeting. Aiming solely at the enemy's C^3I capability (command, control, communication) and at weapons or troops, while minimizing *collateral damage*; this often requires highly accurate *smart weapons*. *See also countervalue targeting.*

counterinsurgency warfare. Political and combat tactics specifically designed for fighting *guerrillas*, mainly by imitating the guerrilla's own small-scale, hit-and-run tactics. It is important to note that this is a broader concept than just military action, encompassing as well political initiatives to win "hearts and minds" and thereby undercut the ability of opponents to win at *guerrilla warfare. See also low-intensity conflict; national liberation, wars of; pacification.*
  Suggested Reading: Michael Shafer, *Deadly Paradigms* (1988).

counterintelligence. Detecting, blocking, turning *double agents, disinforming,* and deliberately deceiving an adversary's spies or saboteurs. Many of the same techniques can be used against *terrorists* or, less happily, *dissidents. See also intelligence.*

countermeasure. Any tactic or technology employed in response to enemy tactics or technology. For instance, if an opponent's *BMD* proposed to shoot down missiles with lasers, a simple countermeasure might be to spin the missiles or give them reflective surfaces.

counterpart funds. Local funds given by an aid recipient to a *donor nation* in exchange for *hard currency* aid. Control of such funds may over time give donors a considerable say in a recipient's national economy through control of large holdings of its currency.

Counter Reformation. The *Catholic* effort to stem, if not reverse, the political and doctrinal changes brought about within Christendom by the *Protestant Reformation*. "Catholic Reformation" is the generally preferred term for serious efforts at self-reform by the *Catholic Church*. These predated the Protestant Reformation and continued for some time thereafter. For this reason, some Catholic historians have sought to blend the Catholic Reformation into the Counter Reformation, the better to smooth away the implied *reactionary* connotations of the latter term. However, the Counter Reformation began later, most clearly with the Council of Trent (1545–1563), and was fundamentally an aggressive reaction to Protestantism and an effort to restore intellectual controls, as in the infamous *Index*, rather than simply an effort at internal Catholic reform. The main players in the Catholic Reformation and the Counter Reformation alike were the papacy, bishops, and clergy, with the *Jesuits* globally prominent as the sword and shield of doctrinal and *missionary* counterattack. It is less clear what role the laity played, though new research in Catholic history is beginning to uncover this long-neglected aspect of confessional history. The movement was also backed by the *Habsburgs* and clashed with a similarly—and in the case of *Calvinism*, perhaps even more so—militant Protestantism. Together, confessional *fanatics* contributed to protracted and highly destructive sectarian wars, which climaxed—but also mostly ended—with the *Eighty Years' War* (1566–1648), the *Thirty Years' War* (1618–1648), and the *Peace of Westphalia* (1648).

Of course, underlying those conflicts—and infusing papal and Conciliar policy on one side, and princely and sectarian responses on the other—were also many and diverse *raisons d'etat*. The deepest international political legacy of the Counter Reformation was in Spain, which had been the most ideological and committed of the Catholic powers. Its retreat into dogma and reaction, expulsion of the Iberian Jews and Moriscos, and close embrace of the spirit of the *Inquisition*—among other things, a persistent resistance to the insights of science and other empirical inquiry—left it ever further behind the general curve of European development, even into the late twentieth century. *See also ecumenism.*

Suggested Readings: C. H. Carter, ed., *From the Renaissance to the Counter-Reformation* (1965); Steven Ozment, *The Age of Reform, 1250–1550* (1981).

counterrevolution. Originally a *Bolshevik* concept, it was in effect anything identified by a reigning *Communist party* as actively opposing, or just passively countering, the principles or policies it laid out. *See also communism; Great Leap Forward; purge; Red Terror; show trials.*

counter trade. A generic term for a variety of exchanges that take place directly, without a transfer of money in return for *goods* or *services*. *See also barter.*

countervailing duty. A tax imposed on imported *goods* said, truly or not, to be unfairly advantaged or *subsidized* by a foreign power as compared with domestic goods, for which subsidies are, of course, seen as entirely reasonable and fair.

countervalue targeting. Aiming at population and economic centers that constitute the "social value" of an adversary. This does not require highly accurate weapons, but does ask for blunted moral sensibility. *See also counterforce targeting.*

coup. The widely used short form of *coup d'etat.*

coup de main. "Blow of the hand." A surprise attack.

coup d'etat. "Blow [aimed] at the [head of government or] state." A sudden strike for power, usually by the military but at times by a revolutionary political party, such as the *Bolsheviks,* in which mass violence is avoided by a small group, which instead strikes quickly and precisely to decapitate the old political leadership from the body politic, seizes the instruments of governance and propaganda, and immediately and publicly portrays itself as the legitimate representative of the *nation* in the hope the rest of the military and the general public acquiesce quickly and accept an extralegal seizure of power. This may be a bloody process or not, depending on the level of resistance. Coups arise from a variety of motivations, including personal ambition or grievance on the part of the *officers corps* or individual coup leaders, general political instability in a given society, or upon the instigation, with the support and in the interest of, an outside power. Failed coups or those opposed by another segment of the military may at times escalate into, or otherwise provoke, *civil war,* as was the case with the *Nigerian Civil War* (1967–1970). This can become an established pattern of governmental changes: from the start of *decolonization* in sub-Saharan Africa in the mid-1950s until the end of the *Cold War* c. 1990, several hundred coups were attempted and many dozens were successful. *See also palace coup; Putsch; rebellion; revolution.*
    Suggested Reading: Edward Luttwak, *Coup d'Etat* (1979).

coup de théatre. "Theatrical stroke [or blow]." An unexpected diplomatic or political foray that captures widespread attention and acclaim. For instance, *Nixon's* stunning trip to China (1972), *Sadat's* courageous visit to Israel (1977), or *Peres* and *Arafat* publicly shaking hands on peace in *Palestine* (1993).

coupling. (1) A synonym for *linkage.* (2) The NATO doctrine of linking a Soviet conventional invasion of Europe to a *strategic nuclear response.*

Courland. A longtime Baltic duchy, established by the Livonian Order. It was long ruled by the Kettler dynasty as a vassal of Poland. In 1726 Russian troops occupied Courland over a succession issue in Poland, but then withdrew. It became a *tsarist* province when it was annexed by *Catherine II*. It was attached to Latvia upon that Baltic republic's independence in 1918. With Latvia, it was annexed to the Soviet Union in 1940, overrun by Nazi Germany in 1941, reattached to the Soviet Union in 1944, and broke free again as part of Latvia in 1991.

Court of St. James. Diplomatic term for the British crown and government, as in the expression "she was appointed Ambassador to the Court of St. James."

covenant. A synonym for *treaty*, but used most often about *multilateral* arrangements; that is, a formal, written agreement among several states specifying mutual legal and political obligations.

Covenant of the League of Nations. That portion of the *Treaty of Versailles*, and other treaties negotiated at the *Paris Peace Conference* (1919–1920), laying out the rules and authority of the *League of Nations*. Its inclusion in the text of the Treaty of Versailles—which was a wholly unnecessary tactical error that must be blamed on *Woodrow Wilson*—had two deeply unfortunate effects: (1) it alienated Germany from the League by making it appear as an instrument for enforcing the hated peace settlement (which it was, in the eyes of the French at least); and (2) it meant the United States never joined the League after "twelve willful men" in the Senate blocked *consent* to the Versailles Treaty.

covert action/operations. Concealed, low-level uses of *agents of influence*, *moles*, *disinformation*, economic incentives (such as bribes, money for foreign political parties or unions or *guerrillas*), information gathering of all sorts and, very rarely, use of direct limited force. *See also intelligence; overt-covert; secret diplomacy; submarine.*

cover-up. An effort to conceal information, scandal, or illegal domestic or foreign policy actions from public scrutiny. *See also Watergate.*

Crécy, Battle of (1346). *See cavalry; Hundred Years' War.*

credentials. *See letter of credence; recognition.*

credibility. The degree to which a state or leader enjoys a reputation for keeping promises (*treaties*, *executive agreements*, and so forth) and for carrying out threats. *See also credibility gap; credible threat; deterrence; prestige.*

credibility gap. The distance between *assured destruction* and the likelihood an adversary would actually be deterred from certain actions by what amounts to a mutual threat to commit suicide.

credible threat. One taken seriously by an adversary because it is believable that the threatened action will be carried out. This is critical in *deterrence*: if a threat is not credible, it is, by definition, not a deterrent. Concerning *nuclear weapons*, credibility about their use may have slipped with the passage of time since *Hiroshima* and *Nagasaki*. It is worrying that perhaps the only thing that could re-establish it would be actual use of nuclear weapons during some future *crisis*.

creeping barrage. *See barrage.*

Creole. "Criollo." (1) Originally, a person of European (white), especially Spanish, ancestry born in the West Indies or Latin America. The discontent of this class with Spanish rule—they were largely excluded from the bureaucracy, so many chose instead a commission in the *militia*—had much to do with Latin America's wars of independence, 1810–1825. (2) More recently, a person of racially mixed ancestry, especially someone of black, Indian, and Spanish background, but including French and African or Belgian and African backgrounds as well. (3) Descendants of freed slaves and early European settlers in Sierra Leone and other European enclaves in colonial Africa. *See also* mestizo.

Suggested Reading: D. A. Brading, *The First America: The Spanish Monarchy, Creole Patriots, and the Liberal State, 1492–1867* (1991).

Crete. Taken from the Venetians by the *Ottomans* in 1669, this Mediterranean island was ruled by Egypt, 1824–1840, upon its capture by *Mehemet Ali*. In 1905, led by Venizelos (the "Lion of Crete"), it seceded from the Ottoman Empire. It was made part of Greece in 1913. It was captured by Germany in 1941 in the first-ever paratroop assault. In 1945 it reverted to Greece.

Crimea. A peninsula jutting southward from the north shore of the Black Sea, and historic homeland of the *Tartars*. Russia paid tribute to the Crimean khans as late as 1683, but in 1687 and 1688 huge Russian armies invaded Crimea. They failed to conquer it, but a new pattern of Russian aggression was established. In the Treaty of Kuchuk Kainarji (1774), Russia finally took the Crimea from the *Ottoman Empire*; it was formally annexed by *Catherine II* in 1783. Sebastopol was the home port of the *Black Sea Fleet*, except during the brief *demilitarization* that followed the *Crimean War*. The Tartars were forcibly deported to Siberia by *Stalin* during and after *World War II*. The Tartars returned from their enforced exile in the late 1980s; they were met by a mixed, and often hostile, reception by Russians and Ukrainians who had moved onto Tartar land in the interim. In the 1950s Russia gave the Crimea to Ukraine, never contemplating that Ukraine might some day split from Russia, as it did with the breakup of the *Soviet Union* in 1991. A *secessionist* movement persisted in calling for reunification with Russia. Modern Crimea has 2.5 million people, of whom 600,000 are ethnic Ukrainians, 300,000 are Tartars, and the majority are ethnic Russians.

Crimean War (1853–1856). The war had roots in the *revolutions of 1848,* and long-standing interfaith rivalries over control and access to the "Holy Places" in *Palestine.* In September 1853, Russia deliberately provoked war with the *Ottoman Empire,* claiming as a *casus belli* the ostensible need to protect Turkey's Christian minority from persecution and to force Turkey to surrender to *Orthodox* control the "keys" to historic Christian Churches in Palestine. Russia's real design was to *partition* the outer provinces of Turkey and compel *Constantinople* to deny access to the Black Sea to other European naval powers. Fear of Russian expansion into Ottoman provinces and the Mediterranean was the root cause of British involvement. London wished to brace the Ottomans in order to bottle up Russia in the Black Sea by closing the *Bosporus* (see *Straits Question*). War broke out between Turkey and Russia in October 1853. British *public opinion* became near-hysterical over early Russian victories; London declared war on Russia in March 1854. France followed suit, so that *Napoleon III* could ingratiate himself with Britain and with French Catholics (who also claimed the "key" to the Holy Places) and overturn the old settlement imposed on France (and his uncle) at the *Congress of Vienna.* Lastly, *Piedmont-Sardinia* declared war on Russia mainly to ingratiate itself with France. Efforts to draw in Austria and Prussia failed.

An Anglo-French invasion fleet arrived after Russia had already agreed to withdraw from *Moldova and Wallachia.* In search of a battlefield outside the Balkans, the combined fleet sailed to the Crimea. Three early battles were won by the Allies: Alma (September 20th), Balaklava (October 25th), and Inkerman (November 5th). Gross and ill-considered misapplication of *sea power* against a great, if backward, *land power* such as Russia ineluctably led to *stalemate* in the form of a futile two-year siege of Sevastopol. The allied cause was not furthered by the fact that the British Army was essentially an unchanged force—in equipment, training, and doctrine—since its last major encounter in warfare, which was *Waterloo.* This lack of preparation and appalling generalship was symbolized for the British by the fiasco of the charge of the Light Brigade into the "valley of death." Thus began a war none of the powers really wanted, in which little other than *prestige* was at stake. *Trench warfare* developed, which portended both the *American Civil War* and *World War I,* with both sides suffering under awful conditions and worse commanders. Other than some naval skirmishes in the Baltic, fighting was limited to the Crimea. This was the first fully modern war, fought on the Allied side at least with the awful new weapons and destructive power of emergent, industrial society. Russian troops were still armed with smooth-bore muskets and were outgunned in all open-field battles. The "butcher's bill" was nearly 600,000 killed on all sides (400,000 of the dead were Russian), with many casualties from disease. Tsar *Nicholas I* died in 1855, and Sevastopol finally fell that September. Now Austria, too, threatened to declare war on Russia—while Sweden and Prussia also posed potential threats. Moscow agreed to terms in February 1856, including limitation of armaments and the *demilitarization* of the Black Sea (which lasted only 15 years).

The war shattered the general consensus underlying the *Concert of Europe*, broke the conservative alliance between Russia and Austria, and put an end forever to the grand pretensions of the *Holy Alliance*. That left Russia an embittered and *revisionist* power, but also one set on a course of internal reform, under *Alexander II*. Austria and France were left mutually isolated vis-à-vis German and Italian nationalist and *irredentist* claims. The Crimean War was thus a step forward for German and Italian unification and toward the long decline in French power, which would see defeat in the *Franco-Prussian War*, lead to near defeat in *World War I*, and to utter humiliation and occupation in *World War II*. The impact on Britain of its hollow victory was rather less: it recommended its military complacency, blithely unaware of what was quietly happening in Prussia (military reform and *modernization*) while frittering away resources on a futile and distant war. The war was complicated (and again, quintessentially modern) as a result of the exacerbating role of democracy; the rising influence of *public opinion*—Catholic in France, liberal and imperial in Britain, nationalist and imperial in Russia; and a command and control revolution in telecommunications, which gave rise to the first-ever war correspondents and near-instant newspaper coverage of its course and allowed micromanagement of battlefield decisions by distant, unqualified civilians. *See also* conscription; jingoism; narodniki; *Treaty of Paris* (1856).

Suggested Readings: Winfried Baumgart, *The Crimean War* (2000); J. Curtiss, *Russia's Crimean War* (1979); A. Seaton, *The Crimean War* (1977); Leo Tolstoy, *Sebastopol Stories* (1855–1856).

crimes against humanity. In a London Agreement signed by the major Allies in 1945, and in several conventions since *World War II*, certain acts were first defined as "crimes against humanity." The formal charge was first made at the *Nuremberg* and *Tokyo war crimes trials* in an effort to elevate the idea of *human rights* to a new plateau by focusing on murderous and other heinous acts against whole populations rather than individuals. In 1994 France convicted a World War II *collaborator* on this charge. Beginning in the 1990s, charges were brought by an international tribunal investigating wars in *Bosnia* and *Kosovo*. The original definition included enslavement, extermination, forcible *deportation*, and *genocide*. In 2001 the Tribunal for the Former Yugoslavia added *rape* to the list of crimes against humanity when it convicted three Serbs for "sexual slavery," the first-ever international convictions on that charge. *See also crimes against peace; war crimes.*

crimes against peace. In a London Agreement signed by the major *Allies* in 1945, certain acts were defined as "crimes against peace." The definition, which was vague and remains controversial, included: "planning, preparation, initiation or waging a war of aggression." Since *aggression* remains ill-defined in law, and because preparations for *self-defense* or *deterrence* may be similar to preparations for offense, many legal thinkers reject this category of international crimes. *See also crimes against humanity;* nullum crimen; *Nuremberg; Tokyo war crimes trials; war crimes.*

crisis. A decisive point in a serious conflict between or among states, with the potential to lead to war if the issues at stake pertain to security, or to some major change in interstate relations, if they concern economic or other nonmilitary conflict. A crisis also represents an opportunity for resolution of the conflict, mainly by focusing the attention of top leaders on it. Some domestic politicians employ the language of crisis to raise fears to a level that makes possible legislative action that resolves a long-standing issue. Only a reckless *diplomat* or *statesman* would employ that technique, because the stakes are so high during a genuine international crisis that such a tactic might well lead to war. In *political science* literature, the term is often laden with additives, such as "decision making," "hegemonic," "systemic," and so on, or dissected into minuscule parts for further analysis. Much effort has been spent by political scientists scribbling arcane analysis of the mechanics of *crisis management* and of *decision-making theory.* For all that, a "crisis" remains a simple metaphor pointing to a hinge moment around which the basic character of events may turn, one way or another, according to the quality of statecraft each participant brings to bear. *See also Agadir; Berlin airlift; brinkmanship; Cuban Missile Crisis; debt crisis; Fashoda; mobilization crisis; Moroccan crisis; Munich Conference; Suez Crisis; tension.*

crisis management. Efforts to control the degree of hostility engendered during a *crisis*, and in particular to abort the tendency toward *escalation.* Theoretical studies of crisis management tend to stress either altering the structure of the confrontation, thereby expanding the time available for analysis and decision making, or somehow adjusting the psychology and perceptions of participants or finding ways to let both sides save *face.* Critics object that such volatile situations cannot be managed by preset schemes or in accord with a flow chart; they must instead be addressed through creative intuition and *diplomacy* and by a willingness for political flexibility. *See also accommodation; conflict management.*

crisis stability. The assumption that the *balance of terror* is such that neither side has any incentive to use *nuclear weapons*, even in a severe crisis.

critical mass. The amount of enriched uranium or *plutonium* needed to sustain a nuclear chain reaction, and so produce an *atomic bomb*.

critical theory (CT). This redundant term denotes a fashionable academic derivative of the Frankfurt School of *Marxism*, which subsequently attracted many non-Marxist adherents as well. CT rejects any epistemology holding that reality exists separate from the observer and is therefore objectively knowable to any real degree. All knowledge about international relations instead merely reflects the biases and power interests of the observer (the usual targets are "racial, class, and economic elites"). Young scholars and students are warned against the attempt to acquire objective knowledge of the reality of international relations, which traditionally was the moral and intellectual raison d'être of the profession. Rather than seek to impartially map out, explore, and explain the *international society* of states and its complex subsystems and mores,—a feat said by CT theorists to be impossible, misconceived, and reinforcing of dominant power structures in academia and society at large—scholars are to directly engage and change the world (even though that too ought to be impossible, if they are unable to understand it in the first place). Such radical chic *relativism* too often leads to polemical harangues, as opposed to scholarly studies, that purport to unmask elites whose pervasive and corrupt power is said to sustain and operate exploitative societies and a fatally unjust *international system*. It is also important to note that CT is thoroughly normative but takes great pains to say it is not, in order to then dismiss the "inherent normative bias" of traditional scholarship on issues of *peace, capitalism,* and *democracy.* There is much intolerance and angry posturing here as well, as in calls for "exposure" of "fellow-traveling" academic approaches, which are identified, more or less prejudicially, as legitimizing and reinforcing irredeemably illicit power structures. In sum, in its epistemological assertion that all knowledge is radically subjective or merely political, critical theory denies the possibility of objective knowledge or the value of other scholarly traditions.

However, in proclaiming that all knowledge is merely political and that only critical theorists are on the "side of the angels"—against illegitimate power—critical theory is revealed as a merely sophomoric (it is not sufficiently serious to be described as a philosophical) moral pose. In this writer's judgment, future intellectual historians are likely to dismiss CT in a single derisive footnote as a last-gasp retreat by certain academics into a relativism that permitted continued avoidance of the messy facts of late twentieth-century international relations. These included situations where individual leaders and even large populations chose atavistic and hard-nationalist political forms, whereas others embraced new-found liberties and the material satisfactions of *free trade* and *globalization*. Nowhere, on the other hand, was there a voluntary embrace of tried-and-failed collectivist notions or any mass preference for radical experimentation over pragmatic progress. Or, historians may write tomes explaining how, at the height of the practical and moral success of liberalism and liberal-internationalism, and having dispatched *fascism* and *communism* over the course of the twentieth century and newly brought hundreds of millions of people to greater personal fulfillment and prosperity than any other societies in history, market democracies yet harbored in their universities a coterie of scholars whose central goal was to inculcate cynicism among students by routinely contrasting the humanly flawed practices of genuinely democratic societies with theoretical utopias, including several forms already demonstrated to have led to real-world dystopias, without either noticing or noting the epistemological difference. Those seriously interested in international history and international relations hence would be well served to do what all statesmen and sober decision makers do on the rare occasions they encounter CT beyond academia: ignore it. *See also boundary*; *classical school*; *Luddism*; *postmodernism*.

Croatia. From 1102, this mainly Roman Catholic area was subordinate to Hungary. It achieved limited *autonomy* after 1868. In 1917, exiled Croat leaders signed the *Pact of Corfu*, leading to Croatia becoming part of the federal state of Yugoslavia. In 1939 Croatian *fascists*, led by Ante Pavelic, launched a terrorist campaign aiming at secession. In 1941 a puppet regime raised by the German invasion accepted *Nazi* and Italian authority and protection and signed the *Tripartite Pact*. Extremists in the *Uštaše* committed wartime atrocities against Serbs, Jews, Muslims, and Communist *partisans*, murdering perhaps half a million. Croatia was forced into Yugoslavia upon its and Germany's defeat in 1945, and *Tito* ordered bloody reprisals against Croat collaborators. In the 1960s a Communist *apparatchnik* and hack historian, Franjo Tudjman (1922–1999), disputed the national mythology of Serbian suffering in World War II and downplayed Croat crimes. By thus revising history, Tudjman emerged as leader of a nationalist revival, 1968–1971, known as the "Croat Spring." Tito eventually crushed the movement and Tudjman was jailed. After his release, he and other nationalist Croats went underground. When multiparty politics re-emerged in Yugoslavia in the late 1980s, Tudjman formed the nationalist Croatian Democratic Union, Croatia's first opposition party in 50 years. On June 25, 1991, the CDU declared Croatian independence, under the provocative flag of the *Uštaše* wartime state. Germany pushed the European Union and NATO to premature recognition of Croat independence, starting a cascade of Balkan recognitions that fed into the *Third Balkan War*. Proclaiming Croatia an ethnic national homeland provoked a rebellion by ethnic Serbs in its province of *Krajiina*, which was supported by Serbia. By the end of 1991 more than 10,000 Croat fighters were dead and a Serb Republic of Croatia was in *de facto* control of Krajiina.

Despite the ongoing civil war, in January 1992 Croatia's independence was *recognized* by the *European Community*, pushed hard by Germany. Croatia supported ethnic Croat militia in their attack on neighboring Bosnia, ostensibly to protect other Croats there from *ethnic cleansing*, but principally to carve up Bosnia in a secret concert Tudjman made with Serbia. In January 1994, as Bosnian Muslims retook lands seized from them earlier in the war, Croatia threatened to intervene, but *NATO* blocked that threat. In December the Serbian *enclave* of *Vukovar* was returned to Croat control after two years of United Nations administration. Fighting in Bosnia ended temporarily with the *Dayton Peace Accords* in 1995. In 1997 Croatia retook additional enclaves from the Serbs.

Cromwell, Oliver (1599–1658). English revolutionary, lord protector of the English Commonwealth. He converted to the Puritan faith after his marriage in 1620. In 1628 he was elected to Parliament, rising to prominence during the "Long Parliament." When the First English Civil War (1642–1646) broke out, he became a leader of parliamentary forces (Roundheads) against King Charles I (1600–1649), organizing his Ironside regiments around strict martial discipline learned from *Gustav II* of Sweden and the moral discipline he believed he had directly from God. Like Gustavus, Cromwell revolutionized warfare by practicing the martial arts ruthlessly, but with an eye to technological changes, in the rate of fire of musketry and the weight of cannon, for instance. He also built a *standing army* based on *conscription*. Often leading from the front, Cromwell bested Royalist forces (Cavaliers) in a series of decisive battles: Grantham (May 13, 1643), Marston Moor (July 2, 1644), and Naseby (June 14, 1645), after which Charles surrendered. Parliament feared the New Army, however, and voted to disband it in 1647. Cromwell now chose the army over democracy, occupied London, and chased his opponents from Parliament. Charles conspired endlessly from his seat of exile on the Isle of Wight, even encouraging the Scots to rise. That rejoined Cromwell's interests and the broader interests of Parliament and launched the Second English Civil War (1648–1649). Once more, Cromwell's New Army was brilliantly successful, pacifying Wales and turning back a Scottish-Royalist army at Preston (August 17–19, 1648). Secured in power, Cromwell pressured Parliament to try and to execute the king. It did so, though with reluctance, in 1649.

The Puritan revolution was now almost complete. After putting down a *mutiny* in the army, Cromwell led a punitive nine-month expedition to Ireland, 1649–1650. He did not enjoy the same easy success in Ireland that he had against the ill-led Cavalier armies, but he won nonetheless. After that, fighting continued against his subcommanders as the Irish reverted to *guerrilla warfare* until 1653. Cromwell's campaign is still remembered by the Irish for its savagery, including deliberate massacre of the entire population of several captured garrison towns, most famously, Drogheda. Scotland rose against him next, starting the Third English Civil War (1650–1651). At its end, Cromwell passed a tough *Navigation Act* in 1651, which aimed at the maritime predominance of the Netherlands and sparked the first *Anglo-Dutch War*, and a century later resonated in England's relations with its American colonies. In 1653 Cromwell famously dismissed the Long Parliament, saying: "You have sat long enough. Let us have done with you! In the name of God, go!" He instituted a military dictatorship and was named Lord Protector of a new Puritan Commonwealth. From 1652 to 1654 he went to war with the Netherlands over commercial interests abroad, even as he still tangled with an obstructionist Parliament at home. In the spreading wake of the *Thirty Years' War*, from which he and ongoing civil conflict had kept England apart, he was seen by many as the protector of Protestant Europe. He made peace with the Protestant Dutch but then allied with Catholic France against Spain, making war on Madrid in 1656. He recalled Parliament to raise war taxes for these conflicts, spurning the offer made by some to crown him as a new English king. Cromwell proved a hard master, but he also set England squarely on the path to becoming a *Great Power*. He modernized its army, expanded its navy, and added several strategic overseas holdings to its ever-expanding empire. Despite his radical Puritanism, he even partly liberalized religious life, permitting new toleration of Catholics, Dissenters, and Jews. Finally, Scotland and Ireland were both tied more closely to England. For all that, he failed as a constitutional revolutionary: Charles II (1630–1685) was restored to the English throne three years after Cromwell's death, displacing the Lord Protector's own son. *See also East India Company; line of demarcation.*

Suggested Readings: R. Cust and Ann Hughes, eds., *The English Civil War* (1997); Ronald Hutton, *The British Republic, 1649–1660* (2000); J. S. Morril, *Oliver Cromwell and the English Revolution* (1990); L. Stone, *Causes of the English Revolution* (1972); James Wheeler, *Cromwell in Ireland* (1999).

crown colony. One that the *metropolitan power* (especially if a monarchy) rules directly, rather than through a local representative legislature. *See also charter colony; Sarawak.*

cruise missile. A guided or remote, air-breathing, pilotless missile that is capable of delivering *conventional* or nuclear ordnance. It may be fired from a ship, aircraft, or *submarine*. It is not a *ballistic missile*. Instead, it hugs terrain using TV, satellite guidance, and inboard computers. Cruise missiles were deployed by *NATO* in the 1980s. A French version was used against British ships by Argentina during the *Falklands War*. Various cruise missiles had a devastating impact on land targets in the *Gulf War* and in punitive attacks against Iraq in 1992–1993. *Clinton* made them his "casualty-free" weapon of choice, at various times firing them into Afghanistan, Iraq, Serbia, and Sudan. *See also terrain contour matching.*

cruiser. A medium tonnage, medium-armored *warship*, capable of high speeds and forward duty to locate the *capital ships* of the enemy fleet, but, unlike simple scouts or destroyers, able to then disengage without being crippled. During most of the twentieth century, a heavy cruiser generally sported eight-inch guns; a light cruiser mounted six-inch guns. This class of ships was first developed to provide a screen for heavier capital ships, but by the late twentieth century had completely replaced *battleships*. With Aegis technology, they performed the additional key function of multiple missile and aircraft defense of *aircraft carrier* battle groups. *See also battle cruiser; cruiser warfare; dreadnought.*

cruiser warfare, rules of. Also known as the rules of commerce raiding. This required that a surface raider (usually a *cruiser*) must give enemy merchant ships fair warning and make provision for the safety of the enemy crew and passengers, before sinking their ship. This could mean transporting them to a *neutral* port, or at least providing lifeboats, food, and water. These rules simply could not be followed by *submarines*, however, because of their vulnerability while on the surface to ramming by any larger surface ship or to fire from armed merchant or escort vessels. Also limiting was their highly restricted space, which did not permit taking *prisoners of war* (or other survivors) on board. This led to great friction between the United States and Germany during *World War I*, culminating in the *Lusitania notes* and American entry into the war in 1917 after Germany's resumption of *unrestricted submarine warfare*. By *World War II*, however, all major navies—including the American—had abandoned the effort to apply cruiser rules to submarine warfare. *See also Karl Dönitz; just war tradition.*

Crusades. The motivations behind the Crusades, which occupied more than 200 years of Latin *Christian* interaction with the *Islamic* world, were deep and complex. They included economic pressures, born of a rising European population and renewed prosperity, and regional competition born of a revival of long dormant trade with and within the Mediterranean. The Crusades also represented a historical reversal—led by its leading warrior-cultures, the Christianized *Normans* and the fanatic *Teutonic Knights*—of 600 years of Asiatic, Arab, and *Viking* invasions of Europe. Now, Western European armies moved from hunkered, castilian defense against invasion to territorial offensive and expansionism, under the cover of service to a common faith. The Crusades also genuinely spoke to apocalyptic religious traditions, sincere religious piety, and a mass penitence movement. So mixed were these populations and motives that scholars point out that it is therefore difficult to tell crusader from Christian pilgrim until about 1200. Crusading offered alternate careers to members of the warrior classes who were needed less at home than before, but whom European society still maintained through its Normanized, *feudal* social and economic structures. Crusades may thus have provided a "safety valve" for advancing societies desirous of becoming more peaceful, increasingly urban, whose population was once again rapidly expanding, and who wished and needed to send abroad dangerous, armed rural men who were no longer required to defend against nomadic invaders.

This rich mix of motives was important in sustaining the crusading spirit over successive generations, as crusading was enormously expensive; to outfit and maintain a single knight and mount might take four years' income. Therefore, it was crucial that crusading was also made spiritually attractive by the *Catholic Church*. Several popes, and perhaps even more the Church as a whole, embraced crusading. The pious were granted remission of sins as crusading was licensed by the clergy as a form of penance. Indulgences thus went to holy warriors, while the more brutal among them also enjoyed the fact that the *just war* restrictions of the Church were waived for those fighting infidels. Reinforcing this sense of religious mission, and underlying the Crusades at a strategic level, was an older geopolitical antagonism to Muslim power and interruption of Mediterranean trade, a related hatred for *corsairs* operated by Muslim states in North Africa, and a new antagonism to Islamic revival in Egypt and Turkey and consequent military pressure brought to bear on fellow Christians in the *Byzantine Empire*.

The First Crusade (the Clermont Appeal) was called in 1095 by Pope Urban II. In 1099 the crusaders sacked Jerusalem, mercilessly putting thousands to the sword in an *atrocity* remembered still in the Middle East—a region that had more than its share of them over the centuries. Yet, at the time the Crusades were seen in the West as an attempt to recover lands lost to Islam during that other warrior faith's first century of *jihad*. In this sense, the Crusades were a failed Christian *holy war* at least partly launched and sustained as an attempt to recover for Christendom lands long lost to the prior Muslim holy war, or jihad. Over time, this belated counterattack retook from Islam the formerly Christian lands of Spain, southern Russia, and most of the Balkans, but was unable to retake North Africa or hold for long the cradle of the Christian faith in the Middle East. As the movement grew, Crusades were also fought in the Baltic, against the Albigensian heresy in France, and against select enemies of the popes in western Europe, and by the Teutonic Knights in northern and eastern Europe.

Initially, the Muslim response to the capture of Jerusalem was tepid, as Muslim power at that time was badly divided among quarrelsome emirates. However, as the Franks (as most crusaders were known to Muslims) foolishly went on to raid and attack the heart of Islam in the *Hejaz*, the Muslim world was roused to counterattack and to a new jihad to expel the crusaders from the region. The Holy City of Jerusalem thus was held and ruled by orders of crusader knights, and known as the Latin Kingdom of Jerusalem, only until 1187, the year the great *Salāh-ed-Dīn*, Sultan of Egypt and Syria, destroyed a Christian army at Tiberias and retook Jerusalem for Islam. The Third Crusade was assembled and led by King Richard I (Coeur de Lion, 1157–1199) of England and King Philip of France. It retook Acre in 1191, but was unable to retake Jerusalem in two advances against it. Small crusader kingdoms remained in the Levant and were established en route on Malta and Cyprus (1197). Also a Latin kingdom was briefly established in *Constantinople* (1204–1261) by crusaders who never made it to the Holy Lands, but attacked and overran parts of the *Byzantine Empire* instead. Other kings and barons with a better sense of strategic direction made it to the Middle East. The great Emperor Frederick II of Germany crusaded to the Holy Land in 1228, but his and other later expeditions never enjoyed the success of the First Crusade. Even as Muslim pressure began to wear down the outlying Crusader states, local conflicts in the fractured West kept would-be crusaders at home to contest for power, so that reinforcements began to thin. For a time Islam and Christianity faced a new and common threat to the region, from the *Mongols*. This did not unite them so much as mutually distract and weaken both civilizations, tie down their military resources, and delay the denouement of the Crusader states.

The era of crusades to the Middle East effectively ended with military failure in the Holy Land and secular depression of Europe's population and economy during the fourteenth century. In 1453 the *Ottomans* captured Constantinople, at last toppling the Byzantine Empire and bringing the Muslim form of holy war, the jihad, deep into Europe itself, for the fourth time. The Spanish Reconquista of Iberia was part crusade, part migration, lasting some 800 years and ending only with the capture of Granada in 1492. The zealous impulse behind the Reconquista influenced Spanish policy for another 150 years after that, driving its fanatic opposition to the *Reformation* and its conquest and conversion of the Americas. Crusading language and perhaps also motivations coursed through Russian propaganda into the nineteenth and even early twentieth centuries, regarding Central Asia and the Turks.

Perhaps the deepest irony still attending to the wars of the Crusades in the Middle East is that they were won by Muslims, many of whom today remember them with a bitterness almost contemporary in its intensity and as precursors to much later European domination of Muslim lands. On the other hand, they were largely forgotten by Europeans, who lost these ancient wars but went on to conquer and dominate most of the rest of the world, and then to fight far more savage and destructive wars with one another. *See also assassin; Age of Exploration; Knights Hospitallers; Knights Templar; Inquisition; just war tradition; Latvia; Lithuania; Livonian Order; Mamluks; Palestine.*

Suggested Readings: Carole Hillenbrand, *Crusades: Islamic Perspectives* (2000); P. M. Holt, *Age of the Crusades* (1986); T. Madden, *Concise History of the Crusades* (1999); Hans Mayer, *The Crusades* (trans. and rev. ed. 1988); Jonathon Riley-Smith, *The Crusades* (1990); Jonathon Riley-Smith, ed., *Oxford History of the Crusades* (1999); Jonathon Riley-Smith, *A History of the Crusades* (2000).

cryptanalysis. The science and study of all procedures and methods of code-making, *ciphering*, and rendering secret writing, and all procedures and methods used in code-breaking and analysis of secret writing.

Suggested Readings: R. Lewin, *American Magic* (1982); Simon Singh, *The Code Book* (1999).

cryptography. All procedures and methods of code-making, *ciphering* and secret writing.

cryptology. All procedures and methods used in code-breaking and analysis of secret writing.

CSBMs. *See Confidence and Security Building Measures; CSCE.*

CSCE. *See Conference on Security and Cooperation in Europe.*

CSIS. Canadian Security and Intelligence Service. It was set up in the 1980s to take over from the *intelligence* division of the RCMP, which had been discredited by a scandal over illegal operations against *separatists* in *Québec* in the 1970s. It is confined to *counterintelligence*, and even then may not act abroad. Its main focus is counterterrorism.

Cuba. This Caribbean island was inhabited by Arawak Indians when it was charted and claimed for Spain by *Christopher Columbus* in 1492. It was conquered, with great brutality and overt *terrorism*, in 1511. One of the conquerors was *Cortés*, who later applied lessons learned in Cuba to his conquest of Mexico. Slaves were imported from West Africa to sustain a gold-mining and plantation economy, as the Indian population succumbed to disease and destitution. Cuba remained a colony until the *Spanish-American War* in 1898, with the exception that the British occupied Havana, 1762–1763. In 1868 a 10-year uprising against Spanish rule began without exciting U.S. opinion. *Slavery* was abolished in 1886. Another rebellion began in 1895, under Jose Marti. By 1898 U.S. opinion favored intervention, which was sparked by the sinking of the U.S. warship *Maine* in Havana harbor. The war forced Spain to renounce all claims to Cuba. Cuban independence was granted with the proviso that the United States retained a right of intervention (the *Platt Amendment*).

U.S. marines accordingly intervened in Cuba in 1906, 1913, 1917, and 1933. In 1934 the United States gave up its right to intervene as part of the *Good Neighbor* policy. In 1934 *Fulgencio Batista* seized power and held it until 1944. He seized it again in 1952 in another coup. He favored foreign investor (including Mafia) interests and ran a corrupt administration. In 1956 a rebel uprising began, led by *Fidel Castro* and *Che Guevara*. With the success of the *Cuban Revolution*, Batista fled in January 1959.

Castro became premier and immediately moved to repress all opposition. In short order, executions began and the count of *political prisoners* rose as it emerged that the regime was thoroughly *Marxist,* though in Castro's case adherence to the doctrine was personalized and appears to have evolved as a self-serving legitimation of his personal rule. Castro *nationalized* much of the economy, mostly without *compensation.* Hundreds of thousands of Cubans fled. Most settled in nearby Florida, where for the next several decades they formed an important lobby stiffening U.S. policy toward Cuba. In 1961 CIA-trained Cubans landed at the *Bay of Pigs* in an attempt to overthrow Castro, who was steadily moving Cuba into the *Soviet bloc* and developing it as a *Communist* state. In 1962 *Kennedy* imposed a trade *embargo,* severely damaging Cuba's economy (the United States was Cuba's natural export market) and pushing Castro even closer to the Soviet Union. In October 1962, the *Cuban Missile Crisis* brought the world to the brink of all-out *nuclear war.* In the early 1970s, U.S.-Cuban relations remained tense over Castro's support for left-wing guerrillas in South and Central America. In 1975 Castro sent troops to fight in civil wars in Angola and Mozambique. In 1977 Castro helped a particularly vicious regime in Ethiopia defeat Somalia. That year, Cuba and the United States established diplomatic contact, but still did not restore full relations. In the *Mariel boat lift* of 1980, 150,000 Cubans left for the United States. This cynical escape valve was opened again by Castro in 1994. In 1983 Cuban military engineers and U.S. troops clashed during the *invasion of Grenada.* Cuba withdrew from Africa when a regional settlement was reached on Namibia and the *revolution* in Ethiopia collapsed. After 1990, with Soviet aid gone, Castro introduced severe rationing but refused to renounce the *Cuban Revolution* or introduce democratic reforms. Throughout the 1990s a two-tiered economy was developed wherein Castro catered to rich tourists who paid in dollars, but kept the rest of the country economically segregated. In 2001 *George W. Bush* reiterated the American commitment to sanctions, but Congress partially eased these nonetheless. In January 2002, Russia ended some 40 years of military presence in Cuba when it withdrew the last of its forces from the island. Note: The United States maintains a naval and marine base at *Guantánamo* Bay.

Cuban Missile Crisis (October 15–28, 1962). This great confrontation arose mainly because—with the recovery and consolidation of Western Europe and Japan into the American camp—the Soviet Union was already clearly losing the *Cold War* in the main theaters of competition. The crisis over missiles in Cuba was nevertheless the major turning point in the Cold War, with each side backing away from direct military confrontation ever after—a fact that over time ensured the peaceful victory of the Western powers. The most dangerous phase of this crisis lasted 13 days, raising global tensions over the possibility of *nuclear war* to their highest point in the Cold War. (*Dean Rusk* talked of going "eyeball to eyeball" with the Soviets.) *U-2* spy planes discovered six Soviet nuclear missile bases under secret construction in Cuba (October 15th). In fact, the Soviets deployed in Cuba medium-range ballistic missiles, intermediate-range ballistic missiles, cruise missiles, Il-28 medium-range bombers with fighter escorts, as well as antiaircraft batteries, battle rockets, and more than 40,000 Soviet troops. Soviet sources later revealed there were 158 strategic and tactical nuclear warheads in Cuba during the crisis, with 42 capable of hitting U.S. targets. *Nikita Khrushchev* appears to have ordered this major deployment to balance the Soviet Union's *deterrent* shortfall in *ICBMs* capable of hitting the United States. The United States had a 17 to 1 advantage in *strategic weapons*, but putting otherwise out-of-range Soviet medium- and intermediate-range missiles in Cuba made them effectively strategic threats to U.S. targets. Khrushchev also entertained a reckless, romantic wish to guarantee the survival of *Castro's* regime subsequent to the *Bay of Pigs invasion*.

After taking a week to decide a course of action, *John F. Kennedy* announced this discovery to the Soviets and the world, warning that use of these missiles would lead to a "full, retaliatory response" by U.S. nuclear forces upon the territory of the Soviet Union itself. While reserving the option of invading Cuba, he chose in the interim to impose a *quarantine* while demanding removal of the missiles (October 22nd). Meanwhile, the *Organization of American States* (OAS) voted unanimously to support the American demand for removal of the missiles. Soviet ships closed on the U.S. *blockade* line and engineers sped up construction of the sites, while U.S. forces prepared to bomb or invade to take out the bases. In private, Kennedy pushed for a compromise, using his brother Robert to negotiate with the Soviets in ways that circumvented even his own advisers. Nevertheless, on several occasions Soviet and U.S. units were engaged and some minor casualties were incurred, though this was not announced at the time. On October 27th a U-2 spy plane was shot down by Cuban forces; other clashes took place along the blockade line. The crisis was resolved by Soviet agreement to withdraw the missiles (October 28th) in exchange for a public pledge by the United States not to invade Cuba, and a more important secret agreement to remove within six months 15 comparable (Jupiter) missiles the United States had based in Turkey. The quarantine was formally lifted on November 21st, as the last of the Soviet missiles departed for Russia.

In 1990–1991 it became clear that the crisis was even more serious than previously thought. A Soviet official said that Russian troops had operational *tactical nuclear weapons* in Cuba at the time and that orders had been issued releasing use of these to the discretion of the local commander (in fact, the order had been rescinded on October 22nd). This implied that had a U.S. invasion taken place it would likely have been met with tactical nuclear weapons, even though use of such weapons within 90 miles of Florida—and against American troops—would almost certainly have required a comparable response, perhaps from Turkey or Europe. Subsequent to the crisis, a mini-

détente developed and down the road both states moved toward acceptance of *assured destruction* and nuclear *arms control*. In the medium run, the Soviet Union after the crisis appeared as a more equal opponent of the United States in the Cold War and greater emphasis was placed on military capabilities, which was the one area in which the Soviet Union could effectively compete. This was an illusion, however: the fundamental and still-advancing superiority of the West on virtually all other political, economic, cultural, and also moral grounds continued slowly and ineluctably to undermine Soviet claims to *legitimacy*, over its empire and ultimately also at home. *See also Monroe Doctrine.*

Suggested Readings: James Blight et al., *Cuba on the Brink* (1993); Ernest May and P. Zelikow, eds., *The Kennedy Tapes* (1997).

Cuban Revolution (1959–1962). It began with a rebel rising led by *Fidel Castro* and *Che Guevara* against the *Batistá* regime. At first, *Eisenhower* reacted calmly to this *Communist* seizure of power, but then he authorized planning for the *Bay of Pigs* operation (which *Kennedy* implemented) to overthrow Castro's revolutionary regime. When Castro became premier in 1960, the revolution moved into a highly repressive stage and development of a *cult of personality* from which it never really emerged. There was large-scale *nationalization* of the economy and an across-the-board shift to the *Soviet bloc*, in part driven by a U.S. *embargo* and diplomatic hostility. That shift actually surprised the Soviets, who were not used to seeing a country turn Marxist without the assistance of the *Red Army*. With the failure of the Bay of Pigs, the *Kennedy* administration—and the United States generally—was humiliated. Kennedy authorized Castro's *assassination*, but several inept attempts by the *CIA* failed, leaving Castro in power and the U.S. embargo in place. The revolution provided literacy and primary health care to many, surpassing most other states in the region in these areas at least. It firmed up this base of domestic support with tenant reform and land redistribution. Its repressive nature never eased, however, and was all that remained as disintegration of the Soviet bloc from 1989 to 1991 ended the huge *subsidies* that for thirty years had artificially sustained Cuba's economy, social welfare system, and the Castro regime. Into the new century, an aging Castro and his stagnant revolution presided over a smoldering but cowed opposition, as the revolution deteriorated into a death watch over an old dictator who would not step aside and could not be opposed.

cuius regio eius religio. *See Peace of Augsburg.*

culpability. In *international law*, a doctrine whereby legal responsibility is established by reference to intentionality or negligence.

cult of personality. Concentration of all political power and authority in a single individual at the head of a *totalitarian* state and near-deification of that person in state *propaganda*. Leaders are portrayed as superhuman in their heroism, knowledge, wisdom, or any other political virtue called upon by the needs of the moment or regime. This serves to sustain them in absolute power, deter even obvious criticism, and legitimate whatever policy shifts and twists they feel compelled to make by reason of necessity or whim. The term appears to have originated with *Nikita Khrushchev's* 1956 *secret speech*. Among the more infamous and pervasive cults of the twentieth century were those of *Hitler, Hô Chí Minh, Kim Il Sung, Lenin, Mao, Mussolini, Pol Pot, Saddam Hussein*, and the father of the genre, *Stalin*. *See also Hirohito; Zhivkov*.

cultural exchanges. Encouragement or sponsorship of private exchanges of artistic, literary, musical, or scientific activities. They may be used to soften *public opinion* and enhance a *rapprochement*, as a form of *propaganda*, or from genuine interest in cultivating superior tastes in the arts and literature. *See also Olympic Games; ping pong diplomacy*.

cultural imperialism. When the values of one nation or social system are deliberately imposed on another, especially a colonized people, as in the policy of *Russification*. Such a conscious policy of cultural extinction through *assimilation* of conquered peoples is usually seen by modern, external observers as morally reprehensible. Its milder forms also provoke *protectionist* policies, such as censorship or *tariffs* against importing cultural goods such as films or mass media. Yet, so-called cultural imperialism more often happens without conscious design. Instead, a strong and dynamic culture may undermine or even threaten to displace a weak or static culture, via international economic and political interaction, cross-cultural processes of communication, and *cultural exchanges*, as in so-called *Americanization*. This phenomenon is therefore increasingly referred to by diplomatic and cultural historians more neutrally as "cultural transmission." *See also capitalism; communism; diffusion; globalization; global village; human rights; imperialism; integration; modernization;* négritude; *pan-Africanism; Philip II; Sinification; Uruguay Round*.

culturalism. The historic dedication of most Chinese not only to their unique institutions but to deeper sources of common norms and values that make up the Chinese way of life. Some scholars compare the rare intensity of this devotion to late developing, but still European-style *nationalism*. Others suggest it unites Chinese civilization in ways more akin to how Latin *Christendom* was unified under the *res publica Christiana*: culturally, but not politically. Perhaps neither analogy holds, given the great difference in the past 500 years of Western and Chinese history. In early modern Europe, local loyalties increasingly focused on *nation-states* because a decentralized and cutthroat *state system* arose from the ashes of *feudalism* and the *wars of religion*. In China, historically the traditional divide was a huge cultural gulf between the highly civilized *Han* and the various barbarian peoples of *Inner Asia*, who occasionally conquered China but even then were always viewed by the Han (if only in private) as culturally inferior.

cultural relativism. *See relativism.*

cultural revolution. (1) A policy adopted by the *Bolsheviks* from the end of the *New Economic Policy*, c. 1928–1932, marked by *Stalin's* edicts against the *kulaks* and in favor of forced *collectivization*, the most deleterious effect of which was the deaths of millions from forced deportation, execution, and *famine*. This shift signaled a return to the spirit of class warfare that had characterized *war communism*. Failures to meet production quotas were blamed not on the central planner who set them too high (Stalin), but on "wreckers," kulaks, and other supposed enlistees in the army of *counterrevolution*. (2) An even more disastrous experience in China, officially known as the *Great Proletarian Cultural Revolution*. (3) Any conscious, official effort by government to harness culture to the purposes of the state, such as in the reorganization of *Shinto* during the *Meiji Restoration* in Japan; or *Nazi* or other right-wing *totalitarian* efforts to make culture an instrument of state power; or for that matter the effort by *Peter I* to make over virtually all of Russian society and institutions.

cultural transmission. *See cultural imperialism.*

curfew. A military or emergency order confining a population to certain zones or hours of public intercourse. A common feature of *occupation*, it may also be used domestically to quell civil unrest or dissent.

Curragh incident (March 1914). A mass resignation (in effect, a *mutiny*) of *Protestant* British Army officers in Ireland, provoked by the prospect of their having to use force to make *Ulster's* Protestant population accept *Home Rule* that was bound to be dominated by the whole island's *Catholic* majority. London backed down, and the outbreak of *World War I* in August rendered the issue moot. Within two years Irish nationalists struck in the *Easter Rising*, and in 1918 the *Irish War of Independence* broke out. British officers tended to see their duty more clearly with regard to those conflicts.

currency. The physical component of a nation's money supply, comprised of bank notes and coins, as well as government bonds. A currency crisis occurs when *exchange rates* fall rapidly even while interest rates are increasing sharply. This may follow, or lead to, loss of confidence in a given currency as a result of excessive debt, high peacetime *inflation*, or high inflation brought about by military spending during wartime.

current account. The record of all financial flows resulting from trade in *goods and services*, including interest, *profits*, and *remittances*. A current account deficit is when exports and financial inflows, from both private and public sources, are exceeded by the value of imports and financial outflows from private and public sources. *See also balance of payments.*

Curzon, George (1859–1925). Viceroy of India, 1898–1905; foreign secretary, 1919–1924. As viceroy, he strengthened the frontier against a nonexistent threat from Russia and then oversaw the invasion of *Tibet* in 1904. His real ambition was to control Persia and the Persian Gulf, but in this he failed. He was a determined social reformer, but was more effective as a builder of *railways* and protector of antiquities. In 1905 he arrogantly and arbitrarily partitioned *Bengal*, rousing massive popular opposition that reverberated in nationalist circles throughout India for many years. He lost the argument with *Kitchener* over who should control colonial policy and the *Indian Army*, and he quit India. After serving as chancellor of the University of Oxford he joined the War Cabinet in 1915. As foreign secretary after *World War I*, he repeatedly lost policy arguments to his prime minister, *Lloyd George*, and he was bitterly disappointed never to become prime minister himself. He had successes too: he blocked French ambitions to create a separate Rhenish state, lent his name to the *Curzon Line*, and negotiated the *Treaty of Lausanne*. He succeeded in public life in spite of a severe back deformity, which he suffered painfully but silently from childhood. *See also Congress Party; Muslim League.*

Curzon Line. A proposal for settlement of the frontier question between Poland and Russia. It was designed to adhere roughly to principles of *self-determination* by excluding from Poland eastern areas populated by non-Poles. Poland rejected the proposal, keeping and expanding those territories in the *Polish-Soviet War* of 1920. In 1939 the Curzon Line served as the *boundary* between *Nazi Germany* and the *Soviet Union* after Eastern Europe was divided in the *Nazi-Soviet Pact*. In 1945 it became the border between the new Poland and a greatly expanded Soviet Union.

customary international law. *See international customary law.*

customs. Duties, or excise tax, imposed by governments or by *customs unions* on imports. Very rarely, duties may be imposed on exports.

customs union. An arrangement among states that lowers, regulates, and "unifies" their *tariffs* vis-à-vis states not in the union. It aims at removal of all barriers to trade between two or more states, in which a common external tariff is kept up against other states. *See also BENELUX; European Economic Area; European Economic Community; free trade area; Mercosur; Zollverein.*

cutting-edge research. Academic *jargon* for whatever is currently fashionable in a discipline or just for "what I am personally interested in" or "presently writing." As an aeronautical metaphor, it fails to appreciate that it is actually the trailing edge of a wing that provides lift.

cybernetic theory. Originally, a communication and control theory concerned with the comparative study of automatic systems. It was first developed in the study of neurology and mechanics. By analogy, cybernetic theory (actually, it is an encrusted metaphor rather than a theory) is applied by some social scientists to so-called automatic, or bureaucratically routine, though still complex, foreign policy decision-making. *See also feedback; decision-making theory.*

Cyprus. A *Crusader* kingdom was set up on Cyprus in the twelfth century, by the *Knights Hospitallers*, where they were later joined by the *Knights Templars*. Cyprus then fell under Venetian sway. In 1571 Cyprus was captured from the Venetians by the *Ottomans*, who held it nominally within their empire until 1914, although it became a de facto British *protectorate* under terms of the *Cyprus Convention* of 1878. When war broke out in 1914, Britain took over the island. It was made a *crown colony* in 1925. Greek Cypriots agitated for *enosis*, or union with Greece, an idea opposed by Turkish Cypriots. This was resisted by the British until after *World War II*, when Cyprus was still seen by Britain as a vital strategic base. This changed after EOKA guerilla violence erupted in 1955 at the instigation of Greece and with the *Suez Crisis* and Britain's retreat from empire. A compromise was reached in 1960 among Britain, Greece, and Turkey, setting up an independent republic with Archbishop Makarios (leader of the enosis movement) as president, 1960–1974. Communal conflict led to insertion of a United Nations *peacekeeping* force in 1964. In July 1974, Greek officers attempted a coup, which forced Makarios to flee and sparked an invasion by Turkey. Turkish troops occupied its northern half, and in 1975 Turkish Cypriots founded a separate government there. Greeks were expelled from the Turkish side of the *green line* drawn between the warring communities. Makarios returned to the presidency of the Greek side in 1975 (he died in 1977).

The *Turkish Republic of Northern Cyprus* declared independence in 1983, but it remained a mere vassal of Istanbul and never enjoyed world *recognition*. By 1994 the UN began to tire of the political stalemate and of its mission: Canada withdrew its troops after 29 years in-country. The *European Union*, on the other hand, moved the Greek part of Cyprus up its membership waiting list.

Cyprus Convention (1878). By this agreement, *Disraeli* secured permission for Britain to station troops on the strategic island of Cyprus, then controlled by the *Ottoman Empire*. In exchange, London guaranteed Turkey from Russian attack.

czar. "Caesar." A mostly archaic spelling of *tsar*.

Czech Legion. A military force of volunteer *prisoners of war* organized by *Tómaš Masaryk* in 1917. It was trapped in Russia by the *Bolshevik Revolution*. It became deeply embroiled in the *Russian Civil War*, drawing in the Western allies as well, as it fought its way out via *Siberia*. One of the declared purposes of the American *Siberian intervention* was to rescue this corp of some 70,000 former allies from *World War I*. *See also Alexander Kolchak*.

Czechoslovakia. Historic *Bohemia* was an electorate within the *Holy Roman Empire*. It subsequently was ensconced within the *Austrian* (later, *Austro-Hungarian*) *Empire*, until the closing days of *World War I*. Along with Moravia and Slovakia it then formed the new state of Czechoslovakia, whose independence was confirmed with *extinction* of the Austro-Hungarian Empire. Led by *Tómaš Masaryk* and *Eduard Beneš*, this small, democratic state joined the *Little Entente* in 1920. In the 1930s it sought security guarantees from the Western democracies as *Nazi* agitators and *fifth columnists* stirred secessionist sentiment in the ethnically German *Sudetenland*. At the *Munich Conference* (September 1938), to which Czechoslovakia was not invited, the Sudetenland was handed over to Nazi Germany by France, Britain, and Italy. *Hitler* then rolled his *Panzers* into the rump of the country in March 1939. Czechoslovakia was divided into *fascist* and *puppet states*, 1940–1945. The *Red Army* liberated it in 1944, and Beneš returned as president. In 1946 he appointed as prime minister the Communist *Klement Gottwald*. In February 1948, a Communist coup forced Beneš to resign, and Gottwald, a harsh *Stalinist*, thereafter took the country deep into the *Soviet bloc*. In 1968 the *Prague Spring* swept through the capital and country, raising the reformist Communist leader *Dubček* to international prominence. Units of the Red Army were joined by forces from four *Warsaw Pact* states (Bulgaria, East Germany, Hungary, and Poland) and crushed the reforms in an unopposed invasion. In 1977 *human rights* campaigners founded *Charter '77* to again press for reform; but its leadership was arrested and the movement driven underground. In 1989 the *velvet revolution* forced the *Communist Party* from power. In 1990 a full restoration of democracy occurred, and *Václav Havel* became president. Regional and ethnic differences then surfaced between Czechs and Slovaks, partly over the speed of adjusting to a market economy, which was favored by most Czechs but not many Slovaks, as most Soviet-style heavy industries were concentrated in Slovakia. The federation suffered extinction by peaceful agreement ("velvet divorce") on January 1, 1993, splitting into the *Czech Republic* and *Slovakia*.
Suggested Reading: Karel Kaplan, *The Short March* (1987).

Czechoslovakia, invasion of (1968). *See Alexander Dubček; Prague Spring.*

Czech Republic. In 1989 regional differences in *Czechoslovakia*, aggravated by demagogic leaders, split Czechs from Slovaks. At issue was disagreement over the proposed pace of adjustment to a full *market economy* from the failed *command economy* of the Soviet period. Czechs, eager to rejoin the West, moved ahead with rapid structural reforms. In *Slovakia* the government hesitated over reform and appeared mainly interested in reviving Slovak ethnic consciousness. The differences ultimately proved irreconcilable and led to the "velvet divorce." A Czech Republic was declared simultaneously with independence of Slovakia after midnight on December 31, 1992, with *Václav Havel* as the new Czech president. During the 1990s Czechs completed a rapid and mostly successful conversion to market economics and methodically developed closer ties to the West at all levels. They immediately applied for the *partnerships for peace* program of *NATO* and for membership in the *European Union*. In March 1999, they were rewarded, as the Czech Republic was admitted to an expanded NATO.

D

Dachau. The first *concentration camp* set up by the *Nazis*, just outside Munich, after their seizure of power in Germany in 1933. It later evolved into one of the *death camps*, with multiple satellite camps surrounding it where most of the actual killing was done. It was also used to house prominent *political prisoners*, including (at various times) former Austrian Chancellor *Schuschnigg*, former French Premier *Léon Blum*, and several out-of-favor or disloyal German generals. Upon its liberation in 1945 by the American Army, many of the citizens of Munich claimed they knew nothing about what had gone on in Dachau. *Eisenhower* was so angered by this denial that he ordered German civilians walked through the camp, so that they could never again disown what had been done within range of the spring breezes that carried the stench of the dead to their homes. *See also Auschwitz; "final solution to the Jewish problem"; Holocaust.*

Dagestan. A small *statelet* in the *Caucasus* region of southern Russia, bordering Azerbaijan to the south and *Chechnya* to the north and west. It is the poorest and most ethnically diverse (there are at least 34 identifiable groups in a population of about two million) of the several Caucasian constituent republics of the Russian Federation. It became strategically important after the *Cold War* because a major *oil* pipeline was built that transversed its territory, connecting the rich oil fields of the Caspian basin to new markets in western Russia and Europe. Its capital, Makhachkala, is a major seaport serving the Caspian trade. Dagestan was badly destabilized by the war that broke out between neighboring *Chechnya* and Russia after the breakup of the Soviet Union. In 1998, violence in Dagestan approached the level of *civil war*.

Dahomey. (1) In the late seventeenth century, an Aja military power called Dahomey arose between Akwamu in Ghana (*Gold Coast*) and the *Yoruba* state of Oyo, to which it paid *tribute* after being invaded and savaged by Oyo *cavalry*, 1726–1730. Dahomey's sustained wars swelled the cargo holds of the Atlantic *slave trade* into the eighteenth century. In the early nineteenth century it continued to supply slaves to coastal traders, though much more grudgingly. Also, when the Oyo state collapsed, Dahomey was able to reassert its independence. The so-called "Amazons" of Dahomey were an all-woman combat unit that began as a bodyguard to the king and evolved into an elite force of some 3,000 female troops. They were engaged in all the kingdom's wars from the mid-nineteenth century. They were destroyed in combat with the French in the early 1890s. (2) The former name of the *Republic of Benin*.

Dáil Éireann. The Irish parliament. *See Anglo-Irish Treaty; Michael Collins; Eamon de Valera; Irish War of Independence.*

daimyo. The *feudal* lords of Japan and their feudatories. Late medieval daimyo (shugo) were slowly displaced by regional warlords (Sengoku daimyo) in the more maturely feudal sixteenth century. These men exercised more power over the peasants and *samurai* and enjoyed greater independence from Kyoto. They were tamed, however, by *Nobunaga* and *Hideyoshi*, and by the *bakufu* under the *Tokugawa shoguns*. As a class, the daimyo were effectively eliminated after the *Meiji Restoration*; their feudatories were reorganized as prefectures in 1871.

Daladier, Édouard (1884–1970). French Radical Socialist premier, 1933, 1934, and 1938–1940. He played second fiddle to *Chamberlain*'s lead at the *Munich Conference*, endorsing *appeasement* but without the same public enthusiasm as his English colleague. He resigned as premier in 1940, but still served as minister of war and as foreign minister. In 1942 he, *Léon Blum*, and General Gamelin were put on trial by *Vichy* for alleged treasonable responsibility for the defeat suffered in the *Battle of France*. The trial was canceled when Blum's brilliant defense turned it into a showcase against Vichy's own extensive *collaboration*. Daladier was then deported to Germany, where he was interned until 1945. He resumed his political career during the *Fourth Republic*, then retired from politics in 1958.

Dalai Lama. The title of the supreme religious leader of Tibetan *Buddhism*, and of Tibet from the seventeenth century (1642) until a failed revolt against Chinese rule in 1959, when the fourteenth Dalai Lama (b. 1935) was forced into exile. He devoted his tenure to keeping Tibet's case for *independence* before *world public opinion*, efforts for which he won the *Nobel Prize* for Peace in 1989. At the *World Human Rights Conference* (1993), China prevented him from addressing official sessions, though in a compromise arrangement he spoke before *NGO* delegates.

Dalhousie, James (1812–1860). Governor-general of India, 1848–1856. An active and confident imperialist, he used *East India Company* troops to conquer the Punjab during the Second *Sikh War*, outright annexed multiple *Princely States* (Satara, 1848; Jaitpur and Sambalpur, 1849; Udaipur, 1852; Jhansi, 1845; Nagpur, 1854; Oudh, 1856), and launched the second *Anglo-Burmese War* in 1852. He was also a builder of irrigation canals, telegraph and postal systems, and important *railways*, and he was a social reformer who tried to stamp out female infanticide, *sati*, *thugi*, and the last remnants of the *slave trade* in India. His governorship appeared to consolidate, morally and territorially, British rule in India. Yet, just one year after his departure the *Indian Mutiny* broke out, in the aftermath of which a number of his policies were reversed as Britain lost its claims to social reform and moral ascendancy in India.

dalits. "Oppressed castes." *See also caste system; Hinduism; untouchability.*

Dalmatia. The Adriatic, coastal region of the Balkan peninsula. It was ruled by *Venice* from across the Adriatic and from 1420 until the late eighteenth century, when it was lost to Venice as a result of the *Napoleonic Wars*. Italy tried to reclaim it at the *Paris Peace Conference* (1919–1920) as the *Austrian Empire* broke up, but was denied. Instead it was incorporated in the new state of *Yugoslavia*. Italy renounced its claim to Dalmatia in 1924 in exchange for control of *Fiume*.
      Suggested Reading: Larry Wolff, *Venice and the Slavs* (2001).

damage. Injury suffered through the *illegal act* of another state, for which *damages* may be exacted.

damage limitation. (1) In warfare: Efforts to reduce the operational impact of enemy fire, such as by using *preemptive strikes* and other *active defense* measures. (2) In *statecraft*: Efforts to reduce the harm to policy or the impact on *public opinion* of an opponent's actions, usually through *propaganda*, or of one's own mistakes (e.g., by blaming a subordinate).

damages. Compensation for *damage. See also* ne judex ultra petita partium.

Daman. *See Portuguese India.*

D'Annunzio, Gabriele (1863–1938). Italian nationalist. A 52-year-old poet who urged war against Austria in 1915; he volunteered when war came and was wounded in combat. In 1919 he led a handful of *fanatics* in the seizure of *Fiume* and held the city for a year in spite of opposition by the other *Allied and Associated Powers*. Fiume had long been coveted by Italian nationalists but was not ceded to Italy as it hoped for at the *Paris Peace Conference*, causing the Italian delegation to storm out of the conference in April 1919. *Mussolini* learned much from D'Annunzio's tactics. They also shared an utter contempt for the Western democracies and for democracy in general. *See also mutilated victory.*

Danton, George Jacques (1759–1794). *Jacobin.* A leader in the radicalization of the *French Revolution,* he supported the September Massacres and voted to execute *Louis XVI.* As head of the Jacobin Club and minister of justice, he repressed the *Girondins* during the *Terror.* When he tried to move the *Committee of Public Safety* toward national reconciliation, and because he was open to accusations of personal corruption, he fell out with the "incorruptible" *Robespierre,* who had him guillotined in his turn. Danton's personal motto: "Audacity, more audacity, always audacity!" This became a favorite saying of *Napoleon I.* Danton's last words: "Show my head to the people, it is worth seeing."

Danubian principalities. Moldavia and Wallachia, which stand astride the strategic mouth of the Danube River and were from the thirteenth century provinces of the *Ottoman Empire.* They were occupied by Russia during the *First Russo-Turkish War* (1768–1774).

Turkey regained Moldovia and Wallachia (the Danubian principalities) in the peace settlement (Treaty of Kuchuk-Kainardji, 1774), but Russia retained the right of intervention in Danubian affairs, effectively establishing a protectorate over the Christian population. Russia tried to make these provinces formal protectorates in 1856, but they were instead given a joint guarantee of *autonomy* by the *Great Powers* in the *Treaty of Paris* (1856). In 1858 they formed Rumania, though still within the Ottoman Empire. Independence was granted in 1878, as Rumania, in the *Treaty of San Stefano.* This was confirmed at the *Congress of Berlin. See Eastern Question.*

Danzig (Gdansk), Free City of. This modern Polish city, located on the Baltic coast, was formerly a German *city-state* and an important member of the *Hansa.* It changed political masters many times. It was formally annexed by Prussia as a result of the *Congress of Vienna* and remained part of Prussia and then Imperial Germany for more than 100 years. It was declared a *demilitarized* and *free city* at the *Paris Peace Conference* in 1919 and placed under the administration of a commissioner appointed by the *League of Nations.* Poland was given charge of its interests in foreign policy, customs, and exports and gained access to the sea through the *Polish Corridor,* which connected Danzig to the main body of Poland. German-Polish relations suffered greatly from this unwieldy arrangement. It became for many Germans a symbol of the hypocrisy of the Paris Peace Conference, which had called for *self-determination* for all nations. In the 1930s the status of *Danzig* became an international question when *Hitler* instructed local *Nazis* to agitate for reunion with Germany. In the West, those who feared that war would result from the crisis and preferred *appeasement* asked, "Who wants to die for Danzig?" On September 1, 1939, Germany attacked Poland, ostensibly to free the "persecuted" German population of the city. That launched *World War II* in Europe. In 1945 Danzig reverted to Poland, which was itself moved north and west by the Soviets, who then expanded into what had been eastern Poland. The city's German population was roughly expelled, and it became ethnically as well as legally a Polish city. Renamed Gdansk, in the 1980s it was the center of anti-*Communist* dissent among discontented workers in the city's shipyards, which gave birth to the *Solidarity* movement that opened the first crack in the Soviet empire. *See also Lech Walesa.*

Daoism. "The path." An animist, mystical, Chinese folk tradition that has for millennia existed both alongside and in contrast to the rigid, elite principles of classical *Confucianism.* Its teachings are based partly on the writings of Laozi (604–521 B.C.E.) and tend to counsel passivity and resignation, rather than moral perfectibility. A central Daoist teaching that was of signal importance in the evolution of twentieth century Chinese political culture and thought was the idea of the "unity of opposites." In the *Han dynasty* the rise of Daoism helped undermine Confucian authority at a time when the state was facing multiple challenges from other sources. In modern times, its worldview possibly helped prepare the way for an easy reception by Chinese *nationalists* and *Communists* alike of the notion that China would emerge from its severe national humiliation to become once more a leading, if not the principal, nation on earth.

Dar al-Harb. "Area of War." In *Islam,* all territory not occupied or ruled by Muslims. For militant Muslims, the term implies that in the fullness of time it will be. The idea dates back to the era of militant Islamic expansion a millennium ago and, except in rare instances, should not be mistaken for a present-day threat to non-Muslims.

Dar al-Islam. "Area of the Faithful (Submission)." In *Islam,* all territory occupied or ruled by Muslims.

Dardanelles. The narrow channel that links the Aegean with the Sea of Marmara and, via the *Bosporus,* connects to the Black Sea. Its status within the tottering *Ottoman Empire* was a major *geopolitical* question of the nineteenth century. Britain kept Russia from passage to the Mediterranean through the Dardanelles, but used them itself during the *Crimean War.* At other times, Turkey denied passage to Britain. During *World War I,* a failed effort to get past Turkish shore defenses with a flotilla of old British and French battleships (February–March, 1915) led to the disaster of troop landings and a bloody battle at *Gallipoli.* Russia gained the right to send warships through in the *Montreux Convention* of 1936. During the *Cold War*, the regular passage of the Soviet *Black Sea Fleet* through the Dardanelles was closely monitored by *NATO*. After 1989 the Dardanelles declined in geopolitical and military importance, as first the Soviet Union, then Russian naval power, decayed, but they remained a potential strategic choke point. *See also Straits Question.*

Darfur. A Central African, cavalry power of mixed Arab-*sudanic* ethnicity. Its population was converted to *Islam* in the mid-seventeenth century and, with the importation of firearms, violently expanded into extensive *slave-raiding* and conquest of pagan tribes to its south.

"Dark Continent." Africa to the nineteenth century; so-called by Europeans as they knew so little about its interior geography and peoples, which raises the question of who was most in the dark. Some later applied the term to Europe in the twentieth century, which witnessed the new barbarities of *total war* as well as a return to older barbarisms such as *ethnic cleansing, genocide,* and *slavery.*

Darlan, Jean Louis (1881–1942). French admiral and *Vichy* leader in Algeria. A willing *collaborator* with *Nazi Germany,* he was in Algiers when Anglo-American forces landed in 1942. He ordered French troops to fire on the invaders, but they had no stomach for more than brief resistance, and many went over to the Allied side. Darlan traded a *cease-fire* for recognition of his authority over Algeria. Shortly after that, he was assassinated.

"dash." In West Africa, the near-standard practice of demanding a bribe as the price of conducting business, obtaining a government license, or avoiding harassment by corrupt local or police officials. *See also* baksheesh; guanxi; la mordida.

Davis, Jefferson (1808–1889). The first, and last, president of the Confederate States of America, or the *Confederacy,* 1861–1865. U.S. representative, 1845–1846; U.S. senator, 1847–1851; 1857–1861. He fought in the "Blackhawk War" under General *Andrew Jackson,* whom he admired, and in the *Mexican-American War.* As U.S. secretary of war, 1853–1857, he oversaw the *Gadsden purchase.* When the *American Civil War* broke out, he hoped to serve as a soldier. Instead, he was elected president. Vain and meddlesome to a grievous fault in military affairs, he repeatedly overruled his generals. *Grant* later wrote of him: "Mr. Davis had an exalted opinion of his own military genius." Davis' diplomacy was based on disastrous, romantic delusions, in particular the idea of *King Cotton.* He was an adamant defender of *slavery,* which he called "a moral and political blessing," and regarded the South as more faithful to original American ideals than the North. At war's end he was captured, shackled, and thrown into solitary confinement at Fort Monroe, Virginia. He lived in quiet, bitter retirement for a quarter century more, always rejecting any responsibility for the bloodshed he had overseen. *See also Zachary Taylor.*

Suggested Reading: William Cooper, *Jefferson Davis, American* (2000).

Dawes Plan (1924). Drafted by Charles Dawes (1865–1951), chairman of the Allied Reparations Commission, and *Joseph Austen Chamberlain*, co-winners of the 1925 *Nobel Prize* for Peace. It stabilized Weimar Germany's runaway economy by developing a reasonable schedule for it to meet *reparations* obligations after *World War I* and authorizing large private loans from the United States, 1924–1929. It thus set in motion a recycling of reparations dollars from Germany to Britain and France, to America in the form of *war debts* payments, and back to Germany as loans. After the Dawes Plan, American investors poured so much money into Weimar Germany to stabilize that developing democracy that it was able to recover fully from the war and avoid paying any net reparations at all between 1924 and 1929. Germany paid its reparations with the money American banks sent its way, then defaulted on the American loans during the *Great Depression. See also Young Plan.*

Suggested Reading: Stephen Schuker, *American "Reparations" to Germany, 1919–1933* (1988).

Dayan, Moshe (1915–1981). Israeli soldier. Chief-of-staff, 1953–1958; agriculture minister, 1959–1964; defense minister, 1967–1974; foreign minister, 1977–1979. He gained much of the credit for the success of Israeli arms in 1967, when he was the main advocate of a *preemptive strike.* However, in the lead-up to the *Fourth Arab-Israeli War,* he made dangerously impolitic remarks about how Israel would remain on the *West Bank* forever, remarks that helped solidify an Arab front favoring war.

Dayton Peace Accords (1995). *Bill Clinton* summoned Balkan leaders to Dayton, Ohio, to impose a temporary settlement in the Bosnia War. Attending were Franjo Tudjman of Croatia, *Slobodan Milošević* of Serbia, and Bosnian Muslim leader Alija Izetbegovic. The Accords agreed to there established a Bosnian Republic that was (on paper, at least) multiethnic and federal and retained Sarajevo as its capital. They also recognized in law, however, what already existed on the ground: *autonomous* regions carved out of Bosnia *de facto* by Bosnian Serbs and Croats, but not permitted to leave the country *de jure,* with just the rump of Bosnia in Muslim hands. This settlement was to be guaranteed by *NATO,* whose forces were to be pulled out by mid-1998. Although this short-term promise was made with vehemence to skeptical NATO publics, no NATO leader seriously believed it could be carried out. In fact, NATO troops were still in-country in 2001, with no clear plans for extraction that would not simply cause the war to resume. In short, with

NATO in occupation of most key points in Bosnia, it became an effective *protectorate*. The agreement also partly confirmed the efficacy of *ethnic cleansing* by sanctioning the new borders and more homogenous regional states to which that practice had led.

D-Day. (1) Any specific date set for launch of a military operation. (2) June 6, 1944. *See also Normandy invasion.*

dead letter drop. In *intelligence* tradecraft, a secure site used to leave messages without actually meeting one's contact.

death camps. The network of mass extermination and *slave labor* camps set up by the *Nazis* during *World War II*, whose ultimate purpose was to kill all the Jews of Europe, as well as several smaller populations of those deemed undesirable by the Nazi hierarchy: common criminals (excluding those many criminals who rose to positions of influence within the Nazi Party itself), *Roma*, Jehovah's Witnesses, "mental defectives," *Communists*, homosexuals, and anyone expressing personal political or moral dissent. The Nazis began planning for a death camp system as early as 1931, as revealed in the so-called "Boxheim papers," two years before *Hitler* seized power in Germany. Immediately upon the Nazi seizure of power in 1933, the *SA* began rounding up "enemies of the state." At first the camps were ad hoc, brutal detention centers, as originally at *Dachau*, rather than overt death camps; but many died anyway, from daily beatings or shootings. And there was systematic murder in the camps as well, right from the start, mainly of people with mental and physical handicaps. The Nazis thereby refined "extermination" techniques that they later used on Jews, by first killing the insane and socially inconvenient, also regarded in Nazi race theory as *Untermenschen*. Most camp inmates wore colored cloth triangles to signify their "crimes": red was for "politicals" (socialists or Communists), pink denoted homosexuals, violet was for religious dissenters, and yellow was reserved for Jews (who were given two triangles and ordered to use them to form the Star of David).

The death camp system as it ultimately developed was designed and run by the *SS*, under the direction of top SS leaders such as *Himmler, Heydrich, Eichmann*, and handpicked SS guards. These men were joined by volunteer SS units of Poles, Balts, Ukrainians, and other non-German *anti-Semites* and *collaborators*.

Most *concentration camps* were organized along military lines and nearly always made use of prisoners to keep basic order at the barracks level. There was a division within the SS as to the best use of Jewish prisoners, which only deepened as the war progressed. Some SS saw the camps as holding pens for huge pools of slaves, who could be rented out to German industry at varying daily rates, to the profit of the SS and the benefit of the war effort. These SS set up slave camps surrounded by dozens of satellite industrial camps, whose production of war materiel grew as Allied bombs destroyed Germany's cities and mainline factories. These SS slave labor camps operated right up to the end of the war. In a perverse way, they competed for Jews with another, much more sinister type of camp: the pure death camps whose sole raison d'etre was to carry out the grand plan for extermination of targeted populations, above all, Europe's 11 million Jews, as had been detailed and agreed at the *Wannsee conference* and in Hitler's order for the *"final solution."* The most infamous death camp was *Auschwitz*, where as many as 1.5 million human beings were methodically murdered in huge gas chambers (capacity 2,000 each) and their remains picked over and then incinerated in specially designed crematoria or buried in mass graves. The average life-expectancy of a prisoner in a slave labor camp was about nine months; many in the death camps, especially women and children and the old, who were specially selected for extermination, died the day of their arrival. At the larger camps, murder targets were set at 15,000 to 20,000 per day. At its height, the Nazi death camp system totaled twenty main camps and as many as 500 satellite camps. The network was so vast, and required so many locomotives, rail lines, and rail carriages to feed its insane and utterly evil appetite, that the *Wehrmacht* repeatedly protested against a major drain of resources away from the war effort. Calculations as to the final toll of the dead vary, but reliable estimates are that at least six million Jews were killed during the *Holocaust*, along with several million more non-Jews from abused and targeted minority populations.

The forced labor camps of the Soviet *gulag archipelago* also amounted to a death camp system at the height of *Stalin's* terror. Indeed, crude death camps appear wherever *genocide* is attempted; inter alia, this happened after 1945 in Cambodia under *Pol Pot* and in Rwanda.

death squads. *Paramilitary* units, often associated with or directly tied to security forces, tasked with elimination of the regime's opponents. The term became current during the *dirty war* in Argentina in the 1970s. It was also used about similar units in El Salvador and elsewhere in Central America in the 1980s. Thereafter, it became a nonspecific term generally applied to this phenomenon wherever it appeared, including retroactively. *See also blueshirts; desaparacidos; Green Gang; Operation Condor; Juan Manuel Rosas.*

debellatio. Elimination of an *international personality* by the utter destruction of its machinery of state.

debriefing. Close scrutiny of the recollected actions and conversations of an *agent* or of a *defector.*

debt. The total money owed by a given state to foreign lenders, whether private banks, international banks, or governments. *See also debt service.*

debt crisis. Unprecedented levels of *Third World* (and other) foreign debt reached by the 1980s. It followed *OPEC* price increases (1973 and 1979) and commodity price falls, which led to massive borrowing to finance *development* plans or to continue consumer *subsidies* and social welfare spending. That was attended by a rising inability of *G-77* and other nations to meet *debt service* obligations. *See also International Monetary Fund; scissors crisis; structural adjustment.*

debt-equity swaps. Exchanging bank debt for equity investment in the local *currency*, with government guarantees. This permits a bank to reduce exposure to possible bad debt, and even convert it into a valuable local asset. The *debtor nation* lowers its overall debt load and obtains needed investment funds.

debt fatigue. The psychological and political process whereby continuing austerity programs designed to reduce debt over time create political, social, and popular resistance to their continuance. It may result in unilateral suspension of *debt service* payments, as happened in 1987 when Brazil and a number of smaller countries announced a *moratorium* on payments. The United States and other Western governments put heavy pressure on Brazil to resume payment, and the banks refused to yield. The moratorium ended with a *debt rescheduling* agreement.

debt-for-nature swaps. Internationally organized *transferable development rights*, wherein *LDCs* agree to designate certain areas for conservation in return for reduced external *debt*. The funds saved may then be used for further conservation or other environmental purposes. *See also debt-equity swaps; environmental security; green loans; sustainable development.*

debtor cartel. Much debated but never tried, this is the notion that *debtor nations* should simultaneously announce a *moratorium* on *debt service* payments, to extract better financing terms or partial loan forgiveness from creditors.

debtor nation. A country that is in *debt* to foreign governments and/or private or international banks.

debt rescheduling/restructuring. When a *debtor nation* and foreign lenders agree to renegotiate existing loans, to draw out the repayment schedule, reduce interest charges, or both.

debt service. The total principal and interest owed on borrowed funds, to be paid over a year; not total debt. The debt service ratio is the amount of export earnings that must go simply to service the debt. *See also London Club; Paris Club.*

Deccan. A great and mostly arid plateau in south India that historically marked a major physical, cultural, economic, and even racial divide in the development of the subcontinent. Its irregular *topography*, with the landscape alternately breaking into mountain ranges and plateaus, explains much of its history of relative historical isolation, resistance to conquest, and small and multiple polities. *See also India; Marathas.*

Decembrist revolt (December 13, 1825). An attempted *coup* in Russia in December 1825, carried out by young, liberal army officers organized into two main conspiratorial groups, with the one in south Russia more radical than the northern group. The revolt was prompted by the accession to power of Tsar *Nicholas I.* It was crushed. Some executions followed, but most plotters—who were all of gentry rank—were exiled to *Siberia.*

decision, battle of. Any decisive battle whose outcome is significant not just in military terms (casualties, damage to the enemy), but politically; for example, *Austerlitz, Trafalgar, Waterloo. See also attrition, battle of; Karl Clausewitz; strategic envelopment.*

decision maker. (1) Any person with the final say in formulating or implementing foreign policy: the *head of government*, principal staff, relevant *cabinet* officers, and senior bureaucratic officials. (2) Any person with the final say in formulating or implementing policy decisions for any major *actor* in international relations, including *international organizations* and/or private concerns such as MNCs. *See also decision-making theory; decision theory.*

decision-making theory. Academic foreign policy analysis that focuses on individual *decision makers.* It is mainly interested in the subjective concerns of decision makers, seeing these as the primary cause of decisions made. It argues that the objective reality within which decisions are made may not be correctly, or at all, perceived by the statesman, and thus has far less explanatory power than a tight focus on the internal dynamics of decision making. A subfield focuses on special strains that are said to apply under the tensions accompanying a *crisis. See also bureaucratic politics; cognitive dissonance; cybernetic theory; game theory; group think; ideology; image; instrumental rationality; misperception; organizational process model; pluralism; rational actor model; standard operating procedures.*

decision theory. A branch of mathematics concerned with optimal choices and cost-benefit analysis where, unlike in *game theory* situations, outcomes of decisions do not depend on the choices of other players but on *exogenous* factors determined by probabilities. Certain academics employ it as a (particularly obscure) variant of *rational choice theory.* No policymaker pays it any attention whatever.

declaration. The usual meaning is a nonbinding statement of policy or intent by one or more states. Even when *multilateral*, these have, at most, quasi-legislative authority under *international law*. For instance, the *Universal Declaration of Human Rights* is seen by some legal scholars as having gained standing in *international customary law* since its adoption in 1948, but others insist it remains nonbinding. There is one important exception to this: some declarations, if undertaken with the clear and overt intention of incurring a binding commitment, may be regarded as having the effective legal force of a *treaty*. *See also resolution.*

Declaration of the Rights of Man and Citizens (1789). *See French Revolution.*

declaration of war. A formal act (under the *Hague Convention III* of 1907) by which one state opens *armed hostilities* with another and claims the rights and privileges of a *belligerent* power. As surprise and *Blitzkrieg* can decide victory quickly, and *aggression* was made formally illegal in the *Kellogg-Briand Pact*, declarations of war were seldom issued after 1930 or they were withheld until after a surprise attack had been made. Thus, Japan struck thrice without a declaration of war: against Russia in 1904, China in 1937, and the United States in 1941; and Germany attacked Poland in 1939 and the Soviet Union in 1941 without warning. After 1945, no war began with a formal declaration. Difficulty in definition of both "aggression" and "war" meant both terms were avoided in the *United Nations Charter. See also armed conflict*; requerimiento; *state of war.*

Declaration on Liberated Europe (1945). A promise of free elections to be held in Eastern Europe after *World War II*, signed by the *Big Three* at the *Yalta Conference*. It was highly controversial during the *Cold War*. Charges were made that the Soviets willfully violated it, and on the hard right in the United States that *Roosevelt* and *Churchill* had somehow betrayed Eastern Europe (were guilty of *appeasement*), even though it is hard to see what they could have done in face of the physical occupation of those lands by the *Red Army.*

"decline of the West." (1) An argument made by German philosopher Oswald Spengler (1880–1936) in a 1922 book of that title, which proposed in *Hegelian* fashion that *democracy* was decadent and already into its inevitable phase of decay and decline. Therefore, he argued in favor of the overthrow of the *Weimar Republic*. He later fell out of favor with the *Nazis*, and his books, too, were banned in Germany—though they were still widely read in the West. (2) A recurring motif among shallower social critics and poseur intellectuals, particularly *conservatives*, who mistake contemporary manifestations of the usual quota of human greed, venality, and ignorance in any society as instead signs of the terminal cultural and moral illness of Western civilization. Whenever encountered, it might be well to recall how long the *Roman Empire* was in "decline," and how many times it revived. Also worth remembering are the words *Adam Smith* once imparted to a young Englishman who was concerned that decay had already started and was fast undermining the pillars of the *British Empire*: "My dear young friend, you must remember that in every great country there is a good deal of ruin." Historically, empires and civilizations have put up with decay, even with being ruined, for quite awhile. *See also end of history.*

   Suggested Reading: Karl Popper, *The Poverty of Historicism* (1957).

decolonization. (1) When an *empire* sheds its colonial possessions. (2) When a *colony* becomes *independent* after a period of rule by a foreign power. The important North American colonies were lost to Britain, 1776–1783; Latin America broke free of Spain and Portugal, 1810–1825. Africa and Asia were mostly decolonized after *World War II*, partly as a result of the long-term effects of the *Great Depression*. Britain, Belgium, and the Netherlands departed with varying degrees of ease, if not grace. The key moment was when Britain left India in 1947. France had difficulty adjusting to loss of empire and hence tried to return by force in *Indochina* until 1954 and to hang on in Algeria until 1962. Of the European powers, Portugal clung to overseas empire second longest: only after its revolution in 1974 were its colonies freed; several collapsed into immediate civil war. Russia (the Soviet Union) was the last European state to leave empire behind, if one discounts the minor territories still attached to France. The Soviet Union surrendered its outer empire of *satellite states* in 1989 and a large portion of its inner empire in 1991, which it had held variously from the seventeenth through the twentieth centuries. The *extinction* of the Soviet Union was thought by many to have completed decolonization, at least concerning European empires. However, there remained significant minority areas within Russia, and the late 1990s saw demands for decolonization of parts of Indonesia, as well as numerous *secessionist* movements in many other countries. And China was still firmly committed to reassembling its old empire at the outer limits (hence, including Tibet) of its historical reach. *See also mandated territories; neocolonialism; self-determination;* uti possidetis.

decommission. To retire a *warship* or an *officer.*

"deepening versus widening" (enlargement). The perennial question faced by the *European Community*, and then the *European Union*: should it concentrate on advancing *integration* of existing members in all its aspects (deepening, as in *Maastricht*) or add new members beyond *les petite riches* (widening) after the *Cold War*—an expansion of the Union to the Russian border? Reunification of Germany was seen by some as requiring widening to internally balance the EU against expanded German influence. Briefly, in the mid-

1990s, the EU proposed a solution of concentric rings of membership: the EU states, other (non-EU) *European Economic Area* states, and dependent east European economies. Eventually it chose deepening; *NATO* chose enlargement. All states waiting in line for membership are required to comply with some 60,000 pages of "acquis communautaires" (formal EU rules and regulations); this greatly slows the pace of change.

de-escalation. Reducing tensions or military readiness; winding a *crisis* or conflict down, level by level.

de facto. "In fact." (1) Existing regardless of legal status, even especially if unlawful. (2) Provisional *recognition* granted to a regime that exists in fact, by virtue of its control of a given territory. *De jure* recognition and full *diplomatic relations* may, or may not, follow. *See also sovereignty.*

default. Failing or refusing to meet one's foreign debt repayment schedule. Most defaults are temporary, pending negotiations on *debt rescheduling. See also debtor cartel; Drago Doctrine.*

Defcon system. The Defense Condition (Defcon) five-stage alert system was set up in 1959 for the U.S. armed forces as a whole, and *Strategic Air Command (SAC)* in particular. The five stages are: Defcon Five: normal peacetime relations and operations; Defcon Four: certain units and crews kept at ready status, but most units remain on stand-down; Defcon Three: all units fully ready; under specific conditions, forward operational units (ships at sea, aircraft in flight) are given limited discretion to use force in self-defense; Defcon Two: strategic units are deployed to search for threats/targets, missiles are readied (silos open, plotted firing solutions entered), with an overall sense of imminent threat of war; and Defcon One: all strategic air units are airborne; missiles are armed, aimed, and ready to fire on a hair-trigger command or upon attack; forward units actively seek out and destroy targets in their threat area. Defcon Two is effectively the highest level of readiness short of actual war. Defcon One would signal that the United States considered itself on the verge of war with a nuclear adversary, in which its strategic forces would likely be used. During the *Cuban Missile Crisis*, the United States reached Defcon Three, with SAC ordered to Defcon Two. Defcon status was also heightened during the *September 11, 2001, terrorist attack on the United States.* At no time to date has the United States gone to Defcon One. The Defcon system had historical counterparts in the form of pre*mobilization* periods called "Period Preparatory to War"; in Germany this was the "State of Danger of War" (Kriegsgefahrzustand); in France it was called "covering operations" (la couvertur).

defeat. When, as a result of war, a state or nation is compelled to concede an opponent's military superiority by *surrender* or otherwise *asking for terms*, with the consequence that its interests in the dispute(s) that led to the war are likely to be gravely harmed or set aside, while its opponent makes major diplomatic, political, *prestige*, and/or economic gains. Most defeats are partial and relative (Germany in *World War I*), though some are absolute (Germany in *World War II*).

In general, a decisive defeat is more likely to discourage efforts to revise the status quo because it clarifies for all participants the reality of their relative *power*. A partial defeat may accomplish that, but can stimulate *revanchism* instead. Thus, criticism of the putative harshness of the *Treaty of Versailles* (as compared to the rehabilitation of Germany and Japan after World War II) might be said to mistake *cause and effect*. That treaty was relatively temperate as compared, for example, to the *diktat* Germany imposed on Russia at *Brest-Litovsk*. It was the absence of a widespread awareness (as represented by belief in the *stab-in-the-back* thesis) of the defeat Germany had, in fact, suffered that sustained subsequent demands for revision of the Versailles Treaty system. Similarly, besides rehabilitation of the *Axis* states after 1945, it was their absolute defeat and deliberate military *occupation* that suffocated any yearning for a military revision of the status quo and blocked those nations from resuming an imperial path. Imported liberal-capitalist institutions and prosperity then were held out as a positive alternative to defeated populations, where the Soviet Union proposed an altogether different, and far less attractive, choice. *See also victory.*

defeat-in-detail. By feinting and maneuvering, to divide a large enemy force into two or more smaller units, then attacking these with locally superior forces of one's own. Each smaller enemy force thus can be fought and defeated before the next is engaged. *Frederick the Great* and *Napoleon*, especially, used this tactic to at times effect victories over more numerous enemy armies.

defeatism. A pervasive attitude of pessimism and anticipation of inevitable *defeat*. It can seriously undermine *national morale*. *See also Maginot spirit; "voting with their feet."*

defection. (1) In *intelligence*: Asking for *asylum* in exchange for being *debriefed* on all one knows about an adversary's operations. (2) In *game theory*: The notion that it may be the most rational choice for a state to defect from cooperation and proceed alone, rather than take the chance that another player will be the first to defect. It has some implications for the idea of a *security dilemma*.

defector. A person who abandons the cause of one country to embrace another—or just for money or from spleen—and who asks for *asylum*. Defectors are a constant, if minor, feature of world affairs. *See also intelligence.*

defense. (1) Resistance of, or all measures taken in preparedness to resist or preempt, a real or anticipated attack. (2) Weapons procurement and deployment, *logistics*, research, training, military *intelligence*, and all other aspects of *war planning*.

defense area. That part of the *high seas* that a *belligerent* declares out-of-bounds to *neutral* shipping.

defense conversion. Changing productive capacity from military to civilian uses. *See also demilitarization; peace dividend.*

defense-in-depth. Establishing several defensive lines, to which one may withdraw in succession to blunt, absorb, and weaken an enemy's attack. Among other states, China and Russia historically used this strategy to great effect against foreign invaders. Russians usually reinforced its impact with *scorched earth*. *See also forward defense; Peter I; retreat from Moscow; Sébastien Vauban.*

Defense Planning Committee (DPC). Founded with *NATO* in 1949, it meets weekly to discuss Alliance business. Unlike the *North Atlantic Council*, which includes all members, France did not participate in the DPC after formal withdrawal from the military side of NATO in 1966. However, in 1993 it began attending to discuss NATO's role in regional *peacekeeping*.

defense spending. The portion of a national budget allocated to military expenditures.

defensive weapons. Weapons whose primary purpose is to defend valued targets by shielding from attack or actively destroying enemy *offensive weapons*. In practice, and depending on the weapon concerned, it is often difficult to see a real distinction other than in the intention with which weapons are actually used. *See also ballistic missile defense; deterrence; dual use; fortification; Maginot Line.*

deficit financing/spending. When a government's total annual expenditures exceed total revenues. Before the twentieth century, this was almost always done to finance a war or a major building project; during the twentieth century, governments increasingly borrowed against future revenues in order to finance domestic welfare spending or to build *infrastructure* and promote *industrialization*. Heroic examples of deficit financing that led to ruin include *Charles V* and *Philip II*, and Imperial Spain's rulers in general, who borrowed against future silver fleets from *Spanish America* in support of their many and protracted wars. *Louis XIV* ruined France's finances in the same manner. Similarly, most of Europe's major combatants were forced to borrow heavily to finance their prolonged efforts in *World War I*, while the United States deficit financed the *Vietnam War*. In nearly all cases this contributed to a major *inflation*. *See also current account deficit.*

defilade. Shielding a position from enemy view, either by using natural cover or *camouflage*.

deflation. A decline in prices, related to a contraction of the money supply and reduced credit. It can produce a vicious circle wherein falling prices encourage delayed consumer spending, which further depresses prices. And it increases real debt. Deflation was an underlying cause, and feature, of the *Great Depression*. In the 1990s Japan was the first industrial economy to suffer deflation in 60 years. *See also inflation.*

deforestation. Denuding an area of its trees and other vegetative covering. It is a contributing cause of the advance of deserts, soil erosion, destruction of coastal *fisheries*, and extinction of species. *See also Kyoto Treaty; Pacific Islands Forum; Sahel.*

De Gaulle, Charles André (1890–1970). French general, war theorist, *resistance* leader, statesman, and first president of the *Fifth Republic*, 1958–1969. De Gaulle fought low in the ranks during *World War I* and was wounded and captured at *Verdun*. He was deeply impressed by the advent of mechanized warfare in the last days of that conflict. He developed a theory of tank tactics in the interwar years and generally sought to modernize the French Army, but his proposals were mostly ignored by his superiors. They were, however, studied closely by German *Panzer* theorists and commanders, such as *Guderian*. De Gaulle was made undersecretary of state for war in the last government of the *Third Republic*, too late to make the changes necessary to prevent defeat. His command was one of the few French units to advance against the Germans during the *Battle of France* (May–June 1940). Determined to prolong the fight, he proposed to *Churchill* a political union of the British and French nations. Refusing to accept defeat or *Vichy*, he fell back to Britain and called upon patriots to rally to his *Free French* movement. In September 1940, he failed to capture Dakar, Senegal, but French Cameroon, Chad, and the French Congo all rallied to him. The French Empire in West Africa thus became the basis of his claim to represent France. He sent Frenchmen to fight Frenchmen in the Levant in 1942, alongside British troops.

A prickly and driven person, who deeply loved France but perhaps disdained most French, De Gaulle got on reasonably with Churchill but had terrible personal relations with *Franklin Roosevelt*, who froze him out of the

North African landings in Algeria in 1942. After patching relations he received Allied recognition and material support. De Gaulle entered Paris a day after it was retaken in August 1944 by a spearhead of Free French forces, thus reinforcing his claim to leadership. He then led the *provisional government* that saw France through the remainder of the war. He worried those French who feared a new *Bonapartism*. Facing resistance, he withdrew to the political sidelines confidently to await his destiny. The parliamentary chaos of the *Fourth Republic*, and a dirty and divisive colonial war in *Algeria*, led to De Gaulle's return to national politics in 1958 as the only figure capable of bridging political divisions that otherwise threatened to lead to civil war. He often governed by appeal to referenda that bypassed the parties and made him an indispensable figure at the center of French politics. He then wrote a strong presidency into the constitution of the *Fifth Republic*, some say to suit the cut of his own gib, and governed France for the next decade. He granted formal independence to most of France's colonies, but ensured that important *neo-colonial* ties still bound them to Paris. De Gaulle's decision to accept Algerian independence in 1962 led to several attempts on his life by the *Organization de l'armée secrèt* (OAS).

In foreign policy De Gaulle sought a "third way" for France and Europe between Moscow and Washington, always on the unspoken assumption that France needed to return to a Great Power role. He looked to reconciliation with Germany and a new Paris-Bonn political axis, and he developed an independent French nuclear force to help provide it and French hegemony over Western Europe. He distanced France from *NATO*'s military wing, but cooperated at other levels. And he twice vetoed Britain's membership in the *European Community*, fearing a rival while arguing that London was not committed to Europe and might act as a Trojan horse for the United States. De Gaulle put his presidency on the line in yet another *referendum* in 1968, on senate and regional reform, after he had already survived unparalleled student riots and labor unrest that nearly toppled his government. After losing the referendum, he resigned (1969). In his deeply patriotic and principled actions during World War II, De Gaulle had rescued a measure of honor for France from the sting of defeat and the shame of *collaboration*. Afterward, he guided the nation through a painful *decolonization* and may well have saved it from both dictatorship and civil war. His constitutional design for the Fifth Republic revealed a deep understanding of the French by producing a synthesis between their republican ideals and their Bonapartist traditions of powerful executive leadership. And he reconciled France with Germany after a century of hostility and three major wars. Whatever the shortcomings of his sometimes petulant anti-Americanism, De Gaulle—along with *Adenauer*—went some way to restoring to France its national dignity, and to a Europe recovering from *fascism* and flirtation with a new Dark Age, a renewed dedication to civilization.

Suggested Readings: Raymond Aron, *An Explanation of De Gaulle* (1965); Charles De Gaulle, *War Memoirs*, 3 vols. (1955–1960; 1984); Charles De Gaulle, *Memoirs of Hope* (tr. 1972); J. Lacouture, *De Gaulle*, 2 vols. (1990–1992).

deindustrialization. A term used to describe the relative loss of manufacturing (*secondary sector*) from advanced industrial economies to *Less Developed Countries,* or from one region to another within industrialized countries, such as from northern England to the south, or the northeastern United States to the southwest. In most cases, such blue-collar jobs are replaced by *service* jobs (jobs in the *tertiary sector*).

de jure. "By right." (1) According to law. (2) In *recognition,* when one state accepts in law the *de facto* status of a new state, as a *subject of international law* with which *diplomatic relations* may be instituted. *See also sovereignty.*

de Klerk, Fredrik Willem (b. 1936). South African president, 1989–1994. The "*Gorbachev* of South Africa," although he headed the Afrikaner *National Party,* the main propagator of *apartheid* for forty years, he dismantled legal apartheid upon taking office, thereby also ending international *sanctions* against South Africa. He released *Nelson Mandela* in 1990, with whom he then worked to further deconstruct the old system. He unbanned the *ANC,* opened multiparty and multiracial talks, and agreed to genuinely free elections for 1994, which he and everyone knew the ANC and Mandela must win. He was awarded the 1993 *Nobel Prize* for Peace, jointly with Mandela. In 1994 he agreed to serve as deputy prime minister in Mandela's "unity government." In 1996 de Klerk withdrew the National Party from the governing coalition. In 1997 he retired from politics. *See also Daniel Malan.*

Delcassé, Théophile (1852–1923). French foreign minister, 1898–1905, 1914–1915; naval minister, 1911–1913. He negotiated an extension of the Russo-French alliance in 1894 and a secret nonaggression pact with Italy in 1902. Driven by a desire to recover *Alsace-Lorraine* for France, he promoted *rapprochement* with Britain over disputes in Africa, such as by backing away from the confrontation at *Fashoda.* Negotiations ultimately led to the *Entente Cordiale* and a fresh foreign policy focus on the problem of Germany. He was forced out of office during the *First Moroccan Crisis* (1905). He helped bribe Italy away from the *Central Powers* into the *Triple Entente* in the *Treaty of London* (1915).

Delhi. Shorthand reference for the new capital of the *Mughal Empire* in India, built in old Delhi in 1648 by Shah Jahan (1592–1666)—who also built the *Peacock Throne* and the Taj Mahal. It was sacked by a Persian army in 1739, when 20,000 were butchered and the Peacock Throne was taken back to Iran.

The British constructed New Delhi starting in 1911 and used it as the administrative seat of their *Rāj* from 1912 onward.

Delhi Sultanate (c. 1200–1526). The original *Muslim* sultanate in India. The universal claim of its title notwithstanding, it was in fact one of several Muslim Indian kingdoms. It was ruled by the Khalji dynasty (1290–1320), then by the Saiyid and Lodi dynasties. It was overthrown by Babur (1483–1530) of Kabul, founder of the *Mughal Empire*.

delict. A breach or offense against *international law*.

démarche. In *diplomacy*, some major change in policy or course of action requiring a significant effort to alter international views and (or) domestic opinion. It may be done to signal a real willingness to negotiate a solution or as *propaganda*.

demilitarization. (1) Placing a country under civilian control. (2) Removing and perhaps also banning weapons, troops, and military infrastructure from an agreed-upon area. (3) Converting military to civilian production. *See also Aland Islands; Antarctica; demilitarized zone; Outer Space Treaty; Rhineland; war termination.*

demilitarized zone (DMZ). An area where no *belligerent* is permitted to keep military equipment or perform military operations. *See also buffer zone.*

demobilization. Returning troops and sailors to civilian life after a war has been won or lost. *See also conscription; mobilization; standing army.*

democracy. In ancient times democracy was a rare thing and not highly regarded. Plato much preferred benevolent tyranny by a philosopher king, and even Aristotle thought democracy amounted to little more than mob rule on a good day. Most classical civilizations—from Pharaonic Egypt, to the *Roman Empire* and the *Byzantine Empire*, to the *Ottomans, Incas, Aztecs*, and various Chinese *dynasties*—were governed by variations of the principle of kingship, usually sanctified by some sense of divine appointment or the *mandate of heaven*. Into modern times, governing principles were more likely to reflect notions of *autocracy* and *absolutism* than representation of the interests of common folk. The *Enlightenment, American Revolution*, and especially the *French Revolution* changed all that, so that modern democracy may be defined as government by elected representatives in accordance with the principle of *majority rule*, legitimized by the theory of *popular sovereignty*, and reinforced by expansive ideas of legal and actual respect for the *human rights* (embracing private property rights as a core proposition) of individuals, and the public rights of all citizens, including ethnic, religious, and social minorities. Thus, although some ancient civilizations—most notably, ancient Athens—experimented with representative government, and European colonial empires permitted representative assemblies to the leading citizens of more developed settler communities, it was really modern *liberalism* that gave birth to mass democracy. Ever since, modern republics have struggled with devising institutions and constitutional forms suited to divers national characters and historical circumstances, which speak as well to the perennial problem of self-governing peoples: the constant need to somehow rejuvenate the civic character of citizens, as memories of the struggle for liberty fade and general complacency sets in.

Along with *fascism* and *communism*, democracy was a central idea at contest in the great ideological wars of the twentieth century. In theoretical terms, most *realist* thinkers argue that, because decision-making processes in democracies are more fractured and complex than in tyrannies, and given the restraints imposed by *public opinion*, democracies find it more difficult to pursue long-term goals and sustain expensive foreign policy efforts. That claim does not take into account the degree to which even democracies continued to regard foreign policy as an executive prerogative and is further belied by the extraordinary success of the democratic bloc that won the *Cold War*, the spread of democratic ideas globally, and transformation of the world economic system through sustained, collective leadership over many decades by democratic, market economy states. By century's end these facts so impressed some social scientists that they began to argue that the triumph of liberal-democracy meant that world politics had already arrived at the *end of history*. Others noted that democracies remained a minority among states and focused instead on debates over the relationship of democracy to *development*, in particular over whether its liberalizing effects were due primarily to expansion of the middle class or the inclusion of labor movements in national political life. The most important debate concerning democracy and international relations continues to be over the widely held *Kantian* proposition that democratic societies are less likely to make *war* upon each other. Whatever its empirical validity, this proposition is now enshrined in international instruments such as the *Charter of Paris* (1990). *See also liberal-internationalism.*

Suggested Readings: Aristotle, *The Politics* (any edition); Robert Dahl, *Democracy and Its Critics* (1989); Mancur Olson, *Power and Prosperity: Outgrowing Communist and Capitalist Dictatorships* (2000); George Sørensen, ed., *Democracy and Democratization* (1998).

Democracy Wall. In 1957, 1978–1979, and 1988–1989, Beijing University students posted criticisms of the Chinese *Communist Party* on a "Democracy Wall." In all instances, after exciting expectations for reform among students and intellectuals with a brief and confused tolerance by the regime, arrests and violent repression put an end to hopes for free expression in China. *See also Tiananmen Square.*

"democratic centralism." In *Marxism-Leninism*, concentration of all *power* in the hands of the top party leadership. It worked by permitting discussion of options until a decision was taken, after which no dissent was tolerated. It was a term used by *Lenin* and his successors, and by *Mao* in China, to conceal from the more naïve in the party the reality of collective, and ultimately personal, dictatorship. *See also Bolsheviks; Mensheviks.*

democratic deficit. The perceived gap between elected representation in the *European Parliament* and actual decision making by non-elected officials within the *European Community*. It progressively narrowed with creation and reform of the *European Union*.

Democratic Party. Founded by *Thomas Jefferson* and *James Madison* in 1792, until 1828 this party was known as the Republican-Democrats. It is surpassed only by the *Conservative Party* in Great Britain as the most successful electoral machine in history. It initially favored agricultural interests nationally, with its southern wing supporting *slavery*. It also opposed establishment of a national bank or any other move toward strong central government. It elected, in succession, Jefferson, Madison, *James Monroe, John Quincy Adams, Andrew Jackson*, and Martin van Buren. In the 1830s it was given a populist twist and newly midwestern focus by Andrew Jackson. It split along north-south lines in 1854 over the expansion of slavery to lands acquired in the *Mexican-American War*, opening the political middle in 1860 to victory by a new party, the *Republicans*, under *Abraham Lincoln*. Still identified with slavery and the south, post–Civil War Democrats were kept out of the presidency until 1884, though they captured the "solid south" after *Reconstruction*. Post-Reconstruction Republicans did not regain control of the Virginia legislature, for example, until 1999. *William Jennings Bryan* led the party to three presidential defeats bracketing the turn of the twentieth century. With Republicans torn apart by the rift between *Taft* and *Theodore Roosevelt* in 1912, *Woodrow Wilson* was elected to the presidency. He put a personal and progressive stamp on the party, the country, and the world during *World War I*. The Democrats were out of the White House, 1920–1932. *Franklin Roosevelt* then completely remade the party, bringing together Catholics, Jews, and Blacks with other constituencies in a broad national coalition. Roosevelt was swept into power as the Republicans were widely blamed for the onset of the *Great Depression*. He held the White House for an unprecedented four terms, passing it to *Harry Truman* upon his death. Then an era of mostly Republican presidents began (*Eisenhower, Nixon, Ford, Reagan, George H. Bush*), punctuated by the foreshortened or failed Democratic presidencies of *John F. Kennedy, Lyndon Johnson*, and *Jimmy Carter*. Yet, for 40 years after *World War II*, with rare exceptions, Democrats retained control of both houses of Congress. Under Kennedy and Johnson they led the United States into the *Vietnam War*, then split so badly over the conduct of that war that their aspiration to the presidency was repeatedly denied over the next two decades. The Democrats retook the White House for a single term in 1976, with Republicans hobbled by the messy end game in Vietnam and by the *Watergate scandal*. They were again shut out of the presidency for twelve years, 1981–1993, until two post–Cold War victories by *Bill Clinton*, 1992 and 1996, wrapped around a stunning 1994 defeat in which the party lost control of the House for the first time in 40 years. The Democratic Party stood firmly behind Clinton, in public, during his impeachment. In a bitterly contested election in 2000 it lost the presidency again, to *George W. Bush. See also social democracy.*

democratic peace. The notable tendency of democracies to threaten or use force against each other less frequently than pairings of other types of states. Although some theorists look to "transparency" and seek to develop elaborate models to explain peace among democracies, this habit is best explained by: (1) shared democratic values such as respect for the rule of law, principles of fair dealing, and protection of minority interests; (2) established means of conflict resolution (negotiation under law) that democracies have tried and tested in their domestic politics; and (3) the fact that during the twentieth century most democracies were allied for geopolitical and ideological reasons against powerful common enemies, and therefore less likely to fight each other. These values and facts best explain their common history and why democracies have resolved disputes with one another more peaceably than with states that do not share their values, with which democracies have often gone to war. *See also Immanuel Kant; liberal-internationalism; zone of peace.*
    Suggested Reading: Immanuel Kant, *Perpetual Peace* (1795).

democratize. To cause to take on the values and characteristics of *democracy*, such as was accomplished through Allied occupation and administration of Austria, Italy, Japan, and West Germany after *World War II* or brought about by local democrats and reformers in numerous East and Central European countries in the aftermath of the *Cold War*.

demography. The study of *population, migration,* and similar patterns, with special regard for national cycles of births and deaths. *See also disease; famine; logistic; Thomas Malthus; population.*

demonetize. (1) To divest a monetary standard of its value. (2) To reduce the available supply of money.

demonstration. (1) A feint, or calculated use of force in one area designed to draw enemy troops in that direction while the real blow falls elsewhere. (2) A calculated *show of force* designed to deter or coerce an opponent from or to some action.

denationalize. To return to private hands a property or enterprise previously controlled by the state. *See also privatization.*

denaturalize. To revoke *citizenship* previously given to a *naturalized* (as opposed to native-born) subject.

denazification. A screening system was set up by the *Allies* in occupied Germany in 1945 to ensure that senior *Nazis* did not escape trial should they be charged as *war criminals*, as well as to remove thousands of lesser Nazis from public office as a prerequisite to reconstructing Germany along *liberal* and *democratic* lines. This led to controversy in the Western *occupation zones* (American, British, and French) when, instead of removing all Nazi Party members from public positions, they were instead classified into four groups according to their degree of commitment to the defeated regime and ideology. Nazi Party membership was thus not taken to mean automatic culpability in Nazi crimes, and unfitness for postwar office was not simply assumed. In other cases (*Krupp*), erstwhile Nazis and their close collaborators were given early release because their skills were needed for economic reconstruction. In the Soviet occupation zone, denazification was more brutal: it included mass executions and deportations by the *NKVD* of party members and SS and *Wehrmacht* officers. In *East Germany*, too, former Nazis were just too numerous, and some too practically useful to the new *Soviet bloc* regime, to permit a total *purge*. (Austria, separated from Germany after the war and occupied discretely, was not officially required to denazify.) In another sense, denazification in Germany is an ongoing process in which promotion of the Nazi Party, its symbols and doctrines, remains illegal and is prosecuted. This special limitation on free speech in a modern democracy is widely accepted within Germany and is understood and supported by foreign powers. *See also reverse course.*

Deng Xiaoping (1904–1997). Chinese Communist statesman. He joined the *Communist Party* (CCP) while a student in France (1920–1925). A veteran of the *Long March*, he rose to become part of the top leadership (deputy premier from 1952; member of the *Politburo* from 1956). He was active in the *purges* of intellectuals and others during the *Hundred Flowers campaign* in 1957. He was appalled by the economic and social destruction and dislocation of the *Great Leap Forward*, though there is evidence he participated in some of its purges and mass campaigns. Still, overall he worked to repair the damage Mao had caused until he was himself purged at the start of the *Great Proletarian Cultural Revolution* (1966). Next came years when his family was also persecuted—his son was thrown from a window by some callous *Red Guards* and was made paraplegic for life. Deng was *rehabilitated* in 1973 and again rose to the top ranks of the CCP. He emerged clearly as the protégé and successor leader of the more pragmatic wing of the CCP then led by *Zhou Enlai*.

Deng's pragmatism and disdain for ideological posturing was famously captured by his widely quoted remark: "It does not matter whether a cat is black or white. As long as it catches mice it is a good cat." That might be instructively contrasted with the Maoist slogan of earlier years, which spoke of "preferring socialist weeds to capitalist seedlings." Deng was therefore purged again, by the *Gang of Four*, after Zhou's death (January 1976) and the *Tiananmen Square incident* (April 4–5, 1976). Out of office, he took refuge in Guangzhou (Canton), where he was protected from any further harm by a loyalist military governor. Deng was rehabilitated, again, in July 1977 and returned to the Politburo to struggle for political control. By 1978 he emerged from that intense succession struggle as first-among-equals within the CCP leadership and instigated a purge of his own, of many vocal followers of the Gang of Four. Deng then moved quickly to take China off the careening course it had endured under the tiller hand of the "Great Helmsman," *Mao Zedong* and those CCP cadres brought into the party during the Cultural Revolution. He pushed instead for full implementation of what he and Zhou Enlai called the *Four Modernizations* of Chinese national life, in agriculture, industry, space (science and technology), and defense. In practice, military expenditure and doctrine was left to last, but caught up quickly after 1990. These Four Modernizations were to be tempered (this was mainly to appease the hardliners in the CCP) by *Four Cardinal Principles*: reliance on *Marxism-Leninism-Mao Zedong Thought*, keeping to the "socialist road," maintaining the *dictatorship of the proletariat*, and upholding the *vanguard* role of the CCP. Whatever the cover language, the changes Deng consistently promoted were openness to domestic market forces and foreign trade, and acceptance of considerable decentralization in national economic affairs, with at least some political decentralization implicit in that process. This reform effort encountered much "conservative" (radical Maoist) resistance from within the CCP and bureaucracy, which clung to policies of *autarky*. Deng pressed ahead, in 1979 approving establishment of several *export processing zones*. By the end of his tenure Deng had significantly opened China to *foreign direct investment* and trade, with huge positive consequences for its people and its engagement with the outside world.

In foreign policy, Deng approved a *friendship treaty* with Japan in 1978 and completed normalization of China's relations with the United States in 1979. That February, he personally ordered the launch of the *Sino-Vietnam War*, or Punitive War, in which the *People's Liberation Army* (PLA) did not fare as well as expected. Also in 1979, he cracked down on the Democracy Wall protestors he had at least implicitly encouraged (old Hundred Flowers campaign habits died hard, it seemed). He became premier of China in 1980, but afterward chose to govern from "behind the throne" by putting a succession of loyal protégées in power. He implemented his own "Rehabilitation Campaign" over nearly five years, partly to secure his political base and in part to restore confidence in the CCP after the depredations and chaos of the Mao decades. This involved partial reconsideration of the legacy of Mao, along the lines of the de-*Stalinization* initiated by *Khrushchev* in his *secret speech.* Officially, the CCP concluded that the "Great Helmsman" had been correct in 70 percent of his decisions, but that he had erred in 30 percent of his leadership policies. Such Jesuitical (or more properly, *Marxist*) casuistry was of course necessary if the whole *legitimacy* of the CCP's role in China was not to be called into question. Nonetheless, by the mid-1980s the Maoist communal principle of economic organization, which had distorted China's development since 1949, had been discarded, and even the cadres of the CCP were keenly debating—though they used much different language—China's prospects for *Smithian growth.* The price of such economic freedom and progress was deemed by the CCP to be continued cultural and political repression. Deng agreed, ordering in tanks and troops to crush the pro-democracy movement in the *Tiananmen Square massacre.*

Despite that appalling episode, and most importantly for the long term health and success of Chinese society, Deng in fact began to turn the country toward greater protection of individuals under a rule of law (albeit, starting from a Maoist baseline of next to zero). Of course, the CCP remained a wholly dictatorial party in the political realm, and in many ways it was still an economic power unto itself. Yet, slow progress was made toward real legal protection of what in the West is widely referred to as "civil society," in a fundamental redefinition of the relationship of the Chinese state to its citizens. Whether such a historic revolution in thinking could be carried through by an ossified party such as the CCP still remained to be seen into the twenty-first century. Promisingly, however, this growing respect for law included a new acknowledgment by China's diplomats of the need to justify and defend their country's legitimate *national interests* in terms of *international law.* At his death, Deng had thus more genuinely modernized—and hence, unlike the great failure Mao, also truly revolutionized—China than any other leader in its modern history and had taken it a long way down the road to final recovery from the ineffable tragedy of its decades in the Maoist wilderness.

Suggested Readings: Richard Evans, *Deng Xiaoping and the Making of Modern China* (1997); Jonathan Spence, *The Search for Modern China* (1990).

denial of justice. *See diplomatic protection; remedy; responsibility.*

Denmark. Originally a *Viking* state, as late as the seventeenth century it controlled parts of Norway, Sweden, and north Germany. In the ninth century, Danish Vikings pressed hard on the Saxon kingdoms of England, first as raiders, then as settlers and conquerors. The Danes eventually converted to *Christianity* as a consequence of these martial contacts and English *missionary* activities. In the eleventh century, Denmark was briefly united with northern England and Norway under King Canute, or Knut (994–1035), a brute of a man who slaughtered hostages and supplicants alike with abandon and who levied the toll of *tribute* known as the "Danegeld," paid by the Saxons, but who in later life mellowed and ruled his united kingdom with some wisdom, if still little mercy. As the nomadic and raiding impulse faded, Denmark settled into the Baltic system of the *Hansa* and the European system of *feudal* vassalage. In 1388 Queen Margaret (1353–1412), daughter of Waldemar IV of Denmark and wife of Haakon VI of Norway, was also offered the crown of Sweden by that country's nobles, who were displeased with their king, Albert of Mecklenberg. She agreed to the offer and invaded Sweden in order to accept it, taking Albert prisoner. In 1397 the *Union of Kalmar* was passed, creating a *union of the crowns*. This lasted with Norway for more than three centuries, but was broken by Sweden in 1523 with the ascent to the Swedish throne of Gustav I. In addition to Norway, the Danes still controlled until 1658 what is today part of southern Sweden.

The *Protestant Reformation* saw most Danes convert to *Lutheranism*. Under Christian IV (1577–1648), Denmark intervened in the *Thirty Years' War* (1618–1648) in 1625, launching the "Danish Phase" of that great conflict. A Protestant coalition failed to form around Denmark, however, and after four years of fighting, which devastated north Germany, Denmark was beaten into submission by the *Habsburgs*. In the seventeenth through eighteenth centuries, Denmark competed overseas with Portugal, England, the Netherlands, and other European powers for control of the West African *slave trade* and maintained slaving and trade forts in Africa into the nineteenth century. Under *Frederick VI* it joined the *League of Armed Neutrality*, then became a French ally in the *Napoleonic Wars*. As one result, it was pounded by the *Royal Navy* at two *Battles of Copenhagen*. At the *Congress of Vienna* (1814–1815), it lost Norway and its north German possessions. It tried to reclaim *Schleswig-Holstein* in a war with neighboring German states in 1848–1849. *Bismarck* forced Denmark to forfeit its claim in a sharp war in 1864. The unification of Germany in 1871 made Denmark acutely vulnerable to German power. It thus remained neutral in *World War I*. It was awarded the northern part of Schleswig in 1920, after a *plebiscite*.

Mainly for strategic reasons, *Nazi Germany* invaded and occupied Denmark, 1940–1944. The occupation was unusually lenient—partly because of the local German commander and partly because, in the Nazi's specious race theory, Danes were considered full *Aryans*. Unlike the Norwegians, the Danes did not establish a *government-in-exile* or present an active initial *resistance* to the occupation. Instead, there was broad collaboration with their occupiers, though under subdued protest. That gave Germany what it wanted: quiet and order in Denmark. On the other hand, King Christian X (1870–1947), to his lasting credit, defied Nazi orders to round up Danish Jews and refused *collaboration* with the more brutal aspects of the occupation. Many Danes followed his lead and successfully hid the majority of the small Jewish community from the *Gestapo*. A resistance movement grew slowly, and an "August Uprising" of strikes and other unrest took place in 1943. In 1944 Iceland declared independence from Denmark, under Anglo-American pressure—it was already in use as an Allied naval base. Liberation came in 1944.

After the war, Denmark became a charter member of NATO. It joined the *EFTA* in 1960 and the *European Community* in 1973. It incorporated Greenland (now *Kalaallit Nunaat*) directly under its constitution in 1953, but granted it *Home Rule* in 1979. Denmark then shook Europe in several *referenda*: in 1992 it turned down *Maastricht* before agreeing to the treaty in a second referendum in May 1993 (which sparked anti–European Union riots in Copenhagen); and in 2000 it voted 53 to 47 percent to reject monetary union. *See also Faeroe Islands.*

Suggested Reading: Gwyn Jones, *Denmark: A Modern History* (1986).

dense pack. Placing nuclear-tipped missiles in clusters, which is cheap but makes them vulnerable, rather than using a wide dispersal pattern, which is costly but safer. *See also fratricide.*

denuclearization. *See Nuclear Weapons Free Zones.*

Department of Defense (DOD). The U.S. department headed by the secretary of defense. It commands the Air Force, Army, Marines and Navy and is headquartered in the *Pentagon*. It is responsible for all matters relating to defense, including procurement and *war planning*. Until *World War II* it was called the War Department.

Department of State. The section of the U.S. federal bureaucracy headed by the secretary of state, responsible for formulating and implementing foreign policy. In fact, its policy suggestions must compete with a wide range of other bureaucratic and political centers of power, such as the president's top advisers, *Congress*, the *Treasury, Defense*, the *National Security Council*, foreign lobbyists, and the personal contacts and political cronies of all the above.

Department of the Treasury. The arm of the U.S. federal government headed by the secretary of the treasury that controls collection, management, and distribution of federal revenues. *See also Federal Reserve; secret service.*

dependence. High *vulnerability* to decisions, policies, interests, markets, and other political and economic events in other countries. Forests have been felled to print *political science* elaborations of this quite straightforward idea. *See also asymmetrical interdependence; complex interdependence; dependency; dependency theory; independence; interdependence; sovereignty.*

dependency. (1) Territorial: A weak, non*sovereign* area subject to rule by a foreign power. (2) Economic: A condition in which key decisions affecting weak national economies are made in foreign capitals and/or financial markets. (3) In *dependency theory*: The condition described in #2 is said to be a product of *imperialism*, and unredeemable and unreformable as long as weak societies remain tied to the *world capitalist system*. *See also associated state; protectorate.*

dependency theory. In this *radical*, political economy view of the *international system*, the *states* are not primary. The nature and operations of what is called the *world capitalist system* are instead the focus of analysis. For analytical purposes, the world is not divided into states, *blocs*, or opposing *alliances*, but into *core*, *semiperiphery*, and *periphery*, as defined by their relationship to the transnational capitalist economy. The central concern is identification of the operations of a putative global capitalist class, and efforts by the periphery to break free of a predicted exploitation of its resources and labor by dominant elites controlling the core, and local elites (the *comprador class*), which are said to cooperate in exploitation. The world financial and trading systems are seen as so corrupt and inherently biased toward the interests of industrial states and the elites that govern them that such institutions are beyond reform. The policy advice of dependency theorists therefore was alternately, withdrawal from the system (*autarky*) or its violent overthrow (*revolution*).

As ahistorical as these theoretical premises and policies were, they gained currency during the *decolonization* phase of the 1960s as the reality of continuing economic dependence by former *colonies* on *metropolitan* powers was contrasted with achievement of real political independence. After a brief flurry of enthusiasm among first-generation *Third World* leaders, the theory faded—everywhere but in "development studies" programs, which continued to propagate it inside the academy.

Subsequently, *developing countries* made proposals that sought to reform rather than overthrow the world economic system. This was so because of the poor prospects faced by radical solutions, but even more because it became clear to responsible leaders that dependency theory seriously underestimated the independent interests of states, overestimated the role of economic considerations as almost the only causal force in world affairs, and blurred and miscast national and cultural differences as always subordinate to class identity. Rhetorically, dependency theory peaked in the late 1970s in the various ambitious proposals that comprised the so-called *New International Economic Order*. Even by the early 1980s a historic transformation was underway in the relationship between developing countries and the major industrial powers, in which both newly recognized (largely as a result of the *debt crisis*, but also because of events unfolding in Russia and China) a mutuality of interest in cooperating to resolve outstanding issues of aid, trade, currency regulation, and international financial transactions. By the 1990s most states that once

tried to fit into the *Procrustean bed* of dependency theory abandoned it and sought instead greater access to global capital and goods markets and to technology, and aspired to membership in regional *free trade* associations, which more fully integrated their national and regional economies with those of other trading states. Some also began to modernize archaic local legal and social structures, which were often the real cause of slow growth and *uneven development*. Predictably, a new academic school then sprang up, styling itself "post–dependency theory," which ponderously pointed out the obvious need to study internal causes of underdevelopment in addition to international structural or systemic factors. A mirror opposite view of world economics is the idea of a global *dual economy*. *See also barter; Council for Mutual Economic Assistance; dependent development; development; imperialism; multinational corporation/enterprise; neocolonialism; neoimperialism; postimperialism; reformism; self-sufficiency; semiperiphery; underdevelopment; uneven development.*
Suggested Reading: Immanuel Wallerstein, *The Modern World System* (1980).

dependent development. The idea that *industrialization* and *modernization* of sectoral areas within the weaker economies in the *South* have the net effect of increasing economic and political dependence on the *North*.

dependent state. One submitting to the legal control of another state. *See also dependency; protectorate.*

dependent variable. *See causation; variable.*

deportation. (1) Expulsion of undesirable *alien*, criminal, or other persons, with or without due process of law. (2) Forcible transfers of whole populations. *See also collectivization; ethnic cleansing; refugees; repatriation; Josef Stalin.*

deportee. A person already, or due to be, deported.

depreciation. A fall in the worth of fixed assets.

depredation. Laying waste, *plundering*, ravaging, and killing; the general condition in which *war crimes* and *atrocities* are likely to take place.

depression. An extended decline in economic activity, rates of production, and investment and a severe contraction of credit, leading to corresponding rises in unemployment and bankruptcies. *See also business cycle; depressions, world; free trade; recession.*

depressions, world. (1) 1873–1896: A severe downturn in finance, trade, prices, and labor markets, felt most keenly in France, but also deeply affecting Great Britain, Germany, Russia, the United States, and all smaller trading nations. It hit India hard as well, contributing to a terrible *famine* in the *Deccan*. (2) 1929–1939 (the *Great Depression*): It was worsened, but not caused, by the stock market crash of 1929 that began on *Black Tuesday*. Controversy still attends the question of its causes, but they certainly included a radical decline in money supply, rapidly falling levels of consumption of industrial products, a prior depression in agricultural markets, the breakdown of the *gold standard*, poor policy responses, speculative excesses in financial markets, and an utter failure of American economic leadership. This may be summed up, in the consensus view of economic historians, as stemming from the core fact that the international financial system erected after *World War I* was inherently unstable. The failure to restore the gold standard led to seriatim major bank failures, which in turn caused a run on other banks. The stock market crash presaged a U.S. recession, which greatly exacerbated the international financial crisis as credit dried up, more banks failed, trade contracted, and *beggar-thy-neighbor* policies ultimately ensued from the governments of all the major economic powers.

The Great Depression's severe, dampening effects on prices and on trade were felt in all economic subfields and in all countries, but most disastrously among the *Great Powers* in Germany. Unemployment levels soared, reaching 17 million in the United States alone, prices severely contracted, banks collapsed, farm income plummeted, and world trade fell off sharply—all made worse by a round of mutually destructive, retaliatory, *protectionist* tariffs set off by the disastrous *Smoot-Hawley Tariff*. A *World Economic Conference* in 1933 failed to secure relief. The Depression soured political relations as well as economic relations among trading nations, including among all the industrial democracies. There were simultaneous and mutually debilitating quarrels over *reparations* and *war debts*, a general closing of national markets, and ultimately a complete collapse of the international economy.

The Great Depression radicalized politics everywhere to some degree, and in key countries such as Germany it was closely related to the rise of *fascist* and *militarist* regimes. *Nazi Germany* was the first major industrial country to recover, pulling out with massive public, especially military, spending programs that pumped *liquidity* into the economy. The United States did not really recover until it too began to spend heavily on military preparedness in the late 1930s. Everywhere, economic depression led to an increase in direct governmental regulation and control of banking, investment, and the economy, as well as efforts at *import substitution* in poorer countries. In China it led directly to several million peasants deaths, as world *cash crop* prices plunged and peasants who had invested all in cash rather than food crops were left with nothing and starved to death. It nearly wrecked colonial economies, by similarly depressing prices for their primary products. This retarded immediate development efforts, but accelerated the pace of *decolonization* after *World War II* by preventing most colonies from achieving financial and tax self-sufficiency and therefore further encouraging war-weary and fiscally bank-

rupt imperial powers to shed the financial burdens of empire. Similarly, it put a sudden halt to a prolonged export-fed boom that most Latin American countries had enjoyed since c. 1850. From then until 1930, Latin America's exports had grown by a factor of ten—an extraordinary growth rate that greatly expanded light manufacturing, early *industrialization*, and a *railway* and steamship transportation revolution in what had been almost wholly agrarian economies. This Latin boom lasted until the Great Depression collapsed world commodity prices and compressed primary product (mineral as well as agricultural) export markets. *See also business cycle; Herbert Hoover; John Keynes.*
Suggested Readings: Patricia Claven, *The Failure of Economic Diplomacy, 1931–36* (1997); Charles Kindleberger, *The World in Depression, 1929–1939* (1973).

depth charge. An explosive dropped overboard by a surface ship to concuss and otherwise damage, surface, or sink a *submarine*. Some are nuclear.

deregulation. Cutting back on heavy and intrusive internal bureaucratic and legislative oversight of private economic activity. This trend began in the 1970s in response to *stagflation* and accelerated in the 1980s, markedly so in the United States and Great Britain, continuing through the 1990s as more *conservative* governments sought to free market forces from centralized regulation and control. *See also* dirigisme; *Ronald Reagan; Margaret Thatcher.*

dereliction. Abandoning legal title to a *territory*.

derogation. Declaring a *reservation* on a clause of a *treaty* (if permitted), so that signature and *ratification* of the whole treaty may proceed without a state being bound or blocked by that one clause.

desaparacidos. "Disappeared ones." First used about unaccounted-for victims of the *dirty war* in Argentina, the term gained currency beyond Latin America as a marker of suspected victims of any *death squad*. *See also Augusto Pinochet.*

desertification. Expansion of desert at the expense of bordering grasslands or other ecosystems better able to sustain agriculture and human and animal settlement. It is a naturally occurring phenomenon but may also be abetted by human activity such as modern mechanized farming, traditional *slash and burn* land clearance, *overpopulation*, using trees from sparsely wooded areas as firewood, and so forth. Desertification is a major problem in Africa especially, but is also of concern in Central Asia and the American West.

desertion. Unlawful abandonment of one's military obligations, especially if from a combat position. Desertion is a widespread—and under reported, for reasons of morale—feature of all wars, but especially those involving large, *conscript* armies. Battles turned on the number of deserters during the *Thirty*

Years' War, and *attrition* by desertion radically thinned the ranks of the Grand Armée that *Napoleon* took into Russia in 1812. During the *American Civil War* masses of troops deserted from both sides. *World War I* was marked by large-scale desertions from most armies. These grew so extensive on the *eastern front* that they severely undermined the Russian war effort in 1917. They also led to *mutinies* in the French and British armies. During *World War II*, among the Western allies alone some 12,000 troops deserted in Italy in 1943–1944. Officially, nearly 20,000 deserted the American Army and another 20,000 deserted the British Army during the course of the war. Desertion was a significant problem for American forces during the *Vietnam War*, undermined the Soviets in Afghanistan, and cratered the Iraqi effort during the *Gulf War*.

Deshima. This artificial island (600 by 200 feet) in *Nagasaki* harbor was reserved for foreigners. It was prepared for the Portuguese in 1636, but given to the Dutch *East India Company* (VOC), which was ordered to move there from Hirado in 1641. Until the late *Tokugawa* era, the Dutch of the VOC were the only Europeans allowed in Japan; only the factor could leave Deshima, and then solely to perform a required annual ceremonial visit to Edo. Nearby was the larger Chinese Quarter, where *Qing* traders resided. For the Tokugawa, trade with the Dutch was relatively unimportant but the station did provide them with key intelligence on the outside world and facilitated the more important China trade. Shipping from Deshima was further restricted in 1715, and again in 1790, mostly to reduce exports of *bullion*. During the *Napoleonic Wars*, the Dutch monopoly was temporarily broken and the Deshima trade was carried by neutral ships, including some American vessels. *See also extraterritoriality; treaty port system.*

desk officer. Within most *foreign services*, an official in charge of coordinating policy and information toward a specific country or region, or overseeing an issue desk such as *human rights* or *arms control*.

despot. A tyrant or *autocrat*. *See also absolutism; despotism; enlightened despotism.*

despotism. The political system and values associated with a *despot*, to wit: absolute authority, arbitrary whim, personal favoritism, vainglory, and often, incompetence or madness. *See also autocracy; enlightened despotism.*

destabilization. Any policy that aims at eroding the popularity and/or perceived *legitimacy* of an opponent regime, including *covert action, disinformation, propaganda, sabotage, sanctions, subversion*, and support for antigovernment insurgents. *See also noise.*

de-Stalinization. (1) The partial lessening of repression within Soviet society after 1953, especially the end of the reign of *terror*, which characterized even personal and family life under the great tyrant, *Josef Stalin*, whose name it remembers. It was a main element of the thaw after the *secret speech* by *Nikita Khrushchev* at a closed session of the 20th Congress of the *Communist Party of the Soviet Union* (CPSU) in 1956. (2) Similar liberalization in any *Soviet bloc* or Soviet-style system. *See also* glasnost; *Hungarian Uprising*; perestroika; *Prague Spring*; *Stalinization*.

destroyer. Originally, "torpedo boat destroyer." A small, fast *warship* originally designed to screen *capital warships* from the threat posed by small, low profile, very fast *torpedo boats*. They also were deployed as *convoy* escorts, as they excelled in *anti-submarine warfare* (ASW).

During *World War I*, destroyers were extensively used to defend major warships and convoys against submarines and torpedo boats, but also took on an offensive role by themselves using speed and torpedoes to attack larger warships, as in a key German destroyer action at *Jutland*. In *World War II*, destroyers and destroyer escorts, smaller destroyers with lighter armor and reduced firepower but enhanced speed, were used by all major navies to protect shipping from submarine attack. After 1943 the Allies combined these ships with escort carriers to form hunter-killer groups, which finished off the *U-boats*.

destroyers-for-bases deal. In 1940 *Franklin Roosevelt* sent fifty *World War I*–vintage destroyers to Britain for use in *convoy* duty, in exchange for leases on several naval bases in the Atlantic. It was a clever way around restrictions on arms sales imposed by the *Neutrality Acts*, and it addressed an immediate and desperate British need in the *Battle of the Atlantic*. In its acquisition of new naval bases, it also spoke to Roosevelt's career-long interest in a permanent expansion of American *sea power*.

desuetude. No longer in being or practice. A legal doctrine holding that, if a *treaty* has been disregarded for some time, it falls into permanent disuse. It is used to give *tacit consent* to termination of a treaty.

détente. (1) Relaxation of international tension; an abatement of hostility, but not resolution of underlying conflict, between antagonistic powers. (2) The reduced tension in American-Soviet *Cold War* relations from c. 1969 to 1975. *See also Willy Brandt; Leonid Brezhnev; James Carter; Henry Ford; Henry Kissinger; Richard Nixon; rapprochement; SALT I and II.*

detention center. A camp or other confined and restricted place where *refugee* claimants or *deportees* are held pending either a hearing of their case or their relocation or *deportation*. *See also concentration camp.*

deter. Discouraging an undesirable or hostile foreign policy action, especially a military attack, by another state through encouraging fear of infliction of grave damage to the interests of that state or of military *retaliation. See also deterrence.*

determinism. (1) Theory, doctrine, or explanation that holds that social and historical phenomena are directly caused by preceding events or the putative laws of god or history, largely unaffected by acts of will, which are themselves determined by unseen structures and forces. Theorists usually deny that their ideas are deterministic. Nonetheless, many theoretical statements about general *causation* reflect an unconscious proclivity toward determinism in thought or language. (2) A disposition to see multiple effects as flowing from a single cause, which is used to explain all change. *See also agent-structure problem; counterfactual; decline of the West; economic determinism; historicism;* post hoc ergo propter hoc; *relativism; structural determinism; volition.*

deterrence. A policy of maintaining a large military, heavy *fortification,* or other effective defenses to discourage in advance an enemy's military from attacking or invading, by threatening to punish any advance and thereby forestall its *aggression.* It works—when it works—by promising to raise the aggressor's costs of success to an unacceptable level, even when the ultimate outcome might still be defeat of the defenders. For example, Sweden might have been overrun by either of its powerful neighbors, Germany and Russia, after the eighteenth century. A sizeable, well-armed military threatened to make any such effort too expensive in lives and national treasure to be worthwhile for those powers. This helped keep Sweden perpetually at peace after 1815. Switzerland similarly deterred attack by bristling with well-armed and trained soldiery, a policy it supplemented by providing *neutral* services to all *belligerents* in times of war. During the *Cold War,* studies of deterrence tended to focus on *nuclear weapons* and promises of *massive retaliation* in the event of aggression, even though *NATO's* conventional forces were also intended as a deterrent to possible *Warsaw Pact* aggression. Even crude fortification may be understood as a basic, indeed classic, deterrent strategy. In this sense, China's *Great Wall,* France's *Maginot Line,* and Belgium's huge frontier forts were spectacular (though unsuccessful) examples of prenuclear deterrence, as were the hundreds of castles that dotted *samurai* Japan and *feudal* Europe and India. Forms of deterrence include *extended, intrawar, minimum,* and *nuclear.* The antonym of deterrence is *appeasement. See also assured destruction; ABM; ballistic missile defense; credibility; humane deterrence; opportunism;* qui desiderat; *retaliation; second strike; war-avoidance strategy.*

deterrent. (1) Any military force capable of forestalling an attack by the credible promise it makes of retaliatory destruction. (2) Any retaliatory threat.

de Valera, Eamon (1882–1975). Irish nationalist; prime minister, 1932–1948, 1951–1954, 1957–1959; president, 1959–1973. De Valera was active in the *Easter Rising*, after which he was arrested and condemned to death (commuted). After his release from prison he was elected to head *Sinn Féin* and to the Dáil Éireann (parliament), which in turn elected him president of the Irish Republic it proclaimed as independent in 1918. He spent two years in the United States raising money for the *IRA*, then returned to play a lead role in the *Irish War of Independence*. He refused to accept the *Anglo-Irish Treaty* (1921) and reluctantly led rump-IRA opposition to *Michael Collins* and *Irish Free State* forces in the *Irish Civil War*. He boycotted the Dáil until 1927, then led his Fianna Fail party to a majority government in 1932. In power, he immediately whittled away at the symbolic restrictions on Irish *sovereignty* of the Anglo-Irish Treaty, abolishing its required oath of allegiance and ending financial payments to Britain. In 1937 he made Ireland an effective republic, under a new constitution, and changed its formal name to *Eire*. He kept Ireland *neutral* during *World War II*, even protesting Anglo-American use of *Ulster* shipyards and as a base of military operations. He was careful to maintain close ties to the Irish *diaspora* in the United States. He was turned out in 1948, but returned as prime minister for most of the 1950s. In 1959 he moved to the presidency. He retired in 1973 and died two years later.
   Suggested Reading: J. O'Carroll and J. Murphy, eds., *De Valera and His Times* (1986).

devaluation. Reducing a *currency's* value relative to other currencies or to the *gold standard*. This is done either by decree where the currency is *soft* and the government *pegs* its value or, in advanced, *hard currency* economies, by a lessening of market support by the *central bank*, which lets markets set *exchange rates* at lower levels. This lowers the price—and thus increases volumes—of exports, raises the cost of imports, reduces consumption, and thereby helps erase the country's *balance of payments* deficit. However, competitive devaluation may result, as nations try to outdo each other's devaluations to gain an advantage for their own balance of payments problem.

developing country/nation. One that has begun the process of exploiting its resources and labor to allow a sustained increase in production and wealth, but has not yet achieved *modernization* in major areas of its national life. It will generally have a low per capita income, compared with developed or *OECD* states, and shortages of capital and skilled labor. In economic terms, a developing economy is one that runs a perennial *balance of payments* deficit, reflecting the fact that it consumes more than it produces, though this may also be true of a *mature economy*. At the start of the twenty-first century, most were located in Africa, Asia, Latin America, the *Balkans*, the *CIS* region, and Eastern Europe. An alternative term, falling into politically correct disuse as a putative pejorative, is *underdeveloped country*. Even older terms, long since in disuse as supposedly insensitive to vital national aspirations, included "poor nations" and "former colonies." *See also Fourth World; LDC; Third World.*

development. There is no consensus about the general meaning of this term, or even which *indicators* should be used to assess or measure it. However, in general it suggests not just economic *growth*, but growth that springs from and reinforces major structural changes in an underlying economy. It suggests economic progression away from subsistence, at the most basic, through creation of regional and national markets, to participation in international trade, to introduction and reliance on the most advanced manufacturing and service industries. More popularly, it refers to building institutions and economic *infrastructure* to steer the general *modernization* of traditional societies. In recent history, development is closely associated with *industrialization* and urbanization. Taking a longer view, development may move in the opposite direction (decline and collapse of failed civilizations), and has done so repeatedly. For the past several centuries, innovations born of *technology* and of *war* have been among the most important factors stimulating accelerating economic development. A controversial, but also nonbinding, Declaration on the Right to Development, adopted by the *United Nations General Assembly* in 1986, proclaimed development as a new *human right*. Theoretical variants include: *autonomous, dependent, reflexive,* and *sustainable development. See also basic needs; capitalism; democracy; dual economy; Human Development Index; International Bank for Reconstruction and Development; International Monetary Fund; institutional matrix; Less Developed Country; Marxism; regional banks; self-reliance; underdevelopment; uneven development.*

Suggested Readings: Amartya Sen, *Beyond the Crisis* (1999); Amartya Sen, *Development as Freedom* (2001).

"devil theories" of war. A (not inaccurate) pejorative for any unsophisticated theory about the causes of *war* that places sole, or at least primary, blame for its outbreak not on historical, economic, or social forces and developments, or on specific decisions, misperceptions, or other blunders by leaders, but instead on secret conspiracies by ostensibly evil-intentioned groups, usually of a different race, religion, or class than the accuser's. The most commonplace variant in the twentieth century, made popular by the playwright G. B. Shaw and a number of influential historians in the 1930s, was that wars were willfully started by the *"merchants of death"* (arms manufacturers) who desired them to create and/or expand markets for their wares. The Nazis held the still more pernicious view that most modern wars, especially those involving Germany, were started by a world conspiracy of Jews; Russian (and other) Christians often placed the blame for the calamity of war on Freemasons; and Communists blamed the captains of *capitalism*, who usually reciprocated the insult. *See also* post hoc ergo propter hoc.

devolution. *See autonomy; Scotland; Wales.*

devolution agreements. Instruments detailing the devolved rights and obligations of *successor states* in cases where a portion of an extant (surviving parent) state achieves *sovereign* independence through a successful *secession.*

Dewey, George (1837–1917). U.S. admiral. He first saw action in the *American Civil War.* He rose in the navy bureaucracy under the sponsorship of *Theodore Roosevelt.* When the *Spanish-American War* broke out, he sailed to Manila, where he destroyed an entire Spanish fleet and captured the city (May 1, 1898) without a single American death and fewer than 10 wounded. He then imposed a *blockade*—including against several German warships— and enforced it while awaiting an invasion force to arrive from the United States. Dewey's victory at Manila made the United States a colonial and Pacific power, to the great surprise and subsequent considerable discomfort of most Americans.

dey. *Ottoman* commanders in *Algiers* and *Tunis.* It was an electoral rather than hereditary office, chosen from among the *corsairs.* It was abolished in Tunis early in the eighteenth century, from which point the *beys* who had long ruled in fact also ruled in name. In Algiers, the reverse happened: in 1711 the dey, military commander of the corsairs, overthrew the bey.

dhow. A generic term for Arab sailing vessels that dominated trade around Africa, Arabia, and the Indian subcontinent before the twentieth century.

diachronic study. *Jargon* for any analysis of a broad phenomenon over a lengthy period, such as a general study of *industrialization* or *war,* as opposed to study of a discrete industry or war.

dialectic. (1) In formal reasoning: Proceeding via a dialogue, or conversation. (2) In Hegelian method: Reasoning in which a *thesis* is opposed by an *antithesis,* forming a higher *synthesis* that serves as a higher thesis, and so on. For Hegel, this was how knowledge must progress, from combinations of partial truths toward higher synthesis or approximation of absolute truth, a form of reified Platonic ideal. *See also end of history; George Hegel; Karl Marx; Marxism.*

dialectical materialism. In *Marxist* usage, the application of the logical model of the *dialectic* to history and the study of the "iron laws" of *class struggle* and social change that supposedly derive from the material basis of reality. Once in power, the mask of materialism has often slipped to reveal the more driving motive force among dedicated revolutionaries: a deep romanticism about human nature and a savage determination to employ whatever means are necessary and at hand to force unwilling people into the *Procrustean* theoretical and societal beds prepared for them by the *revolution*. *See also collectivization; communism; cultural revolution; end of history; Great Leap Forward; kulaks; Karl Marx; Marxism-Leninism; vanguard.*

diaspora. (1) The scattering, through *migration* forced or voluntary, of a people from their original home to far-flung lands, such as happened to Africans, Armenians, Irish, Jews and, for different reasons, Chinese and Russians. (2) The whole body of such people living in new countries.

Díaz, José de la Cruz Porfiro (1830–1915). Eight-time president, and dictator, of Mexico, 1877–1880, 1884–1911. A former muleteer from Oaxaca, Díaz got his start in the 1860s as a military commander on the liberal side, fighting alongside *Juárez* against the French and *Maximilian*. He was in charge of Mexican affairs for so long that the period from 1877 to 1911 is sometimes referred to as the "Porfiriato," or Age of Porfiro. He took power in a *coup* in 1876, had himself elected the next year, and then imposed a (at first brutal) dictatorship on the country. He ruled in collaboration with the landed oligarchy. He kept up good relations with the United States and other *Great Powers*, insulating Mexico from intervention and overseeing a significant rise in *foreign direct investment* and the general *standard of living*, though mainly of the already privileged social classes since Díaz adhered to a coarse social *laissez-faire*. Indians were damaged by his liberal land reforms because they did not have the private capital to purchase plots of formerly communal lands that he broke up and put on the market. He forcibly put down an Indian rebellion in the 1880s. He was overthrown by the *Mexican Revolution* of 1911. He fled to exile in France, where he died and was buried.

dictatorship. A political system where power is exercised arbitrarily by an individual, clique, or party, regardless of the constitutional form and surface appearance of the government. *See also absolutism; autocracy; despotism.*

dictatorship of the proletariat. (1) In *Marxist-Leninist* theory: A transitional phase between the overthrow of the *capitalist mode of production*, the establishment of *socialism*, and the achievement of *communism*. (2) In practice: In the Soviet Union in the 1920s–1930s, a justification of ruthless one-party rule under which opponents of the regime were labeled "class enemies" and *liquidated* and under which *Stalin* and the *Bolsheviks* instituted a *revolution from above* in agriculture and then industry that cost millions of lives. *See also collectivization; five-year plans; kulaks; war communism.*

Diego Garcia. This Indian Ocean island was detached from the jurisdiction of *Mauritius* in 1965 by the British and leased to the United States for use as its major naval and satellite-tracking base in the Indian Ocean. In 1982 Britain agreed to pay *compensation* to former plantation workers deported to make way for the United States base.

Diêm, Ngô Dình (1901–1963). Minister of the interior in *Annam*, 1933; prime minister of the Republic of Vietnam (RVN), 1954 (under *Bao Dai*); president and dictator, 1955–1963. In 1929 he helped suppress a *Communist* uprising. In 1945 he was kidnapped by the *Viêt Minh*, who also killed his brother, an act that left him with an abiding hatred of the Communists. He was appointed prime minister on June 18, 1954. He had a disagreement with Bao Dai and had him removed in 1955. Backed by Washington, he rejected implementation of the *Geneva Accords* and declared independence of the RVN. Diem was a devout Roman Catholic, celibate and puritanical. He had studied at Catholic seminaries in the United States and spent 1953 in a monastery in Belgium. In power, he alienated important anti-Communist groups, including the *Montagnards*, *Buddhists*, and other non-Catholics. He governed autocratically and badly. He survived a *coup* attempt in November 1960, and another in February 1962. Diem was viewed as corrupt and inept by the *Kennedy* administration. He was assassinated in a November 1963 coup, which was at least tacitly authorized by Kennedy just three weeks before his own assassination, even though he probably did not approve of Diem's being killed. Diem's overthrow greatly furthered the growing reality that the *Vietnam War* was becoming an American conflict, rather than a war for the Army of the Republic of Vietnam (ARVN) to fight with American aid.

Dien Bien Phu, Battle of (November 20, 1953–May 7, 1954). The French staked all in the *French-Indochina War* on holding this reinforced military outpost against the *Viêt Minh*. General Henri Navarre hoped to use the garrison as bait to draw the Viêt Minh to its destruction by *artillery* and *air power*. General *Giáp* was determined on a decisive victory, and willing to spend many Vietnamese lives to achieve it. The Viêt Minh were supported by the Soviets and by *Mao Zedong*, who urged the siege on *Hô Chí Minh* and suggested timing it to influence peace talks planned to settle the situation in *French Indochina*. Employing thousands of porters and 800 Chinese trucks, Giáp emplaced artillery and antiaircraft guns in the surrounding jungle hills, from where they pounded the camp for months while Giáp launched *infiltration* attacks and probing assaults with infantry and tanks. He also attacked the air bases on which Dien Bien Phu depended for resupply. The French were cut off in their forward firebase and faced a much stronger enemy than expected (50,000 combat troops and another 50,000 support troops, instead of a single Viêt Minh division). The Viêt Minh launched "human wave" attacks at first, then settled on *trench warfare* and *sappers*, who dug hundreds of miles of assault trenches. In the end, the garrison fell after an all-out *siege* that began on March 13th. The French lost 1,600 dead, 4,800 wounded, and 8,000 prisoners, of whom half later died. The Viêt Minh lost 8,000 dead and 15,000 wounded. This defeat (in which the *French Foreign Legion* was heavily involved) was a major humiliation that convinced Paris to pull out of a losing and over-extended commitment to empire in Southeast Asia. The *Geneva Accords* followed, but so too did the *Vietnam War*.

Suggested Readings: M. Billings-Yun, *Decision Against War* (1988); Võ Nguyên Giáp, *Dien Bien Phu* (1994).

Dieppe raid (August 19, 1942). A large Allied *commando* raid took place near this historic, coastal city of *occupied* France. The raid was intended as a strategic diversion to relieve pressure on the *Red Army* then being brought to bear by *Wehrmacht* and *Waffen SS* advances all along the *eastern front*. It was a disaster: 6,000 men, mostly Canadians under British command, but including a handful of American rangers, were caught on the beaches by well-prepared German defenders. Nearly two-thirds were slaughtered as they stumbled ashore, or later captured. Much was learned from the disaster that would prove useful on *D-Day* and in other seaborne invasions, but at a high and bitter cost. Dieppe was a key event for Canadians: it reinforced a growing nationalist demand that they be allowed to fight under their own commanders, and it more generally encouraged a sense of increased nationhood and political distinction from Great Britain and its Empire. *See also Bernard Montgomery; Louis Mountbatten.*

Diet. The legislative body in Japan.

Difaqane. See Mfecane.

diffusion. The spread of religious or political ideas, cultural values, *technology*, and military skills across borders and among divers peoples, nations, and cultures. It is one of the great themes of world history, speeding up and coalescing in modern times with the changing speed of communications and travel. *See also Buddhism; Christianity; colonialism; Confucianism; diplomacy; Enlightenment; Exploration, Age of; foreign direct investment; French Revolution; haj; Hinduism; human rights; imperialism; industrialization; international law; Islam; modernization; multinational corporation; Protestant Reformation; radio; Renaissance; revolution in military affairs; settlers; sovereignty; technology transfer; tourism; trade route; transnational.*

dignitary. A person with high government or ceremonial rank.

diktat. A harsh, dictated settlement imposed upon a defeated nation; not a compromise peace. For instance, *Brest-Litovsk. See also Carthaginian peace; peace treaty.*

dimension of war. Military *jargon* for the space where combat takes place. Traditionally, this was either on land or at sea. However, the nineteenth and twentieth centuries added several more dimensions: undersea, in the air, in space, and in cyberspace.

Dimitrov, Georgi Mihailov (1882–1949). Bulgarian *Communist*. Charged by the *Nazis* in 1933 as one of those responsible for setting fire to the *Reichstag*, he was acquitted and later became a Soviet citizen. From 1934 to 1943 he was titular director of the *Comintern*. He was installed as Bulgarian premier by *Stalin*, an office he held from 1946 to 1949, and that he used to ruthlessly *sovietize* the country.

Diomede Islands. Two barren islands in the *Bering Strait*, four miles apart and separated by the International Date Line. The big one is Russian and the little one is American, which was more a curiosity than a problem during the *Cold War*.

diplomacy. The art of *negotiation*, comprising the essential activity of all international politics. Diplomacy is the patient quest for compromise resolution of knotty problems in the affairs of nations and states through *representation* of their *national interests* to each other and mutual communication of their policies. Like war, diplomacy is the continuation of politics by other means— only its main means are words not weapons, peaceful interaction not violence, and rational argument and concession rather than the effort to impose one's will on others by *force majeure*. Diplomacy is not divorced from *force*, however: *deterrent* warnings and coercive threats are as much the stuff of diplomacy as affirmative *treaties* or *summitry*. Diplomacy thus relies principally upon persuasion, but also on the precise and calibrated application of *power*, up to and including the use of *force*. The diplomatic system in general aims at achieving limitations on the use of force as a means of resolving disputes among states, but it accepts that circumstances may warrant resort to force, unilaterally or collectively, to defend legitimate international legal and other *sovereign* rights. Still, restraints are more highly valued. They may be self-imposed or mutually assessed through the mechanisms of *international law* and *international society*, so that pragmatic and rule-governed solutions to practical problems become possible and are mutually beneficial.

Harold Nicolson argued that modern diplomatic practice evolved through five distinct periods or styles. It is a depiction worth recalling and utilizing. First came the Greeks. They had no permanent missions, so most diplomacy was by ad hoc conference. Yet, there were developed principles governing *declarations of war, peace treaties, ratification, arbitration, neutrality*, and even certain rudimentary *laws of war*. The *Roman Empire* developed the *jus gentium* to govern relations among Roman citizens and foreigners, and there was respect for elementary *good faith, reciprocity*, and *sanctity* of contracts. Drawing upon contacts between *Venice* and the *Byzantine Empire,* during the Italian *Renaissance* diplomatic practice evolved rapidly and took on its early, but recognizably and characteristically modern, form. The Renaissance witnessed the introduction of regular written instructions to fully accredited and resident *ambassadors*, highly developed ceremonial and ritualized *protocol*, and the crucial breakthrough of the first permanent diplomatic system, comprised of resident missions not just to allied courts but also to potential or real adversaries. *Archives* also were kept by more states to confirm histories of negotiation. *Raison d'état* was elevated to a cardinal principle of statecraft and definition of the ambassadorial mission, replacing older notions of peacefulness and community that had marked the Medieval *res publica Christiana*. Duplicity, short-term agreement (faithlessness), *espionage, subversion*, and bribery became ubiquitous tools of the diplomat. The next move forward came under Cardinal *Richelieu* of France. He was the first statesman attached to a *Great Power* to recognize the Italians were right in viewing negotiation as a permanent activity, and he therefore extended this principle to France's relations with all the Great Powers and to lesser powers as well. He also understood that negotiation should aim at durable arrangements; that the interests of the state were paramount over religion or ideology; that treaties must be treated as sacred if reciprocity is to work; that ambassadors ought not exceed their instructions; and that foreign policy should be conducted by a single, national ministry and by a corps of professional diplomats with access to dependable archives.

Beyond the core Western European countries, the diplomatic system remained primitive into the late nineteenth century, but it was continually expanding nonetheless. For instance, when *Peter I* ascended the Russian throne in 1689, his state had only one foreign mission, in Warsaw. During his reign he established diplomatic relations with all European countries and several in Asia—twenty-three permanent missions in all by 1725. He even sent an emissary to offer his vague protection to Madagascar, though the message never arrived because the ship bearing his envoy sank en route. Elsewhere, the process took much longer: *Qing* China sent its first representatives to Paris and London only in 1871, and to the United States in 1878. Colonial expansion via overseas *imperialism* and then democratic idealism, and a revolution in communications, dramatically altered diplomacy. Europe united the globe through its imperialist thrust and thereby brought non-European peoples into a diplomatic and legal system that was hitherto regional. After *World War I* democratic sensibilities demanded that negotiations be more public, which led to a return to *conference diplomacy* and ultimately to the permanent conferencing of the *League of Nations* and *United Nations*. Insistence on the fiction of interstate *equality*, such as at the *Hague Conferences*, had already eroded the notion that *Great Powers* should have special rights because they have unique responsibilities; this older idea was preserved in the *Security Council*, but erased from the *General Assembly*. The U.S. failure to ratify the *Versailles Treaty*, negotiated personally by a president, shook confidence in the sanctity of contract, as did later Nazi and Soviet practice.

Since the mid-nineteenth century, when cable telegraphs first made near-instantaneous communication possible between national capitals, modern communications technology has lessened the independence and importance of ambassadors and reduced the policymaking role of entire diplomatic services. It has done so by: (1) increasing the role of *public opinion*, including direct *propaganda* appeal to each other's public opinion via means of mass communication (newspapers, *radio*); (2) quickening the *decision-making* process for all concerned; and (3) permitting direct talks between *heads of government* or other *decision makers*. Also contributing to representational confusion during the twentieth century was the rise of *nonstate actors* and the new salience of broad issues requiring international solutions that blurred traditional lines of state jurisdiction and competence. Increasingly, it is the main job of diplomatic services to coordinate complex national policies made by a host of agencies, rather than initiate specific foreign policies on precise issues. Note: An alternate, narrow sense of diplomacy is a synonym for a state's *foreign policy*, as in "Japanese diplomacy toward China." *See also Aix-la-Chapelle;* attaché; chargé d'affaires; *coercive diplomacy; Congress of Vienna; consul; consulate;* embassage; *embassy; envoy extraordinary; gunboat diplomacy; mediation; minister plenipotentiary; nonresident ambassador; plenipotentiary; preventive diplomacy; protocol; Vienna Conventions; and other entries relating to diplomacy below.*

Suggested Readings: R. P. Barston, *Modern Diplomacy* (1988); Edward Gulick, *Europe's Classical Balance of Power* (1955); D. J. Hill, *A History of Diplomacy* (1921); Henry Kissinger, *Diplomacy* (1994); Garrett Mattingly, *Renaissance Diplomacy* (1955); Jan Melissen, *Innovation in Diplomatic Practice* (1999); Harold Nicholson, *Evolution of Diplomatic Method* (1954).

diplomat. An accredited representative of a nation and its foreign policy visiting or resident in a foreign land or resident in the home country but who helps maintain political, economic, and social relations with foreign governments. To Sir Henry Wotten (1568–1639) is attributed the most cuttingly humorous and risqué definition: "An ambassador is an honest man, sent to lie abroad for the commonwealth." That is moderately unfair. It is true that a modest measure of duplicity is often required in diplomacy, and even more the case that a diplomat representing a scheming and conspiratorial government is likely to engage in duplicity beyond even the normal requirements of diplomatic intercourse. At its best and most effective, however, diplomacy assumes and relies upon *good faith*, fair dealing, and a reputation for keeping one's word. *See also representation.*

diplomatic bag. Any receptacle (not necessarily a bag) subject to *diplomatic immunity* from inspection or seizure.

diplomatic corps. (1) The body of resident *diplomats*, from all countries. By tradition, since *Aix-la-Chapelle*, the "dean of the diplomatic corps" is the *ambassador* who has been longest at his or her post, no matter the significance or insignificance of the country represented. (2) All the diplomatic officials and employees of a given state.

diplomatic correspondence. Any official communication traveling in a *diplomatic bag* or otherwise protected under the law of *diplomatic immunity*.

diplomatic courier. An *envoy* charged with delivery of state papers, and enjoying limited *diplomatic immunity* in that task.

diplomatic credentials. *See letters of credence.*

diplomatic immunity. *Extraterritorial* exemption from local civil and criminal *jurisdiction* enjoyed by properly accredited *diplomats*, including freedom from physical search or inspection, from seizure of official property, personal arrest, detention or prosecution for violation of local laws, or obligation to pay local taxes. These exemptions may be waived only by the diplomat's own government. This is rarely, but sometimes, done to permit prosecution for heinous personal crimes. Immunity rights were explicitly laid out in two 1961 *Vienna Conventions*. Note: *Consular* officers do not enjoy these immunities in law, but frequently do as a matter of courtesy and mutual consular convenience. *See also diplomatic protection; herald; hostages; international personality; Spanish Road; state immunity.*

diplomatic instructions. Written instructions to an *ambassador* by the *sovereign* (or government) detailing the goals, negotiating points, degree of latitude permitted in negotiation, and reminding of any and all *vital interests* that must not be compromised. As early ambassadors might be asked to produce their instructions for a host government to read, during the *Renaissance* it became common practice for an ambassador to carry two sets: one to be shown to the host, and another, containing the ambassador's real instructions, which were kept secret. *See also diplomatic powers.*

diplomatic intervention. The effort to persuade, rather than compel, a foreign power to alter some policy or undo some action it has taken toward a third party. *See also diplomatic immunity; diplomatic protection.*

diplomatic note. A formal statement of policy delivered, usually in private and not for publication, directly to a foreign government. It may concern arrangements of mutual interest, in which case it is less than a *treaty* or *executive agreement* but still a statement of official policy. If a protest note, it serves as an instrument of frank understanding. *See also ultimatum.*

diplomatic powers. The specific powers of negotiation granted to an *ambassador*, usually contained in public documents that outline, detail, and strictly limit those powers. Until the seventeenth century, it was common diplomatic practice in Europe to write powers in Latin and on parchment. Diplomatic powers may be highly restricted, especially on matters of great import. Even when a diplomat is allowed to negotiate real substance and sign an agreement, most governments over the centuries have insisted upon later *ratifying* any agreement at the level of *head of state*. For minor issues, full powers to make agreements may be assigned to an ambassador.

diplomatic protection. When a state intercedes on behalf of its own nationals. This is legally permissible only after the individuals concerned have reached *exhaustion of local remedies*. See also *diplomatic immunity*; *passport*; *visa*.

diplomatic protest. A formal objection to some policy or action, for instance, an abuse of *human rights* or an incursion onto one's territory, made to a senior representative of a foreign power. It may, or may not, be *pro forma*. If political, its purpose may be merely propagandistic. However, more usually protests are made as the principal method of enforcing *international law* against minor or irksome breaches. Diplomatic protests against small *delicts* thus are usually accompanied by demands for *compensation*, *restitution*, or, if possible, recovery of the original condition before the offense occurred.

diplomatic recognition. See *recognition*.

diplomatic relations. (1) Formal *recognition*, courtesies, ambassadorial rights and privileges, means of communication, and especially the acknowledgment of *sovereignty* that states extend to one another. These relations can be broken in whole or part to signal deep displeasure with some conduct or policy, but can also remain in place even when states are in conflict, as in the *Gulf War*, when United Nations coalition allies did not sever relations with Iraq. If no formal relations exist, another state may deliver messages, threats and so forth. (2) Formal, government-to-government contact. See also *foreign relations*; *relations officieuses*.

diplomatic revolution (1558). See *Elizabeth I*; *Protestant Reformation*.

diplomatic revolution (1756). For two centuries the *Habsburgs* of Austria were opposed by the kings of France and had allied against France with the monarchs of England. The rise of *Prussia* to *Great Power* status and its seizure of *Silesia* during the *War of the Austrian Succession* changed all that. In 1756 *Maria Theresa* of Austria forged an alliance with Russia and France aimed at defeating *Frederick the Great* and dismembering Prussia. Frederick turned to England, which still opposed France but now was bereft of its Austrian ally.

This realignment lasted through the *Seven Years' War*, but broke down with the *French Revolution* and a wholly new alliance structure and *balance of power* aimed at *containment* of Revolutionary France and later, of the colossal ambition of *Napoleon*.

directed trade. Government intervention that prevents full and open *free trade*. This might be done to consolidate alliance commitments, carry out a *boycott*, or just pander to domestic constituents. A synonym is *managed trade*. *See also protectionism.*

Directory (1795–1799). The five-member executive body that governed France after the overthrow of the *Committee of Public Safety*. Under the Directory, France at first enjoyed major victories against other powers. It also suffered through savage repression of a Catholic revolt in the *Vendée*, the *White Terror*, and then setbacks in the *War of the Second Coalition*. It was first saved by *Napoleon I* ("a whiff of grapeshot") then overthrown by him in the 1799 *coup d'etat* known as *Brumaire*.

direct rule. (1) In colonial administration: When there was no local intermediary (chief, *emir, bey, dey, nawab*) acting as go-between for the colonial governor with the native population. (2) In *Ulster*: The closing of the Stormount Parliament to rule directly from London, as a response to rising *IRA* and other violence in the mid-1970s. It lasted until implementation of a general peace accord in December 1999. *See also indirect rule.*

dirigisme/dirigiste. "Direction." From the French economic theory and practice of state-guided industrial and national *development* that denies that moral phenomena and goals can be radically separated from economics and aims mainly at minimizing collective losses. More broadly, an ethos of elite, bureaucratic prerogative concerning major decisions about national economic and social policy. *See also collectivization; five-year plans; industrialization; Meiji Restoration.*

"dirty float." When a state that publicly says it is letting its currency *float* secretly *intervenes* in the marketplace to influence the direction of *exchange rates*.

"dirty war" (1976–1983). In Argentina, the campaign, replete with *death squads*, carried out by the military against political opposition, 1976–1982. The official estimate of those murdered is 10,000 but some estimates go as high as 25,000–30,000 *desaparacidos*. After the military was humiliated in the *Falklands War*, several top officers were tried and imprisoned for their part in the dirty war. However, in 1986 President Raul Alfonsin passed a remarkably morally retrograde law making *superior orders* an acceptable defense. In 1989 and 1990, President Carlos Menem pardoned almost all officers who had conducted the dirty war, along with some former *guerillas* then in prison. *See also Operation Condor.*

"dirty weapon." A *nuclear weapon* yielding very high *radiation effects. See also clean bomb; radiological weapons.*

disarmament. This term is often inaccurately used as a synonym for *arms control.* It really means the elimination of all offensive arms, either unilaterally (to provide a moral example, as peace activists intermittently suggest); reciprocally as part of a negotiated process; or as a condition of a *diktat* imposed by a victorious power on a vanquished foe, as in the near-complete disarmament of Germany under terms of the *Treaty of Versailles.* According to its charter, the *United Nations* is formally—but is not actually—committed to "general and complete disarmament," which supposedly means that all states one day are to be reduced to levels of weaponry sufficient only to maintain internal order. *Machiavelli* wrote, caustically, of the idea: "Among other evils which being unarmed brings you, it causes you to be despised." *See also armed neutrality; deterrence; demilitarization; peace enforcement;* qui desiderat pacem praeparet bellum.

Disarmament Conference, Geneva (1932–1934). The *Treaty of Versailles* (1919) and later the *Geneva Protocol* (1925) both called for a full *disarmament* conference, but this was delayed until February 1932. The nations finally met in Geneva, with 59 states attending, the largest international gathering to that point in history. The conference was sponsored by the *League of Nations,* but nonmembers such as the United States and Soviet Union also participated. In 1932 the major powers agreed to release Germany from the unilateral disarmament provisions of the Treaty of Versailles by accepting a principle of staged equality in armaments among the *Great Powers.* The conference floundered on French insistence on a prior, general scheme of *international security.* It was beached for good upon the ascent to power of *Adolf Hitler,* who pulled Germany out of the conference and renounced its principles in October 1933. Soon thereafter, the conference broke up.

Disarmament in Europe (CDE) Accord. It arose out of the Stockholm conference of the CSCE, 1984–1986. It sought to reduce the chance of military misunderstanding or miscalculation by introduction of such *CSBMs* as advance notice of *maneuvers* by the *Warsaw Pact* and NATO and on-site weapons and *arms control* inspections. *See also transparency; verification.*

discovery. Historically, a means by which states acquired new *territory* by claiming it as *terra incognita,* usually ignoring claims by any *indigenous people.* Thus, *Christopher Columbus* claimed the Americas for *Ferdinand and Isabella,* a claim divided with Portugal but otherwise upheld by the pope. Not long after the globe was fully mapped, its land surfaces were also fully claimed (except for the *global commons*) by one state or another. To date, the principle of discovery has been earthbound: the United States did not claim the moon when its astronauts landed there in 1969, a self-denial later codified generally in the *Moon Treaty*.

disease. The great epidemic scourges of history—cholera, influenza, leprosy, malaria, plague (the *Black Death*), smallpox, syphilis, yellow fever, and most recently, *acquired immune deficiency syndrome (AIDS)*—have at times shaken states and empires, savaged economies, and contributed to accompanying *famines* and *wars*. The most tragic and remarkable effects were in the Americas, where epidemic diseases brought by the *conquistadores* severely undermined the *Aztec Empire* and contributed to its military and psychological collapse. Subsequently, epidemics led to a complete demographic collapse of the Indian population throughout the Americas, as nonresistant natives first encountered measles, mumps, smallpox, typhus, and the plague, among other diseases. In turn, a quick-killing form of syphilis possibly reached Europe from the Americas c. 1495 (though it is also possible an extant strain of European syphilis mutated). *See also biological warfare; Thomas Malthus; population; World Health Organization.*
   Suggested Readings: Roy Porter, *The Greatest Benefit to Mankind: A Medical History of Humanity From Antiquity to the Present* (1997); Sheldon Watts, *Epidemics and History* (1998).

disengagement. The physical separation of two previously hostile, engaged militaries. This is an essential prelude to ending armed conflict. Note: This may precede, but is different from, and more limited than, *demilitarization.*

disinflation. A downward movement of wages and prices, raising the purchasing power of a *currency. See also deflation.*

disinformation. The deliberate provision of misleading or false information, for example, as part of a *covert operation* to confuse an opponent's political strategy, military *intelligence,* or *counterintelligence* or to poison mass opinion. Disinformation differs from *propaganda* in that it is usually done in secret. *See also biological warfare; Comintern; double cross; Protocols of the Elders of Zion.*

disinvestment. When a firm divests itself of ownership and involvement in an enterprise or project in which it previously had an *investment* stake. In the 1980s the term took on the additional meaning of private *boycott,* with particular application to South Africa: public, and in some cases stockholder, pressure was placed on *multinational corporations* to divest their holdings and plants in South Africa as a way of reinforcing internationally agreed public *sanctions. See also capital flight.*

dispatch. A diplomatic or military communication.

Displaced Person (DP). *See internally displaced person; refugee.*

dispute. Any point of significant legal or political disagreement between or among states. *See also frontier dispute; justiciable dispute; nonjusticiable dispute.*

Disraeli, Benjamin (1804–1881). British author and statesman. *Chancellor of the exchequer*, 1852, 1858–1859, 1867; prime minister, 1868, 1874–1880. A brilliant writer and orator with a rapier wit, on becoming prime minister he famously said: "I have climbed to the top of the greasy pole." He was a strong *protectionist*, opposed to full *free trade* while at the exchequer and later as prime minister. He was also an ardent social reformer and an active *imperialist* and empire builder. He saw the *British Empire* as a major enhancement of British power, yet he did not so much follow an assertive imperial policy as a *grand strategy* as he was led by local and more aggressive imperialists into colonial acquisitions, but also misadventures. He acquired Fiji for the British Empire in 1874. In 1875 he persuaded the Baron *Rothschild* to finance Britain's purchase of a controlling interest in the Suez Canal Co. from the khedive of Egypt. This secured the short route to India, but also dragged Britain deeper into the *Eastern Question* and other swirling controversies in Sudan and elsewhere in the Middle East. He oversaw the crowning of *Victoria* as empress of India the next year. He annexed *Transvaal* to *Cape Colony* in 1877 and extracted Cyprus from the *Ottoman Empire* as the price of his diplomatic support against Russia and for overlooking Turkey's depredations against Bulgarian Christians. He consistently supported the Turks against Russia and played the *Great Game* well in Central Asia. He was able to avoid war over a crisis in Bulgaria and the *Dardanelles* and personally attended the *Congress of Berlin* (1878). After his return he said: "Lord *Salisbury* and myself have brought you back peace—but a peace, I hope, with honor." Disraeli believed firmly in the value of *prestige*, and much of his policy reflected this. He was thus drawn into the *Zulu Wars* (1878–1879) by colonists in Southern Africa, and pulled into the painful and damaging second *Afghan War* (1878–1880) by an overly assertive viceroy. He won Russian confirmation of British interests in the *Straits Question* and achieved the *Cyprus Convention* as well. Military setbacks in Afghanistan and South Africa, and the continuing world depression after 1873, cost him high office in 1880. *See also Neville Chamberlain; William Gladstone; Treaty of San Stefano.*

Suggested Readings: Robert Blake, *Disraeli* (1966, 1987); Robert Blake, *Disraeli and Gladstone* (1969); Richard Shannon, *The Age of Disraeli, 1868–1881* (1992); Stanley Weintraub, *Disraeli* (1993).

dissent. *See Amnesty International; China; dissident; Elizabeth I; fascism; freedom of information; Helsinki Watch; Hundred Flowers campaign; human rights; Saddam Hussein; KGB; liquidation; Nelson Mandela; Mao Zedong; Operation Condor; political prisoner; prisoner of conscience; propaganda; revolutions of 1848; Russia; Andrei Sakharov; samizdat; secret police; Josef Stalin; state of emergency; Tiananmen Square incident; Tiananmen Square massacre; totalitarianism; treason; Yamamoto Isoroku.*

dissenting opinion. When an international justice disagrees with a court's judgment and submits an opinion providing alternate reasoning and/or a different conclusion.

dissident. A person who disagrees with national policy, often suffering persecution as a result. Outside concern for dissenters has grown in recent decades, but still generally leads to nothing more dramatic than *diplomatic intervention.*

Distant Early Warning (DEW) Line. A radar warning system stretching across Alaska and Northern Canada designed to provide early notice of hostile aircraft or missiles traversing the Arctic en route to targets in the United States. For thirty-six years it was under American command and control. From 1988 to 1993, the DEW Line system was phased out, in favor of the more modern *North Warning System*, which also introduced separate national control of bases on American and Canadian territory. The DEW Line was shut down in July 1993. *See also North American Air Defense Command.*

distributive justice. Questions and proposals about allocation of wealth within the global economy, especially as affecting *North-South* relations, based not upon economic *efficiency* but instead derived from considerations of *ethics* and justice. *See also agricultural revolution; aid; development; free trade; green revolution; industrialization; modernization; protectionism.*

Diu. *See Portuguese India.*

diversionary war. One started to deflect public attention from domestic troubles; such as the Argentine *junta's* initiation of the *Falklands War.*

divided states. *See community of nations.*

divide et impera. "Divide and rule." The political maxim of *Niccolo Machiavelli,* and the political practice of many an empire and despot. *See also British Empire; Robert Clive; conquistadores; Inca; Roman Empire.*

divine right of kings. (1) A pre–*French Revolution* political doctrine that held that a *sovereign's* right to rule derived directly from authority proceeding from God, as sanctified by the Church. (2) An ancient ruling device, found in most premodern cultures, wherein sovereigns assert that they rule as instruments of the Deity on earth or, in extreme cases, that they were themselves divinities. *See also absolutism; Byzantine Empire; democracy; Enlightenment; mandate of heaven; popular sovereignty;* res publica Christiana; *Roman Empire.*

division. *See military units; Napoleonic warfare.*

Djibouti. This Horn of Africa territory became a colony (French Somaliland) in piecemeal fashion, 1862–1900. Its population is divided into two main groups: Issas (akin to Somalis) and Afars (akin to Ethiopian tribes).

Ethiopia and Somalia claimed portions of its territory, and there was some interethnic violence before independence in 1977. However, these claims were renounced under international pressure. France keeps a deterrent force in Djibouti nonetheless.

Dobrynin, Anatoli Federovich (b. 1919). Soviet diplomat; ambassador to the United States, 1962–1986. Appointed by *Khrushchev* in March 1962, during the *Cuban Missile Crisis* that October he negotiated secretly with Robert Kennedy the quid pro quo that enabled both sides to save *face* by staggered withdrawals of missiles from Cuba and Turkey. He served as Soviet ambassador during the administrations of *Kennedy, Johnson, Nixon, Ford, Carter,* and *Reagan,* making his among the most familiar faces of the *Cold War.* In 1986 he was recalled by *Gorbachev,* ostensibly to take charge of the international department of the *Communist Party,* but also to clear room for Gorbachev's own choice and a fresh approach to Washington. Dobrynin retired in 1988.

Dodecanese. An island group in the Mediterranean, formerly part of the *Ottoman Empire* but taken by Italy after it defeated Turkey in the *Italo-Turkish War* (1911–1912).

During *World War II,* fierce fighting over the Dodecanese took place, in 1943, with Germans on one side and Italian and British troops on the other. The British failure to seize the islands—a minor replay of *Churchill's* strategy at *Gallipoli*—set back the cause of Turkish entry into the war. The Dodecanese were ceded to Greece in one of the *Treaties of Paris* (1947) and were partly *demilitarized.*

Dodge Plan. A bilateral aid program from the United States to postwar Japan, designed to rapidly rebuild the Japanese economy to make Japan not merely self-supporting, but a bulwark against Soviet political influence in East Asia. It was patterned on the *Marshall Plan*.

dog fight. Aerial combat, so named for its vicious, tangled maneuvering. In the supersonic era, air-to-air missiles rendered such close combat nearly obsolete.

Dogger Bank incident (October 21, 1904). The Russian Baltic Fleet, en route to the Pacific to take part in the *Russo-Japanese War*, fired on British fishing boats in a fog in the North Sea, thinking that they might be Japanese *torpedo boats*. Public opinion in Britain reached a war pitch and was cooled only by formal Russian acceptance of responsibility and agreement to make *reparations*.

dollar convertibility. Under the *Bretton Woods* regime, a commitment of the United States to convert foreign-held dollars into a fixed price of gold, providing *liquidity* and *adjustment* for the whole system.

dollar diplomacy. (1) The use of financial power to promote other *national interests* in a state's foreign policy, through investment or the use of *aid* to gain voting support within the United Nations or in some regional body. (2) The use of foreign policy resources to support the private business interests of a state's citizens. (3) A sometime description of the foreign policy of U.S. President *William Howard Taft* (1909–1913), in which economic incentives were substituted for the use of unilateral force to maintain local stability. This was attempted both in Central America and in policy toward China. *See also Alliance for Progress; Colombo Plan; development assistance; European Recovery Program; Open Door.*

dollar gap. In disuse. The difference between a state's exports and investments in, and what it owed to, the United States. It was important in the post–World War II decades when the U.S. dollar was the unchallenged international monetary standard.

dollarization. Replacing a national currency with the U.S. dollar as, for example, in Ecuador and El Salvador in 2000–2001. In some cases it is a desperation move, aimed at forestalling *hyperinflation*. *See also floating exchange rates; peg.*

Dollfuss, Englebert (1892–1934). Foreign minister and chancellor of Austria, May 1932–July 1934. Suspicious of both left- and right-wing political parties, he tried to govern directly without parliamentary support. He used the army freely against demonstrators, unions, and workers' groups. This played into the hands of the *Nazis*, whom he fatally underestimated: in 1934 he was killed during a Nazi coup attempt. *See also* Anschluss; *Kurt von Schuschnigg.*

domain. (1) The reach or range of *international law*, stopping where it meets, and is curtailed by, the outer edge of territorial *sovereignty*, municipal *jurisdiction*, or denial of *consent.* (2) The area under the sovereign (effective) control of one government, as in "Labrador lies within Canada's domain," or "Burgundy came under the domain of the *Habsburgs.*"

domestic jurisdiction. The range of internal activities undertaken by states that are supposed to be entirely free of the *domain* of international law. In some areas, such as *human rights* and *crimes against humanity*, boundaries between municipal and international law and politics became increasingly frayed during the second half of the twentieth century.

domicile, test of. *See nationality.*

dominant power. This may be a local, regional, or (rarely) global status enjoyed by a powerful state, by which it has no clear rivals and its foreign policy preferences (usually) hold sway.

Dominica. Spanish and French colonizers faced fierce resistance from the island's Carib natives. France ceded Dominica to Britain in the *Treaty of Paris* (1763).

It became a full British colony in 1805. As a member of the *West Indies Associated States*, it was given local autonomy in 1967, gaining full *independence* in 1978. A hurricane devastated its still largely plantation economy the next year. Coup attempts failed in 1980 and 1981. Under Mary Eugenia Charles, prime minister 1980–1995, Dominica took the lead in obtaining support from the OECS for the U.S. *invasion of Grenada* in 1983.

Dominican intervention (1965). In April 1965, in the Dominican Republic a revolt took place led by young army officers seeking to restore deposed President Juan Bosch (1909–2001), a liberal who had been elected in December 1962, but had been deposed seven months later. The group was reported to involve some *Communists* and that sparked U.S. intervention. President *Lyndon Johnson* sent in 23,000 U.S. marines, accompanied by token units from five OAS countries after somewhat reluctant voting support by the OAS. The intervention marked a decided shift in U.S. policy away from the *Alliance for Progress. See also Good Neighbor policy.*

Dominican Republic. It is part of the island of *Hispaniola* and was colonized by Spain after its discovery by Columbus in 1492. It boasts in Santo Domingo the oldest permanent European settlement in the Western hemisphere. The western portion of the island was ceded to France in 1697 and became Haiti. France took the remainder of the island in 1795, but lost it back to Haiti after a successful slave rebellion there in 1801. Spain regained control briefly, 1803–1821. Haiti again took over the eastern half, 1822–1844. In 1844 the Dominican side of Hispaniola broke away from Haiti. Spain returned a third time, 1861–1863. The United States displaced Spain from the hemisphere in 1898 and thereafter sent in marines to directly administer the Dominican Republic, 1916–1924. In 1930 Rafael Trujillo (1891–1961) became president and dictator by electoral fraud and military coercion. He ruled with an iron hand, including ordering the massacre of thousands of Haitians in 1937. *Eisenhower* and *Kennedy* both authorized the *CIA* to arm anti-Trujillo dissidents; he was assassinated on May 30, 1961. There followed a prolonged succession crisis. Juan Bosch (1909–2001) was elected president and served for seven months in 1963 until he was overthrown in a coup. Kennedy briefly severed relations with the new regime. Agitation for Bosch's return to power led to a U.S. invasion in 1965, despite a 1940 treaty in which the United States relinquished a right to intervene. The country thereafter stayed quietly within the U.S. orbit, under Joaquin Balaguer (b. 1907).

In 1994 his 7th consecutive election was judged fraudulent by international observers, but no action was taken, as Dominican help was required to enforce United Nations *sanctions* against neighboring Haiti.

Suggested Reading: Rayford W. Logan, *Haiti and the Dominican Republic* (1968).

Dominion. A class of states within the *Commonwealth* which accepted the British monarch as their *head of state*, as represented by a governor-general. Before *World War II*, they were: Australia, Canada, Eire, Newfoundland, New Zealand, and South Africa. Some post–World War II dominions, such as India, later became republics, accepting the British monarch solely as titular head of the Commonwealth. Others, such as Eire, became republics and left the association. *See also Durham Report; Statute of Westminster.*

domino theory. A strategic metaphor, rather than a *theory*, which views the loss of preponderant influence or control over one *client, colony,* or *satellite state* to an adversary as likely to lead to the loss of adjacent states or colonies, which must fall "like dominoes." At the extreme, it can blind decision makers to the relative insignificance of certain states or stakes. *Philip II* committed Spain to the *Eighty Years' War* (1566–1648) against Dutch rebels, and he and his successors continued that fight long after it was clearly lost, in large part out of fear the effect of concessions might have elsewhere. During the *Great Game*, British statesmen regularly exaggerated the threat to the *British Empire's* defense of India from much-feared Russian moves in the Caucasus and Afghanistan. Similarly, France feared that losing *French Indochina* would unravel its whole empire. During the *Vietnam War*, this metaphor inflated American perceptions of the importance of the Republic of Vietnam (RVN) to the world *balance of power*, though was not as influential as is popularly thought, and thereby contributed to an overcommitment of resources and *political capital* to an area of minor geostrategic significance. On the other hand, Soviet leaders accurately saw their outer empire as a set of potential dominoes where reform in one client state might (and in fact, ultimately did) lead to toppling of their whole, rickety imperial edifice. In turn, that might (and did) threaten the stability of the Soviet Union itself. Until 1989, therefore, Moscow vigorously enforced the *Brezhnev Doctrine*.

Suggested Reading: Frank Ninkovich, *Modernity and Power* (1994).

Dönitz, Karl (1891–1980). Builder and commander of the German *U-boat* fleet, 1935–1945; commander of the Kriegsmarine, 1943–1945. Serving in a U-boat during *World War I*, he was captured and imprisoned in Great Britain in 1918. The *Treaty of Versailles* forbade Germany from building any *submarines*, but Dönitz headed a secret group within the high command that spent the 1920s in U-boat research and planning. When the *Anglo-German Naval Agreement* lifted the U-boat ban, Dönitz oversaw construction of the new fleet. He envisioned a Kriegsmarine made up primarily of his beloved U-boats, but until 1943 was unable to persuade *Hitler* (who was committed to the fantastic *Z-Plan*) or the Kriegsmarine command of this. He replaced Admiral Erich Raeder (1876–1960) as commander of the Kriegsmarine on January 30, 1943, immediately ordered a halt to construction of *capital warships*, and transferred all work and combat crews to submarines. He thereby achieved his dream of a vast submarine fleet (at one point, 300 vessels), organized into *wolf packs*, to hunt down Allied shipping. It was too late: Dönitz's U-boats lost the *Battle of the Atlantic* that same year. He also lost his son, aboard a vanished U-boat. A fanatic *Nazi*, he was named Hitler's successor during the "final days," which he spent with his master deep underground in the Führerbunker in Berlin. With Hitler's suicide, Dönitz was briefly *Führer* of the *Third Reich*, which he formally surrendered to the Allies. He was tried at *Nuremberg* as a major *war criminal*; the principle charge was his order to submarine captains to ignore the rules of *cruiser warfare* and not to stop to rescue crew from ships they sank. He was censured for that order and sentenced to ten years for planning a war of *aggression*—the lightest sentence received by any defendant.

donor country/nation/state. One that gives *aid*.

donor fatigue. When donor governments and populations grow impatient at providing *aid* in face of a lack of *development* progress in recipient nations. This pattern was first noticed in the late 1970s, as *public opinion* and officialdom in *donor countries* became resistant to further outlays of aid without demonstrable improvements in the *infrastructure* and production, and reduction in often gross corruption, of many recipient governments and economies. In

447

part, this was a reaction against the radical demands of the *New International Economic Order*.

Doolittle raid (April 18, 1942). Named for the commander, James Doolittle (1896–1993). This daring, first bombing of Tokyo during *World War II* was conducted soon after *Pearl Harbor* to bring home to Americans and Japanese alike that the United States would not soon or easily quit the war, as some in Japan hoped, and that Japan's *home islands* could and would be reached and pounded by American *air power*. Normally land-based, heavy bombers (B-25s) were instead launched from an *aircraft carrier*, from maximum range, and achieved total surprise. Most planes made it to safety in Nationalist China and eventually returned home; one bomber landed in the Soviet Union, where its crew was interned because Russia was not then at war with Japan; eight crew captured in Japan itself were executed in spite of their status as *POWs* and in violation of the *Geneva Conventions*. The raid stunned the Japanese—*Tōjō* witnessed it from the air en route. It partly provoked *Yamamoto* and the Japanese Navy into the disastrous attack on *Midway*, which changed the course of the Pacific war.

double agent. A *spy* working for two countries simultaneously, who may have real loyalty to one or just be a clever mercenary. In American parlance, an *agent* pretending to work for a foreign *intelligence service* is "a dangle." The Russians call this tactic "a game." *See also false flag recruitment.*

double containment. (1) Any effort to contain more than one regional power at the same time, such as *Edward Grey*'s attempts to contain Germany and Russia before *World War I* or American efforts to contain both Iran and Iraq after 1991 so that neither power was able to gain control of the region's vital *oil* reserves. (2) A widely believed but mostly inaccurate idea that West Germany was included in *NATO* for two vital reasons: to bolster West European defense against the Soviets and to lock Germany itself into a watchful and controlled security setting. This notion, which arose as a post facto explanation of the effect of Germany's membership in NATO, recognized that German military revival was inevitable, but also that it came about under NATO command and with Germany's military integrated with other NATO militaries. Double containment was in some minds at NATO's founding in 1949, but very few saw things that way when the Federal Republic of Germany was admitted in 1955. *See also containment.*

double cross. An intelligence betrayal, taken from the highly successful British *disinformation* campaign against German *intelligence* in *World War II*, code-named "XX."

double government. *See East India Company; indirect rule.*

double standard. When a foreign policy is applied unevenly, across the range of a state's *diplomatic relations*. Thus, economic *sanctions* over *human rights* violations may be applied against one state and not a second because the second is too powerful to be influenced in that way, too unconnected for the sanctions to have any real bite, or too important to other foreign policy goals to risk giving too much offense.

doublethink. In *propaganda*, simultaneous acceptance of mutually contradictory ideas whereby one is preconditioned to ignore what to others appear as obvious contradictions; drawn from the brainwashing process used on Winston Smith ("Everyman") in George Orwell's novel "1984."

double veto. *See veto.*

"dove." American colloquialism for policies that, or persons who, always seek accommodation in the first instance. In its pejorative sense it is used to suggest a predilection for compromise that borders on *appeasement. See also hard line; hawk.*

dowager empress. The widow of an emperor. By Chinese law and tradition, the dowager empress could determine the imperial succession. Some appointed minor children and ruled themselves, through regents. *See also Cixi.*

draft. *See conscription.*

draft dodger. A *conscript* who does not report for service, for whatever reason (American usage). Such a person may or may not also be a *conscientious objector.*

Drago Doctrine. Announced by Argentina's foreign minister Luis Drago in 1902 and backed by the United States, it held that mere *default* on national debt was an insufficient reason for foreign *intervention*, especially by an extrahemispheric power. It was provoked by a *blockade* of Venezuela by several European powers after Venezuela had defaulted on its debt. The United States took direct control of the customs of several smaller countries to ensure payments and forestall additional interventions. *See also Monroe Doctrine.*

dreadnought. An interim class of *battleship* named after the HMS Dreadnought, launched by Britain in February 1906 under the guidance of Admiral *John Fisher.* The heavy armament and "all big guns" of this new warship class (the design eschewed the mix of large- and small-caliber guns common on earlier ships) represented a *revolution in military affairs* that made all older battleships obsolete overnight, not least by introducing mechanical firing computers, rangefinders, and radio for signaling. Fisher recognized this and simply scrapped 154 older ships of the *Royal Navy*. The launch of Dreadnought and later all-big-gun ships threatened to severely weaken Britain's advantage over other major navies in a world naval arms race, at the core of which was the *Anglo-German naval arms race*, since new fleets could be built on roughly even terms in battleships, which were now broadly comparable. Dreadnoughts were in fact built by all major, and several minor, navies from 1906 to 1914, undercutting Britain's policy of keeping to a *two-power naval standard*. In the end, these mighty weapons platforms were hardly used in later naval combat. There was only one major battleship engagement during *World War I*, at *Jutland* in 1916. That war also witnessed the mature emergence of two other classes of warships that would prove dominant over the course of the twentieth century: *submarines* and *aircraft carriers*. *See also battle cruiser; ironclad; Scapa Flow.*

Suggested Readings: R. Massie, *Dreadnought* (1991); P. Padfield, *The Battleship Era* (1972).

Dreikaiserbund (1873–1887). "League of the Three Emperors." A loose system of consultation, and later formal cooperation, among Austria, Germany, and Russia concerning Turkey. It proved a mildly successful effort by *Bismarck* to forestall a French attempt to reverse the defeat it suffered in the *Franco-Prussian War*, by denying France any ally to the east of Germany. It collapsed when Austro-Russian tensions over changes in the Balkans (Bulgaria) led to a war scare during a prolonged crisis, 1885–1888, which outweighed any mutual interests toward Turkey. *See also Reinsurance Treaty.*

Dresden, bombing of (February 13–15, 1945). Dresden escaped much of the destruction of *World War II* until a series of *thousand bomber raids* over the course of February 13–15, 1945. As the last sizeable city in Germany not yet bombed, it was packed with refugees. Allied bombers—British by night, American by day—dropped incendiary bombs in a pattern designed to create a firestorm in the center of the city. This was a deliberate replication of an unintended, but devastating, effect noticed during a prior incendiary bombing of Hamburg. Perhaps 120,000 German civilians died (the figure is disputed, ranging from 35,000 to 150,000). Dresden also housed tens of thousands of Allied *prisoners of war*; those who survived were forced to clear away the corpses after the raid ended. The bombing of Dresden came to symbolize the role that terror bombing had played in the strategic air campaign waged against Nazi Germany. In otherwise comprehensive memoirs, *Winston Churchill* elided over any treatment of the Dresden raid. *See also air power; carpet bombing; strategic bombing.*

Dreyfus affair (1894–1906). Alfred Dreyfus (1859–1935) was a loyal officer in the French Army, who was also Jewish. An investigation into espionage in behalf of Germany was focused wrongly on him, largely as a result of *anti-Semitic* sentiments within the mostly Catholic (and monarchist) *officer corps*.

He was tried, convicted, degraded, and sent to Devil's Island (Guyana) to do hard time. The real traitor was a French Catholic, Major Walsin Esterhazy, who was exposed by a doggedly honest colonel of intelligence, Georges Picquart, and by Dreyfus' brother. In 1897 Esterhazy was acquitted in spite of the evidence, and Picquart's career was blocked for spite for his having exposed the army's anti-Semitic bigotry and its incompetence. The novelist Emile Zola, supported by *Clemenceau* and other leading republicans, wrote a famous letter ("J'accuse") charging the army with anti-Semitism and with neglecting the *national interest* by concealing the true traitor. Zola was then charged with libel and forced to flee into English exile. Dreyfus was retried in 1898, and again found guilty—despite clear exposure of forgeries (by a colonel of Army Intelligence, who committed suicide upon his exposure) in the evidence against him. However, this time Dreyfus was pardoned. In 1906 his name was cleared by the High Court, and his rank was reinstated. Picquart also retrieved his honor, but that of the army was badly tarnished and France was sharply divided. Many Catholics and monarchists closed ranks to defend the military and anti-Semitism; socialists, republicans, and anticlericalists who feared for the republic returned to radical, anti-Catholic policies, just as the great crisis with Germany loomed. In 1998, more than a century after first being falsely accused, Dreyfus was posthumously cleared of all treason by the French Army. *See also Fashoda crisis; Theodor Herzl; Zionism.*

Suggested Readings: Leslie Derfler, *The Dreyfus Affair* (2002); Norman L. Kleeblatt. *The Dreyfus Affair: Art, Truth, and Justice* (1987).

drift-net fishing. The use of huge (some are more than a dozen kilometers long) fishing nets, which are set adrift for hundreds or thousands of miles, riding the ocean currents of the *high seas*. Unlike trawling, drift nets are utterly indiscriminate, scooping up and killing multiple noncommercial fish species, along with those sought after, and catching and drowning dolphins, sea turtles, and even whales. In 1991 the United Nations proclaimed a *moratorium* on drift-net fishing but this was ignored by many nations, notably Italy and Taiwan. The *European Union* first limited nets to 2.5 kilometers then phased them out by 1997.

drug cartels. Private drug production and smuggling operations run out of, at the start of the twenty-first century, Latin American and Asian countries, often into the European and North American markets. Huge profits allowed the cartels to hire private armies, buy local police, silence judges and corrupt politicians, distort entire national economies, and block effective *development* programs among poor peasants. From the 1990s they increasingly became a target of national and international military operations, though to little apparent effect. *See also drug trade; narco-terrorism.*

drug trade. The export of narcotics, or other medicinal substances such as steroids, from one country to another, in the case of illegal drugs via round-about routes and devious means. In the nineteenth century the main importer was China (*opium*) and the trade was openly controlled by Westerners. By the late twentieth century the main importers were Western countries—although the social effects of popular drug use were beginning to be felt glob-ally—whereas the major suppliers were in the *Third World*. The scope of the trade in illegal drugs is difficult to estimate. However, some specialists ranked it as the second largest (after *oil*) export from the Third World to the *OECD* nations. *See also Colombia; drug cartels; East India Company; Opium Wars.*

Druse. A small Middle Eastern sect in *schism* from mainstream *Islam* since the eleventh century, and highly secretive and socially closed as a result. The Druse fought the *Christian* invaders of the *Crusades*, but in later centuries they were mostly left alone in their mountain isolation by the *Mamluks* and then the *Ottomans*. They became blood enemies of the Maronite Christians of Lebanon, whom they first fought in the nineteenth century. They fiercely opposed French colonization of Syria after *World War I*. Although they were defeated in the *Druse rebellion*, they regained some *autonomy* from France. In the twentieth century, Druse fought for Israel, where they are classed sepa-rately from Israeli Arabs, and against Israel, or against anyone else seen as threatening their still cherished, and secretive, independence. They fought intensely with the old Maronite enemy again during the *Lebanese Civil War*. Most Druse now live in Israel, Lebanon, and the Jebel Druz region of Syria.

Druse rebellion (1925–1927). A revolt by the *Druse* against the French *mandate* in southern Syria. The Druse captured Damascus for a time, but in fierce fighting, France reclaimed the city, crushed the rebellion, and drove the Druse fighters back into the hill country. However, the rebellion resulted in limited autonomy for the Druse, until the French departed Lebanon.

Dual Alliance. (1) A secret Austro-German alliance, from 1879, that later became the *Triple Alliance* with the addition of Italy. (2) The Franco-Russian alliance of 1890, reinforced with a military convention in 1893–1894, that lasted until the collapse of the *eastern front* in 1917.

dual containment. *See double containment.*

dual economy. A *liberal* view of political economy that depicts the world economy as divided into two main sectors: a modern, advanced, wealthy, and *industrialized* sector and a premodern traditional sector. In an exactly opposed thesis to that of *dependency theory*, in this view national and regional eco-nomic *development* is seen to advance with, and result from, penetration of the traditional sector by global market forces and *foreign direct investment* flowing from the more advanced sector. Its advocates point to the domestic experience of advanced countries, where similar dual economies existed in earlier epochs, but where many differences in wealth and opportunity were smoothed out over time. *See also dualism.*

dualism. (1) In *international law*: The doctrine that international law and *municipal law* are unrelated. (2) In *development* literature: When urban *modernization* is juxtaposed with rural backwardness and economic neglect. *See also monism.*

dual key. The *NATO* practice, starting in the 1960s, of placing American *nuclear weapons* (warheads) on a second country's launchers with the United States retaining one "key" (set of launch codes), and the host country another. As keys worked only in tandem, actual launch authority had to satisfy command and control concerns of both nations.

Dual Monarchy (Austria-Hungary). It was created in 1867 by the *Ausgleich*, which followed Austria's defeat at the hands of Prussia. This rickety state survived as one of the *Great Powers* into *World War I*, but not beyond. Its breakup was already underway by the end of 1918 and was then sanctioned by the victorious *Great Powers* at the *Paris Peace Conference*. *See also Austrian Empire.*

dual nationality. When an individual has legal *citizenship*, or *nationality*, in two (or more) states. It may result from application of *jus soli* to a child born of foreign parents or of *jus sanguinas* to a child born abroad. *See also Bancroft Conventions.*

dual use technology. Any technology with both military and civilian applications, for example, a boost vehicle/missile launcher, civilian/breeder reactors, advanced computers, bioengineering skills and equipment, and so forth.

Dubček, Alexander (b. 1921). Czechoslovak *Communist Party* leader. He rose to international prominence by supporting the 1968 liberalization movement known as the *Prague Spring* and for promising to reform and deliver "socialism with a human face." That effort was dispatched by force of Soviet arms, and the *Warsaw Pact* invaded Czechoslovakia in July. Dubček was spirited to, and detained in, the Soviet Union until he agreed to publicly renounce the reforms. He was reinstated, briefly served as ambassador to Turkey, then was shunted aside. He reemerged in 1988 as part of the dissident movement calling for real reform and was received as a national hero during the *velvet revolution* of 1989. He was elected to chair a newly and genuinely dem-

ocratic national parliament, 1989–1992, serving it until the breakup of Czechoslovakia.

Dulles, Allen Welsh (1893–1969). A career diplomat from an early age,
Allen Dulles served in a minor capacity with the American delegation to the
Paris Peace Conference. He rose to prominence as head of the *Office of Strategic
Services,* the main American *intelligence* and *covert operations* agency operating
in the European theater during *World War II.* He later helped found and
became first director of the *Central Intelligence Agency.* He was forced to resign
after the disaster at the *Bay of Pigs,* in part because the *Kennedy* administration
needed to deflect blame onto the CIA for the decisions made during the
botched invasion, but also because it was a badly run operation and a major
embarrassment to the nation. His brother was *John Foster Dulles.*

Dulles, John Foster (1888–1959). U.S. statesman. He served on the American delegation at the *San Francisco Conference,* which founded the *United
Nations,* and as U.S. representative to the United Nations, 1946–1950. His
messianic worldview contained a mixture of latter-day *Wilsonianism,* American *exceptionalism,* and personal and *Christian* moralism. His most damaging
delusion was his belief that it was necessary for America to fill all power
vacuums that developed during the *Cold War,* including those left by departing colonial powers in the Middle East and elsewhere, for fear that otherwise
the Soviet Union would do so. That led to strategic overcommitment and,
worse, eventual identification of the United States by local nationalists with
the imperialism of the departing colonial powers. To ensure bipartisan support, *Truman* appointed him to negotiate the *Japanese Peace Treaty.* During
the 1952 presidential campaign, Dulles led a savage *Republican* attack on *containment,* which he portrayed as an immoral policy that abandoned millions
of east Europeans to tyranny. As a conservative internationalist, like *Vanden-
berg* and *Eisenhower,* he actually had more in common with the liberal *Democrats* who first framed containment, and launched the *Marshall Plan* and
NATO, than with the *isolationist* (Taft) wing of his own party. As secretary
of state, 1953–1959, he pragmatically cleaved to containment even as he
adjusted it to a new *strategic doctrine* of *massive retaliation* and continued to
indulge inflated rhetoric about "liberation of the captive nations" of the *Soviet
bloc.* For this he was accused of playing the dangerous game of *brinkmanship.*
Yet, in private, he proposed a joint Soviet-American withdrawal of forces
from Europe in 1953 and a major cut in the defense budget. And, during
the 1953 *Berlin crisis* and again in the 1956 *Hungarian Uprising,* he acted for
the most part with deliberation and restraint. Dulles elevated the role of
personal diplomacy by the secretary of state to a new level, pursuing many
more direct meetings than was then usual with his foreign counterparts and
with other diplomats. It was once thought by his critics that he was highly
independent, even a "rogue secretary," but the archives later showed that

little was done by Dulles in foreign policy without Eisenhower's knowledge and approval. *See also Allen Dulles.*

Suggested Readings: John Foster Dulles, *War Or Peace* (1957); Robert Immerman, *John Foster Dulles* (1999); Frederick W. Marks, *Power and Peace* (1995).

Duma. The Russian parliament, created in the wake of the *Russian Revolution* (1905). It was at best a weak restraint on the tsar. However, when *Nicholas II* tried to dissolve it in 1917, it formed the core of the *provisional government* that replaced him. In 1993 a State Duma replaced the old Soviet parliament after *Yeltsin's* ordered assault on the *White House*, the former Soviet-Russian Parliament.

Dumbarton Oaks Conference (August–October, 1944). A meeting of the *Big Four* to draft the constitution of the United Nations. Most of the major decisions about division of powers, representation, and guiding principles were made here by the *Great Powers* alone. That left minor adjustments and amendments for the *San Francisco Conference* of 1945, with two key exceptions: (1) the scope of the *veto* power of *Permanent Members of the Security Council*; and (2) the question of separate representation for each of the fifteen Soviet republics, over which *Stalin* threatened to scuttle the United Nations. This was later settled by a compromise of giving the Soviets three UNGA seats (Russia, Ukraine, and Belarus). The United States, alone among the Big Four, pushed to include *human rights* in the *United Nations Charter* at Dumbarton Oaks and succeeded—with considerable small power and *NGO* assistance—in inserting human rights language into the United Nations Treaty at San Francisco.

dumping. (1) Selling an *export* below the cost of production to increase market share in order to drive out competitors and thereby create a *monopoly* before later raising prices. It may also be done to clear surplus stock produced by government *subsidies. Anti-dumping laws*, however, are often themselves a disguised form of *protectionism.* (2) Disposing of waste in the *high seas* in an environmentally unsafe manner. This was made illegal by a 1972 marine convention.

Dunkirk evacuation (May 25–31, 1940). At the end of May 1940, Britain organized a desperate withdrawal of some 340,000 British, *Commonwealth*, and allied (nearly 140,000 French) troops, mostly without their equipment, from the beaches of Dunkirk (a coastal French town that was an English prize all through the *Hundred Years' War* and was briefly recaptured by *Oliver Cromwell* in 1656). This massive amphibious retreat was made necessary by a German breakthrough that split the British Army from the major part of the French Army and led to the surrender of Belgium to Germany on May 30th. The evacuation was accomplished only with the aid of hundreds of civilian craft, of all types and sizes, including personal yachts, and by a heroic rear-guard defense by the French Army and selected British and Canadian units. The escape of more than 300,000 men was also made possible by *Hitler's* "stop order": for two critical days he forbade his *Panzer* divisions to pursue the retreating, defeated enemy. The British turned this terrible defeat into an important psychological victory ("the spirit of Dunkirk"), which was crucial in sustaining *national morale* after France too surrendered.

Dunkirk, Treaty of (1947). A defense and security pact between Britain and France that still aimed at the old enemy in Germany rather than the new threat emanating from the Soviet Union. It was superseded by the American policy of rapid rehabilitation of Germany and then by the *Brussels Treaty* and *NATO.*

durable goods. By convention, those expected to last longer than three years, for example, cars and houses.

durbar. Public courts held by the *Moghul* emperors, and later by several governors-general and viceroys of India (1877, 1903, and 1911) to celebrate the ascent to the throne of India by successive British monarchs.

Durham Report. A historic report by Earl Durham (1792–1840), who was sent to Canada in 1838 to address the causes of the *Mackenzie-Papineau rebellion* (1837–1838).
   Durham called for union of the Canadas and establishment of responsible local governments in the major colonies to replace rule by a powerful appointed governor, with foreign policy to remain an imperial prerogative. It was a radical constitutional proposal that, even though not fully implemented, set the *Dominions* (not just Canada) on the road to *autonomy* and enabled the *British Empire* to later evolve into the *Commonwealth.*

Dutch Borneo. A former Dutch colony on *Borneo,* now in Indonesia.

Dutch East Indies. A former Dutch colony, now the major part of Indonesia.

Dutch Guiana. Former name of Suriname.

Dutch New Guinea. Former name of West Irian, now within Indonesia.

Dutch War (1672–1678). This was the first of several great contests between the Netherlands and the engorged ambition and pretensions of *Louis XIV* of France. Louis bribed the English king, Charles II, into a secret alliance (Treaty of Dover, 1670) and allied with Sweden. Then he struck northward. His armies at first made progress, capturing several southern provinces from the

Dutch. They were stopped short of Amsterdam by open dikes and Dutch courage. Meanwhile, a Dutch fleet defeated a combined Anglo-French fleet and prevented any naval flanking move. *William of Orange* took charge of Dutch policy in July 1672. In early 1673 the war widened, as Louis' *aggression* permitted William to deftly assemble the first of several grand coalitions he would lead against France. The Netherlands were now joined by Spain, the *Holy Roman Empire* (such as it was), Denmark, Brandenburg, and several minor German states. More importantly, in 1674 William persuaded England to make peace. On land, the weight of the French Army told the tale in the middle war years, but at sea the Dutch prevailed. A peace settlement was reached at Nijmegen (1678), which left Maastricht with the Netherlands and modified trade relations with France in favor of the Dutch. Louis made minor gains along his border with Spain, and in Lorraine, but was compelled to abandon the *Spanish Netherlands*.

Dutch West Indies. Former name of the *Antilles*.

duties. *See customs*; GATT; *tariffs*.

duties of states. *See state obligations*.

dwarf state. In disuse. *See microstate*.

dyad/dyadic. *Jargon*, meaning "a pair." *See also obscurantism; political science*.

dyarchy. A compromise form of government in India, 1919–1935, that granted limited *autonomy* to the states on specific issues but left the British colonial administration in charge overall. It helped contain post–*Amritsar massacre* violence but ultimately failed to satisfy nationalist demands. *See also India Acts*.

dynastic marriage. Marriage between members of royal households for centuries played a key, even decisive, role in the history of *diplomacy* in nearly every society where kingship forms of government occurred. They were used to cement political *alliances* and to signal major shifts or continuities in policy, and later to build up national, centrally governed, and mostly contiguous territories without necessarily using force, and to ensure political stability through legitimate succession. A widely used aphorism of the fifteenth and sixteenth centuries: "Bell gerant alii. Tu, felix Austria, nube" (Others make war. You, happy Austria [*Habsburgs*], marry).

dynastic war. One prosecuted to expand or extend the narrow interests of a given *dynasty*, usually over rights of inheritance, not that of the general or *national interest.* This was the common form of warfare in Europe well into the seventeenth century.

dynasty. A series of rulers from the same family whose succession is decided by arbitrary hereditary lines rather than suitability or merit. Traditionally, such succession was sanctified by law and ensured *legitimacy.* In modern times, dynasties tend to be *de facto* rather than *de jure,* as *popular sovereignty* has displaced notions of *absolutism* and *aristocracy.* Some dynasties adjusted to these changes and accepted to become figurehead rulers of democratic peoples; others were swept away by hurricanes of war, especially *World War I,* or *revolution. See also Bourbons; dynastic marriage; Habsburgs; Hirohito; Manchus; Ming dynasty; Jawaharal Nehru; Qing dynasty; Romanovs; tanistry; Valois dynasty.*

Dzerzhinsky, Felix (1877–1926). Founder of the *CHEKA* and leading member of the *Bolshevik* inner circle under *Lenin.* He oversaw the *Red Terror* after a failed attempt on Lenin's life and carried out the food seizures and executions that marked *war communism* as much as they had the *Russian Civil War.* He was an early supporter of *Stalin* as successor to Lenin. He was nearly a cult figure within the *OGPU* (later, the *NKVD,* then *KGB*). His austere statue brooded over KGB headquarters in Moscow until 1992, when an angry crowd of former victims, and relatives of victims, forced it to the ground, decapitated it, and otherwise despoiled his memory.

E

Earth Summit. *See United Nations Conference on the Environment and Development.*

East. (1) Historically: Looking from Europe, Asia in general, but especially China (Cathay). (2) During the *Cold War*: a term loosely applied to the *Soviet bloc*, including China before the *Sino-Soviet split. See also Far East; Middle East; Near East.*

East Aden Protectorate. A British possession on the Saudi peninsula, now part of Yemen.

East African Community. From 1967 to 1977 Kenya, Tanzania, and Uganda formed a *common market*. However, this experiment ultimately floundered over their quite different paths to development, and owing to the ascent to power of *Idi Amin* in Uganda.

East Asia. *Northeast Asia* plus *Southeast Asia.*

East Berlin. The Soviet *occupation zone* in Berlin (distinct from the surrounding zone, which formed *East Germany*), 1945–1990, and nominally only, 1990–1994. From 1949 to 1990 it was the capital of East Germany. *See also Berlin airlift; Berlin Wall; West Berlin.*

East China Sea. That part of the North Pacific Ocean lying between China, Japan, Korea, and Taiwan.

Eastern Europe. Bulgaria, Czech Republic, Estonia, Hungary, Latvia, Lithuania, Poland, Rumania, and Slovakia; some usages include Belarus and Ukraine. During the *Cold War* the term was understood to include *Czechoslovakia* and *East Germany* (both states now *extinct*), and the *Baltic States*, which were a (disputed) part of the Soviet Union.

eastern front. In *World War I* and *World War II*, the *frontline* between Russian forces and those of Germany and its minor allies, which at its greatest extent ran for 2,000 miles between the Baltic and Black Seas. The *frontier* between Germany and Russia lacks any significant natural barriers, except for the Vistula River and the impassable (by *armor*) expanse of the *Pripet Marshes* southwest of Moscow. In World War II, Germans fought as their ancient ancestors once had: to exterminate the inhabitants and conquer and resettle the land. This kind of exterminationist warfare had not been seen in Europe since the ravages of the *Mongols*, *Magyars*, and *Teutonic Knights*. The consequent merciless fighting, replete with lack of *quarter* and extermination squads (*Einsatzgruppen*), and the bitter, killing winters, was feared by all troops and became legendary among the armies that fought there as virtual synonym for suffering and death. In both World Wars, *trench warfare* developed on the eastern front. *See also Brusilov offensive; "final solution to the Jewish problem"; Gorlice-Tarnow; Kursk, Battle of; Masurian Lakes; no-man's-land; partisans; Stalingrad, Battle of; Tannenberg, Battle of; Warsaw Rising; Giorgii Zhukov.*
  Suggested Readings: N. Stone, *The Eastern Front, 1914–1917* (1975); Georgi K. Zhukov, *Memoirs of Marshal Zhukov* (1969).

Eastern Orthodox Church. An alternate term for the *Orthodox Church*, or those *Christian* churches that follow the Byzantine rite and Nicene Creed.

Eastern Question. "Who will inherit the non-Turkish provinces of the *Ottoman Empire*, as the center weakens?" With the failure of the Ottoman siege of Vienna in 1683, *Habsburg* Austria began its assault on Turkish power and possessions in Europe. *Peter I* of Russia, too, whittled away at Turkey's Balkan provinces and Central Asian allies—small khanates such as *Kokand* and *Khiva*. Under *Catherine II*, Russia made major gains in the first of the *Russo-Turkish Wars*, playing upon quasi-religious concern for Christians under Muslim authority and playing to the *pan-Slavism* movement. During the nineteenth century the question shifted to one of decay of the Ottoman Empire from within, rather than primarily conquest from without. The Ottoman Empire was deeply wounded, 1804–1817, by Serb revolts and then by the loss of Greece in the *Greek War of Independence*, 1821–1829. In the 1830s *Mehemet Ali* of Egypt, ostensibly an Ottoman vassal, broke away from the sultan's control and became a regional power unto himself. The Eastern Question was further complicated by the competing interests of the Great Powers over the

Straits Question. A major episode was the *Crimean War*, in which Britain and France shored up Turkey against Russia. Internal and Russian pressures on Turkey increased after 1870, contributing to the breakaway of new but unstable states, namely, Rumania (1878) and Bulgaria (1886).

Several powers sought to freeze the Eastern Question with the *Mediterranean Agreement*. It was at the heart of the *Balkan Wars* of 1912 and 1913, and was an underlying cause of *World War I*. It was resolved not with the end of the Ottoman Empire in 1918, but the creation of modern Turkey by *Atatürk* in 1923 and renunciation of the imperial pretensions of the sultans. *See also balkanize; Congress of Berlin; Treaty of Lausanne (1923); Münchengrätz Agreements; pan-Islamicism; Treaty of Paris (1856); Treaty of San Stefano (1878).*

Suggested Readings: Matthew S. Anderson, *The Eastern Question, 1774–1923* (1966, 1987); Gerald Clayton, *Britain and the Eastern Question* (1971).

Eastern Zhou (771–256 B.C.E.). The first Imperial *dynasty* of China, dating from the Zhou move to a new capital at Luoyang in face of an invasion by the Rong. Like the later *Aztec* empire, the Zhou held power through a highly privileged military-religious caste that engaged in human sacrifice. On the other hand, Zhou philosophers included Confucius (551–479 B.C.E.) and his great disciple Mencius (372–289 B.C.E.). From c. 722 to 481 B.C.E. the Zhou lost central control of China to nearly 200 semi-independent, armed, and walled *city-states*. This political chaos, or reorganization, gave rise to a sustained period of city-state conflict culminating in the clash of seven large survivor states during the era of the *Warring States* (403–221 B.C.E.).

Easter Rising (April 24–29, 1916). A *nationalist* insurrection in Dublin by the Irish Volunteers (Irish Republican Brotherhood); forerunner to the *Irish Republican Army* (IRA). It aimed at forcing Ireland's independence by taking advantage of Britain's gravest moment of difficulty: *World War I*. The IRB rebels anticipated coordinated military aid from Germany, which never materialized (a German arms shipment was intercepted by the *Royal Navy)*. British gunboats shelled the heart of Dublin. Within a week, the rising failed, leaving nearly 3,000 killed or wounded. The subsequent execution of nationalist rebel leaders gave yet another Irish generation a round of martyrs ("a terrible beauty is born," in the famous words of W. B. Yeats). That act of legal retribution shifted the country's views and by 1918 provoked further armed resistance, which escalated into the *Irish War of Independence*. *See also Herbert Asquith; Roger Casement; Michael Collins; Eamon de Valera;* Sinn Féin.

East Germany. *See German Democratic Republic.*

East India Companies. (1) The *Netherlands:* Between 1595 and 1601 Dutch traders moved aggressively into south India, Java, Sumatra, and the *Spice*

Islands. The Vereenigde Oostindische Compaagnie (VOC) was chartered in 1602 to maximize and consolidate these penetrations. Initially, it was far better capitalized than its French or English counterparts. In 1605 a Dutch fleet forcibly cleared the Portuguese from the Indian Ocean, and the VOC seized Portugal's share of the Spice Islands at Amboina. In 1609 the VOC operated in Japan, at Hirado. Anglo-Dutch cooperation against the Portuguese and French ended in 1623, when the Dutch judicially murdered 10 English merchants in Amboina. From 1631 to 1641, in the latter part of the *Eighty Years' War*, the Dutch took Pernambuco, Elmina (Ghana), Luanda (Mozambique), Ceylon, Malacca, and *Deshima* (Japan) from Portugal. The VOC thereafter concentrated on the more valuable East Indies, leaving subcontinental India to the French and English. By 1650 VOC wealth and naval power helped make Holland the world's greatest trading nation and a foremost world power. In 1766 and 1791 administrative reforms virtually nationalized the company; after 1815 it reemerged as the Dutch Colonial Office.

(2) *France*: Late to the game of commercial empire in India, the Compagnie des Indies Orientales was founded at the urging of *Jean-Baptiste Colbert* in 1664. Over Dutch opposition, it founded a fortified factory at Surat in 1668. In 1674 it established a base at Pondicherry, on the *Coromandel* coast, and enjoyed considerable martial and commercial success in India under François Dupliex (1697–1764). In 1690 it built a factory near to Calcutta. It took control of Mauritius and Bourbon, in the Indian Ocean, in 1721. It was driven from all but the rump of *French India* as a result of France's loss of the *War of the Austrian Succession* (1740–1748) and the *Seven Years' War* (1756–1763).

(3) *Britain*: "John Company." Far and away the most successful East India Company was English. It received a monopoly charter from *Elizabeth I* on December 31, 1600. It grew to dominate not just trade, but the military and political affairs of the Indian subcontinent, much of southeast Asia, and coastal China. Its first expedition to India, threaded through Portuguese-controlled waters, was in 1608. It established its first "factory" (*entrepôt*) at Surat, in *Mughal* India, in 1619. Thereafter it employed a "factory system" of fortified trading posts, as it competed with the Dutch to control the *spice trade* and with the French to penetrate the Indian interior and control *nawab* allies. It seized Ormuz from Portugal in 1622 and broke violently with the Dutch in 1623 when ten of its officers were murdered in Amboina. In 1640 it received permission to build a fort and factory at a village that later became the metropolis of Madras. Under *Cromwell*, John Company received enhanced state support and broke the Portuguese monopoly in India in 1654. It was recast in 1657 as a joint stock company. It moved its headquarters to Bombay in 1687. Its empire grew slowly but then accelerated after India's collapse into chaos with the final years and then the death of *Aurangzeb*. Internal weakness meant the real threat to company success was from its French rival. However, the overall defeat of France in the War of Austrian Succession (1740–1748)

and the Seven Years' War (1756–1763) was paralleled in India by *Robert Clive*'s exploits, especially the recapture of Calcutta from the nawab of Bengal, at Plassey (June 23, 1757), where he also destroyed French power in India. In 1761 Hindu (*Maratha*) power was smashed by fierce *Pathan* raiders from Afghanistan. In 1764 company troops dispatched the remnants of Mughal power as well. The company fought costly Maratha and Carnatic wars in the 1770s. Using defeated or bribed nawabs as fronts, supporting them with troops and trade in a mixed system of direct administration and *indirect rule*, the John Company emerged as the real power behind the thrones of India, including the latter Mughals.

The *India Act* of 1784 subjected the company to closer control from London. Lord Cornwallis (1738–1805), the losing general at *Yorktown*, took the company into direct administrative and judicial affairs, and under missionary and parliamentary pressure involved it also in land and social reform as well as direct revenue collection. He made its *officer corps* exclusively British, fought in Mysore (1789), annexed the Malabar coast (1792), established the salt monopoly, which *Gandhi* would famously challenge two centuries later, and the *opium* monopoly, over which it would fight two nineteenth-century wars with China. In 1793 it dispatched a famous *Macartney mission* to try to open trade with the *Qing* court, but was rebuffed. Richard Wellesley (1761–1842) and his brother Arthur (later, the Duke of *Wellington*) added enormous new lands to the company's Indian empire, directly and by extending *protectorates* over *Princely States*, thus subduing and pacifying most of India. In 1819 it founded *Singapore* and in 1824 it acquired Malacca from the Dutch. Its monopoly included a hugely profitable *triangle trade* of Indian opium, Chinese porcelains and tea, and British manufactured goods. Its importation of raw cotton to England, the opposition and *protectionism* this engendered, and the new markets it opened, was a spur to the *Industrial Revolution*. In 1834 the company's monopoly was broken, except for salt and opium. Outside India, it fought the *Anglo-Burmese Wars*, the first *Afghan War*, and the *Opium Wars* with China. *Sepoy* regiments of its *Indian Army* supplemented British regular forces fighting elsewhere in the empire, especially in the Middle East. After the governor-generalship of *Dalhousie* (1848–1856), the *Indian Mutiny* broke out and *direct rule* by London was introduced. John Company was dissolved in 1874. *See also Hudson's Bay Company.*

Suggested Readings: Kristof Glamann, *Dutch-Asiatic Trade* (1958); Philip Lawson, *The East India Company* (1993); J. H. Parry, *Trade and Dominion* (1971); John Wills, *Pepper, Guns and Parlays* (1974).

East Indies. A term, never uniformly applied, now in disuse. Earlier it was: (1) a pre*decolonization* term for lower, Southeast Asia; (2) the islands and other territories of the Malay archipelago; and (3) the archipelago of modern Indonesia.

East Pakistan. Now Bangladesh, from 1947 to 1971 it was divided from West Pakistan by 1,000 miles of Indian territory.

East Prussia. Also known as "Ducal Prussia." The historic base of the Order of the *Teutonic Knights*. It was incorporated into *Brandenburg-Prussia* during the Middle Ages. It was invaded by Russia during the *Seven Years' War*, but firmly secured to Prussia in the first *partition of Poland*. A key province in Imperial Germany, it exercised, through its contribution to the officer and diplomatic corps, a disproportionate influence on military and foreign policy. After *World War I* it was separated from Germany by the *Polish Corridor*. After *World War II* it was divided and *annexed* by Poland and the Soviet Union, with most ethnic Germans forcibly deported. *See also Hohenzollern;* Junkers.

East Timor. A long-disputed territory in the eastern extremity of the Indonesia archipelago, comprising about half the island of *Timor*. It was a Portuguese colony until 1975, when it was seized by Indonesia while Lisbon was occupied with *revolution* and readying to shed East Timor and other vestiges of empire in Africa and Asia. That interrupted independence set off a *guerrilla* campaign by the mostly Roman Catholic East Timorese, against union with predominantly Muslim, and Javanese-dominated, Indonesia. The tactics used by Indonesia were brutal, going well beyond *counterinsurgency warfare* to include massive repression of civil and *human rights*, such as massacres of protestors and *torture* of civilians. The malignity and raw exploitation of Indonesia's *occupation* stoked the independence movement while keeping East Timor as underdeveloped as it had been under Portuguese rule. Jakarta claimed that it was making *development* efforts that justified control of the island, an assertion that bore little relation to political and economic reality. Until the *Cold War* ended, the cruel repression of East Timor went largely uncriticized within the United Nations. It was effectively immune from criticism by Third World allies in the *G-77* caucus group and *ASEAN*, even though the United Nations regarded the occupation as illegal and still recognized Portugal as the sovereign administrative power in East Timor. Nor was Indonesia much criticized by Western states, since it was an important ally and seen as a regional bulwark against *communism*.

With the end of the Cold War, both the UN and Western states publicly acknowledged that Indonesia was engaged in near-*genocide* in East Timor. In 1994 a diplomatic row erupted within ASEAN between Indonesia and the Philippines, which hosted an *NGO* conference on the question, over strenuous objections from Jakarta. In 1998 the *European Union* sent an *observer mission* to East Timor, in the wake of the collapse of the *Suharto* regime and rising hope for a negotiated separation of the territory from Indonesia. At first Indonesia stepped up the violence by its army and local militia, but as its economy crumbled during the *Asian financial crisis* of 1997–1998, it agreed to East Timorese independence. A *referendum* in favor of independence was overwhelmingly approved on August 30, 1999, after which Jakarta loosed the *militia* who went on a vengeful killing spree. An international *peacekeeping* mission led by Australia was rushed in to reestablish order, assist with return of refugees, and begin the arduous task of economic reconstruction. All this took place under the auspices and authority of the United Nations, which administered East Timor preparatory to its promised assumption of sovereign independence on May 20, 2002.

Suggested Reading: John Taylor, *East Timor* (2000).

East-West conflict. A colloquial alternative for the term *Cold War*. *See also East; West*.

Eban, Abba (b. 1915). Israeli scholar and statesman. He worked for the *Jewish Agency* before joining the United Nations Special Committee on *Palestine*. He was Israel's ambassador to the United Nations, 1949–1959, and ambassador to the United States, 1950–1959. He served as foreign minister, 1966–1974. He played a key role in gaining UN support for Israel in the 1950s and in formulating foreign policy during the *Third* and *Fourth Arab-Israeli Wars*. He once said *international law* was "the law which the wicked do not obey and which the righteous do not enforce."

Ebert, Friedrich (1871–1925). President of the *Weimar Republic*, 1920–1925. He took power on November 9, 1918, in time to oversee Germany's surrender in *World War I* and the abdication of *Wilhelm II*. A tough-minded *socialist* who appreciated the need for law and order in postwar Germany, he opposed the *Spartacists* and the more radical *Freikorps*. He laid the basis in Weimar of what might well have evolved into parliamentary democracy, but was in fact never able to escape from the shadow of the *Treaty of Versailles*. He then fell victim to Weimar's terrible *hyperinflation*.

EC. *See European Community*.

econometrics. The use of statistical and other mathematical methods in exploring and testing economic propositions. *See also efficiency; parameters*.

Economic and Social Council (ECOSOC). A major United Nations organ coordinating the *specialized agencies*. Its main function is to foster economic and social *development*. Starting in the 1960s it evolved a new emphasis on development of the *Third World*. Its 54 members serve rotating terms and oversee a vast array of programs and commissions, including ones on *human rights* and *refugees*. The *UNDP* and *UNEP* are also run under its auspices. It reports to the *United Nations General Assembly*.

Economic Commissions. The *United Nations* established and maintains several regional commissions devoted to economic and social development of specific regions. The Economic and Social Commission for Asia and the Pacific (ESCAP) was established in 1947 with its headquarters in Bangkok. It helped found the *Asian Development Bank* in 1967. The Economic Commission for Africa (ECA) was founded in 1958. It plays a coordinating and intermediary role with numerous subcommissions and development organizations that have ties to the United Nations, the *International Monetary Fund*, and the *International Bank for Reconstruction and Development*. The Economic and Social Commission for Latin America and the Caribbean (ECLAC) was founded in 1948, with its headquarters in Santiago, Chile. In addition to all regional countries, it includes Canada, the United States, and former colonial powers (France, Great Britain, the Netherlands, Portugal, and Spain). In the 1990s its major concern became hemispheric *free trade*.

Economic Community of West African States (ECOWAS). It was founded in 1975, under Nigerian leadership, to promote regional trade and *development*. It includes both *Anglophone* and *Francophone* West African states. It aims at a *customs union* and at *free trade*, issues on which it has enjoyed only limited success. Nigeria played a less influential role as time wore on, as its own economy fell from OPEC-wealth heights to grossly mismanaged and stolen depths and debts. From the 1990s, ECOWAS tried to assume a regional *peacekeeping* role, sending troops into Liberia and Sierra Leone, where they were sometimes engaged in heavy fighting. *See also Economic Community of West African States, Monitoring Group.*

Economic Community of West African States, Monitoring Group (ECOMOG). A regional *peacekeeping* force sponsored by *ECOWAS* that intervened forcefully in civil wars in Liberia and Sierra Leone in the 1990s. Nigeria played the lead role in the effort to bring both peace and democracy to these regional neighbors, despite at that time suffering under the worst, most oppressive military dictatorship in its own history.

Economic Cooperation Organization (ECO). Founded in the 1960s by Iran, Pakistan and Turkey. It was moribund until after the *Cold War*, when it expanded to comprise ten non-Arab, Muslim countries: the original three, plus Afghanistan, Azerbaijan, Kazakhstan, Kirghizstan, Tajikistan, Turkmenistan, and Uzbekistan. In part, it represented a competitive effort by the original three to provide regional leadership, but it also was quiet acknowledgment of the fact that none of those nations (except perhaps Turkey) stood to gain admittance to the *European Union*.

economic determinism. An analytical tendency that views legal, social, political, and even intellectual forms and phenomenon as ultimately decided by underlying economic factors. An economic determinist is someone who believes that, unless they have arrived at a core economic explanation of some occurrence or circumstance, they have not arrived. *See also Kondratieff cycles; Marxism; Max Weber.*

economic espionage. The use of the tools and resources of *intelligence* to spy on discoveries, trends, and developments of economic, rather than political or military, value. It may be conducted by states or private firms. It implies its antonym, economic *counterespionage.*

economic indicators. *See indicators.*

economic integration. *See integration.*

economic nationalism. *See autarchy; free trade; mercantilism; protectionism; self-reliance.*

economics. The modern field of study concerned with production, distribution, and consumption of *goods and services.* For centuries, political economists were also concerned with politics and sociology, but these subdisciplines have since spun off on their own within academia. Early economists were essentially concerned with the problem of scarcity, and thus with both private and public mechanisms by which decisions were made on the allocation of limited resources in what many saw as, and that for millennia actually was, a *Malthusian* world. Reflecting on this baleful reality, and the dreary conclusions and uneven social consequences of many economic observations and theories, such as those characterizing the *beggar-thy-neighbor* practices of *mercantilism* even under great finance ministers like *Jean-Baptiste Colbert,* Thomas Carlyle famously (though rather unfairly) called economics "the Dismal Science."

However, with the advance of *capitalism* (since c. 1750), and its remarkable capacity to create new forms of wealth, *macroeconomic* theory shifted to a primary focus on the problem of how to sustain *growth* while avoiding sharp cycles of boom and bust in production and consumption. The *Physiocrats* were among the first to break with mercantilism, and thereby greatly influenced the *classical school* of economic liberalism, which was later identified most closely with *Adam Smith.* The field changed again with the advent of full *industrialization.* David Ricardo (1772–1823) developed theories of rent and labor value, which were enormously influential, and the theory of *comparative advantage,* which spurred new thinking about the role of *trade* and prompted some leading states to adopt *free trade* practices. This new economics competed directly with the work of *Robert Malthus,* who clung to an older, more deeply pessimistic view of economic possibilities. It also emphasized scientific inquiry of a form that, over time, led to an academic discipline almost wholly divorced from history and an interest in growth, and instead nearly exclusively concerned with mechanics of *rational choice* by individuals, distribution theory, wages and prices, and *efficiency* of markets.

From the mid-nineteenth century a competing worldview arose based on the work of *Karl Marx*. For all its flaws, Marxist economics remained concerned with historical inquiry into the question of the wealth and poverty of nations. Essentially arguing from *economic determinism*, this school (*Marxism*) rejected classical liberal theory in favor of a radical critique of capitalism that was primarily moral in its inspiration, but that claimed to be rooted in the "scientific logic" of *dialectical materialism*. In the mid-twentieth century, *Keynesianism* interpretations of the *business cycle* and recommendations of new solutions (such as *pump priming*) to the age-old problems of *recession* and *depression* dominated in Western countries, even as the *Soviet Union* and other *Communist* states experimented with *command economies* and instituted such colossal and calamitous socioeconomic experiments as *collectivization* and *five-year plans*. With the breakdown of the old empires after *World War II*, new branches of economics evolved that specialized in problems of *development*. Some were derivations or refinements of classical *liberal* thinking about growth, such as *supply-side* theory and *monetarism*, others (*dependency theory*) were offshoots of older Marxist ideas. New environmental concerns led to ongoing arguments about possible limits to growth and the forms that *sustainable development* might take. By the early twenty-first century, much academic economic theory was highly rarified, as one highly mathematized *microeconomic* speculation was heaped upon another. On the other hand, economics had also become a truly "hopeful science," from which most people expected real help in the progressive betterment of the human condition. *See also absolute advantage; adjustment; agriculture; aid; allocation; Andean Group; anti-dumping laws; arbitrage; Asia Pacific Economic Co-operation; autarky; backwash effect; Baker Plan; balance of payments; balance of trade; Bank of International Settlements; barter agreements; basic needs; black market; Black Tuesday; boom; boycott; Bretton Woods system; buffer stock; buyers' market; capital; capital account; capital flight; capital formation; capital gain; capital goods; capital intensive; capital investment; capitalism; capitalist; capital markets; Caribbean Community and Common Market; cartel; Central American Common Market; central bank; class struggle; collective goods theory; commodity; common market;* Communauté Financière Africaine; *compensation; compensatory financing; competitive advantage; competitiveness; conditionality; consumer price index; convertibility; cost-benefit analysis; Council for Mutual Economic Assistance; counterpart funds; countertrade; countervailing duty; currency; current account; customs union; debt; debt crisis; debt-equity swaps; debt fatigue; debtor cartel; debt rescheduling; debt service; deficit spending; deflation; demonetize; dependency; depreciation; depressions, world; devaluation; developing nation; dirigisme; dirty float; disinflation; disinvestment; distributive justice; dollar convertibility; dollar diplomacy; drug trade; dumping; durable goods; econometrics; economic espionage; Economic and Social Council; economies of scale; economy; elasticity of demand;*

encomienda system; Engel's Law; eurobond markets; eurocurrencies; European Coal and Steel Community; European Currency Unit; European Economic Area; European Economic Community; European Free Trade Association; European Monetary Institute; European Monetary System/Union; European Recovery Program; European Union; exchange controls; exchange rate; Exchange Rate Mechanism; excise; Exclusive Economic Zone; exploitation; export-led growth; export processing zones; expropriation; factor analysis; factor endowments; factors of production; fair trade; final goods; finance; First Tranche; fiscal policy; fixed currency; floating currency; foreign direct investment; foreign exchange; foreign exchange reserve; forward market; free enterprise; free market; free rider problem; free trade area; Free Trade Area of the Americas; fungible; G-5; G-7; G-8; G-10; G-77; GATT; gold rush; gold standard; goods; graduation clause; green loans; Gross Domestic Product; Gross National Product; guanxi; hard currency; hard loan; hot money; human development index; hyperinflation; imperialism; import quotas; import substitution; indicators; Industrial Revolution; inflation; informal sector; infrastructure; input; integration; interdependence; interest rates; intermediate inputs; internalization theory; International Bank for Reconstruction and Development (IBRD); international commodity agreement; International Development Agency; International Finance Corporation; International Fund for Agricultural Development; International Monetary Fund (IMF); investment; invisible trade; Integrated Program for Commodities; International Trade Organization; Kennedy Round; Keynes; Kondratieff cycles; labor; labor theory of value; laissez-faire; land; Latin American Free Trade Association; Latin American Integration Association; law of diminishing returns; leading indicators; leaseholds; Least Developed Countries; liberalism; licensing; linkage; liquidity; managed trade; Manchester school; market economy; Marxism-Leninism; mass production; mature economy; means of production; Mercosur; Ministry of Trade and Industry; mixed economy; MNC/MNE; mode of production; modernization; monetary policy; money market; monopoly; monopsony; most-favored nation; NAFTA; national income; nationalization; natural resources; Net Domestic Product; Net National Product; new protectionism; New International Economic Order; Newly Indus- trialized Countries; Nixon shocks; nontariff barriers (NTBs); official financing; oil; oil shocks; oligopoly; Open Door; orderly market arrangements; Organization for Economic Cooperation and Development; Organization for European Economic Cooperation; Organization of Arab Oil Exporting Countries; Organization of Petroleum Exporting Countries; outputs; patient capital; pegging; petrodollars; planned economy; Plaza Agreement; political economy; portfolio investment; poverty; preferential tariff; price controls; price elasticity; price supports; primary producer; primary products; primary sector; private sector; privatize; product cycle theory; production; productivity; profit; protectionism; protective tariffs; public goods; public sector; quotas; raw materials; reciprocity; reflation; reformism; reform liberalism; refugees; regional banks; remittances; requerimiento; reserve currency; reserves; resources; revaluation; rising expectations; sanctions; scissors crisis; secondary sector; sellers' market; sensitivity; services; short-term capital account; slavery; slave trade; slump; Smoot-Hawley Tariff; social overhead capital; soft currency; soft goods; soft loan; Special Drawing Rights; spice trade; spot market; STABEX; stability; stabilization program; stages of growth; stagflation; stagnation; standard of living; stock; stock exchange; strategic materials; strategic stockpiles; structural adjustment loan; structure; subsidiary; subsidy; Super 301 Procedures; supply; surplus value; sustainable growth; System of National Accounts; takeoff; tariff; tax haven; technology transfer; terms of trade; tertiary sector; textiles; tied aid; tied loan; Tokyo Round; tourism; trade balance; trade barrier; trade routes; turn-key factory; underground economy; uneven development; Uruguay Round; venture capital; visible trade; voluntary export restraints; vulnerability; water; world capitalist system; world system theory; zaibatsu.

Suggested Readings: Derek Aldcroft and Anthony Sutcliffe, eds., Europe in the International Economy, 1500–2000 (1999); William Ashworth, A Short History of the World Economy (1987); J. Foreman-Peck, History of the World Economy (1983); Robert L. Heilbroner, The Worldly Philosophers, 7th ed. (1999); Robert L. Heilbroner and L. C. Thurow, Economics Explained, 2nd ed. (1998); Kenneth Pomeranz, The Great Divergence: Europe, China, and the Making of the Modern World Economy (2000); W. W. Rostow, The World Economy (1978); Paul Samuelson and W. Nordhaus, Economics, 16th ed. (1997); S. Viljoen, Economic Systems in World History (1974).

economic warfare. See blockade; Continental System; famine; sanctions; strategic bombing; total war; unrestricted submarine warfare.

economies of scale. The greater the amount of production (scale) of a given item, the lower the cost per unit will tend to be, as startup, design, and research and development costs are averaged over all units produced. This fact encourages production at large volumes and requires a sizeable home market and/or an assertive export strategy to dispose of any goods in excess of what the national market can absorb. This phenomenon has an impact on arms exports as well as regular goods. For example, if a country wishes to maintain independence of foreign suppliers in its defense industries, it must sell a certain number of fighters (or tanks, or missiles, or whatever) abroad to keep the costs per unit affordable for its own defense needs and production lines rolling. In short, it may be driven to become an arms exporter as well as producer. This has been the case both for small arms producers such as Israel and for larger ones such as France.

economy. (1) The structure of economic life and activity in a country, region, or historical period. (2) The sum total of a nation's economic *resources* and activity, usually measured in terms of GNP.

ecosystem. A biological system of interactions and interdependent processes of a community of organisms and their surrounding environment. Concern for the viability and integrity of natural ecosystems and how they are affected by both domestic and transnational economic activities is a rising issue in global *environmental politics*.

Ecuador. The *Inca* ruled this area for centuries from their base at Quito, the northern administration center of a vast empire that ranged down the Pacific coast of South America. The footless Inca were pushed from control of Ecuador in 1533 by a rival empire, Spain, in the form of an expedition of *conquistadores* formed as an offshoot of *Pizarro's* larger expedition against the Inca in Peru. Ecuador formed part of the composite colony of *New Granada* until detached under a separate captaincy. During the seventeenth century, Ecuador (then known as Quito) became a center of the textile industry. It rebelled in 1809, but was not liberated from Spain until 1822 after the Battle of Pichincha. Thereafter, it was added by *Simón Bolívar* to *Gran Colombia*. It seceded from Colombia in 1830 and afterward kept up a long and sometimes violent boundary dispute with Peru, fighting localized wars over part of the Cordillera del Condor region, known as Tiwintza, in 1941, 1981, and 1995. In 1998 an accord was agreed, ending this dispute. Ecuador alternated shakily between civilian and military dictatorships for many decades, but made halting progress toward democratic rule after 1979. It suffered a rising *national debt* burden from the 1960s onward. In 1987 it unilaterally suspended repayment of its debt, as a result of declining *oil* revenues and *infrastructure* repair costs brought on by a large earthquake. The debt was *restructured*, but Ecuador remained deeply impoverished. Throughout the 1990s it was plagued by *terrorism*, kidnappings for ransom, and rural unrest. In 1997 mass protests against governmental corruption and inefficiency led to a change of government, but little economic improvement. In 1998 a sharp decline in the world price of oil severely cut revenues, while El Niño storms buffeted the coast and damaged much infrastructure. In 2000 an attempted coup, which had some popular support among poor Ecuadoran Indians, was foiled, but led to an extraconstitutional change of government. That was par for the course: from its independence to 2000, Ecuador had no fewer than nineteen constitutions, reflecting an underlying political and social instability that remained unresolved into the twenty-first century. Adding to the chronic turmoil, modern Ecuador's economy rises and falls in tandem with the world price for oil, on which it remains hugely dependent. *See also Galápagos Islands.*

Ecumenical Councils. A series of general church councils called to consider matters of faith and doctrine and to determine what was orthodox belief and what might be condemned as heresy. They are recognized by the *Catholic Church* as providing governing guidance on church doctrine—but only when popes, either at the time or later, decreed findings to be canonical. Many *Protestants* accept the first four as ecumenical, but even so, most do not consider canon law to be binding in preference to direct revelation in scripture or conscience. The first seven Councils are also accepted by the *Orthodox Church*, but from the eighth Council onward Catholics and Orthodox were in effective *schism*, which hardened during later centuries, over the issue of whether conciliar or papal authority was superior and which constituted infallible (guided by God away from error) church teaching.

There have been 21 general councils to date, though starting with Trent (1545–1563) they became councils solely of the Catholic Church. They were the Councils of: Nicaea (325), called by *Constantine the Great*; Constantinople (381), which condemned the "Arian heresy" and affirmed the Nicaean Creed; Ephesus (431); Chalcedon (451), which distanced the *Coptic Church* in Egypt from mainstream Christianity by the decision it took against Monophysitism, which was then deeply dividing the *Byzantine Empire*; Constantinople (553); Constantinople (680–681); Nicaea (787); Constantinople (869), marked by the Photian schism, which ended conciliar cooperation with the Orthodox Church; First Lateran (1123), which discussed organization for the *Crusades*; Second Lateran (1139); Third Lateran (1179), which condemned the Waldensian and Albigensian "heresies," leading to a savage campaign of suppression and *Inquisition* in southern France, in particular; Fourth Lateran (1215), marking the peak of the power and influence of the Medieval Church in West Europe, after which papal power and authority entered its decline; Lyons (1245), which excommunicated Emperor Frederick II and ordered a new Crusade, under St. Louis, against the Saracens and *Mongols*; Lyons (1274); Vienne (1311–1313), during the "Avignon Captivity" of the papacy, which ordered repression of the *Knights Templars* and other presumed or accused heretics; Constance (1414–1418), held during the *Great Schism*, to which it helped put an end and reaffirmed an earlier condemnation as heretical the teachings of Wycliffe and Hus; Basel-Ferrara-Florence (1431, 1438, 1439), which dealt with continuing Hussite rebellion in Bohemia and issues of the *Catholic Reformation*; Fifth Lateran (1512–1517), its planning for a Crusade against the *Ottoman Empire* was disrupted by the beginning of the *Protestant Reformation* in Germany, with the initial protest of *Martin Luther*; Trent (1545–1563), which met to condemn the "errors" of Luther and all other Protestant reformers and thereby set the aggressive tone of the *Catholic Counter Reformation*; it also significantly advanced the Catholic Reformation and revised a large body of doctrine and dogma; *Vatican I* (1869–1870), which is best remembered for decreeing that the pope is infallible when speaking ex cathedra (on matters of faith and morals); and *Vatican II* (1962–1965). Other councils took place during the Great Schism but are not formally recognized and are remembered mostly with great embarrassment. Of the post-schism councils, the most important were Trent, which marked the *Catholic Counter Reformation*; and the two Vatican Councils, the first because it reshaped the role of the modern papacy, and the second because it launched the modern Catholic *ecumenical* movement.

ecumenism. A movement to reunite the world's Christian churches, despite doctrinal differences. In its *Catholic* form, it dates to the second *Vatican Council* (1962–1965). Protestant ecumenism is a less-organized movement. An older term for the ideal of a single, universal church was "catholic," but that did not survive the final split between the *Catholic Church* and the *Orthodox*

Church in 1054 or the *Protestant Reformation*. *See also John Paul II; World Council of Churches*.

Eden, Anthony (1897–1977). British statesman. Foreign secretary, 1935–1938, 1941–1945, 1951–1954; prime minister, 1955–1956. He made a timely resignation from the cabinet in 1938, just before the *Anschluss*, over disagreements with *Neville Chamberlain* on policy toward Italy and over *appeasement* of Nazi Germany. The act made his career and reputation as a tough-minded statesman of principle, even though Eden had done nothing in particular or of use when *Hitler* remilitarized the *Rhineland* and Italy launched the *Abyssinian War*. It also froze his positions in time and place, a fact that proved fatal when he later misapplied the lessons of the 1930s to the Middle East by wrongly viewing *Nasser* as another *Hitler* and bitterly attacking anyone who might offer a rational defense of appeasement. During *World War II* he was a close and important aide to *Churchill*. He then led Britain's delegation to the *San Francisco Conference*. He helped arrange the peace in Korea in 1953 and French withdrawal from Vietnam in the *Geneva Accords* in 1954. However, his 1956 decision to invade Egypt—in concert with France and Israel—set off the *Suez Crisis*, which brought down his government and savaged his reputation.

Suggested Readings: David Dutton, *Anthony Eden* (1997); Robert James, *Anthony Eden* (1987).

Edward I (1239–1307). "Longshanks." *See also England; Scotland; William Wallace.*

Eelam. The proposed name for an independent homeland for the Tamils of Sri Lanka. *See also Tamil Tigers.*

EEZ. *See Exclusive Economic Zone.*

effect. *See causation; variable.*

effective link. A fairly recent (1953) doctrine in *international law* that evolved from efforts to sort out the seemingly endless conflicts and cases that arose from the sometimes incompatible claims to *nationality* of *jus soli* and *jus sanguinis*. It reasonably and logically holds that for nationality to exist there must be an "effective link" between the citizen in question and the state affirming a claim.

efficiency. (1) In economic theory: a measure of the costs of production: *capital*, *labor*, research, and any other costs; and an assumption that prices reflect real, basic information. (2) In statistics and *econometrics*: an evaluation of the relative merits of *parameters*.

Egypt. Conventionally divided into Lower Egypt (Nile Delta) and Upper Egypt (Cairo to Sudan), one of the world's oldest civilizations began in Egypt 6,000 years ago. The great pyramid at Gizeh, symbol of the absolute monarchy invented by Egypt and the vehicle of its unification under the Pharaohs, was built c. 2400 B.C.E. *Nubia* was colonized to above the second cataract of the Nile, c. 2000–1780 B.C.E. In the eleventh century B.C.E., Egypt was disturbed by civil wars and dynastic succession disputes, and Nubia became independent as the Kingdom of Kush. In the eighth century B.C.E., Kush even conquered Egypt and governed it, 770–666 B.C.E., when Egypt was conquered by the Assyrians. After the fall of the ancient empire of the Pharaohs, Egypt was repeatedly conquered: *Persians*, Greeks (under *Alexander the Great*, who moved Egypt's capital from the Nile to a new city, Alexandria, which he founded on the Mediterranean coast), *Romans*, *Byzantines*, and desert *Arabs* all overran it, each leaving behind settlers and distinctive cultural contributions that mixed with the culture and populations already there. The Greeks and Romans fundamentally changed Egyptian history, reorienting it toward Mediterranean trade and civilization, away from its earlier roots in Nilotic Africa.

With the Arabs, who settled in large numbers from the eighth century C.E., came a new faith: *Islam*. Arab *caliphs* (Umayyad and then Fatamid) governed Egypt for 500 years, converting most but not all of its *Coptic* population, which had converted to *Christianity* during the heyday of the Roman Empire, especially after the conversion of *Constantine*. During the *Crusades*, Egypt's governor, *Salāh-ed-Dīn*, used its great wealth to keep the Crusaders at bay and then to recapture *Jerusalem*. Egypt was then ruled by non-Arabs, the Bahri (River) *Mamluks*, 1250–1382, and by the Burji (Citadel) Mamluks, 1382–1517. Thus was established a pattern in Egyptian history in which its great wealth and population enabled ostensibly provincial governors owing allegiance to more expansive empires to nod in the direction of the empire, but rule autonomously. The *Ottoman Empire* conquered Egypt in 1517 and governed it, again sometimes only nominally, until 1914. *Napoleon* invaded in 1798, destroying the Mamluk Army at the Battle of the Pyramids. Britain occupied Egypt until it reverted to Ottoman control in 1802. Under *Mehemet Ali*, founder of modern Egypt, it was *autonomous* of the Ottomans. Under Ali's grandson Ismail (lived 1830–1895; governed as khedive, 1863–1879), Egypt felt growing French influence. This culminated in the building of the *Suez Canal* by a French charter company. Ismail wanted to expand his empire and pushed south from Sudan, waging a losing border war with Ethiopia in the 1870s. His borrowing drove Egypt deep into debt, and he was deposed at European behest in 1879. A military revolt broke out in 1881 over the debt issue, and anti-European demonstrations occurred in 1882. This led Britain to intervene with two armies and to occupy the Canal and Alexandria. After defeating an Egyptian force at Tell al-Kabir, London made Egypt an effective *protectorate*.

Abbas Hilmi II (khedive, 1892–1914) clashed with British administrators as he tried to restore the powers of the khedive and affirm Egypt's autonomy within the Ottoman Empire. Otherwise, progress was made, including completion of the Low Dam at *Aswan*. When *World War I* broke out, *Kitchener* deposed and exiled Hilmi and declared Egypt a formal protectorate. It then served as the major base of British military operations in the Middle East to 1918. A revolt against protectorate status broke out after the war, 1919–1922, after which London still retained control of the Suez Canal and of foreign policy. A 1936 treaty confined British troops in-country to the *canal zone,* and set up a British-Egyptian *condominium* over Sudan. Egypt again hosted British military bases during *World War II*, but after 1946 these were located only in the canal zone. Along with other Arab states, Egypt attacked Israel when *Palestine* was partitioned in 1948, but was beaten back. An anti-British, nationalist military revolt in 1952 overthrew King *Faruk I* and established a republic.

In 1953 *Nasser* became premier; in 1956 he became president, and Egypt tilted toward the Soviet Union, which gave it arms and aid. Nasser introduced radical economic reforms at home, even as he sought to play a lead role on the world stage. Egypt abrogated the Sudanese condominium in 1951, which encouraged Britain to give Sudan independence as a counterweight to Egypt in 1956. Now Nasser began work on the High Dam at Aswan, ordered British troops out of the *Canal Zone,* and *nationalized* the Suez Canal Company. That led to the *Suez Crisis* and the discrete, but related, *Second Arab-Israeli War*. The United States forced Britain and France to withdraw from Suez, and a United Nations *peacekeeping* force was put in place along the Israeli border. In 1958 Nasser attempted *union* with Syria, in the form of the *UAR*. He intervened in Yemen in 1962, but was opposed by both the Saudis and the British. Nasser ordered the United Nations out of Egypt in 1967, precipitating the *Third Arab-Israeli War*, in which Egypt was badly defeated and lost the entire *Sinai*. Next came the *War of Attrition*. Nasser died in 1970.

In 1973 Egyptian president *Anwar Sadat* launched a surprise attack across the Suez Canal, beginning the *Fourth Arab-Israeli War*. Afterward, he moved Egypt into the Western camp in the *Cold War*. In 1977 he flew to Israel, opening *peace talks* that led to the *Camp David Accords* and in 1979 a formal *peace treaty*, which regained Sinai. For making peace, Egypt was expelled from the Arab League, and Sadat was assassinated by Muslim *fundamentalists*. Egypt slowly regained acceptance among Arab states; it was readmitted to the Arab League in 1989. It sent 20,000 troops to fight in the *Gulf War* against Iraq. In 1992 it joined in United States–sponsored peace talks for the whole region and sent troops to aid in the UN relief effort in Somalia. It has long-standing regional rivalries with Iran, Libya, Syria, and Sudan, but is again widely viewed as the natural leader of the Arab world. Internally, it faced fundamentalist objections to its growing *secularism* from the *Muslim Brotherhood*, whose sometime random killing of tourists severely undermined revenues, but who really threatened the regime because through community development they gained significant support among Egypt's millions of poor.

Suggested Readings: H. Idris Bell, *Egypt From Alexander the Great to the Arab Conquest* (1948); M. Daly, ed., *Cambridge History of Egypt*, 2 vols. (1998); P. M. Holt, *Egypt and the Fertile Crescent, 1516–1922* (1966); P. J. Vatikiotis, *A Modern History of Egypt*, 2nd ed. (1980).

Egyptian Islamic Jihad. An *Islamist* organization rooted in the violent traditions of the *Muslim Brotherhood*. It was founded explicitly to overthrow the secular regime in Egypt. Led by Ayman al-Zawahiri, who trained as a doctor, it assassinated *Anwar Sadat* in 1981. Heavily repressed within Egypt thereafter, its leading members fled abroad. In 1988 it merged with *Usama bin Laden*'s Makhtab al Khadimat to form *al Qaeda*, a *terrorist* organization dedicated to fomenting Islamist revolution in all Muslim countries and driving America and Israel from the Middle East. It quickly showed that it was prepared to use any and all tactics to bring this about, in particular sponsoring suicide missions against Western targets. This course of action culminated in its involvement in the *September 11, 2001, terrorist attack on the United States.*

Eichmann, Karl Adolf (1906–1962). SS and *Gestapo* officer; commandant in the *death camp* system. Born in Austria, this door-to-door vacuum cleaner salesman was a lifelong *anti-Semite*. In 1937 he visited Palestine to consult with Arab leaders, but he was expelled as *persona non grata* by the British. Along with *Heydrich*, Eichmann hosted the *Wannsee conference*, which set in motion the genocidal *"final solution to the Jewish problem."* As head of the Department of Jewish Affairs, he oversaw mass deportations of Jews from Germany and Eastern Europe to the death camps. He experimented with various killing methods on Jews and mental patients and closely studied the mechanics of killing to improve the death system at *Auschwitz*, and then replicated it in other camps. He was captured by U.S. forces in 1945, but successfully concealed his identity and several months later escaped to Argentina—like several other Nazis, he used a *Vatican* passport to pass through Allied checkpoints. He was kidnapped by agents of *Mossad* in 1960, smuggled back to Israel, tried, convicted, and executed in 1962. The social philosopher Hannah Arendt observed the calm and apparently detached Eichmann at his trial and concluded that the most remarkable thing about him and similar Nazi functionaries was the "banality" of their personalities and their evil. Israel released Eichmann's personal memoir in 2000, as evidence in a British Holocaust-denial/libel trial.

Eighth Route Army. The name of the Chinese Red Army, later the *People's Liberation Army*, during the *Second Sino-Japanese War* (1937–1945), when it was nominally under the unified command of the *Guomindang*. The other major Communist army during *World War II* were troops designated as the New Fourth Army. Together, by 1945 they put 900,000 troops into the field.

Eighty Years' War (1566–1648). "The Revolt of the Low Countries." The long struggle between Imperial Spain under the *Habsburgs* and the Dutch Republic, led by the House of Orange. Its starting date remains controversial, but is generally accepted as 1566. Driven initially by the personal religious zeal of *Philip II*, it challenged the great compromise of the *Peace of Augsburg*, which Philip's cousin, Maximilian, had just accepted in the *Holy Roman Empire*. Along with the *Wars of Religion* in France, the Dutch Revolt grew to become a broad, European conflict. After 1585 it drew England, under *Elizabeth I*, into a Dutch alliance and an entangling coalition of anti-Habsburg powers. Much of the war was fought at sea, where the English and Dutch "beggars" ultimately prevailed. The Dutch fought hard on land as well, aided by English subsidies and the rapid growth of their more modern economy and financial prowess. Local Dutch liberty was threatened by the personality and the autocratic style of Philip II. He needed a *"revolution from above"* to rationalize administration of his Dutch provinces so as to save the larger empire from financial collapse. That threatened Dutch liberties and brought new taxes and restrictions on commerce, which was the source of Dutch prosperity. Philip's support for the *Counter Reformation* and stern refusal to rein in the *Inquisition* was the final offense. The Dutch Revolt thus began, notably as an effort to preserve traditional liberties and not as a radical revolution, though it was soon fairly radicalized along confessional lines.

Initially, *Catholics* and *Calvinists* alike saw the proposed church reform as royal power impinging on local liberties. The key protest was led by William of Nassau, Prince of Orange (1533–1584), more famously known as William I ("the Silent"), Stadholder of Holland, Zeeland, and Utrecht. In 1566 some 200 nobles took a petition to Brussels, where they were soon dubbed "beggars." Rejection of the petition turned grievance into rebellion, added to by bread riots, which also turned into rebellion. In 1567 the Duke of Alba executed hundreds of nobles and again raised taxes. William, who had been in Germany, invaded with an army of supporters, which Alba defeated only with great difficulty. Holland and Zeeland took the lead in the spreading rebellion, but even Catholic Flanders was restless. In 1572 a fleet of "sea beggar" ships captured the mouth of the Rhine, while "beggar" armies—joined by *Huguenots* exiled from France—held back tough, veteran Spanish troops and German *mercenaries* under Alba. The Spanish response was calculated *terror*: Alba *sacked* and massacred the rebel towns of Mechlen and Naarden. As he prepared to sack Haarlam too, he was halted by a lack of money for the troops. Now began a series of *mutinies*, which hamstrung Philip's war effort—the Spanish Army of Flanders mutinied no fewer than forty-six times between 1572 and 1607. Frustrated officers proposed to break the Dutch dams and sluices and flood the rebel areas, but Philip forbade this on moral grounds. In 1576 the fundamental fiscal crisis that underlay most of Philip's troubles led to one of his periodic royal bankruptcies, and no pay at all for the army in Flanders, which numbered some 70,000 to 90,000 troops and cost 30,000 ducats a day to maintain. This time, it mutinied and sacked Antwerp, in an act of murder and mayhem remembered still in the Low Countries as the "Spanish fury." It was the decisive moment in the war: all 17 Dutch provinces responded with a single will, forming an alliance dedicated to the expulsion of Spanish power from the Netherlands. The religious question that divided Flanders was not easily or peacefully settled, however. Calvinists turned on Catholics until, in 1579, Flemish Catholics turned to Philip for protection. The provinces divided: the ten southernmost formed the Union of Arras and declared for Spain, whereas seven northern provinces formed the Union of Utrecht, a partition reinforced by *ethnic cleansing* of religious minorities on both sides.

Dutch Protestants would not accept a king who could not tolerate their faith. Philip and his successors were incapable of conceding toleration or allowing one part of the empire to break away. And so the war continued, for another six decades. On land, fighting was mostly an affair of sieges, fortification, breeched local canals and dikes, urban occupations, and long waits in winter quarters. There was also the drawn-out and difficult *Spanish Road* to maintain. Along it, decade after decade, infantry reinforcements from Castile wound through Lombardy, *The Grisons*, and the *Rhineland* to the Castra Dei ("God's Camp") in the *Spanish Netherlands*. Often, they detoured to engage in Italian and German wars along the way, before resuming their northward trek to fight the occasional set-piece summer battle in the heavily fortified, confined, and densely populated lands of Flanders. At sea, by 1585 *Elizabeth I* of England had unofficially joined the fray on the Dutch side. In 1588 Philip finally responded with an attempted invasion of England. The failure of the *Spanish Armada* that year seriously weakened Spain's hold, and when Catholic France finally reemerged from its long civil war in the mid-1590s it, too, backed the Dutch revolt against Spanish hegemony. A great contribution to ultimate Dutch victory was made by Maurice of Nassau (1567–1625), who organized a modern, professional army that told the tale on land against the Spanish infantry the way "beggar" and English ships already did on the waters.

Philip III made peace with England in 1604, the year after Elizabeth died. In 1609 the Twelve Year Truce was signed, constituting *de facto*, though not *de jure*, recognition of the Dutch Republic. When the truce ended, all parties (except the English) were drawn into the wider conflict of the *Thirty Years' War*, which was already underway. During this culminating phase of the great conflict with Spain, Dutch *pirates* and *privateers* regularly raided Spanish and Portuguese coastal settlements in Central or South America or the East Indies. The Dutch even sent flotillas around the Horn to raid the west coast of the South American continent in 1624 and again in 1643. From 1631 to 1641 the Dutch *East India Company* (VOC) and the Dutch West India Company together captured Pernambuco, Elmina (Ghana), Luanda (Mozambique), Ceylon, and Malacca from Portugal, which was still locked to Spain until it too rebelled in 1640. In Japan, authorities transferred the Portuguese monopoly at *Deshima* to the Dutch. The VOC also established a base at the Cape of Good Hope to service Dutch ships plying the waters of what had become a transoceanic empire almost to rival Spain's.

All this had enormous consequences for African and world history. Mostly, it meant that Africa was to be drawn into a dynamic world trading system—sadly, mainly via the *slave trade,* which was now largely taken over by the Dutch—by a rising European power with far greater capabilities to penetrate the interior than poorer Portugal had ever been able to exert. And the Dutch presence would attract competitors for African slaves, and then for African empire, in subsequent decades and centuries. Meanwhile, the Portuguese possessions in East Africa were bypassed—Dutch ships sailed further south and east and then turned north to the *Spice Islands*—and Omani power and slaving revived there and in the western Indian Ocean. Peace was not achieved in Europe until 1648, in the *Treaty of Münster.* Spain was left beaten, exhausted, bankrupt, and in terminal decline. The Netherlands emerged confident and expansionist, but abridged in size and already past its prime as a world power, though that was not at all clear at the time, even though the split from southern Flanders (modern Belgium) meant that only a truncated Flanders state emerged from the war. For a century the Netherlands witnessed a glorious Renaissance and created a vast and wealthy world empire, but it was not long before it became clear that it was just too small to hold its own in the ranks of the Great Powers. *See also Maroons; Portugal.*

Suggested Readings: Paul C. Allen, *Philip III and the Pax Hispanica, 1598–1621: The Failure of Grand Strategy* (2000); Jonathon Israel, *Conflicts of Empires* (1997); Jonathon Israel, *The Dutch Republic* (1995); Geoffrey Parker, *The Army of Flanders and the Spanish Road, 1567–1659* (1972); Geoffrey Parker, *The Dutch Revolt,* rev. ed. (1985).

Einsatzgruppen. *See "final solution to the Jewish problem"; Holocaust.*

Einstein, Albert (1879–1955). German physicist and peace activist, most famous for the "Theory of Special Relativity" (1905) and "Theory of General Relativity" (1916). He was awarded the *Nobel Prize* for physics in 1921. A Jew, he was also an enthusiastic *Zionist.* That enraged *anti-Semites* in Germany and he lost his university position in the *Nazi* purge of academia that followed their seizure of power—an anti-intellectual act greeted with enthusiasm by many non-Jewish German professors and students, who eagerly filled the vacated slots. In 1933 Einstein left for America, where he became a professor of physics at Princeton University. That year he coauthored with Sigmund Freud (1856–1939) the *pacifist* pamphlet "Warum Kriege?" ("Why War?"). The Nazis included his books in public burnings of works by Jews, liberals, and others. His impact on world political affairs arose not primarily from his extraordinary scientific achievements and personal activism, but from a letter he wrote to *Franklin Roosevelt* in 1939 spelling out the theoretical possibility of an *atomic bomb*. Einstein had been made aware of this by German chemists, who were then far ahead of American scientists in the pursuit of atomic *fission*. He verified their findings and, pragmatically abandoning his *pacifism* for the duration of *World War II*, informed Roosevelt that Germany was pursuing research that could lead to an atomic bomb and urged that an American program be started. That led to the *Manhattan Project*, which culminated in the attacks on *Hiroshima* and *Nagasaki* and the nuclear arms race of the *Cold War*. On this, the following remark by Einstein is often (mis)quoted: "The unleashed power of the atom has changed everything save our mode of thinking, and we thus drift toward unparalleled catastrophes." After the war Einstein was active in failed efforts to force atomic weapons under international inspection and control. In 1952 he was offered the presidency of Israel, but declined in order to return to his scientific work, in particular the search for a unified field theory to complete the findings of his relativity theory and the insights of quantum mechanics. He once said of the role of theory in physics something he appears to have neglected in his approach to politics: "Elegance is for tailors." Yet, when asked why it proved possible to split the atom but not to prevent the nuclear arms race, he wisely concluded that politics is more difficult than physics.

Eire. The Gaelic name of the Republic of Ireland; it became the official name in 1937, replacing *Irish Free State*.

Eisenhower Doctrine. A policy statement issued by President *Dwight Eisenhower* on January 5, 1957, in the wake of the Anglo-French retreat occasioned by the *Suez Crisis*. It was also affirmed by a joint resolution of Congress. It elevated stability in the Middle East to the level of a *vital interest* of the United States and promised military aid to regional victims of *aggression*. It aimed at forestalling Soviet penetration of the region by justifying an enhanced American presence up to, and including, military intervention. A supporting aim was to stop *Nasser* from expanding his already considerable influence in the region. It was invoked toward Jordan (1957) and Lebanon (1958). *See also Carter Doctrine; Nixon Doctrine; Reagan Doctrine; Truman Doctrine.*

Eisenhower, Dwight (1890–1969). "Ike." U.S. general and statesman. Supreme commander of Allied forces in Europe, 1944–1945; first commander of NATO, 1950–1952; *Republican* president of the United States, 1953–1961. From 1933 to 1939 he served as aide to *Douglas MacArthur* in the Philippines. At the start of *World War II*, his ability was recognized by *George Marshall*, who jumped him in rank over several hundred more senior officers. In 1942 Ike took command of the European Theater of Operations. He oversaw the Allied landings in North Africa, the invasion of Sicily and Italy, and most importantly, *D-Day*, the *Normandy campaign*, and the invasion of Germany that followed. He was surprised by the *Ardennes Offensive*, but recovered and led Anglo-American forces to final victory. He was well-suited to overall command, dealing with rivalries among prickly generals (most notably, *George Patton* and *Bernard Montgomery*) and sacking generals with appropriate ruthlessness when they failed in command. Eisenhower also dealt well with the complex political concerns of powerful civilian leaders such as *Churchill* and *Franklin Roosevelt*, prickly allies such as *De Gaulle,* and far more sinister ones such as *Stalin.* Eisenhower chose not to take *Berlin*, against Churchill's advice, leaving that prize to the *Red Army* in favor of his broad-front strategy, which aimed at destroying German military forces. He got along well with *Zhukov* and other Soviet military leaders during the occupation of Germany.

After the war Eisenhower retired from the military and became president of Columbia University. In 1950 he was recalled by *Harry Truman* to take command of NATO. He then ran for president on a promise to end the *Korean Conflict* ("I shall go to Korea"). After ending that war, Eisenhower rode out the storm of *McCarthyism* at home, though his tardiness in defending honorable Americans, especially George Marshall, against spurious charges left his own reputation and image tarnished. During his first term, Eisenhower was forced to work hard to preserve presidential discretion in foreign policy from the still *isolationist* "Taft wing" of his own party, governing often in cooperation with key Democrats in the Congress. Secretly, he encouraged trade between Japan and China subsequent to the *Chinese Revolution* (1949). He initially opposed the inclusion of West Germany in NATO, but conceded the point by 1955. He worked constantly for nuclear *arms control* but achieved limited success, mostly because of the unreadiness of the Soviet Union to deal from its position of nuclear weakness. Thus, Eisenhower made imaginative proposals such as *Open Skies*—which were accepted decades later when conditions changed for the Soviet Union—only to see them come to naught. A fiscal conservative, he kept *defense spending* low: in percentage terms, his defense budgets were higher than in later years; but that is deceptive, as it fails to take into account an absolute increase but relative decline in defense spending as a result of huge increases in social and other government spending after 1961.

Eisenhower used *John Foster Dulles* to make tough policy declarations and public threats while he himself played the role of senior statesman. His administration relied on *massive retaliation* as its *strategic doctrine* and was prudent about the use of force in peripheral areas: he warned against becoming involved in another land war in Asia. Thus, although his administration provided *logistical* support to the French in Indochina and then to the Republic of Vietnam (RVN), when he left office there were fewer than 600 American advisers in that country and no combat troops. He was not loathe to use force: he supported a coup in Guatemala in 1954, sent marines into Lebanon in 1957, and twice threatened China, possibly with *nuclear weapons*, over *Quemoy and Matsu.* Although he oversaw a significant *arms buildup*, which built upon Truman's and that of the Korean War, it did not approach the levels reached under his successors. That left an opening for *John F. Kennedy* to (falsely) claim in the 1960 election campaign that Eisenhower had permitted a "missile gap" with the Soviet Union to develop. In his Farewell Address, Ike revisited his small-government, Republican roots by warning against the rise of a *military-industrial complex*. His historical reputation rose steadily as archival information led to a reevaluation, but also because of comparisons to the precipitous decline of *Kennedy's* reputation among many historians. Closer to home, Eisenhower successfully oversaw construction of the *St. Lawrence Seaway* and was a principal architect of the U.S. interstate highway system, both of which contributed greatly to the economic boom of the 1950s.

Suggested Readings: Stephen Ambrose, *Eisenhower*, 2 vols. (1984); Robert Divine, *Eisenhower and the Cold War* (1981); Dwight D. Eisenhower, *Mandate for Change: 1953–1956* (1963); Dwight D. Eisenhower, *Waging Peace: 1956–1961* (1965); Richard Immerman and Robert Bowie, *Waging Peace* (1998).

ejus est interpretari legum cujus est condere. "Who has the power to make a law also has the power to interpret it."

El Alamein, Battle of (October 23–November 4, 1942). After earlier defeats by *Erwin Rommel*, the British dug in along a defensive line, heavy with minefields, in front of Alexandria, Egypt. The line stretched from the coastal village of El Alamein to the Qattara Depression, which was impassable by the *armor* of Rommel's Afrika Korps. Behind that line, the humbled British Eighth Army regrouped and rearmed. In August 1942, *Montgomery* assumed command of the Eighth Army. He did not attack as soon as *Churchill* wanted, preferring to ensure overwhelming superiority—particularly in the air—and more sure success. The battle opened with a massive *artillery* barrage, partly aimed at cutting a path through the German minefields, which backed against the British mines. Eighth Army's armor broke through the mine fields on November 1st, and the Afrika Korps—shorn of many of its tanks and transports, and under constant lethal harassment by British fighters and bombers, began to run. Far behind them, in Algeria, Anglo-American forces began to land later that week. This was the first substantial Allied victory over the *Wehrmacht*, soon followed by the even greater German defeat at *Stalingrad*. This great desert battle, fought less than 100 kilometers from Alexandria, was the greatest solo British victory of *World War II*. It turned back the *Axis* threat to Egypt and the *Suez Canal*, cost *Hitler* valuable personnel and equipment (200,000 troops and hundreds of tanks and other armored vehicles), ended *Mussolini's* pretensions to imperial greatness, opened the path to total clearance of the Axis from North Africa, importantly bolstered flagging British and *Allied* morale, and was the necessary prelude to the invasion of Sicily and Italy in 1943 that knocked Italy out of the war. *Winston Churchill* said of it: "This is not the end. It is not even the beginning of the end. But it is, perhaps, the end of the beginning."

élan vital. A mystic concept popular among the French military and public prior to *World War I*, in reference to an elusive "vital spirit," which some theorists hoped would propel French arms to victory in the next war, in spite of the hard facts of higher German demographic growth and the awful logic of *attrition* in modern, industrial warfare which had been revealed, for those with eyes to see, by the deterioration into *trench warfare* of both the *Crimean War* (1853–1856) and the latter stages of the *American Civil War* (1861–1865). As a nineteenth and early twentieth century French military doctrine, the notion of élan vital upheld that since not even full-scale, three-year *conscription* could make the French Army the numerical equivalent of the Imperial German *Reichswehr*, it was essential to cultivate an "offensive spirit" in which sheer national will and raw personal and unit courage would somehow overcome German numerical superiority. This, and the exaggerated memory of *Napoleon* and the Grand Armée as the martial embodiment of the French national spirit, contributed to a "cult of the offensive" within the French military before 1914, which led to utter disaster in the first few weeks of the war as large French units marched or charged into *Alsace-Lorraine*, only to be slaughtered by waiting German *machine guns* and *artillery*—modern weapons capable of crushing even the most elevated human spirit. After experiencing the horrors of trench warfare during World War I, especially the carnage inflicted upon the French Army at *Verdun* (after which French reinforcements bleated like lambs as they arrived at the front), there was little talk in France of "élan vital." Instead, the interwar years were marked by the *defeatest* spirit and defence policy of the *Maginot Line*. *See also Ferdinand Foch; Henri Pétain.*

elasticity of demand. The rate at which demand for *goods* changes in response to changes in price or *supply*. "High elasticity" means that a small change in price or supply leads to a large change in demand; "low elasticity" is the reverse relation. High elasticity can wreak havoc on national budgets and forward economic planning, as operating assumptions may be invalidated almost overnight.

Elba. In the Mediterranean, a small Italian island next to Corsica. *Napoleon I* was exiled there in 1814 with his title intact and an honor guard of 1,000 men. He escaped in 1815, beginning the *Hundred Days*.

elder statesman. (1) In general: A retired or one-time *statesman* called upon to give foreign policy advice to a current policymaker. (2) In Japan: A group of senior politicians who derived great influence over policy from their control of the emperor's Privy Council, especially between 1898 and 1914. *See also* genrō.

El Dorado. The fabled "Kingdom of Gold" of the mythical tribe of "Amazonians." Unfortunately, too many *conquistadors* believed the myth, so thousands of Indians were tortured to death in the belief they were withholding information about its whereabouts. *See also Peru.*

electronic countermeasures (ECM). Jamming and other devices used to confuse enemy radar, signals, and communications or to confuse, trick, and deflect incoming missiles.

elint. "Electronic intelligence." Any and all information gathered in secret by electronic means. Its advocates regard it as highly reliable as compared with *humint* or even *sigint*. Its main drawbacks are that it is extremely expensive to gather information this way and that one can be lulled into a possibly misleading sense of information security.

elite. (1) Of birth: Those who inherit inordinate influence, power, or wealth, but not necessarily any talent. (2) Of merit: The most knowledgeable, skilled, and capable in a given society. (3) Of power: A small, inner circle of persons from government, business, and (far more rarely) academia, who actually make decisions that affect national policy, whether they are formally and legally charged with this task or not. Such persons are usually familiar to each other, are often nonpartisan in a party political sense, and move in and out of senior government and private sector positions with relative ease, if not always with a corresponding grace. *See also aristocracy; Creole; Communist Parties;* Führerprinzip; *junta; military industrial complex; mission, sense of; Friedrich Nietzsche;* nomenklatura; *vanguard.*

elitism. (1) In general: Practice of, or belief in, rule by an *elite,* whether of merit, birth, or power and whether open or secret. (2) In *diplomacy:* The belief that foreign policy should be made and carried out by a special corps of professional diplomats (a *foreign service*); or previously, by an *aristocracy* charged with beliefs of "noblesse oblige" and prepared for the task with a privileged, advanced education. (3) In the *Security Council:* Formal recognition, through *permanent member* status and the *veto,* that *Great Powers* have special obligations in world affairs and that it only follows that they should have special rights as well, to better enable them to fulfill their duty to uphold *international security.* (4) As a pejorative: Commonly used in advanced countries, especially by members of the intelligentsia and other primarily leisured classes, to excuse not listening to people in positions of political authority, or in possession of real knowledge, who actually know what they are talking about on issues of substance. *See also pluralism.*

Elizabeth I (1533–1603). Queen of England, 1558–1603. Daughter of Henry VIII (1491–1547), father of the *Protestant Reformation* in England, and Anne

Boleyn (1504–1536). Given the complexities of the succession to Henry and of her parentage, she barely survived childhood. Then she was implicated in a plot against her half-sister (Wyatt's rebellion, 1554), *Catholic* Queen Mary (1516–1558), and imprisoned in the Tower of London. Lady Jane Grey (1537–1554), her husband, father, and others thought to be involved in the plot, were not treated as leniently. In 1558, Elizabeth succeeded the childless Mary ("Bloody Mary"), wife of *Philip II* of Spain. Philip offered to marry her in order to keep his title as King of England. She demurred—she needed his help against the French—and played him well, leaving him one of many monarchs and princes in the end spurned as suitors for the hand of the "Virgin Queen." Elizabeth initially ascended to the English throne outwardly, though faintly, as a Catholic. Probably inwardly, and certainly politically, she was a Protestant already. Her ascension to the throne, at the age of twenty-five, was greeted with relief by her mostly Protestant population, as, whatever her outward and ceremonial trappings, she ended the persecutions carried out by Mary. Elizabeth then tacked with this wind favorable to her Protestant subjects, recognizing also that England was now part of an increasingly Protestant northern Europe, decreeing that certain Protestant rites displace Catholic rituals in church services (1559). For that, and for later fully establishing Protestantism, she was excommunicated in 1570 by Pope Paul IV, who held her to be illegitimate in any case.

This act by the pope actually ensured that henceforth the cause of Protestantism merged with that of English patriotism, and Elizabeth was seen as champion of both. For centuries, England had allied with Castile against France and Scotland (the "Auld Alliance"), a *balance of power* structure among the Atlantic states whose last gasp was the short-lived *dynastic marriage* of Philip to Mary. Elizabeth's progressive revelation of Protestant sympathies constituted a diplomatic revolution of the first order. It ultimately aligned Protestants in Scotland and England with Dutch rebels waging the *Eighty Years' War* (1566–1648) against Spain. Serious and responsible as a ruler, almost to a fault, before plunging into Europe's confessional warfare, Elizabeth spent a quarter century consolidating her grip on power in face of repeated disloyalty and assassination plots by members of the nobility and by the Catholic former Queen of France, Mary Stuart, Queen of Scots (1542–1587), who was supported by the *Habsburg* powers of Europe and by France. Those plots— over her reign, Elizabeth survived more than 20 known plots to kill her— were brought on partly by the *Wars of Religion* coursing through all European politics, but also by a submerged yet ever-simmering succession problem, which grew as she aged, as it arose from the fact that Elizabeth never married and produced no heir. In the end, having kept Mary Stuart a prisoner for years, with public reluctance and perhaps also private distress, she ordered her great rival's execution (February 8, 1587).

As queen, Elizabeth rationalized England's troubled finances as best a monarch could in that age of limited financial structures and knowledge, improved its administration of justice, and fortified its defenses and commerce. And she reformed the Church of England, completing the long process of making that institution subordinate to the state as the price of *establishment* by the state. She had the foresight to charter the *East India Company*, and reigned over an English cultural renaissance that uplifted the likes of Francis Bacon, Edmund Spenser, and William Shakespeare, when writers and thinkers most everywhere else in Europe were being harried abroad or hounded or even burned by the *Inquisition*. Still, Elizabethan England remained a minor power, distinctly disadvantaged vis-à-vis the *Great Powers* by its small population and the weakness of its army. Elizabeth compensated for her island's weak defenses by building a first-class navy. And she used it often, first to deflect French plans to invade Scotland in support of the Catholic party there (1558, and again in 1560) and, once France succumbed to 30 years of civil war in the Wars of Religion, to support the *Huguenots*. Then she commissioned its many *privateers* to engage a long and profitable, but at first officially undeclared, war at sea with Spain. She was often brilliantly effective in her diplomacy, keeping the pot boiling between England's ancient foe, France, and its new arch-enemy, Spain, so as to keep the influence of both far from her shores. She openly supported the Dutch "beggars" as their fortunes momentarily dimmed in the Eighty Years' War (1585), also dispatching privateers to the Caribbean to troll for Iberian treasure ships and also to Newfoundland to harry and sink the Iberian fishing fleet off the Grand Banks. Sir Francis Drake even raided the Iberian coast itself, taking hostages and desecrating Catholic churches. Philip replied with an *embargo* on all English trade. Then Elizabeth executed Mary Stuart (1587), and Philip answered with war.

Added to Elizabeth's mounting blows against Spain's economic interests and alliance with the Dutch rebels was Philip's belief that it was God's plan that he should annex England. Direct conflict simply no longer could be avoided. In 1588 Elizabeth's new navy, and the weather in the *English Channel*, defeated the *Spanish Armada* sent by Philip to collect an army from Flanders and bring it to England. Elizabeth's generals also defeated Spanish-supported Catholic rebels in Scotland and Ireland, completing the conquest of Ireland. Upon her death, Elizabeth left England more secure and united than she had found it, and set as well on a path of overseas colonization, which would result in its assembling the world-spanning *British Empire* in a later age. Though her many wars left England financially crippled, that was not fundamentally a situation of her choosing and was also a common enough fate of royal finances in an age of constant confessional warfare and expanding and increasingly expensive *standing armies* and navies. Elizabeth was the last Tudor monarch of England. She was succeeded by the son of Mary Stuart, James I (1566–1625), king of England, 1603–1625, and king of Scotland as James VI, 1567–1625. When a later Stuart, in the person of Charles I (1600–1649), tried to repair royal finances with higher taxation, the monarchy was toppled and an English king lost his head. One must suspect that, if in his place, Elizabeth would have found some other way and would have avoided that fate.

Suggested Readings: A. L. Rowse, *The England of Elizabeth* (1950; 1978); A. L. Rowse, *The Expansion of Elizabethan England* (1955); R. Wernham, *The Making of Elizabethan Foreign Policy, 1588–1603* (1980); R. Wernham, *The Return of the Armadas: The Last Years of the Elizabethan War Against Spain, 1595–1603* (1994).

El Salvador. It was part of the *Captaincy-General of Guatemala* until that larger region gained independence in 1821, coincidentally with the independence of *New Spain* (Mexico).

It then broke from Mexico to join a short-lived federal experiment called the *Central American Union, 1824–1838,* but left that troubled association upon its breakup in 1838. During the nineteenth century it was frequently in conflict with neighboring Honduras and Nicaragua or was forced to deal with the spillover effects of *filibusters* and other interventions. From the late nineteenth century it developed as a "*banana republic*," dependent only on coffee exports and world prices rather than on tropical fruits, in which owners of large landed estates dominated the economy in which most Salvadorans remained marginalized, landless peasants. This grave economic and social division also had a racial component, with *Creole* landowners dominating the descendants of conquered Indian tribes. In 1969 El Salvador fought the so-called *Soccer War* with Honduras.

From 1979 El Salvador became a focus of international attention for the first time in its independent history, as it fell into a state of civil war in which American and Soviet funding played a significant role. Some 80,000 Salvadorans died over the next decade. The worst feature of the civil war was the rampaging of *death squads*, mainly associated with the military but operating at arms length from official orders and working instead for powerful private interests. The United States provided large amounts of financial and military assistance to the government, especially after the 1984 election of the relative centrist, José Napoleon Duarte (1926–1990) and the Christian Democratic Party. Duarte led what few moderates there were in El Salvador's 11-year civil war. The guerrillas were an eclectic mix of *Communists*, peasant rebels in search of basic land reform, and native Indians, organized into a common front known internationally by its Spanish acronym, FMLN. They received military aid from Nicaragua, Cuba, and the Soviet Union, but also nonmilitary aid from some Western governments and *nongovernmental organizations*. The war ended in a *stalemate* in the field and political exhaustion on all sides. In 1993 a United Nations *human rights* special committee laid the blame for 90 percent of death squad killings at the feet of the military, with 10 percent attributed to the guerrillas; *State Department* and published CIA documents roughly concurred.

The United Nations mediated the peace settlement in 1991–1993. That was made possible as the collapse of the Soviet Union meant neither Russia nor the United States any longer saw El Salvador as crucial to their *national interests* and worked with the United Nations to end the war. In January 1991, a *cease-fire* was agreed; a formal peace settlement followed in January 1992. The guerrillas were disarmed in five stages, and the armed forces were cut in half. First, each side retreated to preselected sites; next they agreed to stop patrolling; then weapons were turned in to UN officials, and supervised elections were scheduled. Some death squad activity resumed, however, toward the end of 1993. In 1994 internationally supervised elections were held, which returned a broad, right-wing front (ARENA), with the FMLN forming a parliamentary opposition. Land reform followed, again under close international observation, as El Salvador resumed something like normal politics.

emancipation. Granting legal freedom to, or lifting restrictions on, a repressed and exploited class of people, such as Russian serfs (1861), American slaves (1863), or the Eta of Japan (1871). *See also Alexander II; Abraham Lincoln.*

embargo. A refusal to sell *goods* or *services* to another country. (1) Absolute: A declaration by a state prohibiting all goods, shipping, or aircraft from specified countries from entering or leaving its ports or airports. This is an extreme policy, rarely tried, and in this first form only also involves a *boycott*, or refusal to purchase the target state's goods. Examples include *Philip II's* embargo of Dutch and English trade during the first decades of the *Eighty Years' War*, and a decades-long United States embargo of trade with Cuba after the *Cuban Revolution*. (2) Limited: A prohibition, finite in scope and purpose, of specified exports. During the *Cold War* the West banned computer and high technology exports to the *Soviet bloc* through COCOM. *Nuclear states* block the export of nuclear fuel and technology (the *IAEA* monitors this), and advanced military states routinely embargo their latest weapons systems, with exceptions for close allies. *See also blockade; Thomas Jefferson; King Cotton; Abraham Lincoln; quarantine.*

embassage. Archaic: the instructions given an *ambassador*.

embassy. (1) The *diplomats*, staff, and buildings of one state accredited to a foreign government. (2) A mission undertaken by an *ambassador*. *See also consulate; legation; special interest section.*

emergency rule. *See martial law.*

emergency session. When the United Nations calls an unscheduled sitting during a *crisis*. *See also Uniting for Peace.*

emigrant. A person who departs his or her native land intending never again to domicile there. *See also migration.*

emigré community. A group of *emigrants* living in the same quarter, or in close contact, and still with active political interests in the old country. Among the more important of such groups were sizeable numbers of French nobles who fled France for Berlin, Vienna, and Moscow after 1792; various Russian *Marxist* or *anarchist* revolutionaries found in tearooms and salons all over Europe before 1917; *White Russian* communities that fled to Western Europe after losing the *Russian Civil War* in 1920; Cubans in Miami after 1959; various communities of *overseas Chinese*, and so forth. *See also refugees.*

éminence grise. "Gray eminence." (1) Informal salutation of the monk Père Joseph (Francois du Trembley) who served as confidant and adviser to the French statesman *Richelieu*; derived from the color of his monk's robes. (2) From #1, a person with quiet, but especially secret, behind-the-scenes influence over foreign policy.

éminence rouge. "Red eminence." (1) Cardinal *Richelieu*, manipulator of nations and destroyer of the power of *Habsburg* Spain; derived from the color of his cardinal's robes. (2) From #1, an exceptionally independent and powerful adviser on foreign affairs.

emir. A *Muslim* chieftain or prince. *See also sultan.*

emissary. An *envoy* sent from one state to another, especially if on a secret diplomatic mission.

emperor/empress. The title of the male/female ruler of an *empire*; above a king/queen in ceremonial rank.

Emperor System. The Japanese imperial system from the *Meiji Restoration* to the end of *World War II*.

empire. (1) A great political community containing more than one *nation* or *tribe*, yet under the rule of a single *sovereign*. (2) A vast, far-flung *state* comprised of conquered *territories* and/or distant *colonies*. *Nation-states* and empires have often coexisted, uneasily, in history. Since 1500, in addition to state-building by national monarchies, empires were constructed through acquisition of territories that did not fit the classic nation-state model. *See also dynasty; imperialism.*

empirical. Relying on observation or experience; not theoretical. *See also abstract; normative.*

empiricism. (1) A philosophical doctrine that regards all knowledge as derived from sensory experience. (2) An intellectual preference for observation over deduction as the main basis for reasoning. (3) A practice of, and analytical tendency toward, empirical research assumptions and methods.

emplacement. A platform or reinforced position supporting an *artillery* piece.

Ems Telegram (July 13, 1870). A telegram from King of Prussia (later Kaiser of Germany) Wilhelm I to *Bismarck* concerning a meeting he had with the French ambassador at the spa at Ems. Bismarck altered it to appear as if the ambassador had made excessive demands and the king had treated the ambassador with disrespect, and then he released it to the press. French opinion rose to the bait, within a week forcing what Bismarck wanted: the *declaration of war* by *Napoleon III*. That launched the *Franco-Prussian War*, which led to the fall of the *Second Empire*, proclamation at *Versailles* of the Second *Reich*, and two generations of continental dominance by Imperial Germany.

enceinte. (1) The main enclosure in a *fortified* position. (2) A rampart that forms part of a larger fortification. *See also Sébastien Vauban.*

encirclement. When a military force is entirely surrounded and cut off from retreat or contact with supporting units. This may be accomplished by *infiltration tactics* or a *pincer movement. See also* Blitzkrieg; *Stalingrad, Battle of.*

enclave. A small state or portion thereof, or some otherwise culturally or ethnically distinct territory that is surrounded by the territory of another country. For example, *Goa, Lesotho, Nagorno-Karabakh, Walvis Bay,* and *West Berlin,* as well as some *protectorates.* Ethnic enclaves are common. *See also Bosnia-Herzegovina; exclave; Vukovar.*

encomienda. "Entrust system." First introduced by *Columbus* on *Hispaniola,* this was a system of forced, wageless Indian labor (*slavery*, by another name), which later spread throughout the West Indies, and thence to much of Spanish America. Through it, settlers and plantation owners obtained rights to compulsory Indian labor. This was distinguished from outright slavery by a legal veneer that implied that the Spanish "employer" held the physical and spiritual (conversion to *Christianity*) welfare of the Indians "in trust." *Charles V* issued a suppression edict in 1520, but this came too late for the *Aztecs* and other conquered Indian peoples of the Central Mexican Valley, whom *Cortés* impressed into the encomienda system after his invasion and conquest, though he banned Indian labor in mines, which was work for which he thought they were not suited. The Dominicans and *Jesuits* opposed Indian enslavement, and won a legal—though in some ways hollow—victory against these practices in New Laws, promulgated in 1542 after the *missionary* reportage of the Dominican Bartolomé de Las Casas (1474–1566), which abolished formal Indian slavery while affirming the encomienda system in practice. This compromise between conscience and conquest was made because it served the secular purpose of encouraging Spanish settlement throughout the new lands by providing such settlers a guaranteed labor force. An outright ban on encomienda was declared by the crown in 1559, but this was widely ignored in practice.

However, because the crown refused to make Indian labor obligations legally hereditary, the encomienda system could not evolve into permanent or outright slavery and thus slowly died out in most of *New Spain* and *Peru* by c. 1600, though it survived throughout most of the colonial period in Paraguay and Chile, in the latter partly because of continuing and highly successful Indian resistance to conquest in the southern half of the country. Where encomienda faded, it was supplanted in practice by a near-*feudal* enserfment of Indian peasants in a new system of compulsory wage labor (called "repartimiento" in New Spain and "mita" in Peru), which was often accompanied by forced purchase of goods at fixed prices for the *corregidores* (provincial governors), in a system that ensured pitiable wages and perpetual indebtedness. Even this did not suffice to meet colonial labor needs, however, given the rate at which Indians were dying of first exposure to Europe's many and virulent communicable *diseases*. So, the whole complex system of Indian labor was augmented from about the 1570s with debt peonage among "free" Indians and massive importation of African slaves, who were not subject to the New Laws and who for ideological and racist reasons never engaged the same sympathy from the Iberian clergy. Mostly, things grew worse for the Indians over time, as even the few protective Spanish labor laws that existed were largely ignored by *Creole* elites and as deep corruption infected legal and political systems. In many instances, black slaves were used to supervise Indian indentured laborers. *See also* requerimiento.

Suggested Reading: Leslie Simpson, *The Encomienda in New Spain* (1966).

encounter battle. One in which the outcome is decided by the fluid actions of the troops on both sides, acting spontaneously and without direct control by senior commanders, as armies encounter each other in the field.

encroachment. When one state trespasses, especially with military units, across the *border* of another state. This may happen without intent, as when an aircraft is flown in error by a confused pilot; or deliberately, as part of the threat and counterthreat that usually accompanies a *crisis*.

"end of history." At a philosophical level, where it was first pitched, this was a rather hoary effort by neo-Hegelians to stand poor Hegel back on his feet, his having once been famously (and quite rudely) stood on his speculative head by *Karl Marx*, who substituted material interests for reason as the ultimate reality (the Hegelian "Absolute").

The "end of history" thesis became closely identified with American intellectual and essayist, Francis Fukayama, at the moment of Western victory in the *Cold War*. In this context, the "end of history" was the idea that, with the triumph of the democratic states over *fascism* and *communism* in the twentieth century, history has come to its close, that is, history in *Hegel's* sense of an unfolding of contending, ideal forms that mark out the "progress of the consciousness of freedom." Henceforth, public events (wars and other international conflicts) will of course still occur, but there will be no ideal *antithesis* thrown up to contest the triumph of liberal democracy, revealed now as the final *synthesis* of historical processes. At a political level, this fancy (though not wholly fanciful) notion was seen by many—though mainly those already sour on *modernization* and on *capitalist* democracies—as epitomizing a coarse, crowing triumphalism in the West at the end of the Soviet empire. And certainly, its adherents did tend to celebration of the—perhaps only momentarily—unchallenged ascendancy of liberal-market societies and ideas after nearly a century of fierce ideological contest, as well as actual warfare with the radical left. Yet, the "end of history" in its main sense should not be dismissed glibly. Although "never" is a very long time in history, it is in fact difficult to imagine a new, universal challenge being made to the idea that free men and women have an inalienable right to participate in their own governance, including on matters of private economic conduct. Even so, it is almost certainly the case that, as a matter of history, the thesis mistakes the hard-won triumph of Anglo-American material power in the two world wars and the Cold War, which then permitted the reshaping of international relations by the application of material power, for the "inevitable" triumph of the idea of freedom over tyranny. *See also absolutism; autocracy; decline of the West; liberal-internationalism; Marxism; popular sovereignty; shi'ism.*

endogenous factors. Originating from within; elements of an explanation of events said to be internal to the system.

end-user certificate. A document issued by governments to arms-exporting firms that affirms the final destination of the exported arms or munitions. The end-user is certified as a legal purchaser (usually another government), not an illegal buyer such as a *terrorist* or *guerrilla* group or an *embargoed* government. However, many end-user certificates are fakes, and not a few are issued with the connivance of governments for policy reasons or by their officials for private gain.

enemy prisoner of war (EPW). This term came into general and media currency when used by the United States during the *Gulf War*. However, it has not entirely displaced the venerable *prisoner of war (POW)*.

enfilade. A military position in which fire can be directed from along a whole trench or line of troops.

enforcement procedures. Whatever mechanisms, punishments, *reprisals*, or other means of *reciprocity* an agreement says states party to it can use against a transgressor. These may range from nothing, to automatic penalties and fines.

Engels, Friedrich (1820–1895). German socialist, English factory owner, and friend of and collaborator with *Karl Marx* on the 1848 "Communist Manifesto." Before meeting Marx, Engels wrote "Condition of the Working Class in England" (1845). While not an original thinker himself, he supported Marx in his English exile and later was a synthesizer and popularizer of Marxist thought. He was also a noted military critic, who hoped that mass *conscript* armies might become a vehicle of social revolution. On that point at least, he was later proven more insightful than many nineteenth-century *liberals* or *conservatives*.

Engel's Law. Named for German statistician Ernst Engel (1821–1896), this economic (or at least, statistical) "law" holds that as personal or family income increases the proportion of income spent on food declines; as a result, there will be more income available to be spent on other consumer goods.

England. The politically dominant territory on the island of Great Britain. Ancient Britons were only partly conquered by the *Romans*, starting with *Julius Caesar*. The limit of Roman military reach was marked out by a series of defensive walls spanning the island, most famously (but not solely) the Emperor Hadrian's wall, which cut across the country to protect Roman towns and settlements from the "barbarian" tribes to the north. Next came the *Vikings*, who ultimately conquered most of the independent Saxon kingdoms and left Wessex in *tribute* submission to Danish kings to the north, in the Danegeld. Anglo-Saxon England was invaded and defeated by the *Norman* Conquest (1066) under *William I.* Norman kings of England subsequently held vast swaths of territory in France and were not pushed from these until the end of the *Hundred Years' War* (1337–1453).

As their power and population grew, they also sought to conquer and control the rest of the *British Isles*. Edward I "Longshanks" (1239–1307) conquered *Wales* in 1283 and sent armies into *Ireland*; but his effort to control *Scotland* was repulsed by *William Wallace* and his successors.

England only slowly developed as a maritime trading nation. The Wars of the Roses (1455–1485) brought the Tudor dynasty to the throne while decimating the landed nobility. They also freed its minor gentry and merchant classes to fill open political and economic spaces. The English version of the *Protestant Reformation* took peculiar shape, given the marital and monetary interests of King Henry VIII (1491–1547). Its proceeds were applied to repeated and ruinous wars with France (and Scotland), most notably in 1528 and 1544, which kept subsequent English monarchs in relative penury and out of foreign adventures for a half-century. Despite England's smallness and isolation, toward the end of the sixteenth century it began to challenge Catholic Spain commercially and in the New World, even while fighting several *Anglo-Dutch Wars* in the Baltic and North Sea with its most direct commercial rival, the Netherlands. Under *Elizabeth I* it achieved *rapprochement* and then alliance with the Dutch, defeated the *Spanish Armada* in 1588, and led a great coalition against *Habsburg* Spain.

A *union of crowns* and therefore peace along the border was finally achieved with Scotland with James I (1566–1625), king of England, 1603–1625, and king of Scotland as James VI, 1567–1625. England was not drawn militarily into the *Thirty Years' War* except briefly and in a minor way. Instead, it was internally convulsed by a prolonged struggle between crown and parliament, which culminated in a great civil war, social revolution, a regicide, and then *Cromwell's* Puritan republic, all in the 1640s–1650s. Together, the First English Civil War (1642–1646) and the Second (1648–1649) formalized the split between English Anglicans and Protestant dissenters, and it left English, Scots, and Irish Catholics wholly outside a permanently fractured national church and faith. Those were divisions that tore at the social relations and politics of the several peoples of the British Isles for another 200 years; and in the case of relations with Ireland, for 300 years. Indeed, they do so still in *Ulster.* England's next major international engagement came with the *Anglo-Dutch Wars*, from which it emerged well on the path to global naval mastery and after which it began to write many of the rules, to its own great advantage, which later became the *law of the sea.*

England stumbled briefly after Cromwell's passing, with the Restoration of an unpopular monarchy. It rectified this when *William of Orange* mounted the throne in the "Glorious Revolution" of 1688, which also marked a definitive shift in power from the monarch to Parliament. Between 1689 and 1815 England fought seven major wars with France. The first of these occurred immediately upon the ascension of William of Orange, whose coronation ended the long maritime contest between England and the Netherlands and forged instead a key Anglo-Dutch alliance, which ultimately defeated France. After the 1707 *Act of Union* with Scotland, this island *sea power* was more usually referred to as *Great Britain* (constitutionally as the *United Kingdom*) with "England" reserved mainly to refer to domestic and cultural divisions from the Gaelic peoples of the British Isles. Nevertheless, England's role as the heart of the *world power* that Great Britain was becoming was formative not just of English history, but of much of the world as well. As for Ireland, it had been mostly subdued by Elizabeth, and then again by Cromwell. It too was constitutionally joined to England in an Act of Union, but not until 1800.

Great Britain opposed the schemes for aggrandizement of *Louis XIV* and his successors, resulting in several wars that formed a near-seamless whole: *War of the League of Augsburg* (1688–1697), *War of the Spanish Succession* (1701–1714), *War of the Austrian Succession* (1740–1748) and the *Seven Years' War* (1756–1763); with their North American extensions: *King William's War* (1689–1697), *Queen Anne's War* (1702–1713), *King George's War* (1744–1748), and the *French and Indian War* (1754–1760). In these wars Britain contained French power in Europe while destroying it in the Americas and India, greatly expanding the *British Empire* there in the process. The victory in the Americas, however, removed the main bond with thirteen contiguous British colonies there, and the sacrifice of colonial to imperial interests strained relations past the breaking point. The colonies rebelled, launching the *American Revolution* (1775–1783). The expense of fighting a long-distance land war in a continental-sized territory was enormous. Britain fought to preserve its only recently acquired, and hard-won, imperial preferences in America, but lost as a result of two key factors: the scale of the conflict and inability to bring superior force to bear in a decisive way given the *guerrilla* tactics of the Americans; and, more importantly, French, Dutch, and Spanish naval *intervention*. This setback interrupted an otherwise spectacularly successful imperial policy, which continued apace elsewhere. In India, flag and empire followed the commercial lead and troops of the *East India Company*, acquiring support bases along the way in such places as *Aden, Cape Colony, Sudan*, and even *Egypt*. Meanwhile, in *Canada* the *Hudson's Bay Company* ruled a giant *hinterland* of rivers and fur, while the entire continent of *Australia* was claimed in the late eighteenth century and made effectively British in the nineteenth century through *penal settlements*, sheep, and sea power.

Britain was at war with France almost without pause from the radicalization of the *French Revolution* in 1792, through the *Napoleonic Wars*, to the second and final defeat of *Napoleon I* in 1815. Shrugging off the loss of its important North American colonies, which it fought again in the *War of 1812*, it created a second and greater empire in Asia and Africa. In the first half of the nineteenth century, with the *Concert of Europe* helping to keep peace on the Continent but also nicely keeping Britain's rivals apart from one another, Great Britain emerged as the greatest power in the world and ruler of the most expansive and populous empire in history. It did so based on the superiority of the *Royal Navy*, early industrial advantage (it produced 25 percent of world industrial output), and the additional riches of its vast empire; but it also succeeded as a result of the enormous tactical and strategic benefits accruing from an established and successful diplomatic tradition, and a sustained and calculated policy of detachment from Continental entanglements, to whatever degree circumstances permitted. After the *Indian Mutiny*, London instituted *direct rule* in India and sought to complete construction of the *Rāj*, while extending its holdings in Asia in the second half of the nineteenth century as a means of defending its core holdings in India.

As the Concert decayed in Europe in the 1850s, Britain propped up the *Ottoman Empire* against the also-expanding *Russian Empire*, helping to postpone a final answer to the *Eastern Question* by fighting the *Crimean War* and practicing *containment* of Russia in the Mediterranean and during the *Great Game* in Central Asia. Britain's industrial advantage peaked c. 1870. It was thereafter overtaken in industrial production by the United States during the 1880s and by Germany c. 1900. It was also largely outfoxed in the later *scramble for Africa.* The so-called *Pax Britannica* waned along with relative British power at the turn of the twentieth century, mostly because other major countries caught up with or passed Britain economically and technically. Britain was deeply isolated by the *Second Boer War,* and moved to correct this with *Salisbury,* who moved from *splendid isolation* toward *rapprochements* with America, France, and Russia and framed the *Anglo-Japanese Alliance.* Relations with Imperial Germany deteriorated, however, over such episodes as the *Jameson raid,* the *Kruger telegram,* the *Boer War,* and *Agadir,* but especially over the *Anglo-German Naval Arms Race.*

Then came the *mobilization crisis* of July–August 1914 and the cataclysm of *World War I.* While still one of the world's major powers, indeed a *world power,* Britain was so wounded financially (and psychologically) by the Great War that it let Ireland break away in 1922 after the *Irish War of Independence.* And after the *Amritsar massacre* (1919) and the rise of the *Muslim League* and new assertiveness of the *Congress Party* in India, it also began discussions on *Home Rule* for India, as in the *Roundtable Conferences* of the early 1930s. It pursued a shoddy policy of *appeasement* of Nazi Germany until after the *Munich Conference.* Yet, when it had to fight anyway, it did so doggedly. It staggered to a *Cadmean victory* in *World War II,* largely with American and Soviet help.

By 1947 Britain started to let go of its overseas commitments, feeling the strain of *imperial overreach.* It pulled back from the eastern Mediterranean, replaced by the United States as the historic container of Russia in the early *Cold War,* when the Soviets threatened Greece and Turkey. It let India, the "jewel in the crown" of the British Empire, go free, starting a chain reaction of *decolonization* that unraveled in a single generation what had been assembled over 300 years. In the 1950s and 1960s nearly all the rest of the empire followed suit, a loss of stature not concealed by the poor cloth of the Commonwealth. The humiliation of the *Suez Crisis* aside, Britain ceased to act globally—at least, independently of the United States in its major foreign policies—during this period. In July 1967 it declared that it was withdrawing from all commitments "east of Suez," abandoned *Aden,* and withdrew from the Persian Gulf. That led the United States to move into bases in the Gulf to replace British fixed positions.

Still, Britain remained a major nuclear power and a significant player at the United Nations and within NATO and thus continued to "punch above its weight." In 1973 the UK joined the *European Community*, but without embracing full political *union*. The *Falklands War* distracted it from its main security concerns in Europe, while *Margaret Thatcher's* domestic reforms preoccupied it for most of the 1980s. In 1990–1991 it joined the *coalition* that fought the *Gulf War* and stayed to police the *no-fly zones*. It was reluctant to intervene with force in Bosnia or to develop the *WEU* as an alternative to NATO. In the mid-1990s the *Conservative Party* was turned out by the *Labour Party*, which gained the largest majority in the twentieth century. Labour was reelected with a majority in 2001. *See also Agadir; Amritsar massacre; Atlantic Charter; Stanley Baldwin; Arthur Balfour; Jeremy Bentham; Ernest Bevin; Boyne, Battle of; George Canning; Robert Castlereagh; Chamberlain, Joseph; Chamberlain, Neville; Chamberlain, J. Austin; Winston Churchill; Robert Clive; Cold War; colonialism; Commonwealth; containment; James Dalhousie; Benjamin Disraeli; Dreadnought; Durham Report; Anthony Eden; English Channel; European Community; European Union; Falkland Islands; Falklands War; Fashoda crisis; Fenians; John Fisher; Lloyd George; George III; Gibraltar; William Gladstone; gold standard; Gurkhas; Douglas Haig; Home Rule; Imperial Conferences; Imperial Tariff; Indian Army; industrialization; Industrial Revolution; Irish War of Independence; Jacobites; Horatio Kitchener; Liverpool; Frederick Lugard; John Major; mobilization crisis; Louis Mountbatten; Horatio Nelson; New France; Opium Wars; Henry Palmerston; Pax Britannica; penal settlements; William Pitt [the Elder]; William Pitt [the Younger]; George Rodney; Robert Salisbury; Sikh Wars; splendid isolation; Suez Canal; Suez Crisis; Sykes-Picot agreement; Tories; two-power standard; United Kingdom; Victoria; War of Jenkins' Ear; Duke of Wellington; Whigs; Whig history; white man's burden; Harold Wilson; Zulu Wars; and other specific colonies, crises, and wars.*

Suggested Readings: *Cambridge History of the British Empire*, 2nd ed. (1963); *Oxford History of England*, 16 vols. (1936–1993); Muriel E. Chamberlain, *Pax Britannica? British Foreign Policy, 1789–1914* (1988); Muriel E. Chamberlain, *Rise and Fall of the British Empire* (1996); Wm. Roger Lewis, ed., *Oxford History of the British Empire*, 2 vols. (1998); R. Hyam, *Britain's Imperial Century, 1815–1914* (1975).

English Channel. The strait that divides the continent of Europe from England. Less than 20 miles wide at the narrows, along with the *Royal Navy* it helped keep secure the island of *Great Britain* from foreign invaders after the *Norman* conquest of 1066. Although repeated attempts at invasion were made, including various landings in *England, Scotland,* and *Ireland,* no invading army was ever able to land or resupply sufficient forces to succeed. The Channel importantly impeded invasion attempts by *Philip II, Napoleon I,* and *Hitler.* Its strategic importance was made most clear as France fell under the Nazi jackboot and German armor raced for Paris in June 1940. *Churchill* offered Anglo-French *union* and tried to convince the French government to fight on from Great Britain and the outposts of its own empire. *Pétain,* deep in throes of *defeatism,* shot back that Britain might fight on, safe from invasion behind the Channel, which made an excellent antitank ditch, but France could do no more and would *surrender*.

English Civil Wars, First (1642–1646) and Second (1648–1649). *See Oliver Cromwell; England.*

English school (of international relations). *See classical school.*

enhanced radiation weapon. *See neutron bomb.*

Eniwetok. An atoll in the *Marshall Islands* chain. It was the site of U.S. *atomic bomb* tests from 1947 and the first test of a *hydrogen bomb* (1952). It is presently uninhabitable.

enlightened despotism. An eighteenth-century style of government in which absolute rulers refused to surrender formal, legal powers but accepted to govern in practice less arbitrarily and with the welfare of their subjects (at least, the politically influential classes) foremost in mind. It was an unstable transition stage between *absolutism* and *popular sovereignty*. *See also Alexander I; Alexander II; authoritarianism; autocracy; Catherine II; communism; corporatism; democracy; despotism; fascism; Frederick the Great; Napoleon I; Peter the Great; totalitarianism.*

Enlightenment. A deeply humanistic philosophical, cultural, social, and ultimately also political movement in eighteenth-century Europe. Its most famous personalities argued for the elevation of reason and science as the highest standards of knowledge, and against superstition, intolerance, and established religion. This was partly a response to new learning and represented a highly and self-consciously rationalist effort to scientifically determine the "proper order" of society. It was also in part a reaction against the dogmatic and antirational forms Western religious belief had taken during the great upheavals of the *Protestant Reformation* and the *Counter Reformation* of the *Catholic Church*. Lastly, it was a response to the enormous expansion of the destructive power of warfare during the eighteenth century, which had arisen with the *revolution in military affairs* and the development of *standing armies* and navies.

The Enlightenment was unlike the earlier Reformation or the preceding *Renaissance* in several critical respects. Most importantly, those great intellectual ferments had alike aimed at reform of religious life and accommodation of the Church to political and cultural affairs and intellectual inquest. The Enlightenment instead hoped to dissolve religious authority and remove its influence from considerations of public policy, its censorship from all matters of scientific inquiry, and its narrow-minded and doctrinaire clerics from control of public education. To accomplish this, Enlightenment philosophes wielded an often lethal weapon of empirical inquiry against the teachings of the *Christian* Church—whether Catholic or Protestant. They faced widespread lower clerical and popular superstition and higher clerical claims to proprietary revealed truths. Against this fortification of arguments made and accepted century upon century on the basis of the authority of antiquarian writers, or what they saw as the faux rationalism of scholastic reasoning—against Aristotle and Aquinas, in short—Enlightenment thinkers hurled radical new ideas. For instance, they wrote cross-cultural studies that illustrated how non-Christian civilizations, such as the *Confucian*, had prospered and advanced without reference to the putative revelations of the biblical tradition. They then asked, how could this be so, other than by following the light of reason? Nor did the philosophes hesitate to turn their empirical torch on the Bible itself, exposing its historical and heuristic inconsistencies and ridiculing the claims of believers that it was a great compilation of literal truths given by God to humanity—including about the Flood, the origins of species, and the nature of the heavens. This opened vast new areas of criticism and inquiry, much of it historical, including into common justifications for *slavery*, the claims of *absolutism* and the *divine right of kings*, the nature of the state, the relationship between governed and governor in society (the *social contract*), and the actual nature of the physical universe.

Among the Enlightenment's brightest lights were Joseph Addison, Denis Diderot, *Thomas Hobbes*, David Hume, *Thomas Jefferson*, *Immanuel Kant*, John Locke, Montesquieu, Isaac Newton (who did not share in the movement's militant secularism), Joseph Priestly, *Adam Smith*, *Jean-Jacques Rousseau*, and *Voltaire*. It gathered in scores of lesser figures in medicine, natural sciences, philosophy, art, music, and political thought. The Enlightenment was enormously influential in nearly all realms of intellectual life and political affairs, including *war*, which it rejected as irrational, expensive, unnecessary, and immoral, but into which sphere it also trod confidently with the conceits of *Vauban* and development of "rational" *fortification*, siege warfare, ballistics, and other applied military sciences. Its political and intellectual exploration of ideas of natural *human rights* led ineluctably to revolutionary notions of *popular sovereignty*, and in short order this was regarded by subsequent thinkers as the sole basis of political *legitimacy*. That extraordinary change in the way society was conceived, and defended and governed, resonated in the *American Revolution*, did so again far more importantly during the *French Revolution*, and indeed ever after in the forward evolution of *liberalism* and the idea of *democracy*.

Enlightenment thinkers did not have things all their own way. In addition to persecution (Rousseau had to flee Geneva, and Voltaire was unceremoniously stripped, beaten, and expelled from Prussia), a Romantic reaction followed that dismissed as cursory rationalism much Enlightenment thought and ridiculed the Enlightenment for its disregard of the tragic and the darker underside in human motivation and affairs. Thus, not only in its call for the progressive encroachment by reason upon the unknown and for exposure of cherished untruths under the cold light of reason, but also, in its often naïve faith in the triumph of rationality over passion and of reason over ignorance, the Enlightenment was more than just international: it was *cosmopolitan* and thoroughly modern. *See also industrialization; modernization; postmodernism; Maximilien Robespierre; secularism; United Irish Society.*

Suggested Readings: Isaiah Berlin, *Age of Enlightenment* (1956); Immanuel Kant, *"What Is Enlightenment?"* (1784); Peter Gay, *The Enlightenment* (1968); Norman Hampson, *The Enlightenment* (1982); Daniel Roche, *France in the Enlightenment* (1998).

enmity. Ill will between or among nations.

enosis. The demand of Greek Cypriots for *union* with Greece.

entangling alliance. Originally, a warning by *George Washington* to avoid "permanent alliances," thereby keeping America out of the *Napoleonic Wars*—the phrase "entangling alliance" was actually *Thomas Jefferson's.* Later, a near-ritual incantation by *isolationists* about the putative wisdom of not concerning oneself with foreign, and in particular European, affairs. Thus, during *World War I* and in the *Treaty of Versailles*, the phrase "Associated" rather than "Allied" power was used to refer to the United States, in a sop to *public opinion.* The first entangling, that is, peacetime, alliance the United States joined was the *Rio Pact* in 1947, followed by *NATO* in 1949.

Entebbe raid (July 4, 1976). An Israeli *commando* rescue of Jewish passengers of a *hijacked* Air France flight, flown to Entebbe in Uganda with the connivance of *Idi Amin.* The hijackers were all killed, with three Israeli deaths, one an elderly woman left behind and later murdered, possibly by Amin himself and almost certainly on his order. Efforts were made by some in the *United Nations General Assembly* to condemn the raid as a violation of *sovereignty* and *territorial integrity,* but it was defended by others as extended *self-defense.*

entente. An accord between or among states reflecting a shared understanding that they have complementary *foreign policy* and at least temporarily shared *security* goals and interests.

Entente Cordiale **(April 8, 1904).** An agreement between France and Britain that settled minor disputes over fishing and colonial *boundaries,* but most importantly assigned Egypt to Britain's *sphere of influence* and Morocco to that of France. The Entente was not an *alliance,* did not involve the close collaboration of the later *Military Conversations,* and was not aimed at Germany. However, it both cleared and set the stage for full Anglo-French *rapprochement* when Germany's subsequent actions threatened both. It has sometimes been confused with the formal Anglo-French military alliance, which was in fact signed only after the outbreak of fighting in 1914. (Thus, the depiction of *World War I* as caused by a clash of rigid alliances is, at least technically, false.) An *Anglo-Russian entente* was signed on August 31, 1907. It defined spheres of influence in Afghanistan, Persia, and Tibet. It too was not specifically anti-German, though both Russia and Britain wished to block Germany from further influence in the Middle East. These ententes are sometimes melded together and referred to as the *Triple Entente*. *See also Anglo-Japanese Alliance (1902); Fashoda crisis.*

enterprise. A firm organized to pursue commercial activities.

"Enterprise of England." *See Spanish Armada.*

enthrone. To invest with *sovereign* authority.

entrench. To dig into a defensive position, such as foxholes, trenches, or earthen *fortifications. See also siege warfare; trench warfare.*

entrepôt. A city on a major *trade route* where goods are changed from one form of transport to another, such as to or from camel, porter, truck, or rail line, to waiting ships.

entrepreneur. A risk taker who organizes a firm. *See also capitalism; capitalist.*

envelopment. To threaten or attack both flanks of an enemy's position.

Enver Pasha, a.k.a. Enver Bey (1881–1922). Turkish *revanchist* statesman. A leader of the *Young Turks* rebellion in 1908, he became minister for war in 1914. Once the *Ottoman Empire* declared war on Russia, October 31st, 1914, he immediately launched an unsuccessful offensive into the Caucuses. He completely dominated Turkish wartime policy, from which he hoped to restore and even recover to the Empire its many provinces lost in the eighteenth and nineteenth centuries. He fled to Russia in 1918 to avoid imprisonment after Turkey's *surrender*. He was killed during a failed *insurrection* in central *Turkistan* in 1922.

environmental issues (in international relations). *See acid rain; Amazon Basin; Antarctic Treaty System; appropriate technology; Aral Sea; Aswan Dam; Bhopal disaster; biological diversity; Chernobyl; command economy; debt-for-nature-swaps; debt-equity swaps; deforestation; development; desertification; economics; ecosystem; environmental security; Euphrates River; fishing; flag of convenience; Geneva Conventions; Global Environmental Facility; global warming; greenhouse effect; green loans; Greenpeace; Greens; industrialization; information technology; internal affairs; International Bank for Reconstruction and Development; International Maritime Organization; International Monetary Fund; Kyoto Treaty; Navassa; natural resources; new protectionism; nongovernmental organi-*

zations; nontariff barriers; nuclear winter; oil spills; ozone depletion; Pacific Islands Forum; plutonium; Rainbow Warrior Incident; slash and burn; social dumping; state obligations; sustainable development; transferable development rights; United Nations Conference on the Environment and Development; United Nations Environmental Program; water; whaling; West Bank; World Meteorological Organization.

environmental security. The idea that changes to a nation's environment may seriously threaten its national well-being. For instance, a rise in sea levels would cause great harm to island or *coastal states*, especially those such as Bangladesh and Egypt, which have large populations living on low-lying river deltas. Of a different order are questions surrounding defense of nuclear, chemical, or other sensitive facilities from environmental *terrorism*. It remains moot whether environmental security should be seen either as a wholly new concept requiring a basic redefinition of *security* or an addition to the list of traditional security notions and issues. *See also deforestation; ecosystem; Euphrates River; plutonium; water.*

envoy (*envoyé*). *See representation.*

envoy extraordinary (*envoyé extraordinaire*). A *diplomat* next in rank to an *ambassador*, accredited by, but not usually taken to be the personal representative of, a *sovereign* or *head of state*. Diplomats of this rank may also be called *minister plenipotentiary.*

equality. The international right of a *sovereign* entity to be treated as a formal (that is, legal) equal by all other states. Thus, each member state is entitled to one vote in the *United Nations General Assembly* or other international organization that it might voluntarily join and where it is in good standing, no powerful state may legally claim *jurisdiction* over a weak state, and no state is bound by any international law to which it does not *consent.* There are important exceptions to these formal rules: *servitude*, the *veto*, and *weighted voting*, for instance. Equality should be understood as a legal concept that underpins the *international system* and *international law.* Equality does not imply, though many attempts have been made to stretch its meaning in this direction, an equality of rights on issues of economic development or access to resources, or to notions of "fairness" in the world economy, or to mitigation of any other de facto inequality in power, influence, or prosperity. Less formal but much more powerful limitations on equality in practice include the *balance of power* and *war.* *See also classical school; community of nations; international society; Permanent Members of the Security Council; reciprocity; recognition; self-help; Westphalian system.*

Equatorial Guinea. A coastal *enclave*, it includes the offshore island of Fernando Po. It was colonized by Portugal during the late fifteenth century but was ceded to Spain in 1778. It was ruled from Madrid until 1968, when it achieved *independence*. Tensions exist between the more developed island and the poor and backward mainland enclave of Rio Muni. These surfaced horribly during the decade-long tyranny of one mainlander, Macias Nguema Biyongo, who declared himself president for life in 1972. He and others of the Fang tribe embarked on a brutal repression of all dissent and a debasement and corruption of nearly all national life, but with special attention to Fernando Po. In 1976 his brutality led most European settlers to flee. He then expelled tens of thousands of Nigerian migrant workers. In 1979 he was overthrown and executed by his own men. His nephew, Teodors Nguema Mbasogo, replaced him, retaining the one-party system but ruling with less naked brutality. Ostensibly free, multiparty elections were held in 1993, but opposition parties boycotted the process, and fewer than 30 percent of the population voted.

equilibrium. A *balance of power* across a region or the whole *international system*.

equity. The requirement that an international court use fair play, balance, and impartiality in its *judgments*.

equivalence. *See essential equivalence.*

Erfurt conference. A meeting between Tsar *Alexander I* and *Napoleon I* in October 1808. Napoleon wanted a comprehensive settlement with Russia in Eastern Europe and toward Turkey. Alexander, who was secretly told of French plans by *Talleyrand*, was able to evade any commitment. Having failed to placate Russia or secure his eastern flank, Napoleon later struck out at Alexander in 1812. *See also Tilsit, Treaties of.*

Eritrea. Eritrea was first penetrated by Italy in 1883, when the Italian government took over private interests at Assab. It was made an Italian colony in 1890. It was used by *Mussolini* as a base from which to attack Ethiopia in 1935. It was merged into *Italian East Africa, 1936–1942*. It was captured from Italy by the *Allies* during *World War II*, and its subsequent fate handed over to decision by the United Nations upon that organization's creation in 1945. Eritrea was federated with Ethiopia by UN order in 1952, to give that country access to the sea and in fulfillment of Ethiopia's assertion that Eritrea was nothing more than a historic lost province. A *guerrilla* movement developed from 1962, when *Haile Selassie* abrogated the *autonomy* promised Eritrea by the UN agreement within a federal Ethiopia. That act precipitated a rebellion by the predominantly Muslim Eritreans against mainly Christian Ethiopia, which was supported with arms and financing by regional Muslim powers. Fighting continued for decades, contributing to a terrible *famine*, from which it also blocked international relief efforts, and leading to forced *deportations* of Eritrea's civilians during the 1980s by the ruthless *Marxist* regime that had taken control in Addis Ababa in 1974. Eritrea obtained de facto independence after the collapse of the Ethiopian Revolution, as the Ethiopian Army withdrew. In April 1993, a *referendum* produced a 99-percent vote in favor of independence. Eritrea gained *de jure* acceptance from most members of the *community of nations* within the next month and joined the United Nations. It remains one of the world's poorest states: 75 percent of its population in the 1990s was dependent on foreign aid just to survive. Despite these severe handicaps, an extraordinary Eritrean will to independence showed itself again after 1998 when the *Ethiopian-Eritrean War* broke out. Eritrea was badly defeated, but its will to separation from Ethiopia was unbroken.

error. In *international law*, an error of fact (or a deliberate fraud) in the text of a *treaty* may, if discovered, invalidate that treaty. *See also validity.*

escalation. Increasing the level and/or the scope of a military conflict. "Horizontal escalation" involves widening a combat area geographically, instead of stepping up destructive levels of military response. "Vertical escalation" is increasing levels of military response, rather than expanding or widening a combat area. *See also flexible response; massive retaliation.*

escalation control. An idea connected to theories of *limited nuclear war*, in which *escalation* to *strategic nuclear weapons* is carried out in a careful and planned way. Some critics dismiss this notion as both politically and psychologically absurd.

escalation dominance. The effort to keep military superiority over an opponent at all levels of conflict and confrontation, as one moves up the ladder of *escalation* during a conflict.

escape clause. A clause inserted into trade agreements to permit cancellation of agreed *tariffs* after formal *notification*. It is an instrument of qualified *protectionism*.

escort carrier. Small *carriers* used on *convoy* duty during *World War II* as a countermeasure against submarines, but carrying too few planes to undertake large-scale or independent offensive action.

escrow. When a state keeps the assets of another state in a kind of trust account, pending resolution of a *dispute*. For example, after *World War I* the *Allied and Associated Powers* kept in escrow Russian gold that Germany had taken from the *Bolsheviks* under the *terms* of *Brest-Litovsk*. During the 1979–1980 *hostage crisis*, the United States placed in escrow Iranian assets amounting to several billion dollars. This money was returned when Iran agreed to pay *compensation* to American businessmen whose property had been *nationalized* or destroyed.

Eskimo. (1) The native peoples of northern Alaska, whether speakers of Inupiaq or Yupik. (2) An older term, now not always acceptable, to refer to all the Arctic people of Canada, the United States, Greenland, and eastern Siberia, who spoke languages in the Eskimo-Aleut family. *See also Inuit.*

espionage. The use of *elint, humint, sigint,* or other means to discover economic, military, political, and scientific secrets of other countries. *See also intelligence; intelligence services.*

esprit de corps. High morale, or a sense of common purpose, in a nation's military or *foreign service.*

essential equivalence. In *strategy* and *arms control*, treating different weapons systems as effectively equal so that they cancel each other out. For example, *warheads* with larger *yield* on one side might be seen as balanced by more accurate *missiles* on the other.

establish (a religion). To favor one faith over all others in law, and often also with financial support. *See also Buddhism; Oliver Cromwell; Elizabeth I; Lateran Treaties; Orthodox Church; Wars of Religion.*

Estates-General. The consultative body of the *ancien régime* in France. It consisted of representatives of the three "estates" of the old social order: the nobility, the clergy, and the mercantile and urban classes (*bourgeoisie*). It was seldom called into session unless the king needed to raise revenues to wage foreign wars. It was called by *Louis XVI* in 1789, with consequences that shook his throne, then France, and then the world. *See also French Revolution.*

Estonia. One of the *Baltic States*, and a Russian province after 1721, it was occupied by Germany during *World War I*. When German troops withdrew, it declared *independence* and, with Russia deep in civil war until 1920, succeeded in asserting that claim by force of arms. In 1940 it was seized by the Soviet Union under terms of a secret *protocol* to the *Nazi-Soviet Pact*. The United States and some other Western powers refused to *recognize* that annexation as legal and continued to maintain ritualistic, formal *diplomatic relations* with an Estonian *government-in-exile*. Most non-Western states simply accepted Estonia as part of the Soviet Union. In March 1990, its legislature reasserted independence, describing the country as an "occupied nation." D ing the August 1991 coup attempt in Russia, Estonia declared itself fully independent and demanded that Russian troops leave. This was accepted by *Gorbachev*, and Estonia was recognized by the Western states in September, months in advance of the *extinction* of the Soviet Union as a whole. In 1993 Estonia signed a *free trade* agreement with the other *Baltic States*, but its long-term ambition remained membership in the *European Union* and *NATO*. With the latter, it signed a *partnership for peace* agreement.

Suggested Reading: R. Misiunas et al., *The Baltic States* (1983).

estoppel. This legal doctrine underlies *good faith*: states cannot disavow earlier statements made by their representatives or facts they have led other states or *international personalities* to believe.

ethics. Moral principles; that is, ideas about right and wrong conduct (the common usage "morals and ethics" usually raises a distinction without a real difference).

There are four major areas of ethical concern in international relations: (1) use of force; (2) international order and the system of *international law* that helps sustain it; (3) economic or *distributive justice*; and (4) more recently, promotion of *human rights* and obligations to *humanitarian intervention* beyond one's national borders. The *normative* dimension of international affairs cannot be fruitfully studied without reference to the hard realities of the historical and *empirical* dimensions. Nor can it be ignored (as it too often is in *scientistic* and narrow-minded academic studies) if one wishes a complete understanding of international politics. It is a common, even trite, observation among self-appointed *realists* that world leaders cannot afford to be moralists and that morality and politics are things properly considered apart. Yet, it is at least as true that no leader, especially of a *democracy*, makes policy in a moral vacuum. Any sustainable international order must rest on both material and normative compromises among competing interests and principles. If a leader realistically expects to build on a solid and lasting base, this must be recognized. The most successful realists (for instance, *Bismarck* or *Churchill*) understood this and sought to anchor their foreign policies in *prudence* and respect for the complexity of moral interests. Especially within academia, moral reasoning about international politics is also a vital corrective, and a refreshing complement, to more arcane or merely material approaches that concentrate on crude, *quantitative* appraisals of power and interest. Moral reasoning about world affairs is as well a rich and persistent tradition in its own right. *See also aid; anarchical society; community of nations; cosmopolitan values; crimes against humanity; crimes against peace; genocide; Hugi Grotius; Thomas Hobbes; just war tradition; Immanuel Kant; laws of war; liberal-internationalism; moral peace program; Niccolò Machiavelli; Machiavellian; Marxism; nonintervention norm; outlaw state; pacifism; raison d'état; Jean-Jacques Rousseau; realism;*

sanctions; slave trade; slavery; state obligations; terrorism; torture; war crimes; war crimes trials; weapons of mass destruction; world community; world public opinion.

Suggested Readings: Jonathan Glover, *Humanity: A Moral History of the Twentieth Century* (2000); Robert Jackson, *The Global Covenant* (2000); Terry Nardin and D. Mapel, eds., *Traditions of International Ethics* (1992); Cathal J. Nolan, ed., *Ethics and Statecraft* (1995); Thomas Pangle and P. Ahrensdorf, *Justice Among Nations* (1999).

Ethiopia (Abyssinia). An ancient, *Christian* and *feudal* empire, Ethiopia maintained pilgrimage ties to *Jerusalem* even after the explosion of *Islam* in the seventh through tenth centuries cut it off from direct links with the Mediterranean world. Also, it sent to the *Coptic* community of Egypt for Monophysite bishops to head the Ethiopian church. In 1270, when the Solomonid *dynasty* was founded, Ethiopian power reached its zenith. The Solomonids abandoned ancient capitals in favor of peripatetic military encampments that furthered their ambitions for westward expansion at the expense of smaller, pagan kingdoms. Under Emperor Amda Syon (r. 1314–1344), Ethiopia also expanded southward, overrunning several small (and Islamic) "Sidama" slave-trading states and exacting *tribute* from others (Ifat). Solomonid Ethiopia enjoyed mostly peace and prosperity in the fifteenth century. The first Portuguese visited in 1490, when the explorer Pero de Covilhã arrived at court, only to be held prisoner in Ethiopia for the final 30 years of his life. A Portuguese mission that arrived in 1510 was similarly detained. A third came in 1520 and was finally allowed to leave in 1526. The Portuguese were astonished to discover a large Christian state deep within Africa and offered military support.

This became crucial as Ethiopia's position collapsed suddenly, in face of a radical shift in the *balance of power* caused by an invasion of firearms-bearing coastal Arabs, who were in turn supported by the rising power of the *Ottoman Empire*, which was then moving into the Red Sea. In 1529 an outmatched Ethiopian army was crushed in a *jihad*-plunder raid launched by the Muslim coastal state of Adal, which had Ottoman support and access to supplies of Turkish firearms. Much of the country was ravaged until Portuguese musketeers under the command of Vasco da Gama's son responded to an Ethiopian appeal in 1541, allied with Ethiopia, and helped defeat Adal (1542). The Portuguese musketeers remained to train the Ethiopian army, which henceforth purchased guns from the Portuguese. The *Jesuits*—who arrived in 1557 along with more guns—enjoyed brief success by converting King Susenyos to *Catholicism* in 1612, but upon his abdication in 1632 the Monophysite Ethiopian Church was reascendant, and by 1648 the Jesuits were thrown out of the country as Ethiopia entered a period of 200 years of *isolationism*.

Despite Portugal's aid, Ethiopia did not fully recover from the sixteenth-century loss of its Red Sea trade until the nineteenth century. In the meantime, its declining power and early failure against the Arab jihad meant that much of its land was overrun—or infiltrated, or settled, depending on one's point of view—by Oromo peoples (Galla, Somali, and Dankali nomadic pastoralists) from the south and east. In the seventeenth and eighteenth centuries, Ethiopia responded to this long-term threat by bringing Galla into its militia—as the Romans had done with Gauls, Germans, and various other barbarians—and accepted the de facto loss of its outlying provinces. Ethiopia's overall decline and shedding of historic provinces (Amhara, Shoa, Tigre) continued until the fortuitous defeat by *Mehemet Ali* of the *Wahhabi revolt* in Arabia reestablished trade in the Red Sea region. In 1855 Ras Kassa, a half-mad robber chieftain, ascended the throne as Emperor Theodore. In the next dozen years, before he killed himself, he consolidated the core of the old empire. His successor, John IV, took power with British help—in 1867 the British sent a punitive expedition into Ethiopia that devastated Theodore's army, at Aroge. John fended off an Egyptian attack from the Sudan in 1875, in which Egyptian forces were aided by European and American *mercenaries*, and defeated an Italian force at Dogali in 1887. He was killed fighting *Mahdist* invaders from Sudan in 1889. A Shoan warlord now took the throne, Menelik II (b. 1844, r. 1889–1913). He reunited Tigre and Amhara to Shoa, pressed into the Ogaden, and expanded southward into areas earlier overrun by Oromo tribes.

Ethiopia was the only African nation that stayed independent during imperial penetration of that continent. It had resisted the Portuguese for centuries and under Menelik held off an Italian attempt at conquest. After Italy's annexation of neighboring *Eritrea*, which the Abyssinians also coveted, a misread treaty and ongoing border dispute led to a decisive defeat of the Italians at *Adowa* in 1896 in the *First Abyssinian War*. Menelik then turned south, greatly expanding his own empire at the expense of less organized Oromo tribes. Border skirmishes with Italy continued to the 1930s, when the dispute was referred to the *League of Nations*. Italy invaded again in 1935, starting the *Abyssinian War*. Emperor *Haile Selassie* was forced into exile. The League denounced this *aggression*, but imposed only weak *sanctions*. Selassie returned in 1941, with *liberation* by a combined British-Ethiopian force.

Eritrea was taken from Italy and joined to Ethiopia by the United Nations in 1952. When Selassie moved to end Eritrea's *autonomy* in 1962, a revolt broke out. This soon spread to *Tigre* and other provinces. The United States maintained a base at Kagnew, 1962–1974, when Selassie's still largely feudal regime was overthrown by a radical, leftist coup that moved Ethiopia firmly into the Soviet camp and forced the U.S. Navy to a former Soviet base at Berbera, Somalia. Helped by Sudan and Somalia, *guerrilla* campaigns in the provinces of Eritrea and the *Ogaden* continued to destabilize the country. In 1977 large numbers of Cuban troops arrived. They were unable to defeat the Eritrean rebels, but did make headway in the Ogaden and in the *Ethiopia-Somalia War*. In 1984, relief efforts were mounted in response to a terrible *famine*, caused in part by forced *deportations* and made worse by government refusal to allow food into rebel areas. Under Mengistu Haile Mariam (b. 1941)

Ethiopians suffered the *Red Terror*. In 1988 a formal peace was agreed with Somalia. In 1991 a coalition of six guerrilla armies overturned the revolutionary regime, and many of its officials faced charges of *war crimes*. Eritrea's *de facto* independence was accepted by the new government in 1992. The next year its *de jure* independence was accepted, again cutting Ethiopia off from the sea. By 1993 famine had returned to threaten millions. From 1998 to 2000, Ethiopia aggressively pursued victory in the *Ethiopian-Eritrean War*.

Suggested Readings: Mordecai Abir, *Ethiopia in the Era of the Princes, 1769–1855* (1968); Roland Oliver, ed., *Cambridge History of Africa*, vol. 3 (1977); David Phillipson, *Ancient Ethiopia* (1998); Sergew Sellassie, *Ancient and Medieval Ethiopia* (1972).

Ethiopian-Eritrean War (1998–2000). In May 1998, hostilities broke out between Ethiopia and its former province, Eritrea, in a case of armed conflict of the poor versus the poorest, despite the one-time personal friendship and prior good relations of the two presidents. The main *casus belli* was a 2,000–square-kilometer area of disputed border area. Deeper reasons were that Eritrea's successful *secession* turned Ethiopia into a land-locked state and, even more, a centuries-long history of Eritrean vassalage to Ethiopia, which was broken by the former's independence in 1993 but still informally expected by Addis Ababa. In short, it was very much a war about *prestige*. A *cease-fire* was arranged that lasted nine months, but that was really used by both sides to build up their militaries in preparation for a larger conflict. When fighting broke out again in February 1999, casualties on both sides were appalling: early set-piece battles devolved into a form of *trench warfare*, the likes of which had not been seen since *World War I* or the *Iran-Iraq War*. Tens of thousands died. After Ethiopia finally broke the Eritrean lines, a peace settlement was reached in 2000.

Ethiopian-Italian Wars. *See Abyssinian War, First; Abyssinian War, Second.*

Ethiopia-Somalia War (1977–1988). Somalia always claimed the *Ogaden* region of eastern Ethiopia, where mostly ethnic Somalis lived and where local *guerrillas* were already in *rebellion* against Addis Ababa. On July 23, 1977, Somalia invaded. After initial successes, it was pushed back by Ethiopian troops assisted by some 11,000 Cubans and a fair number of *Soviet bloc* advisers. Somalia expelled its own Soviet advisers in November 1977 and sought Western aid instead. In March 1978, its forces were broken. It asked for a *cease-fire* and withdrew. It supported ethnic Somali guerrillas who continued fighting for the next 10 years, during which time some 1.5 million *refugees* poured from the war zone into Somalia, further impoverishing and destabilizing an already poor land. In 1988 terms of a peace settlement that left Ogaden with Ethiopia were agreed.

ethnic cleansing. A term in currency since the start of the *Third Balkan War*, but a practice that has gone on for centuries, accelerating with redefinition of the modern *state* along ethnic lines. It refers to forcible *deportation* and intimidation of a civilian population "pour encourager les autres," that is, forcibly expelling or frightening people from one *ethnic group* into abandoning territory coveted by another. It can include use of terror tactics, mass *rape*, and *summary execution*. At its most extreme it can reach *genocidal* proportions. Among its many examples: forcible deportation west of most of the *indigenous peoples* of North America onto reservations during the *Indian Wars*; the Armenian *genocide* (1915); all Nazi racial policy, by whose strictures millions perished; mass deportations of ethnic Germans from East and Central Europe after *World War II*, in which 14 million ethnic Germans were forced to leave historic German lands (some 2 million died); the human calamity of the *partition* of India in 1947, when 12 million *Hindus*, *Muslims*, and *Sikhs* fled violence by each others' radicals and hundreds of thousands were massacred; elements of *apartheid*; the deportation of Azeris from *Nagorno-Karabakh*; multiple episodes in *Bosnia*, *Kosovo*, and elsewhere in the Balkans in the 1990s; and repeated terror campaigns and genocides in *Burundi* and *Rwanda*. *See also Dayton Peace Accords; ethnocentrism; Holocaust; Idi Amin; Lausanne, Treaty of (1923); Lebensraum; Tamil Tigers; Trail of Tears; war crimes; war crimes trials.*
    Suggested Reading: Norman Naimark, *Fires of Hatred* (2001).

ethnic group. A community that shares language, race, or distinctive religious or cultural values. *See also nation; tribe.*

ethnocentrism. Viewing and judging the world from the narrow perspective of one culture, often taken to be superior, and usually without expression of due empathy for alternate views. (Note: Having "due empathy" for other ethnic groups does not require sinking into *cultural relativism*, just cultivating an honest appreciation of difference and foreign achievement.) As such, any culture may—and most do—produce persons with ethnocentric views. As an exaggerated and often racially or religiously based variant of *nationalism*, ethnocentrism goes well beyond pride in one's nation or culture to imply exclusivity and a blinkered, parochial world view that both magnifies the virtues of one's own group and inflates the vices attributed to other ethnic identities. In its most radical form it is sometimes called "ethnonationalism" and can contribute to aggravated levels of hatred of "the other" that feed into heinous practices such as *ethnic cleansing* or even *genocide*. *See also Afrocentrism; Atlanticism; chauvinism; cosmopolitan values; Eurocentrism; fundamentalism; irredentism; jingoism; négritude; pan-Africanism; pan-Americanism; pan-Arabism; pan-Slavism; racism; xenophobia.*

ethnonationalism. *See ethnocentrism.*

Eupen and Malmedy. A border area between Belgium and Germany, given to Belgium at the *Paris Peace Conference*, retaken by Germany in 1940, and returned to Belgium in 1945.

Euphrates River. It runs through Turkey, Syria, Iraq, and Iran. In the 1980s and 1990s Turkish irrigation and hydroelectric dams significantly reduced the flow volume, raising questions of *environmental security* for downstream states.

Eurasia. *Europe* and *Asia* considered as one geographical and historical entity. *See Heartland.*

eurobond markets. Transactions for bonds held outside the European country of issue.

Eurocentrism. Viewing events from the point of view of *Europe*, its peoples and cultural values. When used as a pejorative, the term implies that a given interpretation grossly exaggerates the relative importance of Europe by always placing its views or interests at the center of world affairs, to the detriment of the interests, world role, and points of view of non-European peoples and cultures. In the postcolonial period, new and explicitly non-Eurocentric histories (and other studies) provided a needed and highly useful corrective to the distorted "victor's history" previously written about Africa, Asia, and Latin America by European observers and scholars with a fondness for empire. However, the charge of "Eurocentrism" is often made too easily, or for mere propaganda purposes, and can itself divert understanding away from an important fact about international history: for 450 years, from c. 1500 to 1945, or from the *Age of Exploration* to the end of *World War II* (when Europe was occupied by two extra-Continental powers), Europe's politics, ideas and values, wars and commercial relations, its *diplomacy*, and its developing tradition of *international law* were of formative and even determining importance in the evolution of the modern world. Therefore, it is not Eurocentric—in the pejorative sense—to point out that until the mid-twentieth century world history itself was Eurocentric—in the geopolitical and Great Power sense—in fact. *See also Afrocentrism; cultural relativism; ethnocentrism.*

Eurocommunism. The post-1962 effort by West European *Communist parties* to establish separate "national paths to *communism*," rather than slavishly follow the *party line* laid out by Moscow, as most had done previously. The trend was first and most strongly evident in Italy, and most resisted in France. The Soviet invasion of Czechoslovakia in 1968 was a turning point, drawing rebukes even from the French. The main tenets were ostensible acceptance of pluralism (socialism constructed on a national not an international basis) and a parliamentary path to a democratic form of *communism*. This switch in tactics did not avert electoral decline in the 1980s, or extinction of this ideological dinosaur by conversion to a softer leftism in the 1990s, after the *Cold War* had ended. *See also internationalism.*

EUROCORPS. It started in 1990 with a Franco-German brigade (unilingual soldiers, bilingual officers). It was pushed hard by the French as the core of an independent (of the United States) European military. In 1993 Belgium joined. Curiously enough, when all else fails, its *lingua franca* is English. Events on the ground in Europe blunted the initial enthusiasm of France for a wholly separate force. In 1993 it was agreed that under specified conditions the EUROCORPS may come under *NATO* command, which may represent a step back toward military *integration* by Paris. It became operational in 1995.

eurocurrencies. Currencies held in accounts outside the country of issue as a medium of international *liquidity*, credit, and exchange, usually free of strong national controls, such as eurodollars, euromarks, and eurofrancs (Swiss).

In 1990 the eurocurrency markets reached $5 trillion. They were overtaken by *European Union* monetary reform and creation of the euro. *See also European Monetary Union.*

Euro-MP. A member of the *European Parliament.*

Europe. A small continent located on the western third of the Eurasian land mass, whose divers peoples and states shaped and dominated the *international system* from c. 1500 to 1945. It is bordered on the north by the Arctic Ocean; on the south by the Mediterranean, Black, and Caspian Seas and the Caucasus Mountains; to the west by Iceland and the Azores; and to the east by the Ural Mountains. For historical and cultural reasons, most political usages exclude Russia even though the western third of that state is geographically a part of Europe. Virtually all usage during the *Cold War* emphatically excluded the *Soviet Union.* Similarly, Turkey is usually excluded, although it was an important European power under the *Ottoman* sultans and retains a portion of the ancient European province of *Rumelia*, surrounding Istanbul (*Constantinople*).

Finally, one sometimes encounters the quixotic exclusion of Britain from Europe, such as in the quaintly nationalistic usage "Europe and Britain." *See also Eastern Europe; Western Europe.*

Suggested Readings: Peter Gay and R. K. Webb, *Modern Europe* (1973); Michael Howard, *War in European History* (1976); Mark Mazower, *Dark Continent: Europe's 20th Century* (1999); Kenneth Pomeranz, *The Great Divergence* (2000); Geoffrey Wawro, *Warfare and Society in Europe, 1792–1914* (2000).

European Atomic Energy Commission (EURATOM). Established in 1958 under the *Treaty of Rome*, it coordinates civilian nuclear research, development, and economic applications. In 1965 it was merged into a single executive with the *ECSC* and the *EEC*, all under the *European Commission*.

European Bank for Reconstruction and Development (EBRD). A regional bank founded to assist post–Soviet era Eastern Europe, especially its private sector, with investment capital for operations that commercial banks judged to be too risky. It was plagued by early scandal over the lavish spending of its first president and management team. In 1994, reforms took hold, and the EBRD expanded lending into the former Soviet region. It often lends to local banks, but may purchase equity in private firms as well.

European Central Bank (ECB). The *central bank* of the *European Union*, created on June 1, 1998, and effectively replacing the *European Monetary Institute*. Together with the national central banks (NCBs) of member countries, it forms the *European System*. Its core charge is to maintain stable prices, especially to prevent *inflation*. *See also European Monetary Union (EMU).*

European Coal and Steel Community (ECSC). It was established in 1952 by a treaty among Belgium, France, Germany, Italy, Luxembourg, and the Netherlands. It was the first major move toward European *integration*, pooling coal and steel resources under a High Authority, which aimed at eliminating *tariffs* on these key industries, but also at political *union*. In 1967 it merged with the *EEC* and *EURATOM*. *See also European Commission; European Communities; European Community.*

European Commission. A quasi-*executive* set up by the *Treaty of Rome* in 1958. At first, it had nine members, one for each of the original six plus additional commissioners for the larger states of France, Italy, and West Germany. Its main duty was to administer the treaty. In 1967 it commenced oversight of *EURATOM* and the *ECSC*, although the latter was still answerable to its own High Authority. The Commission is a vehicle of cooperation among national governments, rather than a *supranational* body. That reality was confirmed in the *Luxembourg Compromise* of 1966, which derailed the fast track toward political *union*. The commission grew weaker with expansion, as complex monetary and other issues fell outside its brief. However, it retains the right to propose legislation for the *European Union*, subject to national approval and consent by the *European Parliament*, oversees the controversial *CAP*, and enforces regulations on competition within the *customs* and *free trade* union.

European Communities (EC). Some, especially in Britain, continue to use this term to make the point that there is not one community, but a galaxy of organizations and functional communities such as *EURATOM*, *ECSC* and the *EEC*. The *European Court of Justice* also maintains this distinction. These three formed the core of the *European Community* in 1965, when they came under a shared *executive* authority (implemented, July 1967). In 1993 the political-terminological debate shifted further, with creation of the *European Union*.

European Community (EC). (1) The collective name of the *European Communities*, beginning with the 1967 merger into a single executive organ of *EURATOM*, *ECSC*, and the *EEC* and the creation of a single Community by 1970. It included the whole complex of *international governmental organizations* related to European *integration*. (2) A looser term referring to the member states working together toward a target of European economic and political *integration*, with federal *union* as the long-term goal. It had six original members: Belgium, France, Italy, Luxembourg, the Netherlands, and West Germany. Britain applied in 1961, but was rejected by a French veto in 1963, and again in 1966–1967. Three other states, Denmark, Ireland, and Norway, had attached their applications to British entry, and these were blocked, too, by *De Gaulle's* opposition to Britain. With De Gaulle's resignation in 1969, the six moved quickly to reopen Britain's application. It joined in 1973; with it came the other three applicants of 1963 and 1966, but Norway balked at the last and decided not to join. In 1981 Greece was admitted, and in 1986 Portugal and Spain joined. In 1987 the *Single European Act* was passed. In the *Maastricht Treaty*, the EC added a higher decision-making layer in the form of the *European Union* (see that entry for an important explanation of Europe's confusing nomenclature). With the end of the *Cold War*, even some traditionally neutral states applied for EC membership: Austria, Finland, and Sweden joined in 1995. However, in 1992, Swiss voters rejected the idea of joining. Norway also was offered membership, but once again rejected it (1994). Most Eastern European and former *Soviet bloc* states applied for membership, along with Malta, Cyprus, and a perennial applicant, Turkey. Other states are attached to the "European Union" at an associate level through the *Lomé Conventions* and the *EFTA*. *See also deepening versus widening*; les petites riches; *Western European Union*.

European Convention for the Protection of Human Rights and Fundamental Freedoms. Launched in November 1950 and in force as of 1953, this is the most advanced of all regional *regimes* on *human rights*. In 1954 it set up protective machinery, including a commission, that permitted individual *petition* to the *European Court of Human Rights*. It has on occasion led to enforceable judgments against *sovereign* governments.

European Council. The name given meetings of the *heads of government* of the *European Union*. These had no official status in the *Treaty of Rome*. After 1974 they became an institutionalized feature of the *European Community* and continued into the *European Union*. Meetings are usually twice per year. It was given legal recognition (without definition of powers) by the *Single European Act*. Its presidency rotates every six months among all members on an equal basis. This can raise very small nations, even Luxembourg, into the world limelight during a time of *crisis* if they happen to be hosting the presidency. After 1974 the Council was the only body that could set targets or guidelines for the Community. Furthermore, it was not tightly bound by *inter se* treaties, and therefore heads of government were free of the authority of both the *European Commission* and the *European Parliament*. In the 1980s the Council evolved from a brake on *integration* to a force pushing for it, as in the *Single European Act* and *Maastricht Treaty*, which modified its relation to the Commission and Parliament.

European Court of Human Rights. Set up in 1950 by the *Council of Europe*, under the *European Convention on Human Rights*, it is based in Strasbourg. It is empowered to make binding decisions in the event complaints cannot be resolved at the national level. The *Council of Ministers* supervises compliance with these decisions, which may also be addressed by the *European Court of Justice*.

European Court of Justice. Its formal name is still "Court of Justice of the European Communities," reflecting its relations with the *ECSC* and *EURATOM* as well as the *EEC* and *European Union*. It was established by the *Treaty of Rome* in 1958. Its seven judges serve six-year terms. It hears *disputes* between members of the several communities, particularly those relating to *treaties*. Its *judgments* are binding, but ultimately have to be interpreted and implemented by national governments and courts. From 1958 to 1994 the Court found against every *European Community* member in some case. By the 1970s it was widely accepted as an important *intergovernmental* instrument.

European Currency Unit (ECU). *See European Monetary System.*

European Defense Community (EDC). It derived from a French proposal for a European army. It met resistance from Britain and Scandinavia, and so was joined only by the six members of the *ECSC* in 1952. Its purpose was to forestall an independent German military by compelling West Germany to base all its military within the EDC, whereas the other members would place only a portion each of their armies under EDC authority. *Adenauer* supported it as a way of quickly rehabilitating Germany. The Soviets tried to block it with an insincere offer of early German unification. The EDC never got beyond the planning stage because it conflicted with *NATO*, but even more because the French parliament ultimately balked at any German rearmament and refused *ratification* of the treaty.

European Economic Area (EEA). It began as a 1988 proposal to extend free market rules, but not full *EC integration*, to the *EFTA* nations. It became entangled with the question of *deepening versus widening*, but still came quietly into effect on January 1, 1994. It is the largest *free trade area* in the world, with 17 member states, 375 million people, and close to $7 trillion collective GDP. In 1992, Switzerland voted, in a *referendum*, against membership. Because of their shared *customs union*, that also denied membership to Liechtenstein. Legal disputes over *European Union* rules against *monopolies* and state *subsidies* led to a compromise: the *European Court of Justice* will rule in the EU zone, and a "surveillance authority" will rule in the EFTA zone. Incongruously, it is located in Switzerland. Three EFTA states (Austria, Finland, and Sweden) joined on January 1, 1995.

European Economic Community (EEC). Established in March 1958 by the *Treaty of Rome*, it created a *customs union* of six nations by 1968 and grew to include 12 members by 1986, with four more slated to join in 1995. It is associated with the members of the *EFTA*, and by the *Lomé Conventions* with states in Africa and the Caribbean. It came under the authority of the *European Commission* in 1967. It is the most important of the three communities that make up the *European Community* (EEC, ECSC, and EURATOM). On the problem of nomenclature, *see European Union*.

European Free Trade Association (EFTA). It was established in 1960 as a counter to the *EEC*, which Britain had not joined. It included Austria, Denmark, Norway, Portugal, Sweden, and Switzerland. It aimed at industrial *free trade* by 1970, but not at political *integration*. It opened a rift within Europe between those eager for *supranational* integration down the road, and a minimalist goal of a set of *sovereign* states sharing free trade and *functional agencies*, but not in any way surrendering national sovereignty. Finland joined, first as an associate member, in 1961; Iceland joined in 1970. In 1973 EFTA lost three members (Britain, Denmark, and Ireland) to the EEC. The EFTA and EEC established a special arrangement in 1972, leading to a wider *free trade area* in 1984. In 1986 Portugal followed other departing states into the *European Economic Community*. In 1989 work began on a treaty of limited union with the EEC. However, the wider events of that year upset the negotiation, raising anew the question of *deepening versus widening*. In 1994 most EFTA states agreed to form the *European Economic Area* with the *European Union*. Norway declined membership.

European Monetary Institute (EMI). It first met in January 1994 and was intended to one day become a *central bank* for the *European Union*. It was essentially a forum where the governors of member central banks sat on a council with ill-defined powers. As new member states joined the EU, their central banks joined the EMI. Its vague mandate was to increase cooperation among Europe's central banks, as Europe moved toward full economic and monetary union. It was superseded by the *European Central Bank*.

European Monetary System/Union (EMS/EMU). The idea of a monetary union was first broached in 1978 as a means of providing some predictability to *exchange rates* through an *Exchange Rate Mechanism* (ERM), whereby *currencies* would be permitted to fluctuate only within a specified range. In addition, a European Currency Unit (ECU) was created to stand beside the various national currencies, and guaranteed by a general fund to which members contributed a share of their gold and financial *reserves*. Under the ERM, each currency was assigned a central rate relative to the ECU. If the floor or ceiling of a permissible range was reached, the *central banks* would *intervene* to keep currencies within the proscribed ranges. This was intended to provide stability, head toward a common *monetary policy*, and prepare the way for full monetary union. In practice, only the second objective was really striven for, until the *Maastricht Treaty* tried to push forward the third, despite German reunification and differential growth undermining the first. The entire EMS idea was brought into question by a monetary crisis in September 1992 and was preserved only by widening the permissible range of currency fluctuation beyond any regulatory meaning (from 2.25 to 15 percent from center). This again raised the prospect of a *two-speed Europe*. In 1995 the *European Council* renamed the ECU the "euro." The *European Central Bank* (ECB) was established in 1998. On January 1, 1999, the third stage of EMU began with fixing of the exchange rates of the currencies of 11 member states. Adoption of the euro as a common currency took place on the same day, with actual coin and notes circulated in lieu of national currencies on January 1, 2002.

European Parliament. Established by the *Treaty of Rome* in 1958, it was to have consultative rights and powers of recommendation within the *European Community*. It later received some minor budgetary powers and theoretically could dismiss the *European Commission*. It ached to become a true parliament for Europe and pushed for an enlarged role based on its claims of democratic legitimacy. This effort was greatly aided by a 1974 decision to hold direct elections to the Parliament. The first took place in 1979. Yet, this popularly elected Parliament was not given more powers. Also, the elections divided Europe, with Social Democrats doing well on the continent just as Britain moved into a more conservative phase under *Margaret Thatcher* and toward a sustained defense of the higher legitimacy of national parliaments. In 1982 *Euro-MPs* held up the EC budget to show displeasure that the *Council of Ministers* had ignored their earlier recommendations. In the end the European Parliament was revealed to have representation, but no power of taxation or decision. Voter participation fell in EC elections, which were often viewed (and fought) merely as midterm comment on national governments. *Maastricht* gave the Parliament more powers within the *EU*, but whether these can be exercised against a prevailing mood of national assertion is moot. In 1994, election turnout was a record low 56 percent, and national voting patterns again were predominant. *See also democratic deficit.*

European Political Community (EPC). An early proposal for comprehensive federation, above the *EDC* and the *ECSC.* It went to ruin along with the EDC when France failed to ratify the latter in 1954. *See also European Union.*

European Recovery Program (ERP). Official name of the Marshall Plan. This program of financial and other economic aid was proposed by Secretary of State *George C. Marshall* in 1947 to formalize and expand U.S. assistance and investment already underway. It came into effect in 1948. To administer it, the *OEEC* was set up. Aid was offered to all European states that had suffered severe damage in *World War II,* including those East European states moving into the *Soviet bloc,* and even the Soviet Union. Czechoslovakia, Poland, and Finland showed interest, but were all compelled by Moscow to decline ERP aid. Thus, the Marshall Plan, originally conceived as an extension of the *Bretton Woods* initiative to peacefully integrate the Soviets and Europe into a revived world trading and financial system, instead evolved into a key component of a larger policy of *containment* of the Soviet Union. The ERP provided global *liquidity* and was a vital catalyst to rapid postwar recovery. It brought Germany and Western Europe into an American-led, international monetary and trading system. And it led to an elevated appreciation, perhaps even an overestimation, of the efficacy of foreign aid as a tool of diplomacy. It did not come merely as American largesse. Recipients were required by Washington to accept much stricter *conditionality* than that laid out by the *International Monetary Fund* (IMF) or *International Bank for Reconstruction and Development* (IBRD). They had to end price controls, balance national budgets, adopt policies to inhibit inflation, accept a stable exchange rate, and begin to liberalize *trade.* Under U.S. encouragement, the ERP was a huge stimulus to European *integration* and *free trade.* It drew to a close in 1952, but was importantly responsible for the fact that, albeit starting from a depressed baseline, the next quarter century saw the highest rates of economic *growth* to that point in European history.
    Suggested Readings: Michael J. Hogan, *The Marshall Plan* (1987); A. Millward, *Reconstruction of Western Europe, 1945–1951* (1984).

European Security and Defense Identity (ESDI). *See Western European Union (WEU).*

European Union (EU). An expansion and extension of the *European Community* (EC), which it superseded without wholly supplanting. Formed by the *Maastricht Treaty* on November 1, 1993, the EU *deepened and widened* the federal structures of the EC and sought unified standards of justice and enhanced police cooperation. It retained the core structures of the EC, but not the same legal personality. Thus, the EC could make agreements that were binding on member states, but not the EU. Yet, it went well beyond the EC by adding to the project of economic and social *integration* and in promising to have the EU, as Maastricht put it, "assert its identity on the world scene, in particular through the implementation of common foreign and security policy including the eventual framing of a common defense policy." In a masterpiece of bureaucratic confusion and slight of hand, Maastricht incorporated what came to be known as the European Community, but that was in fact the older *European Economic Community (EEC)*, into the broader European Union project, and then renamed the EEC—the most important of the three "communities" (*EEC, ECSC, and EURATOM*) that made up the EC—the European Community. For most readers, it is enough to take note that, with rare exceptions, this distinction is lost on the media and, increasingly, also on politicians and citizens, who routinely use "EU" to refer to any one, or all, of the above communities. The EU's aim of more complete European federation provoked early critical reactions against Maastricht in several key countries, especially Denmark. On January 1, 1995, three affluent *EFTA* states joined the EU: Austria, Finland, and Sweden. Norway declined membership. In 2002 its member states were: Austria, Belgium, Denmark, Finland, France, Germany, Great Britain, Greece, Ireland (Eire), Italy, Luxembourg, the Netherlands, Portugal, Spain, and Sweden.

Eurosystem. The collective *central banking* system of the *European Union*, comprised of the National Central Banks (NCBs) and the *European Central Bank (ECB)*.

Euzkadi Ta Askatasuna (ETA). A *Basque* nationalist and *terrorist* organization. It grew less active in the 1990s than it had been in the 1970s or 1980s as a result of Spain's new prosperity, successful democracy, and membership in the *European Union*. Its support fell among Basques once the region received greater *autonomy* in the 1990s, although that did not prevent *hardliners* from continuing a campaign of murder and bombing.

"events data" analysis. Gathering and analyzing information on a range of newsworthy (that is, nonroutine) singular events. Events are chosen according to their salience for transactions among states or societies, whether economic, social, communication, political, diplomatic, or military. The idea is to build a picture (one pixel at a time) of the *international system*, as reflected in its notable, or at least its most public, transactions. This research also seeks to isolate changes that surround *crises*, in the hope of developing a predictive *model*. It has had limited success or utility.

Évian agreements (1962). Secret accords, between *Charles De Gaulle* and the Algerian leadership, that ultimately led to *independence* for Algeria and almost to *civil war* in France. *See also Algerian War of Independence.*

ex aequo et bono. *Judgment* based on fairness rather than black letter law. This idea seeks to go past mere textual judgment to a concept of justice, but can be invoked by an international court only with mutual *consent* of all states party to the case.

examination system (of Imperial China). *See China; Confucianism; and various dynasties.*

exceptionalism (moral). *See manifest destiny; mission, idea of.*

exceptio rei judicatae. When a *judgment* in the same case is had elsewhere, such as a national court or *arbitration* body, this plea ends legal proceedings.

excess of authority. (1) When domestic legal authority is exceeded by a government in pursuit of some international aim; some maintain that this is irrelevant for purposes of *international law* (others disagree). (2) When an international court exceeds its *jurisdiction*, the act invalidates its *judgment*.

exchange. (1) Reciprocal transfer of equivalent sums of different currencies. (2) Transfers of *prisoners of war* between opposing armies or of *spies* between hostile states.

exchange controls. Government interference in the market that sets the *exchange rate*, up to totally fixing rates and refusing to permit conversion or export of a national *currency*.

exchange rate. The price any *currency* will fetch in gold, silver, or credit or in a given *hard currency*. (1) Fixed: When a currency is supported by a government commitment to peg it—to some external *monetary standard* such as gold, silver, sterling, or the U.S. dollar—and keep it at that value regardless of shifts in underlying economic conditions. This is done to provide stability and predictability, but can lead to huge "currency shocks" of sudden value readjustment if the pegged value strays too far from real value. (2) Floating: When the market decides the value of a currency compared with other currencies. A stable system of exchange rates, whether fixed or floating, is vital to international trade and to economic *development* and progress. For example, in Europe before the thirteenth century, "money changers" set exchange rates among a bewildering array of currencies. An explosion of trade occurred in the latter part of the century, however, with the advent of a stable currency whose value gained common acceptance: the gold florin, issued by the Italian *city-state* of Florence, and widely used as the currency of inter-regional and international commerce. Later currencies played a comparable role to the florin, including gold *guineas* (named for the Guinea coast of Africa, from which their gold was taken) during the seventeenth and eighteenth centuries, silver and gold-backed sterling notes in the nineteenth century, and the U.S. dollar in the twentieth century.

Exchange Rate Mechanism (ERM). Created in 1979 by member states eager to reduce *inflation* resulting from the *oil shocks* and from wild fluctuations of European *exchange rates*. The costs of German unification after 1989 placed enormous strains on the system, changing the core economy that had supported it into a new source of instability. In September 1992, a major crisis led to the ejection of the British and Italian *currencies, devaluation* of several others, and a radical shift in exchange rate policy. *See also European Monetary System.*

excise. Tax or duty applied to *commodities*.

exclave. A small territory separate from the main portion of the state to which it belongs, which thereby forms an *enclave* with respect to neighboring lands. The difference from enclave is simply one of point of view: *West Berlin* was an *enclave* within *East Germany*, but an exclave as seen from *West Germany*. *See also Kaliningrad exclave; Nakhichevan; Walvis Bay.*

Exclusive Economic Zone (EEZ). A 200-nautical mile (from the *baseline*) zone of exclusive economic rights granted to *coastal states* by UNCLOS III. In these zones, states control mineral and fishing rights on the *continental shelf* and have obligations concerning marine conservation and pollution. They must permit free passage to international shipping and in all other respects the waters remain part of the *high seas*. EEZ claims overlap, as lines project out from irregular coastlines. Conflicts may be resolved by drawing medians through the zones or by *arbitration*. About one-third of the world's oceans fall within EEZs, including entire seas such as the *Caribbean, Caspian, Mediterranean, Black, Red,* and *Yellow Seas*, among others. Some South Pacific *microstates* potentially control vast EEZs, which can either make them wealthy or set them up as targets of exploitation by larger powers and interests. Competition to claim EEZs around hitherto valueless atolls intensified, which helps explain the UNCLOS-era rise in tension over such hitherto quiet areas as the *Paracels* and *Spratlys*. Several powerful maritime states, including the United States and the United Kingdom, still do not fully recognize such claims because they impinge so heavily on traditional doctrines such as *freedom of the seas*. This suggests that, at a minimum, modifications will have to be made. *See also common heritage principle; fisheries; island; islet.*

exclusive jurisdiction. *See domestic jurisdiction.*

excuse. In *international law*, escaping blame for breach of a legal *rule* or obligation by pleading *force majeure*.

executive. The administrative authority of a state (or *union*, etc.). In the United States this branch of government is under the direct authority of the president.

executive agreement. Agreements between *heads of government* that serve in effect as *treaties* but do not require *ratification*, though they may need enabling legislation, and are more easily revoked. They are usually concerned with mundane matters, such as consular arrangements, but can also be highly significant. American presidents frustrated by the *treaty power* process at times use these to bypass congressional oversight or avoid Senate rejection of a negotiated political or diplomatic settlement, as at *Yalta*. In a sustained campaign, 1952–1954, *conservatives* and *isolationists* failed to amend the U.S. Constitution to put these on the same footing with treaties. *See also deportation; stateless person.*

exequatur. Formal acceptance by one state of a *consular* officer representing another.

exhaustion of local remedies. *See remedy.*

exile. Someone voluntarily living abroad out of declared political opposition to the government of their home country or because they have been expelled from or denied re-entry to their native land. Exile sometimes was enforced internally in huge countries such as China or Russia, as when dissidents or prisoners were sentenced to live in undesirable abodes or territories in *Siberia* or other outer, often desert, provinces. *See Gulag Archipelago; Penal Settlements; transportation.*

existence. Under *international law*, the recognized (and obvious) necessity and reality—some legal theorists also say right—of an *international personality* to continue to exist, barring voluntary *extinction*, in order to enjoy all other *sovereign* rights bestowed by that status.

exogenous factors. Those springing from external causes; elements of an explanation of events that are external to the *system* under study.

expansionism. A policy of *conquest* or *aggrandizement*. *See also aggression; encroachment; imperialism; incursion.*

expatriation. The voluntary renunciation or involuntary revocation of one's *nationality. See also Bancroft Conventions; deportation; exile; naturalization.*

exploitation. (1) Simple usage: using something, such as a *labor* or a *natural resource*, to extract wealth or make a profit. (2) As a moral pejorative: usurping other people's labor or resources to acquire undeserved wealth or make an unfair profit.

Exploration, Age of (c. 1400–1600). *Arabs*, Indians, *Vikings*, and Polynesians all made impressive voyages of discovery at the height of their civilizations. In 1400, *Ming* China was still a great naval power, sending out vast fleets on expeditions of trade and exploration that far exceeded anything Europe then mounted. Having touched the shores of Sri Lanka, Persia, and even distant northern Australia, the Ming pulled back: a great expedition of 1433 to the Middle East and East Africa was the last such Chinese effort, and in 1436 the emperor forbade further journeys or construction of *blue water* ships. It thus fell to Europe's schooners and frigates, not to Chinese junks, to map the oceans and open the world to intellectual and cultural intercourse, as well as to economic exploitation and colonization. The Age of Exploration by Europeans was different from all others, therefore, in having the lasting effect of linking the world's oceans into unified navigational and trading systems.

It was also the second half of a two-part response to the new geopolitical reality of *Islam.* Europe's initial military attempt to reverse the Muslim conquest of the Middle East and North Africa, the *Crusades*, had failed after 200 years of effort and great expenditure of lives and treasure. Now, with an even greater Muslim power rising in the east—the *Ottoman Empire*—Europeans sought a way around the immovable Islamic world to the markets of India and China. The new approach to an old problem was made possible by key navigational innovations, including the magnetic compass, astrolabe and portolan chart, stern-mounted rudders, and triangular lateen sails. Those technological breakthroughs combined with new astronomical knowledge acquired from Muslims via the *Norman* conquest of Muslim Sicily, and Iberian contact with the great scholars of the Emirate of *Granada*, to make maps more accurate and ocean-going navigation somewhat less perilous to crews and investors. The effort was also partly inspired by the famous journals of Marco Polo and visions of Asia as a land of vast wealth, by dreams of mythical empires such as Atlantis or the lost Kingdom of Prester John, and by a more immediate desire to reach the sources of African gold suspected to exist somewhere along the Guinea coast.

By 1375 the Portuguese reached Cape Bojador, 1,500 miles south of *Ceuta.* Concerted voyages of discovery were then made in the African Atlantic by Henry *"the Navigator,"* whose ships reached the Azores in 1427 and rounded Cape Bojador in 1434. Ten years later Portuguese *caravels* reached Cape Verde, and by the time of Henry's death in 1460 they had made landfall 600 miles further south in what is today Sierra Leone. Meanwhile, *Constantinople* fell to the Ottomans in 1453, cutting off the prosperous *city-states* of the Italian *Renaissance* from their historic commerce with Asia—other than *Venice*, which continued to trade in the eastern Mediterranean. The Genoese explorer *Christopher Columbus* was one of many who sailed in search of an alternate route to the east, but the first to do so by sailing west, where he encountered the *New World* in 1492. The next year, the pope drew up a *line of demarcation* dividing the globe between the Catholic crowns of Spain and Portugal. In 1488 Bartolomeu Dias rounded the Cape of Good Hope, and six years later Portuguese ships reached Ethiopia. Vasco da Gama (1469–1524) explored parts of India's coast, 1497–1498 (as had Pero de Covilhã, 1488–1489, but he ended as a prisoner of the Ethiopian court from 1490, for the last 30 years of his life, and so was largely lost to fame and to history). At the same time, the Genoese John Cabot discovered *Newfoundland* and Nova Scotia.

In 1500 Pedro Cabal touched upon the shores of Brazil, pausing to found Veracruz, then continuing with his primary mission to bring a Portuguese war fleet to the Indian Ocean to make good on the discoveries of Vasco da Gama. The next year Amerigo Vespucci mapped the east coast of South America, to the La Plata estuary. On the East African coast, Zanzibar was occupied. Mombasa was sacked in 1505 and once again in 1528, and permanent Portuguese trading forts were set up at Kilwa, Sofala, and in Mozambique and began trading in African *gold* and *slaves*. By 1510 Portuguese war fleets, employing old knowledge of the monsoon winds between Africa and India and mounted cannon on their ships, swept Arab and Indian *galleys* from the East Africa coast and long-established Indian Ocean *trade routes*. In 1513 the isthmus of Panama was traversed by Vasco Nunez de Balboa, the first European to gaze westward on the Pacific. In 1514 the pope granted Lisbon the right to any newly discovered lands to the east; the Spanish therefore hurried to cross the Pacific, looking for a westward route to the *Spice Islands*. Fernão de Magalhães (Ferdinand Magellan) sailed from Seville in 1519 in search of the Moluccas. He skirted South America and survived mutiny, hurricanes, illness, and scurvy, only to be killed by natives in the archipelago later called the Philippines (1521), which his voyage ensured would fall to Spain. The Pacific was then crossed, and the world circumnavigated for the first time, by his second-in-command, Sebastian del Cano, who returned with only one ship and 18 men out of an original complement of 265 crew.

Pacific exploration remained difficult until the 1560s, when the Spanish mapped seasonal circular winds and currents that permitted reliable passage between Asia and the west coast of the Americas, comparable to the seasonal trade winds, which by then were familiar to all ships plying the vibrant and expanding Atlantic trade, in slaves, sugar, fish, and furs. A measure of the difficulty may be seen in the calculation scholars have made that, of the 912 ships Portugal alone sent to the "Indies" from 1500 to 1635, fully 144 were lost before arriving and another 298 never returned, lost to weather, waves, or pirates. Still, by 1600 Europe's naval powers had charted most of the globe, set up forts and trading posts on—and claimed segments of—the coasts of all inhabited continents, and began to penetrate and colonize the interior of the Americas. Portugal alone had 40 forts and factories (*entrepôt*) strung out between East Africa and Japan, serving the trade in *spices, slaves,* and *gold*—and it was already a declining power.

Lesser voyages of discovery included John Davis in the Arctic in 1586 and 1587 and Henry Hudson's ill-fated voyage, 1610–1611. What followed in the seventeenth and eighteenth centuries was a new and raw age of mercantile exploration and exploitation under the several *East India Companies* and similar chartered monopoly houses dedicated to dominating trade with other regions of the East Indies and the West Indies. Accompanying all this were *mercantilist* wars over the international *spice trade* and *slave trade,* then commercial and cultural penetration of continental interiors, and later still, determined and enforced settlement and colonization. Only those north Asian countries located above the main trade routes, which were determined by the prevailing winds, remained outside Europe's growing reach. The turn of Korea, Japan, and China to feel on the throat the tightening grip of Europe's commercial hand awaited the Age of Steam in the mid-nineteenth century. *See also James Cook; Hudson's Bay Company.*

Suggested Readings: C. R. Boxer, ed., *Portuguese Commerce and Conquest in Southern Asia, 1500–1750* (1985); John R. Hale, *The Age of Exploration* (1974); L. Withey, *Voyages of Discovery* (1989).

export. Any *commodity* or *service,* including information and *technology,* sent abroad for sale or exchange. *See also comparative advantage; General Agreement on Tariffs and Trade; trade; World Trade Organization.*

export control. *See embargo.*

Export-Import Bank (EXIMBANK). (1) A U.S. government bank set up in 1934 and reincorporated in 1945. It provides credit to domestic exporters and loans to foreign governments or firms under the condition that the funds must be used to purchase *goods or services* in the United States. (2) Any similar bank devoted to export promotion, set up by any country.

export-led growth. When a national economy, particularly in the *South,* is outward oriented, seeking to capture a share of world markets by *exploiting* its own *comparative advantages* to export *goods or services* and earn *foreign exchange.* More radical critics argued that in the late twentieth century the classical model did not apply to *developing countries* because their exports were tied to existing and distorting world markets, were largely foreign controlled, and might even be causing an overall loss of capital to the national economy.

This led a number of countries to attempt policies of *import substitution*. Whether from despair, *structural adjustment* programs, or sincerely changed conviction born of a wish to emulate the success of the *newly industrialized countries*, by the 1990s virtually all economies that once tried the import-substitution route had turned to encouragement of export-driven *industrialization*. *See also graduation clause; protectionism; Adam Smith; Smithian growth.*

export processing zones (EPZs). Areas set aside by *LDCs* or *NICs* to encourage foreign manufacturing *investment*, local employment, *technology transfers*, and other benefits, by making imports and exports free of *tariffs*. Additional incentives to *foreign direct investment* in these zones might include ready *infrastructure*, cheap labor, and a streamlined bureaucracy. Under *Deng Xiaoping*, the People's Republic of China established similar zones after 1979, but called them "special economic zones." Along the U.S.-Mexico border, they are known as "maquiladoras."

expressio unius est exclusio alterius. "Listing of one thing implies the exclusion of another thing [which is not expressly listed]." Under this principle, for example, an international *human rights* covenant implicitly excludes unlisted rights by clearly listing others.

expropriation. (1) In domestic politics: Government takeover of private property without just compensation. (2) Under *international law*: When one state seizes the property of nationals of another state, or of a private enterprise, without due or just *compensation*. Starting in the late nineteenth century, poorer states in Latin America sometimes resorted to expropriations of key industries or foreign-owned assets, which then provoked *gunboat* interventions by certain of the *Great Powers*. This was also a common legal problem with *Communist* states in the twentieth century, starting with *Bolshevik* Russia and involving decades-long and bitter diplomatic negotiations and court action over compensation owed to Western businesses. Expropriation of the assets of the Suez Canal Company provided both the context and the pretext for the *Suez Crisis. See also nationalization.*

expulsion. A legal device intended as an extreme censure of a miscreant state, which places it outside the company of *civilized states*. The Soviet Union was the only state expelled by the *League of Nations*, for its unprovoked invasion of Finland. Cuba was expelled from the OAS at American insistence. Egypt was expelled from the *Arab League* for making peace with Israel (it was later readmitted).

In the United Nations, a state may be expelled by a simple majority vote of the *United Nations General Assembly*, if after a recommendation of the *Security Council*. The procedure was not even used regarding *Taiwan*, in a most special case involving replacing the Republic of China (Taiwan) with the People's Republic of China (*mainland China*) in the China seat within

the People's Republic of China (*mainland China*) in the China seat within the world body. Instead, the Taiwanese delegation's *letters of credence* were rejected (October 1971), so that the People's Republic could be seated as "China." South Africa was also effectively barred when the UNGA Credentials Committee refused to accredit its delegates, but was never actually expelled from the United Nations over *apartheid*. Similarly, Serbia was suspended—not expelled—by the *OSCE* for its 1990s Balkan *aggression*. *See also suspension; withdrawal.*

extended deterrence. (1) Using threats of nuclear *retaliation* to protect a third party from a nuclear *first strike*, as in the U.S. strategic commitment to Western Europe throughout the *Cold War* and to Japan and South Korea regarding a possible North Korean attack both during and after the Cold War. (2) Any guarantee (not necessarily nuclear) to defend a small power in case of attack, such as that belatedly and ineffectively offered by Britain and France to Poland in 1939. *See also deterrence.*

extermination. *See biological warfare; collectivization; concentration camps; death camps; eastern front; ethnic cleansing; "final solution to the Jewish problem"; genocide; Holocaust; kulaks; liquidation.*

external affairs. A synonym for *foreign affairs.*

external indebtedness. *See debt; debt crisis; debt fatigue; debtor cartel; debt rescheduling; debt service.*

extinction. When one or more *states* absorb the *international personality*, in whole or in part, of another state by *conquest*, complete or partial dissolution of a parent state, *federation*, or *union*. Extinction thus may, and does, occur peacefully and voluntarily, as in the remarkable case of the breakup of the former *Soviet Union*, or it may be accomplished violently through conquest and total absorption and *annexation* of a once-sovereign territory. *See also Act of Union; Austro-Hungarian Empire; Baltic States; Central American Union; Czechoslovakia; debellatio; East Germany; German Confederation; Gran Colombia; Holy Roman Empire; partitions of Poland; Ottoman Empire; state succession; Texas; Tibet; union of sovereign states; Yugoslavia.*

extinctive prescription. When by *consent* or acquiescence the loss of an international legal claim is incurred through failure to assert it over a long period.

extradition. The legal handing over of a fugitive or other person by one state to another, usually under terms of bilateral treaties set up to handle such cases. As states became more genuinely interdependent and *tourism* and general travel increased in the eighteenth and nineteenth centuries, criminals too became international in their movements and often also their crimes. Some were clever enough to commit illegal acts in one *jurisdiction* and then flee to legal safe harbor in another. This produced a common interest among states to establish practical rules for deporting each other's fugitives. Hence, extradition treaties evolved. Originally, they listed specific acts that the contracting states agreed would subject individuals to extradition proceedings. Historically, this early extradition often, even usually, concerned political refugees, would-be revolutionaries, or others thought to be subversive by one or another state. Today, the reverse is true: extradition almost never involves political fugitives and frequently specifically excludes such persons, who may instead enjoy a right of *asylum*. Instead, modern treaties are concerned nearly exclusively with nonpolitical crimes normally dealt with in *municipal law*, from whose jurisdiction a fugitive has fled. It also almost never involves deporting one's own nationals for trial and punishment abroad. An exception to this is the practice of Britain and the United States, which traditionally have been willing to deport their subjects/citizens for trial and punishment in foreign countries. *War crimes* are a special case. Despite their political nature, they are not considered or deemed political offenses under the law, and hence suspected war criminals may be extradited, although in practice this right to extradite may be waived. In the absence of a treaty there is no general legal obligation to extradite a fugitive. For instance, one of the "Great Train Robbers" from England, Ronald Biggs, remained at large for nearly 35 years in Brazil, which had no extradition treaty with Britain, until his money ran out and he went home for medical treatment at the expense of the British state. Indeed, in the absence of a treaty there may not be any legal basis to extradite. Extradition may occur anyway, however, from states less restrained by respect for law or where a regime wishes to curry political favor with a foreign government. Since c. 1975, some states (Canada and others) have refused to extradite even known and vicious criminals unless the receiving jurisdiction (such as a given state of the United States) first agrees not to seek or apply the death penalty. Another special case is when extradition agreements among *belligerents* are automatically suspended in wartime. They are not usually terminated; instead, they resume effect upon completion of hostilities and *ratification* of a *peace treaty*. *See also drug trade; hijacking; International Criminal Police Organization; political offenses; rule of double criminality; terrorism.*

extraterritoriality. (1) A legal exemption of foreign residents or citizens from the *jurisdiction* of local courts. Such special legal rights may derive from mutual agreement to suspend a host state's laws for limited purposes in delimited areas. Thus, a merchant colony set up by the *Hansa* in London enjoyed exemptions from English law (and a measure of self-government) as early as 1281 because it brought to England goods not otherwise available. Similarly, *Christian* merchants from Venice traveling or residing in *Constantinople* were exempted by the *Ottoman Empire* from the *sharia* and other laws that applied to *Muslim* subjects. And the modern *Vatican*, as a result of its cramped size, has buildings elsewhere in Rome where the extraterritorial principle is respected by the Italian state. In this form, extraterritoriality also applies to *embassies* or wherever else *diplomatic immunity* is granted. Extraterritorial claims have also been imposed by *force majeure*. Among more sinister examples were the onerous *capitulations* forced upon China, Japan, and Korea by Western powers (and later, on China and Korea by Japan) during the nineteenth and early twentieth centuries, in the *treaty port system*. (2) Efforts to make one's domestic law apply to one's nationals operating in the territory of other states, as when one country insists that its *multinational corporations (MNCs)* should not permit foreign-based *subsidiaries* to trade with a third country subject to a unilateral *embargo*. The United States, in particular, historically sought to apply its laws to foreign corporations and citizens who wished to conduct business in a third country (such as Cuba, Vietnam, South Africa, or the Soviet Union) with which the United States had other foreign policy issues. Such efforts raised protests from friendly states such as Canada or from the *European Union*, which hosted subsidiaries of American MNCs and accepted COCOM restrictions, but never agreed to certain unilateral U.S. embargoes. *See also Deshima; servitude; territoriality principle; unequal treaties; universality of criminal law; Wanghia, Treaty of.*

extremism. Immoderation in policy or in one's intellectual, political, or social opinions and judgments. *See also chauvinism; fanatic; fundamentalism; ideology; jingoism; prudence; racism; radical; reactionary; secularism.*